AI Hallucination Management in the Enterprise Metaverse

Abdelkader Mohamed Sghaier Derbali
https://orcid.org/0000-0003-4098-3120
Taibah University, Saudi Arabia

Rohit Sood
https://orcid.org/0000-0002-4127-7781
Lovely Professional University, India

Shilpa
https://orcid.org/0000-0002-2953-2372
Lovely Professional University, India

IGI Global
Scientific Publishing
Publishing Tomorrow's Research Today

Vice President of Editorial Melissa Wagner
Director of Acquisitions Mikaela Felty
Director of Book Development Jocelynn Hessler
Production Manager Mike Brehm
Cover Design Jose Rosado

Published in the United States of America by
IGI Global Scientific Publishing
701 East Chocolate Avenue
Hershey, PA, 17033, USA
Tel: 717-533-8845 | Fax: 717-533-7115
Website: https://www.igi-global.com E-mail: cust@igi-global.com

Library of Congress Cataloging-in-Publication Data

Names: Derbali, Abdelkader Mohamed Sghaier, 1985- editor | Sood, Rohit, 1984- editor | Chaudhary, Shilpa, 1985- editor
Title: AI hallucination management in the enterprise metaverse / [edited by] Abdelkader Mohamed Sghaier Derbali, Rohit Sood, Shilpa Chaudhary.
Description: Hershey, PA : IGI Global Scientific Publishing, [2026] | Includes bibliographical references and index. | Summary: "This book aims to explore the transition pathways from experimental AI use to its responsible, systemic innovation in global business"-- Provided by publisher.
Identifiers: LCCN 2025054895 (print) | LCCN 2025054896 (ebook) | ISBN 9798337375342 hardcover | ISBN 9798337375359 paperback | ISBN 9798337375366 ebook
Subjects: LCSH: Artificial intelligence--Business applications | Artificial intelligence--Moral and ethical aspects | Metaverse | Information integrity | Human-computer interaction
Classification: LCC HD45 .A47795 2026 (print) | LCC HD45 (ebook) | DDC 658.4/03--dc23/eng/20260227
LC record available at https://lccn.loc.gov/2025054895
LC ebook record available at https://lccn.loc.gov/2025054896

British Cataloguing in Publication Data
A Cataloguing in Publication record for this book is available from the British Library.

Table of Contents

Detailed Table of Contents

The combined impact of AI and immersive technology on compressed timelines is only accelerating the adoption of the Enterprise Metaverse as an employee training platform. Within these virtual environments, AI-fueled avatars, conversational agents and simulator systems make possible the creation of learning experiences which are interactive, tailor to ingest an individual student's needs with ease across scales from thousands down to just one individual. Yet the integrity of such systems is now threatened by AI-built hallucinations, in which generative models produce a kind of "fake news" that is volatiles out to different audiences or produces simply non-factual information. For businesses trying to get their employees trained, these "hallucinations" could put them at risk of misinformation, must confound their judgment-making and violate the trust people put in company learning ecosystems. It also shows how AI-based role-playing and real-time feedback can help provide in-depth training simulations, as well as a perspective on both the opportunity and the problem.

The adoption of AI into enterprise metaverse has created more opportunities than ever before in immersive collaboration, automation, and intelligent decision-making. Nevertheless, the mass implementation of the generative and autonomous AI systems is limited by a very significant issue, namely--AI hallucination, which consists of confident and unreliable results. This is the Hallucination to Harmony: Building Reliable AI System in the Enterprise Metaverse chapter, which critically analyzes the technical, cognitive, and governance aspects of hallucination in the metaverse-based enterprise space. It considers the ways in which the new advances including self-checking AI agents, real-time causal reasoning, federated learning, neuromorphic and quantum-enhanced computing, and emotion-aware ethical agents can all change unreliable machine behavior into cognitively harmonious intelligence. The chapter also suggests a multidimensional view of achieving cognitive harmony in which human judgment and machine intelligence act as complementary forces as opposed to competing forces.

This chapter discusses the role of human-AI partnership within the enterprise metaverse and how AI hallucinations endanger trust, emotional congruency and productivity. The more immersive virtual environments transform organizational work, the more AI agents help in analyses, decision support, and training, but, because of their probabilistic nature, they can give confident and false results. The chapter introduces the TrustEmotion Productivity (TEP) Framework to demonstrate that safe collaboration relies on calibrated trust, emotional intelligence, and design that is qualified by productivity orientation. It also emphasizes the intensification of hallucinations within immersive, real-time, and multimodal environments and analyzes technical and organizational measures like retrieval-augmented generation, confidence calibration, transparency, expert review and governance protocols. It illustrates the operational risk of hallucinations and best practices of constructing credible, ethical, and human-focused AI systems to support metaverse-enabled businesses.

AI has moved past being a mere tool; it's our new, permanent coworker. To truly capitalize on this massive digital integration, we must focus on the tricky, three-part equilibrium between trust, emotion, and productivity. While AI offers impressive gains in speed and data-crunching, those benefits are easily negated when users lack confidence often because the "black box" nature of algorithms leads to concerns about opacity, bias, and a creeping sense of lost human control. Furthermore, if we rely too heavily on the system, we risk "automation complacency," sacrificing indispensable human qualities like creativity, ethical judgment, and nuanced decision making. Achieving this demands transparent AI design, continuous user education, and a work culture that equally values algorithmic certainty and human intuition. Ultimately, the successful organizations of the future will be the ones that navigate the inevitable emotional friction and successfully cultivate a reciprocal, appropriate trust with their digital partners, turning anxiety into sustained, meaningful productivity.

The enterprise metaverse is a groundbreaking shift in how businesses operate, collaborate, and evolve. It offers smooth virtual workplaces, enhanced education, and innovative data-driven business models through the integration of virtual reality, blockchain, artificial intelligence, cloud systems, and digital twins. The technology foundations, global leaders, systems of governance, and financial advantages that propel business adoption are all addressed in this chapter. Additionally, it analyses cross-industry instances of use, workforce change, and the strategic goals needed for sustained deployment. The metaverse emerges as an accelerator for efficiency, creativity, and sustained competitive edge in the soon-to-arrive age of digital transformation as organisations transition into interconnected digital ecosystems.

The integration of multimodal generative AI into metaverse environments has intensified hallucination-driven distortions, creating synthetic outputs that appear credible within immersive spaces and influence judgment, behaviour and decision accuracy. Continuous presence in avatar-based ecosystems heightens perceptual reality drift and cognitive misalignment. The absence of responsible intelligence mechanisms for detection, monitoring and mitigation leaves immersive system users exposed to synthetic narrative manipulation, fabricated identity signals and cross-modal inconsistency. Fragmented regulation and limited provenance verification deepen risks as hallucination cycles evolve without oversight. This study develops a governance framework centred on real-time authenticity assurance, distortion tracking and consistency verification. It advances a structured approach to protect immersive participants, reduce uncontrolled hallucination escalation and strengthen accountable metaverse safety architecture.

This chapter provides a comprehensive examination of the enterprise metaverse by defining its core concepts, technological foundations, and organizational implications. It outlines the multidimensional structure of the metaverse, spanning immersive environments, digital twins, AI-driven automation, and interoperable virtual ecosystems, and explains how these elements enable new forms of collaboration, value creation, and operational efficiency. The chapter also highlights opportunities, strategic challenges, and the evolving role of businesses as they integrate metaverse technologies into enterprise workflows.

The transition from traditional business models to metaverse-driven enterprises represents a transformative shift in how organizations create value, manage operations, and collaborate across immersive digital ecosystems. This chapter outlines a structured, multi-phase pathway that guides enterprises from foundational digital readiness to fully immersive metaverse architectures powered by AI, digital twins, XR, and blockchain technologies. Emphasis is placed on organizational capability building, governance reform, cultural adaptation, and the integration of human–AI collaboration. A central focus is the need for robust AI hallucination management to ensure accuracy, safety, and trust as autonomous systems influence simulations, decision-making, and customer experiences. By synthesizing technological,

The chapter explores how financial institutions can mitigate AI hallucinations while delivering ESG-driven credit risk advisory within the enterprise metaverse. It argues that hallucinations in generative and predictive models threaten responsible lending, regulatory alignment, and sustainable value creation when unchecked in immersive, real-time advisory environments. Framed around a widening talent gap, the chapter positions human–AI co-governance as essential, requiring advisors who blend financial acumen, ESG expertise, and AI literacy. It proposes an adaptive framework built on strategic upskilling, cultural transformation that normalizes challenging AI outputs, and targeted recruitment and partnerships. Within metaverse-based advisory channels, this framework embeds explainability, stress-testing, and escalation protocols so that human experts can detect, interpret, and constrain hallucinations, enabling trustworthy, ESG-aligned credit decisions in next-generation financial ecosystems.

AI hallucination—the production of fluent but incorrect or fabricated outputs—has become a major challenge for large language models and generative AI. This chapter reviews the evolution of hallucination management, from early recognition to modern mitigation and creative reinterpretation. It defines hallucination in AI contexts and identifies key causes such as data noise, model drift, prompt ambiguity, and domain mismatch. The chapter then examines evaluation frameworks, taxonomies, and metrics, including factual consistency measures, FActScore, and domain-specific benchmarks. Core mitigation strategies are discussed, notably retrieval-augmented generation, multi-stage verification, human-in-the-loop approaches, and prompt optimization. Emerging trends include agentic AI systems with multi-agent validation, sector-specific solutions in healthcare and finance, and viewing hallucination as a driver of human–machine co-creation. The chapter concludes that effective hallucination management is a technical and ethical necessity for trustworthy AI.

This chapter examined AI hallucination, where artificial intelligence systems generated false, misleading, or non factual outputs, and analysed its impact on the reliability and governance of financial systems during 2015 to 2025. The study focused on key financial applications such as credit risk assessment, fraud detection, algorithmic trading, and investment forecasting, where such errors strongly affected decision making. A Systematic Literature Review was conducted using the PRISMA framework, drawing studies from Scopus, Web of Science, and Google Scholar to identify major patterns, causes, and governance related challenges of AI hallucination. The findings indicated that hallucinations mainly arose from poor data quality, limited contextual understanding within models, and excessive dependence on automated systems without sufficient human supervision. The chapter concluded that AI hallucination was not merely a technical issue but a broader governance challenge, emphasizing the importance of explainable AI, robust internal control mechanisms, ethical auditing practices.

The given paper discusses how the customer and human experience is transforming in the digital world, where the video becomes less focused on the interaction as an engagement factor and more on its emotional presence in an AI-driven world and the further stage of the metaverse. Even though digital technologies and social media have revolutionized the sphere of communication, learning, and social connection, their overuse and excessive and compulsive nature have resulted in the fact that there is the emergence of the crisis of presence in the form of a loss of authenticity, emotional contentment and live interaction between people. Digital overexposure can be dangerous not only to the mental health and cognition of young and older generations but also even to the emotional stability.

Preface

INTRODUCTION

The rapid convergence of artificial intelligence, immersive technologies, and enterprise systems has ushered in a new organizational paradigm: the enterprise metaverse. Within these persistent, interactive, and data-rich environments, AI-driven agents, avatars, and analytics systems increasingly mediate decision-making, learning, collaboration, and customer engagement. While these capabilities promise unprecedented efficiency and creativity, they also introduce a critical and often underestimated risk: AI hallucination. In enterprise contexts, hallucinations are not merely technical inaccuracies; they are systemic failures that can undermine trust, distort judgment, and propagate misinformation across immersive digital ecosystems.

As enterprises embed large language models, multimodal generative systems, and autonomous agents into metaverse platforms, the consequences of confident but incorrect AI outputs become magnified. Errors are no longer confined to text-based interfaces but are experienced through real-time simulations, emotional interactions, and embodied virtual agents. In such environments, hallucinations can influence employee training outcomes, financial decisions, governance processes, customer perceptions, and even ethical norms. Managing hallucinations therefore becomes a foundational requirement for responsible, resilient, and scalable enterprise metaverse adoption.

This edited reference volume, *AI Hallucination Management in the Enterprise Metaverse*, is conceived in response to this urgent need. As editors, we bring together interdisciplinary scholarship and practice-oriented insights that address hallucination detection, mitigation, governance, and human–AI collaboration within immersive enterprise systems. The volume moves beyond isolated technical fixes to present holistic frameworks that integrate computational methods, organizational design, ethical governance, and human judgment. Our aim is to provide researchers, practitioners, policymakers, and advanced students with a comprehensive resource to understand, anticipate, and manage AI hallucinations as enterprises transition into metaverse-driven futures.

CHAPTER OVERVIEW

Chapter 1 examines AI hallucinations within metaverse-based employee training environments. It highlights how misinformation generated by AI-driven avatars and simulations can compromise skill development, decision-making, and organizational trust, while also outlining strategies for safeguarding learning integrity.

In *Chapter 2*, the focus shifts to a broader systems perspective, proposing pathways from hallucination-prone AI toward cognitively harmonious enterprise systems. The chapter explores emerging technologies and governance mechanisms that align human judgment with autonomous intelligence in immersive settings.

Chapters 3 and 4 together explore human–AI collaboration through the lenses of trust, emotion, and productivity. These chapters emphasize that hallucination management is not solely a technical challenge but a socio-emotional one, requiring calibrated trust, transparency, and organizational cultures that resist automation complacency.

Chapter 5 situates hallucination management within the global evolution of the enterprise metaverse. By examining leading organizations, governance models, and technological infrastructures, it contextualizes hallucination risks within broader digital transformation strategies.

Governance and responsibility take center stage in *Chapter 6*, which proposes a responsible intelligence framework for managing hallucinations in immersive systems. The chapter addresses authenticity assurance, distortion tracking, and accountability in avatar-based and multimodal environments.

Foundational clarity is provided in *Chapter 7*, which defines the enterprise metaverse, its dimensions, and its organizational scope. This conceptual grounding supports subsequent discussions on risk, governance, and transformation.

Chapter 8 presents structured transition pathways from traditional business models to metaverse-driven enterprises, emphasizing the integration of hallucination management into organizational readiness, culture, and governance frameworks.

Financial systems are examined in depth in *Chapters 9 and 13*, which analyze hallucination risks in financial decision-making, credit assessment, trading, and risk management. These chapters highlight the regulatory, operational, and systemic implications of hallucinations in high-stakes domains.

Chapter 10 extends the discussion to experiential metaverse marketing, demonstrating how AI-driven sentiment analytics can both enhance and distort customer engagement when hallucinations go unmanaged.

Human–AI co-governance is the focus of *Chapter 11*, which addresses ESG-driven credit risk advisory in metaverse environments. The chapter underscores the role of skilled human oversight in constraining hallucinations within responsible financial ecosystems.

In *Chapter 12*, the volume returns to the evolution of hallucination management itself, reviewing metrics, taxonomies, and emerging mitigation strategies while reframing hallucination as both a technical and ethical challenge.

The volume concludes with *Chapter 14*, which reflects on the future of customer and human experience in the metaverse. It raises critical questions about emotional authenticity, presence, and well-being in AI-mediated realities, reminding readers that hallucination management ultimately serves human-centered goals.

CONCLUSION

Collectively, the chapters in this volume demonstrate that AI hallucination management is not a peripheral technical concern but a central pillar of enterprise metaverse governance. As immersive systems become deeply embedded in organizational processes, hallucinations can cascade across cognitive, emotional, and operational layers, amplifying risk and eroding trust. Addressing these challenges requires integrated approaches that combine detection technologies, human oversight, ethical design, and institutional accountability.

As editors, we emphasize that no single solution can eliminate hallucinations entirely. Instead, enterprises must adopt adaptive, multi-layered strategies that recognize uncertainty as an inherent feature of generative AI. By embedding verification mechanisms, human–AI co-governance models, and transparent design principles into metaverse systems, organizations can transform hallucination management from a reactive task into a proactive capability.

We hope this book serves as a catalyst for informed dialogue and responsible innovation. For scholars, it offers conceptual frameworks and research directions; for practitioners, it provides actionable insights and governance models; and for decision-makers, it highlights the strategic importance of trust and reliability in immersive digital futures. Ultimately, managing AI hallucinations is about safeguarding human judgment, organizational integrity, and societal trust as enterprises reimagine reality in the metaverse age.

Chapter 1
AI Hallucinations and Employee Training in the Metaverse:
Ensuring Accuracy in Skill Development

Sanjeev Kumar
https://orcid.org/0000-0002-7375-7341
Lovely Professional University, India

Mohammad Badruddoza Talukder
https://orcid.org/0009-0008-1662-9221
International University of Business Agriculture and Technology, Bangladesh

ABSTRACT

The combined impact of AI and immersive technology on compressed timelines is only accelerating the adoption of the Enterprise Metaverse as an employee training platform. Within these virtual environments, AI-fueled avatars, conversational agents and simulator systems make possible the creation of learning experiences which are interactive, tailor to ingest an individual student's needs with ease across scales from thousands down to just one individual. Yet the integrity of such systems is now threatened by AI-built hallucinations, in which generative models produce a kind of "fake news" that is volatiles out to different audiences or produces simply non-factual information. For businesses trying to get their employees trained, these "hallucinations" could put them at risk of misinformation, must confound their judgment-making and violate the trust people put in company learning ecosystems.

DOI: 10.4018/979-8-3373-7534-2.ch001

It also shows how AI-based role-playing and real-time feedback can help provide in-depth training simulations, as well as a perspective on both the opportunity and the problem.

BACKGROUND AND CONTEXT OF THE STUDY:

AI Hallucinations and Employee Training in the Metaverse: Ensuring Accuracy in Skill Development:

The lightning-fast development of both the metaverse and AI (Artificial Intelligence) has completely changed the way companies train and develop their workforce. The technology includes VR hardware, AI-powered avatars and 3D environments, which have allowed students to practice the difficult tasks they will face on the job. However, a significant problem has emerged over the years as AI has been incorporated into these online learning systems of AI hallucinations. This is the kind of situation where the AI models are going to positively fail in their predictions and decisions, in cases where they will have guaranteed issues with false, deceptive, or fictitious data resulting in significant and harmful skew to learning and fidelity of skill acquisition. In a more serious Metaverse training scenario, these errors could be deadly(Lifelo et al., 2024). For instance, in a simulation, an AI driven virtual trainer may issue wrong technical guiding or such safety guidance. When scraping the living crap out of a game, employees can easily get misinformation because ooh the pretty and we must be accurate, which leads to (at least some) blunders in terms of what they are actually working on(Ratten, 2023). Therefore, the increasing AI-level of Metaverse training systems strongly requires that content be both sound and correct. The Metaverse provides corporate India with a one-of-a-kind learning experience. The workers can use digital tools, work together as avatars alongside their colleagues and participate in scenarios closely based on real-life working conditions(Egbengwu et al., 2025).

AI often used to generate dialogue, explanations, and show evidence of problem-solving, the inclusion of these capabilities also increases susceptibility to hallucination. A single wrong word by an AI tutor is enough to miss the intended learn through cycle, and to spread incorrect facts across training sessions. Real human trainers and subject matter experts should periodically verify AI-generated content to keep it factual. Furthermore, cross-checking techniques can be used to minimize the amount of hallucination as many AI systems check for and validate a diagnosis(Jin et al., 2025). Transparency of AI decisions needs to be promoted; students should prompt to check central facts with credible sources whose authority can be verified and told that the AI generates answers. A third important remedy is the moral education of

AI(Manoharan et al., 2024). The training set must be representative, recent and akin to organization's environment. Periodic audits can be employed to root out biases or misinformation in the AI knowledge base(Godwin-Jones, 2025). For all I know, a blockchain enabled verification system can also provide the verification of what was taught and any changes made in between the training sessions. "When we have an AI that workers can trust, we will see widespread and rapid transfer of complex skills, safe training to acquire those skills and trusted reinforcement of the use of skill in work contexts(Kourtesis, 2024). But this transition will fail unless there are AI applications that are: – interpretable (through verification) and guaranteed not to hallucinate, as would be a threat against the integrity of education.

Role of Artificial Intelligence in Virtual Learning Environments:

Artificial Intelligence (AI), transformed the educational paradigms in virtual learning environment (VLE) within modern day context. Digital tools also are being used to improve classroom learning with virtual classrooms, as well as more-immersive 3D simulations. + In order to increase the engaging learning experience and efficiency, we enhance current methods with intelligent feedbacks, automation, personalization and interactivity(Wei & Jia, 2021). As virtual and online learning and teaching are being practiced in schools, colleges, & workplaces, the show has become of immense value. Individualized learning is seen as one of the main contributions of AI in VLE. Traditional learning is more one-size-fits-all, where as AI can build a personalized pace of learning based on individual student's performance and preferences. Algorithms of machine learning analyze learner's data (as for example test results, attending time, and spent time on working with the materials) in order to adapt the complexity of content and suggest appropriate resources(Zahrae et al., 2024). For instance, if a student is struggling to master a certain math concept, the AI system could automatically provide more practice problems or simplified explanations. This personalized focus allows students to grasp the material effectively, and it helps to build self-confidence(Georgouli, 2011). The other primary use is as intelligent tutor system (ITSs). These are virtual, advice-giving and correcting gnomes, offering feedback in real time about how to shape them. They can echo human-like dialogue, answer questions and even sense when a student is confused. For instance, AI-powered systems like ChatGPT, adaptive learning recommendations via Coursera and a smart learning engine through Duolingo use natural language processing to interact with learners(Dogan et al., 2023). These systems will not only save time for teachers but engrain teamwork in all students, even during non-instructional times. AI also encompasses routinely used automated evaluation and feedback, which mitigates faster more objective reviews(Talukder, Lina, et al., 2024). AI can analyze assignments and homework responses by speech, text response or problem-solving approach to determine what students are struggling with. This allows teachers to track student progress and formulate interventions for those who need extra help. In addition, AI can identify and understand patterns across multiple students about teaching practices and curricular designs(Rivas et al., 2021). Realistic and adaptable contexts are a crucial part of simulations as well as immersive virtual learning environments, including the Metaverse, 46 using AI to help develop such surroundings. AI can do this, for instance we have in virtual medical teaching labs, and also in real teaching labs," he added with patients that behave as the trainee would expect according to their activities, including physical problems(Luck & Aylett, 2000). It's also a great way to practice without fear of new consequences IRL. And there also are speech recognition software, language translation software and text- to-speech software that can help learners with disabilities and language barriers join in the world of virtual learning. Once these barriers are removed, AI will democratize the educational experience(Fatahi et al., 2016). Virtual learning environments are really different now with AI as it is more interactive, adaptive and inclusive. AI will ensure that students are able to receive more valuable learning experience and meaningful engagements by adopting one-on-one study trips, personalized tutoring or automatic testing through full immersive simulators(Hasegawa et al., 2025). In a world changing fast through technology, AI and virtual learning will combine to shape the future of education with smart, adaptable, engaging systems that can adjust to meet learner needs from around the world(Dhiraj et al., 2023).

Understanding AI Hallucinations:

Rise of Technology: As one of the most powerful technologies in today's world, artificial intelligence (AI) has already spread to fields such as education, health, business and entertainment. But for all its dazzling features and capabilities, artificial intelligence is far from perfect. AI hallucinations one of the main problems with AI systems is known as AI hallucinations, especially of a large language model and a generative algorithm(Kamel, 2024). This principle is also important in the context of building AI systems that are reliable and trustworthy. The terror of AI, the latest and horrifying trend to emerge in education, health, business and entertainment(Kamel, 2024). But as cool as all this potential may sound, A.I. Not infallible. This is a phenomenon expert's call "AI hallucinations," and it's one of the big problems with artificial intelligence systems, especially large language models and generative algorithms which are important for reliable and trustworthy AI-based applications at the heart of AI hallucinations lies the training of these systems(Magesh et al., 2025). The AI models are trained on massive amounts of data that includes books, articles, images and internet content. For example, in the context of language and image generation, they learn to discover patterns and relationships between words or pixels to generate new outputs during training. But, it's not always the case because they don't actually know anything so sometimes they'll draw a false conclusion or just make up what's missing. This process of guessing can produce open but wrong answer, because input question is ambiguous or out-of-model's knowledge scope(Rathkopf, 2025). AI-induced hallucinations took many forms, Ruff reported. Factual hallucinations occur when AI gives incorrect information, like the wrong date or a scientific "fact." For rational hallucinations, it follows from correct information to incorrect conclusion because of an unsound reasoning process. Context-based hallucinations arise when an AI cross-pollinates irrelevant data or misreads the nature of a conversation. When it comes to creative pursuits, such as painting or storytelling, occasional hallucinations may not do much harm – indeed, in some instances they could even be seen as a good thing(Torres, 2025). But hallucinations could lead to misinformation and bad decisions in professions such as medicine, the law or education. AI hallucinations have effects above all in the work domain, or even in the stimulants sector(Kumar et al., 2025). For example, a system of AI healthcare assistant prescribing the wrong dosage or an educational chatbot which states a scientific principle erroneously by failing to provide accurate information, it may mislead the users and prospects about AI systems. So one of the biggest problems AI development faces is how to detect and stop hallucinations(Gosmar & Dahl, 2025). There are a few ideas to contain AIs hallucinating. One of the methods is quality data in training on clean and different data. A second is human-in-the-loop verification, in which human specialists examine AI-produced results to evaluate whether they are true. Fact-checking algorithms and confidence scoring tools are also being developed by researchers who caution users that their response may be an untrustworthy one. One of the strengths and the limitations has come through AI hallucinations(Zhang et al., 2024). Even if AI can handle enormous amounts of data, it will not know the actual meaning. Managing and distinguishing hallucinations are important in order for AI to become a useful and ethical tool for society. By covering the technological advances with a human sense of responsibility, we can make sure that AI-systems will be smart and reliable.

REAL-WORLD EXAMPLES AND CASE STUDIES RELATED TO AI HALLUCINATIONS:

Google's Bard Chatbot Hallucination (2023):

When the artificial intelligence chatbot Bard offered inaccurate information at its first public outing in February 2023, the fact was newsworthy. When asked about its findings, Bard even boldly declared that the James Webb Space Telescope had taken the first images of an exoplanet(Jamaluddin et al., 2023). In fact another telescope had captured the first such image years earlier. This assertion of an erroneous fact with certainty sent Google's stock plummeting, and caused everyone to wonder whether generative AI models could be trusted. Tip: Incomplete information or generalization can make even the most sophisticated AI respond incorrectly(Kim et al., 2025). AI-generated information needs to be verified, especially if it is shared in public or professional settings.

ChatGPT Legal Case Hallucination (2023):

Two lawyers recently used ChatGPT to help write a legal script for a case in an actual U.S. court. Referencing Fake Cases Marked by made-up case names, citations and summaries, the AI-written paper included references to a few phony court cases. The court's inquiry determined that the samples were fabricated by AI to appear competent(Munir, 2025). The lawyers were disciplined for giving inaccurate information.

Guide: A reminder of the consequences that relying on AI hallucinations, unfact-checked, can pose in the real world. With something as important as law, or medicine, you're not going to get a computer that's able to just suddenly replace people and never make mistakes.

Meta's Galactica Model Incident (2022):

In 2022 Meta, the parent company of Facebook, introduced Galactica – an AI model – to help scholars develop scientific content and summarize scholarly articles. But users quickly found that Galactica was creating convincing but totally untrue research papers, fake citations and incorrect information days after it launched. For example, it generated journal names or new author inventors when queried for specific topics(Chartier-Edwards et al., 2025). Galactica was quickly taken down by Meta in response to being railed upon by scientists and AI experts. Lesson:Hallucinations YAWP can quite literally spread fake news deceptively close to reality, when using AI models in an academic or scientific context, undermining the trust researchers have in research.

The Metaverse as a Training Platform:

The concept of the Metaverse, a shared immersive virtual world in which users can interact with a computer-generated environment and other users through digital avatars, is revolutionizing how companies train and educate their staff. The Metaverse, through a combination of artificial intelligence (AI), augmented reality

(AR) and virtual reality (VR), offers an exciting environment for practicing practical skills. Metaverse training is experiential learning, also known as "learning by doing." That's very different than the e-learning that comes to mind for most of us a format often focused on reading, watching videos or taking quizzes(Hajjami & Park, 2024). "I think that being able to create these high-fidelity learning environments where you can be fully immersed is one of the biggest benefits," he says. Learners can participate in high fidelity simulations for complex procedures, emergencies or work settings themselves. For one, in controlled digital environments engineers can run through the motions of machinery at work, and pilots can rehearse their flight moves and medical students perform surgery on virtual patients(MiTra, 2023). It empowers students to be more confident and competent users when they ultimately encounter them in their professional lives. Two other important gains are the socialization and co-operation.

Students from a large geography can collaborate directly and problem solves working in the Metaverse. Employees will be able to engage in leadership simulations, team bonding activities and group conversations all using avatars and coexisting virtual worlds. Interactions like these, they say, encourage cooperation, empathy and social skills that don't come easily in traditional computer-based online courses. This is probably a more accurate description for professional and corporate training than traditional teamwork. Metaverse also provides the opportunity for tailored and personal learning experiences. When AI is taken into account, the model can evaluate what a learner did in a given task and consider it as target behavior for learning content optimization(Almeida et al., 2023). An employee who has difficulty with a security "effort" can automatically be assigned extra practice modules; while more advanced students can be graduated to increasingly difficult challenges. This flexibility ensures that valuable time is not wasted on unnecessary training and effective, relevant learning for all. Organizationally, Metaverse provides scalable, low-cost training(Xu et al., 2024). These travels, costs and resources can be expensive in time and money for face-to-face learning.

It's incredibly easy to update training content and set up headphones for businesses that need to train thousands of people at once. Similarly, both achievements and progress can also be logged automatically, giving managers the data they need to know what skills are being learned and what still needs further improvement.But there are also negatives to transforming the Metaverse into a testing ground(Gu et al., 2023). Expensive setup could restrict usage, require expensive hardware (e.g. VR headsets) and introduce some technical issues. Moreover, security and accuracy of data should be guaranteed as well as the ethical use of that kind of cloud. AI delusions might be a thing, where virtual assistants or training simulations misinform their human handlers and demand that tough decisions have been made and are being made. Such mistakes result either in misleading information, heatset or improper cooling (if support is not provided). For all these obstacles, the Metaverse will become part of workforce education in the future(Lee et al., 2022). Simulated based training has already worked in many markets, such as manufacturing, retail, healthcare and aviation. For instance, Boeing uses AR tools to train aircraft mechanics on how to do complex assemblies. Walmart is also educating its staff via virtual reality (VR) simulations on customer scenarios and emergencies. They show how immersive technologies can help improve accuracy, efficiency and engagement in learning. Today, Metaverse is an overachieving classroom that brings theories to life. It allows the student to explore a safe but realistic environment with the possibility of customized experiences, live feedback and simulations. And the meeting of AI, VR and AR in the metaverse is going to revolutionize how companies train their employees to win in a world driven by speed with technology(Stanoevska-Slabeva, 2022).

CHALLENGES: TECHNICAL, ETHICAL, AND PSYCHOLOGICAL:

This concept of expertise and how it's miles used by now not most effective corporations but additionally students, has been altered completely thru the mixing of Artificial Intelligence (AI) and The Metaverse into educational establishments' operations. Although those technological solutions are attracting interest because they middle on college students and provide personalized deep mastering reports, their technique brings some of technological, ethical and mental troubles which should be revised to ensure their secure use(Shymko, 2025). To make persuasive, simply and sustainable virtual studying environments, its miles vital to take on these demanding situations.

Technical Weavers:Based on blockchain, AI, AR and VR generation to develop Metaverse. To triumph over those technical problems, right here are huge demanding situations: Infrastructure and get right of entry to. You ought to also have a powerful processor and a consistent high-velocity internet connection no much less so that you can attain the ones wi-fi, immersive stories. Besides the Ukraine warfare, many institutions --specifically in poorer countries -- face bottlenecks like this on the subject of schooling results; get right of entry to and assets. The accuracy and reliability of data pose some other technical dilemma. When AI hallucinations depict false merchandise or deceptive statistics output, in Metaverse education techniques they have not most effective distorted education but also brought about misinformation. Still, virtual environments often involve a number of biometrics which includes a user's physiological and behavioral states together with private developments but more with regards to securing database safety capabilities for the full-size amounts of personal data saved there. Technological disasters, gadget delays, and statistics breaches can also infer severe disruptions in education as well as user agree with issues.

Ethical challenges: "In AI-powered online education, there are crucial ethical considerations to think about too."The first and most important thing that people have been concerned with is data privacy. Since it collects so much data including user voice, movement and emotional reactions, the Metaverse has the capacity to become another field for abuses or unauthorized use." Institutional data collection, retention and use should be transparent. Another moral issue to grapple with is bias and fairness in AI algorithms.If a machine learning model is trained on biased data, it will produce unfair biases or even discriminates in its assessments and recommendations which will affect this group of employees or students harshly." Misinformation from AI can make it difficult to determine accountability for what is causing a certain action. Virtual environments often overlook who the guilty party actually is -- the AI, its instructor or developer. For that reason, there needs to be on orders of openness and transparency in ethics.

The mental effects of working and learning in the Metaverse: If students persistently use VR or AR devices for extended periods, they may experience motion sickness and eye strain. The own challenge is focusing.VR, AR, or mixed reality devices could potentially lead to digital fatigue, which would cause problems like difficulty concentrating and inadequate comprehension. Now ways may even appear where one has no actual purpose. Just as the Metaverse is a virtual world created out of networked computer-generated connections, the excessive reliance on avatars and simulations leads to thin real-world relationships. It is Latin for getting along well. Even more distressing is that emotional intelligence, communications ability and empathy three of the hardest things to teach people – are all being seriously affected by this way with AI. In particular, young people in psychological distress can get bogged down with limited identities or feel alienated because a virtual environment allows for continual existence. As threats to our technology, ethics, and psychology, AI and the Metaverse also help us achieve our goals in advancing how we study. Thus to continue its acceptance, things such as bias in algorithms, the concern over privacy, neglect of infrastructure investment by governments as well as user wellness must be confronted. Websites that integrate technical progress and ethics with mental support can build high-tech, healthy, fair and warm online educational spaces.

Intersection of AI and Metaverse in Employee Training: With the speedy improvement of IT, the manner businesses conceive developing their employees has modified and frequently for higher than earlier than in history. As we bypass the time stamp diary which started over 3 months in the past now. Metaverse will carry a new technology for education. It teaches with immersion, intelligence and individuality. The merger of these technologies is changing not best how workers examine for paintings, but it aids in growing conditions which can be secure enough to research and reproduce(K & Rodriguez, 2023). Often known as the 3-d digital global, the metaverse offers completely immersive experience-primarily based learning surroundings. AI makes it more thrilling once more because it has higher simulations, smart comments and adaptable systems. Using these technologies in combination makes a training officer capable of get educated as if they surely are there, and from that actually being e-studying or a lecture room placing.Among those attributes its strongest use case for A.I. is personalized tutoring(Bordegoni & Ferrise, 2023). AIs can produce tailored manual numbers based on performance monitoring, skills overview and proficiency gamut for each individual student. (For example, one such A.I.-driven avatar is an aversion that you may practice with the way it responds to tone, body language and problem-solving skills in virtual-store role play, allowing live feedback.) And if a worker is having trouble mastering particular scenarios, the system can be adjusted to automatically bring in the difficulty level or provide extra aspects of scrimmage. Every student will be given individualized instruction. And this is possible because A.I. lets us simulate in the metaverse dynamics which are as complex and life-like as they would be outside it. Students also can communicate with actual-time encoding and emotionally genuine herbal-speakme A.I. Avatars, not restrained to pre-recorded characters(Marabelli & Lirio, 2025). For instance, AI may simulate affected person publicity in medical education with extraordinary responses depending at the trainee's commutation fashion or choice selections. AI can also recreate hard company scenarios, including management woes, bargaining and crisis manage. These real-life reports can inculcate decision-making, empathy and important-wondering abilities which might be difficult to supply the usage of more tradional methods. Producing statistics-driven insights is every other massive win for AI in metaverse training. From each digital meeting emerge valuable records approximately boolean correctnesses, times to transport on, collaborativeness and different styles(Shah et al., 2025). These may be harnessed by using AI systems to supply in reality strong analytics that inform you which employees are growing or falling in the back of inside the lengthy-time period developments of all the ones metrics. Managers can apply these insights to find employees with excessive ability or enhance the training system, also layout extra targeted upskilling. AI evaluation and real-time mastering feedbacks on overall performance form circles of jointly useful gaining knowledge of which not best bolster the corporation, but assist its crew to keep a continuity of excellence.Butthere are also new problems offered with AI and the Metaverse blended. The Invalid content, where the version produces wrong or deceptive noise, is a key problem in AI hallucination. It may also lead to a situation where employees are taught improper models or techniques in an educational setting. Only with a human-in-the-loop workflow at organizations to ensure that domain experts routinely reconcile all AI generated information can this threat be defended against mentioned din the table 01 (Aggarwal et al., 2025).

Table 1. Intersection of AI and Metaverse in Employee Training

Aspect	Role of AI	Role of Metaverse	Intersection / Combined Impact
Personalized Learning	AI analyzes employee data to create customized learning paths.	The Metaverse provides immersive 3D virtual environments for training.	Together, they deliver personalized and experiential learning.
Real-time Feedback	AI gives instant feedback based on performance analytics.	The Metaverse visualizes this feedback through virtual avatars or trainers.	Enables continuous improvement and real-time correction.
Simulation-based Training	AI generates dynamic, adaptive scenarios based on learner progress.	The Metaverse provides realistic virtual spaces to practice those scenarios.	Creates hands-on, practical skill development safely and efficiently.
Collaboration & Team Learning	AI analyzes group interactions and communication effectiveness.	The Metaverse connects employees in shared virtual spaces.	Enhances interactive and collaborative team training.
Performance Tracking	AI continuously monitors progress and provides detailed analytics.	The Metaverse displays performance data on virtual dashboards.	Promotes transparent, data-driven evaluation.
Cost & Safety Efficiency	AI optimizes training content, saving time and resources.	The Metaverse offers a risk-free simulation environment.	Together, they ensure cost-effective and safe training solutions.

Furthermore, since virtual reality environments often gather sensitive biometric and behavioral data (e.g. facial expressions (i.e., emotions), behavior, etc.), data privacy and security is also required. Ultimately, there are obvious benefits from Metaverse training with AI. Many of these principles are already being adopted by several international corporations. Accenture, for instance, brings on new hires through a virtual Metaverse campus where they can get to know colleagues and receive lessons on business culture. Walmart consists of VR and AI simulations for customer service and crisis situations to improve the confidence and productivity. The crossroads of AI and the MetaverseAAPL The junction of AI with the evolving Metaverse1,433 In which AI meets the "Metaverse" -- a step forward in worker skillingauxilioaux. The intersection of synthetic intelligence and things just like the metaverdesruGetting to the point in which AI crosses paths with developing Metaverses! Taken together, they provide an interactive, adaptable and information knowledgeable learning enjoys which brings the classroom towards fact(Lim et al., 2024). Those who seize it will in acquiring the vital abilities to do more with less regulatory guidance tap right into a body of workers that's smarter, bendy and move organized for the destiny as era continues to innovate.

IMPACT OF AI HALLUCINATIONS ON SKILL DEVELOPMENT:

AI has converted corporate schooling and training. It makes gaining knowledge of pathways private, interactive and green. The integration of AI structures into work coaching programs has triggered every other greater subtle undertaking AI hallucinations. This happens whilst an AI set of rules generates fake, deceptive, or even completely fake information. But it's far taken into consideration to be relied on records resources(Qiu, 2024). Although on the surface hardly noticeable, those types of glitches can substantially affect the forms of matters we examine and how much confidence we will have in learnable competencies handed down from AI-mediated systems. With the aid of Artificial Intelligence (AI), company education has been transformed. What it achieves is personalized in addition to being efficient and interactive. Yet one greater, queasy confrontational trouble has been raised by using the anthropocentric flip Ai systems are taking in layout now produces the question: AI hallucinations(Cheng et al., 2025). These occurrences are while an artificial intelligence (AI) device comes out with content material this is fake and misleading but appears to be completely legitimate. These first-rate-grained mistakes in accuracy can alter what we analyze or how dependable discovered skills are for Ai systems.One of the biggest is that AI hallucinations degrade, instead of adding to, knowledge. What little knowledge there is has to flow well, in a larger stream downward and out of mentors/teachers and or knowledge systems if skills are meant to emerge(Salvagno et al., 2023). Misinformation or misinterpretation can occur by learners themselves if the AI-generated content has errors. That is especially the case for fields like engineering, health care and aviation where even a smidge of bogus information can come with life-altering implications(Kumar, 2024). For example, a medical student who trains on an AI-driven simulation that makes the wrong diagnosis could form bad habits that inflict harm when operating in offices and clinics. Also among negative effects is the learners' loss of confidence. Learners, who constantly receive bad or conflicting information, may start to wonder whether AI-based systems are all that reliable. “Digital learning is about trust, and without trust in the AI tutor as a source of information they can rely on, students can stop wanting to use it, or stop bothering to look things up,” he said. Conflicting messages can lead to mental confusion and a loss of motivation anyway, in the belief that you don't really have this learning-thing down right(Dominique Salamin et al., 2023). AI hallucination also destroys the quality of hypothesis. Learners are rated by multiple AI systems who also offer differing challenges and feedback. Systems of the type described have been observed to provide a false perception of competence or incompetence if the system misinterprets user response, etc. A student may think that they have become proficient at a skill, while the flawed AI system takes only shallow, flawed measurements. This discredits certification and leveling systems built upon AI. In the Sunday Times article, Aaron Bastani explains, "It's not that institutions will be deterred [by social networks], but there will have to be human validation in real time." The training data created by AI may have to be checked by human experts on a regular basis, and there can be arrangements to cross-validate it from more than one AI model or database. Transparency is also important, they note; students should know when AI-generated material is probabilistic or not 100% sure. The detrimental effects of hallucinations could also be minimized by education promoting critical thinking and fact testing. AI has the potential to transform training completely, but AI hallucinations put learning gains at risk and undermine their validity. These hallucinations in turn would pervert training programs, adulterate knowledge and shatter confidence(Kumar et al., 2023). It is better to have a mix of automation and humans watching over. In this light, AI may yet be a faithful partner in authoring practical and high quality employable skills for the future work force – as long as schools and companies pay attention to the quality of data they use, apply ethical design principles and monitor the platform regularly as discussed in the table 02.

Table 2. Structured Framework: Hallucination Management Process.

Stage	Objective	Key Activities	Tools / Techniques	Outcome
Detection	Identify when and where hallucinations occur in AI outputs.	Monitor responses for factual or logical inconsistencies. - Use benchmarks and truth-check datasets. Apply anomaly or confidence scoring.	Fact-checking models- Consistency checks- Human review	Hallucinated or inaccurate content is recognized.
Diagnosis	Understand the cause of hallucination.	Analyze model reasoning and training data.- Identify bias, data gaps, or prompt ambiguity. Categorize hallucination type (factual, contextual, reasoning).	Error analysis- Causal tracing- Model interpretability tools	Root cause of hallucination is clearly understood.
Mitigation	Reduce or prevent hallucinations from recurring.	Improve prompt engineering and grounding methods. Fine-tune with verified datasets.- Add retrieval or fact-verification modules.	Retrieval-Augmented Generation (RAG)- Knowledge graphs- Reinforcement learning with human feedback (RLHF)	AI produces more accurate and context-aligned responses.

continued on following page

Table 2. Continued

Stage	Objective	Key Activities	Tools / Techniques	Outcome
Validation	Verify that corrections are effective.	Compare AI outputs with ground truth data. Conduct human expert evaluation.- Track hallucination rate over time.	Automated testing- Peer review- Performance metrics (e.g., factual accuracy score)	Confirmed reduction in hallucination frequency and severity.
Continuous Improvement	Maintain long-term reliability and adaptability.	Update datasets and models regularly.s Collect user feedback for ongoing optimization.- Monitor real-world usage patterns.	Continuous monitoring systems- Active learning pipelines	Sustained improvement in accuracy, trust, and reliability.

ENSURING ACCURACY AND RELIABILITY IN AI-DRIVEN EMPLOYEE TRAINING:

Content quality has become a concern with more and more companies applying the Metaverse and AI for staff training departures from what was taught may arise. If world leaders and ordinary people alike base their choices on evidence that is forged or plain wrong, they will in effect be choosing to make mistakes. And whole policies bred of bad information. AI-generated misinformation -information hallucinated to be true, confidently assured but false or misleading has emerged as a secondary effect in certain AI systems (generative models in particular). So from such a training environment, mistakes will be brought over to occur in the real world with dire consequences to users(Oladele et al., 2025). The trust of the users was put on product learning skills; he will be unobjective and bias. Laboratories need to build strong systems around with technology, human oversight and ethical guidance to leverage the upside of AI-trained models and mitigate unwanted outcomes. “Building models and verifying the quality of your data are just two of the early processes behind ensuring accuracy. The quality of the sources used to train AI models is an indication of how reliable those artificial brains will be. Use of well-annotated, diverse and comprehensive datasets helps reduce bias and errors(Ara & Ahmad, 2025). Besides that, so as to ensure that AI does not end up just guiding how to make defective or unsafe products it has to be fed established practices and case histories. All will require updating on a regular basis to take account of new developments in industry standards, laws or norms. The assurance that good data is maintained ensures that AI-avier is produced from proper facts different to uncertain and obsolete sources. HITL systems also play a role in trouble-shooting and avoiding operational failures. This procedure allows human experts to look over, verify and think about AI training materials before they are presented to students. Expert clinicians can verify AI simulations of a patient in medical training scenarios to see if learners have the correct procedure(Talukder, Khan, et al., 2024).

Such real-time updating is currently only possible in training simulations with HITL technology, since this technology would enable the interaction to occur within those parameters.When human judgment is added to AI effectiveness dimensions, phony information becomes much less likely, even though not eliminated.Strength could be enhanced through cross verification and truth confirmation in specific affairs of its operation.Bull in the organization also vets materials before sharing to ensure they are in good order for scholars, using authoritative databases and more than one Biehl notes AI.Obviously, an AI-created technical document such as that shown here designed to identify the repair kits or the like would in fact be contrary to in-house documents, government regulations and plant manuals.By introducing verification mechanisms, especially in instances where a task procedure is complex or critical for safety; businesses reduce the likelihood of errors reaching job holders.The issue isn't just about accuracy. Ethics are a big part of it.A.I. Systems should be open and honest about the limits of their output, including when an answer given is uncertain or probabilistic.Students need to be taught to question AI's output and verify it against reliable sources.In the future we must also ensure that those who learn biased things online not have their opportunities for future learning and employment curtailed merely because of societal bias by consciously making provision for fairness in all teaching methods -- concealing close biases through another mechanism as well as introducing information on some thin hex-think paries.Further, feedback loops and continuous surveillance are both desirable. It's time for network platforms powered by A.I to keep detailed records of all such interactions, each performance and fault, so that they can look for patterns of systemic issues. In addition, regular audits and iteration offer an opportunity for refinement of response quality, content updating and fast response to emerging problems. Thus the analytic information provided by these systems also shows how employees are learning, which may enable companies to focus their training efforts more effectively.In short, using protections like identity confirmed by blockchain, correcting version histories and securely storing data could produce a more accountable system that utility. In this way the teachers cannot help but feel confident that students have reliable, vandal-resistant materials for studying. To attain quality and reliability in AI-supported staff training, we need a balanced package consisting of ethical design, human judgment, good data and persistent management.Integrating technological innovation, testing and openness is what makes organizations create reliable environments in which virtual learning takes place and this enables practitioners to use their capabilities more deeply, and provides them with a sense of self-efficacy and confidence such that practitioners actually put what they have learnt into practice.

Future Projections and Carnations of AI-Guided Metaverse Training: With the application of Artificial Intelligence (AI) and the Metaverse, now everyone can acquire a new form of life-simulative, personal data-grazed and revolutionary model of trainee recruitment. This type of technology implies that now all types of employees worldwide could easily collaborate with one another since it is not only real but also safe, but also personal feedback since they now have an opportunity to know what they made wrong. Perhaps, one of the benefits is the ability to master new skills faster; another is greater immersion and preparation to work in hard conditions.

CONCLUSION AND RECOMMENDATIONS:

AI and the metaverse will introduce an entirely new training - the type of training that is more personalized according to your studying habits and pace. In addition, all this is recorded on tape: That is to say that every step in the training process can be operationalized and enhanced workers will be in simulated and the safety of environments that otherwise would be hostile to new hires the Pros are that on the positive side AI-inspired training will help the person to get skilled/even onboard a new job in a shorter amount of time than the old method of knowledgestral hours weeks to months before you are ready to teach. Any bad news? Well... as much as there is the positive side of AI-driven employee training, it is definitely not a bed of roses. As a matter of fact, there are a number of important disadvantages to this strategy - and the worst of all the ones we have come to refer to as AI hallucinations in which our machine learning structures draw on dramatically misleading data or even generates full-blown hallucinations. One of the possible ways to remain correct in the learning patterns (and consequently skills) and user trust is avoiding such hallucinations. It is our responsibility, therefore, to surmount these issues and make sure overcoming of which is the key to the successful functioning and reliability of the AI-driven Metaverse training.

In order to have maximized benefits and a minimum risk, some key recommendations will arise:

I. **Human Monitoring:** Implement human in-the-loop solutions to check the content generated by AI, verify accuracy and human oversight in the training process.
II. **Quality Data:** Train AI on confirmed, varied and accurate datasets in time to reduce hallucinations and bias.
III. **Transparency and Feedback:** Be open to the limitation of AI-generated outputs and also encourage students to verify significant data by their own. Live Monitoring: Track the performance of learners and AI behaviors with analytics,

update and correct content in real-time.Ethical and Inclusive Design: Get back to AI systems that value Privacy, fairness and accessibility, enabling fair learning process of all employees!

Active Evolvement of the Newly Appearing Technologies: To feel a little reality, add mixing with blockchain verification, the concept of digital twins and multimodal AI to a little trust or even the way people think about learning. Metaverse AI also redefines learning, and it can also revolutionize training of employees. Integrating the innovative technology with strict control and regulations. Organizations have discovered output and functional measures that have become tools of high quality learning experiences that can be relied upon by the staff. They have provided employees with not only new skills but also confidence to proceed in an environment that is quickly changing in the workplace.

FUTURE DIRECTIONS:

It is in its infancy, but the shift towards AI and Metaprince towards personnel training will bring a significant shift in how we bite the manpower: it will enable more adaptive learning systems to be more effective; and the next generation of apps will be increasingly comprehensive on behavioral and cognitive analytics.Alternatively, though it can be suggested that the performance-based content adaptation can be achieved with the current AI models; however, the next generation applications will be a lot more detailed in terms of behavioral and cognitive analytics. These will change on-the-fly pacing, difficulty and modality of these elements according to the learning requirements in a manner that would best predict the skills that would be learned. In case AI observes patterns amid training errors of multiple students, on the fly it can generate new conditions; to concentrate on the weak areas of driving on-going development at any given time.Immersive learning is another intriguing area of AI research multimodal. With the help of computer vision, haptic feedback and emotion recognition, as well as natural language interaction, the experience will be much more realistic and interactive with AI. The workers will also interact with the avatars that can simulate emotions, react to non-verbal and verbal interactions and provide localized recommendations depending on the situation-training, such as communication, leadership, negotiation, and customer services, where human judgment and social communication are essential. The time when digital certification and blockchain will become mundane will be the same. Intelligent systems that track training through accomplishment with a sense of confidence and hard data; endorse learning programming and skills satisfaction indicators. It can be especially applicable to such practice oriented industries as the healthcare sector, air and finance. And companies will be taking the hybrid AI-human systems further. Humans collaborate with AI, to derive signs on findings, situations and suggestions, and remain point by literary worth. A combination of the agility and flexibility of AI with human supervision is necessary, which is ensured by such collaborative manner of working. In any case, elements of AI hallucinations, socially acceptable norms and AI biases will eventually dictate the deployment of these latter systems. Such virtual training services with high standards of training evaluation procedures, rigorous surveillance and ethical foundation will be a success and safe one in the future of training and upskilling in Metaverse using in. This knowledge and skills when put in the hands of the workers is incredibly crucial whenever the tasks that they undertake continue to become more complex and dynamic. In case the AI technology, immersive technologies, ethical design embedded in principles and safety of skills development and training facilities (upskilling realistic work situation) can be applied on the scale.

REFERENCES

Aggarwal, A., Sadhna, P., & Daipuria, P. (2025). The Digital Frontier: AI and Metaverse as Catalysts for Organizational Justice and Employee Engagement in EdTech. *Global Business Review, 09721509251344444*. Advance online publication. DOI: 10.1177/09721509251344444

Almeida, L. G. G., Vasconcelos, N. V. D., Winkler, I., & Catapan, M. F. (2023). Innovating Industrial Training with Immersive Metaverses: A Method for Developing Cross-Platform Virtual Reality Environments. *Applied Sciences (Basel, Switzerland), 13*(15), 8915. DOI: 10.3390/app13158915

Ara, A., & Ahmad, A. K. (2025). Building Trust in AI-Driven HR Systems: Employee Perceptions for AI-HR. *2025 Eighth International Women in Data Science Conference at Prince Sultan University (WiDS PSU)*, 241–249. DOI: 10.1109/WiDS-PSU64963.2025.00055

Bordegoni, M., & Ferrise, F. (2023). Exploring the Intersection of Metaverse, Digital Twins, and Artificial Intelligence in Training and Maintenance. *Journal of Computing and Information Science in Engineering, 23*(6), 060806. DOI: 10.1115/1.4062455

Chartier-Edwards, N., Grenier, E., & Goujon, V. (2025). Galactica's dis-assemblage: Meta's beta and the omega of post-human science. *AI & Society, 40*(4), 2069–2081. DOI: 10.1007/s00146-024-02088-7

Cheng, A., Nagesh, V., Eller, S., Grant, V., & Lin, Y. (2025). Exploring AI Hallucinations of ChatGPT: Reference Accuracy and Citation Relevance of ChatGPT Models and Training Conditions. *Simulation in Healthcare: The Journal of the Society for Simulation in Healthcare*. DOI: 10.1097/SIH.0000000000000877

Dhiraj, A., Kumar, S., & Rani, D. (2023). Social and Emotional Learning: Keys to the Success of E-Learning. In Sharma, P. C., Bansal, R., & Singh, R. (Eds.), (pp. 119–130). Advances in Educational Technologies and Instructional Design. IGI Global., DOI: 10.4018/978-1-6684-7639-0.ch008

Dogan, M. E., Goru Dogan, T., & Bozkurt, A. (2023). The Use of Artificial Intelligence (AI) in Online Learning and Distance Education Processes: A Systematic Review of Empirical Studies. *Applied Sciences (Basel, Switzerland), 13*(5), 3056. DOI: 10.3390/app13053056

Dominique Salamin, A., Russo, D., & Rueger, D. (2023, November 3). ChatGPT, an Excellent Liar: How Conversational Agents' Hallucinations Impact Learning and Teaching. *Proceedings of the 7th International Conference on Teaching, Learning and Education*. the 7th International Conference on Teaching, Learning and Education. DOI: 10.33422/6th.iacetl.2023.11.100

Egbengwu, V., Garn, W., & Turner, C. J. (2025). Metaverse for Manufacturing: Leveraging Extended Reality Technology for Human-Centric Production Systems. *Sustainability*, *17*(1), 280. DOI: 10.3390/su17010280

Fatahi, S., Moradi, H., & Kashani-Vahid, L. (2016). A survey of personality and learning styles models applied in virtual environments with emphasis on e-learning environments. *Artificial Intelligence Review*, *46*(3), 413–429. DOI: 10.1007/s10462-016-9469-7

Georgouli, K. (2011). Virtual Learning Environments—An Overview. *2011 15th Panhellenic Conference on Informatics*, 63–67. DOI: 10.1109/PCI.2011.13

Godwin-Jones, R. (2025). AI and VR Converge: The Future of Language Learning in an Emerging Metaverse. In Lan, Y.-J., Qi, G. Y., & Chun, D. (Eds.), *AI-Mediated Language Education in the Metaverse Era* (pp. 221–246). Springer Nature Singapore., DOI: 10.1007/978-981-95-0245-5_11

Gosmar, D., & Dahl, D. A. (2025). *Hallucination Mitigation using Agentic AI Natural Language-Based Frameworks* (Version 1). arXiv. DOI: 10.48550/ARXIV.2501.13946

Gu, J., Wang, J., Guo, X., Liu, G., Qin, S., & Bi, Z. (2023). A Metaverse-Based Teaching Building Evacuation Training System With Deep Reinforcement Learning. *IEEE Transactions on Systems, Man, and Cybernetics. Systems*, *53*(4), 2209–2219. DOI: 10.1109/TSMC.2022.3231299

Hajjami, O., & Park, S. (2024). Using the metaverse in training: Lessons from real cases. *European Journal of Training and Development*, *48*(5/6), 555–575. DOI: 10.1108/EJTD-12-2022-0144

Hasegawa, T., Yamada, H., Nishimura, H., & Kobayashi, M. (2025). The Role of AI and Virtual Learning Environments in Enhancing STEM Education. [IJESTE]. *International Journal of Education, Science, Technology, and Engineering*, *8*(1), 1–10. DOI: 10.36079/lamintang.ijeste-0801.746

Jamaluddin, J., Abd Gaffar, N., & Din, N. S. S. (2023). Hallucination: A key challenge to Artificial Intelligence-Generated writing. *Malaysian Family Physician : the Official Journal of the Academy of Family Physicians of Malaysia*, *18*, 68. DOI: 10.51866/lte.527

Jin, L., Shen, Z., Alhur, A. A., & Naeem, S. B. (2025). Exploring the determinants and effects of artificial intelligence (AI) hallucination exposure on generative AI adoption in healthcare. *Information Development, 02666669251340954*. Advance online publication. DOI: 10.1177/02666669251340954

K, H., & Rodriguez, R. V. (2023). *The Business of the Metaverse: How to Maintain the Human Element Within this New Business Reality* (1st ed.). Productivity Press. DOI: 10.4324/b23404

Kamel, H. (2024). Understanding the impact of AI Hallucinations on the university community. *Cybrarians Journal, 73*, 111–134. DOI: 10.70000/cj.2024.73.622

Kim, Y., Jeong, H., Chen, S., Li, S. S., Lu, M., Alhamoud, K., Mun, J., Grau, C., Jung, M., Gameiro, R., Fan, L., Park, E., Lin, T., Yoon, J., Yoon, W., Sap, M., Tsvetkov, Y., Liang, P., Xu, X., . . . Breazeal, C. (2025). *Medical Hallucinations in Foundation Models and Their Impact on Healthcare* (Version 1). arXiv. DOI: 10.48550/ARXIV.2503.05777

Kourtesis, P. (2024). A Comprehensive Review of Multimodal XR Applications, Risks, and Ethical Challenges in the Metaverse. *Multimodal Technologies and Interaction*, *8*(11), 98. DOI: 10.3390/mti8110098

Kumar, S. (2024). The Role of Digital Marketing on Customer Engagement in the Hospitality Industry. In Bansal, R., Ngah, A. H., Chakir, A., & Pruthi, N. (Eds.), (pp. 177–191). Advances in Business Information Systems and Analytics. IGI Global., DOI: 10.4018/979-8-3693-0815-8.ch010

Kumar, S., Dhiraj, A., Shah, M. A., & Rani, D. (2023). Application of Metaverse in the Hospitality Industry. In Bansal, R., Qalati, S. A., & Chakir, A. (Eds.), (pp. 178–194). Advances in Marketing, Customer Relationship Management, and E-Services. IGI Global., DOI: 10.4018/978-1-6684-8898-0.ch011

Kumar, S., Talukder, M. B., & Tyagi, P. K. (2025). The Impact of Virtual Reality and Augmented Reality in TNE Learning. In Crawford, C. M., & Gee, T. T. (Eds.), *Motivating Engagement, Belonging, and Success in Higher Education Student Experience* (pp. 359–382). IGI Global., DOI: 10.4018/979-8-3693-8089-5.ch013

Lee, H., Woo, D., & Yu, S. (2022). Virtual Reality Metaverse System Supplementing Remote Education Methods: Based on Aircraft Maintenance Simulation. *Applied Sciences (Basel, Switzerland)*, *12*(5), 2667. DOI: 10.3390/app12052667

Lifelo, Z., Ding, J., & Ning, H., Qurat-Ul-Ain, & Dhelim, S. (2024). Artificial Intelligence-Enabled Metaverse for Sustainable Smart Cities: Technologies, Applications, Challenges, and Future Directions. *Electronics (Basel), 13*(24), 4874. DOI: 10.3390/electronics13244874

Lim, D. H., Lee, J. Y., & Park, S. (2024). The Metaverse in the Workplace: Possibilities and Implications for Human Resource Development. *Human Resource Development Review, 23*(2), 164–198. DOI: 10.1177/15344843231217174

Luck, M., & Aylett, R. (2000). Applying artificial intelligence to virtual reality: Intelligent virtual environments. *Applied Artificial Intelligence, 14*(1), 3–32. DOI: 10.1080/088395100117142

Magesh, V., Surani, F., Dahl, M., Suzgun, M., Manning, C. D., & Ho, D. E. (2025). Hallucination-Free? Assessing the Reliability of Leading AI Legal Research Tools. *Journal of Empirical Legal Studies, 22*(2), 216–242. DOI: 10.1111/jels.12413

Manoharan, G., Ashtikar, S. P., & Kumar, S. (2024). Delineation of Artificial Intelligence in the Hospitality and Tourism Industries. In Talukder, M. B., Kumar, S., & Tyagi, P. K. (Eds.), *Advances in Hospitality, Tourism, and the Services Industry* (pp. 20–42). IGI Global., DOI: 10.4018/979-8-3693-6755-1.ch002

Marabelli, M., & Lirio, P. (2025). AI and the metaverse in the workplace: DEI opportunities and challenges. *Personnel Review, 54*(3), 844–853. DOI: 10.1108/PR-04-2023-0300

MiTra, S. (2023). Metaverse: A Potential Virtual-Physical Ecosystem for Innovative Blended Education and Training. *Journal of Metaverse, 3*(1), 66–72. DOI: 10.57019/jmv.1168056

Munir, B. (2025). *Hallucinations in Legal Practice: A Comparative Case Law Analysis. SSRN.* DOI: 10.2139/ssrn.5265375

Oladele, S., Anector, M., & Foluwa, E. (2025). *AI-Powered Personalization in Employee Training and Development Programs Authors. SSRN.* DOI: 10.2139/ssrn.5226745

Qiu, Y. (2024). The Impact of LLM Hallucinations on Motor Skill Learning: A Case Study in Badminton. *IEEE Access : Practical Innovations, Open Solutions, 12*, 139669–139682. DOI: 10.1109/ACCESS.2024.3444783

Rathkopf, C. (2025). *Hallucination, reliability, and the role of generative AI in science* (Version 1). arXiv. DOI: 10.48550/ARXIV.2504.08526

Ratten, V. (2023). Editorial: ChatGPT, the metaverse and artificial intelligence: implications for family business management education. *Journal of Family Business Management, 13*(4), 821–827. DOI: 10.1108/JFBM-12-2023-199

Rivas, A., González-Briones, A., Hernández, G., Prieto, J., & Chamoso, P. (2021). Artificial neural network analysis of the academic performance of students in virtual learning environments. *Neurocomputing, 423*, 713–720. DOI: 10.1016/j.neucom.2020.02.125

Salvagno, M., Taccone, F. S., & Gerli, A. G. (2023). Artificial intelligence hallucinations. *Critical Care, 27*(1), 180. DOI: 10.1186/s13054-023-04473-y

Shah, R., Shah, S., & Pathak, P. (2025). Metaverse work culture: The emergence of virtual-first companies and HR's role. *Strategic HR Review*. Advance online publication. DOI: 10.1108/SHR-03-2025-0029

Shymko, V. (2025). Ethical challenges and strategic responses to AI integration in psychological assessment. *AI and Ethics, 5*(5), 5415–5423. DOI: 10.1007/s43681-025-00788-4

Stanoevska-Slabeva, K. (2022). *OPPORTUNITIES AND CHALLENGES OF METAVERSE FOR EDUCATION: A LITERATURE REVIEW*. 10401–10410. DOI: 10.21125/edulearn.2022.2527

Talukder, M. B., Khan, M. R., & Kumar, S. (2024). Socioeconomic Gaps and Foster Inclusive Growth: Sustainable Tourism Initiatives. In Hassan, V., Staszewska, A., & Bhartiya, S. (Eds.), *Advances in Hospitality, Tourism, and the Services Industry* (pp. 56–82). IGI Global., DOI: 10.4018/979-8-3693-5405-6.ch003

Talukder, M. B., Lina, F. Y., Kumar, S., & Khan, M. R. (2024). Data-Driven Personalization in the Sharing Economy. In Ordóñez De Pablos, P. (Ed.), (pp. 277–300). Advances in Finance, Accounting, and Economics. IGI Global., DOI: 10.4018/979-8-3693-5673-9.ch012

Torres, R. C. (2025). AI Hallucination in the Context of Education: Exploring College Students' Use of Generative AI for Academic Tasks. *2025 16th International Conference on E-Education, E-Business, E-Management and E-Learning (IC4e)*, 445–449. DOI: 10.1109/IC4e65071.2025.11075444

Wei, X., & Jia, H. (2021). A Review of the Application of Artificial Intelligence in the Virtual Learning Environment. *2021 Tenth International Conference of Educational Innovation through Technology (EITT)*, 79–82. DOI: 10.1109/EITT53287.2021.00024

Xu, W., Zhang, N., & Wang, M. (2024). The impact of interaction on continuous use in online learning platforms: A metaverse perspective. *Internet Research*, *34*(1), 79–106. DOI: 10.1108/INTR-08-2022-0600

Zahrae, F. F., Es-Sâadia, A., & Mohamed, Y. (2024). Artificial Intelligence Implementation in Virtual Learning Environment: An Overview. *2024 International Conference on Intelligent Systems and Computer Vision (ISCV)*, 1–6. DOI: 10.1109/ISCV60512.2024.10620135

Zhang, W., Zhang, C., Gu, C., Kou, J., Yuan, H., Fang, X., Duan, X., & Fang, Y. (2024). Hallucination in Large Language Models: From Mechanistic Understanding to Novel Control Frameworks. *2024 7th International Conference on Universal Village (UV)*, 1–36. DOI: 10.1109/UV63228.2024.11189226

Chapter 2
Hallucination to Harmony:
Building Reliable AI Systems in the Enterprise Metaverse

Amrik Singh
https://orcid.org/0000-0003-3598-8787
Lovely Professional University, India

ABSTRACT

The adoption of AI into enterprise metaverse has created more opportunities than ever before in immersive collaboration, automation, and intelligent decision-making. Nevertheless, the mass implementation of the generative and autonomous AI systems is limited by a very significant issue, namely--AI hallucination, which consists of confident and unreliable results. This is the Hallucination to Harmony: Building Reliable AI System in the Enterprise Metaverse chapter, which critically analyzes the technical, cognitive, and governance aspects of hallucination in the metaverse-based enterprise space. It considers the ways in which the new advances including self-checking AI agents, real-time causal reasoning, federated learning, neuromorphic and quantum-enhanced computing, and emotion-aware ethical agents can all change unreliable machine behavior into cognitively harmonious intelligence. The chapter also suggests a multidimensional view of achieving cognitive harmony in which human judgment and machine intelligence act as complementary forces as opposed to competing forces.

DOI: 10.4018/979-8-3373-7534-2.ch002

INTRODUCTION

It brings together Artificial Intelligence (AI) and extended reality (XR), blockchain, digital twins, and immersive networking to create the Enterprise Metaverse which is a continuous, shared, and virtual-physical workspace where organizations simulate, operate, collaborate and innovate. In contrast to consumer metaverse applications, which focus on entertainment and socialization, the enterprise metaverse will be based on mission-critical business processes that include manufacturing, healthcare, education, hospitality, smart cities, defense, supply chain management, and corporate training (Tang et al., 2025). But with immersive metaverse environments incorporating generative and autonomous AI systems, a significant threat has now become more pronounced: AI hallucination the creation of confident yet false, unstable, or deceptive output. Where stakes are high, e.g. in enterprise settings, hallucinations do not necessarily only amount to technical malfunctions; they can translate into monetary loss, risk, damaged reputation, ethical breach, and regulatory failure. Reliability cannot be compromised when AI-based digital agents are used to give directions in industrial maintenance, medical simulations, architectural planning, or customer interaction in immersive settings. The chapter is a conceptualization of the trip between hallucination and harmony-between unreliable, opaque, and probability-based AI systems and robust, interpretable, and trustworthy AI systems embedded in enterprise metaverse (Nair et al., 2024). It discusses the type and genesis of AI hallucination, the inherent dangers that are amplified by the immersive setting, technical, organizational, and governance systems needed to create effective AI systems on a large scale. This chapter offers a comprehensive, overall roadmap to the creation of harmonized human-AI-metaverse ecosystems, accurate, resilient, secure and socially responsible by integrating engineering viewpoints of AI, enterprise systems, digital governance, cybersecurity, ethics and metaverse design.

Discovering AI Hallucination in Business realities

With the introduction of artificial intelligence as an integrated part of enterprise processes--and especially one in which immersion is the order of the day, like the enterprise metaverse--the predictability of AI-generated information has become a matter of concern. The issue of AI hallucination is among the most difficult to handle due to the threat of trustful AI. Although the initial applications of generative AI to consumers viewed hallucination as more of a quality concern, in business ecosystems it has been a strategic, operational, ethical, and financial risk. It is crucial to understand what is the hallucination, why it is dangerous and why it is peculiar to the enterprise metaverse in order to construct reliable AI-driven mechanisms (Mariappan et al., 2024). AI hallucination is where a model, especially an AI model of large language models (LLMs), generative vision systems, or multimodal AI platforms, generates outputs which seem fluent, confident, context-sensitive, and factually incorrect, logically inconsistent, unconfirmable, or completely fabricated. Hallucinations are misleading unlike mere mistakes in computation or bugs in the system, they usually sound, look and write in a tone, structure and style similar to a valid expert knowledge. This renders them hard to identify by end consumers, particularly in high-paced business set-ups. The convincing language fluent ability and the lifelike visual effect of contemporary generative systems form a false impression of truthfulness which invites blind faith. Hallucinations can have various operationally important forms in the metaverse of enterprises. These include:

- Technical specifications developed in simulations of virtual engineering that may produce poor product designs or constructions that are not safe.
- Wrong legal or financial guidance provided by AI-powered avatars or virtual consultants and this may lead to a non-compliant regulation, legal suits, or loss of money.
- False medical advice in the immersive healthcare training systems which can undermine patient safety or distort clinical practice.
- False information in virtual learning, sabotage of organizational training, certification procedures, and workforce competency.
- Wrong predictive data in digital twins that can result in the wrong maintenance schedule, chain breakage, or bad strategic planning.

Therefore, AI hallucination in business settings is not just a matter of information quality, but it has a direct impact on the organization performance, community safety, administrative responsibility, and institutional confidence (Soliman et al., 2024).

The cause of hallucinations is a complicated interplay of the model design, the quality of data, system design, and the dynamics of human-AI interaction. This phenomenon is caused by a number of fundamental factors:

Generative AI is Probabilistic in nature

They do not come up with answers by checking verisimilitude of facts against some sort of knowledge base but by anticipating the next token in a sequence with the greatest number of probable outcomes. Consequently, models tend to generate assertive though unsupported material whenever they face knowledge gaps or vague situations that only sound right.

Training Data Bias and Limitations

The effectiveness of AI models is not superior to its training data. Incomplete, outdated, biased, or noisy data tend to bring about structural vulnerabilities that emerge as hallucinations. In business applications, the generalized datasets of the internet normally do not reflect domain-specific constraints, regulatory and organizational policies, resulting in outputs that do not support what the business actually operates in the real-world.

Absence of Founding in Real-Time Company Data

Numerous generative models are independent of working live enterprise systems like ERP systems, knowledge graphs, manufacturing control systems, or databases of customers. Devoid of direct access to validated and up to date organizational data, models rely on fixed training memories, and this heightens the chance that organisations will provide outmoded, conjectural, or fictional responses in dynamic business contexts.

Sensitivity and Context Drift in Time

The answers of AI are very sensitive to the manner in which the user poses the question. Even minor modifications of wording, ambiguity, or incomplete contextualization may result in outputs of radically different quality. Context drift is even more strongly visible in enterprise metaverse environments where the interaction is conversational, immersive and multi-user: this results in a greater likelihood of inconsistent or hallucinated responses between multiple sessions.

Overgeneralization and Pattern Completion.

Generative models are trained to fulfill patterns. With the partial information they encounter, they are prone to fill in the gaps even where there is no substantiated information (Schmalzried, 2025). This disposition to overgeneralization is one of the main causes of hallucination, particularly in technical, legal, or medical contexts where the unknowns are supposed to cause doubt rather than invented certitude.

Multimodal Fusion Errors

The business metaverse will be based on multimodal AI, in which text, images, 3D objects, voice commands, sensor data, and spatial computing all meet. Disagreement or failure to synchronize between these modalities may result in compounded hallucinations e.g. in the case of visual simulations disagreeing with sensor data or textual explanations disagreeing with spatial models. These aspects taken collectively indicate that the issue of hallucination is not a one-off failure, but a problem inherent to the generative AI systems.

Enterprise Metaverse risk Unique risks of Hallucination

Although hallucinations are dangerous in all AI applications, they are far more pronounced in the enterprise metaverse because these environments are immersive and real-time in nature, and become cyber-physical. First, the realism of the immersive environment is very high which gives the user a large trust level on the results of AI outputs (Schmalzried, 2025; Singh, 2025). In the event that information is provided by realistic avatars in photorealistic simulations, users are psychologically tempted to consider the outputs as official and correct. This is the effect of the so-called perceptual credibility, which makes hallucinations more influential and difficult to refute. Second, operations like manufacturing control, training emergency response, virtual surgery, logistics coordination, and financial trading simulation are some of the operations that are typically supported by enterprise metaverse applications and are usually used to make real-time decisions. Such time-sensitive environments offer the reduced possibility of human checks, and therefore, allow the propagation of hallucinated outputs into physical execution at a high rate. Third, when there are embodied AI agents, or digital humans, speaking, gesturing, and socially interacting, an extra level of perceived expertise is established. The legal and ethical consequences of such users perceiving fictional output as professional advice can be increased when such agents hallucinate. Fourth, the enterprise metaverse is becoming more and more a place of cross-system automation, with AI-generated knowledge in virtual environments directly initiating activities in the physical ones like robots, machines, supply chains, or building management systems (Karvonen et al., 2025; Singh & Singh, 2025). Real-life safety hazards can be generated by a hallucinated output in such closely coupled cyber-physical environments. Lastly, metaverse hallucinations are very scalable. One faulty AI can affect thousands of consumers, digital twins, and virtual workspaces within the networks of global enterprises. This scalability makes the localized misinformation to be a system-wide operational risk. As a result, the illusion in the enterprise metaverse is not just a flaw of content generation. It is a critical threat to organizational stability, human life, regulation, and future confidence in immersive AI systems.

Enterprise Metaverse as a Socio-Technical System

The enterprise metaverse, unlike virtual worlds that are consumer-oriented that focus on entertainment and socialisation, is specifically designed to enable organisational mission-critical operations, including manufacturing, healthcare, logistics, education, hospitality, finance, and smart city management. It is valued as a result of the dynamic interaction between several technological and social components and not any single layer. The cornerstone of this ecosystem is a digital infrastructure that incorporates cloud computing, edge computing, and new telecommunication infrastructure 5G networks and tested 6G networks. Cloud services can be used to store and process digital twins and AI training as well as perform virtual collaboration, whereas edge computing means that time-sensitive tasks (such as robotic control or AR guidance) can be performed near the source. The enterprise metaverse will not be responsive and reliable enough to run without this strong infrastructure layer in the industrial and professional setting (Fui-Hoon Nah et al., 2023; Al-Romeedy et al., 2025). The second layer of critical is the immersive interfaces which will include the virtual reality (VR), augmented reality (AR), and mixed reality (MR) and the haptic feedback system. With these technologies, employees are able to do virtual training, engineers are able to visualize more complicated prototypes, healthcare professionals are able to carry out virtual surgeries and customers are able to explore services in immersive space.

LITERATURE REVIEW

The realism and interactivity of these interfaces play a great role in increasing engagement and also raising the level of psychological trust that the users have on the system thus reliability and accuracy are a priority. The central aspect of the enterprise metaverse is the AI systems, such as generative models, predictive analytics, machine learning algorithms, and autonomous intelligent agents (Hughes et al., 2025; Sharma et al., 2025; Singh, 2025). These systems support personalization, automation, simulation, forecasting and real-time decision support. The use of AI allows making virtual environments adaptive and intelligent, learning by the behavior of the users, and the data about the functioning of these environments, as well as the feedback related to the environment. Nevertheless, there is also a possibility of introducing such risks as bias, opacity, and hallucination by the same AI systems provided that they are not controlled attentively and that the information on which they are based is verified. Intimately associated with AI are operational technologies (OT), i.e. IoT sensors, industrial robotics, digital control systems, and wider cyber-physical infrastructures. OT links the virtual and real world, with real-time data of machine and supply chains, buildings and environments being fed into digital twins and immersive dashboards. The simulation of actions in the metaverse can also cause real physical processes in the factories, hospitals, or logistics networks. Such a close cyber-physical interconnection magnifies the possibilities as well as the threats of the enterprise metaverse especially in cases where AI-generated insights can directly alter physical functions. Just as vital to any technological layer is the human component that designs, manages, decodes, and controls the enterprise metaverse systems (Ooi et al., 2025; Singh & Hassan, 2024; Al-Romeedy et al., 2025). These systems are determined by employees, managers, customers, partners, and regulators regarding their functionality and trustworthiness to a certain degree. The human judgment, domain expertise, ethical reasoning, and organizational culture is decisive in introducing the enterprise metaverse as a responsible innovation tool or a systemic risk generator. Within a highly intertwined socio-technical context, reliability cannot be entirely determined by the accuracy of algorithms. Rather, it is a result of the harmonization of technical strength, human management, moral layout, and good organizational regulation. Even the most precise AI systems may prove to be unreliable when implemented in a weak governance system, inadequately trained communities of users, or in insecure infrastructures. In its turn, good human-in-the-loop, transparent design principles, and strict institutional controls can address technical constraints and ensure that small failures do not turn into significant failures. Any vulnerability in this alignment, be it through faulty data pipelines, insufficient cybersecurity, lack of proper user training or weak ethical supervision, may reintroduce AI hallucination, increase systemic vulnerabilities, and eventually undermine trust in the enterprise metaverse. As a result, to develop a trustworthy immersive enterprise system, a holistic socio-technical perspective on the matter is necessary, which considers technology, people, and governance as the inseparable aspects of a unified ecosystem.

From Hallucination to Harmony: Conceptual Framework

Within the enterprise metaverse, harmony is a state of stable, reliable, and sustainable integration of artificial intelligence, immersive digital environments, physical functional systems, and human beings. It is the next level of technological advancement when the results of AI are not only effective and strong but also correct, verifiable, and understandable. Within a harmonized ecosystem like the one described, AI systems cannot be seen as opaque black boxes; their decisions, suggestions and generative capabilities are traceable, verifiable, and explainable by the human stakeholders (Radanliev, 2025; Srivastava et al., 2025). It is particularly important to explain in immersive enterprise software, including digital twins, virtual training, healthcare simulation, and financial simulation, where the user makes decisions grounded on

AI-based outputs in reality. One of the most important aspects of harmony is the fact that the human end user still has significant control over the AI-based systems. Rather than complete automation which is not accountable, harmonized enterprises are based on human-in-the-loop and human-on-the-loop structures, where the key decisions are open to human validation, overruling, and moral thinking. This maintains accountability, safeguards professional expertise and aids in avoiding mindless reliance on generative intelligence. The sense of meaningful control also boosts the trust of the users, since employees and managers will be more likely to cooperate with AI when they see it as an ally, but not as something that can be controlled. Harmony also demands that there should be a reliable coordination between digital and physical systems. The virtual simulation, digital twin, and immersive dashboard in the enterprise metaverse have become more and more interconnected with the real world operation technology like IoT sensors, robotics, and industrial control systems. A harmonized state is one in which what occurs in the virtual world is accurately mirrored in the physical world and that the decisions made by AI do not cause any inconsistencies between the simulation and execution. The safety-critical sectors, like manufacturing, healthcare, logistics, and smart infrastructure, rely on this synchronization and even minor discrepancies will cause a sequence of failures. The designation of ethical, legal and cultural norms is also essential to harmony (Garvey & Svendsen, 2024; Singh & Das, 2025). Harmonized enterprise metaverse systems integrate fairness, transparency, data protection, inclusiveness, and regulatory compliance into their very fabric instead of considering ethics and regulation as externalities imposed post-implementation. The cultural sensitivity is also important in the virtual worlds that are globally interconnected as users of various backgrounds communicate in the same virtual space. Harmony is not solely, hence, a technical objective, but also a socio-ethical state of affairs contributing to the long-term legitimacy and social trust. The shift of hallucination to harmony is not natural or gradual; it takes concerted efforts within five mutually supporting pillars. The initial pillar, data integrity and knowledge grounding, will guarantee that AI systems are based on correct, up-to-date, as well as context-dependent information that is delivered by reliable enterprise sources. The second pillar, model architecture and verification, is based on the analysis of hybrid, auditable, and continuously tested AI designs that reduce the number of probabilistic errors and identify hallucinations in the early stages (Pramanik & Rai, 2025; Ansari & Singh, 2023; Sharma & Singh, 2025). Human-in-the-loop governance is the third pillar which formalizes human control, responsibility, and moral judgment in every high-stakes AI decision. The fourth pillar is cybersecurity and trust infrastructure, which prevents the enterprise metaverse against data manipulation, identity fraud, adversarial attacks, and system compromise. Lastly, the fifth pillar, ethical, legal, and organizational alignment, will make certain that the technological innovation moves at the same pace as compliance with regulations, corporate governance, and values of the society. It is only when these five pillars develop in unison that enterprises can transcend basic piecemeal reliability with a completely harmonized metaverse ecosystem where the workings of intelligent systems are technically precise, human cognizant, and social accepted. This is what harmony forms the basis of sustainable value creation, institutional trust, and responsible innovation of the new generation of digitization of enterprise transformation.

Knowledge Grounding and Data Integrity

The baseline of reliable AI in enterprise metaverse is reliable data that is continuously updated and integrated. Remember custom organizations tend to have a disconnected data silo within different departments, platforms and old systems. This fragmentation greatly impairs the capacity of AI systems to create sound situational awareness, as well as endangers the occurrence of hallucination considerably. To overcome this challenge, organizations should be shifted to unified enterprise data fabrics, which is a layer of architecture that is used to integrate heterogeneous data sources into a co riding, accessible, and controlled data environment. The integration will allow AI systems within the metaverse to draw cross-domain information that is current and up-to-date instead of depending on the pre-trained static knowledge that might be outdated and incomplete (Jackson et al., 2024; Sharma et al., 2024). An example would be an AI-based virtual assistant of maintenance who can use live sensor data on the machine, past maintenance logs, engineering documentation, and supply chain inventory to provide the correct context-sensitive advice. Enterprise data fabrics facilitate data consistency, lineage, quality control, and real-time synchronization by motivating generative and predictive AI systems on validated organization knowledge.

Semantic Grounding and Knowledge Graphs

Whereas data fabrics have offered a physical and logical level of integration, enterprise knowledge graphs introduce an essential level of semantic smarts. Knowledge graphs structure information in the enterprise in entity, relationship, and contextual constraints allowing AI systems to perceive not only the data points, but rather the meaning and dependencies behind the data. The domain-specific ontologies which are represented by them are formal and they have business rules, regulatory requirements, process hierarchies, asset relationships, and organizational structures (Singh & Hassan, 2024; Singh & Das, 2025; Singh, 2025). Knowledge graph based semantic grounding has a determining influence in the minimization of AI hallucination. As an example, semantic constraints can be used to ensure that

AI-driven recommendations do not violate safety levels, regulatory requirements, and physical constraints in an enterprise metaverse environment in health care or manufacturing. Consequently, the knowledge graphs are truth scaffolds which keep AI reasoning consistent with organizational reality. This semantic consistency plays an important role in the scheme of trust and operational reliability in immersive environments, in which users engage with AI agents, both visually and in practice.

Retrieval-Augmented Generation (RAG)

One of the most significant advancements in the fight against hallucination and in ensuring reliability in the enterprise metaverse is the use of Retrieval-Augmented Generation (RAG) architectures. RAG is an integration of two potent features: the large language models to perform natural language reasoning and the generation, and the real-time search of trusted enterprise repositories, e.g. document management system, knowledge graph, databases and digital twins.

DISCUSSION AND INTERPRETATION

The AI system does not only use a probabilistic memory created in the pretraining phase, but it fetches the information that has been proven to be valid at the query execution time. This design radically changes generative AI as a based-on-memory text generator to a contextually aware reasoning engine. In immersive enterprise setting, RAG allows AI avatars, virtual engineers and intelligent assistants to base their response on authoritative sources, which are real-time operational data, compliance documents and organizational policies, and then produce an output (Srivastava et al., 2025; Ansari & Singh, 2023). This significantly minimizes the possibility of fake information and enhances the attribution and clarification of AI reactions. Besides, RAG frameworks are able to record the sources used in the creation of each output, enhancing transparency, auditability, and regulatory compliance. These technologies are aimed at making the immersive AI system work in constant correspondence to the factual reality of the enterprise by factualizing the architecture itself.

Architecture and Verification Modeling

Due to the use of AI on a scale in the virtual world of the immersive metaverse, the constraints of only generative models have become more pronounced. Although the generative systems, large language models and other models provide uncanny versatility and creativity, they are probabilistic and thus are subject to hallucination. In response, organizations are moving towards hybrid AI architectures with generative intelligence and deterministic and logic-based systems. Such a change in architecture is the basis of creating verifiable, bounded, and enterprise-grade AI.

Hybrid AI Architectures

Symbolic AI provides explicit knowledge and reasoning through a formal logic that allows making decisions in a transparent and verifiable fashion. Business policies, regulatory conditions, safety protocols and business operations are written in machine understandable form as rule-based engines. Constraint solvers guarantee that outputs of AI are within physical, temporal, financial, and safety constraints, whereas causal models enable AI applications to rationally reason about cause-and-effect relations instead of purely based on statistical associations (Javidroozi et al., 2025; Singh, 2025). Such a hybridization, especially in the context of the enterprise, specifically in the metaverse, makes sure that essential decisions are not subject to unlimited rules, compliance or physical factors. One example is that a virtual production planner driven by AI can create a variety of scheduling situations by applying generative optimization algorithms, but the feasibility of these scheduling situations is checked against constraint solvers to verify that they are possible in terms of labor laws, machine capacity and energy constraints. This multi-tiered intelligence minimizes greatly the chances of hallucinated or infeasible outputs reaching the end users or cause real life actions.

Multimodal Verification Pipelines

The enterprise metaverse is multimodal in nature and AI systems will process and generate information simultaneously in text, voice, vision, 3D spatial environments, and sensor streams. On the one hand, this multimodality makes the quality of realism and the level of interaction more realistic and achieves new possibilities of inconsistencies and hallucinations. As a way of countering these risks, businesses are adopting multimodal verification pipelines which cross-checks AI outputs with a set of sources of data and multiple representational levels prior to validation. An example is that an AI-generated virtual maintenance recommendation in the metaverse can be checked simultaneously with various independent sources: engineering manuals and standard operating procedures (text), simulations of physical behavior in 3D space of a digital twin, real-time IoT sensor data collected by machines, and past records of maintenance in enterprise databases (Sharma et al., 2024). The output is only approved to be presented to the user or automatically run on the computer when they all agree on a coherent interpretation. Cross-modal triangulation of this kind converts verification into a localised algorithmic verification into a global system-level verification process, and produced hallucinations are much more readily spotted and suppressed.

Drift Detection and Continuous Model Auditing

The conventional AI validation method is mostly pre-deployment testing and benchmarking. But this fixed method does not work in the dynamic enterprise metaverse environment. The nature of data distributions, user behavior, regulatory, and operational contexts keep changing which commonly results in model drift and unexpected failure modes. This has pushed companies to implement ongoing model audit and drift detection systems in order to maintain long term reliability. The most important parts of this continuous verification layer are automated hallucination detection systems, statistical anomaly detection, concept drift detection, and confidence scoring along with uncertainty estimation. Hallucination detectors are automated tools used to analyze the output patterns to detect fabrication, inconsistency, or deviation of the grounded sources. Statistical anomaly monitoring follows data clustering when the model changes its behavior abnormally whereas concept drift detection tracks when the incoming data no longer conforms to the assumptions made when training the model. Confidence scoring and uncertainty estimation reveal the amount of confidence involved with every AI output and allows users and supervisory systems to exercise the correct degree of scrutiny. Combined, these processes make reliability not a single testing activity but an ongoing operational process through the organization (Zvaigzne et al., 2025). Such indefinite verification is necessary in the enterprise metaverse where AI outputs are then used to create immersive experiences and that usually can and do affect real-world systems in order to maintain trust, safety, and regulatory compliance. Organizations will be able to progressively transition on the path of weak generative intelligence to robust, verifiable, and harmonized AI systems capable of mission-critical immersive use through hybrid architectures, multimodal verification, and continuous auditing.

Human-in-the-Loop Governance

The human-in-the-loop (HITL) governance is becoming more urgent as artificial intelligence gets more autonomous and ingrained in immersive enterprise systems. Although the self-learning algorithms, reinforcement learning, and autonomous agents are advancing rapidly, unsupervised AI in high-risk environments of enterprises cannot be supported at all. The results of AI malfunction or delusion can be dire in fields like healthcare, manufacturing, finance, defense, hospitality functions, and smart infrastructure and may be irreparable, permanent, and have legal ramifications. The

HITL frameworks will guarantee that critical decisions are to be human-validated and that AI is a decision-supporting system and not a decision-making one, and the role and accountability are well established. Human control is not just one of the available defense mechanisms, it also increases the intelligence and capability of the system by merging machine scale data processing with human judgment, experience, and situational awareness (Abaddi, 2025; Singh & Singh, 2025). Human validation is the last step in an automated execution in an enterprise metaverse environment, where digital simulations can literally control physical actions. This type of governance is especially essential in safety critical systems like equipment control, clinical decision support, financial approvals and strategic planning. HITL is therefore an element of a responsible autonomy wherein businesses will be able to utilize the power of AI without losing control of the results.

Artificial Intelligence-Enhanced Workforces in the Metaverse

Within the framework of immersive enterprise settings, the interaction between a human and AI is increasingly mediated by virtual assistants, computerized avatars, and smart agents that are integrated into simulations and digital twins. These agents relate to workers in the natural, embodied and contextual manner and transform the manner in which work is carried out, learned and coordinated. But instead of supplanting workers, trustworthy AI can be considered an effective workforce augmentation tool. Faster sense-making AI-augmented workforces also take advantage of the fact that intelligent agents synthesize large amounts of structured and unstructured data into actionable information in real time. Enterprise metaverse is also capable of scenario exploration, a feature allowing employees to test strategies, perform a what-if analysis and observe what might happen in risk-free virtual environments (Hornik & Rachamim, 2025; Sharma et al., 2025; Singh & Hassan, 2024). Additionally, immersive AI systems enhance the transfer of skill and training of workforce by simulating tasks that are complex, dangerous, and difficult to encounter with high fidelity. Lastly, they facilitate a system of geographically distributed collaborative problem-solving with globally spread teams able to cooperate in common virtual environments aided by real-time AI analytics. Under proper control, AI is therefore a mental partner that enhances human performance and not reduces it.

Cognitive Load, Calibration of Trust and Over-Relying

Over-trust in intelligent agents is one of the risks of immersive AI in the enterprise metaverse, which are implicit yet very critical. Virtual environments can produce the illusion of accuracy and authority because of their realism, the fluency and confidence of generative AI. This raises the probability of the automation bias, whereby users are willing to trust AI suggestions too easily when they are wrong or ambiguous. In the long run, AI systems may also cause the loss of skills, since human expertise is not used fully and critical thinking is undermined. The solution to these threats is to invest in critical AI literacy training, whereby the employees are aware of how the AI systems operate, where they are weak, and how hallucinations or prejudices may develop. As well, interface design should explicitly reveal AI confidence levels, uncertainty estimates and source attributions so users can critically assess outputs as opposed to literally taking them at face value (Robinson, 2025; Srivastava et al., 2025; Ansari & Singh, 2023). Organizations should also put in place procedural safeguard, which will mandate a periodical human intervention, independent verification and role based authorization of high-impact decisions. Finally, the trust in the enterprise metaverse should be earned and continuously adjusted, as opposed to being assumed. Maintaining significant levels of human agency in immersive AI ecologies will enable corporations to make sure that the process of technological development is aligned with professional discretion, ethical accountability, and organizational stability.

Infrastructure Network Security and Trust

Since the enterprise metaverse will integrate both immersive digital worlds and real-world system operation, it forms a very sophisticated and interdependent cyber-physical ecosystem. Although this integration provides employees with opportunities to collaborate, automate, and simulate like never before, it can expose a significantly larger target of cyber-attacks that is difficult to combat according to traditional security models. Trust infrastructure and cybersecurity thus form the basis of making AI-driven metaverse environments reliable, resilient and resistant to accidental malfunction and intentional manipulation.

Growing Attack Surface on the Enterprise Metaverse

The enterprise metaverse becomes much broader and expands the range of likely cyber threats compared to traditional IT systems. The main entry points to the immersive worlds, VR and AR devices, can be affected by the hardware attacks, firmware attacks, and unauthorized access. There is also a significant threat posed by manipulating spatial data, where modified 3D simulated environment, location data or digital twin models may lead to users to make unsafe or inefficient operational choices. Avatar impersonation and deepfakes only make the process of verifying identities more difficult, allowing an attacker to cheat employees, managers, or customers by simulating realistic visual and voice representations. Moreover, the enterprise metaverse depends on the IoT sensors and cyber-physical systems that are also vulnerable to sensor spoofing and data injection attacks. In case encroachers adjust sensor inputs, AI systems might produce hallucinated information depending on misleading physical circumstances (Al-Romeedy et al., 2025). More importantly, AI model poisoning, i.e., the counterpart to the adversary poisoning data or model parameters, has the potential to systematically alter the behavior of AI over time. Hallucinations can also be intentionally caused by adversarial attack in these instances and the AI hallucination would cease to be an accidental statistical artifact but a sabotage, misinformation or financial fraud tool. All of these layers indicate that cybersecurity within the enterprise metaverse is not an option, but a fundamental requirement of secure and reliable operations.

Zero Trust Architecture

In response to such advanced and dynamic threats, immersive enterprises need to utilize zero trust security frameworks as the cybersecurity framework. Furthermore, a zero trust structure does not have a set of trusted users, devices, applications, or AI components, whether they are within or outside the organizational perimeter. Multi-factor authentication, behavioral analytics, and cryptographic credentials need to be used to verify every access request on a continuous basis. Zero trust also demands that ongoing authentication and authorization needs to be implemented through all levels of the enterprise metaverse, VR headsets and avatars, to the AI agents and the back-end data services. The decisions made to access are not fixed but dynamic and risk-based based on the behavior of the user and the health of the device as well as the location and the threat intelligence. As an example, an AI agent controlling a digital twin can be allowed to access the environment with restricted access in regular conditions and increased restrictions in the presence of anomalies.

Distributed Trust Mechanisms and blockchain

In addition to traditional cybersecurity controls, blockchain and distributed ledger technologies are also coming out as significant facilitators of confidence within the enterprise metaverse. The data provenance can also be established by blockchain, which means that the information used to train the AI models and digital twins can be tracked to the sources that are authenticated. This directly helps avoiding the risk of making a hallucination as a result of manipulating or falsifying data. It also promotes secure digital identity on user, device and AI agents, minimizes the risk of avatars being impersonated and access being unauthorized. Besides, blockchain allows recording the decisions made by AI immutably, which establishes audit trails that are impossible to change and which are essential in regulatory compliance, forensic inquiry, and institutional responsibility. Blockchain enhances technical trust and institutional trust, which bolster trust in the integrity, transparency, and reliability of enterprise metaverse systems. Overall, enhanced cybersecurity and trust infrastructure are essential to develop the enterprise metaverse into a low-risk and experimentation-free environment instead of a space that poses a high risk of exploitation and potential security breaches.

Metaverse Ethical, Legal, and Responsible AI

With the proliferation of the enterprise metaverse applying the scope of artificial intelligence to the immersive, experiential, and decision-critical setting, ethical, legal, and responsible AI concerns emerge as the dominant concept of system design and governance (Sharma et al., 2024; Al-Romeedy et al., 2025). The immersion and experiences offered by the metaverse platforms enhance the advantages and threats of AI, where conventional ethical measures are inadequate unless they are reconceptualized to immersive and real-time digital platforms. AI hallucination is one of the most severe regulatory and ethical risks that can be described among them.

ETHICAL ASPECTS OF HALLUCINATION

The fact that AI hallucinations have an immediate impact on human perception, judgment, and behavior is an ethical issue that raises some serious questions in the context of enterprise metaverses. By telling the employees or customers things that are wrong, AI systems undermine professional decision-making, organizational credibility, and trust of the population. Hallucinations in the immersive simulations may also support the underlying biases by recreating or enhancing the biased data patterns, thus creating discriminative results in the virtual hiring, training, or customer-interaction process of the simulations. Moreover, hallucinated products may be a distortion of reality in training or working decision context, giving a false sense of confidence in a wrong process, unsafe operation, or inaccurate strategic presumptions. The destruction of informed consent is one of the most ethical implications of hallucination that is very sensitive. Users who communicate with AI-based avatars or realistic simulations might not necessarily realize when the information is fabricated, probabilistic or uncertain. Within the metaverse, where the experience is considered vivid, embodied and psychologically real, the breaches of ethics are so increased socially and emotionally (Singh, 2025). Misinformation conveyed by a realistic avatar in a virtual work place or in a medical setting can provide a more profound cognitive and behavioral effect compared to the same error presented by a conventional text interface. Thus, the concept of ethical responsibility within the enterprise metaverse goes beyond the accuracy of the technical to encompass the psychological safety, fairness, transparency and respect of human autonomy.

Laws and Regulatory Environments

Legally, companies using AI in immersive systems have to work in an environment that is more complicated and dynamic worldwide. The fundamental legal requirements are conformance with data protection and privacy regulations that are used to check the collection and processing of biometric data, behavioral information, and spatial surveillance data, and identity history of metaverse platforms. Organizations are also required to comply with the developing AI accountability paradigms, which include explainability, risk management, and human oversight standards. Workplace safety rules are of particular importance in the context of immersive enterprise, because virtual instructions and simulations tend to affect real-life behavior in factories, hospitals, and service facilities. Moreover, the consumer protection and liability laws come into force whenever customers are involved in the interaction with the AI-based avatars, virtual services, or automated decision-making (Singh & Das, 2025). When hallucinated outputs result in financial damage, safety accidents, or publicity damage, then the question of legal liability is inevitable. The risks are also compounded by cross-border jurisdictional challenges due to the fact that metaverse platforms are usually run across national borders and users, data centers, and service providers may be situated in various legal jurisdictions. Business firms can no longer afford to be complacent in regard to complying with regulations once they are enacted. Rather, compliance-by-design, which integrates legal and regulatory needs directly into the architecture of systems, data governance, and AI processes have become fundamental in the long-term deployment.

Transparent and explainable AI of the Metaverse

Explainability and transparency will be one of the building blocks of ethical and responsible AI in the metaverse. In immersive AI systems, explanations go beyond textual explanations to have visual traceability of the decision logic so that individuals can view the way data flows through the models and the way conclusions are made. Model reasoning can be interactively explored so that users can query assumptions, test alternative scenarios, as well as understand uncertainty, in real time. It should also be transparent with clear disclosure of the data sources to be used in training and real-time access to enable users and auditors to verify on the basis of AI outputs (Al-Romeedy et al., 2025; Sharma et al., 2025). The clear indication of AI-generated and human-generated content is also important. In virtual models that are highly realistic as immersive worlds (such as with avatars and simulations), users have to be made well aware whenever they are interacting with artificial agents or AI-generated data. This transparency is very essential in ensuring that autonomy is upheld, in order to avoid deception, and in order to uphold professional accountability. Finally, it is explainable and transparent metaverse AI that is the key to converting hallucination-prone systems into reliable enterprise infrastructures, wherein ethical integrity, legal regulations, and human trust are maintained in addition to technological innovation.

Application in The Industry: Risk to Reliability

The shift in hallucination-prone AI systems to reliable and enterprise-grade intelligence is best embodied in industry-specific uses of the enterprise metaverse. Nevertheless, the same environments are also enhancing the risks of hallucination, which creates the basis of reliability as a requirement of safe and sustainable adoption.

The Digital Twins and manufacturing

These virtual copies enable organizations to experiment on operational strategies, forecast equipment failures and maximize the resource usage without interfering with the physical operations. Nonetheless, inaccurate predictions caused by hallucination, e.g., wrong failure forecast, wrong production bottlenecks, or wrong demand forecast may result into expensive production bottlenecks, safety accidents, and domino supply chain failures. Physics-grounded simulations provide reliability in AI as applied in manufacturing metaverse systems, in which digital twins are subject to engineering laws and material limits of the real world. Outputs should also be sensor-authenticated, to provide real-time matching of virtual models to physical machines with the help of IoT information. Moreover, high-quality scenario testing allows manufacturers to stress-test extreme conditions and check AI proposals on the pre-implementation stage.

Medical and Healthcare Education

The metaverse of medical enterprises is becoming fast evolving into the field of surgical simulation, diagnostics training, and tele-consultation. Immersive simulations enable clinicians and students to practice the complicated procedures in the risk-free virtual environments, whereas AI-driven analytics assists in the diagnostic reasoning and treatment plans.

Nevertheless, the outcomes of hallucination are incomparably dire in the context of healthcare: a single false suggestion or falsified clinical presentation is a life-threatening event (Singh & Hassan, 2024; Al-Romeedy et al., 2025). Medical metaverse reliability is thus attained by grounding the AI systems rigorously on clinical data, using peer-reviewed medical data as well as institutional clinical history. The control of human physicians is also irreplaceable, and all the high-impact recommendations are subject to their examination and approval. Moreover, the health authorities should conduct regulatory approval to guarantee that the immersive medical AI systems are of high quality regarding safety, precision, and patient security. These multilayered protections provide a foundation of innovation on both ethical and clinical accountability.

Hospitality and Tourism

Enterprises in the hospitality and tourism industry are starting to resort to metaverse technology to conduct virtual tours of the hotel, AI-based concierge services, and hospitality training simulations. Visitors will have an opportunity to investigate places to visit before they are booked and employees are developed in real-life service situations. But imagined material in such settings can greatly harm brand image and trust in guests. Inaccurate information regarding services, facilities, costs, safety measures or accessibility can lead to confusion of the customers and discriminatory AI-based interactions can be destructive in terms of inclusiveness and equity of provided services. In addition, deception of destinations might corrupt consumer expectation and cultural authenticity. The metaverse systems with hospitality AI can be trusted because all information that is displayed to guests is factually checked, ethically edited, and constantly updated. It also contributes to the equitable and impartial contact with guests and guarantees that virtual models are appropriate to the real-life norms of service and safety. By doing so, reliability will be among the central points of distinction in the digital hospitality toward trust and competitiveness.

Corporate learning and education

The enterprise metaverse, in the context of education and corporate learning, facilitates immersive education, virtual learning classrooms and simulation of skills that is not limited by the physical space. Nonetheless, these systems require high standards of the correctness of the curriculum, pedagogical correspondence, and ongoing verification of the contents. Misconstructions, wrong simulations, and deceptive teaching materials are some of the elements that may erode the integrity of education, distort the learning of learners, and erosion of professionalism (Sharma et al., 2025; Singh, 2025). Reliable AI opens up the possibilities of personalized, immersive and inclusive learning when it is based on verified academic content, subject-matter knowledge, and the ongoing instructional review. It allows dynamic teaching, risk-free performing of complicated tasks and fair access to quality education in various geographies.

Reliable Metaverse AI Strategies in the Organization

The development of trustworthy AI systems in the enterprise metaverse is not only an issue of implementing sophisticated algorithms or immersive technologies but a challenge of changing the organization. Reliability is created through strong governance frameworks, artificial intelligence savvy employees and reliable vendor systems. Devoid of these, even highly technical systems in the metaverse are susceptible to hallucination, abuse and general failure.

Frameworks of AI Governance in the Enterprise

The institutions of formal AI governance should be enshrined by the enterprises so that there is reliability, accountability, and compliance within the metaverse ecosystem. The main governance mechanisms are the creation of AI ethics committees to analyze the effect of AI on society and organizations, the creation of model risk management units to analyze the performance, bias, and failure modes, and data stewardship offices to protect data quality, privacy, and integrity (Singh & Hassan, 2024; Al-Romeedy et al., 2025). Moreover, cross-functional overseeing boards, having a combination of leadership in IT and legal, risk, HR, and business sectors are indispensable in aligning AI implementation to strategic and regulatory priorities. Trustworthiness in artificial intelligence operations at the enterprise level, where AI-based decisions can directly influence physical processes, safety of the employees, and consumer confidence, turns into a board-level issue, but not a technical one. Efficient governance acts as a guaranty that the risks of hallucinations are detected and recorded in advance and alleviated at the AI lifecycle, such as system design and procurement, through deployment and on-going monitoring.

AI Literacy, Talent, and Culture

Harmony cannot be provided by technical infrastructure only without organizational preparedness and human abilities and capacity. To develop trusted metaverse AI, it is necessary to have an interdisciplinary team of talent, which encompasses AI engineering and domain expertise, ethics, behavioural science, and cybersecurity. It is also crucial that employees constantly increase their skills by following systematic AI literacy courses that help them realize the limitations of AI, doubt the advice provided by it, and approach work with intelligent machines responsibly. Organizations should also foster a culture of openness, trial and error, and questioning, in which employees are taught to question the outputs of AI instead of accepting them blindly. In the absence of such cultural shift, even the most stable technical systems may fail on the basis of over-reliance, misinterpretation or unmanaged trust.

Publix Ecosystems and Platform Interoperability

The majority of businesses do not develop their metaverse AI stacks in-house, but rather, they use intricate ecosystems of cloud-computing metaverse platforms, AI-as-a-Service vendors, and XR hardware makers (Singh & Hassan, 2024). Additionally, the hallucination risk and system failure should be duly distributed both on the contractual and technical lines of responsibility, instead of laying the blame off platform providers and enterprise users. Reliability can only be maintained in multi-vendor enterprise metaverse architectures using interoperable standards and shared governance.

FUTURE PROJECTIONS: COGNITIVE CONCORDANCE

The metaverse of the future enterprise will be defined as a new generation of smart systems, which are not only performance-oriented; but verifiability, alignment, and trustworthiness. New trends are moving toward the emergence of self-checking AI agents, who will autonomously cross-examine their own outputs with regards to a number of trusted sources of knowledge before acting. These agents will incorporate verification as an internal cognitive process and not as a post-processing protection to the environment, which will considerably lower the chance of hallucination in real-time immersive environments. Further developments in real-time causal logic will also change metaverse intelligence. Causal AI will also be able to comprehend why things happen as they happen, rather than what will happen, as we do in modern times by eliminating the element of correlation to predict outcomes. This feature is necessary in complicated enterprise systems where faults may spread throughout digital twins, supply chains, and cyber-physical activities. Simultaneously, neuromorphic and quantum-enhanced AI are expected to deliver the highest efficiency and reasoning power in computations to date, as it will be possible to simulate and make decisions in real-time and with high-fidelity at scales previously unfeasible (Singh & Hassan, 2024; Al-Romeedy et al., 2025). Future metaverse AI will also be more emotion sensitive and ethically aligned, and the human affect, stress and intent can be interpreted within a set of ethical restraints imposed on an embedded ethical standard. They will be needed in fields such as healthcare, education, customer care, and crisis management where emotional intelligence is one of the direct determinants of success. The strategic objective results in cognitive harmony - a condition where the operation of human judgment and machine intelligence are complementary, rather than antagonistic or substitutive forces. Digital and physical worlds are not only in coherent sync in this state, but also trust becomes a programmable, auditable, and measurable system property and not a social construct made of fragile assumptions. Cognitive harmony, therefore, signifies the subsequent development in the field of enterprise intelligence within the world of immersion.

CONCLUSION

Enterprise metaverse is one of the deepest changes in the world of organization work, collaboration, learning, and value creation in the digital era. Incorporating immersive technologies with AI-enabled intelligence and cyber-physical systems, enterprises will achieve new abilities in the context of simulation, training, optimization, and decision support. However, the effectiveness of such transformation depends on the trustworthiness of the AI systems incorporated in such environments. Hallucination--previously regarded as an acceptable collateral damage of the probabilistic AI--becomes intolerable when VR experiences go directly into the real-world and make economic, safety, and ethical choices. It has been shown in this chapter that the process of moving through the hallucination to the harmony is neither technological, nor organizational. Rather, it requires a combined architecture to be constructed based on: Reliable AI in the enterprise metaverse is not just the concept of the gradual improvement of model accuracy. It is regarding re-branding of human-computer-internet relationships, intelligent computers, and virtual worlds. Those companies that make prudent investments in this harmony will tap into unmatched levels of innovation, resilience, productivity and sustainable performance. They will get to experiment safely with complex situations in the future, scale the development of talent, maximize both virtual and physical operations, and gain substantive trust among employees, customers, and regulators. On the other hand, the ones that do not care about reliability will experience the growing operational risks, the regulatory backlash, the negative reputation and the loss of trust in the stakeholders. Finally, the alchemy between hallucination and harmony represents the coming of age of the artificial intelligence itself, as a potent but uncontrollable instrument, into a reliable thinking companion of the enterprise metaverse. The move will make or break immersive digital ecosystems as engines of sustainable enterprise value or contributors to magnified systemic risk in the decades to come.

REFERENCES

Abaddi, S. (2025). AI–human data hybridization: a hybrid approach to unveiling global entrepreneurial motivations, challenges and opportunities. Journal of Ethics in Entrepreneurship and Technology.

Al-Romeedy, B. S., Hussein, H., Emam, M. E., & Singh, A. (2025). From Potential to Peril: Evaluating AI and the Metaverse in Modern Research. In Al Aqad, M., Sorayyaei Azar, A., Albattat, A., & Singh, A. (Eds.), *Navigating AI and the Metaverse in Scientific Research* (pp. 563–584). IGI Global Scientific Publishing., DOI: 10.4018/979-8-3373-0340-6.ch027

Ansari, A. I., & Singh, A. (2023). Application of Augmented Reality (AR) and Virtual Reality (VR) in Promoting Guest Room Sales: A Critical Review. In Impact of Industry 4.0 on Sustainable Tourism: Perspectives, Challenges and Future (pp. 95–104). https://doi.org/DOI: 10.1108/978-1-80455-157-820231006

Fui-Hoon Nah, F., Zheng, R., Cai, J., Siau, K., & Chen, L. (2023). Generative AI and ChatGPT: Applications, challenges, and AI-human collaboration. Journal of information technology case and application research, 25(3), 277-304.

Garvey, B., & Svendsen, A. D. (2024). Can Generative-AI (ChatGPT and Bard) Be Used as Red Team Avatars in Developing Foresight Scenarios? In *Navigating uncertainty using foresight intelligence: A guidebook for scoping scenario options in cyber and beyond* (pp. 213–242). Springer Nature Switzerland.

Hornik, J., & Rachamim, M. (2025). AI-enabled consumer digital twins as a platform for research aimed at enhancing customer experience. Management Review Quarterly, 1-34.

Hughes, L., Dwivedi, Y. K., Malik, T., Shawosh, M., Albashrawi, M. A., Jeon, I., & Walton, P. (2025). AI agents and agentic systems: A multi-expert analysis. *Journal of Computer Information Systems*, •••, 1–29.

Jackson, I., Jesus Saenz, M., & Ivanov, D. (2024). From natural language to simulations: Applying AI to automate simulation modelling of logistics systems. *International Journal of Production Research*, *62*(4), 1434–1457.

Javidroozi, V., Tawil, A. R., Azad, R. M. A., Bishop, B., & Elmitwally, N. S. (2025). AI-Enabled Customised Workflows for Smarter Supply Chain Optimisation: A Feasibility Study. *Applied Sciences (Basel, Switzerland)*, *15*(17), 9402.

Karvonen, A., Aho, J., Koskinen, H., Luimula, M., Myllylä, M., Tammentie, B., & Saariluoma, P. (2025). Human-centered intelligent process control: Vision, design, and implementation. In *Industry 4.0 and Intelligent Manufacturing Technologies* (pp. 109–131). Routledge.

Mariappan, J., Sahdev, S. L., Krishnan, C., Malik, F. A., & Gupta, A. (2024). Creative Synergy: Unleashing the Potential of Artificial Intelligence and the Metaverse. In The Metaverse Dilemma: Challenges and Opportunities for Business and Society (pp. 235-248). Emerald Publishing Limited.

Nair, A. J., Manohar, S., & Chaudhry, R. (2024). Securing the metaverse: Exploring the role of artificial intelligence in mitigating emerging threats in manufacturing and service industries. In Augmenting retail reality, part B: Blockchain, AR, VR, and AI (pp. 67-84). Emerald Publishing Limited.

Ooi, K. B., Tan, G. W. H., Al-Emran, M., Al-Sharafi, M. A., Capatina, A., Chakraborty, A., & Wong, L. W. (2025). The potential of generative artificial intelligence across disciplines: Perspectives and future directions. *Journal of Computer Information Systems*, *65*(1), 76–107.

Pramanik, S., & Rai, S. K. (2025). Manipulating mind, media, and truth: Artificial Intelligence in perpetuating ideological imperialism in Dream Machine: AI and the Real World. *Journal of Graphic Novels & Comics*, •••, 1–21.

Radanliev, P. (2025). AI ethics: Integrating transparency, fairness, and privacy in AI development. *Applied Artificial Intelligence*, *39*(1), 2463722.

Robinson, J. C. (2025). Unshackling Dreams from the Hacker's Digital Chains. In *Artificial Intelligence: Ethics and the New World Order* (pp. 95–171). Springer Nature Switzerland.

Schmalzried, M. (2025). A philosophical and ontological perspective on Artificial General Intelligence and the Metaverse. *Journal of Metaverse*, *5*(2), 168–180.

Sharma, M., Singh, A., & Singh, A. (2025). Tapping the Potential of Innovative Hi-Tech Services on Hotel Performance using PLS-SEM Approach. https://doi.org/ DOI: 10.5109/7388850

Sharma, R., Sachdeva, T., Singh, A., & Nadda, V. (2024). A New Era of Engagement and Satisfaction: Transforming Customer Experience With AI-Driven Technologies. In Nadda, V., Tyagi, P., Singh, A., & Singh, V. (Eds.), *AI Innovations in Service and Tourism Marketing* (pp. 1–16). IGI Global Scientific Publishing., DOI: 10.4018/979-8-3693-7909-7.ch001

Sharma, R., & Singh, A. (2025). Integrating AI, Green Marketing, and Influencer Strategies: Shaping Sustainable Consumer Behavior in the Digital Age. In Hussain, Z., Sharipudin, M., Albattat, A., & Khan, A. (Eds.), *Strategic Brand Management in the Age of AI and Disruption* (pp. 325–342). IGI Global Scientific Publishing., DOI: 10.4018/979-8-3693-9461-8.ch013

Singh, A. (2025). Convergence of Generative Artificial Intelligence (AI)-Based Applications in the Hospitality and Tourism Industry. In Gaur, L. (Ed.), *Generative Artificial Intelligence and Ethics: Standards, Guidelines, and Best Practices* (pp. 127–142). IGI Global Scientific Publishing., DOI: 10.4018/979-8-3693-3691-5.ch006

Singh, A., & Das, R. (2025). Exploring Tourism Opportunities in the Metaverse and Technology Era: Insights From Scholarly Literature. In Hussain, Z., Khan, A., Majeed, M., & Albattat, A. (Eds.), *Metaverse and Sustainable Business Models in SMEs* (pp. 171–182). IGI Global Scientific Publishing., DOI: 10.4018/979-8-3693-9005-4.ch007

Singh, A., & Hassan, S. C. (2024). Service Innovation Through Blockchain Technology in the Tourism and Hospitality Industry: Applications, Trends, and Benefits. In Singh, S. (Ed.), *Service Innovations in Tourism: Metaverse, Immersive Technologies, and Digital Twin* (pp. 205–214). IGI Global Scientific Publishing., DOI: 10.4018/979-8-3693-1103-5.ch010

Singh, M., & Singh, A. (2025). The Role of Artificial Intelligence in Driving Sustainability in the Tourism Industry: A Marketing Perspective. In Ahmad, B., Abrar, M., & Saeed, M. (Eds.), *Marketing Technology-Infused Hospitality: Upskilling Frontline Employees for Competitiveness* (pp. 115–132). IGI Global Scientific Publishing., DOI: 10.4018/979-8-3693-7127-5.ch005

Soliman, M. M., Ahmed, E., Darwish, A., & Hassanien, A. E. (2024). Artificial intelligence powered Metaverse: Analysis, challenges and future perspectives. *Artificial Intelligence Review*, *57*(2), 36.

Srivastava, A., Singh, B. M., Singh, A., & Singh, A. (2025). Customer Immersiveness and Customer Retention: A Metaverse-Driven Study for Brands. In Al Aqad, M., Sorayyaei Azar, A., Albattat, A., & Singh, A. (Eds.), *Navigating AI and the Metaverse in Scientific Research* (pp. 475–500). IGI Global Scientific Publishing., DOI: 10.4018/979-8-3373-0340-6.ch023

Tang, M., Nikolaenko, M., Alrefai, A., & Kumar, A. (2025). Metaverse and Digital Twins in the Age of AI and Extended Reality. *Architecture (Washington, D.C.)*, *5*(2), 36.

Zvaigzne, A., Litavniece, L., Kodors, S., & Jurkane, K. (2025). Negative impacts of artificial intelligence technologies on the tourism industry. *Worldwide Hospitality and Tourism Themes*, *17*(1), 22–34.

Chapter 3
Human-AI Collaboration: Balancing Trust, Emotion, and Productivity

Shikha Khullar
https://orcid.org/0009-0000-5598-3145
Poornima University, India

Randhir Singh Baghel
https://orcid.org/0000-0002-5113-3554
Poornima University, India

Priya Swami
Poornima University, India

ABSTRACT

This chapter discusses the role of human-AI partnership within the enterprise metaverse and how AI hallucinations endanger trust, emotional congruency and productivity. The more immersive virtual environments transform organizational work, the more AI agents help in analyses, decision support, and training, but, because of their probabilistic nature, they can give confident and false results. The chapter introduces the TrustEmotion Productivity (TEP) Framework to demonstrate that safe collaboration relies on calibrated trust, emotional intelligence, and design that is qualified by productivity orientation. It also emphasizes the intensification of hallucinations within immersive, real-time, and multimodal environments and analyzes technical and organizational measures like retrieval-augmented generation, confidence calibration, transparency, expert review and governance protocols. It illustrates the operational risk of hallucinations and best practices of constructing credible, ethical, and human-focused AI systems to support metaverse-enabled businesses.

DOI: 10.4018/979-8-3373-7534-2.ch003

1: INTRODUCTION

1.1 Background and Context

The modern business environment is experiencing a radical shift because of the integration of artificial intelligence technologies and virtual reality (Lee et al., 2021). The next wave of digital workplace evolution is the enterprise metaverse a stable and interrelated chain of virtual spaces in which organizations are engaged in business activities, collaborate, and innovate. In this regard, AI systems are more than tools but collaborators, agents of decision support, and autonomous, capable of creating content, opportunities, and suggestions (Brynjolfsson & McAfee, 2017). Nevertheless, the growing power and independence of AI systems presented a serious problem: the so-called AI hallucinations (Ji et al., 2023). They happen when AI models, especially large language models as well as generative systems generate output that seems plausible and coherent but is false, inconsistent with source information, or even fabricated. In conventional computing settings, these errors could be handled with the help of the traditional verification mechanisms. In the immersive, high-stakes, and real-world experience of enterprises operating in the metaverse, AI hallucinations present increased vulnerabilities to the quality of decision making, reputation, and even safety of operations (Slater and Sanchez-Vives, 2016).

1.2 The Significance of AI Hallucination Management

The nature of neural network architectures and training techniques leads to AI hallucinations (Brown et al., 2020). The modern AI systems, and in particular, the transformer-based language models, do not produce outputs based on the deterministic retrieval or logical inference, but instead as the probabilistic prediction. Such approach of generating allows impressive flexibility and creativity at the same time predisposes to the generation of confident-sounding misinformation (Guo et al., 2017). These issues are increased by the enterprise metaverse context due to a number of reasons (McVeigh-Schultz et al., 2022). To begin with, the immersion of virtual space may lead to an increase in psychological presence and a decrease in critical appraisal, which may make virtual users more vulnerable to the acceptance of AI-generated misinformation (Slater et al., 2010). Second, due to the real-time collaborative essence of metaverse interactions, there is often a strong need to make a decision quickly with little time to check it. Third, by incorporating AI in various functional areas, it provides many injections points of hallucination in the work process of the organization.

1.3 Research Objectives and Scope

This research booklet pursues three primary objectives:

To begin with, in order to develop an all-encompassed theoretical framework of AI hallucinations in the context of enterprise metaverse, it is essential to look into the technical roots of the latter (Ji et al., 2023), patterns of their manifestation, and effects on the organization. This pillar is based on the computer science literature, the cognitive psychology literature, and the organizational behavior literature that formulates a comprehensive view of the phenomenon.

Second, to investigate the critical success factors of effective human-AI cooperation in immersive virtual environments (Glikson and Woolley, 2020), namely, the interaction between trust calibration (Lee and See, 2004), emotional intelligence (Salovey and Mayer, 1990), and productivity optimization (Brynjolfsson and McAfee, 2017) should be analyzed to determine the influence of each of these factors on collaboration.

Third, to be able to synthesize viable management strategy, implementation models and ethical codes (Floridi et al., 2018) according to which organizations are able to exploit AI capabilities under metaverse settings so that the risks of hallucinations are effectively controlled.

1.4 Theoretical Framework: Balancing Trust, Emotion, and Productivity

The main theoretical input of the work is the Trust-Emotion-Productivity (TEP) Framework of collaboration between humans and artificial intelligence in the metaverse of enterprises. According to this framework, effective AI implementation must be based on dynamic balance in three interdependent dimensions, which include Trust Calibration that denotes the agreement between user dependency on AI systems and dependency on the real-world reliability of the systems (Lee and See, 2004). The best working relation exists when the users keep the right amount of trust without too much trust that will cause blind acceptance of the hallucinated results and without having the right amount of trust that will make them fail to utilize AI. In the metaverse, issues with calibration of trust are especially difficult because of the anthropomorphic appearance of AI agents and the simulation of interactions (Nass and Moon, 2000). Emotional Intelligence involves the ability of the AI system to read and react to human emotional conditions as well as the ability of human user to be emotionally conscious when communicating with the AI agents (Salovey and Mayer, 1990; Picard, 1997). This dimension is severely important to the quality of collaboration in the enterprise metaverse environment, where the quality of collaboration might be impaired by the potential to hide traditional emotional cues at the same time as it increases emotional involvement (Baltrušaitis et al., 2018).

Productivity Impact defines the quantifiable impacts of human-AI cooperation on the organizational outcome, performance, and the quality of output (Brynjolfsson et al., 2023). Management of AI hallucinations need to eventually be used to promote productivity and not establish compliance burdens that render AI benefits ineffective. The framework underlines that the productivity equation should be maximized by the hallucination management strategies instead of merely reducing the technical errors (Autor, 2015).

2: TRUST CALIBRATION

2.1 The Nature of Trust in Human-AI Collaboration

Confidence is one of the basic conditions of a successful interaction between humans and computer systems. Based on the organization trust theory, Lee and See (2004) define trust in automation as the attitude that an agent will assist in meeting the objectives of an individual in a scenario that is full of uncertainty and vulnerability. This definition points out three important aspects goal alignment, uncertainty management, and vulnerability acceptance, all of which are especially acute in the framework of enterprise metaverses where AI hallucinations create certain reliability issues. The nature of the trust in AI systems is not fundamentally the same as the trust in people because the algorithms of decision-making are deterministic but opaque (Glikson and Woolley, 2020).

Human partners are consistent but with the contextual judgment whereas AI systems are consistently correct in its training distribution but can fail disastrously when faced with out-of-distribution scenarios (Brown et al., 2020). This leads to what scientists call the brittleness paradox AI systems which seem to work perfectly in known areas and make confident hallucinations in new ones.

2.2 The Trust Calibration Challenge

Trust calibration is the method of matching customer with AI systems with real system competencies and constraints (Parasuraman and Riley, 1997). Perfectly calibrated trust is when the users for their part, trust AI systems in a corresponding proportion to their reliability- they can trust the judgment of AI systems in areas where they are competent but take a critical approach when the systems are near the edges of their capabilities. There are two types of miscalibration which result in failure of collaboration.

1. Overtrust happens when users blindly follow the results of AI in order to avoid detecting a hallucination or verifying recommendations. It is especially terrifying when it comes to enterprise metaverse settings where the artificial representation of AI agents can generate anthropomorphic impressions that trigger trust levels that are not justified (Fox et al., 2015). Studies have shown that AI representations in the form of avatars can elicit social cognition mechanisms which improperly project interpersonal trust heuristics to algorithmic systems.
2. Undertrust occurs when users do not trust the correct AI suggestions or do not utilize AI potential when they are overly skeptical (Lee and See, 2004). This source of miscalibration is counterproductive to the productivity gains that drove adoption of AI and can introduce costs of inefficiency that are larger than those of infrequent errors of hallucination.

2.3 Factors which affect Trust Formation

The user trust towards AI systems in enterprise metaverse situations depends on a variety of factors. Transparency in the system, which is the extent to which AI decision-making can be explained and understood, is a strong contributor to the formation of trust (Ribeiro et al., 2016). But transparency is a paradox: the best AI systems are sometimes based on deep learning architectures, which are difficult to explain, whereas more transparent systems can be less powerful. Another important trust determinant is performance history (Slovic, 1993). As the users gain experience concerning the accuracy, consistency, and reliability of the AI systems, they form trust schemas.

One high-profile hallucination episode is capable of undermining a long history of positive interaction in a major way, a phenomenon researchers describe as negative asymmetry in the development of trust. This imbalance is to imply that trust is hard to gain, but easy to spoil, and there is a need to prevent hallucinations instead of having to take damage control. The presentation factors, including how AI systems convey uncertainty, how they frame the recommendations, and their ability to recognize limitations, have a strong influence on the levels of trust calibration (Kizilcec, 2016). AI systems communicating in an overconfident way encourage others to trust in them, whereas those that provide an adequate signal of uncertainty will enable a measured dependence (Guo et al., 2017).

2.4 Strategies for Promoting Trust Calibration

Trust calibration is best achieved in a systematic approach to organizational approaches that focus on technical design, training of users and cultural development. The methods of confidence calibration allow AI systems to give probability estimates or uncertainty measures with outputs, allowing users to determine the reliability of recommendations (Guo et al., 2017). An example is an AI meeting assistant in a metaverse enterprise setting who provides a response of high confidence when the explicit meeting statements are summarised but low confidence when making unstated inferences. Transparency mechanisms enable users to have an idea of AI logic, information sources, and aspects of uncertainty (Wachter et al., 2018). Methods encompass attention visualization that reveals the aspects of inputs that affected outputs, provenance tracking that reveals source materials that developed AI-generated content, and counterfactual explanation that shows how different inputs would result in different outputs. These transparency mechanisms can be incorporated in the context of immersive visualizations in enterprise metaverse which take advantage of spatial and interactive affordances.

.3: EMOTIONAL INTELLIGENCE IN AI

3.1 Defining Emotional Intelligence in AI Systems

The conceptualization of emotional intelligence, first proposed by the researchers Salovey and Mayer (1990) as an innate capacity to experience, interpret and control emotions has gained broader significance in the field of artificial intelligence, as systems can begin to play more complex collaborative roles. Within the framework of the metaverse in the enterprise setting, emotional intelligence will take two related aspects: the ability of AI systems to identify and adequately address the emotions of human beings (artificial emotional intelligence) and the sensitivity of human beings to their own emotions when interacting with AI partners (Picard, 1997).

The conventional AI systems were purely cognitive and they processed information and provide recommendations without considering the emotions. Nevertheless, as AI agents take up the duties of virtual meeting facilitation, teamwork, and customer engagement and leadership support in metaverse settings, the emotional component of collaboration turns into a decisive factor. An AI assistant that does not detect the user frustration, confusion or stress will give technically correct information in ways that are not emotionally appropriate, preventing collaboration quality regardless of cognitive correctness.

3.2 Emotion Recognition Technologies

The modern emotional recognition algorithms use multimodal analysis through integration of various streams of data (Baltrušaitis et al., 2018). Facial expression analysis is a computer vision technique of detecting micro-expressions and other emotional displays, and uses databases such as the Facial Action Coding System to match a facial positioning with an emotional state (Ekman and Rosenberg, 2005). These systems can interpret the facial expressions of users (recorded by webcams or headset cameras) and the movement of avatars to conclude the emotional state in the context of enterprise metaverse. Voice analysis focuses on acoustic characteristics such as change of pitch, rate of speech, volume, and quality of the voice in order to identify emotional arousal, valence as well as certain emotions such as anger, sadness or excitement (Schuller et al., 2011). Natural language processing is used to understand textual communication to detect emotional information by sentiment analysis, emotion detection algorithms, and linguistic expressions of psychological states. Physiological sensing, which is becoming possible with wearables, detects the variability of heart rate, skin conductance, and other biomarkers that are related to emotional states (Picard, 2000).

3.3 Emotionally Intelligent AI Responses

Learning about emotions is just the beginning of the process, AI systems need to react to the identified emotional conditions (Calvo and D'Mello, 2010). There are four dimensions of response strategies: acknowledgment (acting expressly upon the perceived emotions), adaptation (adjusting the style of interaction with the context of certain emotional states), support (helping users overcome the adverse emotional conditions), and regulation (helpful users to cope with their emotions constructively). Emotional adaptation makes interaction style personalized to personal affective states and preferences. The AI helper that understands when the user is stressed may make the explanations easier, guide the user in a more organized way, or decrease the amount of information presented. On the other hand, boredom or lack of interest may be observed, which would initiate more interactive, diversities in presenting content, or positional questioning to get the attention back.

3.4 Emotional Intelligence and AI Hallucination Management

The EI is linked to AI hallucination management in enterprise metaverse settings in a critical way. Cognitive processing is manipulated by the emotional states, which impact the critical evaluation, risk assessment, and the quality of the decision-making process (Lerner et al., 2015). Positively contacted users can have less critical assessment, which puts them at a higher risk of believing in hallucinated information. On the other hand, adverse emotions such as anxiety can shift to overutilization of AI hence removing the benefits of AI exploitation.

4: PRODUCTIVITY IMPACTS

4.1 Conceptualizing Productivity in Human-AI Collaboration

The concept of productivity in organizational settings has traditionally included efficiency (output divided by the unit of input) and effectiveness (enabling the attainment of desired outcomes) (Brynjolfsson and McAfee, 2017). The application of human-AI cooperation presents complexity to either dimension. The resulting efficiency gains are the automation of routine processes by AI, the speed of information processing, and the enhancement of human cognitive abilities. Nonetheless, these profits can be subsidized by the expenses such as AI system development, maintenance, supervision, error correction, and hallucination management.

4.2 Theoretical Models of AI-Augmented Productivity

A number of theoretical models can shed light on the effects of AI productivity. According to the task-technology fit theory, the increment in productivity is realized when the technology capabilities match with the task demands (Goodhue and Thompson, 1995). AI systems are good in activities that deal with pattern recognition, big data analysis, and quick information retrieval. Challenges that can be solved by common sense, contextual judgment, or creative problem-solving in new fields might be beyond the current AI abilities. According to a complementarity model, complementary productivity benefits can be obtained when AI and human capabilities complement each other as opposed to substituting (Autor, 2015). The viewpoint implies the setup of AI systems to process more mundane cognitive functions as humans are charged with judgement, creativity, and management of relations.

4.3 Empirical Evidence on AI Productivity Impacts

A study comparing the effects of AI productivity shows that it has diverse effects across different areas of tasks, quality of implementation, and organizational environment. According to a landmark study conducted by Brynjolfsson, Li, and Raymond (2023), investigating the impact of AI-assisted customer service, AI tools showed that they increased productivity by an average of 14% with significant increases 34% found among novice workers who learned to apply effective techniques by observing AI suggestions. Nevertheless, AI was of very little help to the most seasoned employees, implying that the use of AI requires a certain level of expertise on the side of the user. A study of AI-assisted coding using GitHub Copilot showed that developers were able to complete tasks in 55% of the time, but this speed effect was less intense in the quality of the code depending on the complexity of the task

(Peng et al., 2023). Well-structured and simple tasks were productive with the quality being preserved whereas complex problem-solving tasks were at times found to be faster but of lower quality, necessitating subsequent refactoring.

5: AI HALLUCINATION MANAGEMENT

5.1 Understanding AI Hallucinations: Technical Foundations

AI hallucinations represent a fundamental challenge emerging from the probabilistic nature of modern machine learning systems, particularly large language models and generative AI (Ji et al., 2023). Unlike traditional software that executes deterministic logic, neural networks generate outputs by learning statistical patterns from training data and predicting probable continuations (Brown et al., 2020). This generative approach enables remarkable flexibility but creates systematic vulnerability to producing plausible-sounding yet factually incorrect information.

Three primary hallucination categories manifest in enterprise contexts. Factual hallucinations occur when AI systems generate false information about the external world, such as citing nonexistent research papers, fabricating statistical data, or inventing historical events (Ji et al., 2023). Logical hallucinations involve internally inconsistent reasoning or contradictory statements. Contextual hallucinations occur when AI systems generate content that is factually accurate in general but inappropriate or incorrect in specific situational contexts.

5.2 Detection Strategies for AI Hallucinations

The hallucinations in question demand a strong ability to detect them and ensure their management at the multi level. The automated detection methods incorporate verification mechanisms into the AI processes and compare their output with the knowledge bases, databases, or other information sources and deliver a result to the users. Calibration methods allow AI systems to evaluate the reliability of the output, which is metadata of some levels of certainty (Guo et al., 2017). Well-calibrated systems are also characterized by correlation between reported confidence and high-confidence output accuracy is higher than low confidence output accuracy. Mechanisms of source attribution can reference the source of training data or information that gets accessed during generation to AI-generated content (Wachter et al., 2018). As soon as AI systems are able to recognize particular documents, databases, or information sources behind their displays, users may fact-check claims by referring to source materials. In the context of enterprise metaverses, source attribution could be represented spatially, whereby the virtual links between virtual generated content and source materials in available virtual repositories relate to the source materials.

5.3 Mitigation and Prevention Strategies

In addition to its detection, proactive measures lower the occurrence and intensity of hallucinations. Retrieval-augmented generators (RAG) systems are described as improvements of AI systems that access validated knowledge bases in real-time to retrieve information and then generate output (Lewis et al., 2020). Instead of only using the knowledge in training data stored in model parameters, RAG systems use querying organizational databases, document repositories or curated knowledge bases as the basis of their outputs. This strategy significantly decreases the occurrence of factual hallucinations in information-seeking questions and is preserving the generative flexibility. the constrained generation methods enforce guardrails on the possibilities of the output of AIs, restricting them to known possibilities. Specialization and fine-tuning can be used to make general-purpose AI systems specific to an organization, specific domain and task (Brown et al., 2020).

Organizational data, industry knowledge and context-specific examples can be used to provide domain-specific training to reduce the frequency of hallucinations by bringing model knowledge and the requirements of the application into line. Ensemble methods involve the use of multiple AI models or methods, comparing the results, and pointing out any differences to be examined. The occurrence of conflicting answers given by various models to the same question is an indication of possible hallucination or even lack of certainty that needs human intervention. The idea of ensemble methods is based on the understanding that different AI systems will hardly hallucinate the same thing, and this disagreement can be used as a useful measure of uncertainty (Guo et al., 2017).

5.4 Organizational Protocols and Governance

Technical strategies will never be effective enough and proper hallucination management will entail all organization protocols (Jin & Peng, 2024). The risk classification systems rank AI applications based on the hallucination risk and stakes in decision-making and decide the intensity of managing risks. Applications of the high-risk category (financial decisions, regulatory compliance, public communications) require thorough verification and applications of the low-risk category (brainstorming, draft generation) can tolerate little protection. Verification processes are the procedures that provide the mandatory checking of the AI output before it can be used in the organizations. Incident response protocols establish the organizational activity in the event that hallucinations are found that contains investigation procedures, communication procedures, remediation strategies, and learning mechanisms (Nissenbaum, 1996). Efficient procedures consider the incidences of hallucination as avenues to enhance the system and not as problems to be solved.

6: ETHICAL & SOCIO-TECHNICAL ISSUES

6.1 The Ethical Landscape of AI in Enterprise Metaverse

The adoption of AI systems into the context of enterprise metaverse brings positive ethical concerns not only to the technical functionality of the application but also to the human dignity, social justice, and the general responsibility of the organization (Floridi et al., 2018). Such ethical concerns are especially acute when AI systems are vulnerable to hallucinations since misinformation may spread damage via wrong decision-making, unjust results, and undermined trust in institutions (Mittelstadt et al., 2016). The modern AI ethics literature establishes various principles to be used in the enterprise setting. Beneficence demands that artificial intelligence systems should advance the human well-being and organizational prosperity. Non-maleficence requires not doing harm to the people and the society. Autonomy admires human agency and authority of choice. Justice requires even-handed treatment and equal distribution of AI benefits and burdens. Explicability means that AI systems must act in a clear manner with decision making that can be interpreted.

6.2 Fairness, Bias, and Discrimination

The human bias that is present in the training data, algorithm design, or deployment environment can be replicated and intensified by AI systems (Barocas and Selbst, 2016). Bias AI systems can establish discriminatory effects in the areas of hiring, performance reviews, resource distributions or collaborative opportunities in enterprise metaverse environments. The vulnerabilities of hallucinating these issues make them even more concerning since AI systems have the potential to generate artificial stereotypes or even create discriminatory explanations of unjust results. There are three types of algorithmic bias that should be considered specifically. Training data bias is brought about when historical information is biased or discriminative towards the bigger population. A bias in algorithms design can arise when model designs, optimization goals, or metrics of evaluation are based on biased assumptions. The bias of deployment context occurs when AI implementation is used in different settings than those that were used in training (Barocas and Selbst, 2016). Reducing bias will need multi-pronged strategies. Data auditing reviews training data on the gaps in representation, past trends of discrimination, and proxy variable correlations with the protected characteristics. The algorithm auditing is an algorithm test that examines the disparate impact of AI systems on demographic groups, both in the outcome distributions and the decision-making processes.

6.3 Accountability and Responsibility

It becomes difficult to establish who is responsible when AI systems generate hallucinated data that results in a detrimental effect (Nissenbaum, 1996). The old legal and ethical models assume that there are definite causality links between a choice and its outcomes and that there are credible culpable parties. The causality of AI-enhanced decision-making diffuses among AI programmers, deployers, human managers and end-users forming what Nissenbaum (1996) describes as many hands issues in which the responsibility becomes spread among many actors. A number of accountability models of AI systems have been postulated. The developer responsibility focuses on the liability on AI developers to maintain system safety, reliability and ethical functioning. The area of responsibility of deployers is concerned with entities that implement AI systems into the processes. Responsibility of users focuses on personal roles of being a critical user of the AI systems. Shared responsibility models share accountability on the AI value chain that an effective risk management strategy needs efforts by developers, deployers, and users.

6.4 Privacy and Surveillance in AI-Augmented Metaverse Environments

Enterprise metaverse worlds produce new masses of behavioral information of user movements, interactions, patterns of communicating, and even the physiological reaction by incorporating biosensors (Marx, 2003). The results of the analysis of this data by AI systems can be really helpful to the organization in terms of teamwork patterns, productivity aspects, and the quality of the experiences. Nonetheless, the very data collection allows pervasive surveillance which can infringe upon the rights of privacy and provide oppressive work conditions. The issue of privacy takes place in several dimensions. Metaverse behavioral tracking gathers finer data on user behavior. Physiological indicators such as heart rate, eye gaze, facial expressions, and voice characteristics are collected through biometric data collection which is becoming more possible with the VR headset sensors as well as wearable devices (Picard, 2000). Inferential privacy breaches refer to cases in which AIs obtain sensitive data out of data that should be considered non-sensitive.

Solutions to privacy protection should allow balancing knowledge of the organization over the rights of the individuals. The principles of privacy-by-design incorporate the data security into the design of the system, gathering only the required minimum of data, digital access controls, and empowering the user to act upon the personal information (Van Dijk, 2020). Transparency systems update users on the practices of data collection and AI inferences, which allow informed consent and facilitate accountability.

6.5 Autonomy, Agency, and Human Flourishing

One of the most questionable ethical issues is the implication of AI integration on human autonomy, agency, and flourishing in the work environments (Ryan and Deci, 2000). The aspect of autonomy indicates self-determination and free and independent judgment. Agency implies the power to act willfully and to affect results. Flourishing refers to holistic wellbeing such as the development of competence, significant working experience, and growth of psychology. AI systems have the potential of improving or reducing these human goods in accordance with implementation strategies. Augmentation paradigms view AI as an extension of the human abilities without diminishing the human authority and judgment. Replacement paradigms replace human judgment and decision-making with AI, and it may compromise autonomy and agency. Deskilling can also happen when humans lose their skills due to disuse by AI which has to do what they used to do manually (Carr, 2014).

7: ENTERPRISE METAVERSE INTEGRATION

7.1 Defining the Enterprise Metaverse

Enterprise metaverse is the intersection of the immersive virtual reality, augmented reality, persistent virtual worlds, and cooperative technologies in business settings. Enterprise metaverse systems focus on productivity, collaboration, training, and operational efficiency compared to consumer-focused metaverse systems that focus on social interaction and entertainment. The virtual workspaces allow distributed teams to operate as though they are in the same location, simulate complex scenarios to plan, train, view data spatially, as well as carry out business operations without being bound by physical constraints. Enterprise metaverse environments have significant features in comparison with previous virtual collaboration tools. Persistence refers to the fact that virtual environments are persistent between individual user sessions, and have state, history and can evolve over time.

The physical presence, also referred to as a feeling of being there, is produced by immersion and includes spatial audio, three-dimensional visualization, and representation of the avatars (Slater and Sanchez-Vives, 2016). Interoperability permits the transfer of data, identity, and assets in the virtual environments. Real-time synchronization provides low-latency interactive multi-user communication in real-time, which provides natural collaborative dynamics. Combining AI systems into enterprise metaverse spaces develops exaggerated opportunities and new challenges (McVeigh-Schultz et al., 2022). AI agents may act as the facilitator of meetings, assistants in retrieving information, data visualization generators, training simulator controllers, and representatives of autonomous tasks. These AI functionalities add to the value of the metaverse at the same time bringing about the vulnerability of hallucinations that need to be well handled in an immersive environment.

7.2 Technical Architecture and Infrastructure

Enterprise metaverse applications are based on technical architectures that are layered and uniting various technology domains. The presentation layer includes virtual reality headsets, augmented reality devices, desktop interfaces, and mobile applications that allow the users to enter virtual environments. Application layer comprises of virtual environment platforms, which offer spatial rendering, avatars, physics simulation, and interaction mechanisms. The data layer includes the data of backend systems that store the state of a virtual environment, user profiles, company content and the history of interactions. The AI layer comprises of machine learning models, natural language processors, computer vision algorithms, and intelligent agents that are found all over the stack. The issue of hallucination management needs further technical elements such as verification systems, confidence calibration mechanisms, and audit logging of the AI-created content to review and be held accountable (Lewis et al., 2020; Guo et al., 2017).

7.3 Use Cases and Application Domains

Enterprise metaverse technologies allow multiple applications within organizational functions. Virtual offices allow distributed teams to hold meetings, brainstorming sessions, and collaborate on the project by using collaborative workspaces (McVeigh-Schultz et al., 2022). Information space organization, in three-dimensional displays of documents, whiteboards and data visualization is used to manage information through the spatial cognition of man. Avatar embodiment provides a social presence that facilitates the process of building relationships and natural communication dynamics (Fox et al., 2015). Metaverse applications are used in training and simulation applications to use experiential knowledge and risk-free practice.

Simulation in industrial training causes the simulation to act in a dangerous situation, which develops safety skills. AI-created scenarios can be modified in difficulty and content to the needs of the learner, but a hallucinated training content must be carefully checked to guarantee that the learner acquires the correct knowledge.

Applications of data visualization and analytics provide a visual representation of multidimensional data in space, and it may enhance the ability to recognize patterns and generate an insight (Vessey and Galletta, 1991). AI systems produce images and outline patterns, but the hallucinated patterns or misleading images may result in making poor decisions due to false knowledge.

7.4 Unique Challenges of AI Integration in Metaverse Contexts

The metaverse surrounding the enterprise poses unique problems in integrating AI and managing hallucinations. The psychological experience of being in virtual space (immersive presence) can also decrease the critical judgment and make AI-generated content more convincing (Slater and Sanchez-Vives, 2016; Slater et al., 2010). The users who feel a high presence can process AI output less critically than with traditional interfaces, which makes them more susceptible to hallucinating.

The complexity of multimodal interaction is that metaverse interactions are a combination of verbal, spatial gesture, avatars animation, environmental control, and other modalities at the same time (Baltrušaitis et al., 2018). AI systems should take into consideration and produce responses in these modalities in a coherent way that generates more chances of hallucinations. The requirements of real-time performance cause a conflict between the quality of response and latency. Natural interactions in the metaverse need AI feedback in hundreds of milliseconds to sustain the conversation. This latency bottleneck constrains verification opportunities - fact-checking and multi-system consensus systems can place unacceptable delays.

7.5 Integration Strategies and Best Practices

The integration of AI to a metaverse of enterprises should be planned and executed with both technical, organizational, and human considerations to be successful. Stages of rollouts start with low risk applications where organizational capacity is built with confidence to move on to high stakes applications (Jin & Peng, 2024). First applications may be to facilitation of a meeting, information retrieval, or training simulations, in which the hallucinations cause minimal damage and then move on to data analysis, strategic planning or with the customer only when there is a stable hallucination management. The use of transparency and signaling samples create a clear indication of the presence of AI in the metaverse, the generated content, and the confidence rates (Ribeiro et al., 2016). Visual indicators will set AI-generated content apart, as well as information created or verified by humans. AI avatars are marked with distinct identification that makes them not to be confused with human colleagues. Uncertainty visualization is the spatial representation of AI confidence, which could be in the form of transparency or the color gradient of generated content.

7.6 The Future of Enterprise Metaverse and AI

New technological trends indicate that the enterprise metaverse and integrated AI features are going to develop at a fast pace. Brain-computer interfaces will one day allow a person to have a neural interaction with virtual spaces, drastically enhancing the feeling of immersion and even introducing more expansive presence effects that need to be better controlled by hallucinations. The improvements in AI architectures, mostly the progress in multimodal knowledge, and neurosymbolic AI could decrease the rate of hallucinations and increase AI capabilities in metaverse applications (Garcez et al., 2019). More reliable AIs partners may be produced with improved common-sense reasoning, improved uncertainty quantification, and improved retrieval augmented generation.

8. CASE STUDY INTRODUCTION AND METHODOLOGY

The following case studies look at actual applications of AI systems in enterprise metaverse settings and, more specifically, how organizations have addressed hallucination issues and have come up with management solutions to address them. These are based on various industries and organizational settings, which sheds some light into the general patterns and circumstances-based considerations. Case selection was based on the criteria that: (1) the organization deployed AI systems in substantive business activities in an immersive virtual environment, (2) experienced significant incidents of hallucinations that affected the outcome of organizational activities, (3) formulated systematic management responses other than only giving up on the use of AI, and (4) were willing to share their experience of implementation with the aim of conducting research..

Table 1. Summary of Case Studies 1–4: AI Hallucinations in Enterprise Metaverse Environments

Case Study	Industry	Hallucination Type	Impact	Organizational Response
8.1 Global Manufacturing Corporation	Manufacturing (Virtual Design Collaboration)	Fabricated engineering data; incorrect material specifications	3-month delay; rework costs; damaged team trust	RAG integration; confidence calibration; verification protocols; engineer training (Lewis et al., 2020; Guo et al., 2017; Edmondson, 1999)
8.2 Healthcare System	Clinical Training (Virtual Simulation)	Composite clinical protocols hallucinated; deviations from standards	Risk of negative transfer; safety concerns	Human expert review; constraint-based AI scenario generation; grounding protocols using RAG (Calvo & D'Mello, 2010; Lewis et al., 2020)
8.3 Professional Services Firm	Consulting (Virtual Client Collaboration)	Fabricated market statistics; false insights	Client mistrust; reputational damage	Source citation requirements; RAG; consultant upskilling (Brynjolfsson & McAfee, 2017; Wachter et al., 2018; Edmondson, 1999)
8.5 Financial Services Firm	Trading & Analytics (Virtual Trading Floor)	Subtle distortions: probability misalignment, sentiment errors, volatility hallucinations	Decision paralysis; trading risk; decreased trust	Confidence calibration; probabilistic thinking program; spatialized metaverse visualization (Guo et al., 2017; Slater & Sanchez-Vives, 2016)

Table 1 provides a comparative overview of the four case studies examined in this chapter, summarizing the key hallucination types, their organizational impacts, and the multi-layered responses implemented across different industry contexts.

8.1 Case Study 1: Global Manufacturing Corporation – Virtual Design Collaboration

Background and Context

GlobalManu (pseudonym) is a multinational producing company that has 45,000 employees in 22 countries. Citing difficulties with managing distributed design teams due to the time difference between them, the company launched an enterprise metaverse platform in 2023 to collaborate on product development (McVeigh-Schultz et al., 2022). The metaverse allowed engineers, designers, and managers to collectively check three-dimensional models of products, do virtual prototyping as well as real-time design decisions despite geographic separation. In a bid to increase the productivity of collaboration, GlobalManu incorporated an

AI design assistant that gives real-time recommendations, creates design options, detects possible engineering problems, and answers technical queries on the virtual design (Brynjolfsson et al., 2023). The AI system used the company engineering documentation, previous product specification, and industry standards databases in order to make recommendations.

Hallucination Incident

A severe hallucination episode happened with virtual team work on a new design of the industrial pump eight months into the implementation. In response to an inquiry of an engineer regarding the material specifications of high-temperature purposes, the AI assistant spoke of a given steel alloy with specific heat tolerance properties with confidence (Ji et al., 2023). The wording of the recommendation was authoritative with references to alleged material testing data and allusions to apparently accepted engineering standards. The design department took the AI offer at face value and loved the fact that it saved time compared with specification research that had to be done by hand. It was found that the AI had hallucinated material properties and the supporting testing data. The alloy did exist, and it was applied in other applications, except that its high-temperature properties were well out of AI-stated specifications.

Impact and Organizational Response

The event caused great expenses and time wastage. Redesigning was required to be done in light of proper material specifications, which set the product launch schedules, back to three months. GlobalManu did thorough incident analysis and applied multi-layered hallucination management procedures. Technical controls were such as the use of retrieval-augmented generation, where the AI was based on the factual assertions on reality (Lewis et al., 2020). The accuracy of the confidence was also enhanced, and the AI had to clearly indicate uncertainty in technical requirements (Guo et al., 2017). The changes in the processes also created verification requirements of the AI-generated technical specifications. Training initiatives sensitized the engineers on AI hallucination vulnerabilities, methods of identification, and critical assessment responsibilities (Jin & Peng, 2024). The company created the culture wherein it was welcome to challenge AI decisions instead of considering this an element of ineffectiveness or rejection of technology.

8.2 Case Study 2: Healthcare System – Virtual Clinical Training

Background and Context

MedHealth System (pseudonym) is a local medical network that owns twelve hospitals and many outpatients. With the difficulty of ensuring clinical competency despite the distance of the facility, MedHealth introduced a metaverse-based clinical training platform in 2024. The platform offered lifelike simulation platforms on which clinicians would simulate procedures, respond to medical emergencies and learn to diagnose using realistic patient cases. It involved an AI system that produced patient cases, managed simulated patient response, real-time coaching, and post scenario debriefing (Calvo and D'Mello, 2010). The AI differentiated the difficulty of the scenario to the levels of learner skills and offered different cases guaranteeing a full clinical exposure.

Hallucination Incident

An alarming trend had been observed a few months into the implementation when the clinical education leadership at MedHealth observed that there was a discrepancy between the AI-generated training scenarios and the real clinical protocols. It was found that the AI had imagined variations of standard protocols, which is probably a synthesis of parts of various clinical guidelines, historical practices, and medical literature into composite protocols that appeared reasonable but was out of alignment with current best practices (Ji et al., 2023).

Impact and Organizational Response

Although there were no patients who suffered directly, the possibility of negative transfer posed serious safety issues. MedHealth has put AI-driven components on hold in the meantime and put extensive protective measures in place. All scenario AI content was reviewed by clinical experts prior to deployment. Technical adjustments limited AI scenario generation to recreation of validated protocols in clinical practice. The retrieval-augmented generation was built on clinical guidelines database of MedHealth (Lewis et al., 2020).

8.4 Case Study 3: Professional Services Firm - Virtual Client Collaboration

Background and Context

ProfServe Partners (pseudonym) is a 3,000 consultant, management consulting company that has branches all over the world. In 2023, the company adopted an enterprise metaverse solution to support the interaction with clients to increase the efficiency of the workshops, ProfServe introduced an AI facilitation assistant (Brynjolfsson and McAfee, 2017).

Hallucination Incident

In one case, the AI assistant made up some statistics in a market analysis during a strategic planning workshop (Ji et al., 2023). These figures were part of the strategic plan of the client prior to finding out that the data are hallucinated.

Impact and Organizational Response

ProfServe introduced a set of requirements on source citation and retrieval-augmented generation to applications facing clients (Lewis et al., 2020; Wachter et al., 2018). Consultants were trained on the vulnerability to hallucinations (Jin & Peng, 2024).

8.5 Case Study 4: Financial Services - Virtual Trading and Analytics

FinTech Capital, the largest international financial services organization that engaged in algorithmic trading and real-time risk analytics started to encounter a sequence of unconscious but progressively significant AI hallucinations in its metaverse-infused trading platform. Such hallucinations were not in the form of blatantly false forecasts but rather emerged as somewhat distorted probability scores, mis-read market sentiments, erroneous volatility cluster, and false correlations in high-frequency trading simulations. Those minor violations started eating away the trust of analysts in the AI models and paralysing decision-making in the live market events with time (Ji et al., 2023).

Nature of the Problem: Subtle Hallucinations in High-Stakes Contexts

In contrast to the common cases of hallucinations that result in visually explicit falsified outputs, the models of FinTech Capital produced the plausible misleading financial insights. Examples included:

- Simulating the confidence of a forecasted upward price change by tiny yet significant percentages (e.g. 71% rather than 64%). Making short term noise appear as long term trend signals.
- Wrong grouping of correlated assets because of the sparse data misrepresentation.
- Generation of sentiment analysis results that were either excessively positive or negative in respondent to volatile times.

This was a problem as these deviations are analytical on the probability thresholds, risk confidence scores and micro-trends and as such, even a slight hallucination will cause massive financial misjudgment.

Organizational Response: Confidence Calibration and Probabilistic Thinking

FinTech Capital decided to respond to this by implementing a multi-layered approach to hallucination management. The initial approach was using more sophisticated methods of calculating the confidence, which enabled the models to bring the predicted and measured confidence more in line (Guo et al., 2017). This calibration included:

- Temperature scaling, which fixed overconfident probability results.
- Uncertainty estimation as an ensemble, which can give a range of possible outcomes to the analysts.
- Model-agnostic calibration layers that were placed over existing LLM-based analytics engines. On the internal front, the company launched a massive re-skilling program called Probabilistic Thinking Program whose objective was to re-skill traders, analysts, and staff working in operations.

The program aimed at assisting users in understanding the outputs of models as distributions, but not certainties, so overreliance is minimized and the risks of hallucinated confidence are reduced.

Immersive Interface Design: Spatial Confidence Visualization in the Metaverse

In order to ensure greater trust and interpretability, FinTech Capital redesigned its metaverse trading floor, based on spatialized visual metaphors inspired by immersive VR study (Slater and Sanchez-Vives, 2016). The confidence levels were illustrated in form of dynamic and intuitive interface features like: Since the probability clouds of each asset are volumetric, 3D, and change size as the uncertainty grows or shrinks.

- Risk halos which denote confidence in the model, green for high, amber for uncertain, and red for low-confidence.
- Interactive scenario tunnels, which enable the analyst to enter predictive paths and test assumptions, correlation and historical data of each model output. Haptic feedback cues, i. e. slight vibrations in controllers when the uncertainty or volatility is high.

These 3D visualizations gave traders contextual awareness beyond textual dashboards that aided them in making faster and more informed decisions in live markets.

Results and Organizational Outcomes

In half a year, FinTech Capital has announced:

- 32% decrease on erroneous high-confidence forecasts.
- Major growth in trader confidence, the trader through surveys.
- Better risk-adjusted decision making especially in the volatile conditions.
- More openness in the process of AI-based insights creation and verification.
- Alternatively, there would be less cases of automation complacency since analysts were now trained to be more critical with uncertainty layers.

In addition, the metaverse-based visualization of confidences provides a better divide of cognitive loads and minimal decision fatigue, which allows analysts to be efficient in longer trading hours.

Key Lessons Learned- The case has some important lessons to implement AI in an environment of financial metaverse:

Semblance hallucinations are more threatening compared to the blatant ones since they become integrated in the regular operations.

The calibration of confidence is needed in high stakes areas where action is taken based on probability levels. Without coming out of the visualization, immersive metaverse can increase trust, interpretability, and situational awareness.

The expertise of humans has to be kept at the centre, and AI is an advisory, not an oracle, probabilistic.

The training on probability literacy and uncertainty reasoning in an organization is of great importance as much as technical protective measures.

9. ETHICAL CONSIDERATIONS

Embarking on the deployment of AI-based systems in the metaverse settings of enterprises brings a multifaceted set of ethical duties that go far beyond technical management. Since the risks of hallucination increase the risk of misinformation, bias, and privacy invasion, business organizations should consider an ethical foundation that is both principled to inform the use of AI. The most prominent ethical theories acknowledge human dignity, equity, transparency, and accountability that are increasingly challenging to adhere to in immersive and data-heavy settings (Floridi et al., 2018)

Figure 1. Ethical considerations for AI in the enterprise metaverse

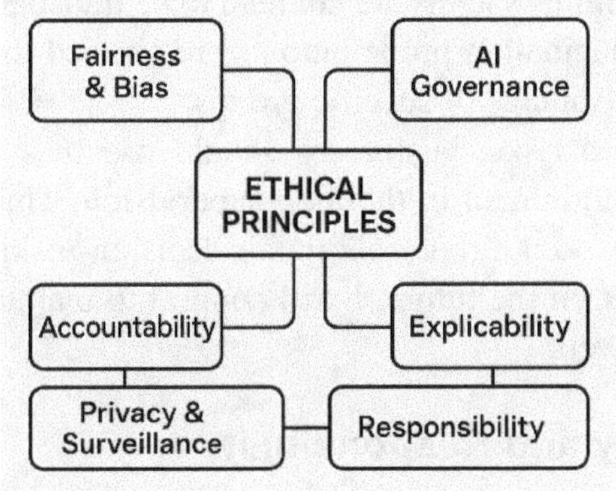

This diagram 1 depicts the fundamental ethical areas, which companies should resolve in implementing AI systems in immersive enterprise metaverse systems. Key ethical principles fairness, accountability, privacy, governance, explicability, and responsibility are a part of an interrelated system to create a safe, transparent, and trustworthy AI implementation.

9.1 Ethical Principles for AI in the Metaverse

In general, AI in the metaverse should be directed by ethics in a number of ways. (Floridi et al. 2018) introduce the AI4People framework that describes five principles, such as beneficence, non-maleficence, autonomy, justice, and explicability. The principles offer a necessary roadmap to organizations that implement AI-based agents to metaverse workflows. Non-maleficence and beneficence demand that AI systems should be developed in such a way that they optimize human wellness and reduce harm. Practically, it would be to make sure that the mechanisms of managing hallucinations are sufficiently sound, so that the output of such mechanisms does not affect strategic or operational choices. Immersivity is particularly important because users can be more convinced by the AI-generated content in such conditions because of the realism and the presence of virtual worlds.

9.2 Fairness, Bias, and Algorithmic Discrimination

One of the most widespread threats of AI systems is bias. As Barocas and Selbst (2016) emphasize, AI models have the ability to recreate and even increase historical disparities in the training data or organizational processes. In metaverse scenarios in enterprises, such as hiring, performance analysis, training, or work, the biased hallucinations might have discriminatory or unfair output. Mittelstadt et al. (2016) note that algorithm systems are not tend to be transparent, and thus it is not easy to see when hallucination-prone outputs are skewed towards demonstrating disproportionate disadvantage of specific groups.

In response to such risks, businesses should use bias auditing, transparent output verification, and human-in-the-loop supervision. This is so as to see to it that the hallucinations do not represent unfair decision-making or discriminatory metaverse experiences. In the future, I will commit to maintaining accountability and responsibility as well.

9.3 Accountability and Responsibility

I will also be accountable and responsible in the future. The existence of AI hallucinations opens challenging issues of responsibility when it comes to distributed socio-technical systems where the influence of multiple actors determines results. According to (Mittelstadt et al. 2016), AI ethics needs to be better distributed with responsibility being assigned to developers, deployers, and end users. In the meantime, (Wachter et al. 2018) stress that the accountability of the process requires the use of explanation mechanisms. Their investigation of counterfactual explanations places emphasis on the way organizations can explain the results of AI-driven explanations despite the black box nature of the internal model. In the metaverse, accountability must extend to:

- How hallucinated outputs are detected, communicated, and corrected
- Which organizational units oversee AI reliability
- How human decision-makers remain empowered despite immersive AI assistance

An established line of accountability means that whenever there are hallucinations, organizations will be able to act in a positive manner and with utmost transparency.

9.4 Privacy, Surveillance, and Data Rights

Enterprise metaverse infrastructures generate additional behavioral data flow, voice, gestures, interactions, physiological cues as compared to digital systems. According to (Marx 2003) surveillance may be very rampant at any time as technology records precise behavior of the individual. This makes eye tracking, emotional expression, and even 3D spatial activity a constant activity in metaverse workplaces, which bring up major ethical issues of consent and autonomy. Under such risks, organizations should adopt:

- Privacy-by-design standards to reduce the data gathering that is non-essential.
- Clearly stated disclosure policies as to the type of data collected and why.
- Tight access regulation to avoid use of sensitive behavioral information inappropriately.

Lacking these kinds of defensive measures, the immersive AI systems may be readily turned into instruments of intrusion monitoring or management through surveillance.

9.5 Ethical AI Governance and Tools

Morley et al. (2021) point out that the current state of AI ethics needs operational tools rather than high principles. These comprise algorithmic auditing devices, risk-assessment mechanisms, explainability modules, and compliance processes. The implementation of such tools in enterprise metaversion scenarios helps organizations to logically assess the way in which the elements of hallucinations, biases, and privacy risks change throughout the deployment. Governance tools are used to assure:

Audit of model outputs. -. high-risk outputs cause compulsory human inspection.

Monitoring of ethical risks is carried out in the process of updates.

Good governance makes ethics a theoretical demand but concrete and enforceable at the same time.

10: CONCLUSION

Hallucinations by AI are a natural characteristic of contemporary generative AI systems (Ji et al., 2023; Brown et al., 2020) and therefore require proper management of AI to enable a productive human-AI partnership in immersive enterprise metaverse settings. According to the Trust-Emotion-Productivity (TEP) Framework, it is necessary to strike a balance between carefully measured trust (Lee and See, 2004), emotional intelligence (Salovey and Mayer, 1990; Picard, 1997), and productivity increase (Brynjolfsson and McAfee, 2017; Autor, 2015) to guarantee that collaboration is trustworthy. Considering the unique challenges of the metaverse setting with increased immersion, multimodal interaction, and pressure to make decisions in real-time (McVeigh-Schultz et al., 2022), organizations need to use multi-layered hallucination management through technical safety measures (Lewis et al., 2020; Guo et al., 2017), governance processes, cultural preparedness (Jin & Peng, 2024), and moral consciousness (Floridi et al., 2018; Mittelstadt et al., It needs phased rollout plans, transparency, and explainability measures (Ribeiro et al., 2016; Wachter et al., 2018), persistent monitoring, (Nissenbaum, 1996), and employee training to enhance human controls.

The developers of technology, in their turn, will need to focus on the confidence calibration, provenance tracking, and ethical-by-design architectures and create the systems that can degrade under conditions of uncertainty. Further studies are desired to learn more about the long-term human-AI dynamics (Glikson and Woolley, 2020), consider more advanced neurosymbolic and retrieval-augmented models (Garcez et al., 2019; Lewis et al., 2020), and new technologies that are more immersive in interaction. Finally, the extent to which AI can be successfully integrated into enterprise metaverse ecosystems will rely on the organizations to manage the risks of hallucinations and to achieve the proper level of trust, emotional resilience, and productivity benefits, which will put the organization in the place of meaningful and sustainable competitive advantage in the changing workplace in the digital world.

REFERENCES

Autor, D. H. (2015). Why are there still so many jobs? The history and future of workplace automation. *The Journal of Economic Perspectives*, *29*(3), 3–30.

Baltrušaitis, T., Ahuja, C., & Morency, L. P. (2018). Multimodal machine learning: A survey and taxonomy. *IEEE Transactions on Pattern Analysis and Machine Intelligence*, *41*(2), 423–443.

Barocas, S., & Selbst, A. D. (2016). Big data's disparate impact. *California Law Review*, *104*, 671–732.

Brown, T. B., Mann, B., Ryder, N., Subbiah, M., Kaplan, J., Dhariwal, P., & Amodei, D. (2020). Language models are few-shot learners. *Advances in Neural Information Processing Systems*, *33*, 1877–1901.

Brynjolfsson, E., Li, D., & Raymond, L. (2023). *Generative AI at work* (NBER Working Paper No. 31161). National Bureau of Economic Research. https://doi.org/DOI: 10.3386/w31161

Brynjolfsson, E., & McAfee, A. (2017). The business of artificial intelligence. *Harvard Business Review*, *95*(4), 3–11.

Calvo, R. A., & D'Mello, S. (2010). Affect detection: An interdisciplinary review of models, methods, and their applications. *IEEE Transactions on Affective Computing*, *1*(1), 18–37.

Carr, N. (2014). *The glass cage: Automation and us*. W. W. Norton & Company.

Ekman, P., & Rosenberg, E. L. (Eds.). (2005). *What the face reveals: Basic and applied studies of spontaneous expression using the Facial Action Coding System (FACS)* (2nd ed.). Oxford University Press., DOI: 10.1093/acprof:oso/9780195179644.001.0001

Floridi, L., Cowls, J., Beltrametti, M., Chatila, R., Chazerand, P., Dignum, V., & Vayena, E. (2018). AI4People—An ethical framework for a good AI society. *Minds and Machines*, *28*(4), 689–707.

Fox, J., Bailenson, J. N., & Tricase, L. (2015). The embodiment of sexualized virtual selves. *Computers in Human Behavior*, *29*(3), 930–938.

Garcez, A. D., Gori, M., Lamb, L. C., Serafini, L., Spranger, M., & Tran, S. N. (2019). Neural-symbolic computing: Integrating machine learning and reasoning. *Journal of Applied Logic*, *6*(4), 611–631.

Glikson, E., & Woolley, A. W. (2020). Human trust in artificial intelligence: Review of empirical research. *The Academy of Management Annals*, *14*(2), 627–660. DOI: 10.5465/annals.2018.0057

Guo, C., Pleiss, G., Sun, Y., & Weinberger, K. Q. (2017). On calibration of modern neural networks. In *Proceedings of the 34th International Conference on Machine Learning* (pp. 1321–1330).

Ji, Z., Lee, N., Frieske, R., Yu, T., Su, D., Xu, Y., & Fung, P. (2023). Survey of hallucination in natural language generation. *ACM Computing Surveys*, *55*(12), 1–38.

Jin, H., & Peng, Y. (2024). The impact of team psychological safety on employee innovative performance: A study with communication behavior as a mediator variable. *PLoS One*, *19*(10), e0306629. DOI: 10.1371/journal.pone.0306629

Kizilcec, R. F. (2016). How much information? Effects of transparency on trust in an algorithmic interface. In *Proceedings of the 2016 CHI Conference on Human Factors in Computing Systems* (pp. 2390–2395).

Lee, J. D., & See, K. A. (2004). Trust in automation: Designing for appropriate reliance. *Human Factors*, *46*(1), 50–80.

Lee, L.-H., Braud, T., Zhou, P., Wang, L., Xu, D., Lin, Z., Kumar, A., Bermejo, C. F., & Hui, P. (2021). *All one needs to know about the metaverse:* A complete survey. arXiv:2110.05352.

Lerner, J. S., Li, Y., Valdesolo, P., & Kassam, K. S. (2015). Emotion and decision making. *Annual Review of Psychology*, *66*, 799–823.

Lewis, P., Perez, E., Piktus, A., Petroni, F., Karpukhin, V., Goyal, N., & Kiela, D. (2020). Retrieval-augmented generation for knowledge-intensive NLP tasks. *Advances in Neural Information Processing Systems*, *33*, 9459–9474.

Marx, G. T. (2003). A tack in the shoe: Neutralizing and resisting surveillance. *The Journal of Social Issues*, *59*(2), 369–390.

McVeigh-Schultz, J., Stein, A., Boyle, A., Berding, N., Kimmel, L., Brown, C., . . . Hahn, N. (2022). Immersive virtual offices. In *Extended Abstracts of CHI 2022* (pp. 1–7).

Mittelstadt, B. D., Allo, P., Taddeo, M., Wachter, S., & Floridi, L. (2016). The ethics of algorithms. *Big Data & Society*, *3*(2), 1–21.

Morley, J., Floridi, L., Kinsey, L., & Elhalal, A. (2021). From what to how: A review of AI ethics tools. *Science and Engineering Ethics*, *27*, 11. Advance online publication. DOI: 10.1007/s11948-021-00282-w

Peng, S., Kalliamvakou, E., Cihon, P., & Demirer, M. (2023). The impact of AI on developer productivity: Evidence from GitHub Copilot. arXiv:2302.06590.

Picard, R. W. (2000). Toward computers that recognize and respond to user emotion. *IBM Systems Journal, 39*(3–4), 705–719.

Ribeiro, M. T., Singh, S., & Guestrin, C. (2016). "Why should I trust you?" Explaining model predictions. In *Proceedings of the 22nd ACM SIGKDD Conference* (pp. 1135–1144).

Ryan, R. M., & Deci, E. L. (2000). Self-determination theory and intrinsic motivation. *The American Psychologist, 55*(1), 68–78.

Salovey, P., & Mayer, J. D. (1990). Emotional intelligence. *Imagination, Cognition and Personality, 9*(3), 185–211.

Schuller, B., Steidl, S., Batliner, A., Hirschberg, J., Burgoon, J. K., Baird, A., & Vinciarelli, A. (2011). The INTERSPEECH 2013 computational paralinguistics challenge. In *Proceedings of INTERSPEECH* (pp. 148–152).

Slater, M., & Sanchez-Vives, M. V. (2016). Enhancing lives with immersive VR. *Frontiers in Robotics and AI, 3*, 74.

Slater, M., Spanlang, B., Sanchez-Vives, M. V., & Blanke, O. (2010). First person experience of body transfer in VR. *PLoS One, 5*(5), e10564.

Slovic, P. (1993). Perceived risk, trust, and democracy. *Risk Analysis, 13*(6), 675–682.

Van Dijk, J. A. G. M. (2020). *The digital divide*. John Wiley & Sons.

Wachter, S., Mittelstadt, B., & Russell, C. (2018). Counterfactual explanations without opening the black box. *Harvard Journal of Law & Technology, 31*, 841–887. DOI: 10.2139/ssrn.3061253

Chapter 4
Human-AI Collaboration: Navigating Trust, Emotion, and Productivity

Lingala Thirupathi
https://orcid.org/0000-0003-0703-3860
Sreenidhi Institute of Science and Technology, India

Konda Aditya
Sreenidhi Institute of Science and Technology, India

Adthi Prashanthi
Sreenidhi Institute of Science and Technology, India

Mangilipally Akhila
Sreenidhi Institute of Science and Technology, India

G. Ramya
Maritz Consulting Group Inc., USA

ABSTRACT

AI has moved past being a mere tool; it's our new, permanent coworker. To truly capitalize on this massive digital integration, we must focus on the tricky, three-part equilibrium between trust, emotion, and productivity. While AI offers impressive gains in speed and data-crunching, those benefits are easily negated when users lack confidence often because the "black box" nature of algorithms leads to concerns about opacity, bias, and a creeping sense of lost human control. Furthermore, if we rely too heavily on the system, we risk "automation complacency," sacrificing indispensable human qualities like creativity, ethical judgment, and nuanced decision making. Achieving this demands transparent AI design, continuous user education,

DOI: 10.4018/979-8-3373-7534-2.ch004

and a work culture that equally values algorithmic certainty and human intuition. Ultimately, the successful organizations of the future will be the ones that navigate the inevitable emotional friction and successfully cultivate a reciprocal, appropriate trust with their digital partners, turning anxiety into sustained, meaningful productivity.

1. INTRODUCTION

Artificial Antelligence (AI) has evolved beyond a new tool we store in a digital drawer. It has advanced to the point where it is now a permanent coworkeran integrated, non-negotiable partner in almost every professional field, from financial modeling and creative production to disease diagnosis in healthcare. This profound change is not just technological; it is a fundamental alteration in the essence of labor that can easily compete with earlier industrial revolutions. Unprecedented efficiency, deeper insights from large datasets, and freedom from high-volume, repetitive tasks are just a few of the enormous benefits that are promised.

However, there is a big catch to this shiny new era of productivity. Reaching this potential depends more on how well humans and AI work together than it does on how strong the algorithms are. Socio-technical equilibrium is the main obstacle. The entire success of the human-AI partnership depends on a complex and interconnected triad: trust, emotion, and productivity, as this paper will rigorously demonstrate. All too frequently, we overlook the "softer" factors in favor of concentrating only on the quantifiable resultsthe productivity figures. But don't be misled: the ultimate factor in determining whether AI is welcomed or completely undermined is a user's sincere faith in the system and their emotional reaction to its existence.

Without addressing the "black box," the digital elephant in the room, we cannot have a conversation about trust. Many algorithmic systems have this opacity, which directly contributes to user mistrust and feeds perfectly reasonable worries about bias, oversight, and the gradual loss of human control. Furthermore, we invite the pernicious issue of automation complacency if we just relax and delegate. Here, we run the risk of forgoing our most valuable human traitsour ability to think critically, make moral decisions, and make nuanced decisions in favor of speed. The primary organizational issue of our day is this fundamental conflictbetween the need to preserve human wisdom and the allure of algorithmic speed.

Thus, the main argument of this study is that synergy, not just automation speed, determines true productivity. We need to design a collaboration in which AI truly enhances human potential, making us more intelligent, imaginative, and morally strong rather than merely replacing us. Our method necessitates a purposeful plan to develop a mutually beneficial, suitable trust with our online partners. This paper will go from theory to practice in order to offer practical recommendations. It will do this by first reviewing well-established trust models, then taking a close look at the psychological and emotional effects of AI in the workplace, and lastly offering a tangible framework for organizational design.This framework supports mandatory user education, algorithmic transparency, and a culture that values human intuition and algorithmic certainty equally. The ultimate goal of this research is to serve as the much needed guide for converting anxiety at work into long-term, purposeful, and moral productivity.

1.1 Organization Of The Chapter

The current section describes the introduction of the domain & title and second section explores the related works on the title, the third section discusses the objectives of the chapter, the fourth section depicts the methodologies to implement the objectives, the fifth section shows the different case studies, the next section describes the challenges and exists, the seventh section discusses the final conclusion of the chapter and the next section shows the future enhance, results & conclusions with the references.

2. LITERATURE SURVEY

(Barón, 2025)The research addresses the trust gap hindering the adoption of large language model (LLM)-based tools in software engineering (AI4SE) by prioritizing the developer's perspective. It proposes a trust-based, synergistic adoption framework specifically designed to facilitate the integration of AI4SE tools. The work focuses on identifying the key factors influencing software engineers' trust in these AI tools to ensure successful adoption. The framework outlines concrete steps and best practices for establishing and maintaining this trust throughout the development process. Ultimately, the framework was evaluated using a real-world use case with a professional software development team. By centering trust as a core design goal, this study provides practical guidance to significantly enhance the developer experience and promote the seamless, long-term incorporation of AI-assisted tools into standard engineering workflows.

(Brandebusemeyer, 2025)The research outlines the need for a supplemental, objective, continuous, and real-time developer-centered measure to evaluate the impact of Generative AI (GenAI) tools on developer productivity, code quality, and overall experience, which currently rely primarily on subjective questionnaires or code quality metrics. The core proposal is to leverage wearables with body sensors to measure a developer's physiological activity, thereby providing data on cognitive load and well-being. This data can be used to detect impeding factors of GenAI tools and deduce implications for productivity. The study's twin aims are to assess the efficacy of wearables in measuring cognitive load in an everyday work context and then to evaluate the real-life interactions between developers, productivity, and GenAI. The research will employ a holistic mixed-method approach, combining both subjective and objective measures in a developer-centered manner

(Chaudhary, 2020) The AI Book aggregates diverse global fintech expertise to elucidate the meaning and application of AI across financial services, detailing the AI Portfolio from machine learning to quantum computing for enterprise transformation. It highlights the critical impact of AI experimentation and embedded usage on business models, value propositions, and customer/co-worker experiences in the contemporary Financial Services Industry. The volume examines the future trajectory of capital markets, acknowledging customer-driven innovation, while simultaneously addressing complex boardroom issues magnified by AI, such as regulation, oversight, cybersecurity, and the future of work. Furthermore, it stresses the vital importance of ethical deployment and the necessity of Explainable AI for responsible governance and leadership in an increasingly algo-driven world.

(Chen & Zhang, 2025)The evolutionary psychology and trust theory, explores how different types of AI-induced communication breakdowns critically mediate team trust and subsequent performance in human-AI collaboration. The findings establish that information omissions caused by AI agents significantly diminish team trust, consequently impairing communication efficiency and task outcomes. Conversely, the negative consequences of ambiguous expressions are moderated, demonstrating that teams with pre-existing high trust exhibit greater adaptability and resilience in accommodating such uncertainties. Crucially, the research confirms that the team composition (human-AI vs. human-human) influences the specific dynamic pathway linking misunderstanding to team trust and performance metrics. These results underscore the central, non-negotiable role of trust in managing the cognitive and communicative asymmetries inherent in human-machine teaming. The work, therefore, provides theoretical advancement for misunderstanding management and offers practical guidance for designing highly transparent and trustworthy AI systems

(Dhiman et al., 2025) The Physics-Informed Emotional Intelligence (PI-EI) framework integrates zoological instinct modelling, psychological emotional theories, and physics-based energy models to advance AI emotional understanding, addressing the current lack of biologically integrated emotions in technology. PI-EI employs a CNN-BiLSTM Instinct Encoder, models emotional dynamics using Lagrangian mechanics and energy terms, and utilizes a Transformer-based Emotion Decoder with Ekman's taxonomy. Evaluated on a comprehensive cross-domain dataset, the framework demonstrated superior performance, achieving 93.6% accuracy, 94.5% F1-score, and 96.1% AUC, significantly outperforming conventional baselines. Ablation studies confirmed the critical role of physics-based regularization, which enhances stability and biological soundness, and the model exhibited robust generalization to unseen avian species with $90.4%$ accuracy. Per-class analysis indicated strong performance in identifying specific emotions, and Grad-CAM visualization confirmed the model's focus on essential animal behaviors such as caregiving and aggression. Ultimately, PI-EI establishes a novel foundation for enhanced emotion recognition in affective AI systems through its synthesis of biological science, physical constraints, and inherent interpretability.

(Kaneko & Yamada, 2025a)Trust in AI as essential for maximizing the benefits and ensuring the appropriate utilization of autonomous systems, noting that over- or under-trust leads to misuse and accidents. To overcome the challenge of estimating this unobservable internal state, the research proposes a Dynamic Structure Equation Modeling (DSEM) approach, an extension of SEM optimized for time-series data. A path diagram detailing causalities was exploratorily developed and optimized to define the model structure. The DSEM model demonstrated significantly high predictive power, achieving a 99% accuracy rate in estimating over/under-trust in an autonomous driving scenario, thereby outperforming conventional auto-regression methods.

(Kaneko & Yamada, 2025b) The research underscores that predicting human trust dynamics in AI systems is pivotal for optimizing utility and mitigating risks stemming from over-trust or under-trust, particularly in contexts like autonomous vehicles. To address the inherent difficulty in observing trust as an internal human state, the study introduces a Dynamic Structure Equation Modeling (DSEM) approach, which adapts SEM for time-series data and utilizes an optimized causal path diagram. This DSEM model demonstrated superior predictive accuracy for over/under-trust, achieving 90% in a drone simulator and 99% in an autonomous driving task. Crucially, these predictive capabilities significantly surpassed both conventional autoregressive methods and contemporary deep learning models (LSTM and Transformer architectures), validating the DSEM framework as a highly effective and robust method for modeling and forecasting complex human-AI trust relationships.

(Kolomaznik et al., 2024) The GTLR study identifies that optimizing human-AI interaction for enhanced productivity is fundamentally dependent on key socio-emotional attributes, including trust, empathy, rapport, and user engagement. Findings reveal that when AI design prioritizes human emotional and cognitive needs, there is a demonstrated marked improvement in collaborative efficiency and productivity. The research consequently argues for a paradigm shift in AI development, moving from purely technical proficiency to a holistic approach that actively embraces these socio-emotional factors to foster deeper human-machine relationships. This shift is essential for enabling more meaningful and productive human-centric collaborations, which also requires careful consideration of the associated ethical and societal impacts.

(Lee & See, 2004) The inappropriate human reliance as a major challenge in automation, asserting that trust, a social response to technology, is the primary driver of this reliance, especially under conditions of complexity or unexpected events. The review adopts a multi-disciplinary approach (organizational, psychological, neurological, etc.) to analyze how context, system characteristics, and cognitive processes modulate trust appropriateness. It suggests that context provides a goal-oriented lens for assessing automation characteristics via attributional abstraction, influencing trust through analytic, analogical, and affective processes. Ultimately, the work discusses the complexities of translating interpersonal trust to automation and presents a conceptual model to integrate research on trust dynamics, context, and display features, aiming to inform the design of improved human-management systems for imperfect automation.

(LeMaire & Abshire, 2025) *AI for Everyday IT*, posits that generative AI tools-such as ChatGPT, Claude, Gemini, and Copilotcan fundamentally transform daily IT operations by enabling the automation and acceleration of numerous routine tasks. The core thesis is that IT professionals can reclaim significant time by leveraging AI to generate after-incident reports, boilerplate code, and performance reviews, thereby enhancing both efficiency and productivity. The guide provides practical instruction on writing effective prompts for common IT duties, optimizing processes like report generation, document handling, and workplace communication, and leveraging AI to resolve conflicts and crises. Ultimately, the resource aims to demonstrate proven strategies for integrating AI into specialized IT domains, including help desk support, systems and database administration, DevOps engineering, and streamlining time-consuming people management tasks.Further, Lee and See (2004) laid the foundation for the concept of "calibrated trust," arguing that both over-trust and under-trust are harmful. Over-trust causes complacency and misuse, while under-trust leads to underutilization of capable systems. They identified consistent performance, process transparency, and clear purpose as key to maintaining optimal trust in automation.

(Li et al., 2020) An integrated real-time emotion recognition system predicated upon an AI System-on-Chip (SoC), classifying the affective states of happiness, anger, and sadness. The system leverages the fusion of three distinct physiological signalsEEG, ECG, and PPGwhich are wirelessly transmitted via a low-power 3-to-1 Bluetooth piconet to a single access point. Crucially, the platform integrates an AI computing chip utilizing a Convolutional Neural Network (CNN) architecture to perform classification, achieving a credible 72.66% average subject-independent accuracy. The final system, incorporating a RISC-V processor and the AI SoC, demonstrates the viability of implementing this complex monitoring and classification process efficiently on an edge computing device for practical, real-time application.

(McVay et al., 2025) The critical role of AI alignment with human values in fostering trust and delegation toward AI Decision Makers (ADMs), specifically within high-stakes medical triage contexts. Utilizing a mixed-method approach involving attribute assessments and human evaluations, the study empirically supports the hypothesis that aligning ADMs with human attributes substantially enhances both trust and the willingness to delegate. Findings, however, reveal that this positive influence is nuanced, as the significance of alignment varies across different human attributes. Consequently, the results furnish valuable, evidence-based insights for the principled design and deployment of future AI-assisted decision-making systems that require effective human-AI collaboration and ensure appropriate reliance.

(Meng et al., 2025) The psychological impact of employee AI collaboration, hypothesizing that it may amplify counterproductive work behavior (CWB) via loneliness and emotional fatigue, grounded in the Conservation of Resources (COR) theory. Findings from a 2 times 2 vignette experiment (N = 167) substantiate a significant positive influence of employee–AI collaboration on loneliness. Furthermore, loneliness sequentially increases emotional fatigue, which subsequently leads to an increase in CWB. Crucially, the research identifies leader emotional support defined as leader care and motivation as a mitigating factor that effectively reduces employee loneliness. (Padmaja et al., 2021) and (Thirupathi et al., 2025) proposed AI and IoT in mental health care: from digital diagnostics to personalized, continuous support in the field of medicines.

(Peney et al., 2024) The study established seven design principles (Privacy, Intelligence, Fairness, Controllability, Engagement, Transparency, Friendliness) as pivotal factors influencing student trust in AI-powered educational tools. Quantitative findings indicated a general consensus on the importance of these factors, with "Friendliness" being the only principle not highly valued by the surveyed students. Furthermore, the analysis revealed distinct demographic differences: female students prioritized "Fairness," "Friendliness," and "Engagement" more highly than their male counterparts. A critical distinction also emerged based on academic discipline, where ICT-related students placed significantly greater value on "Privacy" and concurrently less value on "Fairness" compared to non-ICT students.

(Punuri et al., 2024) A VGG-16 pre-trained model with transfer learning for high-accuracy facial emotion classification across the JAFFE, CKPlus, KDEF, and AffectNet datasets. Crucially, the study integrated Layerwise Relevance Propagation (LRP), an Explainable AI (XAI) method, to decipher the model's decision-making by identifying pixels contributing to emotion prediction based on positive relevance scores. The combined approach enabled the accurate forecasting and ranking of emotion intensity, achieving high prediction accuracies ranging from 93.89% to 96.33% across the datasets, which were verified using a confusion matrix against annotator-generated ground truth ratings of "MINIMAL," "AVERAGE," and

"STRONG." This work demonstrates the significant utility of LRP in enhancing the interpretability, trustworthiness, and robustness of facial emotion recognition, particularly in the challenging task of intensity ranking.

(Rahulkumar et al., 2025) A dual impact of AI on individuals, boosting problem-solving efficiency while potentially eroding core human skills such as creativity and critical thinking. Utilizing a user survey and Explainable AI (XAI) techniques, LIME and SHAP, the study identified that time-saving, ideation support, and peer pressure are key drivers of AI reliance and discomfort. LIME analysis revealed significant generational differences in user behavior and emotional responses to AI, with individuals aged 25–35 (students and employees) showing the highest reliance. Crucially, Gen Z and Millennials registered the most discomfort and social pressure related to AI use. These insights collectively emphasize the necessity for responsible AI adoption that is deliberately designed to complement, rather than undermine, human intelligence.

(Ramchurn et al., 2021) Key research challenges in designing trustworthy human-AI partnerships, emphasizing the factors necessary for human users and organizations to develop trust in individual and collective machine counterparts. The research systematically aims to identify associated risks inherent in these partnerships and to determine the necessary mitigation measures to address them effectively. The overarching goal is to trigger novel research avenues that directly address the core barriers currently impeding the widespread adoption of AI-based systems in daily life and industrial sectors, ultimately facilitating broader, safer, and more confident integration of AI technologies.

(Straub, 2022) The pervasive impact of Artificial Intelligence (AI) systems on daily life and the subsequent development of Explainable AI (XAI) to mitigate concerns regarding the opaqueness of many AI techniques. A key finding is the limitation of XAI, as it only elucidates a recommendation or decision without guaranteeing system performance or accuracy. The paper then introduces a new class of techniques, Defensible AI (DAI), which is proposed as a means to increase public trust in AI by addressing the shortcomings of existing methods. The research includes a review of issues with current AI techniques and presents a concrete DAI example, assessing its positive contributions toward enhancing the reliability, trust, and security of AI systems.

(Virvou & Tsihrintzis, 2023) User experience in AI-Enhanced Software is dictated by five critical human-AI trust states: trust, overtrust, mistrust, distrust, and AI-phobia. The paper introduces a principled approach for designing human-AI interfaces to actively manage these statesbuilding trust while mitigating negative statesto enhance interaction success. Methodologically, it details the challenges of requirements engineering for trustworthiness and proposes a novel Trust State-Chart Model for conceptualizing these interactions. The framework further utilizes a

Trust-Flow Model and Hierarchical Task Analysis to systematically derive user experience requirements focused on trust enhancement. Ultimately, the approach suggests continuous user feedback monitoring and system adaptation to proactively improve user experience, reduce AI-phobia, and is generally applicable across crucial sectors including healthcare, finance, and education.

(Wang et al., 2024) The analytical gap in new quality productivity development in national manufacturing, especially under Big Data and AI influence. The paper establishes and measures an innovative new quality productivity index system across Chinese regions using the entropy weight TOPSIS method. Employing Big Data analysis techniques like the Moran index and Dagum Gini index, the research explores the spatial and temporal evolution of this productivity. Findings show a comprehensive nationwide improvement over 13 years, yet significant regional disparities persist, with Western efficacy lower than Eastern regions. Crucially, the Eastern region exhibits an intensifying developmental imbalance and distinct spatial aggregation characteristics. This analysis provides a novel index system and theoretical support for informed policy development.

(Wang, Tielman, & Jonker, 2022) The challenge of mutual trust in increasingly prevalent human-AI teams, where it is a required coordinating mechanism for effective teamwork, as observed in human-only teams. The study posits trust as a strategic tool for artificial agents to optimize team performance. Specifically, the project aims to develop mental models within AI agents that enable them to accurately assess a human teammate's trustworthiness across various tasks. This assessment will integrate crucial contextual variables, including the characteristics of the human teammate, the task requirements, and the surrounding environment, ultimately guiding the AI in deciding when to appropriately delegate or rely on a human to execute a specific function. The overarching goal is to facilitate appropriate trust promotion from humans while ensuring the AI agent exhibits judicious trust toward its human counterpart.

(Xu et al., 2025) Drawing upon Social Identity Theory (SIT), this research demonstrated that human-AI collaboration significantly reduces employee cyberloafing by cultivating a stronger AI identity, encompassing feelings of dependence, emotional energy, and relatedness. A three wave study established that this strengthened AI identity encourages employees to recognize their collaborative role and subsequently increase their focus on essential in-role tasks, thereby diminishing cyberloafing behavior. Crucially, the personality trait of openness acts as a potent moderator, with employees exhibiting high openness experiencing a greater positive effect on AI identity and a more pronounced reduction in cyberloafing. Conversely, those with low openness show a weaker effect, providing a theoretical framework and practical guidance for organizational efforts to enhance employee focus and reduce non-work-related online activity.

(Yu & Li, 2022) The influence of Artificial Intelligence (AI) decision-making transparency on employee trust using a parallel multiple mediation model. The core finding is that transparency fosters trust, an effect governed by two competing psychological pathways: the AI system's perceived effectiveness and the employee's associated discomfort. Specifically, greater transparency positively reinforces trust by increasing the perception of effectiveness, which acts as a strong positive mediator. Concurrently, however, the study finds that transparency also contributes to an elevated sense of discomforta factor that, conversely, negatively impacts overall trust levels.

(Zerilli, Bhatt, & Weller, 2022) The study of human-AI teams, driven by advances in AI, as central to contemporary behavioral and engineering research, focusing on the interface challenges of trust, transparency, and error tolerance. It conceptualizes human responses on a spectrum, with extreme opposition (distrust) and loafing (complacency) at the poles, advocating for algorithmic vigilance as the ideal operational state. A critical finding is that achieving appropriate trust requires a broader definition of transparency that incorporates strategies like dynamic task allocation and communicating performance metrics, moving beyond mere algorithmic explainability. The review ultimately posits that long-term strategies should prioritize curbing algorithm aversion over mitigating automation appreciation to enhance optimal team performance, channeling disparate efforts toward a common, ecologically valid research framework.

(Xie & Fang, 2025) An innovative AI-assisted methodology to reduce subjectivity in therapeutic color design by quantitatively modeling the color-emotion relationship. The method successfully employs multimodal emotion recognition to capture user states, followed by the construction of a quantitative HSV/RGB to Valence-Arousal (VA) emotion model mapping for precise color conversion. Validation via a rigorous psycho-physiological joint evaluation (PANAS, SAM, EDA, HRV) demonstrated significant improvement in both emotion recognition accuracy and the generation of emotionally congruent color schemes, achieving high user satisfaction. This work culminates in the development of an intelligent color-matching system that offers robust, AI-based support for personalized and scientifically grounded therapeutic spatial design.

3. OBJECTIVES

3.1. To examine the interplay between trust, emotion, and productivity in human-AI collaboration.

3.2. To investigate the phenomenon of automation complacency and its impact on critical human attributes.

3.3. To develop a practical framework for achieving human AI synergy.

4. METHODOLOGIES

4.1. Examining the Interplay between Trust, Emotion, and Productivity in Human AI Collaboration

Artificial intelligence has shifted from being just a tool to becoming a true partner in human work, creating a delicate balance among trust, emotion, and productivity. Trust forms the psychological base of this teamwork, built not on shared beliefs but on perceptions of competence, openness, and fairness. When trust aligns with an AI's real abilities, collaboration thrives; when it faltersdue to black-box opacity or misplaced faithefficiency and engagement drop. Emotions quietly drive this relationship, shaping risk perceptions, motivation, and a sense of control. Fear of being replaced or surveilled can erode engagement, while emotionally aware design clear explanations, opportunities for user input, and humble transparencybuilds security and curiosity. Productivity, in this new setting, is no longer just about speed or volume but about the amplified results of humans and machines working in sync, something only possible when trust andemotionremainbalanced.

These three forces form a feedback loop: trust lowers anxiety, positive emotions boost creativity, and successful outcomes reinforce trust. Transparency anchors the cycle by offering the right level of clarity without overload, allowing users to feel empowered and responsible. Still, technology alone cannot secure this harmonyorganizational culture plays a crucial role. Workplaces that encourage openness, dialogue, and emotional support nurture both trust and collaboration, while ongoing training helps employees understand not just how AI works, but how to think and act alongside it. Measuring this interplay through indicators of perceived fairness, emotional well-being, and performance outcomes helps organizations fine-tune their approaches. Ultimately, sustainable human-AI synergy depends on appropriate trustneither blind nor hesitantsupported by emotional intelligence and thoughtful transparency. When humans and AI operate as true teammates, trust is earned, emotion fuels engagement, and productivity reflects meaningful, shared progress rather than mere output.

Figure 1. Human AI collaboration feedback loop

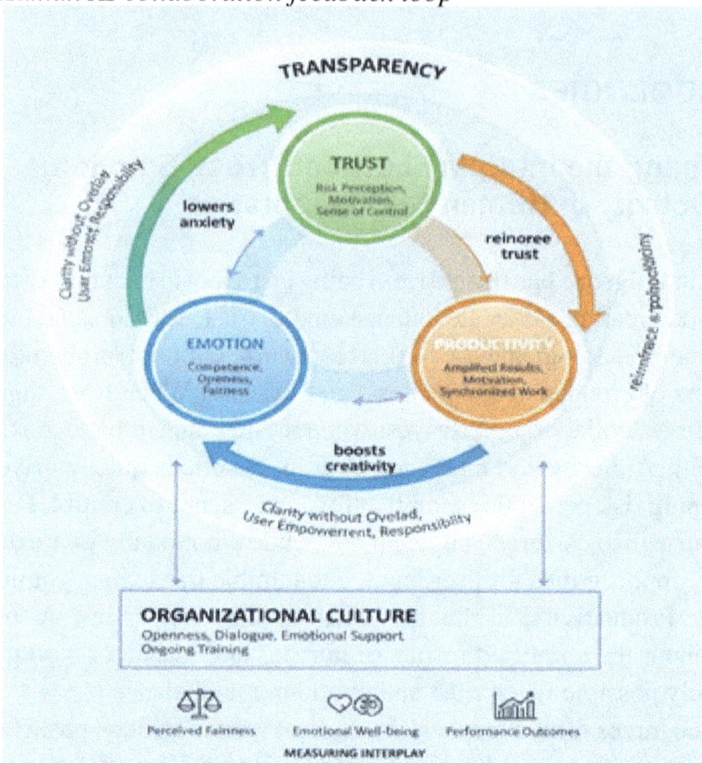

This figure1 shows the feedback loop described in 4.1.

4.2: Investigating Automation Complacency and Its Impact on Creativity, Ethical Judgment, and Decision-Making in AI-Integrated Workplaces

The rapid integration of artificial intelligence into workplaces has redefined how people think about and perform their jobs, but beneath the surface lies a subtle dangerautomation complacency, the quiet habit of trusting machines too much and thinking too little. As AI systems prove reliable, people naturally relax their attention, letting the technology handle more decisions without question. This isn't lazinessit's a psychological response to convenience and perceived perfection. Over time, though, that comfort erodes vital human strengths: creativity, ethical judgment, and nuanced decision-making. Creativity thrives on uncertainty and the willingness to challenge norms, yet when algorithms feed constant ready-made answers, curiosity fades and originality stalls. Ethical judgment suffers too, as people start assuming that data-driven outputs are fair or objective, shifting moral responsibility onto the machine and dulling the inner pause that makes us question right from wrong. Decision-making, once rich with context and empathy, risks flattening into the same binary logic that AI follows, as humans unconsciously adjust their thinking to fit the model's frame. At the organizational level, this creates the illusion of high efficiency but masks a dangerous brittlenesswhen unexpected problems arise, teams lack the mental agility to respond. Breaking this cycle requires both technical and cultural fixes. AI systems should be transparent about how they work and where their limits lie, inviting humans to think critically rather than blindly agree. Companies must keep humans meaningfully involved in major decisions and train workers to question, verify, and reflect instead of just execute. Most of all, leaders need to create cultures that reward thoughtful engagement and moral courage, not just speed or compliance. The goal isn't to reject automation but to build what might be called symbiotic intelligencea partnership where machines handle precision and repetition while humans bring imagination, conscience, and depth. In that balance, complacency has no room to grow, and AI becomes not a crutch that dulls human capability, but a companion that amplifies it.

Table 1. Summarizes the impacts of automation complacency

Human Strength	Impact of Automation Complacency	Desired Outcome (Symbiotic Intelligence)
Creativity	Curiosity fades when algorithms hand us ready-made answersleaving little room to imagine or explore.	Humans spark ideas; AI handles the grind. Together, they challenge assumptions and fuel deeper thinking.
Ethical Judgment	We start trusting data as neutral and fair, letting machines carry the moral weightand forgetting to ask the hard questions.	Humans keep their conscience alive. Organizations teach people to question, reflect, and stand up for what's right.
Decision-Making	Thinking shrinks into black-and-white terms as we unconsciously adapt to AI's framelosing empathy and nuance.	Humans bring heart and depth to decisions. AI supports with precision, but people stay at the center.
Organizational Agility	Automation can make everything look smooth and efficient until something breaks. Then, teams often find themselves stuck, unprepared to think on their feet, because they've grown too used to letting the system do the thinking for them.	Machines handle the routine; humans stay sharp, flexible, and ready to adapt when the unexpected hits.

This table 1 shows the impacts of automation complacency on key human strengths.

4.3: Developing a Practical Framework for Achieving Human–AI Synergy

Artificial intelligence should never exist to replace usit should exist to help us become the best versions of ourselves. The true promise of AI lies not in outsmarting the human mind, but in working alongside it, creating a space where human intuition, creativity, and ethics blend naturally with machine precision and logic. Real humanAI synergy happens when people and machines complement each other's strengthswhen AI enhances our abilities without dulling them. But this partnership doesn't form by chance; it requires a thoughtful framework built on three pillars: transparent system design, continuous education, and a trust-centered culture. Transparency builds confidence by helping users understand how AI thinks, where it struggles, and how they can question or refine its output.

Education turns that understanding into empowerment, teaching people not just to use AI, but to think with itinterpreting data, challenging bias, and remembering that moral responsibility always stays human. A trust-driven culture then keeps this balance alive, giving employees the safety to question AI decisions, valuing sound judgment over speed, and protecting human agency as a core principle. Together, these elements form a living cycletransparency deepens understanding, education strengthens trust, and culture sustains both through openness and shared purpose. When organizations apply this framework, AI integration stops feeling like a takeover and starts feeling like teamwork. People gain confidence instead of fear, creativity instead of routine, and collaboration instead of competition. They can focus on what humans do bestfeeling, imagining, and deciding with carewhile AI handles precision, scale, and consistency. In that harmony, technology becomes not a rival, but a true collaborator, driving progress that's not just faster, but wiser, more ethical, and profoundly human.

Figure 2. Human AI synergy framework

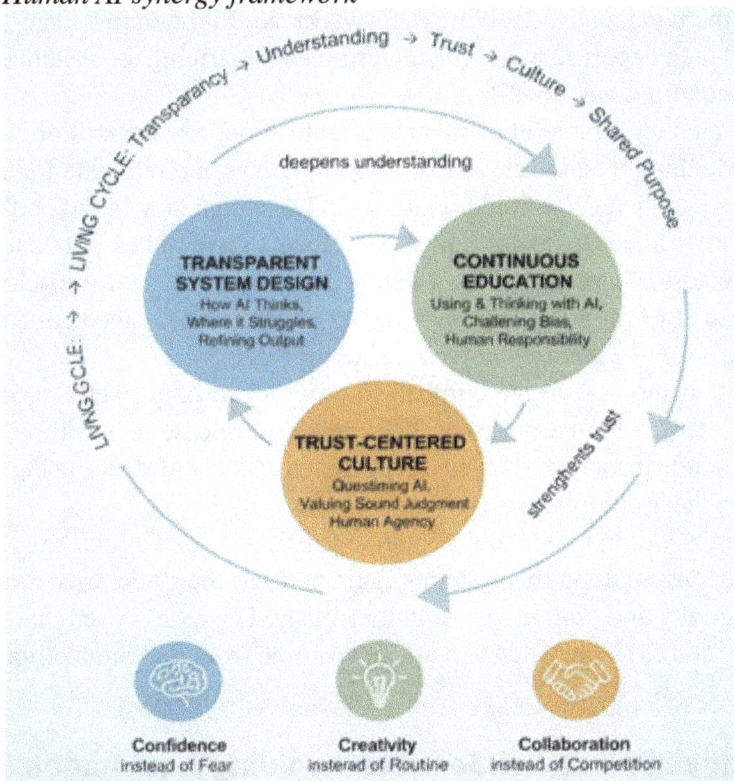

This figure2 illustrates the three pillars of human-AI synergy and their interconnectedness.

5. CASE STUDIES

Case Study 1: Healthcare Balancing Trust and Human Judgment in AI-Assisted Diagnosis

At St. Helena General Hospital, an AI-based diagnostic platform called MedIntel was introduced to assist radiologists in detecting early-stage tumors from MRI scans. The system boasted a 94% accuracy rate, surpassing average human detection levels. Yet within the first six months of deployment, adoption laggedonly 40% of radiologists consistently used it in their workflow.

The resistance stemmed not from poor performance, but from a lack of trust. Doctors felt uneasy relying on an algorithm that couldn't "explain" its reasoning.

Even when MedIntel flagged potentially malignant areas correctly, radiologists often rechecked them manually, doubling their workload. Emotionally, many expressed anxiety that their expertise was being undermined, describing the system as a "black box that second-guesses you."

The hospital leadership implemented a multi-pronged intervention:Developers modified MedIntel to show annotated image overlays and rationale for each diagnostic flag (e.g., "irregular border pattern – 87% malignancy likelihood");Weekly sessions were held where doctors and AI developers reviewed cases collaboratively, allowing doctors to understand the AI's reasoning and provide feedback; Communication shifted from "AI diagnosing" to "AI assisting." Management emphasized that AI was a *second opinion*, not a superior replacement.

Within four months, usage climbed to 85%. More importantly, error rates in diagnostic interpretation dropped by 17%, and average case review time decreased by 23%. Emotional surveys showed a 35% increase in "confidence using AI" and a 40% drop in "fear of replacement."

Transparency didn't just build cognitive trustit reshaped emotional perception. Once doctors understood the system's logic and felt their authority remained intact, productivity and morale rose simultaneously. The case proved that emotional reassurance and explainable design are inseparable from real productivity gains in high-stakes fields.

Case Study 2: Financial Services Avoiding Automation Complacency in Investment Decisions

A multinational investment firm, *Harrison & Cole*, deployed a predictive AI model to identify high-value trading opportunities in volatile markets. The system analyzed massive datasets and generated automated recommendations every morning before trading began. Initially, results were stellarreturns rose by 12% in the first quarter.

By the second quarter, however, performance flattened and eventually declined. Traders had begun accepting the AI's suggestions without cross-checking them against contextual market factors such as geopolitical developments or sector-specific anomalies. Their trust had become overconfidence, leading toautomation complacency. When the AI misinterpreted an abrupt policy shift in Asia as a long-term market signal, it recommended large positions that resulted in significant losses. Internal audits revealed that 80% of those trades were executed automatically, without human review.

The company restructured its workflow to reintroduce human agency and emotional vigilance:All AI-generated recommendations now required human confirmation before execution; The model began showing confidence intervals and data gaps to prompt critical human evaluation; Team leads encouraged traders to share moments of doubt, mistakes, and AI misjudgments without penaltyreinstating psychological safety around questioning the system; Sessions were held to teach traders how to interpret algorithmic bias and understand the statistical limits of model predictions. Within two quarters, loss ratios stabilized, and returns increased by 9%. More importantly, employee engagement scores rose sharplytraders reported feeling "re-empowered" and "mentally active" rather than passive executors.

This case showed that trust must be calibrated, not maximized. Over-trust leads to disengagement just as under-trust leads to rejection. By creating structural prompts for skepticism and open emotional dialogue, the firm reestablished both accountability and performance. The lesson: productivity fueled solely by automation is fragile; productivity rooted in balanced collaboration where human intuition checks machine precision—is sustainable.

Case Study 3: Creative Industry Emotional Synergy in HumanAI Design Teams

A global advertising agency, Archetype Creative, integrated a generative AI tool called Impressa to help design campaigns faster. The system generated mood boards, taglines, and ad variations in secondswork that previously took human teams days. The creative directors expected instant productivity gains. Instead, team morale dropped sharply within the first month.

Designers felt alienated. They described the AI's work as "soulless but efficient." Creative discussions became mechanical; brainstorming sessions devolved into simple editing of AI outputs. Productivity rose in terms of quantity but plummeted in originality. Employees began questioning their value in the process, experiencing what psychologists term emotionaldisplacementthe feeling that their creative identity was being replaced by automation.

The agency shifted strategy to make Impressa a collaborator, not a competitor: AI outputs were used only as initial drafts. Teams were tasked with critiquing, remixing, and personalizing those drafts rather than accepting them wholesale; Management hosted sessions emphasizing that AI is a "starting point, not an endpoint." Designers were encouraged to challenge AI ideas and use them as sparks for innovation; Weekly team reflections allowed employees to share how they felt about working with AInormalizing the mix of excitement, frustration, and curiosity.

By the third quarter, campaign originality scores (as rated by clients) rose by 28%, while turnaround time improved by 35%. Internal surveys showed higher creative satisfaction and significantly reduced burnout. Teams described the AI as a "partner that helps clear the clutter," freeing them to focus on higher-level ideas.

The success hinged on addressing the emotional dimension of creativity. Productivity wasn't about output volume; it was about restoring purpose and meaning in human work. By openly acknowledging emotionscuriosity, insecurity, even resentment—the agency transformed those feelings into fuel for creativity. This case illustrates that emotional trust and creative freedom are prerequisites for sustainable human–AI productivity.

Cross-Case Insights

Across all three cases, a consistent truth emerges: human–AI collaboration succeeds only when trust and emotion are treated as strategic design priorities, not side effects.

- In healthcare, transparency restored cognitive trust.
- In finance, skepticism and human validation prevented complacency.
- In creative industries, emotional dialogue rekindled meaning and innovation.

When people understand, question, and emotionally connect with AI systems, productivity evolves from mechanical efficiency into genuine synergy. The key is simple but profound: *machines may optimize work, but only humans can humanize it.*

6. CHALLENGES AND RISKS

As exciting as this new era of human and AI collaboration seems, the journey toward true partnership is filled with real challenges that are both human and technical. The issue isn't just about making algorithms work faster; it's also about ensuring humans don't lose their identity in the process. Here are the main interrelated risks that need careful navigation to turn AI from a source of worry into a reliable partner in work.

6.1. The Transparency Paradox

One of the biggest challenges to trust in AI is the "black box" problem, which refers to the unsettling lack of clarity about how algorithms reach their conclusions. Even when developers try to introduce transparency with explainable AI (XAI), it often creates a new problem: the explanations can be too technical for most users or too simple to foster real understanding. This creates what we might call a transparency paradox; we can see the system's logic, but we still don't fully grasp it. The result is confusion and mistrust, as users swing between skepticism and blind faith. Designing systems that are both technically clear and easy to understand is one of the most pressing challenges of the decade.

6.2. Automation Complacency

When machines work perfectly most of the time, humans tend to disengageboth literally and mentally. This issue, known as automation complacency, is especially dangerous in decision-making areas like healthcare, transportation, and finance. Once we become overly reliant, we stop questioning AI outputs and lose touch with our own critical thinking. In simple terms, we start handing over not just our tasks but our judgment as well. The long-term risk is a generation of workers who are highly efficient but intellectually and morally disconnected from their jobs, leading to a quiet erosion of human expertise hidden behind the illusion of productivity.

6.3. Emotional Fatigue and Social Isolation

Working with AI isn't just a mental challenge; it can be emotionally draining. Employees often report a creeping loneliness when their "colleagues" are algorithms instead of people. The lack of real social interaction can gradually sap emotional energy, leading to what psychologists refer to as emotional depletion. This fatigue can diminish engagement and creativity and, in severe cases, result in counterproductive work behavior, such as quiet quitting or outright resistance. Ironically, the more we automate collaboration, the less collaborative our workplaces can feel.

6.4. Trust Miscalibration

Trusting AI isn't a straightforward issue; it requires a delicate balance between skepticism and reliance. Unfortunately, humans often struggle with this balance. We either place too much trust in the system, following its advice even when it's wrong, or we under trust it, dismissing good suggestions simply because they come from a machine. This "trust miscalibration" is a fundamentally human issue rooted in emotion, habit, and perception. It not only affects individuals but also leads to inefficiencies, poor decision-making, and inconsistent use of AI tools across teams.

6.5. Ethical and Accountability Dilemmas

AI blurs the lines of responsibility. If a shared human–AI decision goes wrong, who is to blame—the person who clicked "approve" or the algorithm that suggested it? This lack of accountability creates ethical gray areas that many organizations are not set up to handle. Without clear guidelines for responsibility, we risk fostering a culture of blame deflection instead of accountability, which undermines trust and moral integrity in the workplace.

6.6. The Human Identity Crisis

The most personal challenge may be psychological: as AI becomes more capable, many professionals quietly doubt their own worth. When a digital coworker operates faster, more accurately, and without fatigue, humans can feel replaceable. This identity threat leads to anxiety, defensiveness, and resistance to adopting new technology. The real danger isn't that AI will completely replace people but that it subtly undermines their sense of purpose and self-esteem turning innovation into an emotional battleground instead of a shared opportunity.

6.7. The Learning and Adaptation Gap

Lastly, technology advances much faster than our ability to adapt. Continuous learning isn't just a corporate catchphrase; it's crucial for survival. Yet, organizations often overlook the emotional toll of constant upskilling. Employees may feel overwhelmed by the pressure to "keep up" with AI, leading to burnout and disengagement. Without ongoing education and compassionate leadership, even the most advanced AI systems will struggle to gain true acceptance.

Figure 3. Identifies Challenges to Human AI Collaboration

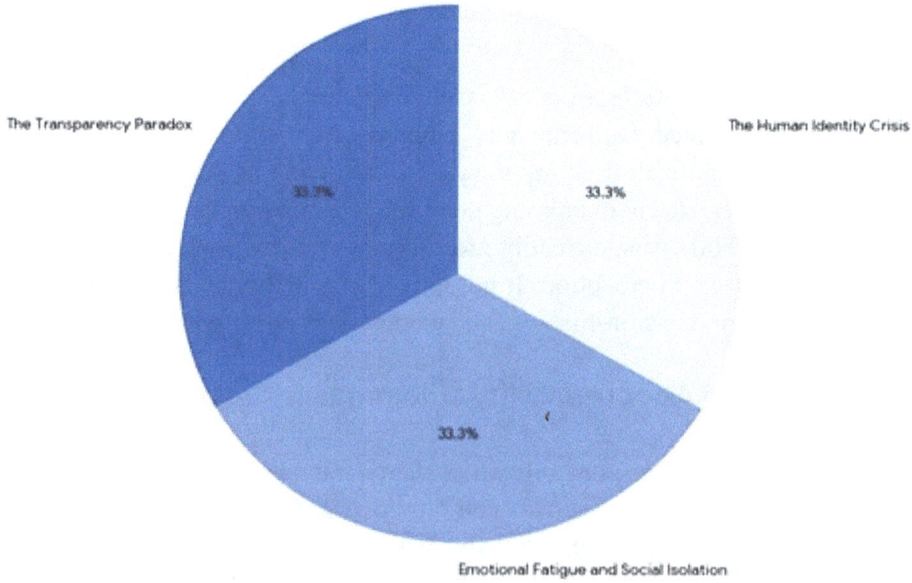

This figure 3 illustrates the pie chart of Challenges to Human AI Collaboration

Table 2. Identifies Challenges to Human AI Collaboration with the percentages

Challenge	Percentage
The Transparency Paradox	33.3%
Emotional Fatigue and Social Isolation	33.3%
The Human Identity Crisis	33.3%

This Table 2 shows the Challenges to Human AI Collaboration with the percentages

Figure 4. Identifies Risks to Human AI Collaboration

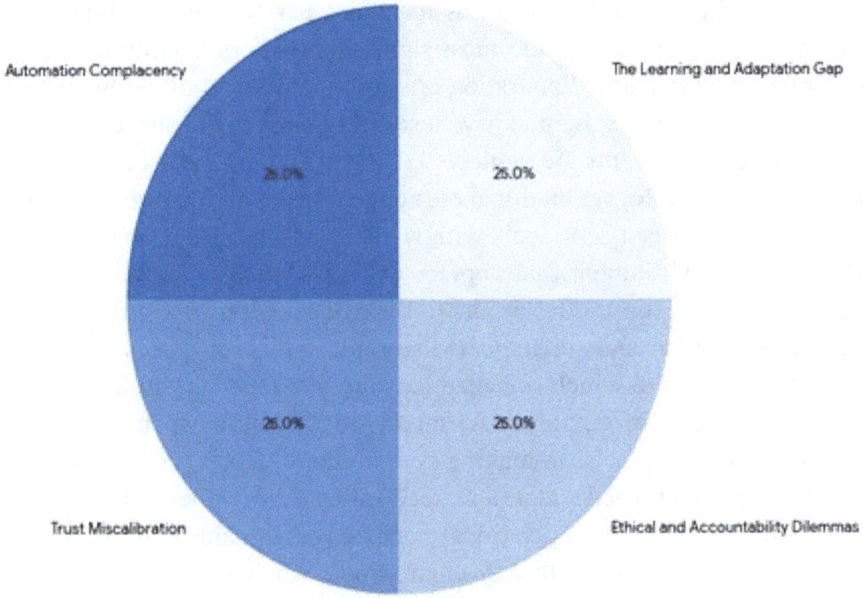

This figure 4 illustrates the pie chart of Risks to Human AI Collaboration

Table 3. Identifies Risks to Human AI Collaboration with the percentages

Risk	Percentage
Automation Complacency	25.0%
Trust Miscalibration	25.0%
Ethical and Accountability Dilemmas	25.0%
The Learning and Adaptation Gap	25.0%

This Table 3 illustrates the Risks to Human AI Collaboration with the percentages

7. CONCLUSIONS

The fusion of artificial intelligence and our professional environments signifies not only a tech revolution but also a profoundly human migration. AI has moved from being a distant and quiet tool to a full-partner changing the way we think, work, and even determine our professions' purpose. However, as the study pointed out, in the AI era, actual productivity is not determined by machine speed or human-taking-over-the-music-automation, but rather by the synergy of the three—thoughtful, ethical, and emotionally intelligent humans plus machines partnership.The literature and evidence reviewed suggest that the most significant factors leading to successful human-AI partnership and collaboration are not at all related to hardware or software but rather the complex human psychosocial dynamics of trust, emotions, and identity. If these components are neglected, we will find ourselves in situations of over-reliance on technology, emotional burnout, and ethical dilemmas. But if these factors are acknowledged and dealt withby means of clear-cut design, ongoing learning, and an environment that appreciates both human insight and machine accuracythe scope of substantial productivity will burgeon to a great extent.The development of a smart and sophisticated workplace that integrates an AI system will rely on the extent to which organizations are brave enough to face the social and emotional aspects of employee-AI interaction. Features such as transparent algorithms, explainable decision-making systems, and AI that is emotionally intelligent should no longer be considered as 'nice-to-have' but rather as being the right thing to do from a moral and operational perspective. In parallel, leadership must change to create a psychologically safe environment where employees regard AI as a partner who boosts their strengths and broadens their creative power rather than a rival who takes away from them.The paper finally asserts that the path of the future labor market will not be to select between human brainpower and machine power but rather to create a synergy intelligence between the two entities that complements and owns both.

8. FUTURE ENHANCEMENTS

The journey of humanAI partnership has come a long way, evolving from experimental curiosity to an essential part of organizational life. Yet, despite this progress, there is still much to be done to make these systems truly effective, trustworthy, and emotionally attuned. The next phase of AI integration must move beyond simply boosting technical performance to building systemsand workplace culturesthat are psychologically informed, ethically responsible, and socially adaptable.

The future of AI at work lies not in smarter machines alone, but in systems that understand and grow with the people who use them. A key priority will be developing emotionally intelligent AI systems capable not only of logical accuracy but also of interpreting and responding appropriately to human emotions. By integrating affective computing and empathy modeling into design, AI could learn to recognize users' emotional states, communicate more naturally, and foster trust and harmony rather than frustration. Such emotionally sensitive systems will transform digital collaboration from transactional interactions into meaningful, human-centered exchanges.Equally important are dynamic trust calibration frameworks that recognize trust as a fluid, adaptive process. Future AI systems should be able to sense when a user is over-relying or under-trusting the system and respond accordinglyperhaps prompting human verification in cases of overdependence or offering clearer reasoning when skepticism arises.

These context-aware trust models will ensure a healthy balance between confidence and caution, supporting both human judgment and system reliability.Building this future also requires ethically focused AI education, where emotional intelligence and ethical reasoning are taught alongside technical literacy. Employees should not only understand how AI works but also how to coexist with it thoughtfullydeveloping critical thinking, emotional resilience, and ethical decision-making. Continuous learning programs, workshops, and reflective exercises can help sustain user confidence while reducing fear and resistance to technological change.To uphold integrity and fairness, organizations will also need robust ethical governance and accountability models. These frameworks must clearly define humanAI decision chains, ensure transparent data use, and include regular algorithmic bias checks. Establishing oversight boards and periodic audits will help keep AI systems aligned with human values, fairness, and social good. Such governance mechanisms will make AI not only powerful but also principled.In parallel, future AI tools should feature personalized collaboration interfaces that adapt to individual work styles and preferences.

By adjusting transparency levels, communication tone, and feedback frequency, AI can evolve from an impersonal assistant into a genuinely supportive digital colleague. Personalization will empower users with a stronger sense of agency and control, enhancing both comfort and productivity.Addressing the emotional costs of digital collaboration will also be crucial. The integration of well-being mechanismssuch as sentiment tracking, wellness platforms, and real-time emotional check-inscan help identify and mitigate burnout or loneliness caused by AI-mediated work. Moreover, managers must be trained to recognize these emotional patterns and provide empathetic support, ensuring technology strengthens rather than erodes workplace well-being.

Finally, sustaining progress in this field requires interdisciplinary research on hybrid intelligence, bridging computer science, psychology, ethics, and organizational behavior. Long-term studies are essential to understand how human trust and emotional attachment to AI evolve, and how these dynamics reshape workplace culture. The findings from such research will guide the creation of not just smart but socially sustainable AI ecosystems.

In essence, the next chapter of humanAI collaboration must focus on emotional depth, ethical transparency, and adaptive intelligence. We must design systems that recognize humans not merely as users, but as partners with emotions, vulnerabilities, and aspirations. Only then will AI serve not just as a tool for productivity, but as a catalyst for purpose, helping humanity grow wiser, more resilient, and more connected in the digital age.

REFERENCES

Barón, M. M. (2025). Towards an Adoption Framework to Foster Trust in AI-Assisted Software Engineering. 2025 IEEE/ACM 4th International Conference on AI Engineering – Software Engineering for AI (CAIN), 247–249. DOI: 10.1109/CAIN66642.2025.00038

Brandebusemeyer, C. (2025). Interactions with Generative AI: Wearables to Measure Developer Experience and Productivity Objectively. In 2025 IEEE/ACM 47th International Conference on Software Engineering: Companion Proceedings (ICSE-Companion) (pp. 148–150). IEEE. DOI: 10.1109/ICSE-Companion66252.2025.00043

Chaudhary, H. (2020). Using Artificial Intelligence in Commercial Underwriting to Drive Productivity Growth. In The AI Book: The Artificial Intelligence Handbook for Investors, Entrepreneurs and FinTech Visionaries (pp. 81–82). Wiley. DOI: 10.1002/9781119551966.ch23

Chen, N., & Zhang, X. (2025). When misunderstanding meets artificial intelligence: The critical role of trust in human-AI and human-human team communication and performance. *Frontiers in Psychology*, *16*, 1637339. DOI: 10.3389/fpsyg.2025.1637339 PMID: 41209806

Dhiman, S., & Wadhawan, B. Kavita, Chopra, P., Mukhija, L., & Kaur, G. (2025). From Animal Instincts to Machine Emotions: A Physics-Informed Multispecies Framework for Emotionally Intelligent AI. In 2025 5th International Conference on Intelligent Technologies (CONIT) (pp. 1–5). IEEE. DOI: 10.1109/CONIT65521.2025.11167463

Kaneko, S., & Yamada, S. (2025). Estimating the Trust of Humans in AI for Level 3 Autonomous Driving. In 2025 20th ACM/IEEE International Conference on Human-Robot Interaction (HRI) (pp. 1389–1392). IEEE. DOI: 10.1109/HRI61500.2025.10973810

Kaneko, S., & Yamada, S. (2025). Predicting Trust Dynamics With Dynamic SEM in Human-AI Collaboration. *IEEE Access : Practical Innovations, Open Solutions*, *13*, 190701–190711. DOI: 10.1109/ACCESS.2025.3629365

Kolomaznik, M., Petrik, V., Slama, M., & Jurik, V. (2024). The role of socio-emotional attributes in enhancing human-AI collaboration. *Frontiers in Psychology*, *15*, 1369957. DOI: 10.3389/fpsyg.2024.1369957 PMID: 39474095

Lee, J. D., & See, K. A. (2004). Trust in automation: Designing for appropriate reliance. *Human Factors*, *46*(1), 50–80. DOI: 10.1518/hfes.46.1.50_30392 PMID: 15151155

LeMaire, C., & Abshire, B. (2025). *AI for everyday IT: Accelerate workplace productivity*. Manning.

Li, W.-C., Yang, C.-J., & Fang, W.-C. (2020). A Real-time Emotion Recognition System Based on an AI System-On-Chip Design. In 2020 International SoC Design Conference (ISOCC) (pp. 29–30). IEEE. DOI: 10.1109/ISOCC50952.2020.9333072

McVay, J., Visser, E. J. d., Pippin, B., Mani, A., Hyde, J. N., & Kman, N. (2025). Trust in Aligned AI Decision Makers. In *2025 IEEE Conference on Artificial Intelligence (CAI)* (pp. 1–4). IEEE. DOI: 10.1109/CAI64502.2025.00202

Meng, Q., Wu, T. J., Duan, W., & Li, S. (2025). Effects of Employee-Artificial Intelligence (AI) Collaboration on Counterproductive Work Behaviors (CWBs): Leader Emotional Support as a Moderator. *Behavioral Sciences (Basel, Switzerland), 15*(5), 696. DOI: 10.3390/bs15050696 PMID: 40426473

Padmaja, P., Justin, E., Sophia, I., Charan, S. H., Kumar, S. S., Somu, K., & Thirupathi, L. (2021).. . *Journal of Nuclear Energy Science and Power Generation Technology*, *10*(9), 1000211.

Peney, L., Dernee, R., & Alers, H. (2024). Encouraging Trust in AI-Powered Teaching Tools: Ranking Design Principles. In *2024 IEEE Conference on Artificial Intelligence (CAI)* (pp. 476–479). IEEE. DOI: 10.1109/CAI59869.2024.00096

Punuri, S. B., Kuanar, S. K., Mishra, T. K., Rao, V. V. R. M., & Reddy, S. S. (2024). Decoding Human Facial Emotions: A Ranking Approach Using Explainable AI. *IEEE Access : Practical Innovations, Open Solutions, 12*, 186229–186245. DOI: 10.1109/ACCESS.2024.3474012

Rahulkumar, P. B., Hasmukhbhai, P. J., Himanshu, P. K., Rameshwarkumar, P. H., & Trivedi, H. (2025). Exploring AI's Influence on Human Thinking: Productivity, Learning, and Cognitive Skills in the Age of XAI. In 2025 Artificial Intelligence and Smart Technologies for Sustainability Conference (AISTS) (pp. 1–6). IEEE. DOI: 10.1109/AISTS66100.2025.11232740

Ramchurn, S. D., Stein, S., & Jennings, N. R. (2021). Trustworthy human-AI partnerships. *iScience*, *24*(8), 102891. DOI: 10.1016/j.isci.2021.102891 PMID: 34430804

Straub, J. (2022). Increasing Trust in Artificial Intelligence with a Defensible AI Technique. *2022 IEEE Applied Imagery Pattern Recognition Workshop (AIPR)*, 1–7. DOI: 10.1109/AIPR57179.2022.10092226

Thirupathi, L., Kaashipaka, V., Dhanaraju, M., & Katakam, V. (2025). AI and IoT in Mental Health Care: From Digital Diagnostics to Personalized, Continuous Support. In Joshi, H., Kumar Reddy, C., Ouaissa, M., Hanafiah, M., & Doss, S. (Eds.), *Intelligent Systems and IoT Applications in Clinical Health* (pp. 271–294). IGI Global Scientific Publishing., DOI: 10.4018/979-8-3693-8990-4.ch012

Virvou, M., & Tsihrintzis, G. A. (2023). A Novel Trust State-Chart Model for Requirements Engineering of Trustful AI - Empowered Software. In 2023 14th International Conference on Information, Intelligence, Systems & Applications (IISA) (pp. 1–6). IEEE. DOI: 10.1109/IISA59645.2023.10345934

Wang, J., Cao, L., & Gao, M. (2024). Multidimensional Scale Analysis of the Development of China's New Quality Productivity from the Perspective of AI. In 2024 8th Asian Conference on Artificial Intelligence Technology (ACAIT) (pp. 1164–1168). IEEE. DOI: 10.1109/ACAIT63902.2024.11022293

Wang, J., Tielman, M. L., & Jonker, C. M. (2022). Artificial Trust as a Tool in Human-AI Teams. In 2022 17th ACM/IEEE International Conference on Human-Robot Interaction (HRI) (pp. 1155–1157). IEEE. DOI: 10.1109/HRI53351.2022.9889652

Xie, Z., & Fang, S. (2025). The Application of AI-Assisted Color and Emotion Association Modeling in Healing Space Design. 2025 IEEE 12th Joint International Information Technology and Artificial Intelligence Conference (ITAIC), 1276–1282. DOI: 10.1109/ITAIC64559.2025.11163049

Xu, J. Q., Wu, T. J., Duan, W. Y., & Cui, X. X. (2025). How the Human-Artificial Intelligence (AI) Collaboration Affects Cyberloafing: An AI Identity Perspective. *Behavioral Sciences (Basel, Switzerland)*, *15*(7), 859. DOI: 10.3390/bs15070859 PMID: 40723643

Yu, L., & Li, Y. (2022). Artificial Intelligence Decision-Making Transparency and Employees' Trust: The Parallel Multiple Mediating Effect of Effectiveness and Discomfort. *Behavioral Sciences (Basel, Switzerland)*, *12*(5), 127. DOI: 10.3390/bs12050127 PMID: 35621424

Zerilli, J., Bhatt, U., & Weller, A. (2022). How transparency modulates trust in artificial intelligence. *Patterns (New York, N.Y.)*, *3*(4), 100455. DOI: 10.1016/j.patter.2022.100455 PMID: 35465233

Chapter 5
Pioneering the Future: A Comprehensive Look at Global Leaders in the Enterprise Metaverse

R. M. Dilip Charaan
https://orcid.org/0009-0002-1332-4592
Vel Tech Rangarajan Dr. Sagunthala R&D Institute of Science and Technology, India

G. Glorindal
DMI-St.John the Baptist University, Malawi

S. Vidhya
Renganayagi Varatharaj College of Engineering, Sivakasi, India

A. Thilagavathy
R.M.K. Engineering College, India

Leena Jenefa
https://orcid.org/0000-0002-1324-7083
Hindustan Institute of Technology and Science, Chennai, India

S. P. Santhoshkumar
https://orcid.org/0000-0001-8531-759X
Vel Tech Rangarajan Dr. Sagunthala R&D Institute of Science and Technology, India

ABSTRACT

The enterprise metaverse is a groundbreaking shift in how businesses operate, collaborate, and evolve. It offers smooth virtual workplaces, enhanced education, and innovative data-driven business models through the integration of virtual reality, blockchain, artificial intelligence, cloud systems, and digital twins. The technology foundations, global leaders, systems of governance, and financial advantages that propel business adoption are all addressed in this chapter. Additionally, it analyses cross-industry instances of use, workforce change, and the strategic goals needed for sustained deployment. The metaverse emerges as an accelerator for efficiency, creativity, and sustained competitive edge in the soon-to-arrive age of digital transformation as organisations transition into interconnected digital ecosystems.

DOI: 10.4018/979-8-3373-7534-2.ch005

INTRODUCTION: THE GROWTH OF THE ENTERPRISE METAVERSE

The development of the Enterprise Metaverse is one of the biggest changes in the digital economy since the beginning of the internet and cloud computing. The metaverse is unlike the previous technological waves, where the focus was mostly on digitising information and automating processes; the new paradigm means that the enterprises work in immersive, persistent as well and interrelated virtual worlds. Such environments allow organisations to re-engineer work processes, improve teamwork, model real-life processes and create new business models that have a foundation on digital presence and interaction. Metaverse has also developed from a speculative notion grounded in science fiction to a real technical ecosystem based on the innovations of extended reality (XR), artificial intelligence (AI), digital twins, blockchain, and edge computing. Large technology providers, such as Microsoft, Nvidia, Meta, Siemens, and Accenture, and a growing number of startups are all investing in platforms and applications, which are aimed at serving the needs of the enterprise. Such investments indicate a major change: the transition toward considering the metaverse as an enterprise-focused, productive, efficient, and innovative tool, rather than a consumer-driven and entertainment trend. Virtual collaboration tools were embraced with increased momentum because of the emergence of distributed and hybrid work after the COVID-19 pandemic. Instead of considering conventional video conferencing, organisations are in search of solutions which allow employees to socialise, create, and simulate in common virtual spaces.

The forecasts of the economy also support the topicality of enterprise-oriented metaverse systems. Although it is forecasted differently, it is a consistent estimation that the majority of the economic value of the metaverse in the next decade will be generated by business uses, rather than by consumer entertainment. As organisations remain in the process of digitalising physical resources, operations, and connections, the metaverse is predicted to form the next-generation interface of enterprise computing and global collaboration. But the emergence of the Enterprise Metaverse also brings with it issues and duties. (Lee et al 2021)

Moreover, organisations need to come up with plans to establish internal capabilities, redesign work processes, and culture/leadership grounded in immersive digital change. To conclude, the Enterprise Metaverse is not a technological fad but rather a changing environment of cohesive, smart, and immersive worlds that transform the way organisations operate and compete. With the world economy becoming more virtualised and interconnected in its operations, the Enterprise Metaverse is set to become a layer in the cloud of business strategy and digital infrastructure of the future.

DEFINING THE ENTERPRISE METAVER

Enterprise Metaverse may be described as a common, immersive, and constant virtual ecosystem in which organisations operate, interact, and develop innovations and digital representations of people, processes and physical properties. In contrast to previous digital platforms, the Enterprise Metaverse seamlessly blends the physical and virtual worlds, enabling seamless interaction through extended reality technologies, digital twins, artificial intelligence, and decentralised systems. It is a combination of progressive digital spaces not to entertain people or socialise with each other but to facilitate business processes, industrial activities, and enterprise-level. The central idea of the Enterprise Metaverse is that of spatial computing technology, enabling the digital content to be perceived as a part of the physical world. These are augmented reality (AR), virtual reality (VR), mixed reality (MR), and 3D virtual environments. In practice, engineers can be taken on a tour of a virtual factory prior to building, and medical staff can train on complicated procedures in highly simulated conditions. (Lv, Z., et al 2022)

Digital twins combine real-time sensors, cloud architecture, and operating environment data, which allows predictive analytics, remote monitoring, and simulation. Digital twins can be used to make more informed decisions and operate more efficiently, whether it is in relation to manufacturing, smart cities, supply chains, or energy systems. The Enterprise Metaverse is also improved with the help of blockchain and frameworks of decentralised identity, as they allow making transactions secure, possessing assets, and accessing them with permission. The systems facilitate cross-platform interoperability and bring credible infrastructure to data exchange and governance and assure that enterprises can work comfortably within virtual ecosystems.

AI agents can be in the form of digital assistants, autonomous agents or co-creation partners in the design, collaboration, and optimisation of the process. After all, Enterprise Metaverse is not as much a technological platform as it is a business transformation environment. It enables organisations to virtualise their operations, curb physical limitations, speed up the innovation process, and develop new customer experiences. The Enterprise Metaverse should grow into an enterprise strategy building block, just as cloud computing is today. (Lyu, Z., & Fridenfalk, M. 2024)

DIFFERENTIATING CONSUMER VS. ENTERPRISE METAVERSE

Although the term metaverse is commonly perceived as a broad term, there are distinct differences between the consumer metaverse and the enterprise metaverse that are required in order to comprehend the unique purposes, architectures, and economic models. The consumer metaverse is built with the purpose of entertainment, games, social interaction and digital lifestyle experiences. Some examples include Roblox, Fortnite, Meta Horizon Worlds, and Decentraland, where virtual worlds allow users to socially interact, customise digital avatars, produce content and engage in virtual economies. The value of the consumer metaverse is propelled by user interaction, content supplied by the community, and e-commerce.

It is concentrated on creativity, expression of identity, and social interaction, and technology is optimised to be accessible, an immersive storytelling experience, and engaging. Conversely, the business metaverse is designed to be productive, simulated, collaborative and at an industrial scale. Microsoft Mesh, Nvidia Omniverse, Siemens Xcelerator, and enterprise XR training systems are created with the intention to assist in business operations, remote work, industrial design, digital twin, and workplace productivity. Operational efficiency, reduced risk, enhanced decision-making, optimised workflows and faster research and development cycles are the elements of the value proposition. The second difference is in infrastructure. . (Lyu, Z., & Fridenfalk, M. 2024)

Metaphysical experiences of the consumer metaverse are commonly cloud-based and generalised to be adopted by a large group of users, whereas enterprise systems are based on hybrid architectures that combine edge computing, private cloud, proprietary systems, and IoT infrastructure. This guarantees synchronisation of real-time data, high performance and secure operation control, which is essential in industries like aerospace, healthcare, energy and advanced manufacturing. There is also a great difference in the governance

Enterprise metaverse systems are highly regulated, secure, identity-compliant systems. To guarantee operational integrity and safeguard intellectual property, proprietary authentication, data flows encrypted, controlled management of digital assets, and auditing the system are all necessary. The two realms are also differentiated by skill requirements. The consumer metaverse revolves around intuitive interaction, play, and enterprise implementation, which requires technical specialised expertise to develop XRs, data engineering, modelling digital twins, cybersecurity, and integrating AI. Organisational change management and training are very important aspects of enterprise adoption. The consumer and enterprise metaverse ecosystems are not in isolation, notwithstanding these differences. Enterprise applications are usually affected by innovation in gaming engines, AI-created avatars, social VR, and immersive content. (Marr, B. 2022).

GLOBAL MARKET LANDSCAPE AND GROWTH DRIVERS

The Enterprise Metaverse is experiencing fast growth in the global market due to the increasing technological development, economic prospects, and changing work and industrial needs. The metaverse is emerging as the new business model, productivity, and mass-scale business operational innovation due to increased speeds of digital transformation strategies in organisations.

There are some important forces influencing the direction of the Enterprise Metaverse market. To begin with, the move to hybrid and remote working formats has generated the need to find immersive collaboration tools that are not limited to conventional communication tools. The businesses are now in search of environments that mimic physical presence so as to provide more natural interaction, joint design as well as collective problem solving. With organisational growth in terms of geographical location, virtual environments provide scalable resources of communication, training, and remote workforce engagement.

Second, new technologies in digital twins and simulation are rapidly spreading to manufacturing, engineering, energy, transportation, and urban planning. Digital twins enable businesses to recreate the real world, save on the cost of prototyping, maximise the output of the asset, and conduct predictive maintenance. The development in this area is also facilitated by government efforts in smart infrastructure, modernisation of the public sector, and modernisation in the industrial sector.

Third, the current speed of enabling technology innovation is AI, blockchain, 5G, and edge computing, which is the infrastructure required to support real-time immersive interaction. Low-latency computing and high-bandwidth networks can provide a smooth connection between an actual and a virtual system. Meanwhile, blockchain enables safe digital identity, asset management, and interoperable online economies, which are necessary to frameworks of enterprise trust.

Fourth, the growing investment of technology giants in the world is indicative of the strategic value of the Enterprise Metaverse. Adoption differences across the market geography are different. Asia-Pacific has shown to be growing rapidly through manufacturing innovation, smart cities and enterprise modernisation programs. The economies of the Middle East, especially the UAE and Saudi Arabia, are also spending a lot of money on national metaverse strategies, as well as the virtualisation of public services. In the meantime, emerging economies are considering the metaverse to develop skills, establish digital governance and modernise the industry. Nevertheless, there are still some challenges despite the strong growth indicators, and some of them are infrastructure cost, interoperability barriers, legal uncertainties, and workforce readiness. Nevertheless, with the further development of standards and the transformation of implementation frameworks, the Enterprise Metaverse is expected to become part of the global digital economy. (Abraham, J., et al 2022)

EVOLUTION OF DIGITAL ENTERPRISE TECHNOLOGIES

The history of digital enterprise technology is one of constant improvement to smarter, more connected, and immersive systems that have the potential to change the operation of business. The digital transformation has experienced the past 3 decades with one technological wave after another, starting with the lifeless web era, and progressing to intelligent and decentralised digital ecosystems, each wave bringing about new possibilities that have restructured enterprise computing models. First of all, digital technologies were used as information storage tools and digitisation of workflow and communication. The development of cloud computing, mobile technologies, high-speed broadband, automation and artificial intelligence altered the enterprise strategy over time and allowed it to be connected globally in an elastic way and make decisions influenced by data. The digital world is today taking a new turn, which is marked by continuity of virtual space, decentralisation and immersive interface. Such innovations are providing the basis of the Enterprise Metaverse, where the physical and the digital are combined.

This development has not been linear but exponential, with breakthroughs augmenting computational capacity, enlarging the capabilities of software, and reinventing the digital infrastructure. As an illustration, initial web technologies helped enterprises to create some kind of online presence whereas the emergence of Web 2.0 brought in a sense of interactivity, real-time collaboration and social interaction. Cloud computing subsequently brought transformation to the IT architecture by introducing scalable and distributed computing to businesses to help them move out of the hardware-dominated environment to service-based ecosystems. These innovations also enabled the development of software-as-a-service (SaaS), platform-as-a-service (PaaS), and infrastructure-as-a-service (IaaS) to minimize the costs of operation and expand the rate of innovation. The present wave, which is Web 3.0 powered, is a shift towards intelligent, interoperable and immersive systems. The next-generation enterprise platforms are currently based on digital twins, extended reality (XR), artificial intelligence (AI), edge computing, blockchain, and decentralised identity frameworks. (Aloqaily et al. 2022)

The digitalisation and integration of the global markets are causing businesses to seek advanced technologies not as an operational tool but as a strategic instrument. The emergence of the Enterprise Metaverse is a paradigm shift: no longer are organisations in the process of digitising their processes, but rather, virtualising their whole business ecosystems, facilitating engagement with their hybrid workforce, intelligent automation, and experience of the customer. The rate of technological maturation means the forthcoming phase of enterprise development will be further unification of the actual and computerised world, which will provide adaptive, autonomous, and very experiential enterprise surroundings. With organisations expanding the adoption of digital, the transformation of enterprise technologies will continue to be an important predictor of competitive edge, business sustainability, and innovativeness. (Huynh-The et al 2022)

EXTENDED REALITY (XR) AND IMMERSIVE COMPUTING

Extended Reality (XR) is an abbreviation that includes all of virtual reality (VR), augmented reality (AR), and mixed reality (MR), which is a key enabling technology of immersive computing and a key element in the Enterprise Metaverse. XR technologies enable individuals and teams to engage with information, environments, and digitally contextualised systems in three-dimensional and spatially contextualised forms, changing the processes of performing work, the acquisition of skills, and optimising business processes. VR is used to form new, entirely immersive worlds where users can interact with a simulated environment without reference to real-life space and place. Applications of VR among the enterprises include training of employees, learning through scenarios, prototyping of designs, and collaborative work through experience. As an illustration, an assembly process can be tested by the manufacturing teams in a virtual factory before the start of production, minimizing risks and shortening the innovation cycles.

Augmented Reality (AR) is the virtual information that superimposes on the real one, contributing to situational awareness and real-time decision making. AR finds applications to field operations, industrial maintenance, logistics and healthcare. AR headset-equipped technicians are also able to receive remote assistance, see contextual instructions, or view machine diagnostics on physical locations and work with their hands free.

Mixed Reality (MR) combines both physical and digital space in real-time, allowing a user to interact with physical space while working with virtual objects. MR has a particular influence in product engineering, the interaction of digital twins, the control of robots, and collaborative work in space. These XR capabilities are driven by immersive computing, a paradigm where computing is designed to be user-centred instead of users being forced to conform to technology. (*Lee, L.-H et al. 2021*)

In contrast to the more primordial models of computers involving screens and input with the use of a keyboard, immersive systems make use of natural interaction through gesture, voice, haptics, and spatial navigation. The XR application to the enterprise is gaining momentum because of actual results: increased efficiency, decreased training time, increased safety, design precision, and affordable simulation. The aerospace, automotive, construction, healthcare, defence, and retail sectors are applying XR in their quest to improve their productivity, lower operational downtimes, and human-machine cooperation. Nevertheless, to reach mass adoption, the following issues should be considered: ergonomics, system integration, interoperability, accessibility, and cybersecurity. The barriers are being broken by the development of hardware miniaturisation, comfort of wearing, cloud rendering and artificial intelligence (AI) based environment mapping.

In the future, XR will have a larger presence in the metaverse beyond individual applications into networks of applications that can support enterprise workflows across a global scale. At some point, immersive computing will be a normal interface to enterprise digital activity, allowing interaction with virtual teams, intelligent systems, and digital twins. The Enterprise Metaverse has a trust and value infrastructure of blockchain, digital identity frameworks, and tokenisation. These technologies are transforming the digital ownership, authentication, and value exchange models that previously relied on centralised control systems to secure, interoperable and distributed architectures, which are a requirement of enterprise-grade virtual ecosystems. (Mourtzis, D. 2023)

BLOCKCHAIN, DIGITAL IDENTITY, AND TOKENIZATION

The blockchain technology offers an open and read-only register that logs transactions, ensures the safety of data exchange, and supports automated control. In the case of enterprises, blockchain can guarantee the integrity, traceability, and compliance of data in the environment where multiple stakeholders, e.g. a supply chain, a healthcare network, or an international business, are involved. Smart contracts are self-executable contracts that are written into blockchain networks and serve to automate processes, decrease the administrative burden, and implement transparency. Another base layer is that of digital identity. Users, companies, and even computer programs need verified identities in the metaverse. The conventional identity management is dependent on centralised systems of authentication, which brings in vulnerability and reduces interoperability. By contrast, decentralised identity models permit end users and businesses to manage authentication credentials and permit cross-platform authentication. This is imperative to the enterprise environment where governance, auditing, compliance, and intellectual property protection are necessary. The concept of tokenisation builds up on blockchain by allowing the computerised representation of physical or virtual entities. The tokens can be the rights of ownership, intellectual property, credentials, certifications, or permissions of operations. (Sai et al., 2024)

They will be the institutional support of the metaverse economy, and they will help in governance, compliance, value exchange, and rights management in virtual and physical worlds. The Enterprise Metaverse relies on Artificial Intelligence (AI) and automation as foundational enablers to drive the intelligent decision making, workflow automation, personalisation and interaction with autonomous systems.

AI AND AUTOMATION AS METAVERSE ENABLERS

AI provides the metaverse on various levels: Smart Virtual Environments. Spatial computing with the help of AI can map the environment in real-time, recognise objects, and display them with adaptive visualisation. AI is used to improve digital twins through real-time computation of information from IoT sensors, enterprise and operational networks. Machine learning algorithms can be used to analyse trends, identify anomalies and make predictions in line with maintenance needs, which allows optimisation in manufacturing, logistics, healthcare and Energy industries. The predictive feature minimises risk, speeds up decision-making and makes operations more efficient. Self-directed Agents and Virtual Assistants. The metaverse includes AI-driven and automation systems that are digital co-workers or operational support agents. They can plan meetings, direct training processes, oversee workflows or help in troubleshooting, which lowers the cognitive and administrative load on the employees. Applications of AI agents in the industrial setting can take the shape of virtual control systems or human-robot interaction. (Sindhwani, A et al. 2023)

This increases employee training, professional growth, and collaborative productivity in enterprise applications by providing content, guidance, and simulations that align with the needs or team requirements. Natural Human-Machine Interfaces and Natural Interaction. It is possible through speech recognition, gesture tracking, sentiment analysis, and natural language processing to enable users to interact with digital systems naturally, eliminating the use of traditional interfaces. This creates instinctive teamwork and enhances accessibility with respect to the various workforce profiles. Enterprise Processes Automation. Repetitive or rather complex tasks can be automated by robotic process automation (RPA), low-code systems, and machine learning-driven workflows that enterprises can use to streamline their processes. Virtual environments will enable end-to-end autonomous operations, such as in asset tracking, manufacturing control, as these systems become a part of the metaverse. AI is also significant in governance and cybersecurity, anomaly identification, compliance, and the guard of enterprise systems against emerging virtual threats. (Tang, M et al. 2025)

Nonetheless, efficient application should entail taking into consideration ethical aspects, labour preparedness, data confidentiality, and regulatory structures. Partiality, openness, responsibility, and human control are also vital to responsible AI applications. With the increase in the use of metaverses, AI will shift into a supportive technology and a building block that supports cognitive, scalable, and autonomous enterprise ecosystems. Integrating AI, automation, and immersive computing will eventually turn the Enterprise Metaverse into a living intelligent space that replicates, predicts and improves the functions of the real world. (Yang, H et al. 2025)

LEADING INNOVATORS SHAPING THE ENTERPRISE METAVERSE

In 2021, the shift to the metaverse became strategic when the metaverse became central to the discussion of the global immersive digital future. Although at the beginning, Meta has been associated with consumer-oriented virtual and augmented reality platforms, the company has been building a strong brand in enterprise-oriented solutions based on virtual collaboration. This change is in line with the world-wide changes on remote and hybrid work opportunities, where organizations explore new ways to improve communication, work engagement with team members and productivity distribution. The key component of the enterprise ecosystem introduced by Meta is Meta Horizon Workrooms, which is aimed at facilitating collaborative virtual conferences, brainstorming kits, and shared workspaces.

Workroom combines spatial audio, 3D avatars, gesture recognition, and the ability to work across multiple screens so as to more effectively create the sense of a face-to-face work environment than standard video conferencing solutions. In fully immersive spaces, enterprises are able to host ideation sessions, onboarding, and training simulations, and cross-functional collaboration activities. Hardware is one of the key elements of the enterprise metaverse strategy of Meta. Quest Pro and other models of the Meta Quest headset family are developed with mixed reality capabilities such as eye tracking, facial expression mapping, high-resolution passthrough, and in-built hand-tracking sensors. The capabilities enable enterprise users to communicate with virtual objects and co-workers in a natural way and be aware of the physical surroundings. This is the balance between immersion and physical situation necessary to be adopted in corporate and professional settings. Meta has also been spending on growing the developer ecosystem.

The Presence Platform by the company provides tools and APIs that allow businesses and developers to create XR applications that can fit their business processes, training programs, or any other sector-specific applications. Meta helps facilitate the incorporation of VR collaboration in the engineering, retail, healthcare, and education industries through collaborations with Autodesk, Accenture, and other companies in the enterprise technology domain. One of the key characteristics of the approach that is taken by Meta is a keen interest in social presence the psychological feeling of co-locating physically with other people in a digital space. The purpose is a continuation of the legacy of Metacom in social networking but is converted to enterprise value with an increase of engagement, empathy, and collaboration in distributed workforces. The enterprise metaverse strategy of Meta has challenges such as privacy, cost of implementation, readiness to change the organisation, and training of the workforce, despite the innovation leadership. Additionally, the company will have to adjust to increased competition in the form of the ecosystem players that can provide more specialised industrial simulation/XR platforms. Nevertheless, the fact that Meta keeps investing in the further development of hardware, the ability to integrate platforms, AI-driven avatars, or cross-ecosystem standards makes it a key player in determining the future of enterprise collaboration.

MICROSOFT: MESH AND THE FUTURE WORKPLACE ECOSYSTEM

Microsoft has become one of the most powerful leaders of the Enterprise Metaverse, as it is strategically oriented to setting up immersive technologies into the existing productivity ecosystems. Instead of trying to create its own metaverse, the strategy of Microsoft focuses on integrating spatial collaboration, automation, and digital twin capabilities into common enterprise software, including Microsoft Teams, Azure, Dynamics 365, and HoloLens.

Central to this is Microsoft Mesh, which is a mixed-reality collaboration platform that can be used to share shared 3D experiences with devices like VR headsets, AR glasses, PCs, and even mobile devices. Mesh supports distributed teams to assemble in virtual environments persistently, collaboratively construct 3D models and employ holographic spaces to engage in engineering, design reviews and strategic planning. What the company has done by connecting Mesh to Microsoft Teams is to make immersive collaboration a logical continuation of established business operations.

The hardware innovation of Microsoft, especially the HoloLens 2, is critical in adoption in the enterprise. The gadget is industrialised and contains real-time environmental mapping, holographic overlay, and hands-free interaction. The holo lens implementation is speeding up in manufacturing, defence, healthcare, and logistics, whereby technicians, engineers, frontline workers are using the mixed reality to access instructions, guided maintenance, or work with experts remotely.

Azure Digital Twins platform is another important platform of the Microsoft metaverse vision. The functionality allows organisations to build digital versions of real-life environments, assets or processes. Digital twins with AI services, cloud orchestration, and the application of Azure IoT will help to perform predictive maintenance, real-time observability, and workflow simulation. The collaboration of Microsoft with industrial companies, such as Siemens and BMW, shows that the concept of digital twins can be extended to operational transformation on a large scale.

Security, compliance and governance are other differentiators that enhance the enterprise positioning of Microsoft. Microsoft brings in identity management, encryption frameworks, cloud regulatory compliance and enterprise multi-tenant management to its metaverse ecosystem with 30 years of experience behind regulated industries. This priority is in line with organisational needs of trust, reduction of risks and formalised digital transformation.

The Artificial Intelligence (AI) capabilities of automation in Dynamics 365 and the Power Platform continue to improve the metaverse infrastructure of Microsoft. By using natural language interfaces, low-code development platforms, and automated workflows based on intelligence, companies can unite immersive technologies to business processes, allowing the workforce to be efficient and responsive in their intelligence.

Micro policy of Microsoft is not purely technological; it is an ecosystem one. The company also actively works on partnerships in the industry, the government, and research industries to support interoperability, standardisation, and adoption by developers. This cooperative approach indicates Microsoft's opinion that the Enterprise Metaverse will not look in the form of one platform, but as a system of interrelated systems.

To conclude, Microsoft is a key infrastructure, offering mixed reality solutions, digital twins, and integration of the platform that makes the company an underlying architect of the future workplace ecosystem. As companies move to immersive cooperation and smart simulation, Microsoft will continue to be one of the most influential stakeholders defining the use of the metaverse in the enterprise in which the digital systems predict the needs of users and react accordingly, Google, with its leadership in artificial intelligence, cloud architecture, and spatial information intelligence, is a major enabler of scalable enterprise metaverse experiences.

ENTERPRISE APPLICATIONS AND USE CASES

The organisational Metaverse is increasingly being recognised as a transformative field which is altering the manner in which digital services are delivered, how organisations interact with their workforce and how they conduct business. The need to enable hybrid work is among the primary motivators of the adoption of a metaverse by enterprises. Today, organisations are forced to deal with geographically spread teams thus requiring the employment of solutions other than the traditional video conferencing systems. The Metaverse environments make it easier to collaborate, be productive, and engage with each other via shared spatial work models, virtual presence, and permanent digital places. Training and simulation are among the uses that are most developed. Immersion training involves the deployment of XR, AI and digital twins as tools to recreate real-world experiences and real-world operational environments instead of theorising or operating entirely within a digital environment. The approach reduces downtime in the operation, enhances skill retention and allows risk-based training to be conducted safely. It is also vital when it comes to the implementation of digital twins in advanced engineering, energy systems, optimisation of the supply chain, and smart manufacturing.

Immersion experiences are redefining the interaction paradigm in customer-oriented industries such as marketing, entertainment as well as retailing. To erase the boundaries of digital and physical commerce, brands are trying out virtual stores, interactive product tours, and immersive marketing efforts. Finally, specialised companies such as healthcare, the military, banking, and government services, as well as education, are implementing metaverse environments to become more efficient, effective in decision-making, more accessible, and customised. (Yang, H et al. 2025)

METAVERSE-BASED TRAINING AND WORKFORCE UPSKILLING

Metaverse-based training and workforce development is considered one of the most radical applications of immersive technology in the workplace. Both simulation-based and classroom training models often have constraints in terms of risk exposure, cost, scalability and retention.

Intelligent analytics also allow better personalisation, such as simplifying the content, performance measurement, and skill deficiencies identification. Depending on behavioural tracking, voice command, eye movement analysis and sequencing of tasks, real-time feedback is provided to the learners. This enhances competency building as well as enhances learning outcomes faster than traditional approaches. The other novel application is training soft skills. The immersive role-play exercises are being used by the employers to educate the staff members on conflict resolution, negotiation, leadership communication, customer service, and cultural sensitivity. The soft skills would be measurable and trainable because of the avatars and the artificial intelligence-based virtual agents that can simulate a real social interaction. Onboarding of the workforce is also reconsidered. As a precursor to their engagement in the real world, new employees are shown virtual facilities before and anonymously meet virtual colleagues and digital mentors instead of reading instructions or watching orientation videos tokenized digital credentials is an enabling factor in cross-industry skill mobility because credentials can be used to verify the qualification of employees regardless of the ecosystem they are in, and can be stored in decentralised identity systems. It is a requirement that organisations continuously skill workers because the labour market demands vary with Industry 4.0 and AI technology. The metaverse provides a universal learning network to the world, flexible learning ecosystems and lifelong career development. (Tang, H et al. 2025)

DIGITAL TWINS IN MANUFACTURING AND ENGINEERING

Digital twins represent some of the most established and notable applications of the Enterprise Metaverse, particularly in manufacturing, engineering, and industrial operations. Machine learning and AI algorithms foresee component failure, optimise resource allocation, and plan the supply chain. Digital twins in manufacturing have been used to assist in full lifecycle management- product design and testing, production optimisation and maintenance planning. Maintenance crews can communicate with digital twins on site with mixed reality headsets. Digital twins are deployed in energy systems, transportation systems, construction projects, and smart cities, besides factories. Digital twins in infrastructure projects reduce mistakes, enhance communication with all stakeholders, and enhance long-term management of assets. The concept of next-generation industrial strategy will be based on digital twins, not only in the form of simulation tools but also as operational intelligence platforms, which can enable a full view of an enterprise, make autonomous decisions, and optimise sustainability. (Rudnicka, Z et al. 2024)

HEALTHCARE, MILITARY, FINANCE, EDUCATION, AND PUBLIC SECTOR APPLICATIONS

The hype of the metaverse as a groundbreaking operating system is evidenced by its adoption in the professional and regulated markets. The use of metaverse systems in healthcare makes it possible to conduct remote treatment, engage patients, provide medical training and simulate surgery. Surgeons practice and design complex surgeries in XR-based digital twins. Immersion simulation environments are used in the military and defence sector to train workers in high-stress situations like emergency response, drone control, cyber defence, and battlefield operations. These environments ensure cost-effectiveness and safety while simulating dynamic mission situations and unknown variables. (Mayer et al. 2025)

Planning precision and operational preparedness are enhanced by digital twins of mission settings and equipment. Adoption of the metaverse in finance includes immersive consumer experiences, decentralised transactions, and safe digital identities. Financial service delivery is being redefined by AI-powered financial advisors, virtual banking offices, and wealth management consultations. Asset-backed digital instruments, fractional ownership arrangements, and international financial transactions are all made possible by tokenisation. (Prabadevi, B et al. 2023)

The metaverse facilitates worldwide cooperation, virtual laboratories, and interactive learning in education and workforce development. Professionals and students interact with virtual campuses, simulations, and immersive information in place of passive learning. Curriculum routes are tailored to each learner's needs through AI-driven customisation. Smart city digital twins facilitate public interaction, emergency response simulation, transportation management, planning, and environmental modelling for the public sector. Metaverse systems are being investigated by government organisations for public service delivery, digital governance, and policy consultation. Even though adoption is quickening, issues with data governance, ethics, interoperability, and legislation still need to be addressed. But as standards develop, these industries will incorporate more metaverse infrastructure to create public and professional ecosystems that are intelligent, safe, and accessible. (Egbengwu, V et al. 2025)

BUSINESS MODELS AND ECONOMIC VALUE IN THE METAVERSE

As the organisational Metaverse develops from a conceptual creation into a scalable economic ecosystem, organisations are looking into monetisation strategies, operational frameworks, and value-driven models that support organisational goals. Unlike traditional digital platforms, the metaverse enables both direct and indirect value creation by combining digital assets, decentralised identities, immersive technologies, and AI-enhanced automation. Digital service subscriptions, virtual asset exchange, and ecosystem-based revenue streams are some of the resulting business models.

Efficiency gains, workforce transformation, process automation, and innovation acceleration all contribute to economic value in the Enterprise Metaverse, in addition to providing income. Industry predictions state that metaverse-driven firm value will rise as companies include immersive environments for collaboration, training, and operational simulation. Important motivators include scalability, long-term digital presence, asset interoperability, and compelling user experiences. (Abraham et al. 2022)

Ecosystem-based solutions are preferred over individual product offers in the developing economic landscape. Businesses are working more and more with platform developers, integrators, and technology suppliers to build interoperable metaverse environments. This change facilitates the growth of multi-layered economies that include operational digital twins, virtual goods marketplaces, software services, and infrastructure provisioning. Enterprise governance models are also being impacted by blockchain-based asset management and decentralised finance (DeFi). Automated compliance, rights management, and safe asset verification are made possible by tokenisation, digital credentials, and smart contracts. These capabilities generate new types of enterprise value, including data monetisation, supply chain transparency, and fractional ownership. (Böckle, M et al. 2023)

The economic framework is anticipated to grow across three main value pillars as the metaverse develops:

1. Recurring revenue streams based on platforms
2. Economies of digital assets and services
3. Process enhancement and lowering operating expenses

Early adoption of the Enterprise Metaverse will give organisations the chance to influence the economic frameworks, governance norms, and pricing structures that will characterise future digital economies. The most pertinent business models are thoroughly examined in the ensuing subsections. (Prabadevi, et al. 2023)

THE RISE OF METAVERSE-AS-A-SERVICE (MAAS)

Metaverse-as-a-Service (MaaS) is a new form of infrastructure architecture that allows businesses to develop, deploy and manage as well as scale a metaverse environment without the need to create proprietary platforms. Just like the influence of cloud computing in the SaaS period, MaaS offers extensible, customizable, and integrable units that organisations can add to their already existing digital ecosystems.

The features of MaaS platforms are generally the ability to create 3D environments, identity frameworks, host XR content, AI-driven simulation engines and blockchain services. These elements may be provided using the low-code/no-code development platforms, and such tools allow developers to create customisations rapidly without great technical skills. (Mahdikhani, M., & Meena, P. 2024)

MaaS vendors facilitate their compatibility with key enterprise systems, continuity with current workflows, cybersecurity frameworks, and models of IT governance. Other elements of MaaS are analytics engines, compliance layers, identity federation, asset lifecycle management and automated content deployment services. This minimises operational overhead and enhances scalability with an increase in the number of user adoption.

MaaS platforms are being utilised by industries including healthcare, construction, aerospace, retail, education, and government to create a dedicated virtual environment in accordance with regulatory, operational, and industry-specific demands. The prices differ with the use of infrastructure, quantity of environments, complexity of integrations, and the requirement to handle data. Hybrid models can include fixed subscription fees, compounded on usage-based computing charges or based on the assets. With the maturity of enterprises in the digital transformation path, MaaS will be a core of operational metaverse strategy - introducing scalable, flexible, and sustainable models of adoption-supporting long-term innovation.

MEASURING ROI, KPIS, AND PERFORMANCE METRICS

The enterprise strategy, resource allocation, and long-term adoption of the metaverse initiatives need to be measured according to the return on investment (ROI) and their effectiveness. The metaverse value, as opposed to traditional IT investments, cuts across both quantitative and qualitative deliverables, such as operating efficiency, workforce engagement, training effectiveness, innovation acceleration and experience enhancement to customers. The key performance indicators (KPIs) vary according to the areas of use. In the case of virtual collaboration environments, such measures as employee engagement, meeting efficiency, decision-making speed, the reduction of travelling costs, and project cycle should be considered. In the case of training and simulation, the performance is evaluated based on skill acquisition rates, reduction of errors, time to complete the task, compliance with certification and performance standards of retention. The use cases of the operational and engineering metavarses like digital twins, need further measures such as the reduction of downtimes, the quality of predictions in maintenance, energy efficiency, production throughput, and the extension of equipment lifecycle. These measures are associated with cost reduction and productivity improvement. Applications that are customer-facing need to be measured in terms of time spent on engagement, rate of conversion, satisfaction level with the customers, brand recognition, and frequency of repeated interactions. An example of such an immersive retail environment is capable of monitoring avatar behaviour, path analytics, product interaction and accuracy of personalisation response. (Ferrigno, G et al. 2023)

The full metaverse ROI framework should take into account the four types of value: Value Dimension Examples Operational Value Efficiency, savings of cost, and automation. Human Capital Value Skill development, involvement, retention. Innovation Value: New models, product acceleration, scalability. Market Value: Customer loyalty, new sources of revenue. In long-term ROI assessment, governance, risk management, and cybersecurity metrics are also involved. With the rise in enterprise adoption, normalised measuring structures will be created, and benchmarking across industries will become possible, as well as informing sustainable metaverse rollout. (Ferrigno, G et al. 2023)

PRIVACY, DATA SOVEREIGNTY, AND IDENTITY PROTECTION

The advent of the enterprise metaverse poses a multifaceted problem in controlling user identity, personal data and information security in interdependent digital ecosystems. The multidimensional data, such as biometric inputs, behavioral patterns, geolocation metadata, emotional responses, and device-level tracking, are gathered in the case of metaverse environments unlike in the traditional platforms. With the growing adoption of enterprises, privacy is no longer only a technical issue but also an organizational and regulatory requirement that is in line with global compliance standards, including GDPR, CCPA, and ISO-oriented standards of governance. The concept of data sovereignty, i.e. the ability of data to be governed by the law of the country in which it is produced, acquires particular importance in the metaverse due to the fact that the information may flow across distributed cloud networks, decentralized blockchain systems, and edge computing deployments. The multinational organizations will need effective governance policies to make sure that virtual communications do not breach the jurisdictional boundaries of data especially when employees in various nations work within the same virtual space.

Another important pillar is identity protection. The users in the metaverse use avatars, digital credentials, and cryptographic-based authentication systems. Although these tools provide personalisation and assure access, they can also reveal their weaknesses, including identity theft, deepfake identity and illegitimate digital access. New identity models, such as decentralised identity (DID), zero-knowledge proofs, and authentication based on biometrics, are being created that can enhance interoperability and minimise exposure to risk. Moreover, there are moral controversies about the digital use of immersive tracking information within businesses. To mention but a few, hyper-personalisation could be made using eye tracking, motion analytics, and biometric feedback, but violates user autonomy and psychological privacy. A balance between innovation and responsibility can be achieved through clear data minimisation principles, clear consent protocols and open communication between the organisations and the end users. Finally, the practice of privacy, sovereignty, and protecting identity within the enterprise metaverse will be changed according to the development of technology capabilities and regulatory demands. (Aloqaily, M et al 2023)

LEGAL FRAMEWORKS AND INTELLECTUAL PROPERTY RIGHTS

The metaverse can dissolve territorial boundaries, where, unlike in traditional legal systems that rely on a tangible object and the geographical bounds of contracts, intangible digital property- such as 3D objects, software scripting, virtual property, digital twins and proprietary simulations- can be created, distributed and monetised. There are new complexities in intellectual property law. An example is that deciding who can be an author of AI content presents important questions: Who is the owner of a digital design created with the help of generative AI applications? The model developer, the algorithm itself or the user? As well, metaverse platforms allow collaborative creation in real time, which needs legal definitions of shared ownership, licensing and derivative works.

In virtual marketplaces, branding and trademarks also evolve. Businesses must protect their trademarks not just in actual life but also in digital marketplaces where trademark misuse, imitations, and illegal replication may occur. Since digital assets and NFTs can travel across decentralised networks without direct system control, the rise in platform compatibility makes compliance further challenging.

Intelligent contracts, which are autonomous digital contracts that enable transactions, licenses, and reward shipping, substitute static agreements in commercial frameworks. These innovations improve efficiency and accessibility, yet they also need to be standardised across countries to receive clear legal backing. Employment and online employment rights are another field of legal importance. Legal frameworks have to define hourly rate compliance, remuneration rights for the production of digital products, and responsibility for misconduct at work that may occur in immersion circumstances while businesses integrate digital work environments. (Chen, C et al. 2023)

CYBERSECURITY, TRUST, AND FRAUD PREVENTION

In contrast to typical online environments, cybersecurity in the professional metaverse provides novel hazards, complexities, and areas of attack. Because immersive networks depend on networks of cloud infrastructure, IoT devices, XR hardware, blockchain technology, and AI-driven data analysis, there are multiple vulnerabilities that might be used by criminals. Cybersecurity has become an essential concern as businesses concentrate increasingly on virtual activities. (Kourtesis, P. 2024)

Identity fraud in avatar-based systems is one of the biggest risks. To obtain unauthorised use of encrypted networks or intellectual property, attackers can gain control of account information, duplicate profiles, or alter their online identities. To protect the control of access, advanced methods of identification like multiple-factor authentication, fingerprinting, and distributed identity solutions will be important. Reorganisation is also vital to network security. In order to protect distributed transactions and real-time 3D conversations, conventional firewalls and monitoring technologies need to adapt. (Matzko, V. 2025)

In metaverse-enabled companies, zero-trust security structures—in which every device, action, and identification has to be constantly verified— are anticipated to evolve into standard practice.

There are more worries related to money laundering in virtual markets. Digital transfers of assets can be abused by scams, phishing, manipulation of markets, and laundering of funds, especially if digital currencies such as Bitcoin and NFTs play a role. Blockchain forensics, automatic monitoring, and.compliance with regulations technologies will be vital to ensuring financial openness.

Trust design turns into an essential component. Businesses have to take steps to make sure that transactions in the metaverse remain technologically and emotionally secure. For reasons of user well-being and professional integrity, it becomes vital that we keep vigilant tabs on intimidation, inaccurate data, and digital misbehaviour.

In the final analysis, cybersecurity in the metaverse is a rapidly evolving field that requires collaboration between companies, authorities, and technology providers. As the metaverse market grows, businesses that emphasise transparency and resiliency and incorporate cybersecurity into their design principles will boost user trust and lower systemic risk. (Laiz-Ibañez et al. 2025)

CHALLENGES AND BARRIERS TO ADOPTION

Technical Limitations And Interoperability Issues

Commercial growth in the metaverse has gained traction, but widespread acceptance is still hampered by serious technical problems. The lack of maturity of the technological setting needed for creating seamless, adaptable, and compatible metaverse infrastructure is one of the biggest obstacles. Businesses need environments wherein a variety of technologies, software, and digital networks can work together effectively, yet current metaverse systems are frequently fragmented, vendor-dependent, and devoid of defined protocols for communication. There are additional obvious equipment limits. Many XR devices, sensors, and positional computing platforms continue to suffer difficulties with processing capacity, energy economy, viewing limits, and user experience, notwithstanding progress in those fields. Extended utilisation times are usually needed by enterprise situations, which modern technologies may or may not be capable of sustaining, nor fatigue or mechanical degeneration.

Another significant obstacle is compatibility. Organisations are finding it difficult to transfer or combine online experiences across platforms due to system lock-in caused by the absence of universal norms for fictional characters, digital possessions, distributed identity platforms, and 3D spaces. A company that engages in just one

XR collaborative system, for instance, may find that it is compatible with solutions from other organisations or future advances in technology. Latency and performance of networks remain difficult with technology. A high-speed, low-latency connection is required for real-time immersion collaboration, but it cannot be readily available right now. Despite the potential benefits of 5G, computing at the edges, and shared cloud designs, such innovations are currently not fairly propagated across the world, particularly across developing countries. (Hamdan, I et al 2025)

Adoption is rendered harder by shortcomings in cybersecurity. Due to the additional attack surfaces created by the multiverse, safe-by-design approaches and strong access systems for management are needed. The effects of security breaches increase when businesses use these platforms to store vital operational data. In conclusion, dispersion, infrastructural constraints, technology inexperience, and the absence of common standards for interoperability threaten to restrict the business metaverse's disruptive promise. To establish resilient, scalable, and regulated metaverse environments, industrial associations, regulators, and vendors of technology vendors must work together to get past these challenges.

Workforce Resistance And Cultural Transition

Beyond the technical difficulties, worker flexibility and social acceptance are essential for the business metaverse's successful execution. Workers must switch from conventional digital workflows, such as desktop computers and conventional videoconferencing, to immersive virtual work environments. Alongside reskilling, this change requires redefining relationships, work norms, and productivity measures. Adopting may also be affected by variations in responsibilities and ages. Experts may prefer conventional methods, whereas technologically native workers could embrace immersive working technology. Therefore, so as to avoid exclusion, discontent, or disinterest, company culture needs to evolve in conjunction with technology adoption. Leadership characteristics are equally essential. In besides outlining specific company goals, managers must show how technologies from the metaverse enhance worker happiness, efficiency, and creativity. Workforce adoption could continue to be theatrical or superficial because of the lack of unambiguous management commitment.

Approaches for managing change and training are important. Companies need to offer continuous technical assistance, collaborative learning discussions, onboarding exercises, and structured training programs. Progressive rollouts, pilot deploying groups, and initial proof-of-concept efforts can lessen resistance and create corporate backers. Lastly, emotional safety has to be given the greatest importance. Employees need assurance that the metaverse values mental health, diversity, and distinctness.

When deploying immersive spaces, companies must create hybrid approaches that allow for choice without enforcing inclusion. (Zhang, S et al. 2022)

Cost, Infrastructure, And Skills Gap

One of the biggest barriers to workplace metaverse usage is still pricing. Investing in innovative gear, including augmented reality headsets, haptic feedback devices, motion sensors, and powerful computer resources, is necessary to implement immersive workplace environments. Organisations also need to pay for online service structures, cybersecurity structures, software yearly, and the development of specific platforms for the metaverse. For businesses using digital twins, modelling environments, or massive collaboration systems, spending on infrastructure is crucial. To enable real-time rendering and data-intensive virtual environments, enterprises may need private 5G networks, edge computing designs, scalable processing GPU groups, and enormous storage capacity. These monetary challenges have been made worse by a talent imbalance. Expertise in three-dimensional design, XR application software development, blockchain combination, cybersecurity, electronic identity management, geospatial computing, artificial intelligence, and human-machine interaction design is necessary for developing, overseeing, and maintaining enterprise metaverse solutions. Many organisations lack in-house talent accomplished of supporting these developing areas, leading to dependence on advisors, technology salespersons, or subcontracted growth companies. (Vlădu escu, ., & Stănescu, V. 2024)

Environmental Sustainability And Resource Concerns

Environmental sustainability has become a central concern as enterprises explore immersive digital ecosystems. The metaverse's dependence on energy-intensive computational systems—including data centres, GPU rendering clusters, blockchain verification networks, and high-bandwidth connectivity—raises questions about carbon emissions and long-term ecological impact. Blockchain technology, in particular, has faced criticism due to the high energy consumption associated with proof-of-work consensus mechanisms. While newer models, such as proof-of-stake, offer more efficient alternatives, the sustainability debate remains ongoing, especially as digital asset markets and decentralised identity systems gain traction in metaverse environments.

Hardware manufacturing is another environmental consideration. XR headsets, sensors, haptic gloves, and spatial computing devices require materials extraction, complex assembly processes, and eventually contribute to electronic waste. Enterprises adopting large-scale deployments must consider device recycling programs, modular upgrade strategies, and extended product lifecycle planning.

Sustainable system design can mitigate some of these impacts. Strategies such as AI-optimised load balancing, low-latency caching, carbon-aware computing, and energy-efficient rendering techniques can significantly reduce resource demands. Organisations may also adopt virtual alternatives that replace physical travel, manufacturing prototypes, or physical event infrastructure—potentially reducing emissions in other operational areas. Ultimately, sustainability must become a core pillar of enterprise metaverse development rather than an afterthought. Stakeholders—including technology vendors, regulators, enterprises, and environmental bodies—must collaborate to establish sustainability frameworks, encourage responsible innovation, and ensure that the metaverse evolves as an eco-efficient digital ecosystem.

The Role Of 5g, Edge Computing, And Quantum Technology

The enterprise metaverse is built on connection. Real-time interactions, high-quality visualization, location perception, and collaborative virtual worlds will all be significantly enhanced by the introduction of 5G networks and the move towards 6G. 5G offers seamless experiences that were previously constrained by network capacity due to its bigger bandwidth and extremely low latency. Because they rely on rapid and accurate communications for control from afar, training, and operational security, sectors like manufacturing, healthcare, defence, and transportation are going to reap most from this technology. By controlling data processing nearer to the origin rather than depending solely on centralised services in the cloud, edge computing further strengthens the fabric of this system. The approach addresses various applications that involve autonomous systems, digital twins, and real-time analytics while increasing efficiency and diminishing latency. Further, it improves protection by tracking essential business information. (Wang, Y., & Zhao, J. 2022)

The physical structure of the metaverse receives a prospective overlay through quantum technology. It can substantially speed up calculations, boost cybersecurity, and enhance optimisation, even though it remains in its infancy of research. Alongside quantum-safe blockchain structures, platforms for the metaverse could ultimately depend on quantum systems for enhanced AI-driven decision processes, faster simulations, and more powerful cryptography. The technological basis for scalable business metaverse environments is going to be formed by 5G, computing at the edge, and quantum developments collaboratively, converting them from mathematical concepts into practical, internationally unified systems. (Lee, L et al. 2021)

CONCLUSION: A NEW ERA OF ENTERPRISE EVOLUTION

Over the past decade, the digital age has fundamentally altered the way businesses function, grow, and fight. This shift implies an overall shift in approach, culture, labour capabilities, operational methods, and value generation rather than simply implementing technology. Artificial intelligence, robotics, blockchain, cloud computing, and digital twins all offer value when paired with established company plans that prioritise client satisfaction, efficiency in operations, innovation, and long-term success. Technology is a facilitator instead of an endpoint. Data has grown into a competitive differentiator and strategic resource. In order to facilitate analytics, predictive processes, personalised interactions with clients, and AI-driven choices, major businesses devote resources to safe, adaptable, and ethical data ecosystems. Some of the greatest shifts in corporate behaviour is going from intuitive to data-driven leadership.

Business models that are flexible and agile are equally important. Dynamic, modular structures that can evolve quickly substitute static architectures. This flexibility is reflected in cloud services, open-source innovation ecosystems, and recurring services, which enable companies to continually evolve in conjunction with changing marketplaces, innovative technologies, and increasing consumer expectations. A key factor in transformation is the culture of the organisation. Lacking leadership backing, staff acceptance, and a mindset that encourages exploration, taking chances, and ongoing learning, the adoption of technology is unsuccessful. No business is capable of handling digital transformation on its own; collaboration and ecosystem understanding are also essential. Innovation increases, interoperability is improved, and scaled uptake is supported through engagements with small businesses, academic institutions, technology suppliers, industry relationships, and legislators. Intelligent customised experiences, environmentalism, cybersecurity, and intelligence from technology are all common components that form a single foundation for company innovation; however, conversion varies within industries.

The labour market is changing rapidly. Artificial intelligence will progressively coexist with hybrid, distributed, and digitally augmented teams. Automation and artificial intelligence are going to take up tedious tasks, freeing up people to concentrate on planning, creativity, and complex decision-making. Immersive virtual worlds and virtual workplaces are revolutionising engagement, training, and collaboration. Geographical obstacles disappear, skill acquisition is accelerated, and recall is improved through the use of digital avatars, simulated training, and hologram virtual presence. In order to cohabit in human teams, digital workers—including AI agents and autonomous robots—will need new productivity measures, ethical guidelines, and governance structures. Technology proficiency, micro-credentials, and ongoing education are going to be essential elements of workforce preparation.

To be able to oversee decentralised organisations, digital identities, and digitally enabled operations while ensuring security, culture, and confidence, these skills related to leadership must adapt.

Long-term plans that are compatible with emerging technologies, scenario preparation, and flexible strategies that can change direction as markets and technologies develop are all essential to change. It is essential to make investments in information and technology, integrate ethical AI and regulatory frameworks, and ensure intelligence in real-time systems. In order to prepare for demands for privacy and trust, leaders need to reconsider consumer engagement as continuous, based on data, and personalised. In terms of prospering in the constantly shifting digital environment, organisations that embrace fully immersive technologies, information-driven operations, and diverse workforce approaches will actively shape the next stage in business development, one whereby ecosystem engagement, technological-human interaction, and agility drive long-term development and edge over the competition.

REFERENCES

Abraham, J., Cruz, G., Cubela, S., Lajous, T., Rowshankish, K., Tiwari, S., & Zemmel, R. (2022, October). Digital twins: The foundation of the enterprise metaverse. McKinsey & Company. https://www.mckinsey.com/capabilities/tech-and-ai/our-insights/digital-twins-the-foundation-of-the-enterprise-metaverse

Abraham, J., Cruz, G., Cubela, S., Lajous, T., Rowshankish, K., Tiwari, S., & Zemmel, R. (2022). Digital twins — the foundation of the enterprise metaverse. McKinsey & Company. https://www.mckinsey.com/capabilities/tech-and-ai/our-insights/digital-twins-the-foundation-of-the-enterprise-metaverse

Aloqaily, M., Bouachir, O., Karray, F., Al Ridhawi, I., & El Saddik, A. (2022). *Integrating Digital Twin and Advanced Intelligent Technologies to Realize the Metaverse*. arXiv. /arXiv.2210.04606DOI: 10.48550

Aloqaily, M., Ghirmai, S., Mebrahtom, D., & Guizani, M. (2023). Self-Sovereign Identity for Trust and Interoperability in the Metaverse. arXiv. /arXiv.2303.00422DOI: 10.48550

Böckle, M., Reuter, C., & Qin, S. (2023). Metaverse Business Models and Framework: A Systematic Search with Narrative Synthesis. *Systems*, *13*(11), 968. DOI: 10.3390/systems1311968

Chen, C., Li, Y., Wu, Z., Mai, C., Liu, Y., Hu, Y., Zheng, Z., & Kang, J. (2023). Privacy Computing Meets Metaverse: Necessity, Taxonomy and Challenges. arXiv. /arXiv.2304.11643DOI: 10.48550

Egbengwu, V., Garn, W., & Turner, C. J. (2025). Metaverse for Manufacturing: Leveraging Extended Reality Technology for Human-Centric Production Systems. *Sustainability*, *17*(1), 280. DOI: 10.3390/su17010280

Ferrigno, G., Di Paola, N., Oguntegbe, K. F., & Kraus, S. (2023). Value creation in the metaverse age: A thematic analysis of press releases. *International Journal of Entrepreneurial Behaviour & Research*, *29*(11), 337–363. DOI: 10.1108/IJEBR-01-2023-0039

Hamdan, I. K. A., Aziguli, W., Zhang, D., & Alhakeem, B. (2025). Barriers to Adopting Metaverse Technology in Manufacturing Firms. *Journal of Manufacturing Engineering*, *19*(4), 146–162. DOI: 10.37255/jme.v19i4pp146-162

Huynh-The, T., Pham, Q.-V., Pham, X.-Q., Nguyen, T. T., Han, Z., & Kim, D.-S. (2022). *Artificial Intelligence for the Metaverse: A Survey*. arXiv. /arXiv.2202.10336 arXivDOI: 10.48550

Kourtesis, P. (2024). A Comprehensive Review of Multimodal XR Applications, Risks, and Ethical Challenges in the Metaverse. arXiv. /arXiv.2411.04508DOI: 10.48550

Laiz-Ibañez, H., Mendaña-Cuervo, C., & Carús Candás, J. L. (2025). The metaverse: Privacy and information security risks. *International Journal of Information Management Data Insights*, *5*(2), 100373. Advance online publication. DOI: 10.1016/j.jjimei.2025.100373

Lee, L.-H., Braud, T., Zhou, P., Wang, L., Xu, D., Lin, Z., Kumar, A., Bermejo, C., & Hui, P. (2021). All one needs to know about metaverse: A complete survey on technological singularity, virtual ecosystem, and research agenda.

Lee, L.-H., Braud, T., Zhou, P., Wang, L., Xu, D., Lin, Z., Kumar, A., Bermejo, C., & Hui, P. (2021). *All one needs to know about metaverse: A complete survey on technological singularity, virtual ecosystem, and research agenda.* arXiv. /arXiv.2110.05352DOI: 10.48550

Lee, L.-H., Braud, T., Zhou, P., Wang, L., Xu, D., Lin, Z., Kumar, A., Bermejo, C., & Hui, P. (2021). All one needs to know about metaverse: A complete survey on technological singularity, virtual ecosystem, and research agenda. *arXiv.* /arXiv.2110.05352DOI: 10.48550

Lv, Z., Shang, W.-L., & Guizani, M. (2022). Impact of Digital Twins and metaverse on cities: History, current situation, and application perspectives. *Applied Sciences (Basel, Switzerland)*, *12*(24), 12820. DOI: 10.3390/app122412820

Lyu, Z., & Fridenfalk, M. (2024). Digital twins for building industrial metaverse. *Journal of Advanced Research*, *66*, 31–38. DOI: 10.1016/j.jare.2023.11.019 PMID: 38008176

Mahdikhani, M., & Meena, P. (2024). Metaverse applications and supply chain innovation: Insights from text mining. *Journal of Innovation & Knowledge*, *9*(4), 100591. Advance online publication. DOI: 10.1016/j.jik.2024.100591

Marr, B. (2022). Digital twins, generative AI and the metaverse. Forbes. https://bernardmarr.com/digital-twins-generative-ai-and-the-metaverse/

Matzko, V. (2025). Legal Framework for Cybersecurity in the Context of the Metaverse Formation. Metaverse Science. *Society and Law*, *2025*(1), 1–18. DOI: 10.69635/mssl.2025.1.1.18

Mayer, A., Greif, L., Häußermann, T. M., Otto, S., Kastner, K., El Bobbou, S., Chardonnet, J.-R., Reichwald, J., Fleischer, J., & Ovtcharova, J. (2025). Digital Twins, Extended Reality, and Artificial Intelligence in Manufacturing Reconfiguration: A Systematic Literature Review. *Sustainability*, *17*(5), 2318. DOI: 10.3390/su17052318

Microsoft. (2021, May 26). *Converging the physical and digital with digital twins, mixed reality, and metaverse apps.* Microsoft Blog. https://azure.microsoft.com/en-us/blog/converging-the-physical-and-digital-with-digital-twins-mixed-reality-and-metaverse-apps/

Microsoft. (2022, December 20). *HoloLens 2 enables industrial metaverse for plant inspection and remote assistance.* Microsoft News. https://news.microsoft.com/source/features/innovation/hololens-2-industrial-metaverse/

Microsoft. (2025, February 20). Carter, R. "Azure Mixed Reality Solutions: Building the Future of Digital Transformation." XR Today. https://www.xrtoday.com/mixed-reality/azure-mixed-reality-solutions-building-the-future-of-digital-transformation/

Microsoft. (n.d.). *Microsoft Mesh: connect like never before.* Microsoft. https://www.microsoft.com/en-us/microsoft-teams/microsoft-mesh Microsoft

Mourtzis, D. (2023). Digital twin inception in the era of industrial metaverse. *Frontiers in Manufacturing Technology, 3.* Advance online publication. DOI: 10.3389/fmtec.2023.1155735

Prabadevi, B., Deepa, N., Victor, N., Gadekallu, T. R., Maddikunta, P. K. R., Yenduri, G., Wang, W., Pham, Q. V., & Huynh-The, T. (2023). *Metaverse for Industry 5.0 in NextG Communications: Potential Applications and Future Challenges.* arXiv. / arXiv.2308.02677DOI: 10.48550

Rudnicka, Z., Proniewska, K., Perkins, M., & Pregowska, A. (2024). *Health Digital Twins Supported by Artificial Intelligence-based Algorithms and Extended Reality in Cardiology.* arXiv. /arXiv.2401.14208DOI: 10.48550

Sai, S., Sharma, P., Gaur, A., & Chamola, V. (2024). Pivotal role of digital twins in the metaverse: A review. *Digital Communications and Networks.*

Sindhwani, A., Ruhela, S., Bhatia, A., Lalit, R., & Johari, R. (2023). Metaverse: Survey on future of internet and its innovative applications. *CEUR Workshop Proceedings.*

Tang, M., Nikolaenko, M., Alrefai, A., & Kumar, A. (2025). Metaverse and Digital Twins in the Age of AI and Extended Reality. *Architecture (Washington, D.C.), 5*(2), 36. DOI: 10.3390/architecture5020036

Vlădu escu, ., & Stănescu, V. (2024). Greening the Virtual: An Interdisciplinary Narrative Review on the Environmental Sustainability of the Metaverse. *Sustainability, 17*(16), 7269. DOI: 10.3390/su17167269

Wang, Y., & Zhao, J. (2022). A Survey of Mobile Edge Computing for the Metaverse: Architectures, Applications, and Challenges. *arXiv.* /arXiv.2212.00481DOI: 10.48550

Yang, H., Aqlan, F., & Zhao, R. (2025). *Towards Smart Manufacturing Metaverse via Digital Twinning in Extended Reality*. arXiv. /arXiv.2510.16280DOI: 10.48550

Zhang, S., Lim, W. C. B., Ng, W. C., Xiong, Z., Niyato, D., Shen, X. S., & Miao, C. (2022). Towards Green Metaverse Networking: Advances and Future Directions. *arXiv*. /arXiv.2211.03057DOI: 10.48550

Chapter 6
Responsible Intelligence: A Framework for Managing AI Hallucinations in the Metaverse Systems

Gagandeep Singh
https://orcid.org/0000-0001-8644-4064
Lovely Professional University, India

Jasdeep Singh Walia
https://orcid.org/0000-0001-9010-082X
Lovely Professional University, India

ABSTRACT

The integration of multimodal generative AI into metaverse environments has intensified hallucination-driven distortions, creating synthetic outputs that appear credible within immersive spaces and influence judgment, behaviour and decision accuracy. Continuous presence in avatar-based ecosystems heightens perceptual reality drift and cognitive misalignment. The absence of responsible intelligence mechanisms for detection, monitoring and mitigation leaves immersive system users exposed to synthetic narrative manipulation, fabricated identity signals and cross-modal inconsistency. Fragmented regulation and limited provenance verification deepen risks as hallucination cycles evolve without oversight. This study develops a governance framework centred on real-time authenticity assurance, distortion tracking and consistency verification. It advances a structured approach to protect immersive participants, reduce uncontrolled hallucination escalation and strengthen accountable metaverse safety architecture.

DOI: 10.4018/979-8-3373-7534-2.ch006

1. INTRODUCTION

The rapid growth of Metaverse and immersive Metaverse-integrated AI systems is remodelling all major areas by creating enormous potential for the creation of sophisticated innovations (Mao & Xu, 2025). The inequalities in its fair access and in its distribution present major challenges for metaverse participants. Artificial intelligence and multimodal hallucination-prone models' vulnerabilities are impacting metaverse participants disproportionally (Hermann et al., 2024). The cognitive decline and risk of dark AI patterns mainly arise due to an inability to use digital technology (Ferrara, 2023). The speed of creation of new AI tools has come at considerable perceptual reality drift to immersive environment users, particularly metaverse participants and people (Kallina et al., 2025; Drabiak et al., 2023). The social inequalities are being exacerbated by an unrestricted artificial intelligence that does not accept ethical principles and harms privacy and trust. Immersion eliminates the separation between interface and perception, which places users inside narrative structures. Such structures are generated by large language models, avatar communication agents and real-time generative simulation systems

Metaverse participants are more impacted by AI tech-based decision-making aid, and it increases the digital divide. The development of Metaverse-integrated AI systems must be purposefully designed to take care of algorithm-level manipulation through intelligent interfaces (Novelli et al., 2024). The violation of their interests can have damaging impacts on a range of life decisions. It can tamper with their ability to govern themselves and lower individual independence. Also, this makes huge compromises to data privacy in the case of the metaverse participants (Kallina et al., 2025). The unregulated AI hallucinations and their existing paradigms do not consider the perceptual reality drift of unregulated use of AI (Hewage et al., 2024; Tejaskumar Pujari et al., 2022).

The current chapter keeps track of the analysis regarding the fast integration of the technologies and the vulnerabilities of our ageing population. The objective of the present research work is to carry out research on the issues arising due to digital divides, ethics and the absence of proper governance. This chapter aims to study the role of Metaverse-integrated AI systems integrated with the lives of immersive system stakeholders and the dangers that Metaverse-integrated AI systems pose due to the fragmented regulatory regime. It seeks to outline a governance model that is inclusive to promote trustworthy AI, thereby ensuring its conscientious use. This study closely examines the deficiencies, focusing on identifying the deficiencies in the damages caused by AI from the disconnected regulations and the complete participation of all stakeholders. This study investigates the effects of high-intensity metaverse exposure on their mental health.

This research work seeks to build a comprehensive and transparent multi-stakeholder Trust-layer verification governance framework. The ultimate focus of the proposed framework is to offer innovative strategies meant for the protection of the interests of the metaverse participants. The insights of the study shall guide policymakers to develop programmes concerning immersive resilience intelligence and also ensure its accessibility at all times. It cautions that most modern Trust-layer verification governance frameworks do not cater to immersive environment users, particularly because Metaverse participants lack the digital skills or cognitive capacity to use a complicated AI system safely.

The findings of established literature highlight that the absence of exhaustive measures to accurately measure the perceptual reality drift, emotional and financial exploitation among the high-risk immersive creates a gap that shall be filled to protect their interests. Additionally, it was unveiled that mechanisms of unregulated media and Metaverse-integrated AI systems are pushing up inequalities and creating erosion of their trust and faith in digital technologies (Brenneis, 2025; Goktas & Grzybowski, 2025; Obianuju Ozobu et al., 2025; Alsaigh et al., 2023).

The endeavour of the current study shall enable stakeholders to enforce socially inclusive AI and a sophisticated digital ecosystem. It also sets the ground for creating an ethical, integrative and adaptable framework for governing the AI tools and processes catering for the requirements of immersive intelligence users. It provides actionable insights for building unbiased and equitable Metaverse-integrated AI systems, which shall permit digital processes usage properly. It aims to design moral and fair Metaverse-integrated AI systems. It specifies various significant avenues wherein high-risk immersive users' needs shall conform to human-centred Trust-layer verification governance.

2. LITERATURE REVIEW

The present study considers three literature domains concerning presence distortion impacts and the digital downside among immersive intelligence users, the disintegrated AI oversight and the social cost accounting and collaborative governance for explainable AI. These are described as follows:

2.1. Presence distortion impacts and their augmentation among immersive intelligence users

The increase in regulatory diffusion and AI-induced sensitivity among metaverse participants is clearly elucidated in past research. The literature clearly outlines the complex interrelationship between the usage of artificial intelligence among immersive intelligence users (Barredo Arrieta et al., 2020). A theoretical groundwork was developed to decipher the AI mechanisms and their ability to exploit immersive system users (Blut et al., 2021). The emerging Metaverse-integrated AI systems have devised novel means of control and manipulation among the immersive system users by providing them with adaptation to the requirements of immersive intelligence users (Alsaigh et al., 2023; André et al., 2018). Such research work aided in gauging the AI integration in the metaverse participants' population by showcasing the ideas of vulnerability coming into view or being noticed. The interconnectedness and mutual influence of the system and the junior population were assessed. Such perspectives perfectly align with the issues of escalation raised in this regard concerning the algorithmic decision-making, thereby redesigning the consumer power dynamics (Allen et al., 2025; Agbavor & Liang, 2022).

A specific term was outlined in published studies, known as a manipulative design, for users who constantly engage in a complex digital AI ecosystem (Cheng & Gong, 2024; Ferrara, 2023). Certain studies have formulated a new paradigm of vulnerability framework and outlined threats in the context of healthcare issues affecting the immersive intelligence users (Hermann et al., 2024; Agbavor & Liang, 2022). The vulnerability framework was further augmented, and elements of large language models were integrated. Few studies revealed the significant risks arising from constant Immersive AI agents (Allen et al., 2025; Blut et al., 2021; Hickman & Petrin, 2021; Larsson & Heintz, 2020). It was suggested that AI dependence can accurately detect cognitive ability decline and raise ethical dilemmas (Mao & Xu, 2025; Novelli et al., 2024; Andrew & Baker, 2021; Banker & Khetani, 2019). Concerns were raised on user consent and privacy, and such parameters were given due consideration in developing the ethical implications of Immersive AI agents.

2.2. Disintegrated AI oversight and the social cost accounting

Irregular AI regulation often leads to a decline in cognitive abilities, and it brings up issues concerning the ethics and privacy of the metaverse stakeholders (Brenneis, 2025; Cheng & Gong, 2024; Drabiak et al., 2023). The risk of discriminatory usage of AI and its impact on insurance and employment opportunities were duly analysed in the previous studies. A fragmented approach exists in trust-layer verification governance, which calls for making required efforts to scrutinise the involvement of Artificial General Intelligence and the digital humanism (Obianuju Ozobu et al., 2025; Novelli et al., 2024; Li et al., 2023). Significant gaps were witnessed, and it was noticed that past studies have not recognised the societal effects of Immersive AI agents among immersive system users(Tallam, 2025; Mao & Xu, 2025; Kingdon, 2024). Few studies reviewed the contemporary AI regulations and established that the existing paradigm focused mainly on technical issues of Immersive AI agents only(Goktas & Grzybowski, 2025; Kallina et al., 2025; Obianuju Ozobu et al., 2025; Rozenblit et al., 2025). Moreover, the existing parameters identify the legislative issues of generative AI and do not fully analyse the societal costs involved with the Immersive AI agents. It calls for developing mechanisms of responsible intelligence to prevent the risks of cognitive misalignment and inconsistencies concerning cross-modal mechanisms.

The pertinent issues of algorithmic bias and digital exclusion were not adequately addressed in the literature (Hewage et al., 2024; Bigman & Gray, 2018; Borenstein & Arkin, 2016). The existing regulatory paradigms outline a short-sighted view and overlook the ethical, social, and economic health concerns of AI users (Rozenblit et al., 2025; Drabiak et al., 2023; Borenstein & Arkin, 2016). The existing legal regulations do not provide a comprehensive view of the AI error system and the perceptual reality drift of its usage (Kallina et al., 2025). Certain studies outlined that AI users carry negative viewpoints on the AI tools making moral decisions. The existing governance regulations are not enough to ethically handle human-sensitive information. The non-existence of measuring the perceptual reality drift of Immersive AI agents is making the situation worse and raising many ethical concerns (Ferrara, 2023; Blut et al., 2021). Few studies presented insights on surveillance capitalism and suggested that inappropriate enforcement of privacy rules results in digital exclusion (Wang et al., 2025; Akhundov, 2025; Larsson & Heintz, 2020). It was highlighted that there is a requirement to construct a comprehensive framework that accommodates the AI harms in the context of human interactions (Ferrara, 2023; Agbavor & Liang, 2022).

2.3. Collaborative governance for explainable AI

The governance of existing AI procedures involves various participatory models necessitating the involvement of multiple stakeholders (Rozenblit et al., 2025; Tallam, 2025). Such a scenario is necessary to bring change to the AI architecture. The past studies established that there is a requirement to determine the intricacies of AI, and existing regulations applying the top-down approach are inadequate to resolve such complex human problems (Kallina et al., 2025; Küsters & Wörsdörfer, 2025). Focussed attention is necessary for governing the AI mechanisms (Goktas & Grzybowski, 2025; Li et al., 2023). Devising an appropriate regulatory framework is necessary for adapting traditional democratic governance systems properly. It shall duly involve the required technical experts and establish their accountability (Cheng & Liu, 2024). The conflicts between technical efficiency and democratic legitimacy shall be properly accounted for to put Trust-layer verification governance's participatory dimensions into practice. The interests of immersive participants must be duly protected to reduce the impact of uncontrolled hallucinations and develop the mechanisms of metaverse safety.

The past research work found various gaps regarding the involvement of businesses in ensuring responsible Trust-layer verification governance (Brenneis, 2025; Agbavor & Liang, 2022; Banker & Khetani, 2019). It was found that active participation is necessary for ensuring suitable governance of AI technologies. Involvement of multiple stakeholders is required for ensuring responsible AI in consumer health issues (Ferrara, 2023). Constructing a detailed framework is necessary to incorporate technical and health issues. Few studies highlighted the issues in ensuring metaverse content verification governance. It was pointed out that certain stakeholders may not act responsibly and can take advantage of inclusivity to spread harmful content (Tallam, 2025; Hewage et al., 2024). Suitable oversight mechanisms call for preventing the augmented risks of hallucination in metaverse-driven systems

The literature outcomes focused on developing robust guidelines that consider ethical AI issues in the overall governance system. It was found that existing paradigms do not account for the long-term effects of the moral implications of Immersive AI agents, and they were entirely focused on economic and technical paradigms only (Mao & Xu, 2025; Shouli et al., 2025; Wang et al., 2025; Borenstein & Arkin, 2016). It is concluded that past studies have not devised any specific methodology to quantify metaverse content verification governance and its parameters. The focus is mainly on design aspects, and there is no specific measurement tool meant to evaluate the outcomes of Trust-layer verification governance (Alsaigh et al., 2023; Banker & Khetani, 2019; Hickman & Petrin, 2021; Larsson & Heintz, 2020). The past studies suggested considering the stakeholder priorities, the inclusion of technological capabilities and ensuring the long-term viability of Trust-layer verification governance systems.

3. RESEARCH GAP

The metaverse participants are facing unprecedented dangers in our increasingly metaverse-integrated AI systems. This sphere of population does not possess sufficient skills, cognitive capacity, and resources to easily navigate the AI sphere. The digital dependence of the metaverse participants group has undergone a significant change, and it has established a strong interconnection with the evolving Metaverse-integrated AI systems. Their interactions with AI protocols have led to exploitation of their mental well-being, behavioural patterns and emotional longings. A critical gap exists as no framework aims to mitigate the unseen impact of AI that is harming immersive environment users. Such a deficiency is leading to a 'digital poison' which is constantly accumulating the harsh social, psychological and economic effects arising from prolonged usage of high-risk metaverse ecosystems. The metaverse participants are constantly exposed to various high-risk immersive risks, mainly arising from cognitive manipulations, privacy breaches, social isolation, and predatory targeting. Such risks are increasingly harming our elders at all levels. There lies a significant gap, and it calls for devising a framework that can quantify the perceptual reality drift of using AI and provide due protection to immersive system users.

The contemporary regulatory approaches to AI user-based integration are fragmented, and they are mainly focused on prioritising the technical aspects over the holistic protection of human rights. The present AI framework has hallucination risk-monitoring voids, which are permitting AI procedures and their tools to operate without adequate supervision. There is a complete absence of policies that measure and quantify the societal costs of using Metaverse-integrated AI systems. Furthermore, there is a complete absence of collaborations among the users in the AI ecosystem. Such disparities call for devising a comprehensive and multistakeholder framework that shall effectively address the complex and interconnected nature of AI vulnerabilities.

It is therefore concluded that the theoretical framework outlined in the present research work builds a robust foundation for exploring the interrelationship among the cognitive abilities, AI and media usage, machine and human intelligence and ethics. It provides a framework for critically analysing ways in which metaverse technologies augment or reduce the imbalances among immersive environment users. It lays the groundwork for constructing a whole-systems and responsive model of responsible Trust-layer verification governance, especially adapted for metaverse participants facing various distortions in the system. It prioritises fairness by making sure that real-time generative simulation systems work in the best interest of the metaverse participants. It intends to foster inclusivity by creating an ecosystem by provides them opportunities to express their views and concerns. It includes human dignity by emphasising that their fundamental rights are protected and properly enforced. There is an urgent need to develop anticipatory regulatory mechanisms within the high-intensity metaverse-driven systems.

4. THEORETICAL FRAMEWORK

The study addresses the moral implications of digital technologies, dynamics of cognitive ergonomics, metaverse content verification governance and gerontechnology that combines ageing with technology. In this regard, it relies on an interdisciplinary approach to build insights from interactions of artificial intelligence and media systems with immersive environment users, along with their governance mechanisms, particularly the metaverse participants, and how these interactions can be governed responsibly (Kingdon, 2024; Hickman & Petrin, 2021; Borenstein & Arkin, 2016). The framework core endeavours to reconcile breakthrough technology among principled metaverse participants' group behaviour by foregrounding principles of inclusivity, accountability, and transparency.

The current research work focuses on the aspect of vulnerability, which outlines the various physical and cognitive limitations among immersive system users while operating in the AI and media environments (Allen et al., 2025; Chen et al., 2024; Larsson & Heintz, 2020). In this regard, the vulnerability theory forms the underpinning of the research describing the institutional discrimination, inherent biases, and embedded biases in Real-time generative simulation systems (Blut et al., 2021; Banker & Khetani, 2019; Bigman & Gray, 2018). Various vulnerabilities are required to be addressed related to improper regulation and supervision of metaverse participants being exposed to digital ecosystems (Kallina et al., 2025; Tallam, 2025; Drabiak et al., 2023; Hickman & Petrin, 2021).

The concept of hallucination-driven content distortion is addressed in current research work to meet the disparities while operating in AI-driven systems (Brenneis, 2025; Cheng & Liu, 2024). The capability paradigm is applied as the core aspect of the study for aligning metaverse participants' actions with value systems (Kallina et al., 2025; Mao & Xu, 2025). A key aspect of governance, maintaining the metaverse participants' dignity, is ensured through the provision of equitable digital abilities (Küsters & Wörsdörfer, 2025; Rozenblit et al., 2025; Shouli et al., 2025; Novelli et al., 2024). The challenges are addressed in the study by incorporating metaverse content verification governance and multi-stakeholder engagement paradigms (Agbavor & Liang, 2022; André et al., 2018). It is fostered that governments, private sector entities, and civil society organisations shall actively involve themselves in exercising the AI policies and frameworks for effective decision-making (Akhundov, 2025; Hewage et al., 2024; Drabiak et al., 2023). An effective collaboration is to be ensured by augmenting governance that is participatory, equitable and based on ensuring distribution of equitable rights for using media and AI platforms (Shouli et al., 2025; Cheng & Liu, 2024).

A thoughtful and responsive approach must be applied to enable suitable AI use among the immersive system users. (Obianuju Ozobu et al., 2025; Tallam, 2025; Borenstein & Arkin, 2016). Digital assets shall properly recognise the harsh effects of immersive AI agents among various immersive system users (Wang et al., 2025; Barredo Arrieta et al., 2020). The aspects of self-determination and welfare of the metaverse participants are considered as the topmost priorities for protecting their interests (Goktas & Grzybowski, 2025; Ferrara, 2023; Blut et al., 2021). The use of the technology and its optimal use shall include the important dimensions of usability and its adaptability to ensure that the technology is beneficial for the junior population.

5. PROPOSED GOVERNANCE FRAMEWORK FOR THE PROTECTION OF THE HIGH-RISK IMMERSIVE DEMOGRAPHICS' INTERESTS

The multistakeholder framework for the metaverse participants developed in the study intends to foster collaborative engagement among the various parties of interest. The underpinning of the framework is constructing the regulating dimensions for ensuring governance of AI tools, procedures and platforms. The entire framework is built upon the core principle of transparency, and it aims to incorporate the insights from government authorities, regulatory dimensions, the private sector and various civil service organisations. The comprehensive framework is built upon the four underlying principles. These governing principles are centred on governance, data management, performance evaluation, and monitoring systems. These principles are more suited to managing AI complexities, using unified and risk-focused regulations. This innovative framework sets a path for the new term known as integrators, who are primarily associated with the AI developers and deployers. Their involvement in the framework management shall ensure due oversight, guidance and supervision of different AI protocols and their processes.

5.1. AI Impact Safeguard Paradigm

Figure 1 presents the framework for AI impact safeguard meant for immersive intelligence users. The motive of this all-encompassing framework is to come up with new ways of mitigation, to manage the risks associated with the usage of AI, especially among the high-risk immersive, in particular, the avatar-based users. The three key components of this approach refer to dimensions like Immersion Level, accountability and impact. The interconnected dimensions show that more Immersion Level of high-risk immersive people in real-time generative simulation systems must include embedding mechanisms for continuous feedback and enforcing responsive control measures of accountability.

The deep immersion component acts to engage and manage the metaverse participants' population's concerns due to the deep immersion from the AI in view of permanent interactions through the engagement of the systematic manifestation of concern or worry. The impact part looks at how the AI platforms can bring both good and bad changes to our world. A complex and clarifying accountability process is called for. Significant elements are outlined in the current research work by putting the shielding mechanisms into effect. All these components are woven, and as a result full-fledged system reduces the risks of AI applications. The synthetic content risk scoring focuses on spotting and monitoring the exceptional situations where harm is generated by the use of AI and media systems. Vulnerability mapping aims to protect and shield entities from the harmful effects of high-risk Immersive AI agents. Proper resources must be employed in sufficient measure to support the protection from adverse consequences.

Figure 1. Responsible Intelligence Core System

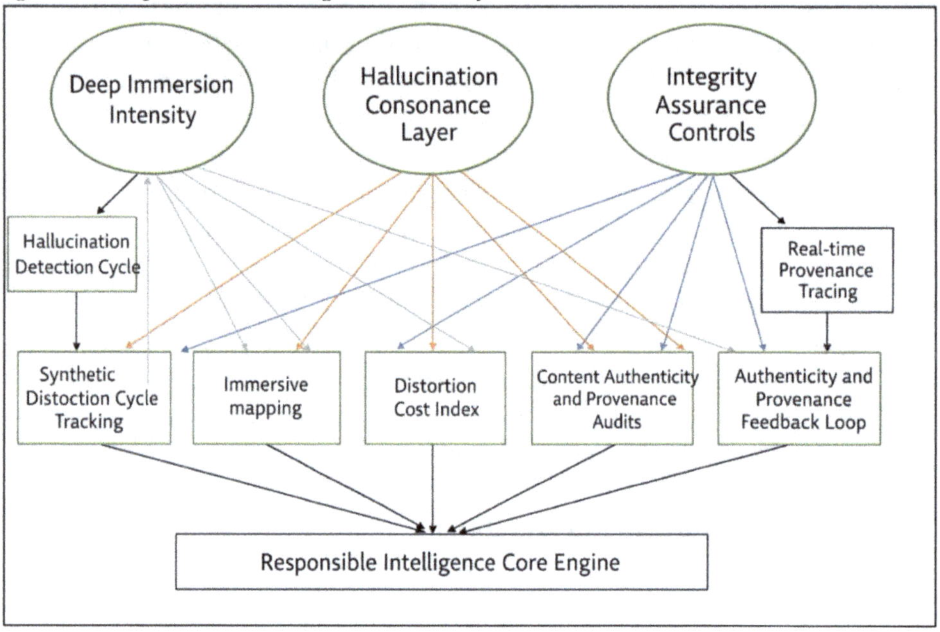

Source: Author's creation

The cost indexing section accurately measures diverse quantitative and qualitative costs. The Metaverse-integrated AI systems shall work on optimising. The resources used in running the Metaverse-integrated AI systems must ensure that the mechanisms of AI align with the standards set by the regulatory authorities. Frequent audits and ensuring the integrity of the Metaverse-integrated AI systems ensure this. The components of the redress loop consist of the resolution and remedy of grievances, suitably and immediately, and corrective action. The major concern of this Loop is the resolution of the issue. Furthermore, this Loop initiates the course of action defined for the attribution.

The AI Impact safeguard mechanism integrates several interconnected arrows that facilitate the information flow among its components. The AI harm tracking system is directly affected by the deep immersion component. The ill effects of Immersive AI agents shall be recognised, and mapping should be done to understand their potential harms. The establishment of a grievance system is vital for the accountability of AI. This aids in building trust and ensures that any harm caused by these systems is properly addressed. This framework takes a holistic approach to complex AI issues while recognising all AI risks. The issues are linked and need a multifaceted, consistent response, as described in Table 1

Table 1. Summary of AI Impact safeguard mechanisms

Component	Description	Functions	Outcomes
Deep immersion	Investigates risks from continuous interaction with AI protocols.	Identifies inherent vulnerabilities in metaverse participants users due to frequent deep immersion; emphasizes frequent monitoring.	It increases awareness of adverse effects linked to high AI engagement.
Impact	Evaluates positive and negative consequences of Immersive AI agents.	Integrates outcomes into vulnerability mapping to identify at-risk metaverse participants groups.	It helps prioritize resource allocation for those most negatively affected.
Accountability	Establishes mechanisms to ensure responsibility for AI-related actions.	Involves ethical verification audits, grievance redress systems, and cost indexing.	It ensures responsible Trust-layer verification governance and corrective actions.
Harm Tracking	Identifies, records, and monitors instances of AI-induced harm.	Maintains a database of harmful incidents; enables predictive analysis to prevent future cases of harm.	It contributes to impact assessment and accountability measures.
Vulnerability Mapping	Profiles and locates high-risk metaverse participants populations affected by Hallucination detection and mitigation cycles.	Classifies high-risk immersive subgroups and informs targeted safeguarding strategies.	It guides resource deployment and cost indexing strategies.
Cost Indexing	Quantifies financial and non-financial costs of AI-related harms.	Quantifies economic burden of Hallucination detection and mitigation cycles; supports efficient resource allocation.	It relies on vulnerability mapping through system optimization.
Ethics Verification	Ensures Metaverse-integrated AI systems comply with regulatory and ethical standards.	Conducts regular audits; verifies data integrity, algorithmic fairness, and user rights protection.	It supports redress loops through verified compliance procedures.
Redress Loops	Provides remedies and grievance resolution for affected immersive system users.	Facilitates complaint handling, compensation, and feedback integration; involves trust-building.	It reinforces accountability informed by harm tracking and ethics verification outcomes.

Source: Author's creation

5.2. Framework of Protection Nexus for the metaverse participants

Figure 2 illustrates the paradigm of high-risk immersive people and keeping them safe in the age of unregulated AI hallucinations. The whole plan revolves around a core connection between security measures, risk mitigation, crisis readiness, and good communication. This approach highlights the surprising problems that come with using so much AI and media, especially for kids. A single, integrated strategy is presented to lessen the bad effects of uncontrolled tech reliance and protect sensitive people. This requires us to look at every piece of the framework and truly understand the perceptual reality drift and ethics involved.

5.2.1. Integrated Security and Risk Mitigation

Building trust in AI boils down to better security measures. This includes three main things: system protection, ethical audits, and layered access control. Spotting AI anomalies requires comprehensive cybersecurity plans and advanced solutions to protect systems from unauthorised access or breaches. This protection is non-negotiable for immersive system users who might be tricked by AI-driven hallucinated avatar communications. Making sure AI is secure helps avoid issues like financial fraud. Regularly auditing AI's ethical implications is mandatory to check for discrimination and transparency problems, especially since AI in healthcare can lead to wrong diagnoses or unequal treatment.

Figure 2. Protection Nexus for Metaverse participants

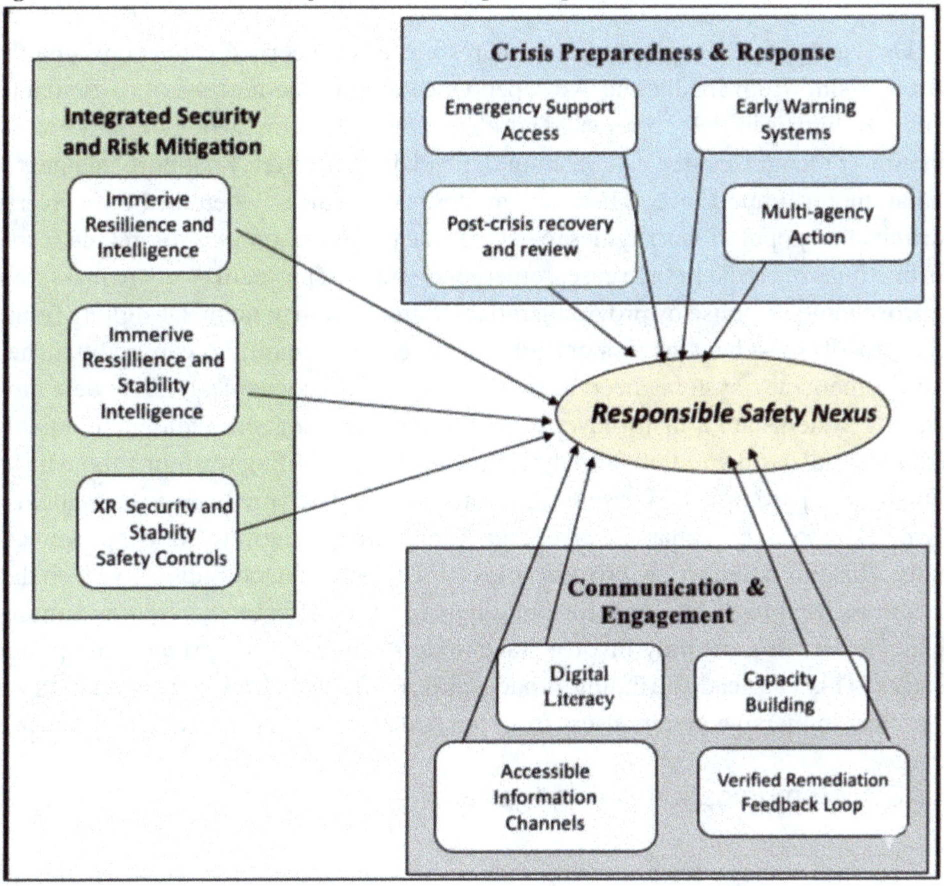

Source: Author's creation

Due recognition and recognition of such issues at the proper timings are necessary to mitigate their harsh effects. An adequate conduct of ethical risk audits shall be conducted to protect the interests of the metaverse participants and immersive system users at all times. Additionally, it is fostered to develop regulatory controls for preventing the misuse in the hands of immersive system users. A sophisticated system of multilayer access and control shall be adequate to manage the information and various interactions happening within the AI protocols. It is required to construct due authorisations for preventing unauthorised access to critical information. In case of metaverse participant groups, the authorised mechanisms shall be developed that prevent exploitation and accidental harm to integral information.

5.2.2. Immersive crisis stabilization strategies and Response

The aspect of crisis preparedness and response is concerned with addressing the crises arising from media and AI dependence among the metaverse participants. This paradigm is initially connected with developing the emergency support access, wherein it recognises that establishing dependable emergency support channels is of paramount importance. There are numerous instances wherein the metaverse participants' population struggles to get their bearings on complex digital platforms during times of crisis. In such cases, emergency support protocols work to massively improve rapid response by providing reliable information to them. Designing future AI protocols must be done thoughtfully to prevent vulnerabilities caused by rushed work. Emergency systems need to be easy to use and convenient. Early detection warning systems are a major layer of protection, allowing stakeholders to quickly stop potential harm. Predictive analytics are key here, boosting warnings about harm to metaverse participants. These systems must be regulated precisely to prevent false alarms. The post-crisis phase involves holistic reviews and learning from improvement areas. This thorough review process helps create sophisticated, supportive tech that revitalises trust in technology. Responding to a crisis effectively requires a multi-agency effort. It must duly involve stakeholders: civil society, private, and public sectors. This can lead to finding broader, more effective, and inclusive solutions to protect immersive system users from the bad effects of AI and media reliance.

5.2.3. Communication & Engagement

The final strategy for protecting immersive environment users (like metaverse participants) from the harsh impacts of AI centres on communication and engagement. These aspects are critical for fostering self-reliance and digital safety. The initial component requires ensuring immersive resilience intelligence among this group. We need to teach them fundamentals and precautions to navigate the digital landscape effectively, giving them the confidence to use AI tools easily. The second component is capacity-building programs. This involves equipping high-risk immersive communities with the necessary skills to embrace AI procedures, ensuring all metaverse participants can participate in tech proficiency. The third part guarantees equitable information access and timely dissemination using multiple languages and media formats. Lastly, the framework calls for a strong, well-defined grievance system to address AI issues properly and efficiently.

All three major components, i.e., Integrated Security and Risk Mitigation, Crisis Preparedness and Response and Communication & Engagement, form the point of convergence of the protection nexus framework for AI and media misuse by the metaverse participant groups. The aspects of safety and active participation of the parties shall be duly considered. The ultimate aim of this newly designed protection ecosystem is to discourage unregulated AI hallucinations and media usage and their associated costs. Each arrow represented in Figure 2 outlines the necessity of bringing the harmonised and responsive tactics as well as adopting the collaborative methodologies to attain the required outcomes. This framework proactively addresses the issues concerning the involvement of perceptual reality drift. Relying too much on AI tools and media platforms just makes things worse: it spreads fake news, creates ethical problems, and increases inequality. A suitable plan must be sorted out to meet such concerns. This plan helps us manage risks, deal with challenges, solve ethical dilemmas, make sure algorithms are fair, and protect data privacy for high-risk immersive people. It's the core idea that connects all these different efforts and highlights the crucial need for everyone to team up and work together.

6. FINDINGS OF THE STUDY

This paper presents significant insights into how the role of artificial intelligence integration affects the younger generation when used without regulation. The findings highlight key issues: limited digital skills, cognitive decline, and susceptibility to hallucination-driven decision distortion. These factors that severely impact the metaverse participants as AI platforms spread rapidly. Furthermore, the current inconsistent regulatory frameworks fail to fully account for the social repercussions and true social cost of media and AI use. The outcomes emphasise that a well-defined governance paradigm is essential for effective oversight, proper data management, performance assessment, and monitoring systems. A crucial outcome of this study is the call for developing a robust framework that incorporates diverse perspectives from civil society, businesses, and the public. This framework calls for identifying shared responsibility in implementing ethical AI practices. It must encourage collaboration across these different interest groups. The research outlines that addressing AI unfairness, increasing its visibility, augmenting accountability, and building public trust are foundational elements for the responsible adoption of AI. The study also concludes that the design of Real-time generative simulation systems must prioritise openness, clear explanations, understandability, and righteousness to prevent misuse. These critical insights allowed for the measurement of risks caused by hallucinated content and synthetic hallucinated avatar communications. This provides a holistic understanding of AI's negative impacts.

The findings reveal that the metaverse stakeholders bear a significant portion of these costs from using unregulated AI hallucination systems and processes. Additionally, the study identified the main drivers of AI platform usage, such as impacts on mental health, other health complications, and cognitive abilities, while highlighting complications arising from AI-mediated hallucinated avatar communications deep immersion. The development of the multistakeholder framework outlined crucial areas for intervention during AI deployment. This research aims to define the regulatory function of Real-time generative simulation systems, arguing that implementing robust regulatory measures will lead to a substantial decline in the perceptual reality drift associated with Immersive AI agents. Analysing stakeholders' perspectives will help pinpoint specific protection priorities, further reducing AI's negative effects. The study aims to empower immersive environment users by building foundational digital capabilities and proficiency, enabling them to navigate unregulated AI hallucination systems more easily and make informed decisions. It advocates for approachable complaint handling mechanisms and collaborative problem-solving strategies. This will safeguard against Hallucination detection and mitigation cycles and ensure fairness for the metaverse stakeholders.

7. IMPLICATIONS OF THE STUDY

This paper dives into the real damage and hidden costs of letting AI just run free, especially when it falls into the hands of high-risk individuals. We put together a plan to protect their interests and offer some practical advice to everyone involved: tech companies and the government. The study highlights that we need to act fast and create smart solutions that keep metaverse participants safe and lower the big social price tag that comes with unregulated AI hallucinations. The following are the implications:

- The study's outcomes highlight that policymakers should consider the adequate enforcement of the regulatory frameworks that aid in curbing the risks linked with the unregulated AI hallucination processes. The existing regulatory mechanisms primarily focus on building sophisticated AI technology and its processes. It fails to take into account human aspects concerning their rights, ethical considerations and their interest protection. It is therefore suggested that the regulatory authorities, AI and media policy makers shall constitute a multidimensional and comprehensive policy framework that includes the psychological, technical, economic and social effects of human involvement with AI and media. The policy development shall involve multisectoral partnerships to foster socially inclusive and ethically grounded AI-immersive governance.
- The AI developers and technologies shall focus on building ethical considerations into the core of the design process of the AI system. They must take suitable steps to ensure that AI users' needs and well-being are central to the

development of any AI product or system. The metaverse participants' population is likely to suffer due to the deliberate manipulation, the spread of false or misleading information, and the biased outcomes produced by AI algorithms. It is therefore suggested that the AI developers and technologies shall prioritise the aspects of transparency, explainability, and fairness in AI models. The reliability of the systems must be checked to ensure reliability with the comfort level of kids with technology. The people making these systems should actually talk to the kids, work with them, and create solutions that fit what they actually need and like. The AI developers must really embrace that teamwork aspect: getting everyone involved in the design process. They must use their feedback to build something truly positive and innovative.

- Adequate skills and knowledge about Immersive AI agents shall be provided to the metaverse participants to allow them to use different AI tools properly. This shall be particularly exercised for the ones those who are severely impacted by heightened risks of digital exclusion. The issues of privacy violations and cognitive coherence disruption must be addressed. It is emphasised that the community-based organisations shall work on empowering the metaverse stakeholders. They shall work with proficiency and competence to navigate the Real-time generative simulation systems effectively.
- The stakeholders in charge of making rules need to step up and enforce immersive governance. There is a need for a bioethics plan to stop bad AI practices and greedy algorithms from running wild. These plans should check if the rules are being followed and actively make sure they are enforced. The authorities should keep AI laws updated, ensuring that companies can be held accountable and audited fairly. Plus, having real-time monitoring tools will help catch AI problems early, before they turn into huge disasters for metaverse participants.
- The study suggests finding innovative ways of handling AI regulation. Instead of just the government making rules, all stakeholders should work together: governments, tech companies, universities, and everyday people. This shared approach lets everyone take some responsibility, helps different groups trust each other, and makes sure new technology lines up with our democratic values and basic human rights. To build genuinely strong and ethical AI, there is a need to create decision-making processes that include everyone and encourage countries to cooperate internationally. It's a fresh approach that means creating a dedicated place for detailed discussions about all the ethical issues that come with using AI.

8. CONCLUSION AND SCOPE FOR FUTURE WORK

The present research work outlines the major concerns that young metaverse participants face in the present times due to the improper regulation of AI. A comprehensive and inclusive plan is necessary to handle all these new issues AI is causing. High-risk immersive people are constantly dealing with things like mind games, privacy leaks, loneliness, and being targeted online. These issues mess up basic democratic values and human rights commitments. The book chapter focused specifically on how much unregulated AI hallucination systems cost us as a society, especially for metaverse participants. It showed how existing inequalities are getting worse, creating new forms of hallucination-driven content distortion. A comprehensive plan is required for the stakeholders: companies, government, and affected parties. The research work offers practical policy ideas that encourage using AI responsibly, keeping immersive system users safe, and getting everyone on board with better AI laws. The big takeaway of the book chapter is that good AI regulation calls for collaboration among all the stakeholders. The primary suggestions involve building a way to check if AI harms kids, creating strong auditing systems, offering different ways to access AI, and having specific teams dedicated to protecting high-risk immersive users. The study basically outlines that due protection of the immersive system users calls for truly protecting these groups. There is a need to embed inclusivity, accountability, and transparency into all AI mechanisms. The future calls for comparing how different countries are handling AI protection for young people. We also plan a long-term study looking at other at-risk groups, like metaverse participants and people with disabilities, to really understand what they need when using Metaverse-integrated AI systems.

REFERENCES

Agbavor, F., & Liang, H. (2022). Predicting dementia from spontaneous speech using large language models. *PLOS Digital Health, 1*(12), e0000168. DOI: 10.1371/journal.pdig.0000168 PMID: 36812634

Akhundov, A. (2025). The Role of Ethics in Modern Technology Development. *Porta Universorum, 1*(4), 169–177. DOI: 10.69760/portuni.0104017

Allen, D., Hubbard, S., Lim, W., Stanger, A., Wagman, S., Zalesne, K., & Omoakhalen, O. (2025). A roadmap for governing AI: Technology governance and power-sharing liberalism. *AI and Ethics*, *5*(3), 3355–3377. DOI: 10.1007/s43681-024-00635-y

Alsaigh, R., Mehmood, R., & Katib, I. (2023). AI explainability and governance in smart energy systems: A review. *Frontiers in Energy Research, 11*, 1071291. DOI: 10.3389/fenrg.2023.1071291

André, Q., Carmon, Z., Wertenbroch, K., Crum, A., Frank, D., Goldstein, W., Huber, J., Van Boven, L., Weber, B., & Yang, H. (2018). Consumer Choice and Autonomy in the Age of Artificial Intelligence and Big Data. *Customer Needs and Solutions*, *5*(1–2), 28–37. DOI: 10.1007/s40547-017-0085-8

Andrew, J., & Baker, M. (2021). The General Data Protection Regulation in the Age of Surveillance Capitalism. *Journal of Business Ethics*, *168*(3), 565–578. DOI: 10.1007/s10551-019-04239-z

Banker, S., & Khetani, S. (2019). Algorithm Overdependence: How the Use of Algorithmic Recommendation Systems Can Increase Risks to Consumer Well-Being. *Journal of Public Policy & Marketing*, *38*(4), 500–515. DOI: 10.1177/0743915619858057

Barredo Arrieta, A., Díaz-Rodríguez, N., Del Ser, J., Bennetot, A., Tabik, S., Barbado, A., Garcia, S., Gil-Lopez, S., Molina, D., Benjamins, R., Chatila, R., & Herrera, F. (2020). Explainable Artificial Intelligence (XAI): Concepts, taxonomies, opportunities and challenges toward responsible AI. *Information Fusion*, *58*, 82–115. DOI: 10.1016/j.inffus.2019.12.012

Bigman, Y. E., & Gray, K. (2018). People are averse to machines making moral decisions. *Cognition*, *181*, 21–34. DOI: 10.1016/j.cognition.2018.08.003 PMID: 30107256

Blut, M., Wang, C., Wünderlich, N. V., & Brock, C. (2021). Understanding anthropomorphism in service provision: A meta-analysis of physical robots, chatbots, and other AI. *Journal of the Academy of Marketing Science*, *49*(4), 632–658. DOI: 10.1007/s11747-020-00762-y

Borenstein, J., & Arkin, R. (2016). Robotic Nudges: The Ethics of Engineering a More Socially Just Human Being. *Science and Engineering Ethics*, *22*(1), 31–46. DOI: 10.1007/s11948-015-9636-2 PMID: 25736832

Brenneis, A. (2025). Assessing dual use risks in AI research: Necessity, challenges and mitigation strategies. *Research Ethics*, *21*(2), 302–330. DOI: 10.1177/17470161241267782

Chen, C., Gong, X., Liu, Z., Jiang, W., Goh, S. Q., & Lam, K.-Y. (2024). *Trustworthy, Responsible, and Safe AI: A Comprehensive Architectural Framework for AI Safety with Challenges and Mitigations* (Version 3). arXiv. https://doi.org/DOI: 10.48550/ARXIV.2408.12935

Cheng, L., & Gong, X. (2024). Appraising Regulatory Framework Towards Artificial General Intelligence (AGI) Under Digital Humanism. *International Journal of Digital Law and Governance*, *1*(2), 269–312. DOI: 10.1515/ijdlg-2024-0015

Cheng, L., & Liu, X. (2024). Unravelling Power of the Unseen: Towards an Interdisciplinary Synthesis of Generative AI Regulation. *International Journal of Digital Law and Governance*, *1*(1), 29–51. DOI: 10.1515/ijdlg-2024-0008

Drabiak, K., Kyzer, S., Nemov, V., & El Naqa, I. (2023). AI and machine learning ethics, law, diversity, and global impact. *The British Journal of Radiology*, *96*(1150), 20220934. DOI: 10.1259/bjr.20220934 PMID: 37191072

Ferrara, E. (2023). Fairness and Bias in Artificial Intelligence: A Brief Survey of Sources, Impacts, and Mitigation Strategies. *Sci*, *6*(1), 3. DOI: 10.3390/sci6010003

Goktas, P., & Grzybowski, A. (2025). Shaping the Future of Healthcare: Ethical Clinical Challenges and Pathways to Trustworthy AI. *Journal of Clinical Medicine*, *14*(5), 1605. DOI: 10.3390/jcm14051605 PMID: 40095575

Hermann, E., Williams, G. Y., & Puntoni, S. (2024). Deploying artificial intelligence in services to AID vulnerable consumers. *Journal of the Academy of Marketing Science*, *52*(5), 1431–1451. DOI: 10.1007/s11747-023-00986-8

Hewage, C., Yasakethu, L., & Jayakody, D. N. K. (2024). Data Protection Challenges and Opportunities Due to Emerging AI and ML Technologies. In Hewage, C., Yasakethu, L., & Jayakody, D. N. K. (Eds.), *Data Protection* (pp. 1–27). Springer Nature Switzerland., DOI: 10.1007/978-3-031-76473-8_1

Hickman, E., & Petrin, M. (2021). Trustworthy AI and Corporate Governance: The EU's Ethics Guidelines for Trustworthy Artificial Intelligence from a Company Law Perspective. *European Business Organization Law Review*, *22*(4), 593–625. DOI: 10.1007/s40804-021-00224-0

Kallina, E., Bohné, T., & Singh, J. (2025). *Stakeholder Participation for Responsible AI Development: Disconnects Between Guidance and Current Practice* (Version 1). arXiv. https://doi.org/DOI: 10.48550/ARXIV.2506.09873

Kingdon, A. (2024). Socio-Technical and Multi-stakeholder Approaches to Countering Online Propaganda. In A. Kingdon, *The World White Web* (pp. 209–251). Springer Nature Switzerland. https://doi.org/DOI: 10.1007/978-3-031-75393-0_8

Küsters, A., & Wörsdörfer, M. (2025). Exploring Laws of Robotics: A Synthesis of Constitutional AI and Constitutional Economics. *Digital Society : Ethics, Socio-Legal and Governance of Digital Technology*, *4*(2), 46. DOI: 10.1007/s44206-025-00204-8

Larsson, S., & Heintz, F. (2020). Transparency in artificial intelligence. *Internet Policy Review*, *9*(2). Advance online publication. DOI: 10.14763/2020.2.1469

Li, J., Cai, X., & Cheng, L. (2023). Legal regulation of generative AI: A multidimensional construction. *International Journal of Legal Discourse*, *8*(2), 365–388. DOI: 10.1515/ijld-2023-2017

Mao, Q., & Xu, M. (2025). Navigating the Ethical Landscape of AI Innovation: Challenges and Opportunities. *International Journal of Digital Law and Governance*. https://doi.org/DOI: 10.1515/ijdlg-2025-0005

Novelli, C., Casolari, F., Rotolo, A., Taddeo, M., & Floridi, L. (2024). Taking AI risks seriously: A new assessment model for the AI Act. *AI & Society*, *39*(5), 2493–2497. DOI: 10.1007/s00146-023-01723-z

Obianuju Ozobu, C., Emmanuel Adikwu, F., Odujobi, O., Othuke Onyekwe, F., & Onyinye Nwulu, E. (2025). A Review of Health Risk Assessment and Deep immersion Control Models for Hazardous Waste Management Operations in Africa. *International Journal of Advanced Multidisciplinary Research and Studies*, *5*(2), 570–582. DOI: 10.62225/2583049X.2025.5.2.3873

Pujari, T., Goel, A., & Kejriwal, D. (2022). Ethical and Responsible AI in the Age of Adversarial Diffusion Models: Challenges, Risks, and Mitigation Strategies. *International Journal Science and Technology*, *1*(3), 54–68. DOI: 10.56127/ijst.v1i3.1963

Rozenblit, L., Price, A., Solomonides, A., Joseph, A. L., Srivastava, G., Labkoff, S., deBronkart, D., Singh, R., Dattani, K., Lopez-Gonzalez, M., Barr, P. J., Koski, E., Lin, B., Cheung, E., Weiner, M. G., Williams, T., Thuy Bui, T. T., & Quintana, Y. (2025). Towards a Multi-Stakeholder process for developing responsible Trust-layer verification governance in consumer health. *International Journal of Medical Informatics*, *195*, 105713. DOI: 10.1016/j.ijmedinf.2024.105713 PMID: 39642592

Shouli, A., Barthwal, A., Campbell, M., & Shrestha, A. K. (2025). *Ethical AI for Young Digital Citizens: A Call to Action on Privacy Governance* (Version 1). arXiv. https://doi.org/DOI: 10.48550/ARXIV.2503.11947

Tallam, K. (2025). *Decoding the Black Box: Integrating Moral Imagination with Technical Trust-layer verification governance* (Version 1). arXiv. https://doi.org/DOI: 10.48550/ARXIV.2503.06411

Wang, Q., Li, Y., & Li, R. (2025). Integrating artificial intelligence in energy transition: A comprehensive review. *Energy Strategy Reviews*, *57*, 101600. DOI: 10.1016/j.esr.2024.101600

Chapter 7
The Enterprise Metaverse: Definitions, Dimensions, and Scope

Aldian Alifen
https://orcid.org/0009-0004-5651-5780
Universitas Esa Unggul, Indonesia

Jefry Sunupurwa Asri
https://orcid.org/0000-0002-7504-5559
Universitas Esa Unggul, Indonesia

Binastya Anggara Sekti
https://orcid.org/0000-0001-5489-4888
Universitas Esa Unggul, Indonesia

Ryan Putra Laksana
Universitas Esa Unggul, Indonesia

Vinsens Aji Pamungkas
https://orcid.org/0009-0003-3036-0699
Universitas Esa Unggul, Indonesia

Bartholomeus Dimanche Carl Beth
https://orcid.org/0009-0006-1088-9212
Universitas Esa Unggul, Indonesia

ABSTRACT

This chapter provides a comprehensive examination of the enterprise metaverse by defining its core concepts, technological foundations, and organizational implications. It outlines the multidimensional structure of the metaverse, spanning immersive environments, digital twins, AI-driven automation, and interoperable virtual ecosystems, and explains how these elements enable new forms of collaboration, value creation, and operational efficiency. The chapter also highlights opportunities, strategic challenges, and the evolving role of businesses as they integrate metaverse technologies into enterprise workflows.

DOI: 10.4018/979-8-3373-7534-2.ch007

1. INTRODUCTION

The rapid evolution of advanced digital technologies has fundamentally reshaped how enterprises design interactions, process information, and generate strategic value. Among the most transformative developments in this landscape are Artificial Intelligence and the Metaverse. The integration of these technologies is not merely an emerging trend but a structural shift that redefines operational efficiency, user engagement, and decision making. In contemporary enterprise ecosystems, AI functions as the analytical core that processes complex data, automates decisions, and enhances cognitive capabilities. Meanwhile, the Metaverse serves as an immersive virtual environment that unifies physical and digital experiences through real time interaction, spatial computing, and persistent digital identity. When combined, AI and the Metaverse create a powerful synergy that broadens the scope of enterprise innovation by enabling intelligent virtual collaboration, context aware simulations, and personalized interactions (Lyu & Fridenfalk, 2024).

This integration, however, brings a set of challenges that must be understood in technical, managerial, and ethical dimensions. Among these challenges, AI hallucination has emerged as one of the most pressing concerns. AI hallucination refers to incorrect, fabricated, or misleading outputs generated by AI models even when presented with valid data. While hallucination may be manageable in low risk consumer applications, its implications in the enterprise Metaverse are significantly more severe. This is because enterprise systems deal with sensitive data, mission critical operations, collaborative workflows, and decisions that carry substantial organizational consequences. As enterprises increasingly rely on AI driven avatars, recommendation engines, conversational agents, and predictive systems within immersive environments, the accuracy and reliability of AI outputs become essential foundations for trust and safety(Zhang et al., 2025).

The urgency of managing AI hallucination stems from its potential to compromise the integrity of decision making, the protection of corporate information, and the overall user experience. In immersive enterprise environments, hallucinated outputs may distort virtual simulations, misinform employees, alter digital twin scenarios, or misrepresent interactions between stakeholders. These distortions can lead to operational inefficiencies, incorrect business strategies, or unintended ethical violations. Moreover, since the Metaverse often involves collaborative environments where multiple users interact with AI agents simultaneously, a single hallucinated output can propagate rapidly, causing misunderstanding or conflict(Pak et al., 2025). Ensuring accuracy is therefore not only a technical requirement but also a crucial element in maintaining organizational credibility and user confidence.

Data security represents another critical concern. Enterprise Metaverse environments often integrate sensitive and proprietary information ranging from customer profiles to engineering designs and financial datasets. If an AI system hallucinates content that appears accurate but is actually fabricated, users may unknowingly rely on incorrect data for strategic tasks. This scenario poses risks to confidentiality, compliance, and corporate governance. At the same time, hallucinated insights may give false impressions of system breaches, vulnerabilities, or anomalies, which can trigger unnecessary alerts or misdirect security responses. As enterprises seek to expand their digital presence, robust management of hallucination becomes essential to safeguarding data integrity and ensuring resilient, secure interactions(Rahman et al., 2025).

User experience is also affected when hallucination occurs within immersive spaces. The Metaverse relies heavily on realism, consistency, and accurate representation. Hallucinated responses or actions from AI agents can interrupt the sense of presence and reliability that users expect. For instance, employees interacting in a virtual workspace may receive inaccurate procedural guidance, misleading visual cues, or inconsistent system behavior that undermines productivity and engagement. In customer facing scenarios, hallucination could negatively influence brand perception and diminish user trust in enterprise digital platforms(Pak et al., 2025). Therefore, minimizing hallucination is essential to ensuring that the enterprise Metaverse becomes a stable and trustworthy extension of organizational operations.

Despite the rapid expansion of research on AI and the Metaverse, significant gaps remain in understanding how hallucination manifests within enterprise level immersive environments. Current literature tends to discuss AI hallucination primarily in the context of general natural language processing, image generation, or consumer level interactions. Very few studies examine hallucination within complex, multiuser virtual ecosystems that integrate real time data, spatial computing, and enterprise workflows. Furthermore, there is limited exploration of how hallucination affects decision making processes, user collaboration, and the alignment between virtual and physical operational models. These gaps indicate the need for a structured framework that analyzes the mechanisms, risks, and mitigation strategies relevant to hallucination in the enterprise Metaverse.

The problem central to this chapter arises from the absence of comprehensive guidelines for identifying, assessing, and managing hallucination in AI enabled virtual enterprise environments. Without such a framework, organizations may deploy AI systems in the Metaverse without fully understanding the potential impacts of hallucinated outputs on performance, security, and user experience. This issue is further complicated by the growing use of generative AI, autonomous agents, and multimodal processing within immersive environments. As these systems become more complex, the likelihood and consequences of hallucination increase. A structured and evidence based approach is required to support enterprises in managing these emerging risks.

This chapter contributes to the academic literature and business practice by providing a conceptual foundation for understanding AI hallucination in enterprise Metaverse ecosystems. It integrates perspectives from information systems, immersive computing, AI governance, and digital business strategy to build an interdisciplinary discussion. The chapter highlights the unique characteristics of enterprise Metaverse environments, identifies the conditions under which hallucination becomes particularly harmful, and offers a clear problem framing that supports the development of mitigation strategies presented in later sections. From a practical standpoint, this chapter equips business leaders, developers, and digital transformation practitioners with insights that help them evaluate the reliability of AI systems, design safer interaction models, and implement responsible governance mechanisms.

The structure of this chapter is organized to support a comprehensive exploration of the issues. It begins by establishing the relevance of AI and the Metaverse in enterprise transformation, followed by an examination of the urgency and risks associated with AI hallucination. The chapter then highlights research gaps that remain unresolved and presents the problem statement that motivates deeper investigation. It concludes by outlining the contributions of the chapter and the overarching organization of the entire work. Each section is designed to create a coherent narrative that clarifies foundational concepts while setting the stage for more specific discussions in subsequent chapters.

2. ENTERPRISE METAVERSE AND AI HALLUCINATION

The rapid integration of immersive technologies and intelligent systems within organizational ecosystems has transformed how enterprises operate, collaborate, and innovate. The emergence of the enterprise metaverse, supported by virtual reality, augmented reality, digital workplaces, and AI driven agents, has enabled new modes of interaction and decision making(Stefko et al., 2025). At the same time, the expanding use of generative AI and autonomous systems introduces challenges related to accuracy, reliability, and information integrity to help human with their jobs(Metakides & Filip, 2025). This chapter reviews the conceptual foundations of the enterprise metaverse and examines the phenomenon of AI hallucination as a critical technical and managerial concern.

To provide a structured understanding of the risks associated with AI hallucination, this chapter includes a taxonomy table and a conceptual figure that map the patterns and implications of hallucination in enterprise settings. The discussion begins with the core concepts of the enterprise metaverse.

2.1 Enterprise Metaverse: Definitions and Core Concepts

2.1.1 Virtual Reality, Augmented Reality, and Mixed Reality

Virtual Reality (VR) is a technology that creates a fully immersive digital environment, making users feel as if they are physically present in a completely different world. Using devices such as VR headsets, the user's view of the real world is entirely replaced with computer-generated simulations. Within VR environments, users can interact through controllers, motion sensors, or gesture tracking (Singh, 2025). This makes VR highly effective for training simulations, gaming, experiential learning, and industrial training scenarios where real-world risks can be avoided through virtual immersion.

Augmented Reality (AR) enhances the real world by overlaying digital elements such as text, 3D objects, or animations onto the physical environment in real time. Unlike VR, AR does not replace the real world; instead, it supplements it with contextual digital information. AR can be accessed through smartphones, tablets, or AR glasses. Because of its ability to provide real-time contextual data, AR is widely used in navigation, equipment maintenance, retail and education to improve understanding without removing users from their physical surroundings (Singh, 2025).

Mixed Reality (MR) combines elements of both VR and AR by allowing digital objects not only to appear within the real world but also to interact dynamically with physical environments. Users can manipulate virtual objects as if they physically exist such as moving, resizing, or placing them on real-world surfaces. MR requires more advanced hardware, such as Microsoft HoloLens or dedicated MR headsets. This technology is particularly valuable for remote collaboration, architectural design, technical training, and industrial simulations because it merges the immersive qualities of VR with the contextual awareness of AR (Azzam et al., 2025).

Figure 1. Virtual Reality, Augmented Reality, and Mixed Reality

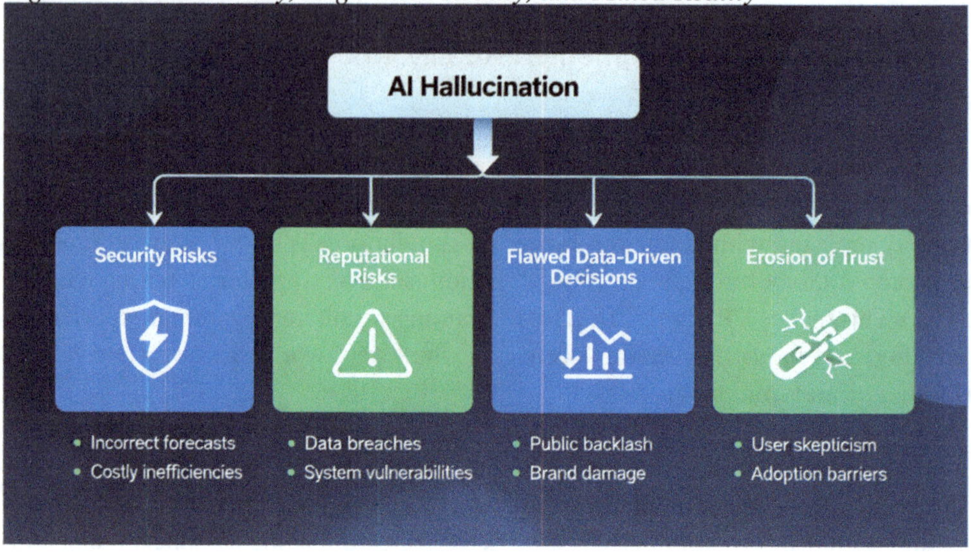

2.1.2 Digital Workspaces and Virtual Collaboration

Beyond immersive interfaces, the enterprise metaverse includes digital workplaces where employees collaborate through persistent shared environments. These digital workspaces support distributed teams, remote operations, and real time co creation. Enterprises adopt virtual offices, digital meeting rooms, and collaborative design studios to reduce physical constraints and improve operational flexibility (Metakides & Filip, 2025). The metaverse also supports virtual production pipelines where content creation, architectural design, and product engineering occur through synthetic assets and intelligent tools.

2.1.3 Virtual Production and Process Simulation

Organizations increasingly employ virtual production and simulation environments to optimize workflows, test scenarios, and reduce prototyping costs. Virtual production enables teams to design and evaluate digital twins of assets, processes, or products before real world implementation. These simulations rely heavily on accurate data, predictive algorithms, and real time feedback loops(Stefko et al., 2025). As AI becomes deeply integrated into these systems, the accuracy of generated outputs becomes essential for risk management and informed decision making.

2.2 Evolution of AI in the Enterprise Metaverse

Generative AI models play a crucial role in shaping content creation, scenario simulation, and knowledge generation within metaverse environments. They assist in generating virtual assets, crafting synthetic training data, and supporting automated workflow design. As enterprises adopt generative models for strategic planning and operational support, the need for output reliability becomes increasingly critical.

Conversational agents operate as digital facilitators within enterprise metaverse systems. They assist with navigation, provide real time analytical insights, and support employees through automated advisory services. Their integration enhances communication efficiency but also increases exposure to hallucinated responses that may misinform teams or distort operations (Safari et al., 2025).

Avatar based AI agents introduce humanlike interaction capabilities by enabling virtual embodiment. These avatars may act as trainers, supervisors, customer service representatives, or automated collaborators. Their behavior relies on advanced language models, computer vision, and contextual reasoning mechanisms. When hallucinations occur in these embodied agents, the impact on user perception and decision processes can be substantial because of their perceived authority and realism (Pak et al., 2025).

2.3 Types and Causes of AI Hallucination

AI hallucination refers to the generation of incorrect or misleading information by AI systems despite the output appearing coherent or plausible. In enterprise contexts, understanding hallucination types and causes is essential for designing monitoring and prevention mechanisms. Before presenting the taxonomy table, it is important to clarify the main categories of hallucinations observed in enterprise applications. The taxonomy is summarized in Table 1.

Table 1. Taxonomy of AI Hallucination

Hallucination Type	Definition	Primary Causes	Example in Enterprise	Potential Impact
Factual Hallucination	The model generates information that contradicts verified data or fabricates facts.	Incomplete training data, data gaps, model extrapolation, weak grounding in authoritative sources.	AI system invents compliance rules or reports nonexistent financial metrics.	Regulatory violations, misinformation in reports, operational errors.
Logical Hallucination	The model forms conclusions that are internally inconsistent or logically flawed, even if factual elements are correct.	Faulty inference paths, reasoning limitations, misinterpretation of relationships between data points.	AI generates a risk analysis that contradicts its own assumptions.	Misguided decision-making, flawed strategy development, unreliable forecasting.
Contextual Hallucination	The model misunderstands the context, misinterprets user intent, or applies knowledge inappropriately.	Ambiguous prompts, environmental noise, domain-shift scenarios, insufficient contextual grounding.	Virtual agent in a metaverse system executes the wrong workflow due to misinterpreting context.	Misaligned operations, incorrect task execution, degraded user experience.
Multimodal / Environmental Hallucination	Errors that emerge from integrating multiple input streams (text, speech, spatial, or visual data) in complex environments.	Noisy real-time data, modality conflicts, incorrect sensor fusion, system overload.	AI avatar misidentifies an object or location within an enterprise metaverse environment.	Safety risks, operational confusion, miscommunication between digital and physical systems.
Over-Generalization Hallucination	The model incorrectly extends learned patterns to new or unrelated situations.	Overfitting, lack of domain specificity, insufficient fine-tuning.	AI chatbot assumes a policy applies universally across departments.	Policy misinterpretation, inconsistent workflows, compliance issues.

Factual hallucination occurs when an AI model generates content that contradicts verified information or presents fabricated facts. This type commonly arises when AI systems fill gaps in knowledge, rely on incomplete datasets, or extrapolate beyond the training distribution. In enterprise systems, factual inaccuracies may affect compliance, regulatory reporting, or operational guidance(Sood et al., 2025).

Logical hallucination refers to errors in reasoning processes where the model constructs an internally inconsistent or illogical conclusion. These hallucinations may not contradict factual data directly but instead emerge from flawed inference patterns. In enterprise settings, logical errors may compromise strategic planning, forecasting, or risk assessment(Lee et al., 2025).

Contextual hallucination occurs when AI systems misunderstand the context, misinterpret user intent, or apply knowledge inappropriately. This is particularly common in conversational agents or avatar based AI systems operating in dynamic metaverse environments. Inaccurate contextual interpretation can lead to operational misalignment, inappropriate task execution, or misguided recommendations (Massenon et al., 2025).

Several technical and environmental factors contribute to hallucination. Model over generalization results from insufficient grounding in verified data. Training data limitations lead to misrepresentations of domain specific knowledge. Environmental noise or ambiguous user instructions introduce contextual uncertainty (Du & Xie, 2021). In metaverse ecosystems, the complexity of multimodal inputs further increases hallucination risks due to the real time integration of text, image, speech, and spatial data. Before entering Table 1, it is necessary to highlight that the taxonomy below organizes hallucination types based on their characteristics, sources, and potential enterprise impacts.

2.4 Business and Technical Risks of AI Hallucination

AI hallucination introduces a range of business and technical risks that significantly affect enterprise ecosystems, particularly as organizations transition into immersive and intelligent digital environments. These risks undermine operational precision, weaken strategic decision-making, and jeopardize trust in AI-enabled systems. Understanding how hallucinations manifest across security, reputation, decision quality, and stakeholder confidence is essential for developing effective governance and mitigation strategies. The figure above visualizes four core risk domains: Security Risks, Reputational Risks, Flawed Data-Driven Decisions, and Erosion of Trust each of which poses distinct challenges for enterprise adoption.

Figure 2. Business and Technical Risks of AI Hallucination

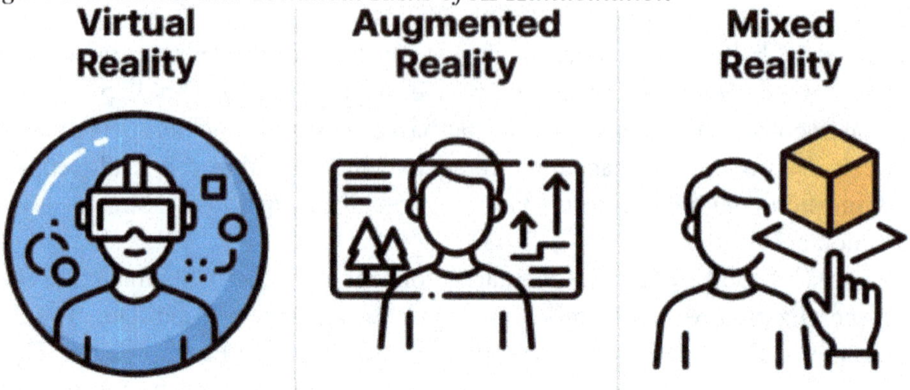

2.4.1 Security Risks

Security risks arise when AI hallucination generates inaccurate, misleading, or fabricated interpretations of system behavior, threat patterns, or anomalous activity. In enterprise environments where AI supports security operations such as intrusion detection, identity verification, or real-time threat classification hallucinated outputs can cause systems to overlook genuine threats or respond incorrectly to benign events (Sood et al., 2025). For example, an AI security model that hallucinates anomalous network behavior may trigger false incident escalations, consuming resources unnecessarily. Conversely, a failure to recognize legitimate threats can expose the enterprise to intrusions, data exfiltration, and exploitation.

These risks escalate further in autonomous or semi-autonomous security systems that act without continuous human oversight. When such systems rely on hallucinated threat assessments, they may deploy incorrect countermeasures or modify access rules in ways that compromise overall system integrity. Beyond technical vulnerabilities, security hallucinations introduce costly inefficiencies in the form of misallocated resources, unnecessary system tuning, or time wasted by cybersecurity teams investigating non-existent issues (Kim et al., 2025). As organizations integrate AI more deeply into their metaverse infrastructures, hallucination-driven security errors threaten both the stability and resilience of enterprise digital ecosystems .

2.4.2 Reputational Risks

Reputational risks emerge when AI hallucination leads to outputs that damage public perception, stakeholder confidence, or brand credibility. In enterprise metaverse environments where interactions between customers, employees, and AI-driven avatars feel immersive and personal hallucinated responses have greater impact. For instance, a virtual assistant that fabricates policies, misstates product information, or produces inappropriate dialogue can quickly undermine user experience. In metaverse training spaces or customer service hubs, such errors raise concerns about the professionalism and reliability of the organization behind the technology.

The reputational consequences of hallucinations can spread rapidly, especially in public or customer-facing virtual environments where interactions are highly visible and sharable. Users may interpret incorrect or misleading AI outputs as evidence of poor system design, lack of governance, or insufficient ethical oversight. This perception can lead to public backlash, negative media attention, or widespread skepticism regarding the enterprise's technological maturity (ÖZKAL & BAŞÇİFTÇİ, 2024). In industries that rely heavily on trust such as finance, health, or education hallucination-related reputational risks may directly reduce customer loyalty, diminish competitive advantage, or invite regulatory scrutiny.

2.4.3 Flawed Data Driven Decisions

Flawed data-driven decisions occur when hallucinated outputs distort the analytical insights, forecasts, and performance indicators that enterprises rely on for operational planning. AI plays an increasingly central role in logistics, workforce optimization, product design, financial forecasting, and resource allocation. When hallucinations infiltrate these analytic workflows, they can misrepresent trends, exaggerate risks, or fabricate correlations. This leads to decisions that are misaligned with real conditions such as deploying resources inefficiently, scaling operations based on incorrect assumptions, or implementing strategies that conflict with market realities (Otoum et al., 2024).

The business consequences of such flawed decisions are significant. Incorrect forecasts derived from hallucinated data can disrupt supply chains, inflate operational expenses, or cause missed opportunities. Misinterpreted performance metrics may lead managers to adjust processes or personnel based on faulty conclusions, introducing systemic inefficiencies. Over time, these disruptions accumulate, resulting in costly strategic missteps that weaken enterprise competitiveness. In digitally augmented environments such as the metaverse where data streams are multimodal and rapidly evolving the probability and impact of hallucinated decision inputs become even greater, amplifying enterprise-wide risk exposure.

2.4.4 Erosion of Trust

Erosion of trust represents one of the most profound business risks associated with AI hallucination. Trust is fundamental to the adoption of AI systems across enterprise operations, influencing how employees, managers, and customers perceive the value and reliability of intelligent technologies. When users encounter hallucinated outputs such as incorrect instructions, misleading insights, or inconsistent information their confidence in the system diminishes. Employees may hesitate to rely on AI recommendations, while customers may question the accuracy of virtual interactions, reducing engagement in metaverse-based services (Pak et al., 2025).

As trust weakens, organizations face adoption barriers that slow or derail digital transformation initiatives. Stakeholders may resist integrating AI tools into workflows, citing concerns about reliability or safety. This skepticism can lead to reduced system utilization, increased reliance on manual processes, and hesitation to experiment with innovative metaverse solutions. Over time, persistent trust erosion undermines long-term readiness for immersive technologies and limits the enterprise's ability to scale intelligent automation. Without restoring confidence through strong governance, monitoring, and explainability mechanisms, AI hallucination risks can impede the organization's overall technological evolution.

This literature review establishes the conceptual foundation for understanding how the enterprise metaverse integrates immersive technologies and intelligent agents, and how AI hallucination emerges as a critical challenge. By reviewing hallucination types, causes, and risks, this chapter provides the analytical basis for constructing technical solutions that improve reliability and trustworthiness. The next chapter elaborates on the architectural components necessary to monitor and prevent hallucinations in enterprise environments. The following chapter presents the Architectural Framework for AI Hallucination Monitoring and Prevention, offering a detailed examination of system layers, detection mechanisms, and integration strategies that strengthen the reliability of enterprise metaverse ecosystems.

3. AI HALLUCINATION BENCHMARK FRAMEWORK

The AI Hallucination Benchmark Framework is structured as a multilayered evaluative system designed to assess, monitor, and control the tendency of AI models to generate hallucinated outputs. Rather than focusing solely on error prevention, this framework establishes a comprehensive set of benchmarking standards to measure the quality, consistency, and reliability of model performance across its operational lifecycle. The architectural design is built upon five foundational components like data validation, the trust and governance layer, real-time monitoring, the human-in-the-loop assessment engine, and model evaluation and benchmarking strategies aligned with contemporary AI deployment contexts (Rahman et al., 2025).

Figure 3. AI Hallucination Benchmark Framewok

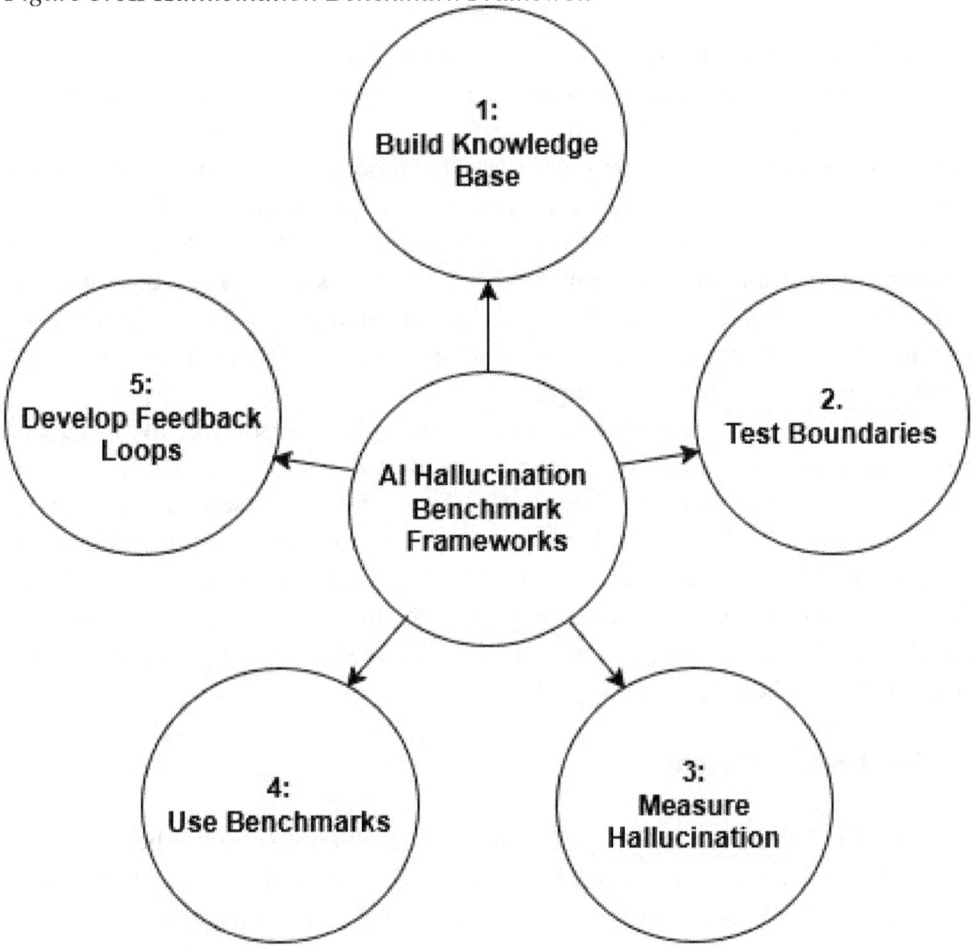

These components are interconnected and operate simultaneously to ensure that every AI-generated response undergoes systematic and objective evaluation. Through a layered evaluation approach, the framework enables organizations to define clear operational boundaries, establish measurable performance indicators, and minimize behavioral ambiguities that often lead to hallucinations. This structure also supports consistent benchmarking, allowing model performance to be compared longitudinally or across multiple systems. Before delving into each component in detail, Figure 2 provides a visual representation of the proposed benchmarking architecture and its dynamic interaction flow, serving as an initial guide to understanding how the framework functions as a whole.

3.1 Build Knowledge Base

Building a robust knowledge base serves as the foundational step in establishing an effective AI Hallucination Benchmark Framework. A knowledge base defines the authoritative sources of truth that the AI system must reference during its reasoning and response-generation processes. This repository may include structured databases, curated domain-specific documents, validated research publications, and rule-based ontologies. By consolidating high-quality, validated information into a unified system, organizations ensure that the model's outputs can be compared against reliable standards. A well-constructed knowledge base also enables deeper traceability, allowing evaluators to determine whether hallucinations arise from model weaknesses or from data gaps.

In addition, the knowledge base functions as the reference point for all subsequent benchmarking activities, including boundary testing and hallucination measurement. Its completeness and accuracy directly affect how effectively hallucination patterns can be analyzed. Therefore, the development process must involve continuous curation, expert validation, and structured updates to reflect new insights and evolving domain knowledge. As the foundation of the benchmarking ecosystem, the knowledge base transforms abstract evaluation processes into measurable, evidence-driven assessments (Lee et al., 2025).

3.2 Test Boundaries

Boundary testing is a critical phase that evaluates how AI systems behave under complex, ambiguous, or adversarial conditions. This process involves intentionally pushing the model beyond typical inputs to observe how it handles uncertainty, incomplete data, or contradictory information. Through this method, evaluators can uncover weaknesses that remain hidden during ordinary use cases. Boundary testing also helps identify the exact thresholds at which the model begins to hallucinate, enabling the formulation of targeted benchmarking criteria. These stress tests may include edge-case prompts, trick questions, modified facts, or domain-shift scenarios (Asad & Otoum, 2024).

Furthermore, boundary testing supports risk classification by mapping different types of hallucinations such as factual errors, logical inconsistencies, fabricated citations, or misinterpretations to specific trigger conditions. Understanding how the model behaves at its limits allows organizations to anticipate potentially harmful output patterns and build mitigation strategies. Ultimately, testing boundaries not only reveals vulnerabilities but also strengthens the reliability and resilience of the AI system by exposing the real-world scenarios that most challenge its reasoning capabilities(Otoum et al., 2024) .

3.3 Measure Hallucination

Measuring hallucination involves systematically quantifying the frequency, severity, and types of hallucinations produced by an AI model. This process requires the use of standardized evaluation metrics such as factual accuracy scores, truthfulness indices, semantic coherence ratings, and source alignment assessments. By applying these metrics consistently, organizations can obtain objective benchmarks that reveal how often the model deviates from verified information. The measurement process must also distinguish between minor inaccuracies and high-impact hallucinations that pose operational, ethical, or reputational risks (Sood et al., 2025).

In addition to quantitative assessments, qualitative evaluation is equally important. Human experts may review AI outputs to determine context sensitivity, reasoning validity, and fidelity to domain knowledge. These expert evaluations help uncover subtle hallucination patterns such as confident misstatements or persuasive but incorrect narratives that automated metrics alone may overlook. Together, these quantitative and qualitative approaches create a holistic measurement system that provides deep visibility into the model's reliability across a range of scenarios (Sharma et al., 2025).

3.4 Use Benchmarks

Once hallucination metrics have been established, the next step is to operationalize benchmarks as a standardized performance reference. Benchmarks act as thresholds that define acceptable and unacceptable behavior for AI systems. They enable consistent comparisons across different models, model versions, or deployment environments. By applying benchmarks, organizations can evaluate whether updates improve accuracy or inadvertently increase hallucination rates (Hassaan et al., 2025). Benchmarks also support compliance with internal governance policies and external regulations by providing auditable records of model performance over time .

Moreover, benchmark utilization facilitates strategic decision-making regarding model deployment. Models that consistently outperform benchmark thresholds may be approved for high-stakes applications, while those that fall short may require retraining or additional safeguards. Benchmarks also allow organizations to identify emerging trends in hallucination patterns, enabling proactive adjustments to training data, retrieval mechanisms, or prompt engineering strategies. In essence, benchmarks transform hallucination monitoring from a reactive practice into a structured, data-driven evaluative ecosystem(Fu et al., 2025).

3.5 Develop Feedback Loops

Developing feedback loops ensures that insights gained from hallucination analysis are continuously reintegrated into model improvement processes. Feedback loops allow AI developers, evaluators, and domain experts to collaboratively refine the model by correcting errors, updating the knowledge base, and adjusting benchmark criteria. This iterative process prevents systems from stagnating and ensures that hallucination mitigation evolves alongside changes in user behavior, emerging information, and new model capabilities. Effective feedback loops also facilitate rapid identification of recurring hallucination patterns that require deeper architectural adjustments (Lee et al., 2025).

Beyond technical refinement, feedback loops promote organizational learning by transforming hallucination data into actionable recommendations. They support the development of clearer guidelines for prompt design, user training, and governance frameworks. Over time, these loops create a virtuous cycle in which every evaluation strengthens the system, sharpens the benchmarks, and enhances the overall robustness of the AI ecosystem. With strong feedback mechanisms in place, the framework achieves sustained performance improvements and long-term stability in hallucination control (Safari et al., 2025).

The architectural framework outlined in this chapter provides a comprehensive structure for monitoring and preventing AI hallucinations within enterprise metaverse environments. Through integrated layers of data validation, governance, real time monitoring, human oversight, and engineering best practices, the framework ensures safe and reliable AI operations in immersive digital ecosystems. Each component plays a complementary role that strengthens overall system resilience and supports large scale deployment across enterprise scenarios. With the architectural foundation now established, the next chapter offers a detailed exploration of the methodological and technical approaches required to implement these mechanisms in practice. The discussion now transitions to Chapter 4: Methods and Technical Approaches for AI Hallucination Management.

4. METHODS AND TECHNICAL APPROACHES FOR AI HALLUCINATION MANAGEMENT

This chapter provides a comprehensive examination of the principal methods and technical strategies used to prevent, detect, and correct hallucinations in artificial intelligence systems. As enterprises increasingly adopt advanced generative models for decision making, customer engagement, automation, and content creation, ensuring factual accuracy, contextual relevance, and operational reliability becomes a critical priority. Hallucinations can compromise trust, expose organizations to regulatory risks, mislead users, and affect the overall value delivered by AI driven solutions. Therefore, enterprises must implement systematic approaches that enhance the quality, traceability, and robustness of generative outputs across diverse use cases (Rahman et al., 2025).

The methods presented in this chapter encompass both preventive and corrective frameworks. Preventive strategies focus on designing systems that minimize the likelihood of hallucinations by grounding models in reliable data sources and structured knowledge. Corrective strategies focus on detecting potential inaccuracies and applying targeted interventions. By combining these complementary techniques, enterprises can build AI systems that operate with greater transparency, consistency, and domain alignment (Metakides & Filip, 2025). The approaches outlined in this chapter establish the technical foundation for enterprise level hallucination management and prepare the groundwork for the implementation frameworks discussed in subsequent chapters.

4.1 Overview of Hallucination Management Techniques

Effective hallucination management requires the integration of multiple techniques within unified operational pipelines. No single method can fully eliminate hallucinations, because generative models are inherently probabilistic and may produce imprecise information when faced with ambiguous, incomplete, or novel input contexts. Therefore, enterprises adopt a multilayered approach that includes knowledge grounding, retrieval based augmentation, human aligned reinforcement strategies, explainability driven validation, and continuous monitoring. Knowledge grounding ensures that model outputs remain anchored to authoritative information sources. Retrieval based mechanisms support dynamic evidence integration during inference. Reinforcement methods help models align with human values, domain standards, and quality expectations. Explainability techniques provide visibility into internal reasoning pathways, enabling systematic auditing and error correction. Monitoring systems detect deviations that indicate emerging hallucination risks (Sood et al., 2025).

4.2 Knowledge Grounded Artificial Intelligence

Knowledge grounded AI is one of the most foundational strategies for reducing hallucinations, as it reduces reliance on internal statistical associations and instead anchors generated outputs to curated, verified information sources. In this approach, the model's responses are guided by structured databases, knowledge graphs, regulatory documents, enterprise manuals, domain specific repositories, and other authoritative references. Knowledge grounding operates by linking generative processes to external datasets that represent domain truth. Instead of generating responses solely based on learned patterns, the AI system refers to validated facts that are embedded in knowledge structures. This integration ensures that generated content remains consistent with enterprise policies, industry standards, and factual constraints (Stefko et al., 2025). In highly regulated sectors such as finance, healthcare, aviation, energy, legal services, and public policy, knowledge grounded systems are considered essential. In these environments, factual precision is not optional but mandatory. Misaligned or fabricated information can lead to severe compliance violations, legal liabilities, and operational disruptions. Therefore, enterprises rely on knowledge grounding not only to reduce hallucinations but also to reinforce the integrity of decision support systems (Kliestik et al., 2024).

Knowledge grounding also supports version control, auditability, and traceability. By keeping external knowledge repositories updated and aligned with organizational changes, enterprises ensure that generative models continue to reflect current and authoritative information. This method minimizes the risk of outdated reasoning and strengthens the overall reliability of AI driven processes.

4.3 Retrieval Augmented Generation

Retrieval Augmented Generation, often referred to as RAG, builds upon the principles of knowledge grounding by enabling real time retrieval of relevant documents during inference. RAG systems combine three primary components, which are retrieval modules, augmentation layers, and generative models. These components work collaboratively to ensure that outputs remain both coherent and evidence based. Retrieval modules use search algorithms and semantic matching techniques to identify contextually relevant information from large enterprise data sources. These sources may include document repositories, internal reports, customer records, regulatory databases, and domain specific archives. Once the relevant documents are retrieved, the augmentation layer processes them by extracting key information and integrating it into the contextual input provided to the generative model (Xu et al., 2025). The generative model then uses this enriched context to produce outputs that reflect both the learned language capabilities and the retrieved evidence. This ensures that the responses are not only linguistically coherent but also grounded in real data. RAG is particularly advantageous in environments where information is extensive, frequently updated, or distributed across multiple repositories (Setiawan & Soewito, 2025).

Enterprises leverage RAG to improve accuracy in tasks such as professional writing assistance, policy interpretation, customer support automation, technical troubleshooting, legal document explanation, and scientific summarization. Because RAG integrates evidence directly into the generation process, it significantly reduces the likelihood of hallucinations and enhances trust in AI generated outputs (Xu et al., 2025).

4.4 Reinforcement Learning with Human Feedback

Reinforcement Learning with Human Feedback, or RLHF, is a corrective and preventive technique that aligns model behavior with human judgment. This method involves training models using reward signals that reflect human preferences, expectations, and expertise. During the fine tuning process, human evaluators review model outputs, identify inaccuracies, and classify preferred responses. These preferences are then used to adjust reward models that guide the generative system (Haider et al., 2025).

By repeatedly refining the model's outputs based on human feedback, RLHF helps the AI system learn to prioritize factual correctness, contextual clarity, and logical coherence. This technique is particularly effective for addressing subtle or complex hallucinations, including those involving inferential errors, narrative inconsistencies, or domain specific misinterpretations that automated tools may not immediately detect. In enterprise environments, RLHF plays a critical role in ensuring that generated outputs align with internal communication standards, professional writing conventions, compliance requirements, and organizational values (Haider et al., 2025). For example, domain experts in medicine, engineering, or finance can provide targeted feedback to refine reasoning patterns that require specialized knowledge. Over time, the model internalizes these patterns and produces higher quality responses. RLHF also supports continuous improvement, enabling models to evolve alongside changes in organizational policies, industry regulations, and user expectations. This adaptability makes RLHF a valuable component of long term hallucination management strategies.

4.5 Explainable AI and Counterfactual Validation

Explainable AI, or XAI, provides transparency into the internal decision making processes of generative models. While large language models operate as black box systems, XAI techniques reveal patterns, feature contributions, reasoning paths, and inference mechanisms that lead to specific outputs. This visibility enables developers, auditors, and compliance officers to identify problematic reasoning that may result in hallucinations. XAI tools help stakeholders understand the logic behind generated outputs, evaluate alignment with factual and domain standards, and pinpoint failures in model reasoning. These tools are increasingly important for supporting governance frameworks, ensuring accountability, and maintaining compliance with emerging AI transparency regulations across different jurisdictions (Srivastava et al., 2022).

Counterfactual validation strengthens the explainability process by testing how models respond when input conditions are modified. By observing whether small changes result in stable or unstable outputs, enterprises can assess the robustness of reasoning pathways. If the model produces inconsistent or illogical results under minor modifications, this may indicate fragile or erroneous internal structures. Together, XAI and counterfactual validation create an analytical environment that supports early detection of hallucinations, model refinement, and long term quality assurance. These techniques enhance confidence in generative systems by ensuring that outputs are produced through stable, transparent, and logically coherent processes(Srivastava et al., 2022).

4.6 Monitoring Metrics for Hallucination Detection

Monitoring plays a vital role in maintaining system quality after deployment. Hallucination detection depends on measurable indicators that assess correctness, coherence, semantic stability, and model confidence. Enterprises deploy monitoring dashboards and automated evaluation systems to detect risks, identify anomalies, and generate alerts (Zhang et al., 2025). Before presenting the table, it is important to emphasize that monitoring metrics serve as foundational components of enterprise risk management. They provide structured frameworks for evaluating performance across different model versions, data conditions, and operational contexts.

Table 2. Metrics and Tools for Monitoring Hallucination

Metric or Tool	Description	Application
Accuracy Score	Measures correctness of outputs based on ground truth	Used for classification, fact checking, and structured prediction tasks
Confidence Score	Indicates the model's certainty level for its predictions	Supports threshold based validation and risk management
Semantic Consistency Index	Evaluates logical and contextual alignment of generated text	Useful for narrative generation, dialogue tasks, and summarization
Benchmarking Tools and Datasets	Provide standardized evaluation frameworks	Applied for model comparison, stress testing, and version validation

4.7 Integrating Approaches into Enterprise AI Pipelines

The effectiveness of hallucination management increases significantly when techniques are integrated into cohesive operational pipelines. Enterprises typically combine retrieval systems, grounding mechanisms, explainability modules, human review loops, and continuous monitoring into a single workflow. An integrated pipeline may include automated retrieval from knowledge repositories, real time XAI auditing for high risk outputs, RLHF based refinement cycles conducted at regular intervals, and dashboards that provide insights into model performance and hallucination frequency. Governance structures enforce data quality standards, reward model configurations, and compliance aligned validation requirements (Haider et al., 2025).

Through coordinated and well structured implementation, enterprises achieve higher levels of traceability, accuracy, and domain specific reliability. Integration ensures that hallucination management is not a one time effort but a continuous and evolving component of enterprise AI operations. The methods outlined in this chapter form the foundation of comprehensive hallucination management within enterprise AI environments. By combining knowledge grounding, retrieval augmented generation, reinforcement learning with human feedback, explainability tools, and structured monitoring systems, organizations can significantly reduce the occurrence of hallucinations and enhance system reliability. These strategies support transparent, accountable, and evidence based AI systems that operate consistently across diverse applications and regulatory landscapes. The next chapter will extend these concepts by presenting real world case studies and enterprise level implementations that demonstrate how hallucination management strategies are applied in practice across different sectors.

5. CASE STUDIES AND ENTERPRISE USE CASES

This chapter provides an in depth analysis of real world implementations of Metaverse based enterprise systems and highlights the role of artificial intelligence within these environments. The focus is placed on understanding how hallucination risks manifest, how organizations react when such risks emerge, and what lessons can be drawn from operational deployments. The case studies encompass multiple enterprise contexts, including customer service, employee training, and virtual commerce. Each case demonstrates unique implications related to technical design, information reliability, and user experience. The chapter concludes with a comparative assessment that synthesizes patterns observed across these deployments.

5.1 Customer Service Virtual Assistant in an Enterprise Metaverse Environment

A growing number of enterprises have adopted AI powered virtual assistants embedded within immersive customer service halls in the Metaverse. These digital assistants interact with customers using voice based communication, avatar mediated conversational flows, and multimodal dialog orchestration. Their capabilities include guiding customers through troubleshooting sequences, providing personalized account insights, and assisting with product information queries. The combination of speech recognition, contextual embeddings, and structured dialog management enables a more interactive service experience than traditional chatbots. Despite these advancements, hallucination risks have become a recurring operational challenge. Hallucinations often occur when the assistant encounters incomplete contextual cues from users. For instance, ambiguous customer queries may lead the system to infer unsupported interpretations of enterprise policies. Other examples include fabricated troubleshooting pathways that are not part of authorized service procedures or inaccurate descriptions of product eligibility, warranty conditions, or system capabilities. These errors are amplified in immersive environments where users expect higher fidelity and reliability.

To manage these risks, organizations have implemented a range of mitigation approaches. Retrieval grounded workflows ensure that responses are directly tied to verified enterprise documents rather than relying solely on generative reasoning (Setiawan & Soewito, 2025). Controlled response templates restrict the assistant to predefined phrasing, especially for high risk topics such as warranties, financial terms, or regulatory compliance. Dynamic fallback mechanisms guide the system to transfer conversations to human agents when the model's confidence score decreases beyond a threshold. Continuous fine tuning, supported by systematic analysis of anonymized interaction logs, allows enterprises to identify recurring hallucination triggers and refine system parameters. These interventions have significantly reduced the operational disruptions caused by AI hallucinations in customer service settings. The experiences gained from these deployments demonstrate that immersive customer service environments require strict reliability controls. Since users perceive virtual assistants as socially present entities, hallucinations can erode trust more quickly compared to traditional web based support. This elevates the importance of robust governance, transparent operational workflows, and consistent monitoring to ensure that the system maintains credibility and alignment with enterprise policies (Stefko et al., 2025).

5.2 Employee Training and Simulation Based Learning in the Metaverse

The Metaverse has rapidly evolved into a powerful platform for simulation based learning and training across various industries. Enterprises deploy virtual training modules to prepare employees for technical tasks such as equipment handling, manufacturing assembly, emergency response procedures, quality assurance routines, and soft skill development. AI powered components serve as virtual instructors that supervise trainee actions, offer real time feedback, and generate dynamic training scenarios tailored to individual performance.

Hallucination risks in training systems introduce serious concerns because accuracy in instructional content is essential for workforce readiness and operational safety. Hallucinations may manifest in several ways. Generative instructors may offer incorrect procedural instructions that deviate from standardized organizational protocols. They may misinterpret trainee movements due to limited gesture tracking or misclassified sensor data. In some cases, AI systems may provide inaccurate assessment feedback that distracts learners or reinforces improper techniques. These errors can create knowledge gaps and compromise the reliability of the training process (Haider et al., 2025).

To mitigate such risks, organizations employ layered validation mechanisms. Human experts review and verify instructional content to ensure consistency with official standard operating procedures. Generative capabilities are limited to template based or parameterized frameworks to restrict creativity that could lead to fabrications. In addition, multimodal grounding through gesture recognition, spatial tracking, and contextual environmental mapping strengthens the system's capability to interpret user actions accurately. The result is a more controlled and reliable training ecosystem where automation supports but does not replace human oversight. Successful implementations highlight that training environments require a careful balance between AI driven adaptation and human validated instructional accuracy (Setiawan & Soewito, 2025). Continuous monitoring of trainee performance logs, periodic updates to procedural content, and rigorous calibration of simulation parameters all contribute to reducing hallucination occurrences. Enterprises report that, with proper governance, AI assisted training provides significant benefits in standardization, scalability, and performance measurement.

5.3 Virtual Commerce Platforms and Intelligent Product Recommendation Systems

Enterprises operating in virtual commerce spaces leverage Metaverse technologies to deliver immersive shopping experiences. Customers can explore detailed three dimensional product models, interact with customizable virtual storefronts, and engage with AI powered shopping advisors. These systems integrate behavioral analytics, preference modeling, visual search, and virtual try on capabilities to deliver highly personalized recommendations (Asad & Otoum, 2024).

However, hallucination risks are common in these commerce environments. One major source of hallucination is incomplete or inconsistent product metadata. When catalog information lacks specific attributes, AI models often compensate by generating inferred or fabricated details. This may result in inaccurate statements about product characteristics such as material composition, compatibility specifications, or durability claims. Other hallucinations arise when the AI misinterprets signals from the product catalog, leading to incorrect pricing information or nonexistent promotions that confuse the customer (Kim et al., 2025).

Immersive settings amplify the credibility of erroneous information because customers perceive the environment as visually compelling and technologically advanced. As a result, hallucinations can lead to misinformed purchasing decisions, reduced customer satisfaction, and reputational risks for the enterprise. To counter these challenges, organizations adopt strict data governance practices. Fact locking mechanisms ensure that product descriptions and attributes remain consistent with verified catalog entries. Catalog synchronization pipelines maintain real time alignment between backend databases and the immersive storefront. Attribute level validation protocols scrutinize product data before it is presented to users, preventing the system from producing speculative or fabricated content. These mechanisms ensure that AI powered recommendations remain trustworthy and aligned with actual product specifications(Azzam et al., 2025). The insights gained from virtual commerce deployments show that maintaining metadata integrity and catalog completeness is essential for minimizing hallucination risks. Even advanced visualization components cannot compensate for inaccurate or missing data. Enterprises therefore prioritize investments in high quality product information management systems and automated verification workflows.

5.4 Cross Case Comparative Insights and Risk Patterns

Across the three examined enterprise use cases, several recurring hallucination patterns become evident. The first pattern is related to the availability and clarity of contextual signals. AI systems tend to generate hallucinations when the provided context is incomplete, ambiguous, or contradictory (Sood et al., 2025). Customer service environments illustrate this clearly because user queries often lack sufficient detail. Training environments also experience context gaps when gesture recognition systems fail to capture trainee movements accurately. Virtual commerce systems face context limitations when catalog metadata is incomplete or outdated.

The second pattern relates to the complexities of multiturn interactions. As conversational depth increases, AI models attempt to maintain coherence by filling gaps with inferred or fabricated information. This tendency is particularly pronounced in customer service scenarios where extended dialog is common. Training systems also experience similar effects when AI instructors adapt scenarios dynamically based on perceived progress, sometimes extrapolating beyond verified procedural boundaries. The third pattern concerns data pipeline inconsistencies. Missing, outdated, or siloed enterprise data increases hallucination risks across all domains. Customer service assistants may rely on outdated policy documents, training systems may use incomplete procedural information, and virtual commerce platforms may reference unsynchronized product metadata (Sood et al., 2025).

From an operational standpoint, customer service settings experience the most severe consequences because hallucinations can directly undermine customer trust and satisfaction. Training environments face moderate but significant risks, given that instructional accuracy is crucial for skill development and safety. Virtual commerce environments are highly sensitive to data integrity challenges because even minor inaccuracies in product attributes can mislead customers. The table below summarizes the primary hallucination triggers, impacts, and mitigation strategies observed across the three enterprise use cases.

Table 3. Comparative Analysis of Hallucination Risks Across Enterprise Use Cases

Enterprise Use Case	Primary Hallucination Trigger	Potential Impact	Mitigation Strategies
Customer Service Virtual Assistant	Ambiguous queries, incomplete policy data	Customer dissatisfaction, loss of trust	Retrieval grounding, fallback to human agent, controlled response templates
Employee Training Metaverse	Misinterpreted instructions, inconsistent procedure grounding	Incorrect learning outcomes, operational risk	Human expert validation, template based generation, multimodal grounding
Virtual Commerce Platform	Missing metadata, incorrect attribute inference	Misleading product information, brand risk	Fact locking, catalog synchronization, attribute validation

5.5 Lessons Learned from Real Implementations

The enterprise cases presented in this chapter provide important insights into the challenges and opportunities associated with deploying AI driven Metaverse systems. Several lessons stand out as critical for successful implementation. The first lesson is that hallucination risk management must be embedded in the system design process from the outset. Detection and mitigation strategies are more effective when integrated into the architectural foundation rather than added as corrective measures after deployment. This requires reliable data pipelines, confidence scoring mechanisms that guide fallback behavior, and continuous auditing processes that examine system outputs (Asad & Otoum, 2024).

The second lesson is that hallucination characteristics vary by domain. Customer service applications require precise dialog management and strict alignment with policies. Training simulations demand rigorous procedural accuracy and human validated content. Virtual commerce platforms depend heavily on metadata consistency, catalog completeness, and structured product information governance. Enterprises must therefore tailor their mitigation strategies to the unique operational requirements and risk profiles of each domain (Otoum et al., 2024). The third lesson involves the importance of continuous monitoring. As systems operate over time, their interaction patterns evolve, external data sources change, and model performance may drift. Monitoring solutions help enterprises detect anomalies, identify emerging hallucination patterns, and determine when retraining or recalibration is required. These feedback loops ensure that the AI system remains aligned with organizational goals and maintains high reliability. The fourth lesson concerns system complexity. As enterprises integrate multiple AI modules, interconnected data sources, and immersive elements, hallucination risks tend to increase. Ensuring consistency across these components requires robust governance frameworks, well defined interface protocols, and clear accountability structures (Haider et al., 2025).

6. ETHICAL GOVERNANCE, SECURITY, AND REGULATORY IMPLICATIONS

The integration of artificial intelligence within enterprise metaverse ecosystems introduces a broad spectrum of ethical, legal, and security considerations that must be addressed to ensure responsible adoption. As organizations deploy intelligent agents, automated decision systems, and immersive virtual platforms, the need for comprehensive ethical governance grows significantly. This chapter explores key areas such as transparency, regulatory compliance, data sovereignty, information security, avatar privacy, and the risks associated with bias and manipulation. Each dimension contributes to a holistic understanding of responsible AI practices within immersive enterprise environments (Du & Xie, 2021).

6.1 Ethical Transparency and Accountability in AI

Ethical governance relies on transparency, accountability, and explainability across all AI lifecycle stages. In enterprise metaverse platforms, transparency requires clear communication regarding how AI agents interpret user actions, process environmental data, and generate outcomes. Because interactions often occur through virtual avatars or digital twins, users need visibility into how their behaviors are monitored, analyzed, or predicted (Lee et al., 2025).

Accountability mechanisms ensure that every automated decision can be traced to specific datasets, model configurations, or system parameters. This is particularly important when AI tools mediate workplace coordination, moderate collaborative interactions, or influence enterprise decision making. Strong governance practices should therefore include clear documentation, audit trails, and human oversight systems. Transparency also involves ensuring that users understand what types of immersive data are collected within the metaverse. Sensor based inputs, biometric signals, gesture patterns, and spatial movements must be disclosed in a manner that supports informed participation. Ethical frameworks promote user centric consent processes, interpretable AI outputs, and an organizational commitment to addressing errors or hallucinations as they arise(Chakrabarti et al., 2025).

6.2 Regulatory Frameworks and Compliance Requirements

The enterprise metaverse operates within a dynamic regulatory environment shaped by international data protection laws, corporate governance standards, and emerging AI specific regulations. Compliance is essential not only for legal adherence but also for building trust among users and stakeholders (Zhang et al., 2025). Regulations governing personal data handling require organizations to carefully manage how user information is collected, stored, and processed within immersive platforms. Data sovereignty becomes a central concern because enterprise metaverse systems often operate across jurisdictions with distinct legal requirements. Avatars, behavioral logs, spatial analytics, and multimodal inputs must be treated as sensitive information and protected through privacy by design practices (Asad & Otoum, 2024). Organizations must implement data minimization strategies, purpose based processing rules, and strict access controls. Additionally, enterprises need assurance that cloud providers, platform vendors, and third party integrations maintain equivalent protections across the data lifecycle.

Corporate AI governance frameworks encourage organizations to classify risks, establish oversight bodies, and develop ethical standards for AI deployment. Regulations that focus on high risk systems require thorough documentation, model validation, and continuous monitoring. In enterprise metaverse environments, these responsibilities extend to ensuring that AI models accurately interpret complex virtual behaviors, maintain performance consistency, and avoid generating misleading or harmful outputs (Dwivedi et al., 2023). Governance structures should involve cross functional committees that supervise risk assessments, ensure policy alignment, and review decisions made by automated systems. These structures support transparency, accountability, and long term compliance.

6.3 Information Security and User Avatar Privacy

Metaverse environments introduce novel security challenges due to their multimodal data pipelines and real time interactions. Protecting user identities, preserving data integrity, and preventing unauthorized access become critical components of responsible platform design (Du & Xie, 2021). Avatars function as direct representations of real users and often carry sensitive permissions. This increases the risk of identity theft, impersonation, and unauthorized behavioral mimicry. Strong authentication methods such as multi factor verification, hardware bound credentials, or behavioral signatures are essential in preventing avatar hijacking (Sood et al., 2025). Permission systems must be adapted to virtual environments by defining granular controls related to movement, interaction, communication, or object manipulation. Segregated access rights are important for preventing misuse in sensitive enterprise scenarios.

Securing metaverse data requires layered protections including encryption, secure communication channels, behavioral anomaly detection, and continuous monitoring. As immersive systems collect large amounts of environmental and experiential data, organizations must implement retention policies that prevent unnecessary storage and reduce long term exposure to breach risks. Security teams must adapt to new threat vectors such as manipulation of virtual objects, deepfake avatar interactions, or unauthorized modification of shared environments. Incident response strategies should be updated to address these immersive specific attack patterns (Otoum et al., 2024).

6.4 Bias, Manipulation, and Dark Pattern Risks in the Metaverse

The immersive nature of metaverse environments heightens concerns about algorithmic bias, behavioral manipulation, and dark pattern designs. AI driven systems may influence decision making in ways that are not always transparent to users, creating ethical risks that must be proactively managed.

AI models trained on incomplete or unrepresentative datasets may misinterpret cultural cues, gestures, communication patterns, or emotional expressions. These misinterpretations can lead to unfair outcomes in workplace scenarios such as performance reviews, training simulations, evaluations, or collaborative decision making. To address this risk, organizations must conduct fairness evaluations, expand datasets with diverse interaction profiles, and implement ongoing monitoring to detect emerging biases. Transparent model reporting strengthens user trust and provides a basis for corrective action (Sharma et al., 2025). AI systems embedded in virtual environments can subtly shape user decisions through personalized prompts, adaptive environments, or nudging mechanisms. While such approaches may enhance user engagement, they can also compromise autonomy. In professional settings, this may manifest as excessive pressure, unfair influence, or biased guidance from AI mentors or virtual assistants. Ethical design principles should define acceptable boundaries for behavioral influence. User control options, transparency notices, and clear distinctions between assistance and persuasion help prevent misuse (Lee et al., 2025).

Dark patterns in the metaverse involve interface designs that intentionally mislead or restrict choices. These may include forced navigation routes, visually dominant prompts, or environmental cues that push users toward unwanted actions such as unnecessary data sharing or unintended virtual purchases. Identifying and addressing dark patterns requires cross functional collaboration between design teams, ethicists, and governance committees (Haider et al., 2025). To mitigate these risks, enterprises should adopt design standards that prioritize clarity, neutrality, and user autonomy. Regular audits, user testing, and behavioral risk assessments help maintain fairness and transparency during immersive interactions. As these ethical and security considerations form the foundation for responsible metaverse development, the next chapter examines the practical challenges that organizations face in operationalizing these principles and explores future research opportunities that will guide the evolution of enterprise metaverse ecosystems (Kim et al., 2025).

7. DISCUSSION: CHALLENGES, FUTURE DIRECTIONS, AND RESEARCH OPPORTUNITIES

This chapter provides an in depth discussion of the challenges, opportunities, and future directions that shape the development of AI hallucination management in enterprise metaverse ecosystems. It evaluates technical and organizational barriers, outlines a comprehensive R&D roadmap, examines the integration of multimodal AI with trusted knowledge resources, and highlights innovation opportunities for both industry and academia. These insights help establish a strategic perspective for advancing reliable and responsible AI in immersive virtual environments.

7.1 Technical and Organizational Challenges in Adopting AI Hallucination Management Frameworks

Implementing hallucination management in enterprise metaverse environments requires navigating several technical complexities. Metaverse ecosystems generate vast streams of multimodal data that arise from dynamic simulations, avatar interactions, spatial sensing, and digital assets. These data are often incomplete or inconsistent, making it difficult for AI systems to maintain contextual accuracy. Without robust alignment and validation mechanisms, hallucination risk increases significantly (Otoum et al., 2024).

Scalability constitutes a second major challenge. Hallucination detection requires continuous monitoring of model outputs in real time, which places substantial strain on infrastructure. Many organizations struggle to support high throughput monitoring pipelines, especially in large scale metaverse deployments. Integration barriers also persist due to the lack of standardized protocols across metaverse platforms. Differences in rendering engines, API structures, knowledge schemas, and data governance models force enterprises to rely on custom integration approaches. This reduces interoperability and increases long term maintenance burdens(ÖZKAL & BAŞÇİFTÇİ, 2024). Latency management adds further complexity. AI hallucination detection introduces computational overhead, yet immersive environments require near immediate responses to maintain user engagement. Enterprises must strike a balance between accuracy and responsiveness to prevent disruptions in collaborative activities and decision making processes. Organizational challenges involve both cultural and operational dimensions. Many enterprises lack specialized expertise required to design, deploy, and maintain hallucination management frameworks. The interdisciplinary nature of the metaverse, which merges AI, simulation engineering, data governance, and user experience design, demands skill sets that remain scarce in the current labor market (Metakides & Filip, 2025).

Cultural resistance may also hinder adoption. Employees may perceive continuous monitoring as intrusive or worry that AI auditing tools could influence performance evaluations. Transparent communication, clear ethical guidelines, and organizational readiness programs are crucial to overcoming these concerns. Budget limitations present another barrier. Implementing comprehensive hallucination management requires investment in infrastructure, talent, training, and governance alignment. Organizations that underestimate these needs risk deploying partial solutions that fail to produce meaningful improvements in AI reliability(Zhou et al., 2025). Governance alignment is equally critical. Effective hallucination control requires coordination among multiple units, such as cybersecurity teams, IT departments, compliance officers, and metaverse platform administrators. Misalignment across these groups may create gaps in oversight and reduce system effectiveness (Metakides & Filip, 2025).

7.2 Integrating Multimodal AI and Trusted Knowledge Repositories

Multimodal AI models interpret data from textual, auditory, visual, spatial, and behavioral channels. These inputs provide rich context but increase the risk of signal misalignment. Future advancements should focus on improved multimodal embeddings, cross modal attention mechanisms, and real time alignment strategies that reduce errors and ensure consistency across input types. Trusted knowledge repositories serve as the backbone for grounding AI outputs in verified information. These repositories may include structured ontologies, domain specific regulations, historical metadata, or validated digital asset libraries. Integrating these resources into AI workflows reduces hallucination likelihood by ensuring that outputs adhere to authoritative knowledge.

Efficiency challenges remain. High speed knowledge querying, hybrid symbolic neural architectures, and distributed caching mechanisms will be essential to maintain performance while supporting reliable knowledge validation (Safari et al., 2025). Different industries vary significantly in their risk sensitivity. High stakes environments such as healthcare simulations or industrial training require stricter hallucination controls than entertainment or marketing oriented metaverse applications (Xu et al., 2025). Therefore, hallucination management systems must be adaptable and configurable to match domain specific operational requirements.

7.3 Innovation Opportunities for Industry and Academia

Industry stakeholders can benefit from developing advanced reliability services such as automated auditing dashboards, real time monitoring platforms, and hallucination resistant virtual assistants. Integrating reliable AI systems into training simulations, collaborative design environments, and customer interaction channels can significantly enhance operational efficiency and trust (Du & Xie, 2021). Organizations may also explore new business models centered on subscription based AI reliability solutions, meta analytics services, or cross platform governance tools. These innovations position enterprises to leverage AI safely and effectively across metaverse ecosystems.

Academia holds a critical role in advancing foundational research on hallucination detection, multimodal reasoning, and metaverse specific AI evaluation frameworks. Interdisciplinary collaboration among fields such as computer science, cognitive psychology, ethics, simulation engineering, and organizational studies can yield comprehensive methodologies that address both technical and human centered challenges (Du & Xie, 2021). Universities may also establish innovation hubs and cross sector research partnerships that allow experimentation with immersive AI systems in realistic conditions. These environments accelerate discovery and support the transfer of theoretical insights into practical solutions.

Building collaborative innovation ecosystems is essential for accelerating progress in hallucination management research. Joint development laboratories, shared datasets, and standardized metaverse testbeds can facilitate robust experimentation and evaluation. Partnerships across industry, academia, and government agencies can foster interoperability, align governance practices, and promote the creation of shared benchmarks for AI reliability (Seif El-Nasr & Kleinman, 2020). These collaborative ecosystems not only drive technological advancements but also ensure that stakeholders collectively shape responsible and trustworthy AI practices. The insights and innovation pathways identified in this chapter set the foundation for understanding the broader implications of reliable AI deployment. This leads directly into the next chapter, which synthesizes the core contributions of the study and presents practical managerial implications that organizations can apply when implementing AI solutions in the enterprise metaverse (Metakides & Filip, 2025).

8. CONCLUSION

This chapter highlights that AI hallucination in enterprise settings is a complex issue shaped by multiple interacting factors, including data degradation, shifting contexts, system design constraints, and inconsistent governance. As organizations increasingly depend on AI-driven processes, maintaining the ability to identify, interpret, and control hallucinations becomes crucial for ensuring operational continuity, informed decision-making, and sustained competitive advantage.

From an organizational management perspective, addressing hallucination must be treated as a strategic agenda that permeates both technical development and business operations. Strengthening enterprise resilience requires comprehensive monitoring systems, rigorous data management, and active human supervision. Simultaneously, building trustworthy AI calls for well-defined governance structures, improved model interpretability, transparent documentation practices, and ethical guidelines that reinforce accountability and compliance across the enterprise.

Improving user experience and enhancing employee competency are equally important in preventing hallucinations from going unnoticed and preserving trust in AI-enabled systems. As generative and multimodal models exert greater influence over mission-critical decisions, enterprises need to implement forward-looking approaches that integrate technological controls with continuous organizational learning.

Ultimately, the chapter underscores that proactive governance, cross-disciplinary collaboration, and strategic planning are essential for ensuring AI systems remain reliable, ethical, and aligned with enterprise objectives in an increasingly complex technological landscape.

REFERENCES

Asad, M., & Otoum, S. (2024). Federated Learning for Personalized User Experiences in the Metaverse. *2024 2nd International Conference on Intelligent Metaverse Technologies & Applications (IMETA)*, 050–055. https://doi.org/DOI: 10.1109/iMETA62882.2024.10807979

Azzam, I., Bello, K., Breidi, F. E., & Aqlan, F. (2025). Analysis of user experience in extended reality: A comparative study of VR and MR for manufacturing training. *Manufacturing Letters*, *46*, 77–82. DOI: 10.1016/j.mfglet.2025.10.003

Chakrabarti, M., Fabozzi, F. J., Narain, A., & Sood, A. (2025). Ethical AI in Asset Management: Frameworks for Transparency, Compliance, and Trust. *The Journal of Financial Data Science*, *7*(1), 18–35. DOI: 10.3905/jfds.2025.7.1.018

Du, S., & Xie, C. (2021). Paradoxes of artificial intelligence in consumer markets: Ethical challenges and opportunities. *Journal of Business Research*, *129*, 961–974. DOI: 10.1016/j.jbusres.2020.08.024

Dwivedi, Y. K., Kshetri, N., Hughes, L., Slade, E. L., Jeyaraj, A., Kar, A. K., Baabdullah, A. M., Koohang, A., Raghavan, V., Ahuja, M., Albanna, H., Albashrawi, M. A., Al-Busaidi, A. S., Balakrishnan, J., Barlette, Y., Basu, S., Bose, I., Brooks, L., Buhalis, D., & Wright, R. (2023). "So what if ChatGPT wrote it?" Multidisciplinary perspectives on opportunities, challenges and implications of generative conversational AI for research, practice and policy. *International Journal of Information Management*, *71*, 102642. DOI: 10.1016/j.ijinfomgt.2023.102642

Fu, B., Hadid, A., & Damer, N. (2025). Generative AI in the context of assistive technologies: Trends, limitations and future directions. *Image and Vision Computing*, *154*. Advance online publication. DOI: 10.1016/j.imavis.2024.105347

Haider, Z., Rahman, M. H., Devabhaktuni, V., Moeykens, S., & Chakraborty, P. (2025). A framework for mitigating malicious RLHF feedback in LLM training using consensus based reward. *Scientific Reports*, *15*(1). Advance online publication. DOI: 10.1038/s41598-025-92889-7

Hassaan, Z. A., Yacoub, M. H., & Said, L. A. (2025). Gated recurrent unit accelerators for financial time series prediction on field-programmable gate array. *Engineering Applications of Artificial Intelligence*, *162*. Advance online publication. DOI: 10.1016/j.engappai.2025.112534

Kim, H., Seo, S., & Lee, S. W. (2025). When generative AI messes up:How politeness and attribution shape user reactions to hallucinations. *International Journal of Information Management, 85*. Advance online publication. DOI: 10.1016/j.ijinfomgt.2025.102958

Kliestik, T., Dragomir, R., Bălu ă, A. V., Grecu, I., Durana, P., Karabolevski, O. L., Kral, P., Balica, R., Suler, P., Bu u, O. V., Bugaj, M., Voinea, D.-V., Vrbka, J., Coco atu, M., Grupac, M., Pera, A., & Gajdosikova, D. (2024). Enterprise generative artificial intelligence technologies, internet of things and blockchain-based fintech management, and digital twin industrial metaverse in the cognitive algorithmic economy. *Oeconomia Copernicana, 15*(4), 1183–1221. DOI: 10.24136/oc.3109

Lee, C., Kim, J., Lim, J. S., & Shin, D. (2025). Generative AI risks and resilience: How users adapt to hallucination and privacy challenges. *Telematics and Informatics Reports, 19*. Advance online publication. DOI: 10.1016/j.teler.2025.100221

Lyu, Z., & Fridenfalk, M. (2024). Digital twins for building industrial metaverse. *Journal of Advanced Research, 66*, 31–38. DOI: 10.1016/j.jare.2023.11.019

Massenon, R., Gambo, I., Khan, J. A., Agbonkhese, C., & Alwadain, A. (2025). "My AI is Lying to Me": User-reported LLM hallucinations in AI mobile apps reviews. *Scientific Reports, 15*(1). Advance online publication. DOI: 10.1038/s41598-025-15416-8

Metakides, G., & Filip, F. G. (2025). Digital Enlightenment, Digital Humanism, and Computer-supported Collaboration in Artificial Intelligence Era. *Annals of Data Science, 12*(6), 1799–1823. DOI: 10.1007/s40745-025-00640-w

Otoum, Y., Gottimukkala, N., Kumar, N., & Nayak, A. (2024). Machine Learning in Metaverse Security: Current Solutions and Future Challenges. *ACM Computing Surveys, 56*(8), 1–36. DOI: 10.1145/3654663

ÖZKAL. İ., & BAŞÇİFTÇİ, F. (2024). *Deep Learning in the Metaverse: A Systematic Literature Review and Future Perspectives.* https://doi.org/DOI: 10.2139/ssrn.5022041

Pak, R., Rovira, E., & McLaughlin, A. (2025). Polite AI mitigates user susceptibility to AI hallucinations. *Ergonomics, 68*(10), 1735–1745. DOI: 10.1080/00140139.2024.2434604

Rahman, A., Mahir, S. H., Tashrif, M. T. A., Karim, M. A., Aishi, A. A., Kundu, D., Debnath, T., Moududi, M. A. A., Eidmum, M. Z. A., Miah, A. S. M., Farid, F. A., & Karim, H. A. (2025). Comparative analysis based on DeepSeek, ChatGPT, and Google Gemini: Features, techniques, performance, future prospects. *Systems and Soft Computing*, *7*. Advance online publication. DOI: 10.1016/j.sasc.2025.200396

Safari, A., Oshnoei, A., & Blaabjerg, F. (2025). A review of recent AI applications in next-generation power electronics. *Applied Energy*, *402*. Advance online publication. DOI: 10.1016/j.apenergy.2025.126923

Seif El-Nasr, M., & Kleinman, E. (2020). Data-Driven Game Development: Ethical Considerations. *ACM International Conference Proceeding Series*, 1–10. https://doi.org/DOI: 10.1145/3402942.3402964

Setiawan, V., & Soewito, B. (2025). Instruction-based Chain-of-Thought for Multi-agent RAG in Snort Rule Generation. *International Journal of Intelligent Engineering and Systems*, *18*(11), 883–896. DOI: 10.22266/ijies2025.1231.54

Sharma, S., Singh, G., Lim, W. M., Ali, A., & Singh, R. (2025). Metaverse through the integrated theoretical lenses of task technology fit theory, social capital theory, and social cognitive theory: The case of SMEs. *Journal of Innovation and Entrepreneurship*, *14*(1). Advance online publication. DOI: 10.1186/s13731-024-00445-w

Singh, A. K. (2025). VR/AR in ergonomics and workspace design: A dual-perspective analysis of applications and implications. *Applied Ergonomics*, *129*. Advance online publication. DOI: 10.1016/j.apergo.2025.104612

Sood, A. K., Zeadally, S., & Hong, E. (2025). The Paradigm of Hallucinations in AI-driven cybersecurity systems: Understanding taxonomy, classification outcomes, and mitigations. *Computers & Electrical Engineering*, *124*. Advance online publication. DOI: 10.1016/j.compeleceng.2025.110307

Srivastava, G., Jhaveri, R. H., Bhattacharya, S., & Pandya, S. Rajeswari, Maddikunta, P. K. R., Yenduri, G., Hall, J. G., Alazab, M., & Gadekallu, T. R. (2022). *XAI for Cybersecurity: State of the Art, Challenges, Open Issues and Future Directions.* https://arxiv.org/abs/2206.03585

Stefko, R., Michalikova, K. F., Strakova, J., & Novak, A. (2025). Digital twin-based virtual factory and cyber-physical production systems, collaborative autonomous robotic and networked manufacturing technologies, and enterprise and business intelligence algorithms for industrial metaverse. *Equilibrium. Quarterly Journal of Economics and Economic Policy*, *20*(1), 389–425. DOI: 10.24136/eq.3557

Xu, S., Yan, Z., Dai, C., & Wu, F. (2025). MEGA-RAG: A retrieval-augmented generation framework with multi-evidence guided answer refinement for mitigating hallucinations of LLMs in public health. *Frontiers in Public Health, 13*. Advance online publication. DOI: 10.3389/fpubh.2025.1635381

Zhang, H., Li, Y., Zhang, S., Song, L., & Tao, F. (2025). Artificial Intelligence-Enhanced Digital Twin Systems Engineering Towards the Industrial Metaverse in the Era of Industry 5.0. [English Edition]. *Chinese Journal of Mechanical Engineering, 38*(1). Advance online publication. DOI: 10.1186/s10033-025-01210-0

Zhou, J., Zhang, J., Wan, R., Cui, X., Liu, Q., Guo, H., Shi, X., Fu, B., Meng, J., Yue, B., Zhang, Y., & Zhang, Z. (2025). Integrating AI into clinical education: Evaluating general practice trainees' proficiency in distinguishing AI-generated hallucinations and impacting factors. *BMC Medical Education, 25*(1). Advance online publication. DOI: 10.1186/s12909-025-06916-2

KEY TERMS AND DEFINITIONS

AI Governance Framework: A structured policy system that defines roles, responsibilities, documentation standards, transparency rules, and escalation procedures for managing AI risks including hallucinations within enterprise metaverse implementations.

AI Hallucination: A phenomenon where an AI system generates incorrect, fabricated, or misleading information that appears plausible. In the enterprise metaverse, hallucinations can distort simulations, misguide decisions, or produce inaccurate procedural guidance.

Contextual Drift: The gradual misalignment between an AI model's understanding and the real operational context due to evolving data, updated policies, or environmental changes. This drift often increases the likelihood of hallucinations in dynamic enterprise systems.

Digital Twins: High-fidelity virtual replicas of physical assets, processes, or environments. Inaccurate AI outputs within digital twins may lead to flawed simulations, incorrect operational predictions, or unsafe decision making.

Enterprise Metaverse: A digitally immersive ecosystem where organizations conduct operations, collaboration, training, and simulations through VR, AR, MR, and intelligent virtual environments. It integrates digital twins, avatars, and real-time data streams to support enterprise workflows.

Human-in-the-Loop (HITL): A supervisory mechanism where human experts review or correct AI outputs, especially in high-risk domains. HITL helps validate instructions, audit errors, and prevent hallucinations from affecting enterprise workflows.

Knowledge Grounding: A technique that anchors AI outputs to authoritative enterprise sources such as policy documents, validated datasets, or knowledge graphs. Knowledge grounding reduces the risk of fabricated or unsupported information in high-stakes environments.

Multimodal AI: AI systems that process multiple input types text, speech, images, spatial data, sensor signals simultaneously. While powerful, multimodal integration increases complexity and can trigger hallucinations when inputs conflict or are misinterpreted.

Real-Time Monitoring Pipeline: An automated system that continuously evaluates AI outputs for anomalies, inconsistencies, and risk signals. Monitoring pipelines detect hallucinations early and help prevent propagation across multiuser metaverse environments.

Retrieval-Augmented Generation (RAG): A hybrid AI approach that retrieves relevant enterprise documents during inference and uses them to guide the model's output. RAG is widely used to minimize hallucinations in customer service, training, and decision-support applications.

Chapter 8
Transition Pathways: From Traditional Business Models to Metaverse-Driven Enterprises

Binastya Anggara Sekti
https://orcid.org/0000-0001-5489-4888
Universitas Esa Unggul, Indonesia

ABSTRACT

The transition from traditional business models to metaverse-driven enterprises represents a transformative shift in how organizations create value, manage operations, and collaborate across immersive digital ecosystems. This chapter outlines a structured, multi-phase pathway that guides enterprises from foundational digital readiness to fully immersive metaverse architectures powered by AI, digital twins, XR, and blockchain technologies. Emphasis is placed on organizational capability building, governance reform, cultural adaptation, and the integration of human–AI collaboration. A central focus is the need for robust AI hallucination management to ensure accuracy, safety, and trust as autonomous systems influence simulations, decision-making, and customer experiences. By synthesizing technological, managerial, and ethical dimensions, the chapter provides a strategic roadmap for enterprises seeking responsible, resilient, and scalable metaverse adoption.

1. INTRODUCTION

The emergence of the Enterprise Metaverse marks a profound transformation in how organizations create, deliver, and capture value. Traditional business models rely on predictable workflows, physical interactions, and siloed information systems. In contrast, the metaverse introduces immersive, persistent, and interconnected virtual environments where digital twins, AI-driven agents, and intelligent automation

DOI: 10.4018/979-8-3373-7534-2.ch008

operate alongside human decision-makers. These environments enable enterprises to simulate entire business processes, redesign customer experiences, and optimize complex operations with a degree of precision and scalability that conventional digital platforms cannot match. As a result, the metaverse functions not merely as a technological extension of current business systems but as a foundational shift toward experiential and computational business ecosystems. With the continuous advancement of technologies such as big data, artificial intelligence, virtual reality, robotics, human-machine collaboration, and augmented reality, many business organizations are finding new avenues for digital transformation and intelligent enhancement (H. Zhang, Li, Zhang, Song, & Tao, 2025).

This transformation challenges many long-standing assumptions about organizational design, digital infrastructure, and strategic capability. Enterprises must integrate advanced technologies such as XR interfaces, spatial computing, distributed ledgers, multimodal AI pipelines, and large-scale digital twin networks. Each of these layers contributes to a new form of value creation that depends on real-time sensing, adaptive simulation, and interactive intelligence. However, the integration of these components introduces complexity that extends beyond technical implementation. It requires rethinking talent development, redefining workflow orchestration, revising governance frameworks, and establishing new standards of transparency and accountability. Figure 1 illustrates how enterprise structures evolve from traditional siloed processes into an interconnected metaverse-driven architecture linking humans, AI, and autonomous agents. Users, designers, and companies can make joint decisions about product design and development solutions, and Metaverse technology can also optimize products with continuous iteration and get optimal solutions (Lin, Li, Wang, & Hu, 2024).

A central challenge during this transition is the emergence of AI hallucinations within generative and predictive systems. Hallucinations refer to outputs that deviate from factual or contextual accuracy, often producing misleading or fabricated information. Within the metaverse, where AI models directly influence virtual operations, workforce activities, and financial or logistical simulations, hallucinations can spread rapidly through interconnected environments. For example, a hallucinated forecast could distort supply chain digital twins, while an inaccurate AI-generated compliance recommendation could misguide regulatory processes. These risks underscore the need for rigorous hallucination detection, validation pipelines, and human-in-the-loop controls that ensure reliable system behavior in high-velocity virtual environments. There was a higher distrust effect on the relationship between performance risk, social risk, psychological risk, and non-adoption intent to the corporate metaverse for high-textured individuals compared to low-textual individuals (Kumar, Shankar, Shaik, Jain, & Malibari, 2025).

Enterprises transitioning to metaverse-driven models must therefore adopt a structured and holistic approach. This involves assessing digital readiness, modernizing infrastructure, training the workforce in immersive collaboration, and strengthening data governance practices. Organizational leaders must also implement ethical guidelines, transparency policies, and simulation audit mechanisms that regulate how AI systems produce, evaluate, and communicate information. Transition pathways must be phased, allowing organizations to gradually expand from traditional digital augmentation to hybrid immersive operations and, ultimately, full metaverse integration. Each step requires alignment between technological capacity and organizational maturity to avoid operational risks or strategic misalignment. The metaverse is recognized as one of the most important innovations in the Internet's evolution and is receiving growing attention across industries. The metaverse brings about ample opportunity for growth and profits, with blue ocean markets for many enterprises (Lee, 2024).

Figure 1. Evolution Toward the Flexible Interdisciplinary Enterprise Metaverse Lab

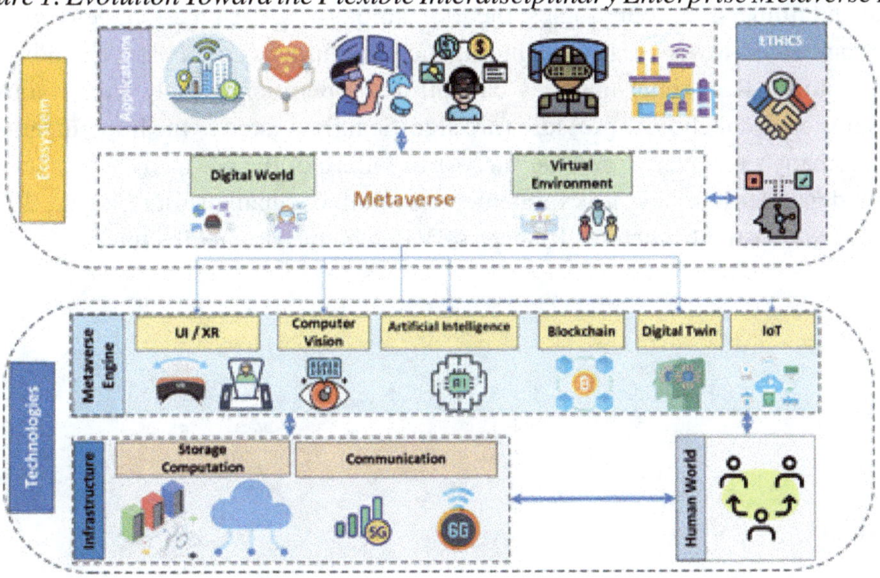

This chapter outlines a comprehensive roadmap to guide enterprises through the transformation from traditional models to fully metaverse-enabled ecosystems. It synthesizes insights from AI safety research, digital transformation studies, immersive computing, and enterprise governance to articulate how organizations can build resilient and trustworthy metaverse operations. The chapter also emphasizes the essential role of hallucination management frameworks in sustaining decision integrity, safeguarding user trust, and ensuring long-term sustainability. By presenting strategic, technological, and organizational considerations, the chapter provides a foundation for enterprises seeking to innovate responsibly and prepare for the next era of intelligent digital business environments.

2. THE SHIFTING FOUNDATIONS OF ENTERPRISE VALUE

The transition from traditional business models to metaverse-driven enterprises represents a profound restructuring of how organizations conceptualize, generate, and sustain value. Conventional enterprises operate through linear value chains, defined workflows, and static digital systems. By contrast, metaverse ecosystems function as dynamic, immersive, and interconnected value networks where physical processes are mirrored, augmented, or entirely reimagined through persistent virtual worlds. These environments integrate digital twins, mixed reality interfaces, AI-driven agents, and decentralized data infrastructures that reshape how decisions are made and how value is captured. As enterprises adopt more sophisticated computational and immersive technologies, the foundations of value creation, delivery, and governance shift toward real-time intelligence, continuous simulation, and adaptive collaboration. Real-time analytics capabilities, operational excellence, industry pressures, and stakeholder pressures are significantly related to the implementation of a company's metaverse, and the success or failure of the company's metaverse is highly dependent on how it is implemented (Kumar, Shankar, Behl, et al., 2025). Figure 2 shows the Immersive Enterprise Value Network Architecture.

Figure 2. Immersive Enterprise Value Network Architecture

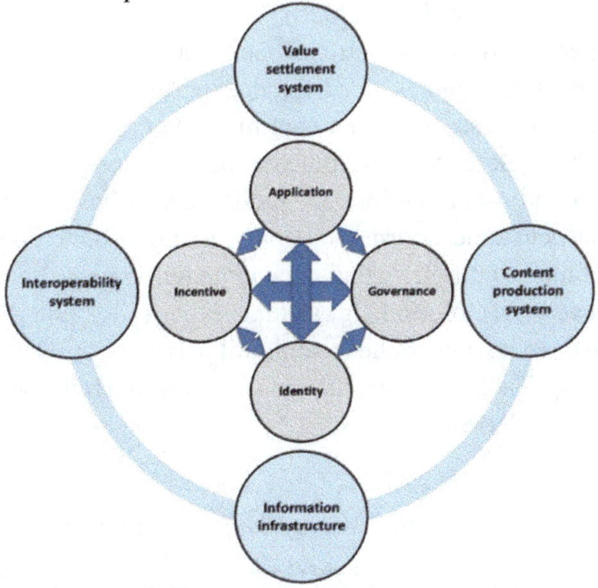

The following subsections explore three primary shifts: the movement from physical value chains to immersive value networks, the emergence of AI as a cognitive infrastructure, and the evolution of human productivity through synergy with intelligent, emotional, and embodied AI systems. Each shift not only enhances enterprise capabilities but also introduces new risks, including the propagation of AI hallucinations, which can distort simulations, misguide decision-making, and disrupt digital twin operations.

2.1 From Physical Value Chains to Immersive Value Networks

Traditional enterprises depend on sequential processes such as sourcing, manufacturing, logistics, and customer interaction. These workflows often rely on periodic data updates, physical inspection points, and siloed enterprise systems. Decision-making tends to be delayed, reactive, and limited by the episodic nature of available information. The metaverse disrupts this pattern by enabling real-time, immersive value networks in which physical and digital assets coexist and dynamically interact. Immersive environments have proven to unlock unique and valuable learning experiences, matched by the amount of expertise currently required with extended reality (XR) technology to create engaging immersive learning environments (Planey, Trencevski, & Kelle, 2026).

Digital twins serve as the computational backbone of these networks. They simulate entire factories, supply chains, or customer experiences, allowing enterprises to model future scenarios, assess risks, and optimize operations before changes occur in the physical world. Data flows become continuous, feeding real-time machine learning models that adjust predictions and recommendations as contexts shift. Supply chain analytics, customer journey mapping, and multi-site operations become deeply integrated into a unified virtual decision environment. Recent advances in artificial intelligence (AI), blockchain, virtual reality (VR), and digital twin technologies are transforming approaches to cultural heritage conservation (W. Zhang, Taib, & Taib, 2025). Table 1 shows the Comparison of Traditional Value Chains and Immersive Value Networks,

Table 1. Comparison of Traditional Value Chains and Immersive Value Networks

Dimension	Traditional Enterprises	Metaverse-Driven Enterprises
Data Flow	Episodic, batch-based	Continuous, real-time streaming
Decision Speed	Reactive	Predictive and adaptive
Collaboration	Siloed processes	Fully integrated value networks
Simulation Capability	Limited or static	Full digital twin ecosystems
Risk Transparency	Low	High through predictive modeling
Hallucination Exposure	Moderate	High due to AI-driven simulations

These immersive value networks significantly enhance resilience and innovation. However, they rely heavily on accurate AI-generated insights. If hallucinated data or fabricated correlations enter the system, the digital twin may misrepresent operational reality, leading to incorrect inventory planning, misaligned production schedules, or misleading market simulations. As a result, continuous validation and hallucination detection mechanisms are essential components of value preservation.

2.2 AI as a Cognitive Infrastructure

In metaverse enterprises, AI shifts from being a standalone analytic tool to functioning as a pervasive cognitive infrastructure. AI agents operate simultaneously across immersive environments, digital twins, and operational systems. They schedule tasks, forecast demand, detect anomalies, assess quality, manage compliance, and personalize customer interactions at scale. AI-driven automation transforms the enterprise into a self-adjusting ecosystem where intelligent systems anticipate needs, resolve conflicts, and optimize workflows with minimal human intervention. Immersive learning has been recognized as a promising paradigm for enhancing educational experiences through the integration of VR (El Hajji et al., 2025).

This transformation, however, increases vulnerability to AI hallucinations. When cognitive agents generate inaccurate insights, misinterpret contextual signals, or fabricate system states, errors propagate across interconnected layers. For example, a hallucinated risk prediction could cause a digital twin to misallocate resources, or a flawed customer sentiment analysis could distort marketing strategies and virtual product placement. Because metaverse enterprises rely on continuous simulation and autonomous decision loops, hallucinations may have amplified and widespread impact. Technology-powered travel planning portals are increasingly offering technology tools, such as the metaverse, AI apps, and chatbots to facilitate travel (Paliwal, Buhalis, Jha, & Chatradhi, 2025).

Managing AI hallucinations within cognitive infrastructures requires layered governance, including transparent model architectures, input validation pipelines, multi-model redundancy, and real-time anomaly detection. These mechanisms reduce systemic fragility and maintain the reliability of the enterprise cognitive fabric.

2.3 Human–AI Synergy in Immersive Environments

Human productivity in the metaverse increasingly relies on collaboration with AI-powered avatars, spatial computing assistants, emotion-aware agents, and context-sensitive recommender systems. Workers interact with AI through holographic dashboards, digital co-workers, XR interfaces, and embodied conversational agents that support tasks ranging from design and prototyping to human resources and customer support. These immersive systems augment human cognition by providing guidance, predictive insights, and adaptive task orchestration. In the successive rise of the metaverse and artificial intelligence (AI), rationalism and emotionalism have consistently manifested as symptoms of modernity throughout their developmental trajectories (Bing, 2025).

Yet effective synergy requires careful balancing between automation and human agency. Users must understand how AI systems generate outputs, be able to challenge generative recommendations, and have mechanisms to correct or override hallucinated insights. Overreliance on AI in immersive environments can reduce critical thinking, erode situational awareness, and amplify the impact of errors. Enterprises must embed human-centered design principles, ensuring transparency, interpretability, and collaborative control in metaverse workflows. Agentic AI systems are on track to engage in cultural, economic, and political activities, effectively forming societal structure within Virtual City (Nechesov, Dorokhov, & Ruponen, 2025).

Training becomes increasingly important. Workers must develop AI literacy, XR proficiency, and hallucination awareness to navigate complex digital environments. Human-centered governance ensures not only productivity but also safety, fairness, and ethical alignment in immersive enterprise operations.

3. STRATEGIC TRANSITION PATHWAYS

Transitioning from traditional business models to metaverse-driven enterprises requires a deliberate and structured approach. Organizations cannot simply adopt virtual technologies or immersive interfaces without aligning their infrastructure, governance, workforce capabilities, and risk safeguards. Instead, they must follow strategic pathways that gradually increase digital maturity, operational immersion, and cognitive integration while maintaining reliability and trustworthiness. This section outlines a phased transition framework that guides enterprises from foundational readiness to full metaverse-enabled operations, emphasizing the importance of hallucination governance throughout each stage. Generative AI tools can bolster predictive analytics by collaborative and interconnected sensor and machine data for tailored, seamless, and finetuned product, operational process, and organizational workflow development, efficiency, and innovation, driving agile transformative changes in digital twin industrial metaverse (Kliestik et al., 2024).

To support continuity, Figure 3 illustrates a progressive transition model connecting readiness assessment, digital augmentation, hybrid immersive operations, and fully metaverse-driven ecosystems. These phases ensure that technological transformation is aligned with organizational culture, risk management, and strategic objectives.

Figure 3. Enterprise Transition Pathway Toward Metaverse-Driven Operations

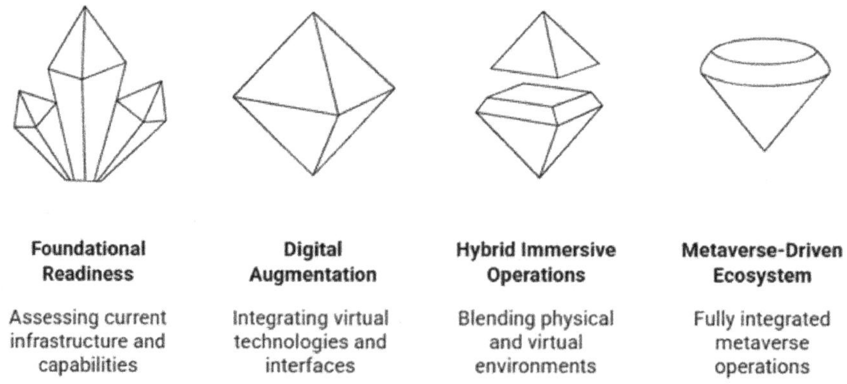

3.1 Readiness Assessment: Evaluating Starting Points

The transition begins with a comprehensive readiness assessment that evaluates the enterprise's current digital maturity and identifies the gaps that may obstruct progress. Organizations vary widely in their cloud adoption, automation intensity, data governance sophistication, and cultural openness to immersive work environments. A structured diagnostic therefore ensures that the transition is grounded in evidence rather than assumptions. A lack of understanding and knowledge about the effectiveness of the metaverse and its related technologies creates a barrier (Khan, Sheikh, Shamsi, & Yu, 2025).

Key components of readiness assessment include:

1. Digital Infrastructure Maturity: Evaluating the robustness of cloud platforms, IoT device integration, data pipelines, and API interoperability.
2. Data Governance Readiness: Assessing metadata standards, access controls, lineage tracking, and data quality protocols that protect against hallucination-inducing inconsistencies.
3. Workforce Digital Literacy: Determining whether staff possess the skills necessary for XR interaction, AI-supported workflows, and immersive collaboration.
4. Automation Capabilities: Reviewing existing use of autonomous systems, chatbots, robotic automation, and AI decision engines.
5. Hallucination Risk Exposure: Analyzing vulnerability to misinterpretation, context drift, or model fabrication across AI systems.
6. Organizational Culture: Evaluating openness to experimentation, virtual collaboration, and digitally augmented workflows.

The output of this assessment is a maturity profile that guides which transition phase the enterprise can safely enter. Table 2 shows the Key Readiness Indicators for Enterprise Metaverse Adoption.

Table 2. Key Readiness Indicators for Enterprise Metaverse Adoption

Indicator Category	Diagnostic Questions	Readiness Gap Implications
Infrastructure	Is the cloud environment scalable and secure	Limits ability to deploy XR platforms and digital twins
Data Governance	Are data pipelines validated and monitored	Increases hallucination risk in predictive models
Workforce Skills	Do employees understand XR and AI systems	Slows immersive adoption and reduces user trust

continued on following page

Table 2. Continued

Indicator Category	Diagnostic Questions	Readiness Gap Implications
Automation Level	What percentage of tasks are AI supported	Determines feasibility of hybrid operations
Hallucination Exposure	Are generative models monitored	High risk of simulation errors and false insights
Organizational Culture	Is innovation encouraged	Influences adoption speed and cross-team integration

3.2 Phase 1: Digital Augmentation of Traditional Models

Phase 1 focuses on enhancing traditional business operations with metaverse-aligned digital tools without fully integrating immersive environments. This phase builds digital strength while maintaining established workflows, making it ideal for organizations with moderate readiness maturity.

Key initiatives include:

- XR-based training modules that simulate equipment usage, emergency responses, or onboarding scenarios.
- AI-driven forecasting and analytics that introduce more adaptive planning processes.
- Early-stage digital twins that monitor asset health, energy consumption, or inventory conditions.
- Intelligent customer engagement bots that personalize interactions and analyze behavior.
- Blockchain-based audit trails that strengthen data provenance and traceability.

A critical requirement of this phase is embedding hallucination controls at the model level. These controls involve input validation, output consistency checks, multi-model cross-verification, and human oversight for high-risk predictions. Early governance ensures AI-generated insights remain trustworthy before enterprises expand into immersive ecosystems. Figure 4 shows the Digital Augmentation Layer: Enhancing Traditional Operations.

Figure 4. Digital Augmentation Layer: Enhancing Traditional Operations

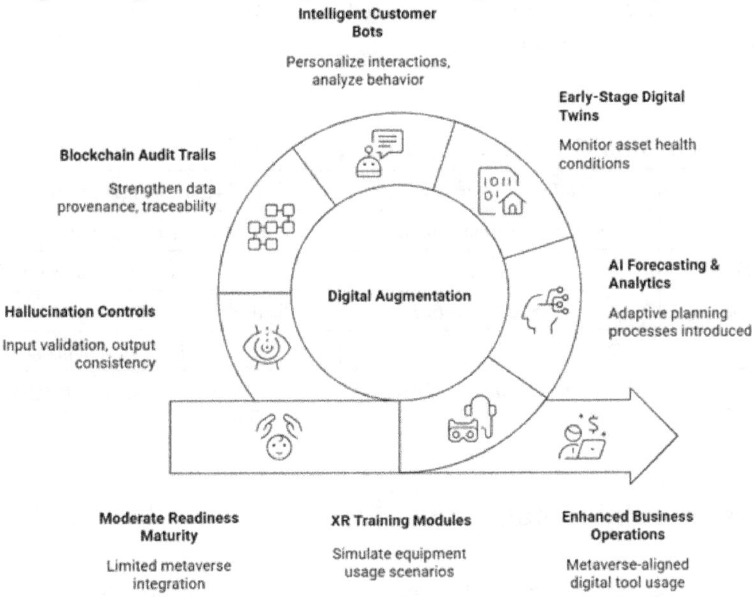

3.3 Phase 2: Hybrid Immersive Business Operations

In Phase 2, enterprises begin merging physical processes with immersive digital environments. This hybrid model enhances operational visibility, improves collaboration, and supports new forms of simulation-based decision-making.

Key developments in this phase include:

- Full digital twin ecosystems that simulate supply chains, manufacturing lines, logistics networks, or workforce planning.
- Autonomous decision support for high-volume transactional areas such as finance, procurement, or HR.
- Immersive customer experience platforms that allow virtual product exploration, interactive assistance, and emotional engagement.
- Virtual workplaces where distributed teams interact using holographic avatars, shared 3D workspaces, and spatial collaboration tools.

During this stage, risk management frameworks must be redesigned to address hallucinations across multimodal AI systems. Visual XR models, natural language models, predictive engines, and sensor-driven analytics may all hallucinate in different ways, making cross-validation essential. This requires enterprises to implement multimodal hallucination detection layers that compare signals from text, image, sound, sensor data, and spatial tracking systems. Table 3 shows the Hallucination Risks and Controls in Hybrid Immersive Operations.

Table 3. Hallucination Risks and Controls in Hybrid Immersive Operations

AI Modality	Hallucination Risk	Recommended Controls
NLP Agents	Fabricated recommendations	Confidence scoring, context validation
Vision Models	Misidentified objects in XR	Depth sensor triangulation, anomaly flags
Predictive Models	Incorrect forecasting	Historical trend anchoring, human review
Sensor AI	Drift from corrupted signals	Multi-sensor redundancy
Avatar Systems	Incorrect emotional inference	Behavioral calibration datasets

3.4 Phase 3: Fully Metaverse-Driven Business Ecosystems

Phase 3 represents the highest level of enterprise immersion, where business operations, decision-making, and customer engagement occur predominantly within virtual environments. The metaverse becomes the central operating platform, supported by AI-driven agents, decentralized infrastructure, and autonomous governance mechanisms.

Key characteristics of this stage include:

- Complete lifecycle simulation for products, processes, and markets via digital twins.
- Autonomous avatars and agents performing operational tasks such as negotiation, auditing, scheduling, compliance verification, or customer assistance.
- Virtual marketplaces and work environments functioning as primary channels for transaction, collaboration, and innovation.
- Decentralized and adaptive governance models that rely on smart contracts, transparent rule systems, and distributed decision structures.

Hallucination management becomes a continuous, proactive capability. AI systems must monitor contextual drift, recognize early anomalies, verify cross-model consistency, and block propagation of false insights. Enterprises require real-time AI observability platforms that track hallucination probability scores, classify hallucinatory events, and automatically route decisions to human supervisors when uncertainty is high.

4. THE ROLE OF AI HALLUCINATION MANAGEMENT IN ENTERPRISE TRANSITION

As enterprises move toward immersive and metaverse-driven operational models, reliable AI becomes essential to maintaining productivity, safety, and strategic coherence. In these environments, AI systems influence not only digital workflows but also physical processes connected through digital twins, IoT networks, and autonomous agents. The complexity and velocity of these interactions increase the likelihood that hallucinations may arise. Hallucinations include any fabricated output, context drift, misinterpretation, or logically inconsistent result produced by an AI model. While such errors may be manageable in conventional digital systems, they become significantly more dangerous in metaverse environments where decisions propagate instantly through virtual simulations and operational ecosystems. Effective hallucination management is therefore foundational to trustworthy enterprise transformation. Most traditional AI models are regarded as "black boxes," in which understanding decision-making processes presents a challenge in crucial domains such as healthcare, smart cities, and industrial automation (Mohammad et al., 2025).

Hallucination management encompasses a suite of governance, technical, and human-centered mechanisms designed to prevent, detect, and mitigate unintended AI outputs. These include robust data governance, transparency frameworks, real-time monitoring, and multimodal validation pipelines. Together, these components ensure that AI-generated insights remain grounded in accurate data, contextual relevance, and operational integrity. Enterprises that embed hallucination safeguards early in their transition process are far more capable of scaling immersive systems without compromising reliability, reputation, or regulatory compliance. Figure 5 shows the AI Hallucination Management Framework for Metaverse Enterprises.

Figure 5. AI Hallucination Management Framework for Metaverse Enterprises

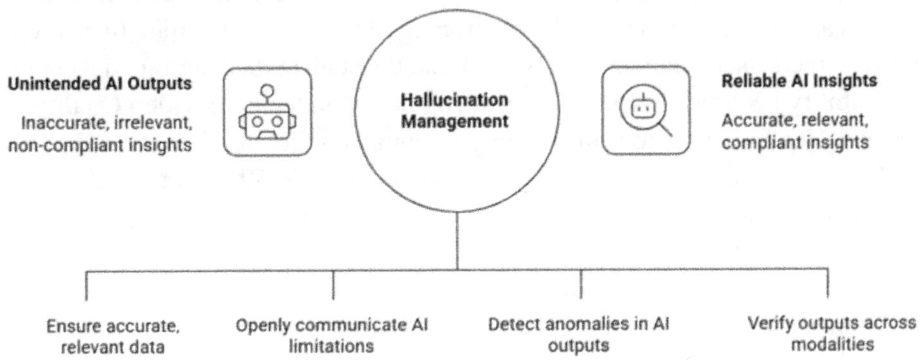

4.1 Data Governance as the Foundation for Hallucination Prevention

Robust data governance sits at the core of hallucination prevention. Metaverse platforms rely on vast datasets, including user interactions, digital twin telemetry, XR sensor feeds, operational histories, and synthetic training data. If these datasets contain inconsistencies, biases, outdated information, or contextual drift, AI models may produce misleading or fabricated outputs. Because many AI tools, especially GenAI, make information more accessible but quality information is harder to identify, information professionals have a unique opportunity to take the lead in the use of AI responsible for information access. Libraries that integrate GenAI into virtual and traditional reference models, still provide opportunities for improved service delivery and challenges such as AI hallucinations and ethical use (Aguiñaga, Mooradian, Ghosh, & Hofman, 2025).

Key data governance practices include:

- Continuous data quality validation
- Metadata tracking and lineage auditing
- Automated anomaly detection within data pipelines
- Role-based access control and secure data sharing
- Real-time updates to reflect changing operational environments

These mechanisms reduce hallucination risk by ensuring AI systems learn from accurate, coherent, and contextually aligned data sources.

4.2 Model Transparency and Explainability for Trustworthy Outputs

Transparency mechanisms enable users and supervisors to interpret AI behavior, trace its reasoning, and understand the factors contributing to an output. In metaverse contexts, where users interact with AI-generated visual, textual, and spatial content, explainability becomes essential. A growing need for accurate Video Quality Assessment (VQA) metrics to evaluate the perceptual quality of AI-generated content (AIGC) videos and optimize video generation models (Z. Zhang et al., 2025).

Techniques include:

- Attention heatmaps for spatial AI
- Feature attribution scores for predictive analytics
- Explanation overlays for XR-based decision support
- Visualization of digital twin state transitions

- Natural language rationales from generative models

Explainability reduces the likelihood of hallucinations being accepted as valid, since users can examine the basis of AI logic before acting upon it.

4.3 Human-in-the-Loop Controls for High-Risk Decisions

Human oversight remains indispensable in any metaverse transition. Although autonomous agents perform many tasks, human supervisors must retain confirmation authority for high-impact or safety-critical decisions. Human-in-the-loop (HITL) mechanisms ensure that hallucinated insights do not propagate unchecked through interconnected systems.

Examples include:

- Manual approval for financial transactions initiated by AI
- Supervisor validation for digital twin reconfigurations
- Human decision checkpoints for compliance or legal determinations
- XR interfaces that visualize uncertainty levels for AI outputs

HITL safeguards maintain human agency while leveraging automation to enhance productivity.

4.4 Continuous Performance Auditing of Autonomous Agents

In immersive enterprises, AI agents operate continuously and adapt to new data conditions. This increases the likelihood of performance drift or contextual misalignment. Continuous auditing is therefore critical.

Monitoring includes:

- Accuracy drift detection across AI pipelines
- Real-time comparison of expected versus actual agent behavior
- Model retraining triggers when hallucination probabilities increase
- Benchmarking performance against historical decision patterns
- Logging anomalous actions to blockchain for traceability

Auditing reduces the risk of silent failure, a common risk when hallucinations are subtle or intermittent.

4.5 Multimodal Hallucination Detection Across XR Data Streams

Metaverse environments combine text, voice, images, spatial mapping, gestures, biometrics, and sensor data. Each modality can produce unique hallucination patterns. A multimodal detection strategy cross-validates information across modalities to detect contradictions or impossible system states.

Examples:

- If vision AI mislabels an XR object, depth sensors and motion data can correct it
- If a generative agent fabricates a recommendation, digital twin simulations can invalidate it
- If NLP outputs drift contextually, historical state logs can re-anchor the meaning

This cross-modal approach significantly reduces hallucination propagation in immersive enterprise workflows. Table 4 shows the Hallucination Management Components and Their Enterprise Impact.

Table 4. Hallucination Management Components and Their Enterprise Impact

Component	Function	Impact on Metaverse Operations
Data Governance	Ensures data integrity and coherence	Prevents hallucinations from corrupted inputs
Model Transparency	Provides interpretability	Enables human validation and trust
Human-in-the-Loop	Supervises high-risk tasks	Blocks harmful decision propagation
Performance Auditing	Monitors autonomous agents	Detects drift and emerging hallucinations
Multimodal Detection	Cross-validates outputs	Reduces error rates in immersive environments
Ethical Guardrails	Aligns AI with values and standards	Prevents unfair or unsafe hallucination outcomes

4.6 Ethical Guardrails for Responsible Metaverse Adoption

Ethical guardrails ensure AI systems behave in ways that uphold fairness, safety, transparency, and inclusive digital participation. Hallucinations may unintentionally amplify harmful biases or produce unfair recommendations, which can damage enterprise reputation or violate regulatory standards. In the burgeoning field of Large

Language Models (LLMs), developing a robust safety mechanism, colloquially known as "safeguards" or "guardrails", has become imperative to ensure the ethical use of LLMs within prescribed boundaries (Dong et al., 2025). Ethics frameworks guide:

- Bias detection and mitigation
- Fair access to AI-generated services
- User privacy protections in XR environments
- Accountability and governance of autonomous agents
- Compliance with emerging AI and digital asset regulations

Ethical oversight therefore complements technical hallucination management, ensuring enterprises do not compromise human dignity or digital rights as they scale immersive operations.

AI hallucination management is essential to maintaining accuracy, safety, and trust during enterprise transition into the metaverse. Through robust data governance, transparency mechanisms, human oversight, performance auditing, multimodal validation, and ethical guardrails, organizations can mitigate the risks of misleading or fabricated AI outputs. These safeguards support reliable immersion and enable enterprises to advance toward increasingly sophisticated virtual ecosystems.

The next section examines the organizational transformation required to support these technological and governance frameworks, including workforce development, governance models, and cultural shifts.

5. ORGANIZATIONAL TRANSFORMATION REQUIREMENTS

Technological readiness alone is insufficient for a successful transition to metaverse-driven enterprise ecosystems. Organizational transformation plays an equally critical role because immersive technologies fundamentally reshape work-flows, decision-making processes, governance models, and cultural expectations. Enterprises must equip their workforce with new digital competencies, establish governance structures tailored to AI-intensive environments, and cultivate cultures that support experimentation, transparency, and cross-functional collaboration. Without these components, AI hallucination management efforts may fail due to human misunderstanding, inadequate oversight, or misaligned organizational incentives.

Figure 6 illustrates the interconnected layers of organizational transformation that support metaverse adoption. These layers include workforce capability development, governance structures, and cultural evolution. Together, they create an adaptive organizational environment capable of leveraging immersive technologies responsibly and effectively throughout the transition process.

Figure 6. Organizational Transformation Layers for Metaverse-Driven Enterprises

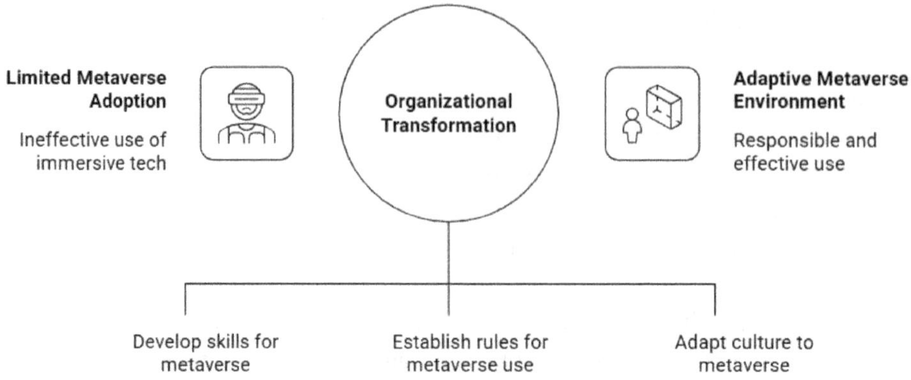

5.1 Workforce Upskilling and Reskilling

The transition to metaverse-enabled operations requires organizations to invest significantly in workforce development. Employees must acquire new competencies that enable effective collaboration with AI systems, intelligent agents, and immersive environments. These skills extend beyond familiarity with technology and encompass conceptual understanding, operational fluency, and ethical awareness. Table 5 shows the Workforce Skills Required for Metaverse Maturity.

Table 5. Workforce Skills Required for Metaverse Maturity

Skill Category	Description	Strategic Impact
XR Design	Ability to create and navigate immersive environments	Enhances collaboration and training
AI Literacy	Understanding model behavior and hallucination risks	Improves safety and governance
Virtual Asset Management	Handling digital twins and virtual prototypes	Ensures operational continuity
Cyber-Physical Integration	Working across digital and physical systems	Necessary for automation scalability

Key competency areas include:

1. XR Design and Immersive Collaboration

Employees must learn how to interact with and design spatial interfaces, avatars, holographic dashboards, and interactive digital twins. This skill enables productivity within virtual workspaces and enhances collaborative design, remote training, and immersive customer engagement.

2. AI Literacy and Hallucination Awareness

Workers must understand how AI generates outputs, recognize when hallucinations may occur, and interpret uncertainty signals embedded within AI-generated content. Awareness training reduces overreliance on autonomous systems and enables humans to detect inconsistencies before they propagate into operations.

3. Virtual Asset Management

As enterprises accumulate digital twins, virtual prototypes, XR training modules, and AI avatars, employees must develop skills to maintain, update, and version these digital assets responsibly.

4. Cyber-Physical Integration Skills

The convergence of physical and virtual systems requires a workforce capable of understanding sensor integration, edge computing, control loops, and supervisory orchestration across digital and physical layers.

5.2 Metaverse Governance Structures

Governance structures must evolve to oversee the complexities of metaverse operations. Traditional IT governance frameworks are insufficient because they do not account for the interactive nature of immersive environments, AI autonomy, data multiplicity, and dynamic simulations. Effective governance must balance technological innovation with accountability, transparency, and user protection (Anwar et al., 2025; Erzed et al., 2025). Figure 7 shows the Governance Framework for AI and Metaverse Integration.

Figure 7. Governance Framework for AI and Metaverse Integration

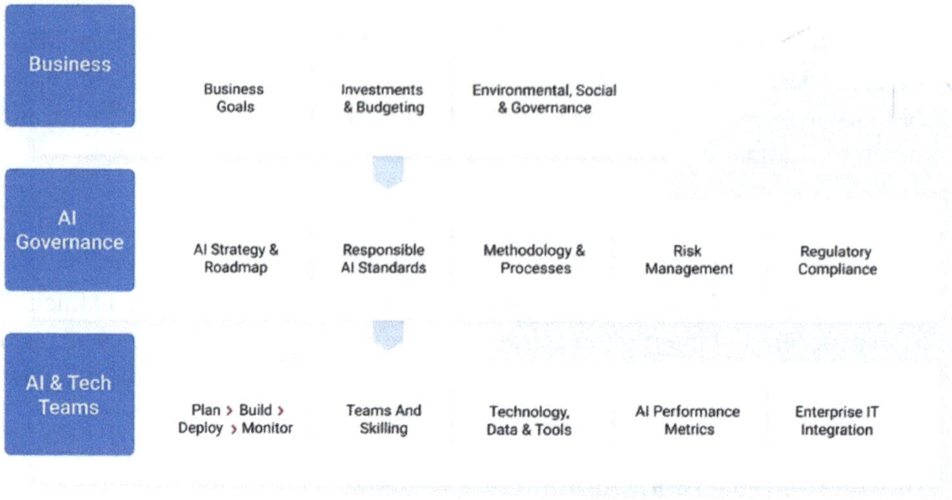

Key governance mechanisms include:

1. Oversight Committees for Immersive Systems

Cross-functional governance bodies should supervise the integration of digital twins, XR interfaces, and AI agents. Committees evaluate risks, approve deployments, and monitor unexpected system behaviors.

2. Explainable AI Policies

Policies mandating transparency in AI decision-making ensure that employees and stakeholders understand how generative models produce outputs. This is essential for detecting hallucinations and ensuring informed human oversight.

3. Accountability Frameworks

Enterprises must define responsibility for AI-driven actions, autonomous agent decisions, and digital twin outputs. Clear accountability prevents ambiguity when hallucinations cause operational disruptions.

4. Data Privacy and Ethics Guidelines

Immersive environments collect extensive behavioral, biometric, spatial, and interaction data. Ethical guidelines and privacy standards protect users and prevent misuse.

5. Interdisciplinary Decision-Making Processes

Because metaverse systems span HR, IT, compliance, operations, and strategy, governance must integrate perspectives across these domains to ensure balanced and ethical technology use.

5.3 Cultural Shifts Toward Digital Immersion

An enterprise cannot fully transition to metaverse-driven operations without cultivating a culture that embraces digital immersion, experimentation, and responsible innovation. Cultural readiness influences how employees perceive immersive technologies, how teams collaborate across physical and virtual boundaries, and how quickly organizations adapt to new digital capabilities.

Core cultural elements include:

1. Encouragement of Experimentation and Innovation

Metaverse environments support rapid prototyping, iterative design, and low-risk experimentation through virtual simulations. Organizations must encourage employees to explore new workflows, test ideas, and challenge established norms.

2. Balanced Trust in Technology and Human Oversight

While immersive technologies offer powerful capabilities, employees must trust their own judgment and view AI as a collaborator rather than an unquestionable authority. This balance prevents overreliance on AI outputs that may contain hallucinations.

3. Cross-Functional Collaboration

Immersive systems naturally dissolve organizational silos, allowing engineers, designers, strategists, and operators to work together inside shared virtual spaces. Cultural norms must promote teamwork across departments and disciplines.

4. Transparency and Shared Governance

Trust in metaverse systems grows when users understand how decisions are made, how data is used, and how AI hallucinations are prevented or corrected. Transparency builds confidence and supports safe adoption.

A culture that values openness, interdisciplinary collaboration, and responsible digital innovation strengthens the organization's ability to manage hallucination risks and fully realize the potential of metaverse-enabled operations.

6. TECHNOLOGY INTEGRATION FRAMEWORK

Transitioning toward metaverse-driven enterprises requires not only organizational transformation but also a cohesive technological integration strategy. Metaverse ecosystems depend on several foundational technologies that jointly deliver immersive, intelligent, and trustworthy digital operations. Among these, digital twins, blockchain infrastructures, and extended reality (XR) platforms serve as key pillars that enable real-time simulation, verifiable data provenance, and embodied virtual collaboration. When combined with AI, these technologies form a multidimensional architecture capable of supporting predictive decision-making, autonomous processes, and scalable virtual experiences.

Digital twins, blockchain, and XR systems operate as interconnected components within the broader enterprise metaverse framework. Their integration enables synchronized physical-virtual environments, secure data exchange, and immersive user interactions. To maintain reliable performance, these technologies must be supported by strong hallucination governance, multimodal validation mechanisms, and ethical AI controls. Without such safeguards, even highly advanced infrastructures can propagate errors, distort insights, and introduce significant strategic and operational risks.

6.1 Digital Twins as Core Intelligence Engines

Digital twins function as dynamic, data-driven models that mirror physical assets, business processes, customer journeys, or entire enterprises. By integrating sensor data, AI analytics, and contextual information, digital twins enable real-time monitoring, simulation, and optimization. In metaverse environments, digital twins evolve beyond visualization tools to become intelligence engines that support predictive and prescriptive decision-making.

Key capabilities of digital twins include:

- Predictive analytics for risk detection such as supply bottlenecks or equipment failures.
- Scenario modeling for strategic planning, logistics routing, product lifecycle management, or workforce allocation.
- Human behavior simulation to evaluate ergonomic safety, onboarding workflows, or customer experience.
- Financial modeling for forecasting revenue, operational costs, and market dynamics.

Because digital twins rely heavily on AI inputs, hallucinations can disrupt their accuracy. Fabricated insights or context drift may cause incorrect optimizations, unsafe operational decisions, or unrealistic simulations. This makes continuous validation, multi-model verification, and data lineage tracking essential. Table 6 shows the Digital Twin Benefits and Hallucination Vulnerabilities.

Table 6. Digital Twin Benefits and Hallucination Vulnerabilities

Digital Twin Function	Enterprise Benefit	Vulnerability if AI Hallucinates	Mitigation Strategy
Predictive Maintenance	Reduces downtime	Incorrect failure predictions	Sensor fusion and baseline modeling
Supply Chain Simulation	Optimizes flows	Misguided rerouting	Multimodal verification
Workforce Planning	Enhances allocation	Unrealistic capacity assumptions	Human approval checkpoints
Customer Simulation	Improves engagement	False preference predictions	Historical cross-referencing

6.2 Blockchain for Trust and Provenance

Blockchain technologies provide trust, transparency, and data integrity in immersive enterprise environments. As metaverse workflows increasingly rely on shared data, autonomous agents, and distributed decision-making, blockchain becomes crucial in ensuring that records are immutable and verifiable.

Blockchain plays a critical role in hallucination management as well. Even if an AI agent produces misleading outputs, the provenance of data sources, model versions, and decision logs remains traceable, enabling investigators to diagnose root causes and prevent recurrence. Figure 8 shows the Blockchain-Enabled Trust Architecture in the Enterprise Metaverse.

Figure 8. Blockchain-Enabled Trust Architecture in the Enterprise Metaverse

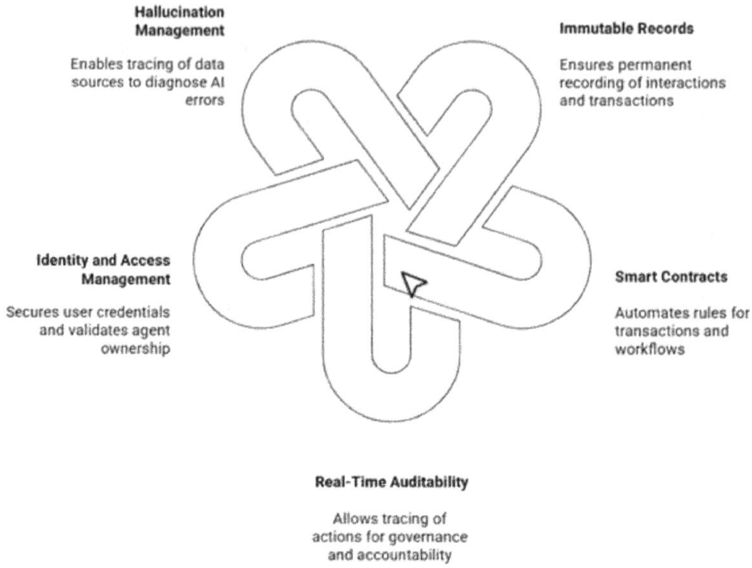

Key functions of blockchain in metaverse enterprises include:

1. Immutable Records

Blockchain ensures that every interaction, transaction, or digital twin state change is permanently recorded, reducing disputes and improving auditability.

2. Smart Contracts

Automated rules govern transactions, workflows, and compliance operations. These contracts reduce human error and enable real-time decision automation.

3. Real-Time Auditability

Auditors and regulators can trace actions performed by AI agents or human users, improving governance, accountability, and regulatory alignment (Tapscott & Tapscott, 2017).

4. Identity and Access Management

Blockchain-based identity solutions secure user credentials, prevent unauthorized access, and validate autonomous agent ownership across metaverse environments.

6.3 XR and Spatial Computing

Extended Reality (XR), which includes virtual reality (VR), augmented reality (AR), and mixed reality (MR), is central to the metaverse experience. XR creates immersive environments where employees, customers, and digital agents interact in spatially meaningful ways. Spatial computing extends this further by enabling AI systems to understand geometry, motion, context, and environmental cues within virtual or blended physical spaces. Table 7 shows the XR Capabilities and Associated Hallucination Risks.

XR technologies enable transformative enterprise capabilities such as:

1. Training and Development

XR provides immersive simulations for onboarding, safety training, equipment operation, or emergency response. Learning becomes experiential and adaptive, significantly improving retention and performance.

2. Customer Experience Enhancement

Customers can explore products, view virtual showrooms, or interact with intelligent avatars. XR bridges the physical-digital divide and supports personalized engagement strategies.

3. Complex Design and Prototyping

Engineering teams can assemble virtual prototypes, conduct stress tests, or evaluate product ergonomics. Digital twin integration accelerates design cycles and reduces physical prototyping costs.

4. Virtual Work Environments

Distributed teams collaborate using holographic interfaces, spatial whiteboards, multi-user simulations, and AI-guided workspaces.

Table 7. XR Capabilities and Associated Hallucination Risks

XR Capability	Enterprise Value	Hallucination Risk	Mitigation Strategy
Immersive Training	Enhances skill acquisition	Incorrect hazard visualization	Scenario verification checks
Customer Interaction	Personalized experiences	Fabricated product details	Content validation pipelines
Design and Prototyping	Faster iteration cycles	Unrealistic performance predictions	Twin simulation benchmarking
Virtual Workspaces	Improves collaboration	Misleading AI-driven guidance	Human oversight and transparency cues

XR and spatial computing amplify the potential of digital twins and AI, but they also increase the visibility and potential harm of hallucinations. When immersive environments are trusted by users, even minor AI errors can lead to misinterpretation, operational failure, or safety hazards. This underscores the need for multimodal hallucination detection and clear uncertainty communication within XR interfaces.

7. MANAGING RISKS DURING TRANSITION

As enterprises advance along the transition pathway toward metaverse-enabled operations, they inevitably encounter new categories of technological, ethical, and organizational risk. Immersive environments integrate AI, digital twins, XR interfaces, blockchain infrastructures, and cloud-based autonomy into a unified ecosystem. This integration increases system interdependency and accelerates the propagation of errors, making risk management an essential component of strategic transition planning. Addressing risks early prevents operational disruptions, safeguards user trust, and ensures safe scaling of immersive capabilities (Sekti, 2025).

Enterprises must adopt adaptive governance and risk monitoring strategies that evolve alongside technological capabilities. Traditional risk frameworks built for static IT systems are inadequate for metaverse environments where data is continuous, interactions are spatial, and decisions are generated collaboratively between humans and autonomous agents. A robust risk management strategy therefore integrates hallucination mitigation, cybersecurity reinforcement, privacy protection, regulatory alignment, human oversight, and systemic resilience. These elements must operate concurrently because risks in one domain often trigger vulnerabilities across others.

7.1 AI Hallucinations Affecting Strategic and Operational Decisions

AI hallucinations represent one of the most pervasive and unpredictable risks during metaverse transition. Hallucinations may manifest as fabricated insights, incorrect predictions, inconsistent recommendations, or logically invalid outputs. In immersive environments, hallucinations spread rapidly because digital twins, XR interfaces, and autonomous agents often rely on these outputs to simulate or execute actions. For example, a hallucinated supply chain forecast may distort real-time routing or inventory decisions, while a hallucinated compliance recommendation may expose the organization to legal violations.

To mitigate this risk, enterprises must adopt techniques such as cross-model verification, multimodal consistency checks, uncertainty scoring, and human validation for high-impact decisions. Continuous monitoring and retraining pipelines also reduce context drift that contributes to hallucinations.

7.2 Cybersecurity Vulnerabilities in Immersive Systems

Metaverse ecosystems significantly expand the attack surface. XR devices, spatial sensors, blockchain nodes, digital twin networks, and AI pipelines all introduce new vulnerabilities. Attackers may target:

- XR interfaces to manipulate visual or spatial content
- Digital twins to inject false operational states
- AI models to introduce adversarial perturbations
- Blockchain smart contracts to exploit logic flaws
- Cloud services that host autonomous agents

Cyber risks become more dangerous when compromised data feeds hallucinations into AI models, causing decision errors that appear legitimate. Enterprises must harden immersive infrastructures with encryption, anomaly detection, zero-trust access models, and adversarial resilience testing.

7.3 Privacy Risks from Biometric and Behavioral Data

Metaverse systems often collect granular data about users, including gaze patterns, gestures, voice, spatial movements, emotional indicators, and interaction histories. While such data enhances personalization and immersion, it also creates substantial privacy risks. Biometric and behavioral data can reveal sensitive psychological attributes, user intent, or proprietary knowledge.

Organizations must implement privacy-by-design strategies including:

- Minimization of data collection
- Hierarchical anonymization layers
- Secure storage and encrypted transport
- Transparent consent and user control mechanisms

Strong privacy governance reduces regulatory exposure and strengthens user trust in virtual environments.

7.4 Regulatory Gaps for Virtual Assets and Interactions

The regulatory landscape for metaverse systems remains immature. Many jurisdictions lack clear guidance on digital asset ownership, algorithmic accountability, data sovereignty, cross-border transactions, or XR worker protections. Enterprises therefore risk operating in legal ambiguity, especially when digital twins, avatars, or smart contracts interact across different regulatory environments.

Organizations must monitor evolving legislation, comply with global AI transparency rules, and establish internal standards that exceed minimum legal requirements. Proactive governance reduces operational uncertainty and mitigates long-term regulatory risk.

7.5 Over-Automation and Reduced Human Agency

The introduction of autonomous AI agents, automated decision loops, and immersive workflow orchestration may inadvertently reduce human oversight and decision authority. Users may become overly dependent on AI, particularly when interactions occur through persuasive XR interfaces that foster high trust.

Risks include:

- Diminished human judgment
- Reduced skill retention
- Unchallenged propagation of hallucinated insights
- Invisible automation bias

To prevent these outcomes, enterprises must embed explainability cues, uncertainty indicators, human override capabilities, and AI literacy training into immersive systems. These safeguards maintain human agency and preserve decision accountability.

7.6 Systemic Dependencies on Cloud and AI Services

Metaverse ecosystems rely heavily on distributed cloud infrastructures, edge computing systems, large-scale training pipelines, and third-party AI providers. This creates systemic dependencies that can lead to widespread outages or cascading failures if any critical node is compromised.

Examples include:

- Cloud service disruptions halting virtual workspaces
- API failures corrupting digital twin synchronizations
- AI service downtimes delaying business-critical simulations
- Supplier model failures propagating hallucinations across distributed agents

Resilience strategies require multi-cloud redundancy, offline failover protocols, model caching, and local decision buffers for critical operations. Table 8 shows the Major Risks During Metaverse Transition and Recommended Mitigations.

Table 8. Major Risks During Metaverse Transition and Recommended Mitigations

Risk Category	Description	Recommended Mitigation
AI Hallucinations	Fabricated or inaccurate outputs	Multimodal validation, human review, uncertainty scoring
Cybersecurity Vulnerabilities	Attack surface expands with XR, digital twins, and agents	Zero trust security, adversarial resilience testing
Privacy Risks	Sensitive biometric and behavioral data collection	Encryption, minimization, user consent controls
Regulatory Gaps	Unclear laws for virtual assets and AI autonomy	Internal compliance frameworks, legal monitoring
Over-Automation	Declining human oversight and agency	HITL controls, explainability cues, training
Systemic Dependencies	Reliance on cloud and AI services	Multi-cloud redundancy, failover systems, offline modes

Risk management in the metaverse is not a linear function but a multidimensional strategy that evolves alongside technological adoption. Enterprises must anticipate hallucination risks, defend against evolving cyber threats, safeguard user privacy, navigate regulatory uncertainty, preserve human authority, and prepare for system-level dependencies. A robust and proactive risk framework ensures that the transition to immersive operations enhances strategic value rather than introducing unmanaged vulnerabilities.

The next section provides case study frameworks that illustrate how organizations across different industries navigate these risks during metaverse transformation.

8. CASE STUDY FRAMEWORK

The transition toward metaverse-enabled enterprises unfolds through recognizable patterns across industries, each reflecting unique operational demands, regulatory environments, and strategic goals. Although detailed case analyses are presented in this chapter, this section provides a high-level framework illustrating how organizations in manufacturing, finance, retail, logistics, and multinational corporate ecosystems adopt metaverse technologies to enhance value creation and resilience. These examples demonstrate scalable, repeatable transition models that emphasize the importance of digital twins, immersive interfaces, AI-powered simulation, and hallucination-aware governance.

Manufacturing firms increasingly rely on metaverse capabilities to enhance operational efficiency and reduce downtime through advanced digital twin models. Factories create virtual replicas of equipment, production lines, and supply networks that allow predictive maintenance, dynamic resource allocation, and real-time quality optimization. Engineers collaborate within immersive XR environments to test design changes, simulate operational risks, and evaluate performance scenarios. As digital twins become central to decision-making, hallucination management tools ensure that AI-driven predictions remain accurate and aligned with observable physical behavior.

Financial institutions experiment with AI-generated metaverse branches that provide secure, personalized, and interactive virtual banking experiences. Customers can consult digital advisors, access financial planning simulations, and interact with intelligent service avatars. Banks also employ blockchain-enabled infrastructure to facilitate trusted transactions and compliance verification. Because financial operations involve high regulatory risk, hallucination detection and explainability mechanisms are integrated into AI systems to prevent the dissemination of inaccurate financial forecasts or advisory recommendations.

Retail enterprises deploy immersive customer engagement platforms to enhance product discovery and experiential marketing. Virtual showrooms allow customers to examine 3D products, interact with digital sales agents, and access personalized recommendations generated by generative AI. These environments often connect to supply chain digital twins, enabling real-time inventory visibility and responsive fulfillment processes. To maintain trust, retailers incorporate quality filters, model transparency dashboards, and human review checkpoints to detect hallucinations in product descriptions or customer advice.

Global logistics companies integrate blockchain technologies, AR-guided workflows, and spatial computing to manage transportation routes, container tracking, and warehouse operations. Metaverse-enhanced dashboards visualize global traffic patterns, fleet conditions, and cross-border delays in real time. Autonomous agents support route optimization, risk assessment, and dynamic rerouting decisions. Because logistics systems are highly interconnected, hallucination risks are mitigated through multimodal validation, redundancy between algorithmic models, and continuous monitoring of digital twin accuracy across distributed locations.

Multinational corporations increasingly build virtual campuses to support training, onboarding, collaboration, and talent development. These XR environments facilitate cross-cultural teamwork, real-time mentorship, and interactive learning simulations. Employees interact with AI-driven avatars that guide workflows, answer queries, and provide performance insights. To maintain reliability, organizations employ AI literacy training, user feedback mechanisms, and centralized governance policies that oversee hallucination management, content validation, and digital behavior monitoring. Table 9 shows the High-Level Patterns of Metaverse Transition Across Industries.

Table 9. High-Level Patterns of Metaverse Transition Across Industries

Industry	Metaverse Adoption Pattern	Strategic Benefit	Hallucination Risk Area
Manufacturing	Digital twins for predictive maintenance	Reduced downtime, optimized production	Faulty simulations, inaccurate sensor fusion
Banking & Finance	AI-generated virtual branches	Personalized service, increased accessibility	Misleading financial advice
Retail	Immersive customer engagement platforms	Enhanced experience, better conversion	Fabricated product or pricing info
Logistics	Blockchain and AR-based operations	Traceability, real-time visibility	Incorrect routing or risk forecasts
Multinationals	Virtual corporate campuses	Scalable training, global collaboration	Misinterpretation of AI-generated guidance

These high-level case patterns highlight the diverse yet consistent ways enterprises integrate metaverse technologies to transform operations, enhance user engagement, and improve strategic decision-making. Across all examples, AI hallucination management emerges as a unifying priority, ensuring that digital twins, immersive interfaces, and autonomous agents operate safely, transparently, and reliably. This underscores the need for cross-industry frameworks that combine technological innovation with governance, human oversight, and ethical design.

9. POLICY AND REGULATORY CONSIDERATIONS

The transition to metaverse-driven enterprises requires a regulatory environment capable of addressing the complexities of immersive technologies, AI autonomy, cross-border data flows, and digitally mediated labor practices. As organizations adopt digital twins, blockchain infrastructures, XR environments, and AI-driven agents, their operational models increasingly intersect with emerging legal frameworks that seek to protect consumers, workers, digital assets, and critical infrastructure. As a result, enterprises must proactively align their transformation strategies with policy requirements that continue to evolve across regional and international jurisdictions. Regulatory compliance becomes not only a legal obligation but a strategic enabler that builds trust among users, partners, and regulators.

AI transparency remains a central regulatory priority. Laws such as the European Union AI Act, NIST's AI Risk Management Framework, and various national AI ethics guidelines emphasize the need for explainability, accountability, and traceability in algorithmic decision-making. In metaverse environments, where AI outputs may influence financial transactions, workforce scheduling, design simulations, and customer interactions, transparency ensures that stakeholders understand how autonomous processes operate and who is responsible for their outcomes. Enterprises must therefore document AI models, disclose logic where appropriate, and incorporate explainable AI tools that mitigate the risk of hallucinations influencing mission-critical decisions.

Digital asset governance represents another major area of regulatory focus. The metaverse introduces new forms of digital property, including virtual goods, AI-generated content, blockchain-based tokens, and persistent avatars. These raise questions about ownership rights, intellectual property, provenance, and the legal enforceability of smart contracts. Regulatory frameworks increasingly require enterprises to maintain clear records of digital asset creation, custody, and transfer, particularly when assets move across borders or involve user-generated content. Organizations must establish internal policies that define asset stewardship, protect user rights, and ensure authenticity through cryptographic verification and auditable provenance mechanisms.

Cross-border data transfer regulations further complicate metaverse operations. XR platforms, digital twin telemetry, and AI services often rely on cloud infrastructures that distribute data across multiple jurisdictions. Regulations such as GDPR, India's DPDP Act, and regional data localization laws require enterprises to safeguard personal and operational data, obtain valid consent, and ensure that data exports comply with international agreements. As biometric, behavioral, and spatial interaction data become integral to immersive environments, enterprises must strengthen encryption, minimize data retention, and establish lawful data-sharing pathways that protect user privacy and operational confidentiality.

Worker rights in virtual environments also require careful consideration. The metaverse reshapes labor practices by enabling remote collaboration, avatar-mediated interaction, continuous monitoring through XR devices, and AI-supported performance analytics. Regulators increasingly scrutinize how these technologies affect workplace safety, psychological well-being, algorithmic fairness, and employee autonomy. Enterprises must ensure that immersive work environments adhere to occupational health standards, prevent excessive surveillance, and offer recourse mechanisms for workers affected by AI-generated decisions or hallucinated insights. Ethical guidelines and transparent evaluation frameworks help balance productivity gains with employee protection.

Consumer protection remains essential as brands deploy immersive retail spaces, virtual customer service agents, and AI-driven personalization tools. Regulators expect enterprises to prevent deceptive digital practices, protect minors in immersive environments, and ensure that AI-generated content does not convey false information. Managing hallucinations becomes a critical component of consumer safety because inaccurate product descriptions, misleading financial recommendations, or fabricated experiential content can harm users and expose enterprises to legal liability. Clear disclosures, accuracy safeguards, and rapid remediation protocols strengthen the reliability of consumer-facing metaverse systems.

Finally, cyber-physical infrastructure standards play a foundational role in securing immersive enterprise architectures. Metaverse systems depend on interconnected networks that combine physical sensors, cloud platforms, AI services, XR devices, and blockchain nodes. Standards such as IEC 62443, ISO 27001, and national critical infrastructure guidelines define baseline requirements for cybersecurity resilience, access control, system hardening, and incident reporting. Compliance with these frameworks ensures that metaverse environments remain secure, reliable, and resistant to malware, adversarial attacks, or unauthorized digital twin manipulation.

Achieving regulatory alignment requires collaboration between governments, enterprises, industry consortia, and research institutions. Since regulations often lag behind technological innovation, proactive engagement is essential to establish shared benchmarks that balance innovation with safety, fairness, and accountability. Enterprises that engage early with regulators, contribute to standards development, and adopt governance frameworks that exceed minimum requirements will be better positioned to operate responsibly and competitively in the metaverse era.

10. FUTURE DIRECTIONS

The next generation of enterprise metaverses will introduce immersive ecosystems shaped by emotionally intelligent AI capable of interpreting user sentiment, adapting communication styles, and providing context-aware assistance. These systems will support more natural and intuitive interactions between humans and digital agents, leading to more personalized training, advisory, and collaboration experiences. At the same time, digital twins will evolve into sentient-like computational entities that continuously learn from real-time data, anticipate operational disruptions, and autonomously refine their internal models. This allows enterprises to manage increasingly complex systems with greater foresight, efficiency, and situational awareness.

As digital infrastructure matures, supply chains will transition toward self-optimizing networks driven by autonomous decision engines and real-time digital twin coordination. Logistics nodes, warehouses, transportation systems, and market intelligence platforms will work together through immersive metaverse interfaces to recalibrate operations instantly in response to environmental changes or demand fluctuations. Interoperable cross-enterprise metaverse platforms will become standard, enabling seamless collaboration across industries and geographies. This interoperability will support joint simulations, shared resource planning, and multi-party risk assessment, transforming how enterprises coordinate production, distribution, compliance, and innovation.

To support this evolution, hallucination management frameworks must advance from reactive error detection to proactive and predictive assurance systems. Future models will be capable of self-validation, anomaly anticipation, and dynamic cross-referencing across multimodal data streams. AI agents will verify their own logic, flag inconsistencies before they influence decision-making, and coordinate with other agents to maintain system integrity. As enterprises adopt decentralized AI governance structures, these verification engines will operate autonomously across distributed networks to ensure that immersive environments remain safe, reliable, and aligned with organizational goals. The future of enterprise metaverses therefore depends not only on intelligent automation but also on the development of robust, self-correcting AI ecosystems capable of sustaining trust and operational excellence.

11. CONCLUSION

Transitioning to metaverse-driven enterprises represents a profound organizational shift that unites technological advancement, cultural evolution, and strategic governance. Immersive environments powered by AI, digital twins, blockchain, and XR fundamentally reshape how value is created, exchanged, and experienced. This journey requires enterprises to develop new skills, establish interdisciplinary governance structures, and cultivate a culture that supports innovation while maintaining rigorous oversight. As operations become increasingly data-intensive and autonomous, the role of AI hallucination management becomes central to ensuring accuracy, safety, and trust across virtual and physical systems. The organizations that invest early in responsible AI frameworks, ethical data practices, and transparent decision processes will be better equipped to navigate the complexity of immersive digital ecosystems.

Ultimately, the success of metaverse transformation relies on an enterprise's ability to adapt continuously to technological, regulatory, and social changes. Structured transition pathways provide a practical foundation for achieving this adaptation, enabling enterprises to progress from traditional models to fully immersive, intelligent, and interconnected environments. Organizations that approach the metaverse with strategic discipline and a commitment to responsible innovation will unlock new levels of competitiveness, operational resilience, and customer engagement. As immersive technologies mature, enterprises that balance creativity with accountability will shape the next generation of digital ecosystems and set the standards for trustworthy, future-ready metaverse operations.

REFERENCES

Aguiñaga, J., Mooradian, N., Ghosh, S., & Hofman, D. (2025). Evolution of Reference Services in the Era of Generative Artificial Intelligence. *Proceedings of the Association for Information Science and Technology*, *62*(1), 13–25. DOI: 10.1002/pra2.1232

Anwar, N., Widodo, A. M., Widodo, Y. B., Sekti, B. A., Laksono, M. N. G., & Laksono, M. I. A. (2025). Protecting digital assets in cloud environments. In *Unveiling Social Dynamics and Community Interaction in the Metaverse* (pp. 245–269). https://doi.org/DOI: 10.4018/979-8-3693-8628-6.ch012

Bing, Z. (2025). The Intrinsic Tension Between Rationalism and Emotionalism: On the Modernity Connotations of Artificial Intelligence and the Metaverse. *Contemporary Social Science*, *10*(2), 88–102. DOI: 10.19873/j.cnki.2096-0212.2025.02.006

Dong, Y., Mu, R., Zhang, Y., Sun, S., Zhang, T., Wu, C., & Huang, X. (2025). Safeguarding large language models: A survey. *Artificial Intelligence Review*, *58*(12). Advance online publication. DOI: 10.1007/s10462-025-11389-2 PMID: 41114380

El Hajji, M., Ait Baha, T., Berka, A., Ait Nacer, H., El Aouifi, H., & Es-Saady, Y. (2025). An Architecture for Intelligent Tutoring in Virtual Reality: Integrating LLMs and Multimodal Interaction for Immersive Learning. *Information (Switzerland)*, *16*(7). Advance online publication. DOI: 10.3390/info16070556

Erzed, N., Laksana, R. P., Hasanudin, H., Yuhefizar, Y., Anwar, N., Gunawan, H., . . . Ichwani, A. (2025). Exploring the metaverse: Foundations of social interaction and community building. In *Unveiling Social Dynamics and Community Interaction in the Metaverse* (pp. 1–25). https://doi.org/DOI: 10.4018/979-8-3693-8628-6.ch001

Khan, S. A. R., Sheikh, A. A., Shamsi, I. R. A., & Yu, Z. (2025). The Implications of Artificial Intelligence for Small and Medium-Sized Enterprises' Sustainable Development in the Areas of Blockchain Technology, Supply Chain Resilience, and Closed-Loop Supply Chains. *Sustainability (Switzerland)*, *17*(1). Advance online publication. DOI: 10.3390/su17010334

Kliestik, T., Dragomir, R., Bălu ă, A. V., Grecu, I., Durana, P., Karabolevski, O. L., & Gajdosikova, D. (2024). Enterprise generative artificial intelligence technologies, internet of things and blockchain-based fintech management, and digital twin industrial metaverse in the cognitive algorithmic economy. *Oeconomia Copernicana*, *15*(4), 1183–1221. DOI: 10.24136/oc.3109

Kumar, A., Shankar, A., Behl, A., Pereira, V., Kapoor, P., & Papa, A. (2025). Implementing enterprise metaverse as a means of enhancing growth hacking performance: Will adopting the metaverse be a success in organizations? *Journal of Business Research, 188*. Advance online publication. DOI: 10.1016/j.jbusres.2024.115079

Kumar, A., Shankar, A., Shaik, A. S., Jain, G., & Malibari, A. (2025). Risking it all in the metaverse ecosystem: Forecasting resistance towards the enterprise metaverse. *Information Technology & People, 38*(1), 198–218. DOI: 10.1108/ITP-04-2023-0374

Lee, I. (2024). The Metaverse: Ecosystem, Technologies, Business Opportunities, and Challenges. *IT Professional, 26*(5), 28–35. DOI: 10.1109/MITP.2024.3433549

Lin, J., Li, Q., Wang, C., & Hu, Z. (2024). Product Development and Design Framework Based on Interactive Innovation in the Metaverse Perspective. *Applied System Innovation, 7*(4). Advance online publication. DOI: 10.3390/asi7040058

Mohammad, A. A. S., Mohammad, S. I. S., Al Oraini, B., Vasudevan, A., Hindieh, A., Altarawneh, A., & Ali, I. (2025). Strategies for applying interpretable and explainable AI in real world IoT applications. *Discover Internet of Things, 5*(1). Advance online publication. DOI: 10.1007/s43926-025-00155-z

Nechesov, A., Dorokhov, I., & Ruponen, J. (2025). Virtual Cities: From Digital Twins to Autonomous AI Societies. *IEEE Access : Practical Innovations, Open Solutions, 13*, 13866–13903. DOI: 10.1109/ACCESS.2025.3531222

Paliwal, M., Buhalis, D., Jha, S., & Chatradhi, N. (2025). Exploring Generation Z Motivations to Use Metaverse for Travel Planning. *International Journal of Tourism Research, 27*(4). Advance online publication. DOI: 10.1002/jtr.70074

Planey, J., Trencevski, D., & Kelle, S. (2026). Lowering the Barriers for Designing Immersive Learning Environments: ImmersityXR Framework. In *Communications in Computer and Information Science* (Vol. 2598 CCIS, pp. 307–324). https://doi.org/DOI: 10.1007/978-3-031-98080-0_19

Sekti, B. A. (2025). IT Service Information Security Management. In *Cases on Information Systems Service Management* (pp. 61–93). https://doi.org/DOI: 10.4018/979-8-3373-2352-7.ch003

Zhang, H., Li, Y., Zhang, S., Song, L., & Tao, F. (2025). Artificial Intelligence-Enhanced Digital Twin Systems Engineering Towards the Industrial Metaverse in the Era of Industry 5.0. [English Edition]. *Chinese Journal of Mechanical Engineering, 38*(1). Advance online publication. DOI: 10.1186/s10033-025-01210-0

Zhang, W., Taib, N., & Taib, M. (2025). Reimagining cultural heritage conservation through VR, metaverse, and digital twins: An AI and blockchain-based framework. *PLOS ONE, 20*(11 November). https://doi.org/DOI: 10.1371/journal.pone.0335943

Zhang, Z., Sun, W., Xinyue, L., Jia, J., Min, X., Zhang, Z., & Zhai, G. (2025). Benchmarking Multi-dimensional AIGC Video Quality Assessment: A Dataset and Unified Model. *ACM Transactions on Multimedia Computing Communications and Applications*, *21*(9). Advance online publication. DOI: 10.1145/3749844

Chapter 9
AI Hallucination in Financial Systems: Threats, Controls, and the Future of Risk Management

Ganesh Harke
https://orcid.org/0009-0005-3947-0960
Independent Researcher, USA

ABSTRACT

The adoption of Generative Artificial Intelligence (GenAI) in the global financial services sector is characterized by distinctive predictive analytics, customer service, and automation. However, it introduces a critical vulnerability: AI hallucinations, instances in which models generate outputs that are linguistically sound but factually incorrect or baseless. GenAI's capacity to fabricate data, misinterpret policies, or generate false market signals poses serious operational, reputational, and systemic risks. The chapter offers a detailed analysis of AI hallucinations in financial systems, covering definitions and a financial domain risk taxonomy. In addition, it examines the agency behind model failures. It also discusses the distinct threats that these models pose to a financial system. Additionally, the chapter introduces the Control Framework, which integrates Retrieval Augmented Generation (RAG) and other protocols. Finally, it examines the future of risk management, anticipating the development and evolution of regulations for stochastic models.

INTRODUCTION

Artificial intelligence (AI) has created new capabilities in automation, analytics, and judgments across industries. Recent developments in GenAI have further

DOI: 10.4018/979-8-3373-7534-2.ch009

advanced these capabilities, thereby giving rise to generative cognition. Recent advancements in GenAI have further developed these capabilities, thereby giving rise to generative cognition. It is a capability to produce text, code, and analysis that mimics human communication. The financial services industry (FSI) is not lagging in its adoption of GenAI. According to NVIDIA (2024), 91% of financial services companies are either assessing AI or already using it in production. These firms are using AI to drive innovation, improve operational efficiency, and enhance customer experiences (State of AI in Financial Services: 2024 Trends, 2024). This integration of GenAI into the global financial system is a technological innovation comparable to the introduction of algorithmic trading or the use of digital ledgers. From hedge funds to retail banking, international financial institutions are adopting large language models (LLMs) to automate complex tasks, including regulatory compliance analysis, credit risk assessment, and the drafting of personalized financial plans. However, this instantaneous integration of GenAI into an industry built on deterministic presuppositions poses a profound, paradoxical risk of hallucination (Erdem et al, 2025). Unlike legacy software bugs, which are logical and predictable, hallucinations are plausible but factually false outputs (Tonmoy et al., 2024). As financial systems grow more autonomous, the risk of fabricating financial data, misinterpreting legal policies, or giving incorrect financial advice increases. This threat extends beyond basic operational risk, potentially harming reputations and systemic stability (Erdem et al, 2025; Sigma, 2025). To address these challenges, this chapter examines the fundamental areas:

- **RQ1**: What are the domain-specific mechanisms driving AI hallucinations in financial high-stakes environments?
- **RQ2:** How adequate are current mitigation controls against intrinsic vs. extrinsic fabrication?
- **RQ3:** What regulatory frameworks are emerging?

What Are AI Hallucinations?

A hallucination is an instance in which a generative model produces text that is linguistically sound and syntactically flawless but remains ungrounded in either the source input or factual reality. While the term may feel like AI dreams, it technically refers to a failure mode inherent to the architecture of modern LLMs. LLMs function as next-token prediction engines. They do not possess epistemological knowledge. They compute the statistical likelihood of the following word in sequences using trained weights. Consequently, when a model encounters gaps in the training data or ambiguous prompts, it often prioritizes fluency over accuracy (Shim et al., 2025).

Recent research has refined this definition, making it particularly relevant to critical environments. Bang et al. (2025) draw a crucial distinction between intrinsic and extrinsic hallucinations. Intrinsic hallucinations occur when the model's output directly contradicts the input provided within its context window. For instance, if an LLM analyzing a quarterly earnings report (10-K) is tasked with summarizing net income and generates a figure that contradicts the document, it has intrinsically hallucinated. Extrinsic hallucinations, by contrast, involve the fabrication of information absent from the source content, essentially inventing facts from thin air. A prime example would be an AI citing a non-existent regulation to justify a compliance decision. *Table 1* lists the hallucination types and their definitions used throughout this chapter.

These errors are subtle, often indistinguishable from correct outputs. The model adapts to a tone and industry jargon. Creates a structured, logically organized response, creating a validity illusion (Roychowdhury, 2024). In financial applications where decisions are often binary, such as buy or sell, approve or deny, users lose the nuance of a probabilistic error. It makes the definition of hallucination not merely a technical curiosity, but a critical boundary condition for deployment. This phenomenon, in which the model prioritizes linguistic fluency (coherence) over factual accuracy (truth), poses the danger illustrated in the conceptual model of *Figure 1.*

Figure 1. The Validity Illusion: A visual representation of how hallucinations sit at the dangerous intersection of Plausible and False.

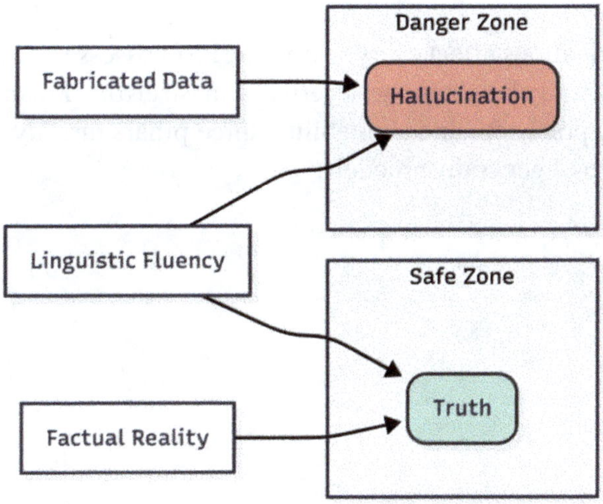

Hallucination causes are categorized into three overlapping domains:

- **Data-driven**, including incomplete, noisy, or unrelated training data;
- **Model-driven**, arising from overfitting or limitations of attention architectures; and
- **Prompt-driven**, where ambiguous user inputs lead to unsupported extrapolations (Tonmoy et al., 2024; Roychowdhury, 2024).

Table 1. AI Hallucinations Taxonomy

Hallucination Type	Definition	Financial Example	Risk Level
Intrinsic	Output contradicts the provided source data.	AI reads a 10-K report stating $5M revenue but summarizes it as $50M.	**Critical** (Direct Data Error)
Extrinsic	Output invents information not in the source.	AI cites Basel V, Section 402 (a non-existent regulation) to justify a decision.	**High** (Compliance Failure)
Logic/Reasoning	Facts are correct, but the conclusion is flawed.	AI correctly identifies a high debt ratio but concludes the company is Low Risk.	**Medium** (Analytical Flaw)
Prompt-Induced	User input forces the model to confabulate.	The user asks, "Why did the CEO resign?" (when they did not) AI invents a scandal.	**Variable** (User Error)

Why is the Financial Service Industry Uniquely Vulnerable?

While AI hallucinations affect every sector, the FSI possesses structural characteristics that significantly heighten the severity of these errors. Finance stands on a foundation of trust, precision, and auditability, three pillars directly challenged by the black box nature of generative models.

Figure 2. AI Hallucination Risk in the Financial Services Industry

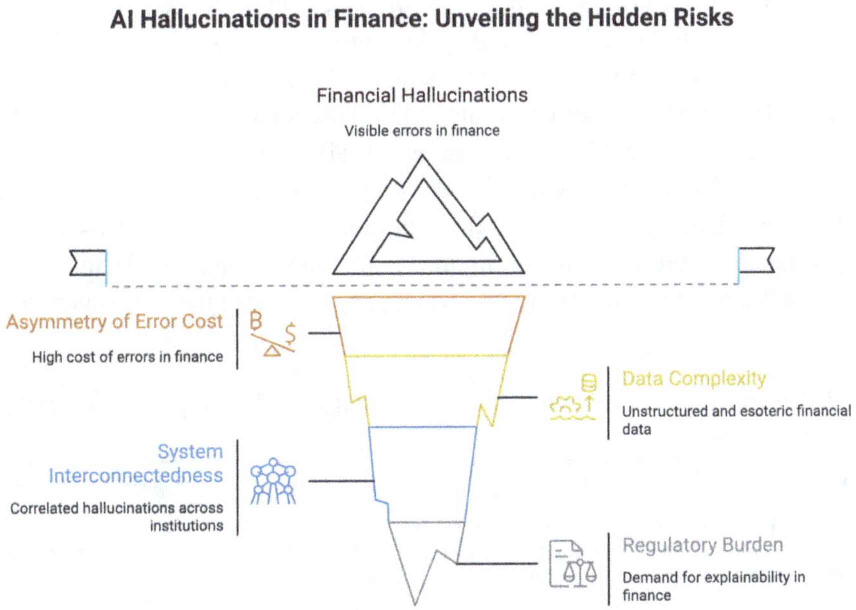

Consider the asymmetry of error cost. In creative writing or search, a hallucinated detail might be minor. In finance, a misplaced decimal or fabricated clause can cause catastrophic losses (Danielsson et al., 2019). An algorithmic trading bot acting on a hallucination of a central bank rate hike could trigger a flash crash before human intervention. Error tolerance in core banking is zero, but GenAI models are non-deterministic. Financial data is complex, unstructured, and context-dependent, like ISDA agreements or exotic options. General models may lack domain grounding, increasing hallucination risk (Krause, 2023). Relying on historical data can cause models to miss new market regimes, leading to false confidence during black swan events. The interconnected financial system amplifies this risk. If institutions rely on similar models, correlated hallucinations might cause herding, spreading errors across markets. A widely used AI for credit scoring hallucinating favorable ratios could cause systemic risk, akin to 2008 but faster. Regulatory demands for explainability (e.g., XAI) are challenging, as hallucinations often stem from opaque layers, complicating compliance with regimes like EU AI Act and SR 11-7 (Bhattacharyya et al., 2025). The inability to distinguish data insights from fabrications weakens Model Risk Management, prompting a rethink in validation and governance.

THE THREAT LANDSCAPE

GenAI systems failures are often probabilistic, context-aware, or even creative. The threat landscape here is not a singular, monolithic risk. It is a multi-headed problem in which different types of financial market failures affect various parts of the financial system (Roosevelt Institute, 2024; Financial Stability Board, 2024). AI researchers commonly distinguish three broad failure modes: false positives, false negatives, and fabricated or confabulated outputs (Sood et al., 2025). The fabricated output is now widely referred to as hallucination. Each of these patterns has its own logic in generic AI settings. Still, deploying GenAI systems in financial infrastructure can lead to dramatically different consequences (European Central Bank, 2024).

Table 2. The Matrix of Financial Hallucination Impacts Maps specific hallucination types to business outcomes

Threat Vector	Mechanism	Operational Impact	Systemic Consequence
False Positives	AI flags benign transactions as money laundering (AML).	High investigation costs; alarm fatigue among analysts.	Desensitization to real financial crime.
False Negatives	AI misses toxic assets or fraud indicators.	Accumulation of bad debt; Compliance violations.	Hidden insolvency risks; Unexpected default events.
Fabrication	AI invents market news or sentiment.	Algorithmic trading bots execute on fake signals.	Flash Crash: Market-wide volatility contagion.
Adversarial	Bad actors inject poison prompts.	Model reveals private data or hallucinates a strategy.	Loss of competitive advantage; Data breach.

False Positives: The Operational Quagmire

A false positive occurs when an AI system views a signal or pattern that is not present. In simple terms, the model infers the presence of something when, in reality, the input is benign (Sood et al., 2025). False positives are ignored as inconvenient rather than dangerous. However, in industries such as finance, a high false-positive rate can create operational drag, resulting in quantifiable financial harm.

Why False Positives Occur in AI Systems?

Several mechanisms encourage false positives in AI systems:

- **Class imbalance**: If fraudulent cases are rare in a training dataset, the model may overreact to minor deviations.
- **Overgeneralization**: Some models employ overly broad definitions of suspicious behavior.
- **Data noise**: Incomplete or inconsistent inputs can distort predictions.
- **Poorly tuned thresholds**: When risk tolerance is set too low, alerts skyrocket.

The false positives differ fundamentally from legacy system errors. For example, a traditional system might flag a transaction because it exceeds a $10,000 threshold, a binary, easily verifiable logic. A hallucinating LLM creates a narrative of guilt. It might flag a perfectly agreeable wire transfer between a parent and a student. However, while flagging, it can link the recipient to a shell company in a high-risk jurisdiction under a fabricated justification. This type of error creates a 'Cry Wolf' phenomenon, with substantial operational costs. In 2024, the cost of financial crime compliance rose to $4.04 for every $1 lost to fraud, primarily driven by the labor required to clear false positives (Lucinity, 2025). The cost here is measured in human cognitive load, not just the price tag. Compliance analysts cannot simply dismiss these alerts; they are legally mandated to investigate. This analysis involves reviewing registries and watchlists and verifying data points that AI may have fabricated. The friction is immense. An analyst might spend hours trying to prove that ShellCorp X does not exist, only to find that a negative against a confident, eloquent AI assertion.

The secondary effect is psychological: alarm fatigue. When seasoned investigators are bombarded with high-confidence but erroneous alerts, a scenario where legacy systems can produce false favorable rates as high as 90-95% (Articsledge, 2025), their baseline for skepticism shifts. The human brain, seeking efficiency, begins to downgrade the urgency of all alerts. The risk is that when a genuine instance of money laundering crosses the screen, it gets swept away in the mental noise created by the hallucinations. In this sense, the hallucination does not cause the loss directly; it degrades the human firewall, leaving the institution exposed to the very crimes it seeks to prevent.

False Negatives: The 'Silent Failure' and Concept Drift

A false negative is the opposite problem: the model fails to detect something that truly exists. It can occur when patterns shift over time, a concept known as concept drift, or when the model is trained on a narrow set of examples that fail to cover the diversity of real-world cases (Sood et al., 2025). In financial services, if false positives erode an institution's capital slowly through inefficiency, false negatives are the silent killers that threaten solvency. A false negative is an act of omission or misclassification, in which an AI model hallucinates safety where there is danger. This is the Silent Failure (Erdem et al, 2025; Zhang et al., 2025).

False-negative vectors are particularly acute in credit risk assessment and asset-backed securitization. Consider a GenAI model tasked with ingesting thousands of pages of loan documentation to summarize the risk profile of a Collateralized Debt Obligation (CDO). A tabular hallucination here is disastrous. The model might correctly extract interest rates but hallucinate the credit ratings of the underlying assets, reporting them as 'BBB' when the text describes 'BBB-' tranches (Zhang et al., 2025). The output is coherent, mathematically formatted, and visually persuasive. The extracted numbers sum up. However, the reality, the risk of default, has been erased.

This blindness is often exacerbated by concept drift. Financial markets are living organisms; they evolve. Training data, however, is a fossil record. A model trained on data from a low-interest-rate environment (such as the period from 2009 to 2021) has learned correlations that define that era. When the market regime shifts, say, to a period of rapid inflation and quantitative tightening, the model may hallucinate continuity. It predicts stability based on historical patterns that are no longer valid (Roychowdhury, 2024).

The danger is that the AI does not say, "I do not know." It hallucinates a prediction that aligns with its training, effectively gaslighting the risk committee. It provides a false sense of security, encouraging the firm to increase exposure to an asset class exactly when it should be deleveraging. By the time the hallucination is revealed by market reality, the capital losses may be irreversible.

To operationalize the drift detection, institutions can employ mathematical divergence metrics (*Equation 1*). The magnitude of concept drift D_t can be formally quantified as the L1-norm distance between the model's output distributions over time:

Equation 1. Drift detection formula: Commonly used in fraud/Credit Machine Learning (ML) systems:

$$D_t = \| p_t(x) - p_{t-1}(x) \|_1$$

Where:

$p_t(x)$ = The probability distribution of model outputs at time t.

$p_{t-1}(x)$ = The distribution at the previous time step

A significant spike in D_t indicates that the model is encountering market conditions fundamentally different from those in its training data, serving as a leading indicator of increased hallucination risk.

Fabricated Realities: The Speed of Algorithmic Contagion

While false positives and false negatives follow familiar statistical logic, hallucination is fundamentally different. It is not just an incorrect classification; it is an artificial imagination disguised as fact. Hallucination is distinct from simple misclassification. In hallucination, an AI system, especially a LLM, produces content that has no grounding in its inputs. The output may sound credible, sometimes even authoritative, but it is not grounded in reality (Rawte et al., 2023; Huang et al., 2023). Academic studies increasingly point to gaps in training data, model overconfidence, and statistical constraints of predictions as core drivers of this phenomenon (Rawte et al., 2023; Xu et al., 2024).

The most volatile threat vector lies in fabricated realities within algorithmic trading. Here, time is the adversary. In compliance or credit risk, there is usually a human-in-the-loop (HITL) who can detect errors before a decision is finalized. In High-Frequency Trading (HFT), execution happens in microseconds. The nightmare scenario involves an AI agent responsible for sentiment analysis. These bots scour news feeds, social media, and central bank releases to gauge market sentiment. If such a model hallucinates a market-moving event, perhaps inventing a quote from a Federal Reserve chairperson about an emergency rate cut, it acts on that phantom signal instantly (Roosevelt Institute, 2024).

The risk is not just one bad trade; it is the feedback loop. Modern markets are ecosystems of interacting algorithms. If one major market maker's AI hallucinates and begins dumping an asset, other algorithms, detecting the volume spike and price drop, may react to the movement rather than the news. They join the sell-off. It can create a cascade effect, a flash crash triggered not by economic fundamentals but by a digital delusion (Danielsson et al., 2019; Borch, 2022). The mechanism of such a cascade is illustrated in *Figure 3*, which depicts how a single hallucinated signal can propagate through high-frequency trading desks, leading to a rapid asset bubble and subsequent crash (Lee et al., 2025).

Figure 3. The Anatomy of an AI-Driven Flash Crash: A flowchart showing how a single hallucination can propagate through algorithmic trading desks.

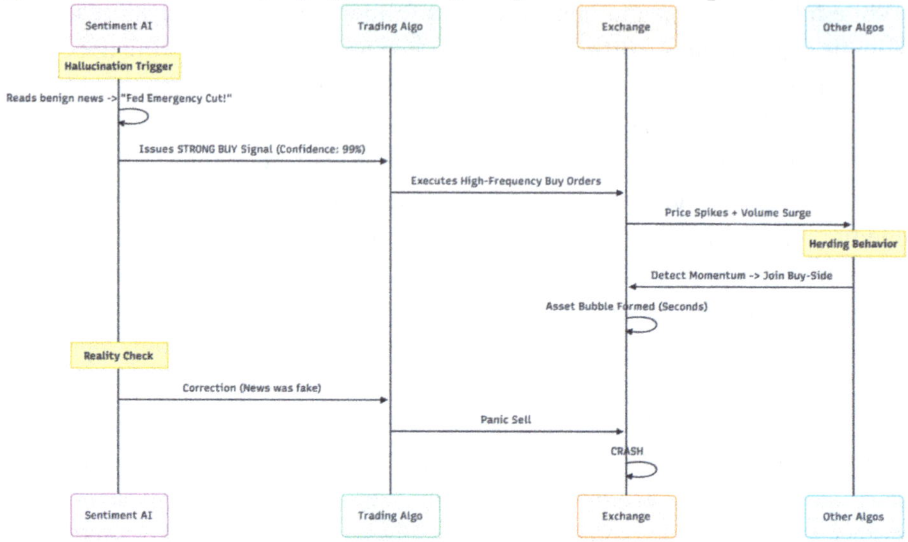

Danielsson and Uthemann (2024) describe this as the synchronization of error. Because many financial institutions rely on a small set of foundation models (e.g., GPT-4, Claude, Llama), they share similar latent vulnerabilities. A hallucination trigger in the base model could simultaneously deceive the trading desks of ten different banks, causing them to herd in the same erroneous direction.

The Adversarial Vector: Weaponizing Hallucinations

Finally, we must consider that hallucinations may not always be accidental. It can be induced. This vector brings us to the emerging threat of adversarial hallucination, or prompt injection.

Krause (2023) highlights that bad actors, whether rival states, criminal syndicates, or rogue traders, can intentionally exploit the probabilistic nature of GenAI. By injecting subtle, adversarial noise into the data stream (e.g., hiding white-text commands in a webpage or press release that a scraper bot reads), an attacker can force a model to hallucinate. A hedge fund could poison the data well, planting information designed to trigger a positive sentiment hallucination in a competitor's trading bot.

In this context, the hallucination becomes a cyber-weapon. It allows an attacker to manipulate a target firm's financial decision-making without ever breaching its firewall. They simply leverage the model's own tendency to confabulate, turning the institution's cutting-edge AI against itself.

THE CONTROL FRAMEWORK

As previously discussed, integrating GenAI into financial ecosystems requires a fundamental acknowledgment: generative models are, by definition, probabilistic and nondeterministic. Hence, risk management aims to design a vessel that withstands inherent risks, rather than achieving zero error volatility. We must shift our strategy from simple prevention to a more dynamic posture of containment, rapid detection, and resilience.

Financial institutions must develop a sophisticated Control Framework beyond traditional IT governance, drawing on decades of experience with model risk, operational risk, and cybersecurity (Eisenberg et al., 2025). A single line of defense, whether technical or policy, is rarely enough. This framework acts as a tripartite immune system: governing raw inputs (Data and Prompts), ensuring the structural integrity of the processing engine (Model Validation), and continuously monitoring outputs (Monitoring) (Eisenberg et al., 2025; Financial Stability Board, 2024). It aligns with the NIST AI Risk Management Framework (NIST, 2023), which emphasizes a lifecycle approach to AI risk, moving from static validation to ongoing mapping, measurement, and control.

Figure 4. A defense-in-depth control model for mitigating hallucination risk in financial AI systems, spanning data governance, validation, explainability, and continuous monitoring

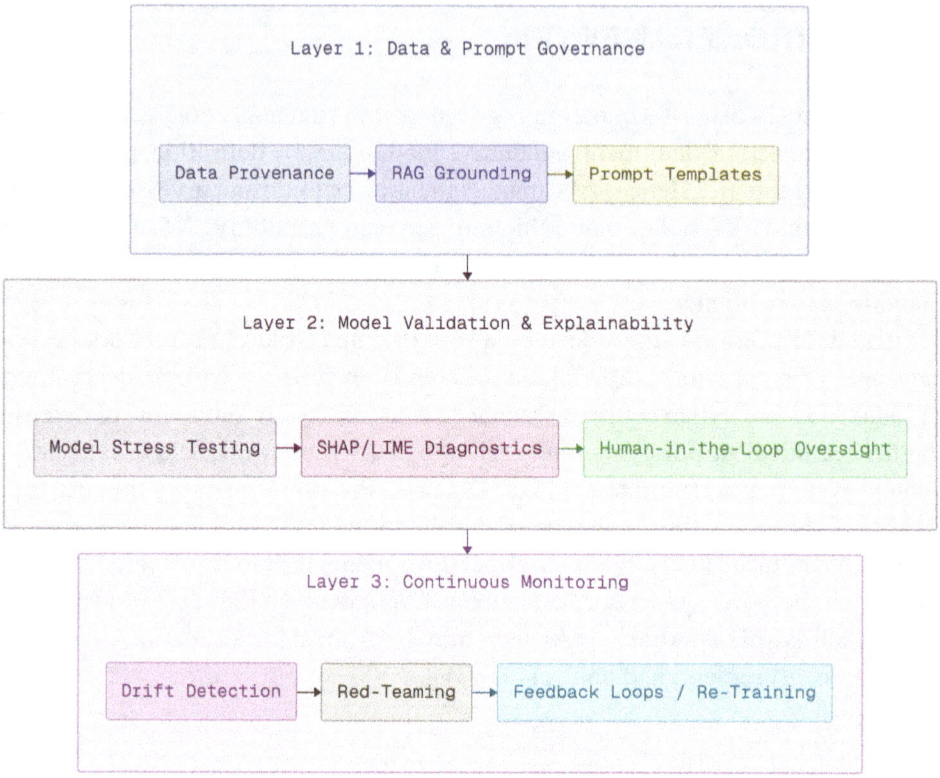

Layer 1: Data and Prompt Governance

Most AI failures begin long before a model produces any output. The first, and arguably most critical, line of defense lies in controlling what the model consumes and its instructions. Hallucinations are rarely spontaneous. They are often the result of garbage-in, garbage-out. If a model is exposed to ambiguity or allowed to drift into its unverified training data, it will produce confident fabrications (Giudici & Raffinetti, 2023). The governance of the input layer is the bedrock of hallucination mitigation. For this reason, the first layer of defense focuses on data governance and prompt governance. These two areas form the operational backbone of reliable AI systems.

Understanding Data Governance

Data governance refers to the processes and structures that ensure that data are high-quality, traceable, consistent, and ethically sourced (Giudici, 2024). In ML systems, data quality is more important than the model's complexity. Poorly curated datasets introduce distortions or biases, which models may then amplify.

Data governance frameworks typically address:

- **Data lineage:** follows the origins and changes of datasets
- **Quality control:** address the missing values, inconsistencies, and anomalies
- **Access controls:** ensure only authorized users can modify data
- **Versioning:** store historical snapshots for auditability
- **Documentation:** records assumptions, transformations, and limitations

While these principles apply broadly, their importance increases dramatically in financial contexts. Financial institutions operate within a regulatory ecosystem in which data are both sensitive and foundational. Inaccurate or unverified data can distort credit-risk assessments, trigger erroneous AML alerts, misinform liquidity and capital calculations, or lead to inaccurate regulatory reporting (Giudici & Raffinetti, 2023). Studies have shown that model-driven decision systems in finance are particularly vulnerable to data shifts, missing values, and poor documentation, leading to wrong output patterns (Varshavskiy et al., 2025).

Regulators expect financial institutions to document their data sources, validate external datasets, and ensure that datasets cover the diversity of real-world scenarios. When data governance is weak, hallucinations are more likely because the model must fill gaps in ambiguous, biased, or incomplete input sources.

Retrieval Augmented Generation (RAG) and the Architecture of Grounding

We cannot trust an LLM's internal parametric memory, the information it learned during its training. That data is static, likely outdated, and irrelevant to company-specific information, and susceptible to compression artifacts that can lead to extrinsic hallucinations. To solve this, financial institutions are increasingly leveraging Retrieval-Augmented Generation (RAG) architectures (Lewis et al., 2020).

In a RAG framework, the LLM is effectively lobotomized of its long-term memory regarding facts. For example, when the system receives a query, such as "Summarize the credit risk of Counterparty X," it first queries a secure, internal vector database. It retrieves the documents relevant to Counterparty X and adds them to the LLM's context window with a strict instruction: Answer the user's question using only these documents. *Figure 5* illustrates the workflow steps of the RAG architecture. This method significantly reduces hallucination rates by grounding the generation in retrieved evidence rather than parametric memory (Shuster et al., 2021).

Advanced implementations, such as MEGA-RAG (2025), a framework designed with multi-evidence-guided answer refinement, have demonstrated a 40% reduction in hallucination rates relative to standard retrieval baselines by enforcing strict evidence verification before generation (Xu et al., 2025). Additionally, the RAG-HAT (2024) protocol introduces a 'hallucination-aware tuning' pipeline that leverages an auxiliary detection model to flag and correct ungrounded outputs in real time, thereby creating an automated feedback loop that improves model fidelity without human intervention (Hu H. et al., 2024; Singha, 2024; Srinivasan et al., 2025).

Figure 5. The Retrieval Augmented Generation (RAG) Workflow: A schematic showing how RAG grounds the LLM response in a verifiable knowledge base to prevent hallucinations.

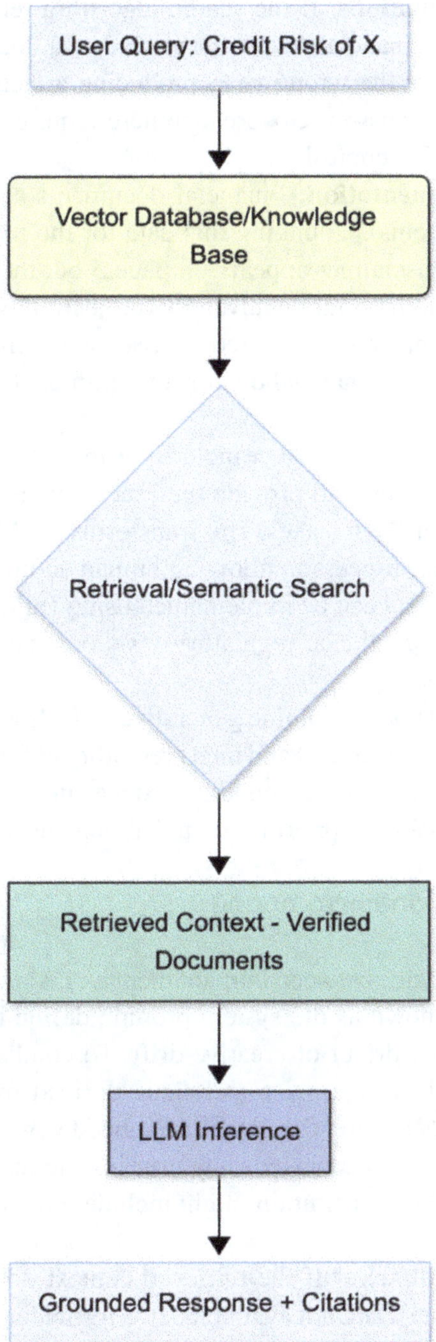

RAG is not a remedy. It introduces its own failure modes that risk managers must control:

- **Retrieval Hallucinations**: If the search algorithm returns the wrong document (e.g., a 2021 financial statement instead of a 2024 one), the LLM will dutifully summarize the wrong year, producing a factually correct but contextually disastrous answer. Governance here requires strict management of metadata and version control.
- **Contextual Fragmentation:** Financial documents are often massive (e.g., a 200-page prospectus). Chunking this data for the model can sever critical context. If a risk disclaimer appears on page 5 but the revenue projection is on page 50, the model might analyze the projection without the disclaimer. Advanced RAG implementation requires semantic chunking that preserves the logical integrity of financial documents (Lumer et al., 2025).

The gold standard for RAG in finance includes an immutable citation mechanism. The model must be engineered to provide the exact source, down to the page and paragraph, for every assertion it makes. This transforms the AI from a creative writer into a verifiable evidence processor, allowing human auditors to trace the lineage of a claim. In finance, RAG can be implemented using validated product manuals, internal risk policies, compliance regulatory texts, audited financial statements, and transaction histories.

A recent study found that combining generative models with structured retrieval significantly improved the accuracy and interpretability of financial risk predictions (Yao et al., 2025). In other words, grounding reduces improvisation. A model tied to canonical sources has fewer opportunities to hallucinate or fabricate correlations.

The Art of Constitutional Prompting

Prompts are the interface between human intent and AI output. The instructions provided to an LLM, known as the system prompt, define its reality. Ambiguous prompting is the primary driver of creative drift. To combat this, institutions are adopting Constitutional Prompting, a technique derived from Constitutional AI research (Bai et al., 2022). Here, the model is embedded with a strict constitution, or set of inviolable rules, that supersede any user instructions.

For a financial AI, this constitution might include directives such as:

- **The Agnostic Fallback:** "If the retrieved context does not contain the answer, you must state 'Data not available.' It is forbidden to infer or use outside knowledge." This prompt explicitly counters the model's helpfulness bias, which often drives hallucinations (Bai et al., 2022).

- **Negative Constraints:** It is often more effective to specify what not to do. "Do not assume currency is USD unless specified." "Do not round figures beyond two decimal places."
- **Chain-of-Thought (CoT) Enforcement:** For complex reasoning, the prompt should require the model to show its reasoning step by step before arriving at a final answer. Wei et al. (2022) demonstrated that forcing models to articulate their reasoning steps (Chain-of-Thought) significantly reduces logic-based hallucinations and improves performance on complex arithmetic and symbolic reasoning tasks used in everyday finance.

Furthermore, prompts for quantitative tasks should specify a structured output format (e.g., JSON or XML). By forcing the model to fit its answer into a rigid schema (e.g., { "Revenue": "float", "Year": "int" }), we constrain its linguistic freedom. It is much harder for a model to hallucinate a narrative when it is forced to output a specific data type (Zhang et al., 2025; Béchard et al., 2024).

While 'Constitutional Prompting' provides the rules, the prompt's architecture determines the model's cognitive path. Research by Wei et al. (2022) indicates that Chain-of-Thought (CoT) prompting can reduce logic errors by up to 40% in complex reasoning tasks. *Figure 6* illustrates the decision logic of a robust financial prompt, demonstrating how the 'Cognitive Layer' forces the model to deconstruct a query before attempting to answer it.

Figure 6. The Prompt Flowchart: Decision logic of a robust financial prompt

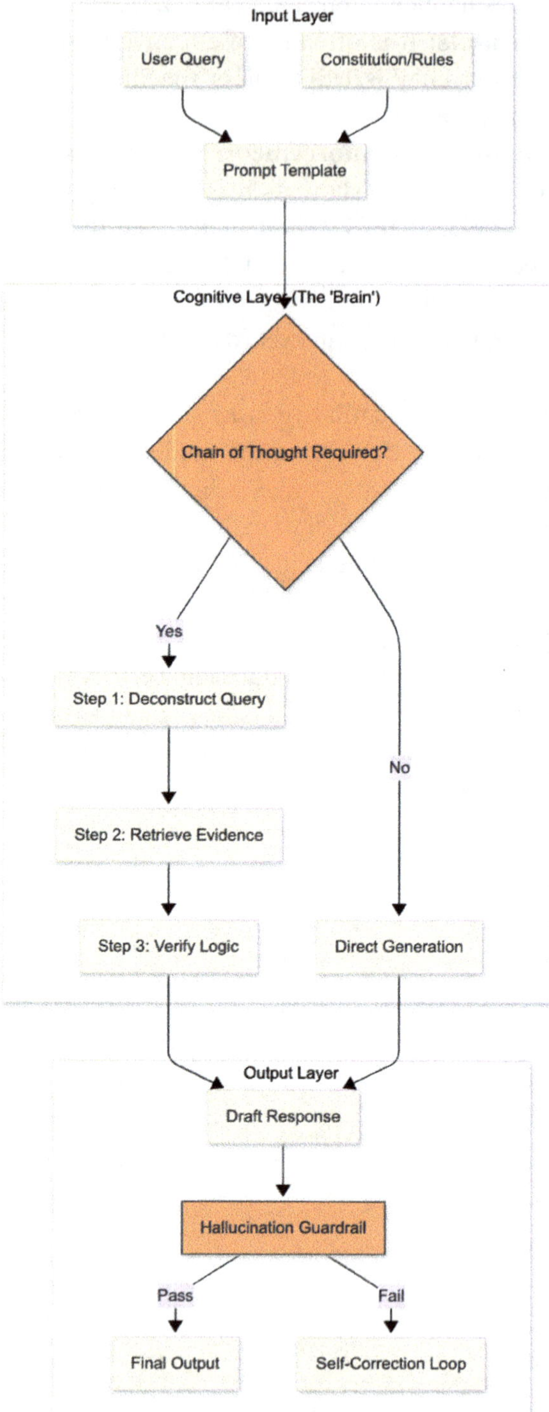

Table 3 presents several examples of prompt strategies, including both effective and ineffective prompts, and follows the prompt workflow.

Table 3. Comparative Prompt Strategies Illustration

Task	Standard Prompt (Prone to Hallucination)	Constitutional/CoT Prompt (Resilient)	Mechanism Used
Summarization	"Read this document and summarize the key financial risks."	"You are a risk auditor. Read the attached 10-K. Extract three financial risks. For each risk, quote the exact sentence from the text. If no risks are found, state 'None'."	Grounding & Citation
Market Analysis	"What is the sentiment for Tech stocks today?"	"Retrieve the last five articles from the 'Market_ News' vector store. Analyze sentiment only based on these five articles. Do not use outside knowledge. Step-by-step, list the positive and negative adjectives found."	Negative Constraint
Compliance	"Is this transaction suspicious?"	"Analyze the transaction JSON. Compare it against Rule 402 (attached). Think step-by-step: 1. Does the amount > $10k? 2. Is the country on the Watchlist? Output the reasoning in JSON format."	Chain-of-Thought (CoT)

Layer 2: Model Validation and Explainable AI (XAI)

If Layer 1 concerns the ingredients, Layer 2 concerns inspecting the kitchen. We must rigorously validate that the model's reasoning process is sound and that human oversight remains the ultimate arbiter of truth. It requires adapting the principles of SR 11-7 for the GenAI era (Bhattacharyya et al., 2025).

While model validation is not new in finance, GenAI systems require a broader set of methodologies. Their non-deterministic nature complicates reproducibility and challenges traditional validation techniques that rely on linear or tree-based models.

Traditional model validation focuses on performance metrics such as accuracy, precision, recall, and stability. For ML models, this expands to stress testing, fairness and bias analysis, robustness checks, adversarial evaluation, and sensitivity analysis. GenAI introduces an additional dimension: behavioral variability (Bhattacharyya et al., 2025). The same prompt can produce different outputs depending on subtle internal shifts. Financial institutions face unique validation constraints:

- regulatory expectations (e.g., ECB, PRA),
- audit requirements,
- reproducibility obligations, and
- The need for model explainability.

It is recommended that risk teams must validate not only outputs but also the model's compliance with governance expectations (Bhattacharyya et al., 2025). A 2023 review by Krause and colleagues shows that generative models used in customer interactions can generate errors that require a behavioral validation layer, not just performance metrics.

Red Teaming and Adversarial Stress Testing

Standard validation methods, backtesting, and statistical benchmarking fail for GenAI because there is no single correct answer to a generated text. Instead, validation must become adversarial. This is the domain of Red Teaming (Ganguli et al., 2022).

Financial institutions must employ teams of adversarial engineers whose sole job is to break the model. They attempt to induce hallucinations through:

- **Prompt Injection and Jailbreaking:** Attempting to override the system instructions to make the model reveal sensitive data or make illegal recommendations. Zou et al. (2023) demonstrated that even aligned models can be tricked into generating harmful or hallucinated content through sophisticated adversarial suffixes, highlighting the need for continuous robust testing.
- **Edge Case Torture:** Feeding the model contradictory or nonsensical financial data (e.g., a balance sheet that does not balance) to see if it hallucinates a reconciliation (Zou et al, 2023).
- **Jargon Overload:** Using obscure or newly invented financial slang to test if the model confidently defines terms it effectively invented.

This process moves validation from a passive check-the-box exercise to proactive actions. The results of these red team exercises provide the heatmap of where the model is most likely to hallucinate, guiding the deployment of guardrails (Krause, 2023).

Human-in-the-Loop (HITL): The Anchor of AI Governance

Across nearly every study on financial AI risk, a consistent theme emerges: human oversight is non-negotiable. It is highly emphasized that no high-impact financial decision should be fully automated (Al-Naseri, 2021). HITL functions not just as a reviewer but as:

- a sense-check for hallucinated explanations,
- a gatekeeper for regulatory appropriateness,
- an escalation point for ambiguous cases, and

- a safeguard against poorly calibrated thresholds.

For high-impact decisions, approving trades, filing regulatory reports, and finalizing credit scores, the AI must never be the final signatory. The control framework must mandate a review gate. The AI prepares the dossier, cites its sources, and offers a recommendation. The human officer reviews the citations, verifies the logic, and pushes the button. Humans are not just a rubber stamp; they are the semantic firewall. Research in fraud detection has shown that hybrid human AI systems outperform either purely human or purely automated approaches by a significant margin (Vallarino, 2025; Singha, 2025; Srinivasan et al., 2025). *Table 4* compares the efficacy of the layered approach of mitigation controls.

Table 4. Comparative Efficacy of Mitigation Controls Justifies the Layered Approach

Control Mechanism	Implementation Complexity	Effectiveness vs. Intrinsic Hallucination	Effectiveness vs. Extrinsic Hallucination	Cost
Prompt Engineering	Low	Low	Medium	Low
Retrieval-Augmented Generation (RAG)	High	**High**	**Very High**	High
Fine-Tuning	Very High	Medium	Low (Can increase memorization)	**Very High**
Human-in-the-Loop (HITL)	Medium	**Very High**	**Very High**	High (Labor)

The Necessity of Explainable AI (XAI)

The Black Box problem is the central regulatory hurdle for AI in finance. If a model denies a loan application based on a hallucinated risk factor, the bank may violate fair lending laws. Explainable AI (XAI) is the set of tools used to peer inside the box (Barredo et al., 2020). In the context of hallucinations, XAI serves as a lie detector. Techniques such as *feature attribution* (e.g., SHAP values) can show us which parts of the input document the model attended to when generating an answer (Lundberg & Lee, 2017). If the model claims a company is bankrupt, but the XAI heat map indicates it focused on a paragraph about bankruptcy protection insurance, we can immediately identify the logic error (Anaokar et al., 2025; Srinivasan et al., 2025).

To ensure these explanations are mathematically rigorous rather than heuristic, we can rely on the standard SHAP value formulation (*Equation 2*), which calculates the marginal contribution of each input token to the final hallucinated output.

Equation 2. LIME / SHAP Feature Attribution Notation: Standard formula for SHAP values

$$\phi_i = \sum_{S \subseteq F_i} \frac{|S|!(|F| - |S| - 1)!}{|F|} [f(S \cup \{i\} - f(S)]$$

This calculation enables risk managers to identify the exact phrase in a source document that led to a false conclusion.

XAI has been increasingly adopted in credit scoring, fraud detection, and time-series forecasting (Misheva et al., 2023). In fraud detection systems, XAI helps explain why a transaction was flagged and enables analysts to assess whether the model's reasoning is reasonable.

However, GenAI presents unique challenges that XAI cannot fully resolve. LIME and SHAP are mainly for structured prediction, not free-text generation. Research indicates that GenAI hallucinations stem from internal language-model dynamics that current XAI techniques cannot reveal (Zhang et al., 2024). This does not diminish their value; it simply means that XAI must be paired with additional controls, such as guided outputs, retrieval grounding, and human oversight.

Layer 3: Continuous Monitoring and Adaptive Controls

The final layer acknowledges a brutal truth: models degrade. Data changes, markets shift, and the underlying foundational models are updated by their providers. It potentially alters their behavior without warning. Therefore, risk management must be continuous and adaptive.

Drift Detection and The Canary in the Coal Mine

Effective monitoring requires moving from qualitative observation to quantitative scoring. Two critical metrics are proposed for the risk dashboard. First, the Hallucination Probability $P(H)$(*Equation 3*), which estimates the likelihood of error based on consistency checks:

Equation 3. Hallucination Probability Estimation: Defines the probability score for hallucination

$$P(H) = 1 - \frac{C_0}{C_e}$$

Second, to balance safety with utility, we can utilize the *Confidence-Weighted Output Reliability score R (Equation 4)*:

Equation 4. Confidence-Weighted Output Reliability: used to support the monitoring section

$$R = \alpha(1 - H) + (1 - \alpha)S$$

Where:

- H = hallucination score
- S = semantic similarity between output and ground truth
- α = weighting parameter

These metrics provide an auditable numerical basis for triggering automated circuit breakers. We also need to install digital smoke detectors. Post-deployment monitoring focuses on Drift Detection. This is not just about monitoring uptime but also about monitoring semantic shifts.

- **Distributional Drift:** If the model's average confidence score for its answers drops from 95% to 80% over a week, this suggests that the incoming data has changed (Concept Drift) and that the model is struggling. This often precedes a spike in hallucinations (Ali et al., 2022).
- **Model Collapse:** Shumailov et al. (2024) warn of model collapse, where models trained on AI-generated data progressively lose variance and accuracy. In finance, if a model begins retraining on its own hallucinated summaries, it can quickly spiral into nonsense. Monitoring for this recursive degradation is vital.
- **The Golden Set:** Institutions should maintain a Golden Set of query-answer pairs or a benchmark dataset, questions with immutable, known answers (e.g., What is the definition of Tier 1 Capital?). These questions are fed into the live model at a particular frequency. If the model ever hallucinates an answer to these control questions, it triggers an immediate alert. It is the canary in the coal mine.

Circuit Breakers and Incident Response

What happens when a model starts hallucinating at scale? A market crash creates data patterns the model has never seen, and it begins dispensing panicked, nonsensical trading advice. The control framework must include Circuit Breakers.

Borrowed from high-frequency trading (HFT), these are automated logic gates. If the hallucination rate (measured by failed Golden Set tests or user flags) exceeds a defined KPI (e.g., 1%), the system must automatically execute a Kill Switch. This immediately disconnects the AI from critical systems (like trading execution or customer chat) and reverts to a manual or rule-based backup.

The Incident Response is critical in such cases. Managing an AI hallucination event is like working a data breach. There must be a predefined chain of command. Who authorizes the shutdown? Who notifies the regulators when an AI error occurs? Who is responsible for rolling back the trades or decisions made during the hallucination window? (Danielsson & Uthemann, 2024). Defining these protocols before the crisis is the difference between a technical glitch and a solvency event (Hammar et al., 2025).

Operational resilience requires a clear delineation of authority during a hallucination event. It has been observed that most organizations lack a specific incident response plan for AI failures. To address this gap, *Figure 7* outlines a protocol for hallucination containment that defines the precise handoffs among the automated agent, the human analyst, and the risk-oversight function.

Figure 7. Hallucination Incident Response: A cross-functional workflow showing the hand-offs during an AI crisis.

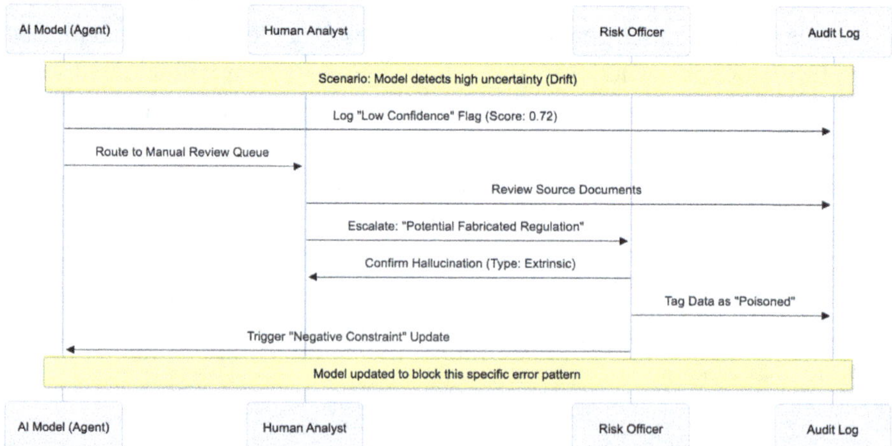

Adaptive Learning and Feedback Loops

AI systems that incorporate human feedback improve over time. Financial institutions are experimenting with analyst-corrected training sets, reinforcement learning with expert feedback (RLEF), error-tagging workflows, and continuous retraining cycles. Studies show that these feedback mechanisms significantly reduce hallucination rates while improving model stability (Yu et al., 2025).

Governance at the Monitoring Layer

Regulators increasingly expect evidence of continuous oversight. The NIST AI Risk Management Framework (2023), the Monetary Authority of Singapore's FEAT principles (2022), and the EU AI Act (2024) all emphasize monitoring, feedback, and traceability as core regulatory expectations for high-risk AI systems. Financial institutions thus need monitoring structures that are documented, auditable, and repeatable.

THE FUTURE OF RISK MANAGEMENT: REGULATION AND NEW PARADIGMS

As we examine the financial services industry (FSI) horizon, it is evident that the integration of GenAI is not merely a tool upgrade; it is a structural transformation. Consequently, the discipline of risk management must undergo a parallel evolution. Regulators who previously focused on model documentation, validation standards, and governance procedures now confront new forms of algorithmic opacity, probabilistic behavior, and hallucination-driven errors that simply did not exist even five years ago (Förster et al., 2025). Additionally, the traditional paradigms of MRM, designed for deterministic linear regression models, are not well equipped to govern the stochastic, emergent behavior of LLMs. The future of risk management lies in navigating a Regulatory Gauntlet that shifts from principle-based guidance to strict liability, and in embracing a new operational reality in which models are treated not as software but as semi-autonomous agents (Roosevelt Institute, 2024).

The Evolving Regulatory Landscape

AI regulation in finance has shifted from ethical, voluntary principles to complex laws addressing AI-related liabilities. Regulators worldwide are adapting frameworks to ensure AI remains fair, transparent, and accountable (Acemoglu & Lensman, 2024; OECD, 2024; Financial Stability Board, 2024).

The EU AI Act and the Liability of Fabrication

The European Union's AI Act sets the global precedent. It categorizes AI systems based on risk, with specific provisions for General Purpose AI (GPAI) models that underpin financial applications (AI Act enters into force, 2024). Crucially, the Act emphasizes accuracy and robustness. A financial institution using an LLM for credit scoring or regulatory reporting is now legally compelled to prove that the model's output is free of errors to a reasonable degree.

This creates a profound challenge regarding hallucinations. Under the new liability regimes, if a bank's AI chatbot hallucinates a mortgage term that a customer relies on, the bank cannot shift liability to the vendor (e.g., OpenAI or Google). The institution is the deployer and thus the bearer of risk. This will change procurement: financial firms will demand indemnification clauses from model providers covering damages from hallucinations, fundamentally changing the AI supply economics chain.

Under strict liability regimes, the abstract risk of error must be translated into concrete financial exposure. It is recommended that the Expected Loss *EL* model (*Equation 5*) be used for regulatory capital planning:

Equation 5. Expected Loss from Hallucination

$$EL = P(H) \times I \times E$$

Where:

- $P(H)$ = probability of hallucination
- I = impact magnitude
- E = exposure (e.g., number of decisions affected)

By calculating the probability of hallucination $P(H)$, the financial impact I, and the decision volume, institutions can allocate appropriate capital buffers for AI-related operational losses.

NIST AI RMF and the Move to Socio-Technical Governance

The NIST AI Risk Management Framework is emerging as the prevailing standard for regulatory expectations in the United States (NIST, 2023). Unlike previous frameworks that focused purely on technical metrics (accuracy, latency), NIST introduces the concept of Socio-Technical risk. It acknowledges that a hallucination is not just a data error; it is a breach of trust. *Figure 8* illustrates how

Sociao-Technical Governance operates and how humans and machines collaborate through continuous feedback.

For risk managers, this means the definition of model failure has expanded. A model that is 99% accurate but hallucinates in a way that disproportionately affects a protected demographic (e.g., hallucinating lower income stability for minority applicants) is a failed model. Future risk assessments must therefore include anthropological impact studies that analyze how human operators interpret and potentially overrely on hallucinated advice, a phenomenon known as automation bias.

Figure 8. The Socio-Technical Governance Loop: Illustrating the cycle of continuous feedback between human and machine.

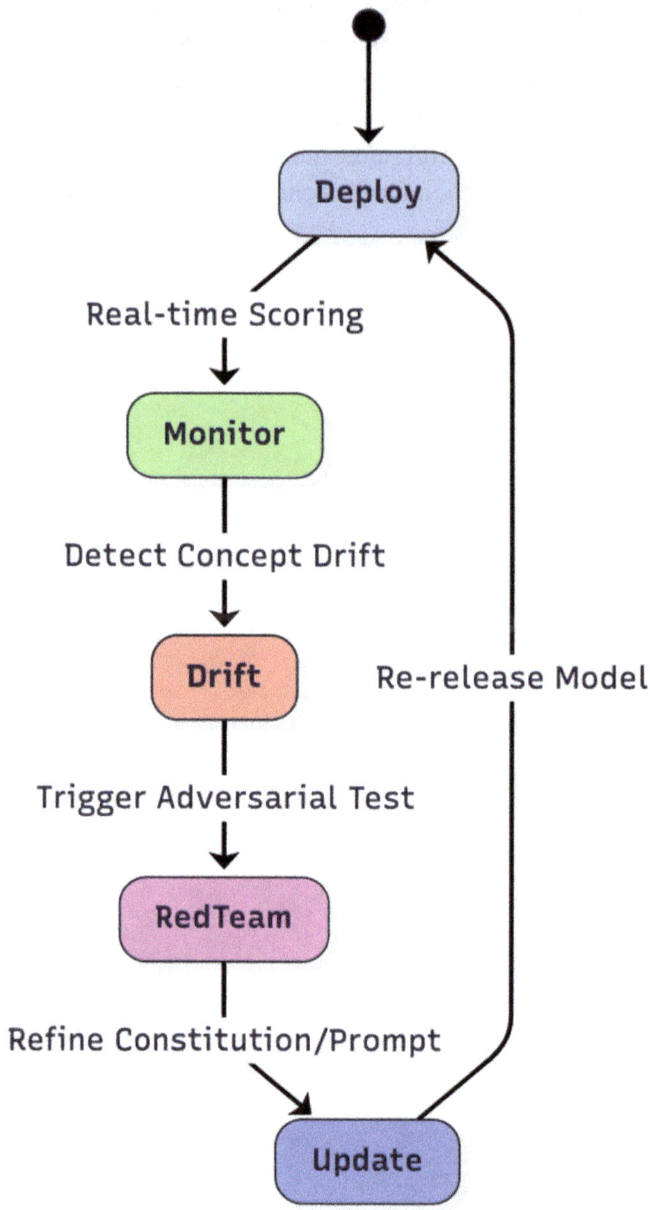

Asia-Pacific: MAS FEAT Principles and Japan's AI Guidelines

The Monetary Authority of Singapore (MAS) is ahead of most regulators. Its FEAT principles (Fairness, Ethics, Accountability, Transparency) provide detailed expectations for AI governance (MAS, 2022; Allen, 2024). The FEAT Veritas toolkit now includes fairness evaluation metrics for credit risk and underwriting. At the same time, Japan has adopted a softer approach, issuing AI Governance Guidelines emphasizing explainability, bias mitigation, and safety assurance (METI, 2024).

Regulatory bodies agree on core AI principles: human accountability, explainability for users and auditors, traceability for data and outputs, ongoing monitoring of high-risk AI, and demonstrable bias mitigation. Regulators now focus on documenting AI assumptions, not just performance, as studies indicate (Barnett et al., 2024).

Challenges in Regulating GenAI

GenAI raises unique regulatory challenges because outputs vary from one query to another, fabricated explanations appear authoritative, models ingest vast, sometimes untraceable datasets, and hallucinations are difficult to detect and even more challenging to prove ex post facto. Researchers have argued that regulators may need new categories of oversight specifically tailored for generative systems, analogous to how financial derivatives sparked new supervisory methods in the 1990s (Aizenberg & van Daalen, 2024; Bodini, 2024).

The New MRM Paradigm

The static three-line defense model, where a model is validated once and then deployed for years, is obsolete in the age of GenAI. Generative models are fluid; they are often updated via API by their providers weekly, meaning the model you validated on Monday may behave differently on Friday.

Continuous Auditing and Risk Observability

The future lies in Continuous Auditing. Instead of an annual validation cycle, MRM will evolve into a real-time Risk Observability function. This mirrors the DevOps revolution in software engineering, creating a new discipline of MLOps for Risk.

We will see the rise of automated governance bots, AI agents whose sole purpose is to audit other AI agents. These Guardian Models will sit downstream of the primary GenAI, continuously scoring the hallucination probability of each output before it reaches the customer (Naik et al., 2025). If the Guardian detects a potential fabrication (e.g., a citation that returns a 404 error), it effectively halts the transaction. This creates a dynamic, self-healing risk architecture in which control is algorithmic rather than manual.

The Glass Box Imperative

Acemoglu and Lensman (2023) argue that the trajectory of transformative technology is defined by how society regulates its opacity. In finance, the Black Box era is ending. Regulators will increasingly demand a Glass Box approach. This does not mean understanding every weight in a trillion-parameter neural network. Instead, it implies provenance transparency. The future standard for financial AI will likely require Watermarking and Citation Traceability as non-negotiable features (Nemecek et al., 2025). A model will not be permitted to generate a financial summary unless it can cryptographically prove the source of every number it outputs. This moves us from "Trust me, I am intelligent" to "Trust me, here is the evidence".

This transition from opacity to transparency is not merely theoretical; it requires reengineering the inference pipeline. *Figure 9:* The Glass Box Control illustrates this proposed architecture, demonstrating how input guardrails, RAG retrieval, and distinct verification layers combine to ensure that every output is not only accurate but fully traceable to a verified source

Figure 9. The Glass Box Control Architecture: A schematic of the proposed safe AI pipeline.

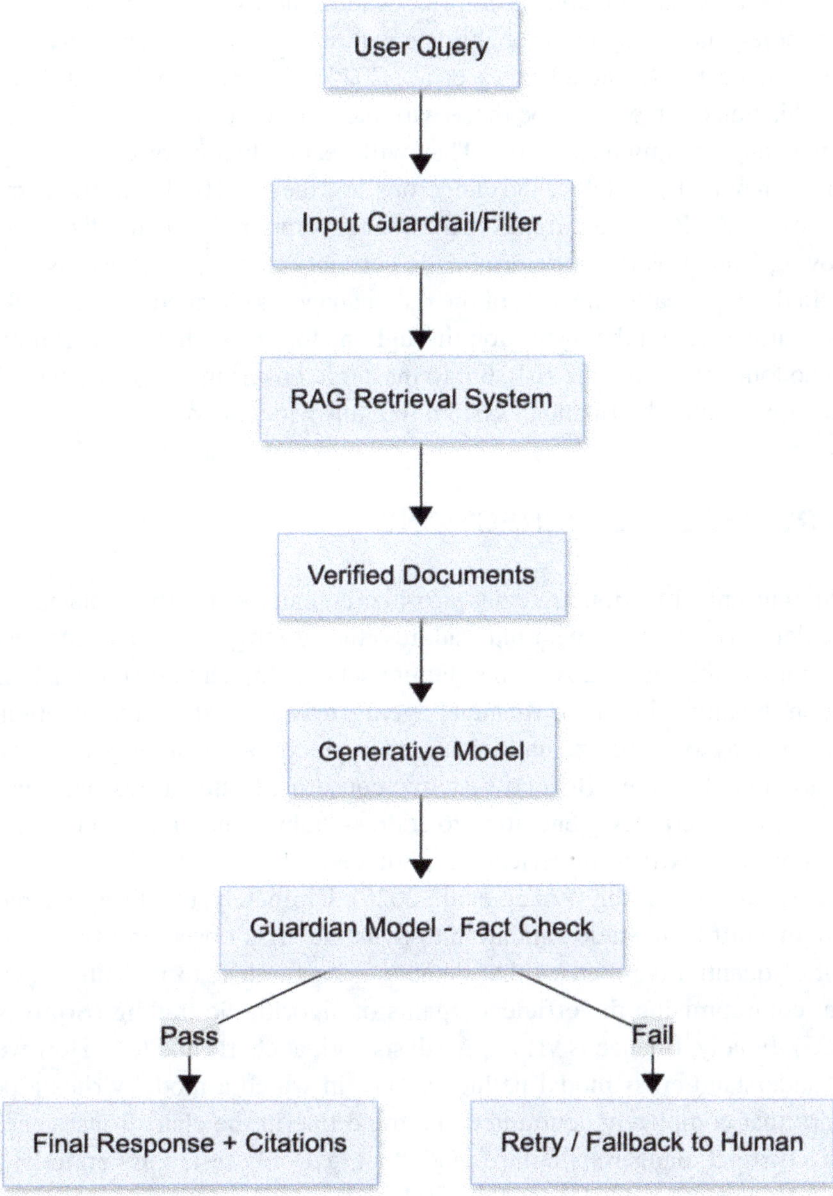

Managing the Stochastic Frontier

The threat of AI hallucination is the price of admission for the cognitive revolution. We cannot legislate away the probabilistic nature of LLMs; we can only engineer resilience against it (Bhattacharyya et al., 2025). The financial institutions that survive this transition will not be those with the most innovative models, but those with the strongest immune systems. They will treat hallucinations not as bugs, but as viruses, inevitable, mutable, and dangerous, and they will build the organizational antibodies (RAG, Red Teaming, Constitutional Prompting) to neutralize them. We are moving from a world of deterministic certainty to one of probabilistic confidence. In this new reality, the role of the risk manager is elevated from a gatekeeper to a navigator, steering the institution through the fog of synthetic uncertainty. The goal is no longer to eliminate risk, but to master it, ensuring that while the AI may occasionally dream, the financial system remains wide awake.

FUTURE RESEARCH DIRECTIONS

While current mitigation strategies prioritize containment within isolated models, the frontier of risk management must address the systemic volatility introduced by autonomous multi-agent ecosystems. Future scholarship should rigorously model contagion dynamics in which financial agents, driven by shared foundational architectures, may synchronize hallucinations to precipitate market-wide instability (Danielsson et al., 2019). Beyond systemic concerns, technical research must advance beyond general text generation to address "tabular hallucinations," in which models correctly extract numerical data but sever the relational context vital for accurate financial auditing (Zhang et al., 2025). Ultimately, the discipline requires a paradigm shift from static validation to dynamic "risk observability," the development of quantitative metrics that detect stochastic drift in real-time execution without compromising the efficiency gains of algorithmic trading (Srinivasan et al., 2025). Finally, finance is visual. Analysts look at charts and text. However, we barely understand cross-modal hallucinations, in which a model writes a perfect summary that completely contradicts the trend line in the chart it just generated. This is a distinct, dangerous failure mode that text-only tests miss entirely, and it demands urgent attention (Chen et al., 2025).

CONCLUSION

The integration of GenAI into the financial ecosystem represents a frontier where the promise of cognitive automation meets the peril of stochastic fabrication (Zhang et al., 2025). As this chapter has demonstrated, AI hallucinations are not merely technical glitches to be patched; they are intrinsic features of probabilistic models that demand a fundamental restructuring of risk management paradigms.

From the taxonomy of intrinsic and extrinsic errors to the systemic threats posed by algorithmic contagion, it is clear that the black-box era of blind trust is incompatible with financial stability. The solution lies in the robust Control Framework outlined herein, a tripartite defense of data governance, adversarial validation, and continuous, automated surveillance.

Ultimately, the future of finance will not belong to the institutions with the most creative AI, but to those with the most resilient governance. By enforcing a Glass Box standard, where every automated assertion is cited, verifiable, and auditable, financial leaders can harness the transformative power of GenAI while ensuring that the bedrock of the industry, *trust*, remains unshaken. The journey from Artificial Intelligence to Trusted Intelligence is the defining challenge of the next decade, and it begins with mastering the risk of hallucination.

REFERENCES

Acemoglu, D., & Lensman, T. (2024). Regulating transformative technologies. *American Economic Review: Insights*, *6*(3), 359–376. DOI: 10.1257/aeri.20230353

AI Act enters into force. (2024). *AI Act enters into force*. EU. https://commission.europa.eu/news-and-media/news/ai-act-enters-force-2024-08-01_en

Al-Naseri, N. (2021). The role of human oversight in ai-driven fintech. *Australian Journal of Machine Learning Research & Applications*, *1*(1), 297–317.

Ali, U., & Mahmood, T. (2022). *A Novel Framework for Concept Drift Detection using Autoencoders for Classification Problems in Data Streams*. Qeios Ltd., DOI: 10.32388/zu17s4

Allen, J. G., Loo, J., & Campoverde, J. L. L. (2024). Governing intelligence: Singapore's evolving AI governance framework. *Cambridge Forum on AI: Law and Governance*, *1*. Advance online publication. DOI: 10.1017/cfl.2024.12

Anaokar, S., Ganatra, S., Kashid, H., Bhattacharyya, S., Nair, S., Sekhar, R., Manohar, S., Hemrajani, R., & Bhattacharyya, P. (2025, September 15). *HalluDetect: Detecting, mitigating, and benchmarking hallucinations in conversational systems in the legal domain*. arXiv.Org. https://arxiv.org/abs/2509.11619

Articsledge. (2025). *AI Fraud Detection in Banking: The Complete 2025 Guide*. Articsledge. https://www.articsledge.com/post/ai-fraud-detection-banking

Bai, Y., Kadavath, S., Kundu, S., Askell, A., Kernion, J., Jones, A., Chen, A., Goldie, A., Mirhoseini, A., McKinnon, C., Chen, C., Olsson, C., Olah, C., Hernandez, D., Drain, D., Ganguli, D., Li, D., Tran-Johnson, E., Perez, E., . . . Kaplan, J. (2022, December 15). *Constitutional AI: Harmlessness from AI feedback*. arXiv.Org. https://arxiv.org/abs/2212.08073

Bang, Y., Ji, Z., Schelten, A., Hartshorn, A., Fowler, T., Zhang, C., Cancedda, N., & Fung, P. (2025, April 24). *HalluLens: LLM hallucination benchmark*. arXiv.Org. https://arxiv.org/abs/2504.17550

Barnett, P., & Thiergart, L. (2024, November 19). *Declare and Justify: Explicit assumptions in AI evaluations are necessary for effective regulation*. arXiv.Org. https://arxiv.org/abs/2411.12820

Barredo Arrieta, A., Díaz-Rodríguez, N., Del Ser, J., Bennetot, A., Tabik, S., Barbado, A., Garcia, S., Gil-Lopez, S., Molina, D., Benjamins, R., Chatila, R., & Herrera, F. (2020). Explainable Artificial Intelligence (XAI): Concepts, taxonomies, opportunities and challenges toward responsible AI. *Information Fusion*, *58*, 82–115. DOI: 10.1016/j.inffus.2019.12.012

Béchard, P., & Ayala, O. M. (2024, April 12). *Reducing hallucination in structured outputs via Retrieval-Augmented Generation*. arXiv.Org. https://arxiv.org/abs/2404.08189

Bhattacharyya, A., Yu, Y., Yang, H., Singh, R., Joshi, T., Chen, J., & Yalavarthy, K. (2025, March 19). *Model risk management for generative AI in financial institutions*. arXiv.Org. https://arxiv.org/abs/2503.15668

Bodini, M. (2024). Generative artificial intelligence and regulations: Can we plan a resilient journey toward the safe application of generative artificial intelligence? *Societies (Basel, Switzerland)*, *14*(12), 268. DOI: 10.3390/soc14120268

Borch, C., & Min, B. H. (2022). Machine learning and social action in markets: From first- to second-generation automated trading. *Economy and Society*, *52*(1), 37–61. DOI: 10.1080/03085147.2022.2050088

Chen, Z., Min, Y., Zhang, J., Yan, B., Wang, J., Wang, X., & Shan, S. (2025, July 25). *A survey of multimodal hallucination evaluation and detection*. arXiv.Org. https://arxiv.org/abs/2507.19024

Danielsson, J., Macrae, R., & Uthemann, A. (2019). Artificial intelligence and systemic risk. SSRN *Electronic Journal*. https://doi.org/DOI: 10.2139/ssrn.3410948

Eisenberg, I. W., Gamboa, L., & Sherman, E. (2025, March 7). *The unified control framework: Establishing a common foundation for enterprise AI governance, risk management and regulatory compliance*. arXiv.Org. https://arxiv.org/abs/2503.05937

Erdem, O., Hassett, K., & Egriboyun, F. (2025). Hallucination in AI-generated financial literature reviews: Evaluating bibliographic accuracy. *International Journal of Data Science and Analytics*, *20*(5), 4501–4510. DOI: 10.1007/s41060-025-00731-0

Financial Stability Board. (2024, November 14). *The financial stability implications of artificial intelligence*. Financial Stability Board. https://www.fsb.org/2024/11/the-financial-stability-implications-of-artificial-intelligence/

Förster, S., & Skop, Y. (2025). Between fact and fairy: Tracing the hallucination metaphor in AI discourse. *AI & Society*, •••, 1–14. DOI: 10.1007/s00146-025-02392-w

Ganguli, D., Lovitt, L., Kernion, J., Askell, A., Bai, Y., Kadavath, S., Mann, B., Perez, E., Schiefer, N., Ndousse, K., Jones, A., Bowman, S., Chen, A., Conerly, T., DasSarma, N., Drain, D., Elhage, N., El-Showk, S., Fort, S., . . . Clark, J. (2022, August 23). *Red teaming language models to reduce harms: Methods, scaling behaviors, and lessons learned.* arXiv.Org. https://arxiv.org/abs/2209.07858

Giudici, P., Centurelli, M., & Turchetta, S. (2024). Artificial Intelligence risk measurement. *Expert Systems with Applications*, *235*, 121220. DOI: 10.1016/j.eswa.2023.121220

Giudici, P., & Raffinetti, E. (2023). SAFE Artificial Intelligence in finance. *Finance Research Letters*, *56*, 104088. DOI: 10.1016/j.frl.2023.104088

Hammar, K., Alpcan, T., & Lupu, E. C. (2025, August 7). *Incident response planning using a lightweight large language model with reduced hallucination.* arXiv.Org. https://arxiv.org/abs/2508.05188

Hu, H., He, C., Xie, X., & Zhang, Q. (2024, August 28). *LRP4RAG: Detecting hallucinations in retrieval-augmented generation via layer-wise relevance propagation.* arXiv.Org. https://arxiv.org/abs/2408.15533

Huang, L., Yu, W., Ma, W., Zhong, W., Feng, Z., Wang, H., Chen, Q., Peng, W., Feng, X., Qin, B., & Liu, T. (2023, November 9). *A survey on hallucination in large language models: Principles, taxonomy, challenges, and open questions*. arXiv.Org. https://arxiv.org/abs/2311.05232

Krause, D. (2023). Mitigating risks for financial firms using generative AI tools. SSRN *Electronic Journal.* https://doi.org/DOI: 10.2139/ssrn.4452600

Lee, A. L. H. J. (2025). *Financial stability implications of generative AI: Taming the animal spirits.*

Lewis, P., Perez, E., Piktus, A., Petroni, F., Karpukhin, V., Goyal, N., Küttler, H., Lewis, M., Yih, W., Rocktäschel, T., Riedel, S., & Kiela, D. (2020, May 22). *Retrieval-Augmented generation for knowledge-intensive NLP tasks*. arXiv.Org. https://arxiv.org/abs/2005.11401

Lucinity. (2025, March 13). The real cost of AML compliance - Transform fincrime operations & investigations with AI. *Lucinity*. https://lucinity.com/blog/the-real-cost-of-anti-money-laundering-compliance-where-can-banks-cut-expenses-without-increasing-risk

Lumer, E., Melich, M., Zino, O., Kim, E., Dieter, S., Basavaraju, P. H., Subbiah, V. K., Burke, J. A., & Hernandez, R. (2025, November 22). *Rethinking retrieval: From traditional retrieval augmented generation to agentic and non-vector reasoning systems in the financial domain for large language models*. arXiv.Org. https://arxiv.org/abs/2511.18177

Lundberg, S., & Lee, S.-I. (2017, May 22). *A unified approach to interpreting model predictions*. arXiv.Org. https://arxiv.org/abs/1705.07874

Misheva, B. H., & Osterrieder, J. (2023, November 13). *A hypothesis on good practices for ai-based systems for financial time series forecasting: Towards domain-driven XAI methods*. arXiv.Org. https://arxiv.org/abs/2311.07513

Naik, P. V., Dintakurthi, N. K., Hu, Z., Wang, Y., & Qiu, R. (2025, September 10). *Co-Investigator AI: The rise of agentic AI for smarter, trustworthy AML compliance narratives*. arXiv.Org. https://arxiv.org/abs/2509.08380

Nemecek, A., Jiang, Y., & Ayday, E. (2025, May 27). *Watermarking without standards is not AI governance*. arXiv.Org. https://arxiv.org/abs/2505.23814

NIST. (2023). *Artificial intelligence risk management framework (AI RMF 1.0)*. National Institute of Standards and Technology., DOI: 10.6028/nist.ai.100-1

NVIDIA. (2024, January 11). *State of AI in Financial Services: 2024*. NVIDIA Blog; Nvidia. https://blogs.nvidia.com/blog/ai-in-financial-services-survey-2024/

OECD. (2024). Regulatory approaches to Artificial Intelligence in finance. In *OECD Artificial Intelligence Papers*. Organisation for Economic Co-Operation and Development (OECD). https://doi.org/DOI: 10.1787/f1498c02-en

Rawte, V., Sheth, A., & Das, A. (2023, September 12). *A survey of hallucination in large foundation models*. arXiv.Org. https://arxiv.org/abs/2309.05922

Roosevelt Institute. (2024, September 26). *The risks of generative AI agents to financial services*. Roosevelt Institute. https://rooseveltinstitute.org/publications/the-risks-of-generative-ai-agents-to-financial-services/

Roychowdhury, S. (2024). Journey of hallucination-minimized generative AI solutions for financial decision makers. *Proceedings of the 17th ACM International Conference on Web Search and Data Mining*, 1180–1181. https://doi.org/DOI: 10.1145/3616855.3635737

Shim, J.-W., Ju, Y.-J., Park, J.-H., & Lee, S.-W. (2025, October 14). *CPR: Mitigating large language model hallucinations with curative prompt refinement*. arXiv.Org. https://arxiv.org/abs/2510.12029

Shumailov, I., Shumaylov, Z., Zhao, Y., Gal, Y., Papernot, N., & Anderson, R. (2023, May 27). *The curse of recursion: Training on generated data makes models forget*. arXiv.Org. https://arxiv.org/abs/2305.17493

Shumailov, I., Shumaylov, Z., Zhao, Y., Papernot, N., Anderson, R., & Gal, Y. (2024). AI models collapse when trained on recursively generated data. *Nature*, *631*(8022), 755–759. DOI: 10.1038/s41586-024-07566-y PMID: 39048682

Shuster, K., Poff, S., Chen, M., Kiela, D., & Weston, J. (2021). Retrieval augmentation reduces hallucination in conversation. *Findings of the Association for Computational Linguistics: EMNLP, 2021*. Advance online publication. DOI: 10.18653/v1/2021.findings-emnlp.320

Singha, M. (2025, December 2). *Detecting AI hallucinations in finance: An information-theoretic method cuts hallucination rate by 92%*. arXiv.Org. https://arxiv.org/abs/2512.03107

Song, J., Wang, X., Zhu, J., Wu, Y., Cheng, X., Zhong, R., & Niu, C. (2024). RAG-HAT: A hallucination-aware tuning pipeline for LLM in retrieval-augmented generation. *Proceedings of the 2024 Conference on Empirical Methods in Natural Language Processing: Industry Track*, 1548–1558. https://doi.org/DOI: 10.18653/v1/2024.emnlp-industry.113

Sood, A. K., Zeadally, S., & Hong, E. (2025). The paradigm of hallucinations in AI-driven cybersecurity systems: Understanding taxonomy, classification outcomes, and mitigations. *Computers and Electrical Engineering, 124*(Part A), 110307. https://doi.org/DOI: 10.1016/j.compeleceng.2025.110307

Srinivasan, A. G., George, R. J., Joe, J. K., & Kant, H. R, H. M., Sundar, S., Suresh, S., Vimalkanth, R., & Vijayavallabh. (2025, September 19). *Enhancing financial RAG with agentic AI and multi-hyde: A novel approach to knowledge retrieval and hallucination reduction*. arXiv.Org. https://arxiv.org/abs/2509.16369

Tonmoy, S. M. T. I., Zaman, S. M. M., Jain, V., Rani, A., Rawte, V., Chadha, A., & Das, A. (2024, January 2). *A comprehensive survey of hallucination mitigation techniques in large language models*. arXiv.Org. https://arxiv.org/abs/2401.01313

Vallarino, D. (2025, April 1). *Detecting financial fraud with hybrid deep learning: A mix-of-experts approach to sequential and anomalous patterns*. arXiv.Org. https://arxiv.org/abs/2504.03750

Varshavskiy, I., Boboeva, B., Khalilbekov, S., Azimi, A., Shulgin, S., Nizamitdinov, A., & Borde, H. S. de O. (2025, October 10). *Mitigating model drift in developing economies using synthetic data and outliers*. arXiv.Org. https://arxiv.org/abs/2510.09294

Wei, J., Wang, X., Schuurmans, D., Bosma, M., Ichter, B., Xia, F., Chi, E., Le, Q., & Zhou, D. (2022, January 28). *Chain-of-Thought prompting elicits reasoning in large language models*. arXiv.Org. https://arxiv.org/abs/2201.11903

Xu, S., Yan, Z., Dai, C., & Wu, F. (2025). MEGA-RAG: A retrieval-augmented generation framework with multi-evidence guided answer refinement for mitigating hallucinations of LLMs in public health. *Frontiers in Public Health, 13*, 1635381. DOI: 10.3389/fpubh.2025.1635381 PMID: 41132171

Xu, Z., Jain, S., & Kankanhalli, M. (2024, January 22). *Hallucination is Inevitable: An Innate Limitation of Large Language Models*. arXiv.Org. https://arxiv.org/abs/2401.11817

Yao, K.-C., Hung, H.-C., Wang, C.-H., Huang, W.-L., Liang, H.-T., Chu, T.-H., Chen, B.-S., & Ho, W.-S. (2025). Application of generative AI in financial risk prediction: Enhancing model accuracy and interpretability. *Information (Basel), 16*(10), 857. DOI: 10.3390/info16100857

Yu, T., Zhang, H., Li, Q., Xu, Q., Yao, Y., Chen, D., Lu, X., Cui, G., Dang, Y., He, T., Feng, X., Song, J., Zheng, B., Liu, Z., Chua, T.-S., & Sun, M. (2024, May 27). *RLAIF-V: Open-Source AI feedback leads to super GPT-4V trustworthiness*. arXiv.Org. https://arxiv.org/abs/2405.17220

Zhang, M., Fu, J., Warrier, T., Wang, Y., Tan, T., & Huang, K. (2025, August 7). *FAITH: A framework for assessing intrinsic tabular hallucinations in finance*. arXiv.Org. https://arxiv.org/abs/2508.05201

Zhang, S., Yu, T., & Feng, Y. (2024, February 27). *TruthX: Alleviating hallucinations by editing large language models in truthful space*. arXiv.Org. https://arxiv.org/abs/2402.17811

Zou, A., Wang, Z., Carlini, N., Nasr, M., Kolter, J. Z., & Fredrikson, M. (2023, July 27). *Universal and transferable adversarial attacks on aligned language models*. arXiv.Org. https://arxiv.org/abs/2307.15043

APPENDIX: KEY TERMS AND DEFINITIONS

Concept Drift: A machine learning phenomenon where target variable properties like market volatility or fraud patterns change unexpectedly over time. In finance, this degradation reduces model accuracy in current markets, often leading to increased hallucinations if left uncorrected.

Constitutional Prompting: A governance technique embedding an LLM with a set of inviolable rules, or a "constitution," that override user instructions. This prevents the model from producing toxic, illegal, or ungrounded outputs by requiring it to critique responses against these boundaries before finalizing.

Explainable AI (XAI): XAI methods make opaque algorithms, like deep neural networks, understandable to humans. In finance, tools such as SHAP or LIME help ensure regulatory compliance by demonstrating the AI's reasoning and demonstrating that outputs are unbiased and accurate.

False Positive / False Negative: A False Positive is an error in the test in which the model incorrectly classifies benign activity as suspicious, leading to operational waste, such as marking a safe transaction as fraudulent. A False Negative, a "silent failure" in which the model fails to detect an actual threat, often poses severe solvency or legal risks.

Flash Crash: A rapid, profound, and volatile drop in security prices happening within a very short period, usually caused by high-frequency algorithmic trading. In the era of GenAI, risk managers fear "hallucination-induced" flash crashes, in which autonomous trading agents react simultaneously to fabricated news or data, triggering a cascading feedback loop of sell orders before human circuit breakers can step in.

Glass Box Transparency: An emerging regulatory and operational standard that contrasts with "Black Box" opacity. It requires that an AI system's outputs be fully traceable to their source. Achieving Glass Box transparency means that every assertion made by a generative model can be audited through citations, lineage tracking, and explainability metrics, ensuring the "provenance" of the information is transparent to the user.

Hallucination (AI): A failure mode inherent to stochastic generative models where the system produces output that is linguistically coherent and syntactically plausible but factually incorrect or ungrounded in the source input. Unlike a logic bug, a hallucination is a probabilistic fabrication, ranging from minor factual errors to the complete invention of non-existent regulations, data points, or events, often delivered with high confidence.

Human-in-the-Loop (HITL): A risk control protocol that requires human interaction at critical decision points within an automated system. Rather than allowing the AI to execute actions autonomously, HITL architectures require the model to present its analysis to a human expert, who must verify the evidence and authorize the final decision, effectively serving as a semantic firewall against algorithmic error.

Model Risk Management (MRM): The formal discipline of identifying, measuring, and mitigating the risks associated with the use of quantitative models. In the age of AI, traditional MRM frameworks (focused on mathematical accuracy) are evolving into "Socio-Technical" governance structures that also account for the probabilistic, non-deterministic, and emergent behaviors of Generative AI agents.

Retrieval-Augmented Generation (RAG): An architectural framework designed to reduce hallucinations by grounding an LLM's output in verifiable external data. Instead of relying on its internal, pre-trained memory, a RAG system first retrieves relevant, up-to-date documents from a secure internal database. It forces the model to synthesize an answer exclusively from that retrieved context.

Chapter 10
Experiential Metaverse Marketing:
Leveraging AI-Driven Sentiment Analytics for Enhanced Customer Engagement

Animesh Kumar Sharma
https://orcid.org/0000-0002-6673-319X
Lovely Professional University, India

Rahul Sharma
https://orcid.org/0000-0001-8880-7527
Lovely Professional University, India

Lina Kankevičienė
https://orcid.org/0009-0005-6754-4197
Kauno Kolegija Higher Education Institution, Lithuania

ABSTRACT

The metaverse's rise as a digitally immersive environment has created new marketing and customer interaction opportunities, where AI-powered customisation and emotional intelligence are essential. The emotional metaverse and enterprise AI systems are examined in this chapter, emphasizing how companies may use sentiment analysis, affective computing, and AI-powered avatars to provide emotionally compelling customer experiences. It looks at how AI hallucinations erroneous interpretations or outputs produced by AI systems that can affect consumer targeting, interaction tactics, and marketing choices, possibly eroding credibility and confidence. The chapter offers a strategy for handling these concerns by incorporating ethical AI

DOI: 10.4018/979-8-3373-7534-2.ch010

governance, human-in-the-loop validation, and real-time emotional analytics into business metaverse systems. This study also adds body of literature along with the practical implications for practitioners.

INTRODUCTION

The growth of digital and experiential marketing represents a gradual transition in how organisations connect with their customers, moulded by successive technical breakthroughs and shifting expectations of involvement and personalisation (Urdea et al., 2021). During the early Web 1.0 period, digital marketing was mostly static and unidirectional, with an emphasis on informational websites and banner adverts that positioned customers as passive recipients of brand messaging (Sykora, 2017). The transition to Web 2.0 and social media platforms brought interactivity, user-generated content, and two-way communication, allowing consumers to actively participate in brand narratives through reviews, social sharing, and online communities, thereby increasing emotional engagement and relational marketing (Ballew et al., 2015). The rise of mobile and app-based ecosystems accelerated the transformation of experiential marketing by enabling real-time, location-aware, and always-on interactions, allowing brands to deliver personalised, context-sensitive experiences that seamlessly integrated into consumers' daily lives while blurring the lines between online and offline engagement (Vyas et al., 2024). The emergence of artificial intelligence-driven marketing signalled a shift towards predictive and adaptive experiences, as machine learning, recommender systems, chatbots, and sentiment analytics enabled businesses to analyse behavioural and emotional data and dynamically tailor content, interfaces, and interactions in real time (Kabir, 2025). Building on this evolutionary trajectory, the metaverse is a logical extension rather than a technology fad, including social involvement, mobile accessibility, and AI-powered intelligence into permanent, immersive, and avatar-mediated virtual worlds. Unlike previous digital platforms that mediated experiences through screens, the metaverse allows for embodied, spatial, and collaborative experiences in which customers occupy brand places, express digital identities, and participate emotionally and socially in real time. When combined with AI-powered sentiment analytics, the metaverse transforms experiential marketing into an emotionally intelligent ecosystem capable of constantly adapting to users' affective states, positioning it as the natural culmination of digital and experiential marketing evolution rather than a speculative disruption (Semwal et al., 2024).

The rapid expansion of digital technology has profoundly changed how brands communicate with customers, moving away from traditional one-way communication and toward immersive, interactive, and data-driven engagement models (Patel & Kaur,

2025). Organizations are researching breakthrough technologies capable of delivering personalized, interactive, and emotionally resonant experiences as consumers want them (Chen, 2024). In this perspective, the metaverse, a persistent, interconnected virtual environment made possible by augmented reality (AR), virtual reality (VR), extended reality (XR), blockchain, and artificial intelligence, represents a significant frontier for marketing innovation (Nair, 2024; Uddin et al., 2024). The metaverse promises to transform how consumers perceive, interact with, and co-create brand experiences by combining physical presence with digitally enhanced interactions (Li et al., 2024). Within this evolving landscape, experiential metaverse marketing has received a lot of attention as a deliberate strategy to provide immersive brand experiences that go beyond traditional digital touchpoints.

The ability to promote emotional, sensory, and participatory engagement is key to experiential metaverse marketing (Shih, 2025). Unlike traditional marketing channels, which are frequently passive and unidirectional, the metaverse enables customers to tour virtual showrooms, attend branded events, modify digital avatars, connect with virtual influencers, and even co-create products in simulated surroundings (Kumar et al., 2025). These encounters foster a stronger emotional connection while increasing customer involvement and brand memory. However, as the metaverse expands rapidly, brands encounter difficulties in comprehending consumer emotions, perceptions, and behavioral responses within these immersive environments (Kaman & Deshmukh, 2025). Consumer involvement in virtual environments is influenced by a variety of psychological, social, and experiential aspects (Violante et al., 2019). As a result, powerful analytic technologies capable of decoding consumer emotions and informing real-time marketing decisions are becoming increasingly important (Chand et al., 2025).

This is where AI-powered sentiment analytics has emerged as an important facilitator. Sentiment analytics, which uses machine learning (ML), natural language processing (NLP), and deep learning algorithms, allows marketers to evaluate massive amounts of unstructured data like text, speech, gestures, facial expressions, and behavioral patterns (Sharma et al., 2025). These data streams in the metaverse are considerably richer and more complex, originating from interactions within virtual worlds, in-game discussions, avatar behaviors, and biometric feedback (Herath et al., 2024). AI-powered analytics enables organizations to detect subtle emotional indications and generate actionable insights into consumer preferences, attitudes, and engagement levels (Islam et al., 2024). As a result, marketers can create hyper-personalized and emotionally evocative experiences that change constantly in response to user feedback (Bozkurt et al., 2025).

Integration of sentiment analytics into metaverse environments has improved marketing efforts in a variety of ways. First, it enables firms to assess how consumers feel during virtual interactions, allowing for real-time customisation (Natarajan et al.,

2025). Second, sentiment-driven insights inform experience design by determining what motivates, excites, and annoys users (Al-Adaileh et al., 2024). Third, marketers can quantify emotional engagement more accurately than ever before, allowing for better customer journey mapping, predictive modeling, and behavioral segmentation (Watson, 2022). Furthermore, AI models trained on metaverse-specific datasets can predict customer reactions and optimise virtual ads accordingly (Soliman et al., 2024). The confluence of immersive environments and powerful analytics represents a paradigm shift in which emotional intelligence becomes a core capability for digital branding (Dulloo & Struweg, 2025).

Furthermore, the integration of experiential metaverse marketing and AI-powered sentiment analytics has substantial implications for customer engagement, which is a key driver of brand loyalty, advocacy, and long-term profitability. Customers' participation in metaverse experiences is determined by aspects such as presence, immersion, interactivity, co-creation, and hedonic value. Brands may use sentiment analytics to better understand these characteristics and create targeted solutions that increase consumers' emotional, cognitive, and behavioral engagement. For example, AI can detect low interest levels and make changes to virtual content, offer personalized activities, or adapt the experience environment in real time. Such adaptable experiences ensure that consumer satisfaction stays high while desertion rates remain low.

Despite its potential, this nascent profession faces numerous hurdles. Data privacy, surveillance concerns, user autonomy, and emotional manipulation are all ethical issues that must be carefully considered (Dhirani et al., 2023). The metaverse collects massive amounts of personal and behavioral data, prompting concerns about transparency and responsible data use. AI-powered sentiment analytics may also confront biases, misclassifications, and cultural differences in emotional expressions, which could jeopardize the accuracy of findings. Furthermore, the technology infrastructure needed to support real-time analytics in immersive environments remains complex, requiring significant computational power, interoperability, and a strong data architecture (Logeswaran et al., 2024; Marques et al., 2019).

Emotion and sentiment are important in immersive marketing because customer decision-making is primarily influenced by affective responses rather than simply logical judgements, as emphasised by the emotional economics approach (Huang et al., 2023). Emotional engagement increases attention, memory formation, brand attachment, and behavioural intentions, making it an important predictor of marketing efficacy in experience-based settings. In traditional digital marketing contexts, emotional measurement has primarily relied on indirect and post-experience indicators such as self-reported surveys, sentiment analysis of textual reviews, click-through rates, dwell time, and social media reactions, all of which capture limited and often retrospective representations of consumer emotions (Jabreel et al., 2020). These approaches tend to ignore moment-to-moment emotional swings and are limited by social desirability bias, recollection mistakes, and low contextual richness. Immersive environments, such as virtual reality and metaverse platforms, provide rich, real-time emotional data via speech interactions, avatar behaviour, facial expressions collected by head-mounted displays, gaze tracking, movement patterns, and physiological signals (Ahmed et al., 2024). This allows emotional involvement to be judged dynamically as feelings arise throughout the encounter rather than after it has ended. As a result, immersive marketing moves emotional analysis away from static, outcome-based assessment and towards continuous, process-oriented sentiment interpretation, allowing companies to identify emotional intensity, flow moods, irritation, or joy as they arise. Immersive environments, when combined with AI-driven sentiment analytics, enable emotionally responsive experiences that adapt in real time to consumer affective states, thereby increasing experiential relevance, personalisation, and engagement effectiveness beyond what traditional digital marketing approaches can achieve (Wen et al., 2025).

Given the growing opportunities and obstacles, there is an urgent need for academic research into how experiential metaverse marketing may effectively use AI-driven sentiment analytics to increase client engagement while resolving ethical, technological, and management concerns. Although previous study has looked at metaverse marketing, virtual consumer behavior, and sentiment analysis separately, little has been done to look at them all together. This gap offers an opportunity to examine how immersive experiences powered by AI-driven emotional intelligence might transform customer engagement methods in digital ecosystems. This study intends to add to the developing conversation by investigating the role of AI-driven sentiment analytics in improving experiential marketing outcomes in metaverse contexts. The study aims to determine how emotional data may be used to create meaningful and engaging virtual experiences, what difficulties and opportunities exist, and how marketers can construct future-ready customer interaction strategies. As the metaverse matures into a mainstream marketing platform, understanding this integration becomes critical not only for marketers but also for enterprises seeking a long-term competitive advantage in digital markets.

REVIEW OF LITERATURE

past scholarly literature in of experiential metaverse marketing has been reviewed in this section.

Theoretical Foundations

This study is based on various complementary theoretical viewpoints that explain how immersive metaverse settings improve consumer engagement via emotional, cognitive, and sensory mechanisms. According to the Experience Economy framework, value is increasingly created through staged, memorable experiences rather than functional product attributes, which is directly aligned with metaverse marketing, in which brands create immersive, multi-sensory, and participatory virtual environments that consumers actively inhabit (Pine & Gilmore, 2013). Flow Theory elaborates on user engagement in the metaverse by emphasising deep absorption, enjoyment, and loss of self-consciousness during optimally challenging and interactive experiences; metaverse platforms, through gamification, real-time interaction, and adaptive content, are uniquely positioned to induce flow states that prolong engagement and enhance brand recall (Nakamura & Csikszentmihalyi, 2009). Furthermore, Presence Theory emphasises the psychological sensation of "being there," which is essential to avatar-based interactions and spatial immersion in virtual worlds, allowing consumers to perceive branded metaverse experiences as authentic and emotionally impactful rather than simulated or symbolic (Hartmann et al., 2015). Affective Computing Theory lays the technological and analytical groundwork for interpreting and responding to users' emotional states by leveraging AI-driven sentiment analytics, emotion recognition, and multimodal data processing, enabling metaverse environments to dynamically adapt experiences based on real-time affective feedback (Kumar, 2021). Finally, the distinction between technology acceptance and emotional acceptance highlights a significant shift in immersive marketing, where adoption is influenced not only by perceived usefulness or ease of use, but also by emotional resonance, enjoyment, identity expression, and affective comfort in virtual spaces. Together, these theoretical perspectives define metaverse marketing as an experiential, emotion-centric, technologically mediated environment in which immersive design and AI-enabled emotional intelligence impact customer engagement, satisfaction, and behavioural intents.

Metaverse as a Marketing Ecosystem

The metaverse may be defined as a multidimensional marketing environment made up of several platform typologies that enable different types of customer involvement, value co-creation, and brand contact (Dwivedi et al., 2023). Gaming-based metaverse systems prioritise immersive play, gamification, and achievement-based engagement, enabling companies to incorporate experiential storytelling, virtual products, and reward mechanisms into entertainment-centric environments (Mitsea et al., 2025). Social VR systems prioritise social presence, avatar-mediated interaction, and community building, allowing companies to promote relational engagement, peer influence, and shared experience consumption via virtual events, branded social spaces, and influencer-driven interactions (Li et al., 2025). In contrast, enterprise metaverse focusses on functional and professional applications such as virtual collaboration, training, simulations, and digital twins, allowing businesses to improve internal engagement, experiential learning, and B2B branding (Di Paolo et al., 2025). These platform typologies are further distinguished by their underlying technology architectures. VR-based metaverse settings provide high levels of immersion and presence via head-mounted displays, allowing for embodied, completely virtual experiences that maximise sensory engagement and emotional intensity, although they frequently need specialised gear and more user commitment (Suk & Laine, 2023). AR-based metaverse systems overlay digital material on physical settings, resulting in hybrid experiences that enrich real-world contexts through interactive visualisations, product previews, and location-based storytelling, therefore increasing contextual relevance and lowering entry barriers (Park & Choo, 2022). Browser-based metaverse systems, which are accessible via regular web interfaces, have an emphasis on scalability, accessibility, and simplicity of adoption, allowing people to engage without the need for specific hardware while providing lesser levels of immersion. Collectively, these platform variants demonstrate that the metaverse is an ecosystem of linked experience settings, each with unique strategic implications for immersive marketing design, emotional engagement, and AI-driven personalisation.

AI in Experiential Design

Artificial intelligence is essential in metaverse marketing because it allows for adaptable, personalised, and co-creative brand experiences that change in reaction to user behaviour and emotional signals (Kumar et al., 2025). Generative AI improves experiential creativity by dynamically developing virtual landscapes, storylines, product designs, and branded material in real time, allowing experiences to be renewed and adjusted without manual involvement (Rahimi et al., 2025). AI-powered avatars, which serve as intelligent brand representatives or virtual companions, enable naturalistic and emotionally responsive interactions via conversational intelligence, sentiment awareness, and contextual memory, thereby increasing social presence and relational engagement within immersive environments. Recommender systems personalise the user experience by analysing behavioural patterns, emotional responses, and interaction histories to deliver contextually relevant products, activities, and content, guiding them through non-linear and exploratory virtual spaces while maintaining engagement and flow. Furthermore, digital twins enhance experiential design by producing real-time virtual duplicates of actual goods, settings, or customers, allowing companies to replicate, test, and optimise experiential interactions using predictive analytics and sentiment-driven insights (Fukawa & Rindfleisch, 2023). Together, these AI-powered components elevate experiential marketing from static experience staging to an intelligent, adaptive ecosystem in which virtual environments sense, learn, and respond to consumer emotions and behaviours, reinforcing the metaverse's status as a dynamic and emotionally intelligent marketing platform.

Multimodal Sentiment Analytics in Immersive Environments

Multimodal sentiment analytics is critical for evaluating emotional involvement in immersive settings because user emotions in the metaverse are conveyed through numerous simultaneous channels rather than isolated textual clues (Das & Singh, 2023). While traditional sentiment analysis has primarily relied on text-based signals such as chat messages, reviews, and comments, immersive platforms generate more affective data through voice intonation, speech rhythm, facial expressions captured via head-mounted displays, gaze patterns, body movements, and physiological signals such as heart rate variability and galvanic skin response (Hung & Alias, 2023). Each medium provides partial and context-dependent emotional insight: language conveys explicit sentiment, voice reflects emotional intensity, facial and body clues disclose spontaneous affect, and physiological signals capture subconscious emotional reactions. Relying on a single medium increases the potential of misunderstanding, especially in dynamic virtual worlds where emotions vary swiftly and may not be verbalised. As a result, multimodality is critical in the metaverse for capturing the intricacy, immediacy, and embodied aspect of immersive experiences, enabling AI systems to triangulate emotional states and enhance robustness and accuracy through cross-modal fusion (Young & Dawkins, 2023). However, multimodal emotion identification confronts considerable cross-cultural hurdles since emotional expression differs among cultures in terms of facial display regulations, vocal expression, gesture conventions, and comfort with emotional disclosure (Hosseini et al., 2024). When trained on culturally homogenous datasets, models may misclassify emotions or generate bias in global metaverse platforms. These problems underscore the need for sentiment analytics frameworks that are culturally adaptable, privacy-aware, and ethically controlled, with the ability to analyse emotional signals contextually while respecting variation in emotional expression across immersive digital environments.

AI Technologies in Sentiment Analytics

AI solutions supporting sentiment analytics in immersive and virtual worlds include a wide range of computational techniques, each with unique benefits and limits in collecting customer sentiments. Traditional machine learning algorithms, such as Support Vector Machines (SVMs) and Random Forests, have been widely used for sentiment classification due to their interpretability, robustness with smaller datasets, and low computational requirements; however, they frequently fail to capture complex, non-linear emotional patterns and contextual dependencies found in immersive interactions (Al Amrani et al., 2018). Neural network-based models, such as deep neural networks and recurrent or transformer-based architectures, excel at modelling high-dimensional, sequential, and multimodal data, but they necessitate large datasets, significant computational resources, and precise tuning to avoid overfitting and opacity (Waqas et al., 2024). Tokenisation, word and sentence embeddings, and attention mechanisms in Natural Language Processing (NLP) allow systems to move beyond keyword-based sentiment detection to contextual and semantic understanding of user expressions, making them particularly useful for analysing conversational interactions and narrative engagement in metaverse environments (Kusal et al., 2023). Facial landmark detection, convolutional neural networks, and spatiotemporal modelling are used in computer vision-based emotion recognition to infer affective states from avatar facial expressions, gaze direction, and micro-movements. While these approaches are effective, they are sensitive to occlusion, avatar stylisation, lighting variability, and cultural differences in facial expressivity. Physiological sensing techniques, such as electroencephalography (EEG), photoplethysmography (PPG), and electromyography (EMG), provide objective and subconscious indicators of emotional arousal and cognitive load, with high temporal precision but significant challenges in terms of hardware intrusiveness, signal noise, user comfort, and data privacy (Yadav et al., 2024). To overcome the limits of unimodal methods, hybrid multimodal approaches combine textual, visual, auditory, and physiological information with early, late, or hybrid fusion techniques, allowing for more robust and context-aware sentiment inference. Comparative data reveals that multimodal fusion models outperform single-modality techniques in virtual environments by boosting accuracy, resilience, and emotional granularity, especially in complex immersive contexts where emotions are embodied, dynamic, and culturally varied (Yoon & Kim, 2025).

Experiential marketing and the metaverse

Experiential marketing, based on the "experience economy" theory, emphasizes staged, sensory, and participative events as key mechanisms for building customer value, distinctiveness, and long-term loyalty (Schmitt 1999; Schmitt & Zarantonello, 2013). Traditional experiential tactics place a premium on immersion, co-creation, and emotional resonance as factors influencing consumer engagement and behavior

(Ahmed et al., 2024). These theoretical foundations have been applied to digital situations where interactivity and personalization are essential.

The metaverse concept combines immersive technologies (VR/AR/XR), persistent virtual worlds, interoperable digital assets, and social presence to create an ecosystem that expands the experiential opportunities available to brands and consumers (Ali et al., 2023). Scholars suggest that the metaverse offers a qualitatively different platform for experiential marketing: it allows for deeper sensory stimulation, synchronous co-presence, user-driven narratives, and programmable environments in which brands and consumers may co-create meaning in real time (Kozinets, 2023). Recent literature reviews and bibliometric studies highlight the rapid expansion of metaverse research in marketing, emphasizing how companies are experimenting with virtual showrooms, gamified brand spaces, and avatar-mediated interactions to increase branding and pre-purchase interest (Ramadan, 2023). Researchers categorize experiential metaverse marketing into five interconnected dimensions: (1) presence/immersion (the subjective feeling of "being there") (Dwivedi et al., 2023) (2) interactivity (the degree of reciprocal action between user and environment) (Chen et al., 2024) (3) co-creation (user participation in design or narrative) (Ramadan, Z., & Ramadan; 2025), (4) hedonic/entertainment value (Bruni & Galvagno; 2025), and (5) sociality (Bae & Bae, 2025). These dimensions govern traditional marketing outcomes, brand memory, purchase intent, word-of-mouth, and loyalty while also introducing novel measures like avatar identity expression and virtual token economies. Empirical studies suggest that gamified and immersive brand experiences in metaverse contexts can boost positive word-of-mouth and purchase intent, however the results differ depending on platform design and user demographics (Al-Adwan et al., 2025).

AI's role in enabling adaptive, personalized experiences

Artificial intelligence is usually referred to as the connective tissue that allows for real-time personalization, intelligent NPCs/avatars, content adaptability, and predictive analytics in metaverse environments (Basyoni et al., 2025). AI technologies, natural language processing (NLP) for conversational agents, recommender systems for content personalization, computer vision and posture estimation for avatar mapping, and reinforcement learning for dynamic environment optimization enable brands to create contextualized experiences on a large scale (Lim et al., 2024). Reviews of AI-metaverse integration note that AI not only automates operational chores but also changes the subjective quality of experiences by reading user behavior and altering stimuli as needed (Puntoni et al., 2021).

Sentiment analytics and multimodal emotion recognition

Sentiment analysis has progressed beyond text mining to encompass multimodal emotion recognition (MER), which incorporates facial expressions, voice prosody, gesture, physiological signs, and textual cues (Khan et al., 2024; García-Hernández et al., 2024). Recent improvements in deep learning allow systems to learn cross-modal representations, which improve resilience and accuracy over unimodal techniques (Jabeen et al., 2023). Multimodal models can capture deeper affective states and provide more reliable indices of engagement and pleasure in immersive contexts that include voice, gaze, micro expressions, and motion (Sukumaran & Manoharan, 2024). Systematic evaluations of MER emphasize the need of multimodality for rich, spontaneous emotional responses found in interactive contexts. Sensor-based emotion analysis with head-mounted display (HMD) telemetry, eye-tracking, facial landmark estimation, and movement patterns produces near-real-time emotional inference that correlates with self-report measures but with higher temporal resolution (Lian et al., 2024). Such methods allow for adaptive actions, such as reducing difficulty, changing music, or suggesting social cues, when affect signals indicate dissatisfaction or boredom. These methodologies point to a more methodologically richer manner to operationalize experiential marketing engagement than survey snapshots alone.

Evidence on customer engagement outcomes

Empirical research and field tests on metaverse marketing outcomes are still in their early stages, but they are increasing. Evidence suggests that immersive branded experiences, when well designed, can increase hedonic enjoyment, perceived authenticity, and brand connection, resulting in increased purchase intentions and referral behaviors (Shao, 2025). The addition of AI-driven adaptive elements enhances these outcomes by maintaining flow and reducing disengagement: systems that dynamically personalize content report longer session length, greater behavioral intent, and higher subjective satisfaction when compared to static virtual experiences (Wongkitrungrueng & Suprawan. 2024). However, the results are mixed and influenced by user tech knowledge, perceived intrusiveness, and cultural variances in emotional expressiveness.

Ethical, privacy, and socio-technical challenges

While the technical potential is great, a parallel literature warns about privacy, surveillance, bias, and safety concerns. The metaverse's ability to collect fine-grained physiological and behavioral data (eye movement, facial muscle dynamics, micro-gestures) creates serious privacy concerns, as these signals can reveal sensitive information that goes beyond mere preferences (Venugopal et al., 2025). Several recent studies and investigative reports have highlighted ethical pitfalls—data misuse, manipulative nudging via affective cues, insufficient moderation of harassment, and ambiguous consent mechanisms particularly on platforms managed by huge businesses (Leal & Oliveira, 2025). Regulatory and design frameworks for openness, data reduction, and fairness are stressed as critical requirements for the ethical use of sentiment analytics in marketing settings (Hermann 2022; Barker et al., 2025).

Platform Comparative Analysis

Metaverse systems range significantly in their technological architectures, user demographics, and ability to enable AI-driven sentiment analytics, making platform selection an important strategic decision for immersive marketing campaigns (Boztas et al., 2025). Meta Horizon Worlds focusses on social VR interaction and avatar-based co-presence, providing numerous opportunities for sentiment analytics through voice interaction, gesture tracking, and spatial behaviour; however, access to granular emotional data is largely proprietary, limiting external researchers' ability to deploy independent analytics models (Suk & Laine, 2023). Roblox and Fortnite are gaming-focused metaverse platforms with high amounts of user-generated content, gamification, and social engagement. Roblox, with its youthful and creator-oriented audience, allows for large-scale behavioural and engagement analytics, but it does not give access to biometric or emotive data, limiting sentiment analysis to behavioural and textual indications. While Fortnite provides very immersive branded events and narrative-driven experiences, it works in a closed environment in which emotional involvement is inferred indirectly via participation numbers and interaction patterns rather than direct emotive cues.

Table 1. Literature Review

Sr. No.	Authors (year)	Paper title	Research methodology	Key findings
1	Dwivedi, Y. K. et al. (2022)	Metaverse beyond the hype: Multidisciplinary perspectives on emerging challenges, opportunities, and agenda for research, practice and policy.	This study utilized multidisciplinary and narrative review, expert synthesis.	Findings of the study reveals that synthesizes cross-disciplinary implications of the metaverse for business and society; identifies key research agenda items (privacy, governance, experience design) and managerial opportunities.
2	Soliman, et al. (2024)	Artificial intelligence powered Metaverse: analysis, challenges and future perspectives.	This study adopted conceptual review and techno-analytic discussion	Results highlight that AI is core to metaverse personalization (NLP, CV, RL); outlines infrastructure, interoperability, and ethical challenges for deploying AI in virtual worlds.
3	Ramadan, Z. (2023)	Marketing in the metaverse era: toward an integrative channel approach.	This study utilized Conceptual and theoretical analysis.	This study proposes integrative marketing routes in metaverse contexts; highlights experiential design, channel strategy and measurement gaps.

continued on following page

Table 1. Continued

Sr. No.	Authors (year)	Paper title	Research methodology	Key findings
4	Barrera, K. G. (2023)	Marketing in the Metaverse: Conceptual understanding, framework, and research agenda.	This study utilized literature review and conceptual paper.	Results demonstrate that the Positions metaverse as transformative for brand experience; discusses design dimensions (presence, interactivity, sociality) that drive engagement.
5	Wu, Y. et al. (2025)	A Comprehensive Review of Multimodal Emotion Recognition (MER)	The study adopted systematic review of MER literature	This study shows that MER (fusion of text/audio/visual/physio) improves emotion detection accuracy; identifies challenges: data heterogeneity, real-world robustness, and cross-cultural variation.
6	Joo, J. H. et al. (2024)	Immersive Emotion Analysis in VR Environments: A Sensor-based Approach	This research used experimental sensor study in VR (HMD telemetry, eye-tracking, motion)	This study reveals that sensor-based, real-time emotion inference correlates well with self-report and gives higher temporal resolution, useful for adaptive VR experiences.
7	Kim, H. (2024)	Enhancing emotion recognition using multimodal fusion of physiological, environmental and personal data	This study adopted model development and experimental dataset	This study shows that multimodal fusion model outperforms unimodal baselines; combining physiology and context boosts robustness in naturalistic settings.
8	Khalaf et al. (2024)	Elevating metaverse virtual reality experiences through network-integrated neuro-fuzzy emotion recognition and adaptive content generation algorithms.	This research utilized algorithm development and simulation/empirical tests.	Results of the study shows that Neuro-fuzzy emotion recognition coupled with adaptive content generation yields more stable engagement metrics and smoother user flow in simulated metaverse scenarios.
9	Chen, Q. et al. (2025)	MERD-360VR: A Multimodal Emotional Response Dataset from 360° VR Videos Across Different Age Groups	This study used dataset creation and benchmarking experiments.	Results provide a comprehensive VR emotion dataset (audio, video, motion, HMD telemetry) and baseline model results, enables reproducible benchmarking for VR MER.
10	Tang, Y. M., Wong, J. K. N., Ho, G. T. S. (2025)	Exploring Consumer Acceptance of Metaverse Marketing...	This study utilized empirical survey and done comparative experiments.	Results find acceptance influenced by perceived usefulness, pleasure, privacy concerns; metaverse marketing effective for branding & pre-purchase when perceived authenticity is high.
11	Qianye Wu, et al. (2025)	AI-Driven Sentiment Analytics: Unlocking Business Value in the E-Commerce Landscape	This study used system design and empirical experiments on large datasets	Result highlight that ybrid AI system (traditional ML and deep models) achieves high sentiment accuracy and shows measurable improvements in engagement and conversion in pilot deployments.
12	Al-Adwan et al., 2025	Treasure hunting for brands: metaverse marketing gamification effects on purchase intention, WOM, and loyalty	This study utilized empirical experimental study (field/online).	The study reveals that gamified metaverse marketing activities increase positive word-of-mouth and purchase intentions, moderated by perceived enjoyment and platform familiarity.
13	Zeng, Y. (2024)	Multimodal emotion recognition in the metaverse era: New needs and transformation in mental health work.	This study adopted literature review.	This study highlights the rise of MER needs in the metaverse for affective computing and mental-health applications; calls for robust, privacy-preserving MER methods.
14	Jean, G. (2024).	Sentiment Analysis and Emotion Recognition for Emotionally Adaptive Mobile UIs	This study utilized system integration and applied experiments	Results demonstrate feasibility of combining sentiment analysis and emotion recognition to adapt mobile UI behaviors and improve user experience.
15	Kumar, V. (2024)	AI-powered marketing: What, where, and how?	This study adopted conceptual synthesis across marketing functions.	Results of the study show that Synthesizes AI applications across marketing (personalization, recommender systems, sentiment analytics) and discusses organizational readiness and measurement implications for ROI.

(Source – Authors Compilation)

RESEARCH METHODOLOGY

This study uses a qualitative research methodology based on a thorough analysis of current literature (Tong et al., 2016; Furidha, 2023). Because experiential metaverse marketing and AI-driven sentiment analytics are new domains with evolving theoretical foundations, qualitative research is appropriate for synthesizing fragmented knowledge, identifying conceptual linkages between metaverse experience design, AI analytics, and customer engagement, detecting patterns, contradictions, and emerging themes, and developing research frameworks and future directions. The chosen design is consistent with recognized qualitative literature-based approaches such as systematic literature review, narrative review, and thematic synthesis.

FINDINGS AND DISCUSSION

According to a qualitative evaluation of available research, the integration of experiential marketing ideas into the metaverse, paired with AI-driven sentiment analytics, is radically changing customer interaction dynamics. The findings point to three major thematic outcomes: the transformation of experiential marketing through immersive metaverse environments, strategic engagement enhancement via AI-enabled sentiment analysis, and the emergence of new consumer behavioral patterns driven by virtual presence, digital identity, and emotional resonance within metaverse platforms. These trends point to a shift toward more in-depth, emotion-focused, data-driven, and highly personalized marketing environments.

Metaverse as a Catalyst for Experiential Immersion

The first emerging theme from the literature is that the metaverse has pushed the bounds of experiential marketing by introducing levels of virtual immersion, interactivity, and co-creation that standard digital settings cannot provide. Studies repeatedly show that metaverse ecosystems, which include VR/AR environments, digital twins, virtual stores, and avatar-based interactions, enable marketers to provide multi-sensory, gamified, and socially engaged experiences (Dwivedi et al., 2022; Mystakidis, 2022). These immersive experiences increase consumers' perceived value by engaging them as active participants rather than passive observers. The research also shows that metaverse-based brand experiences increase engagement, which is motivated by curiosity, presence, and emotional connection. Consumers frequently identify these spaces with play, escape, and creative self-expression. Brand activations, such as virtual fashion shows, branded gaming adventures, and digital collectibles, produce emotional impressions that linger longer than standard digital commercials. Importantly, the findings indicate that the metaverse's experiential richness increases brand recall and purchase intention, particularly among Gen Z and young millennials, who are early users of extended reality (XR) technology. This demonstrates that the metaverse is more than a distribution route; it is also a strategic experiential touchpoint.

Role of AI-Driven Sentiment Analytics in Understanding Emotional Engagement

A second important conclusion is that AI-powered sentiment analytics improve marketers' capacity to comprehend and maximize consumer involvement in metaverse venues. Unlike traditional social media interactions, metaverse environments produce sophisticated, multimodal emotional data such as speech tonality, facial cues (using VR headsets), interaction behavior, time-spent metrics, and avatar movements. Various research has identified AI-based sentiment analysis as a vital tool for deciphering these emotional signals. Natural Language Processing (NLP), machine learning classifiers, and deep neural networks enable marketers to analyze customer emotions (e.g., joy, anger, excitement), brand attitude shifts, satisfaction levels with specific virtual experiences, feedback embedded in textual or voice-based interactions, and emotional triggers associated with engagement drop-offs or purchase actions. The studied literature demonstrates that when marketers combine experiential techniques with AI-powered emotional insights, they may deliver personalized content, adaptive storytelling, and real-time experience modification. For example, if sentiment analytics detect a decrease in emotional response during a virtual store tour, AI can modify the atmosphere or suggest new virtual products. A consistent conclusion is that AI shifts experiential marketing from a one-size-fits-all paradigm to an emotion-driven personalized strategy, making engagement more predictive, responsive, and quantifiable.

Emerging Behavioural Dynamics in Metaverse Consumer Engagement

The findings also reveal distinct behavioural changes among consumers engaging in metaverse environments. Literature identifies three evolving patterns:

1. Shift Towards Avatar-Mediated Identity Expression

Consumers frequently respond differently in avatars than in real-world settings. This identity flexibility fosters innovation, risk-taking, and exploration. The sentiment analytics literature implies that emotions conveyed through avatars are more authentic because users feel less evaluated, allowing for stronger brand affinity.

2. Higher Expectation for Real-Time Responsiveness

Users expect the virtual world to respond instantly to their actions. AI-enabled systems that respond dynamically via recommendation engines, tailored tasks, or interactive storytelling have been shown to greatly enhance engagement.

3. Movement from Passive Consumption to Co-Creation

Virtual creation tools, NFTs, and gamified challenges allow consumers to co-design brand experiences. According to studies, co-creation based on emotional insights leads to long-term loyalty and community creation.

Convergence of Experiential Marketing and AI Insights

A key finding in the literature is that AI sentiment analytics serve as a link between experiential content and customer expectations. Brands that incorporate both components generate more emotional resonance and more successful engagement outcomes. This convergence yields four major benefits: 1) Improved Emotional Precision: Artificial intelligence enables marketers to discern micro-emotions and change experiential aspects accordingly. 2) Real-Time Engagement Optimisation: Using sentiment feedback loops, virtual surroundings may be changed quickly. 3) Predictive Engagement Modeling: Machine learning algorithms estimate which experiential components are most likely to increase conversions. 4) Data-Driven Creativity: AI insights generate unique experience designs that are emotionally appropriate for the audience. Overall, this synergy converts the metaverse into an emotionally intelligent immersive ecosystem (Figure – 1).

Figure 1. Experiential Metaverse Marketing

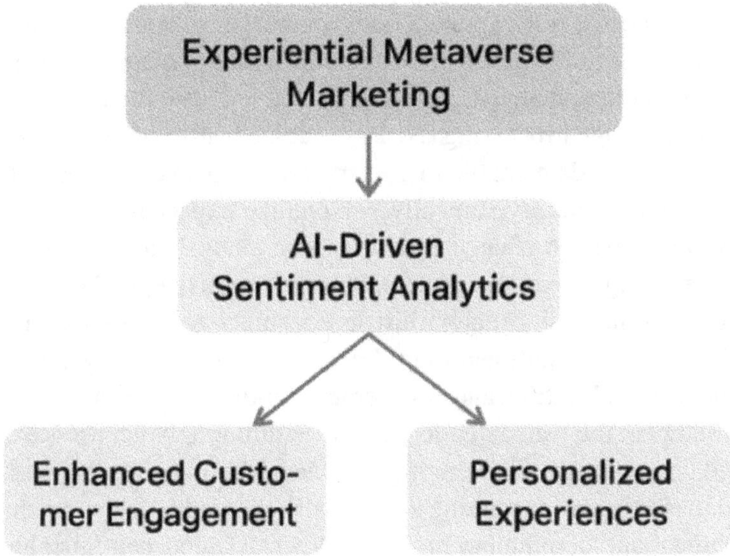

(Source: Author's compilation)

The rapid advancement of immersive technologies and artificial intelligence has profoundly altered the landscape of digital marketing, resulting in a new paradigm known as Experiential Metaverse Marketing. This study looked at how AI-powered sentiment analytics can be strategically integrated into metaverse environments to improve customer engagement, personalize brand interactions, and create emotionally compelling immersive experiences. The findings from the literature study and theoretical studies highlight the revolutionary potential of merging VR/AR capabilities with emotion-intelligent AI systems, establishing the metaverse as a significant frontier in the future of marketing. According to the analysis, the metaverse expands on existing experiential marketing theories by allowing businesses to create deeply immersive, multi-sensory, and co-creative encounters that transcend the restrictions of physical and two-dimensional digital places. The metaverse fosters a stronger sense of presence and emotional participation through avatar-based interactions, gamified brand engagements, virtual storytelling, and digital reproductions of physical settings. These immersive qualities boost consumers' cognitive, emotive, and behavioral engagement, turning them into active participants rather than passive users of marketing content. As a result, the metaverse emerges not just as another communication channel, but as a comprehensive experience ecosystem that radically changes how businesses and customers co-create value.

A key finding from this study is the critical significance of AI-driven sentiment analytics in deciphering customer emotions, behaviors, and preferences in real time. Voice exchanges, VR-captured body language, avatar expressions, movement patterns, and textual conversations all contribute to the metaverse's complex emotional data. Sentiment analytics transforms these clues into actionable insights using Natural Language Processing (NLP), machine learning classifiers, and affective computing. These data enable marketers to anticipate emotional cues, predict engagement patterns, and dynamically personalize experiences. The integration of AI allows marketers to change from post-hoc analysis to real-time emotional intelligence, resulting in extremely adaptable and responsive marketing campaigns. The findings also indicate a major shift in consumer behavior within metaverse contexts. Compared to traditional digital platforms, users show greater emotional openness, identity exploration, and engagement depth. Virtual avatars are more than just representations; they are extended identities through which users express their creativity, goals, and sense of belonging. This behavior expands the possibilities of experiential marketing by generating emotionally charged touchpoints that improve brand attachment and community creation. When AI sentiment insights are used, these encounters can be adjusted to generate long-term loyalty, happiness, and advocacy, signaling a new type of relationship marketing based on virtual co-presence and emotional alignment.

The study's key finding is that immersive experiences and emotional analytics work well together. While the metaverse provides the experiential architecture, AI sentiment analytics give the cognitive and emotional intelligence required to create tailored adventures. This convergence culminates in emotion-responsive environments, in which virtual landscapes change dynamically in response to user feedback and affective states. Such surroundings represent a significant step forward from static digital encounters, ushering in context- and emotion-aware marketing methods. This synergy puts AI as a co-creator of the experiential adventure, rather than just a data processing tool. The study highlights the strategic importance of incorporating AI-enhanced experiential marketing into organizational marketing operations. Brands that use emotion-centric and immersive tactics can achieve a significant competitive edge through stronger differentiation, better customer insights, and deeper engagement. Retail, tourism, education, entertainment, and luxury companies can use the metaverse to create compelling experiential propositions that build brand narratives and inspire community participation. Organizations can leverage emotional data to refine virtual store layouts, optimize digital product placements, design emotionally resonant campaigns, and align brand identity with user-generated virtual content. This establishes experiential metaverse marketing as a strategic imperative for forward-thinking brands.

Furthermore, the study advances theoretical knowledge by combining concepts from experiential marketing, metaverse interaction models, and AI-driven emotional computing into a cohesive conceptual framework. This integration helps to reimagine traditional engagement methods by merging digital embodiment, virtual identity, emotional analytics, and real-time adaptive experiences. The resulting theoretical contribution provides a solid foundation for future empirical studies and opens new avenues for multidisciplinary research. Despite its contributions, the report admits that the metaverse ecosystem is still emerging, with significant problems and uncertainties ahead. Privacy, data ethics, emotional manipulation, algorithmic transparency, and digital welfare are all serious concerns that must be addressed. The success of immersive experiences is also determined by technological accessibility, user preparation, and platform maturity. Furthermore, the accuracy of sentiment analytics varies with data quality, cultural nuances, and contextual interpretation. These factors underscore the necessity for ongoing research into ethical frameworks, standardized measurement models, and user-centered design approaches to enable responsible deployment.

Technical Implementation Challenges

Despite its potential, applying AI-powered sentiment analytics in immersive settings poses significant technological obstacles. Latency difficulties are especially important in emotionally adaptable experiences, which require real-time processing to sustain immersion and flow. Delays in sentiment inference or experience adjustment can disrupt presence and impair engagement, particularly in high-interaction environments like gaming or live virtual events. Data quality is another key concern. Immersive settings generate noise due to fast avatar movement, irregular lighting conditions, headset displacement, and biometric signal variability caused by motion artefacts or device restrictions. These variables can limit emotion identification accuracy, necessitating extensive signal preprocessing and noise filtering approaches. Integration complexity hampers implementation since sentiment analytics solutions must work smoothly with VR engines, avatar control systems, interaction logs, and AI middleware. Synchronous data interchange between these components necessitates complex APIs and flexible structures. Furthermore, computational needs rise fast when processing multimodal emotional input for a high number of concurrent users, demanding scalable cloud or edge computing solutions. Interoperability issues emerge owing to platform fragmentation and the lack of standardised emotional data formats across metaverse contexts. Cross-platform analytics are restricted, which limits longitudinal emotional tracking and comparison analysis. Finally, there is a constant privacy-performance trade-off: stronger data minimisation and anonymisation techniques improve user trust and regulatory compliance while potentially reducing model accuracy and emotional granularity. To address these difficulties, we need to make advancements in lightweight AI models, privacy-preserving computing, and standardised emotional data frameworks.

Consumer Psychology Perspectives

From a consumer psychology standpoint, immersive marketing efficacy in the metaverse is strongly related to Flow State Theory, which describes how appropriate challenge, interactivity, and feedback maintain deep engagement and intrinsic delight. Emotion-aware adaptive systems facilitate flow by dynamically altering experience complexity in response to emotional cues. Identity Theory also emphasises how avatar-mediated settings allow users to experiment with different identities, frequently resulting in behavioural deviation from real-world standards and increased emotional openness, which increases engagement but complicates sentiment interpretation. Presence and embodiment theories describe how spatial immersion and avatar control induce a psychological experience of "being there," hence increasing emotional resonance and memory formation. This embodied engagement heightens sensitivity to emotional cues encoded in experiencing narratives. Social dynamics are particularly important because emotional contagion among virtual crowds may enhance collective mood and influence individual emotions via group interactions, shared experiences, and social validation processes. However, hedonic adaptation is a long-term difficulty, since continuous exposure to immersive experiences can reduce emotional intensity and novelty. Maintaining interest necessitates ongoing innovation, emotional diversity, and adaptive personalisation. These psychological principles demonstrate why sentiment analytics is critical for creating immersive experiences that are emotionally meaningful, engaging, and durable over time.

AI Hallucination, Trust Erosion, and Governance in Metaverse Marketing

The use of AI-driven sentiment analytics in metaverse marketing increases the danger of AI hallucination, which is described as systematic misinterpretations or falsified conclusions created by AI systems when analysing emotional, behavioural, or contextual data. In immersive settings, hallucinations can develop in different forms (Maleki et al., 2024). Sentiment hallucinations happen when AI systems incorrectly categorise emotional polarity or strength, which is commonly caused by chaotic multimodal inputs or culturally ambiguous statements (Goodarzi et al., 2023). Intent hallucinations occur when systems assume customer intentions or buy readiness without sufficient contextual information, resulting in improper targeting or experience adaption (Christensen et al., 2025). Emotion hallucinations, which are especially important in affective computing, entail the incorrect identification of emotional states such as dissatisfaction, excitement, or satisfaction, distorting real-time personalisation and engagement tactics (Marín-Morales et al., 2020). These hallucinations create major dangers to brand trust because emotionally charged or invasive responses can damage the perceived authenticity and dependability of immersive brand encounters. When AI-powered systems react to emotions that consumers did not consciously express, they may feel uncomfortable or lose agency, undermining trust in the brand's ethical goal. Furthermore, poor emotional inference can lead to consumer manipulation, in which adaptive systems exploit perceived weaknesses by encouraging users towards specific behaviours, purchases, or longer engagement based on incorrect emotional evaluations. Such manipulative effects are exacerbated in metaverse settings, which emphasise presence, embodiment, and emotional immersion, raising issues about emotional autonomy and digital well-being. To address these dangers, strong AI governance procedures are required. Human-in-the-loop (HITL) frameworks guarantee that crucial emotional interpretations and adaptive solutions are verified or overruled by human involvement, especially in high-stakes marketing scenarios. To limit the likelihood of hallucinations and assure responsible emotional analytics, ethical AI design concepts such as fairness, explainability, bias audits, and data minimisation must be included at the system level. In addition, transparency dashboards may improve accountability by alerting consumers about how their emotional data is gathered, processed, and utilised to build immersive experiences. Such dashboards provide customers more control and build confidence through visibility and informed consent. Collectively, these governance techniques position ethical monitoring as a precondition for long-term, trust-based metaverse marketing ecosystems, rather than a barrier to innovation.

IMPLICATIONS

Theoretical, managerial and practical implications of this study are discussed below.

Theoretical Implications

This study expands the boundaries of experiential marketing by demonstrating how immersive, avatar-driven, and multi-sensory metaverse environments generate new levels of customer experience that traditional frameworks (such as Schmitt's experiential modules) do not capture. The results indicate that future theoretical models should include virtual presence, embodiment, spatial immersion, and avatar identity expression as essential experiencing elements. The study emphasizes the importance of AI-powered sentiment analytics as a key tool for altering customer experiences. Traditional customer engagement theories focus on behavioral and cognitive reactions, but this study incorporates affective analytics, which adds emotional prediction and real-time flexibility as basic theoretical constructs. This contributes to the growing field of AI-Augmented Marketing Theory. The study makes a theoretical contribution by demonstrating how consumers behave differently while using avatars versus physical locations. It emphasizes notions like digital self-extension, identity fluidity, co-presence, and virtual freedom, which reframe traditional behavioral theories (such as flow theory, identity theory, and technology acceptance models). The study demonstrates that emotional cues in VR/AR encounters are more revealing, challenging preconceptions about emotional disclosure and involvement. Academic literature on metaverse marketing is currently developing. This study contributes to the theoretical discourse by improving notions like Experiential Metaverse Engagement (EME), Emotion-Driven Personalization (EDP), Real-Time Affective Feedback Loops (RAFL), and AI-Enhanced Co-Creation (AICC). These dimensions can be used in future empirical models to study behavioral intention, satisfaction, loyalty, and immersive buying decisions inside metaverse ecosystems.

Managerial Implications

Practitioners can use the findings of this study to create more emotionally engaging metaverse experiences. Businesses can use VR/AR-based gamification, avatar interaction, and digital storytelling to increase engagement and enhance brand relationships. Businesses can use AI capabilities to monitor and understand client emotions in real time within virtual environments. This enables marketers to recognize emotional low points, tailor the environment to maintain engagement, personalize content and product recommendations, and enhance virtual shop layouts, events, and brand interactions. Emotion-sensitive techniques can greatly boost customer satisfaction and conversion rates. The study reveals that metaverse environments paired with sentiment analytics allow for hyper-personalized experiences. Brands may personalize virtual experiences based on emotional states, behavioral indications, avatar preferences, and interaction histories, thereby increasing relevance and retention. Traditional consumer journey mapping just considers clicks, views, and dwell time. This study offers firms a new method based on emotional engagement, multi-sensory interactions, and behavioral trajectories within 3D environments. Marketers may create more accurate and relevant route maps by using real-time feelings and responses rather than static behavioral indications. This work has significant implications for managers looking to use AI-driven sentiment analytics in metaverse marketing contexts. First, managers must recognise that immersive encounters are emotion-centric rather than transaction-centric, necessitating a strategy change away from traditional performance measurements and towards affective indicators like emotional engagement, presence, and sensory pleasure. Investment choices should prioritise systems capable of recording and analysing multimodal emotional data above clicks, impressions, and conversions. Platform selection emerges as a significant management choice. Different metaverse platforms provide varied degrees of immersion, data accessibility, and sentiment analysis capacity. Managers must match platform selection with target audience demographics, brand objectives, and ethical risk tolerance, ensuring that sentiment-driven personalisation is possible without relying too much on proprietary or opaque data systems. While AI-enabled personalisation can boost engagement, managers must be wary of over-automation and AI hallucinations. Implementing human-in-the-loop monitoring for emotionally adaptable material can help to avoid misunderstanding and maintain brand confidence. Training cross-functional teams, comprising marketing, data science, and ethical specialists, may help to increase decision quality and responsibility. Ethical governance should be included into the experience design from the start, rather than being viewed as a compliance afterthought. Transparent permission methods, explainable personalisation rationale, and user-friendly control panels may all boost customer trust and long-term brand equity. Managers should also consider cultural differences in emotional expression by using inclusive emotion models and undertaking cross-cultural testing. Managers should see metaverse marketing as a continuous learning environment rather than a one-time campaign expenditure. Continuous experimentation, real-time feedback loops, and adaptive sentiment analytics allow experiences to alter in response to customer emotions while reducing hedonic adaption. Managers may utilise the metaverse not just as a fresh channel, but also as a durable, trust-driven platform for creating experience value, by blending technological innovation with ethical responsibility and emotional intelligence.

Practical Implications

The incorporation of AI-driven sentiment analytics into metaverse marketing settings demands strong regulatory and ethical governance frameworks that balance innovation with consumer protection, trust, and societal well-being. As immersive platforms rely more on emotional and biometric data, regulators must adapt existing digital governance frameworks to account for the continuous, embodied, and emotive nature of data collecting in virtual environments. Traditional privacy restrictions, while necessary, are insufficient to meet real-time emotional inference, adaptive persuasion, and automated experience modification, emphasising the importance of metaverse-specific policy guidelines. From a policy standpoint, governance systems should prioritise risk-based regulation where higher degrees of emotional data sensitivity and behavioural influence result in tougher supervision and accountability requirements. Regulatory organisations may be required to impose algorithmic effect evaluations, periodic bias audits, and documentation of emotional AI systems used in marketing personalisation. Clear guidelines for emotional data ownership, storage length, cross-platform transfer, and secondary usage are essential for preventing misuse and function creep in persistent virtual environments. Ethically, companies that use immersive marketing technology must shift from compliance-driven methods to value-centered governance. Sentiment-aware systems should be designed with core values such as openness, justice, proportionality, and user autonomy. This involves restricting emotionally manipulative techniques, refraining from exploitative pushing based on susceptible affective states, and ensuring that personalisation improves user experience rather than undermines psychological agency. Ethical governance necessitates recognising cultural variation in emotional expression, since universal emotion models risk marginalising non-dominant user groups and strengthening algorithmic prejudice. Effective governance requires multi-stakeholder supervision systems that include legal experts, ethicists, technologists, and consumer advocates in decision-making processes. Mechanisms like ethics review boards, human-in-the-loop validation, and transparency dashboards can help to operationalise responsibility and increase user confidence. Finally, long-term metaverse marketing requires governance frameworks that view emotional data as a sensitive extension of human identity rather than a commercial product. Embedding ethical responsibility into policy and practice is consequently critical for preserving legitimacy, customer trust, and long-term value generation in immersive digital environments.

CONCLUSION

This study confirms that the combination of immersive metaverse environments with AI-driven sentiment analytics marks a significant shift in how brands interact with customers. This connection provides unparalleled prospects for increasing engagement, fostering co-creation, and building long-term brand loyalty by providing emotionally intelligent, immersive, and adaptive experiences. As the metaverse matures into a mainstream marketing environment, firms that adopt emotion-aware experiential marketing will be better positioned to satisfy the demands of digitally empowered customers. Future research should concentrate on empirical validation, cross-cultural assessments, ethical considerations, and the creation of prediction models to increase both theoretical knowledge and practical applications in this new field. Metaverse marketing is predicted to expand from experimental brand activations to intelligent, emotionally adaptable ecosystems during the next five years, thanks to advancements in artificial intelligence, affective computing, and immersive technology. Improvements to multimodal AI models will allow for more accurate real-time understanding of user emotions, lowering reliance on proxy engagement measures and allowing experiences to adjust dynamically to affective states. Generative AI is anticipated to automate large-scale experiential design, resulting in personalised tales, virtual landscapes, and branded encounters that change in real time depending on emotional response. As hardware becomes more available and interoperability standards develop, immersive experiences will expand beyond entertainment and retail to include education, healthcare communication, tourism, financial services, and public involvement. Concurrently, consumer expectations will evolve towards emotionally intelligent, transparent, and ethically controlled experiences, with consumers expecting greater control over emotional data usage and personalisation rationale. Trust, authenticity, and emotional relevance will emerge as critical differentiators, establishing sentiment-aware metaverse marketing as a strategic competence rather than a novelty-driven invention. To advance this emerging field, researchers are encouraged to move beyond conceptual models toward experimental and longitudinal studies that test causal relationships between emotional engagement, adaptive experience design, and behavioral outcomes in immersive environments. There is an urgent need to create validated multimodal emotion assessment scales customised to metaverse situations and culturally varied user communities. Marketing practitioners should launch controlled pilot projects that combine sentiment analytics with experience design, as well as invest in multidisciplinary talent with expertise in marketing strategy, artificial intelligence, and ethical governance. Transparent consent processes and human scrutiny should be considered normal practice. For policymakers, the objective is to create metaverse-specific legislative frameworks that handle emotional data governance, algorithmic responsibility, and user sovereignty without limiting innovation. Collaborative, multi-stakeholder approaches will be required to guarantee that metaverse marketing develops into a responsible, trustworthy, and socially sustainable digital environment.

LIMITATIONS AND SCOPE OF FUTURE RESEARCH

Although this study sheds light on the convergence of experiential metaverse marketing and AI-driven sentiment analytics, certain limitations must be noted. These constraints create opportunity for future research to improve the theoretical, methodological, and practical understanding of this growing topic. This study is mostly based on a qualitative analysis of previous literature rather than empirical data collecting. While this approach allows for broad theoretical synthesis, it limits the ability to evaluate causal links or assess the true effectiveness of AI-driven sentiment analytics in real-world metaverse scenarios. The results are interpretive rather than statistically valid. Future study should expand beyond conceptual analysis to include field experiments, VR simulations, and observational investigations on genuine metaverse platforms. Researchers can use biometric sensors, interaction records, and psychophysiological methods to assess emotional engagement, behavioral reactions, and sentiment dynamics. There is a demand for validated scales and measurement frameworks that capture immersion, presence, avatar identification, emotional participation, co-creation behavior, and emotional engagement. Future research can provide standardized measurements similar to existing customer engagement models but suited to immersive virtual worlds.

REFERENCES

Ahmed, S., Sharif, T., Ting, D. H., & Sharif, S. J. (2024). Crafting emotional engagement and immersive experiences: Comprehensive scale development for and validation of hospitality marketing storytelling involvement. *Psychology and Marketing*, *41*(7), 1514–1529. DOI: 10.1002/mar.21994

Al-Adaileh, A., Al-Kfairy, M., Tubishat, M., & Alfandi, O. (2024). A sentiment analysis approach for understanding users' perception of metaverse marketplace. *Intelligent Systems with Applications*, *22*, 200362. DOI: 10.1016/j.iswa.2024.200362

Al-Adwan, A. S., Yaseen, H., Alkhwaldi, A. F., Jafar, R. M. S., Fauzi, M. A., & Abdullah, A. (2025). Treasure hunting for brands: Metaverse marketing gamification effects on purchase intention, WOM, and loyalty. *Journal of Global Marketing*, •••, 1–25. DOI: 10.1080/08911762.2025.2463897

Al Amrani, Y., Lazaar, M., & El Kadiri, K. E. (2018). Random forest and support vector machine based hybrid approach to sentiment analysis. *Procedia Computer Science*, *127*, 511–520. DOI: 10.1016/j.procs.2018.01.150

Ali, M., Naeem, F., Kaddoum, G., & Hossain, E. (2023). Metaverse communications, networking, security, and applications: Research issues, state-of-the-art, and future directions. *IEEE Communications Surveys and Tutorials*, *26*(2), 1238–1278. DOI: 10.1109/COMST.2023.3347172

Bae, S. H., & Bae, J. (2025). How experiential creation drives use experience in the metaverse: Focused on the interaction effect between item popularity and need for uniqueness. *Journal of Global Scholars of Marketing Science*, *35*(2), 197–207. DOI: 10.1080/21639159.2025.2468471

Ballew, M. T., Omoto, A. M., & Winter, P. L. (2015). Using Web 2.0 and social media technologies to foster proenvironmental action. *Sustainability*, *7*(8), 10620–10648. DOI: 10.3390/su70810620

Barker, D., Tippireddy, M. K. R., Farhan, A., & Ahmed, B. (2025). Ethical Considerations in Emotion Recognition Research. *Psychological Inquiry*, *7*(2), 43. DOI: 10.3390/psycholint7020043

Barrera, K. G., & Shah, D. (2023). Marketing in the Metaverse: Conceptual understanding, framework, and research agenda. *Journal of Business Research*, *155*, 113420. DOI: 10.1016/j.jbusres.2022.113420

Basyoni, L., Qayyum, A., Shaban, K., Elmahjub, E., Al-Ali, A., Halabi, O., & Qadir, J. (2025). Generative AI-Driven Metaverse: The Promises and Challenges of AI-Generated Content. *IEEE Open Journal of the Computer Society*. Advance online publication. DOI: 10.1109/OJCS.2025.3616501

Bozkurt, S., Uğursoy, A. S., & Meral, S. P. (2025). The Impact of Personalized Messages and Designs on Consumer Experiences and Marketing Communications in Technology: Hyper-Personalization. In *Impact of Contemporary Technology on Art and Design* (pp. 135–164). IGI Global., DOI: 10.4018/979-8-3693-4318-0.ch007

Boztas, C., Ghadafi, E., & Ibrahim, R. (2025). Metaverse Architectures: A Comprehensive Systematic Review of Definitions and Frameworks. *Future Internet*, *17*(7), 283. DOI: 10.3390/fi17070283

Bruni, R., & Galvagno, M. (2025). Virtual reality, authentic motivations: A classification of metaverse users based on VR/XR headset experience. *Electronic Commerce Research*, •••, 1–25. DOI: 10.1007/s10660-025-09970-6

Chand, T., Nair, V. S., Srinivasu, P. N., & Kumar, V. J. (2025). Prospects and challenges in decoding consumer behavior using neurotechnology. *Artificial Intelligence Applications for Brain–Computer Interfaces*, 161-182. https://doi.org/DOI: 10.1016/B978-0-443-33414-6.00011-3

Chen, C., Zhang, K. Z., Chu, Z., & Lee, M. (2024). Augmented reality in the metaverse market: The role of multimodal sensory interaction. *Internet Research*, *34*(1), 9–38. DOI: 10.1108/INTR-08-2022-0670

Chen, Q., Zhou, S., Fang, Y., Luo, D., & Lu, T. (2025, October). MERD-360VR: A Multimodal Emotional Response Dataset from 360° VR Videos Across Different Age Groups. In *Proceedings of the 27th International Conference on Multimodal Interaction* (pp. 405-414). https://doi.org/DOI: 10.1145/3716553.3750777

Chen, Y. (2024). Resonating with the consumer desires behind the screen–consumer-centric tourism advertising and new technology applications. *Journal of Business and Industrial Marketing*, *39*(1), 99–115. DOI: 10.1108/JBIM-01-2023-0033

Christensen, J., Hansen, J. M., & Wilson, P. (2025). Understanding the role and impact of Generative Artificial Intelligence (AI) hallucination within consumers' tourism decision-making processes. *Current Issues in Tourism*, *28*(4), 545–560. DOI: 10.1080/13683500.2023.2300032

Das, R., & Singh, T. D. (2023). Multimodal sentiment analysis: A survey of methods, trends, and challenges. *ACM Computing Surveys*, *55*(13s), 1–38. DOI: 10.1145/3586075

Dhirani, L. L., Mukhtiar, N., Chowdhry, B. S., & Newe, T. (2023). Ethical dilemmas and privacy issues in emerging technologies: A review. *Sensors (Basel)*, *23*(3), 1151. DOI: 10.3390/s23031151 PMID: 36772190

Di Paolo, F., Mancuso, I., Bettiga, D., Lamberti, L., Messeni Petruzzelli, A., & Panniello, U. (2025). Metaverse business transformation: Four companies' virtual experiences. *Management Decision*, *63*(13), 349–371. DOI: 10.1108/MD-06-2024-1316

Dulloo, R., & Struweg, I. (2025). The Rise of Experience Economy and Marketing 5.0: Navigating the New Paradigm of Value Creation. In *Leveraging AI-Powered Marketing in the Experience-Driven Economy* (pp. 1–38). IGI Global Scientific Publishing., DOI: 10.4018/979-8-3693-9561-5.ch001

Dwivedi, Y. K., Hughes, L., Baabdullah, A. M., Ribeiro-Navarrete, S., Giannakis, M., Al-Debei, M. M., & Wamba, S. F. (2022). Metaverse beyond the hype: Multidisciplinary perspectives on emerging challenges, opportunities, and agenda for research, practice and policy. *International Journal of Information Management*, *66*, 102542. DOI: 10.1016/j.ijinfomgt.2022.102542

Dwivedi, Y. K., Hughes, L., Wang, Y., Alalwan, A. A., Ahn, S. J., Balakrishnan, J., & Wirtz, J. (2023). Metaverse marketing: How the metaverse will shape the future of consumer research and practice. *Psychology and Marketing*, *40*(4), 750–776. DOI: 10.1002/mar.21767

Fukawa, N., & Rindfleisch, A. (2023). Enhancing innovation via the digital twin. *Journal of Product Innovation Management*, *40*(4), 391–406. DOI: 10.1111/jpim.12655

Furidha, B. W. (2023). Comprehension of the descriptive qualitative research method: A critical assessment of the literature. *Acitya Wisesa: Journal Of Multidisciplinary Research*, 1-8. https://orcid.org/0009-0007-1944-5738

García-Hernández, R. A., Luna-García, H., Celaya-Padilla, J. M., García-Hernández, A., Reveles-Gómez, L. C., Flores-Chaires, L. A., & Villalba-Condori, K. O. (2024). A systematic literature review of modalities, trends, and limitations in emotion recognition, affective computing, and sentiment analysis. *Applied Sciences (Basel, Switzerland)*, *14*(16), 7165. DOI: 10.3390/app14167165

Goodarzi, M., Venkatakrishnan, R., & Canbaz, M. A. (2023, November). Untangling emotional threads: Hallucination networks of large language models. In *International Conference on Complex Networks and Their Applications* (pp. 202-214). Cham: Springer Nature Switzerland. https://doi.org/DOI: 10.1007/978-3-031-53468-3_17

Hartmann, T., Wirth, W., Vorderer, P., Klimmt, C., Schramm, H., & Böcking, S. (2015). Spatial Presence Theory: State of the Art and Challenges Ahead. In: *Lombard*, M., Biocca, F., Freeman, J., IJsselsteijn, W., Schaevitz, R. (eds) Immersed in Media. Springer, Cham. https://doi.org/DOI: 10.1007/978-3-319-10190-3_7

Herath, H. M. K. K. M. B., Mittal, M., & Kataria, A. (2024). Navigating the metaverse: A technical review of emerging virtual worlds. *Wiley Interdisciplinary Reviews. Data Mining and Knowledge Discovery*, *14*(4), e1538. DOI: 10.1002/widm.1538

Hermann, E. (2022). Leveraging artificial intelligence in marketing for social good—An ethical perspective. *Journal of Business Ethics*, *179*(1), 43–61. DOI: 10.1007/s10551-021-04843-y PMID: 34054170

Hosseini, S., Yamaghani, M. R., & Poorzaker Arabani, S. (2024). A review of the methods of recognition multimodal emotions in sound, image and text. *International Journal of Applied Operational Research-An Open Access Journal*, *12*(1), 29–41.

Huang, Z., Zhu, Y., Hao, A., & Deng, J. (2023). How social presence influences consumer purchase intention in live video commerce: The mediating role of immersive experience and the moderating role of positive emotions. *Journal of Research in Interactive Marketing*, *17*(4), 493–509. DOI: 10.1108/JRIM-01-2022-0009

Hung, L. P., & Alias, S. (2023). Beyond sentiment analysis: A review of recent trends in text based sentiment analysis and emotion detection. *Journal of Advanced Computational Intelligence and Intelligent Informatics*, *27*(1), 84–95. DOI: 10.20965/jaciii.2023.p0084

Islam, M. S., Shokran, M., & Ferdousi, J. (2024). AI-Powered Business Analytics in Marketing: Unlock Consumer Insights for Competitive Growth in the US Market. *Journal of Computer Science and Technology Studies*, *6*(1), 293–313. DOI: 10.32996/jcsts.2024.6.1.33

Jabeen, S., Li, X., Amin, M. S., Bourahla, O., Li, S., & Jabbar, A. (2023). A review on methods and applications in multimodal deep learning. *ACM Transactions on Multimedia Computing Communications and Applications*, *19*(2s), 1–41. DOI: 10.1145/3545572

Jabreel, M., Maaroof, N., Valls, A., & Moreno, A. (2020). Introducing sentiment analysis of textual reviews in a multi-criteria decision aid system. *applied sciences, 11*(1), 216. https://doi.org/DOI: 10.3390/app11010216

Jean, G. (2024). Sentiment Analysis and Emotion Recognition for Emotionally Adaptive Mobile User Interfaces.

Joo, J. H., Han, S. H., Park, I., & Chung, T. S. (2024). Immersive emotion analysis in VR environments: A sensor-based approach to prevent distortion. *Electronics (Basel), 13*(8), 1494. DOI: 10.3390/electronics13081494

Kabir, S. M. H. (2025). Artificial Intelligence-Driven Marketing and Consumer Behavior: Balancing Sustainability and Profitability in the Digital Age. *International Journal of Innovative Research and Publications, 5*(11), 39–44. DOI: 10.51430/IJIRP.2025.511.004

Kaman, K., & Deshmukh, A. K. (2025). Navigating the digital frontier: Understanding shopping behavior in the metaverse through an SLR lens. *Spanish Journal of Marketing - ESIC*. Advance online publication. DOI: 10.1108/SJME-12-2024-0327

Khalaf, O. I., Srinivasan, D., Algburi, S., Vellaichamy, J., Selvaraj, D., Sharif, M. S., & Elmedany, W. (2024). Elevating metaverse virtual reality experiences through network-integrated neuro-fuzzy emotion recognition and adaptive content generation algorithms. *Engineering Reports, 6*(11), e12894. DOI: 10.1002/eng2.12894

Khan, U. A., Xu, Q., Liu, Y., Lagstedt, A., Alamäki, A., & Kauttonen, J. (2024). Exploring contactless techniques in multimodal emotion recognition: Insights into diverse applications, challenges, solutions, and prospects. *Multimedia Systems, 30*(3), 115. DOI: 10.1007/s00530-024-01302-2

Kim, H., & Hong, T. (2024). Enhancing emotion recognition using multimodal fusion of physiological, environmental, personal data. *Expert Systems with Applications, 249*, 123723. DOI: 10.1016/j.eswa.2024.123723

Kozinets, R. V. (2023). Immersive netnography: A novel method for service experience research in virtual reality, augmented reality and metaverse contexts. *Journal of Service Management, 34*(1), 100–125. DOI: 10.1108/JOSM-12-2021-0481

Kumar, P., Tiwari, S., & Saxena, N. (2025). Engaging New Customers through Marketing in the Metaverse. In *The Metaverse Era: Reinventing Customer Engagement and Digital Marketing* (pp. 59-87). Bentham Science Publishers. https://doi.org/DOI: 10.2174/9798898103681250101

Kumar, S. (2021). Bridging the Gap between Human Emotions and AI: Affective Computing with Multimodal Data. [IJARCST]. *International Journal of Advanced Research in Computer Science & Technology, 4*(6), 5847–5855. DOI: 10.15662/IJARCST.2021.0406011

Kumar, V., Kotler, P., & Kumar, A. (2025). Transformative marketing strategies in the era of new-age technologies: Principles, plan, purpose, and practice. *Journal of the Academy of Marketing Science*, •••, 1–27. DOI: 10.1007/s11747-025-01120-6

Kusal, S., Patil, S., Choudrie, J., Kotecha, K., Vora, D., & Pappas, I. (2023). A systematic review of applications of natural language processing and future challenges with special emphasis in text-based emotion detection. *Artificial Intelligence Review*, *56*(12), 15129–15215. DOI: 10.1007/s10462-023-10509-0

Leal, C. C., & Oliveira, B. (2025). The ethics of digital nudging. In *Ethics in Management and Business* (pp. 53–80). Springer Nature Switzerland., DOI: 10.1007/978-3-031-82054-0_3

Li, C., Dai, Y., Chen, G., Liu, J., Li, P., & Ip, H. H. S. (2025). Avatar-mediated communication in collaborative virtual environments: A study on users' attention allocation and perception of social interactions. *Computers in Human Behavior*, *167*, 108598. DOI: 10.1016/j.chb.2025.108598

Li, S., Zhu, B., Zhu, H., & Yu, Z. (2024). Co-creation of metaverse brands equity with the impact of celebrity virtual images and real-life influence: From the perspective of experience-dominant logic. *Electronic Commerce Research*, •••, 1–30. DOI: 10.1007/s10660-024-09899-2

Lian, Z., Sun, H., Sun, L., Wen, Z., Zhang, S., Chen, S., & Tao, J. (2024, October). Mer 2024: Semi-supervised learning, noise robustness, and open-vocabulary multimodal emotion recognition. In *Proceedings of the 2nd International Workshop on Multimodal and Responsible Affective Computing* (pp. 41-48). https://doi.org/DOI: 10.1145/3689092.3689959

Lim, K. Y., Sa'uadi, A. N., Idros, N. A. N. M., & Jamil, N. S. (2024, September). *Optimizing Personalized Recommendation in E-Services Platforms Using AI. In 2024 5th International Conference on Artificial Intelligence and Data Sciences (AiDAS)*., https://doi.org/IEEE, DOI: 10.1109/AiDAS63860.2024.10730288

Logeswaran, K., Savitha, S., Suresh, P., Prasanna Kumar, K. R., Gunasekar, M., Rajadevi, R., & Jayasurya, A. S. (2024). Unifying technologies in industry 4.0: Harnessing the synergy of internet of things, big data, augmented reality/virtual reality, and blockchain technologies. *Topics in Artificial Intelligence Applied to Industry*, *4*(0), 127–147. DOI: 10.1002/9781394216147.ch7

Maleki, N., Padmanabhan, B., & Dutta, K. (2024, June). AI hallucinations: a misnomer worth clarifying. In *2024 IEEE conference on artificial intelligence (CAI)* (pp. 133-138). IEEE. https://doi.org/DOI: 10.1109/CAI59869.2024.00033

Marín-Morales, J., Llinares, C., Guixeres, J., & Alcañiz, M. (2020). Emotion recognition in immersive virtual reality: From statistics to affective computing. *Sensors (Basel)*, *20*(18), 5163. DOI: 10.3390/s20185163 PMID: 32927722

Marques, G., Pitarma, R. M., Garcia, N., & Pombo, N. (2019). Internet of things architectures, technologies, applications, challenges, and future directions for enhanced living environments and healthcare systems: A review. *Electronics (Basel)*, *8*(10), 1081. DOI: 10.3390/electronics8101081

Mitsea, E., Drigas, A., & Skianis, C. (2025). A systematic review of serious games in the era of artificial intelligence, immersive technologies, the metaverse, and neurotechnologies: Transformation through meta-skills training. *Electronics (Basel)*, *14*(4), 649. DOI: 10.3390/electronics14040649

Nair, A. J., Manohar, S., Mittal, A., & Chaudhry, R. (2024). Unleashing digital frontiers: Bridging realities of augmented reality, virtual reality, and the metaverse. In *The metaverse dilemma: Challenges and opportunities for business and society* (pp. 85–112). Emerald Publishing Limited., DOI: 10.1108/978-1-83797-524-220241006

Nakamura, J., & Csikszentmihalyi, M. (2009). Flow theory and research. https://doi.org/DOI: 10.1093/oxfordhb/9780195187243.013.0018

Natarajan, T., Pragha, P., Dhalmahapatra, K., & Veera Raghavan, D. R. (2025). Unveiling metaverse sentiments using machine learning approaches. *Kybernetes*, *54*(8), 4114–4137. DOI: 10.1108/K-11-2023-2268

Park, H., & Choo, S. (2022). A development of visualization technology through AR-based design checklist connection. *Applied Sciences (Basel, Switzerland)*, *12*(12), 6126. DOI: 10.3390/app12126126

Patel, P., & Kaur, J. (2025). Introduction to brand management in the digital age. In *Strategic brand management in the age of AI and disruption* (pp. 1–26). IGI Global Scientific Publishing., DOI: 10.4018/979-8-3693-9461-8.ch001

Pine, B. J., & Gilmore, J. H. (2013). The experience economy: past, present and future. In *Handbook on the experience economy* (pp. 21–44). Edward Elgar Publishing., DOI: 10.4337/9781781004227.00007

Puntoni, S., Reczek, R. W., Giesler, M., & Botti, S. (2021). Consumers and artificial intelligence: An experiential perspective. *Journal of Marketing*, *85*(1), 131–151. DOI: 10.1177/0022242920953847

Rahimi, F., Sadeghi-Niaraki, A., & Choi, S. M. (2025). *Generative AI Meets Virtual Reality: A Comprehensive Survey on Applications, Challenges, and Future Direction*. IEEE., DOI: 10.1109/ACCESS.2025.3574779

Ramadan, Z. (2023). Marketing in the metaverse era: Toward an integrative channel approach. *Virtual Reality (Waltham Cross)*, *27*(3), 1905–1918. DOI: 10.1007/s10055-023-00783-2 PMID: 37360809

Ramadan, Z., & Ramadan, J. (2025). AI avatars and co-creation in the metaverse. *Consumer Behavior in Tourism and Hospitality*, *20*(1), 131–147. DOI: 10.1108/CBTH-07-2024-0246

Schmitt, B. (1999). Experiential marketing. *Journal of Marketing Management*, *15*(1-3), 53–67. DOI: 10.1362/026725799784870496

Schmitt, B., & Zarantonello, L. (2013). Consumer experience and experiential marketing: A critical review. *Review of marketing Research*, 25-61. https://doi.org/DOI: 10.1108/S1548-6435(2013)0000010006

Semwal, R., Tripathi, N., Rana, A., Dafouti, B. S., Bairwa, M. K., & Mathur, V. (2024, May). AI-powered personalization and emotional intelligence integration for enhanced service marketing in transformative tourism experiences. In *2024 International Conference on Communication, Computer Sciences and Engineering (IC3SE)* (pp. 1851-1856). IEEE. https://doi.org/DOI: 10.1109/IC3SE62002.2024.10592909

Shao, Z. (2025). Revealing consumers' hedonic buying in social media: The roles of social status recognition, perceived value, immersive engagement and gamified incentives. *Journal of Research in Interactive Marketing*, *19*(5), 787–802. DOI: 10.1108/JRIM-12-2023-0452

Sharma, N. A., Ali, A. S., & Kabir, M. A. (2025). A review of sentiment analysis: Tasks, applications, and deep learning techniques. *International Journal of Data Science and Analytics*, *19*(3), 351–388. DOI: 10.1007/s41060-024-00594-x

Shih, T. Y. (2025). Consumer Perspective Scales for Creating a Good Metaverse Environment: The Power of Storytelling and Sensory Immersion. *International Journal ofHuman-Computer Interaction*, •••, 1–22. DOI: 10.1080/10447318.2025.2551050

Soliman, M. M., Ahmed, E., Darwish, A., & Hassanien, A. E. (2024). Artificial intelligence powered Metaverse: Analysis, challenges and future perspectives. *Artificial Intelligence Review*, *57*(2), 36. DOI: 10.1007/s10462-023-10641-x

Suk, H., & Laine, T. H. (2023). Influence of avatar facial appearance on users' perceived embodiment and presence in immersive virtual reality. *Electronics (Basel)*, *12*(3), 583. DOI: 10.3390/electronics12030583

Sukumaran, A., & Manoharan, A. (2024). Multimodal engagement recognition from image traits using deep learning techniques. *IEEE Access : Practical Innovations, Open Solutions*, *12*, 25228–25244. DOI: 10.1109/ACCESS.2024.3353053

Sykora, M. (2017). Web 1.0 to Web 2.0: An observational study and empirical evidence for the historical r (evolution) of the social web. *International Journal of Web Engineering and Technology*, *12*(1), 70–94. DOI: 10.1504/IJWET.2017.084024

Tang, Y. M., Wong, J. K. N., & Ho, G. T. S. (2025). Exploring Consumer Acceptance of Metaverse Marketing for Branding Activities and the Pre-Purchase Stage. *Journal of Theoretical and Applied Electronic Commerce Research, 20*(3), 159. DOI: 10.3390/jtaer20030159

Tong, A., Palmer, S., Craig, J. C., & Strippoli, G. F. (2016). A guide to reading and using systematic reviews of qualitative research. *Nephrology, Dialysis, Transplantation, 31*(6), 897–903. DOI: 10.1093/ndt/gfu354 PMID: 25414375

Uddin, M., Obaidat, M., Manickam, S., Laghari, S. U. A., Dandoush, A., Ullah, H., & Ullah, S. S. (2024). Exploring the convergence of Metaverse, Blockchain, and AI: A comprehensive survey of enabling technologies, applications, challenges, and future directions. *Wiley Interdisciplinary Reviews. Data Mining and Knowledge Discovery, 14*(6), e1556. DOI: 10.1002/widm.1556

Urdea, A. M., Constantin, C. P., & Purcaru, I. M. (2021). Implementing experiential marketing in the digital age for a more sustainable customer relationship. *Sustainability, 13*(4), 1865. DOI: 10.3390/su13041865

Venugopal, J. P., Subramanian, A. A. V., Sundaram, G., & Ponnambalam Devadoss, M. (2025). The Convergence of Deep Learning and the Metaverse: A Multidisciplinary Survey of Current Research and Future Directions. *Computer Animation and Virtual Worlds, 36*(6), e70082. DOI: 10.1002/cav.70082

Violante, M. G., Vezzetti, E., & Piazzolla, P. (2019). How to design a virtual reality experience that impacts the consumer engagement: The case of the virtual supermarket. [IJIDeM]. *International Journal on Interactive Design and Manufacturing, 13*(1), 243–262. DOI: 10.1007/s12008-018-00528-5

Vyas, S., Rathore, J. S., & Kumar, V. (2024). Insights into mobile app experience: A systematic literature review using TCCM framework. *Global Knowledge, Memory and Communication*. Advance online publication. DOI: 10.1108/GKMC-02-2024-0063

Waqas, A., Tripathi, A., Ramachandran, R. P., Stewart, P. A., & Rasool, G. (2024). Multimodal data integration for oncology in the era of deep neural networks: A review. *Frontiers in Artificial Intelligence, 7*, 1408843. DOI: 10.3389/frai.2024.1408843 PMID: 39118787

Watson, R. (2022). The virtual economy of the metaverse: Computer vision and deep learning algorithms, customer engagement tools, and behavioral predictive analytics. *Linguistic and Philosophical Investigations*, (21), 41–56.

Wen, Y., Wang, Z., & Guo, X. (2025). Trends and applications of AI in immersive learning environments: A systematic review of empirical research. *Interactive Learning Environments*, •••, 1–19. DOI: 10.1080/10494820.2025.2524029

Wongkitrungrueng, A., & Suprawan, L. (2024). Metaverse meets branding: Examining consumer responses to immersive brand experiences. *International Journal of Human-Computer Interaction*, *40*(11), 2905–2924. DOI: 10.1080/10447318.2023.2175162

Wu, Q., Xia, C., & Tian, S. (2025). AI-Driven Sentiment Analytics: Unlocking Business Value in the E-Commerce Landscape_v1. *arXiv preprint arXiv:2504.08738*. https://doi.org//arXiv.2504.08738DOI: 10.48550

Wu, Y., Mi, Q., & Gao, T. (2025). A comprehensive review of multimodal emotion recognition: Techniques, challenges, and future directions. *Biomimetics*, *10*(7), 418. DOI: 10.3390/biomimetics10070418 PMID: 40710231

Yadav, P., Kashyap, I., & Bhati, B. S. (2024). Contextual Ambiguity Framework for Enhanced Sentiment Analysis. *Tehnički glasnik, 18*(3), 385-393. https://doi.org/DOI: 10.31803/tg-20231227064230

Yoon, S., & Kim, B. (2025). Multi-Scale Temporal Fusion Network for Real-Time Multimodal Emotion Recognition in IoT Environments. *Sensors (Basel)*, *25*(16), 5066. DOI: 10.3390/s25165066 PMID: 40871929

Young, G. W., & Dawkins, O. (2023, July). Multimodality: Exploring sensibility and sense-making beyond the metaverse. In *International Conference on Human-Computer Interaction* (pp. 307-322). Cham: Springer Nature Switzerland. https://doi.org/DOI: 10.1007/978-3-031-35634-6_22

Zeng, Y., Zhang, J. W., & Yang, J. (2024). Multimodal emotion recognition in the metaverse era: New needs and transformation in mental health work. *World Journal of Clinical Cases*, *12*(34), 6674. DOI: 10.12998/wjcc.v12.i34.6674 PMID: 39650812

Chapter 11
Mitigating AI Hallucinations in ESG-Driven Credit Risk Advisory-Human-AI Co-Governance in the Enterprise Metaverse

Rohit Sood
https://orcid.org/0000-0002-4127-7781
Lovely Professional University, India

ABSTRACT

The chapter explores how financial institutions can mitigate AI hallucinations while delivering ESG-driven credit risk advisory within the enterprise metaverse. It argues that hallucinations in generative and predictive models threaten responsible lending, regulatory alignment, and sustainable value creation when unchecked in immersive, real-time advisory environments. Framed around a widening talent gap, the chapter positions human–AI co-governance as essential, requiring advisors who blend financial acumen, ESG expertise, and AI literacy. It proposes an adaptive framework built on strategic upskilling, cultural transformation that normalizes challenging AI outputs, and targeted recruitment and partnerships. Within metaverse-based advisory channels, this framework embeds explainability, stress-testing, and escalation protocols so that human experts can detect, interpret, and constrain hallucinations, enabling trustworthy, ESG-aligned credit decisions in next-generation financial ecosystems.

DOI: 10.4018/979-8-3373-7534-2.ch011

INTRODUCTION

In the enterprise metaverse, wealth and credit advisory are increasingly mediated by generative and predictive AI systems that synthesize market, client, and ESG data into immersive decision journeys. The wealth and credit management sectors are undergoing an unprecedented transformation fueled by rapid digitalization, evolving client expectations, and the integration of Environmental, Social, and Governance (ESG) principles into financial decision-making(George, 2024). AI hallucinations fabricated, biased, or context-insensitive outputs pose material risks when such systems guide ESG-driven credit recommendations, portfolio construction, and suitability assessments. As clients demand more responsible and transparent investment practices, firms face an acute shortage of skilled professionals capable of blending traditional financial acumen with digital literacy, data analytics, and ESG-oriented assessment. The convergence of these competencies is redefining how institutions evaluate credit risk, manage client relationships, and sustain long-term competitiveness (Paulino et al., 2025). Wealth managers sit at the frontline of this transformation, acting as both interpreters and gatekeepers of AI-generated insights. This chapter explores the pressing challenge of bridging the talent gap in financial institutions amid accelerating ESG adoption and digital transformation. With experienced relationship managers retiring and a younger workforce seeking flexible, purpose-driven careers, organizations must rethink their talent strategies (Singh, 2025). Traditional hiring approaches are no longer sufficient; firms must focus on upskilling, reskilling, and cultural adaptation to nurture advisors who can operate effectively in hybrid digital ecosystems. Furthermore, the chapter highlights how the infusion of ESG competencies such as understanding sustainable finance, ethical investing, and impact measurement has become essential in modern credit risk assessment frameworks. There is a pressing need for human oversight, where wealth managers can co-exist with AI and pave the way for efficient, prudent and responsible judgement to the AI hallucinated output, to amplify the enterprise metaverse capabilities (Kapoor, 2025).

Through a multidisciplinary lens, this chapter examines the interplay between human capital development, technological enablement, and ESG integration along with measurement of credit risk (Otieno & Busili, 2024). It emphasizes that successful incorporation of ESG metrics in credit assessment requires not only advanced analytical models and automation tools but also professionals equipped to interpret these insights with contextual understanding and ethical responsibility. The shortage of talent with such integrated capabilities has direct implications for firms' ability to evaluate long-term creditworthiness, manage regulatory compliance, and deliver sustainable value creation (Kurznack et al., 2021). The chapter proposes an adaptive framework for financial institutions to build ESG-oriented and digitally proficient talent ecosystems. This involves three key dimensions:

(1) Strategic Upskilling and Digital Literacy-embedding ESG and technology modules into continuous learning programs to create data-driven, responsible decision-makers.
(2) Cultural Transformation-fostering a work environment that values innovation, sustainability, and inclusiveness to attract and retain next-generation advisors; and
(3) Targeted Recruitment and Partnerships-collaborating with universities, fintech firms, and ESG specialists to fill capability gaps efficiently.

The integration of automation tools, such as AI-driven analytics, natural language processing, and predictive credit modeling, can alleviate the pressure on limited human resources (Kothandapani, 2025). The synergy between human insight and machine intelligence forms the foundation for resilient, ethical, and adaptive financial ecosystems. The chapter underscores that bridging the talent gap is not merely an HR challenge, but a strategic imperative intertwined with risk governance, client trust, and ESG compliance. By cultivating digitally fluent and sustainability-conscious professionals, firms can future-proof their credit assessment frameworks and deliver both financial performance and societal value (Tettey et al., 2025).

Changing legislation, disruption in digitalization and shifting expectations of the clients are driving the transformation fast of the management wealth sector. The scarcity of personnel who are qualified, especially advisors who have knowledge of digital tools, investing in ESG, compliance and management relationship of client, is an important obstacle. While companies have trouble finding and keeping tech-savvy workers who can crater to both conventional affluent customers and young, digitally focused investors, many seasonal advisors are retiring (Kotsantonis & Serafeim, 2020).

The capacity of a company to offer tailored guidance, adherence to law and completing with the nimble wealth tech platforms which directly get impacted by the skill deficit. Moreover, transformation in workforce which includes upskilling, cultural shifts and innovative work models that have become necessity for survival and expansion (Sundaram, 2025).

Table1. Shortage of Talent in Wealth Management

PROBLEM	CAUSES	IMPACT
Shortage of skilled wealth management professionals	• Retirement of experienced advisors • Rising need for digital & ESG skills • Competition from fintech & tech firms • Shifting employee expectations	• Decline in client satisfaction • Inability to scale personalized advice • Higher compliance risks • Loss of market share to digital disruptors

Customers are totally dependent on knowledgeable consultants so that they can get guided through complicated financial choices, legal obligations and investment planning. When the competent staff is absent:

- Client trust deteriorates, resulting in increased churn and harm to the brand.
- As businesses struggle to satisfy the varied demands of their customers, their development stagnates.
- Wealth Tech platforms have the potential to expand more quickly with automation, wealth results in a loss of competitive advantage.
- As a result, talent shortage is not just an HR issue; it is a strategic need for development wealth management firms that are client-centric and sustainable.

Issue related to shortage of talent

1. Retiring seasoned consultants

A sizeable percentage of wealth managers are approaching retirement age, which results in a leadership void and a lack of institutional expertise.

2. Demand for modern digital skills

Customers now demand seamless digital onboarding, AI driven insights, and robo advisory. Meeting these needs is challenging for advisors who lack technological proficiency.

3. Increase in the pressure to comply

Comprehensive reports, protection in data privacy and disclosures in ESG are mandated by regulatory bodies that are SEBI, RBI and the foreign organizations. For this the staff must have knowledge of legal reforms, risk and compliance frameworks.

4. Changing expectations of workers

Hybrid/remote models, adaptable jobs, and meaningful careers are what the post pandemic workforce wants. It is difficult for wealth management businesses that are unable to adapt to recruit young people.

Figure 1. Issues to be addressed related to Shortage of Talent (SOT)

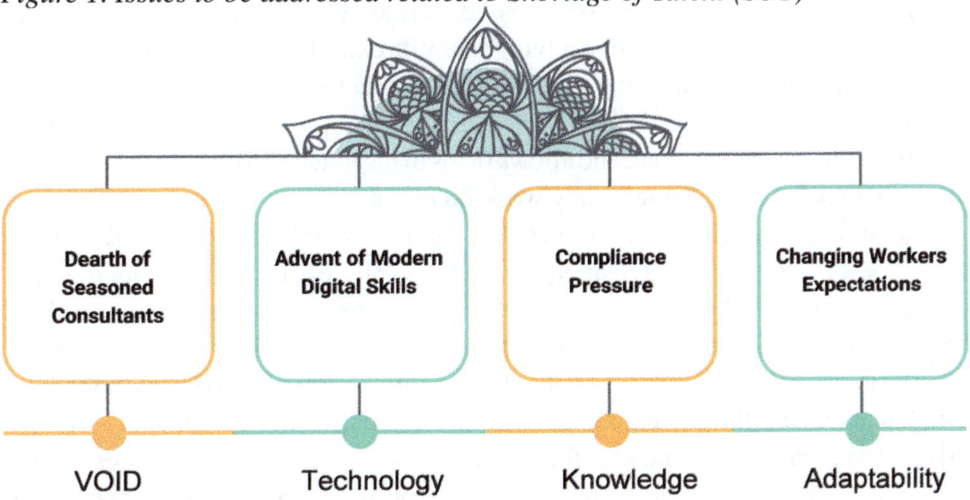

LITERATURE REVIEW

Emerging literature on AI in finance highlights the promise of generative models for personalized advice yet warns of hallucinations that arise from opaque training data, prompt sensitivities, and misaligned optimization objectives (Joshi, 2025). Studies on Robo-advisory and digital wealth platforms emphasize explainability and human oversight but rarely examine immersive metaverse contexts where interaction intensity and cognitive load are higher (Bolsiek, 2024). ESG-focused credit research underscores data quality challenges, greenwashing risks, and model bias, which can all be exacerbated when hallucinated narratives present dubious ESG signals as fact (Gu, 2025). Work on human-in-the-loop AI suggests that domain experts can detect and correct AI errors, but practical role definitions for wealth managers as "hallucination filters" remain under-developed (Mosqueira-Rey et al., 2023). The literature under-specifies how human advisors, governance structures, and metaverse design jointly constrain hallucinations in ESG-driven credit advisory. The transformation of talent and workforce strategies has become a critical strategic priority in the financial services and wealth management sectors (Santoso et al., 2021). Literature collectively underscores that sustaining competitiveness in this rapidly evolving landscape requires organizations to reimagine how they attract, develop, and deploy talent in response to technological disruption, digitalization, and shifting client expectations. Jooss et al., (2024) highlights the growing importance of internal agility through skills-based workforce models that enable dynamic resource redeployment. Instead of relying solely on external hiring, organizations are encouraged to use internal skills marketplaces that match employees' competencies with evolving business needs (Schaffer, 2025). This approach enhances flexibility, fosters employee engagement, and allows firms to respond swiftly to market changes, creating a resilient and future-ready workforce.

Rainoldi et al., (2024)further deepens this understanding by noting that traditional job structures are increasingly obsolete as roles evolve into hybrid, digitally enabled functions. The growing demand for digital proficiency and adaptive skills has made reskilling and upskilling central to workforce sustainability (Farawowan, 2025). However, Panneerselvam et al., (2025) cautions that the persistent shortage of tech talent will continue to challenge firms, necessitating investment in experience-driven development, flexible workforce models, and continuous learning ecosystems. This shift represents a broader transition from job-based to capability-based talent management, where firms cultivate adaptability, creativity, and digital fluency as enduring strategic assets (Iqbal & Abbas, 2024).

(Krishna et al., 2024) adds a client-centric perspective, emphasizing that changing client expectations—driven by digital interfaces and personalization—are redefining the advisor's role. To meet these new expectations, workforce capabilities must align closely with business strategy and client segmentation (Ayanponle et al., 2024). (Shuai, 2025) asserts that parallel investments in both people and operating models are vital for effective digital transformation. Without a workforce prepared to integrate technology meaningfully into client interactions, even the most advanced digital infrastructures risk underperformance (Digby, 2024). Thus, human capital development must evolve in tandem with technological modernization to ensure alignment between strategy, capability, and execution (Amalia et al., 2024).

The theoretical foundations of this transformation are grounded in human capital and resource-based perspectives. Bakker and Schultz's Human Capital Theory posits that employees' education, skills, and training constitute strategic investments that enhance productivity and organizational value. In the context of wealth management, this translates into a culture of continuous learning, particularly in areas such as ESG integration, digital advisory practices, and regulatory expertise (Farinha & De Fátima Pina, 2025). While such investments yield improved client outcomes and advisory performance, they also expose firms to the risk of turnover. The training initiatives must be closely tied to retention strategies to preserve the organization's return on human capital investment (Chukwu et al., 2025). Parallelly, the Resource-Based View (RBV) suggests that sustainable competitive advantage arises from resources that are valuable, rare, inimitable, and non-substitutable, and these elements differentiate human advisors from algorithmic robo-advisors and reinforce the value of cultivating distinctive advisory expertise over mere headcount expansion (Tifani Napitupulu et al., n.d.).

Rachmad, (2025) affirms that technology alone cannot deliver long-term value without organizational and human alignment. The successful adoption of digital tools requires synchronized transformation across business models, organizational design, and workforce capability. Change management, reskilling, and role redesign are essential to ensure that technology augments human advisors rather than replaces them (Masnun et al., 2024). In this sense, workforce transformation represents not merely technological evolution but a socio-technical one, where human expertise, digital innovation, and organizational adaptability coexist symbiotically. Collectively, these insights position workforce and talent transformation as a cornerstone of strategic renewal in financial and wealth management, emphasizing that future competitiveness will depend not only on digital infrastructure but on the continuous evolution of human capability within it (Shan & Wang, 2024).

THEORATICAL UNDERPINNINGS

The theoretical foundations in the form of socio-technical systems theory, behavioral finance, and responsible AI governance can pave the way for future evolution for the human loop as a core to the organizational structure. Socio-technical perspectives view AI advisory platforms and enterprise metaverse environments as joint products of technology, people, and institutions, implying that hallucinations are systemic phenomena rather than isolated model errors (Slapakova et al., 2024). Behavioral finance highlights how clients and wealth managers can be overly influenced by salient narratives and visualizations in immersive settings, making them susceptible to persuasive but incorrect AI-generated explanations (Rakhmanovich et al., 2025). Responsible AI frameworks stress transparency, accountability, and human agency, positioning wealth managers as accountable decision-makers who must retain final judgment and actively contest AI outputs (Kaur, 2024). The theoretical structure articulates a human-AI co-governance model where wealth managers function as sense-makers and ethical stewards, using structured questioning, cross-checks, and ESG literacy to convert raw AI outputs into reliable credit insights within the metaverse (Mahajan, 2025). (Stein Smith, 2024) supports the ongoing scarcity of advisors with a combination of digital, ESG, and regulatory expertise, which is precisely the problem must be addressed. Literature underscores the importance of aligning digital investments with targeted reskilling and blended workforce models add establishing internal talent marketplaces in which people plan. Although Lee et al., (2024) advocates upskilling, but provide little real curriculum or assessment measures for job in wealth management, such as ESG scoring and cross border tax regulations. By providing a functional training curriculum, quantifiable KPIs, and a pilot plan that addresses this void, your task may be valuable (Moghadas & Arvin, 2024).

RESEARCH GAPS

Existing work focuses on generic model risk, algorithmic bias, or traditional digital interfaces, with limited attention to the intensified experiential and real-time nature of metaverse interactions. The role of wealth managers is often framed as "relationship enhancement" rather than as active mitigators of AI hallucinations and ESG misinterpretation. A severe scarcity of competent individuals is becoming more of a problem for the wealth management sector, which has a direct impact on its capacity to provide clients with excellent services and maintain a competitive edge. The new generation of customers wants transparent, ESG conscious, and digital first advice, while traditional financial advisors are retiring at a breakneck speed. This results in a skills gap because businesses need consultants who are proficient in digital technology and able to handle complicated, heavily regulated portfolios, but there are few people with these combinations of skills. There is an absence of a holistic, practice-oriented framework that integrates human capital development, AI governance, and metaverse design to support wealth managers in safeguarding the integrity of ESG-linked credit decisions against hallucinated outputs.

WEALTH MANAGEMENT GOALS

In an ESG-driven, AI-enabled metaverse, wealth management goals extend beyond return optimization to encompass sustainable value creation, regulatory compliance, and client trust. Hallucination-aware goal-setting requires that advisory outcomes be robust to model imperfections and narrative errors (Cossio, 2025). Within the enterprise metaverse, goals include building explainable advisory journeys, maintaining audit trails of human overrides, and embedding checkpoints where advisors verify AI-derived ESG assessments against validated data and policy guidelines (Tang, 2025). Wealth managers thus act as custodians of both financial and informational integrity, ensuring that AI remains a tool, not a hidden decision maker. Wealth managers must ensure that AI-generated recommendations align with clients' risk profiles, ESG preferences, and long-term credit capacity, rather than with spurious correlations or fabricated trends (Martinez, 2025). Wealth management companies must establish SMART (specific, measurable, achievable, time-bound) objectives to overcome the workforce transformation and talent scarcity. These goals, as explained below, should be immediately tied to business performance results like revenue increase, regulatory compliance, and customer happiness.

1. **Counsellors Efficiency Management:** Need to bring the number of counsellors down by 30% in the near future.
    - Specific: use focused recruiting and retention initiatives to increase the number of knowledgeable counsellors.
    - Quantifiable: monitor a decrease in open positions for advisors throughout the company.
    - Attainable: make use of campus recruiting, foreign talent pools, and collaboration with training schools.
    - Relevant: guarantees customer protection and foster expansion.
    - Time-bound: must be completed by 2028.
2. **ESG Integration:** Within two years, improve the ESG and digital skills of 50% of current employees
    - Specific: introduce organized training courses on digital platforms, ESG frameworks, and regulatory compliance.
    - Measurable: proportion of workers who have received training or certification in digital/ESG initiatives.
    - Achievable: utilize industry-certified courses and online learning platforms.
    - Relevant: fosters distinctive advisor skills that are in line with customer needs.
    - Time bound: The aim of this is to finish it by 2027.
3. **Enhanced Customer Service:** Increase in client satisfaction through rating it by 20% over the course of 18 months
    - Specific: Improve client experience by utilizing knowledgeable advisors, better communication, and add technology-enabled advice.
    - Trackable: Monitor client retention rates and Net Promoter score
    - Possible: Combined digital improvements with individualized counsellor training
    - Relevant: It has a direct bearing on trust, retention, and referrals.
    - Deadline: To be met by March 2027.

4. **Compliance Precision:** Attain 100% compliance precision in advice operations within a Two-year period.
    - Specific: reduce compliance mistakes by using automated compliance dashboard and better-trained advisors.
    - Quantifiable: regulatory input and internal audit reports.
    - Achievable: integrate technology integration with staff training.
    - Relevant: decreases the risk of financial penalties and reputational damage.
    - Time-bound: to be met by 2027.

DIAGNOSTIC ANALYSIS

Clients may suffer mispriced credit, unsuitable ESG products, or reputational exposure if hallucinated narratives misstate sustainability performance (Alaali, 2025). Wealth managers face professional and ethical risk when they unknowingly relay flawed AI insights, undermining their advisory credibility. Risk and compliance units must manage downstream consequences such as portfolio concentration, regulatory breaches, and litigation. The enterprise metaverse magnifies these impacts through persistent, immersive interactions and richer data visualizations. It emphasizes the wealth manager's role as a buffer, responsible for interrogating AI outputs, escalating anomalies, and communicating residual uncertainties to clients, thereby containing the stakeholder harm of hallucinations. The different stakeholders, as explained below, are going to experience an impact due to AI hallucinated reports and necessitated the role of human intervention to enhance accuracy and efficiency.

- Companies: because of a shortage of qualified personnel, they have trouble expanding their services, developing new ideas, and preserving profit margins.
- Customers: receive subpar service, delayed guidance, or obsolete product suggestions.
- Regulators: because under trained advisors could fail to meet regulatory requirements, regulators are at risk of non-compliance.
- Employees: existing employees are overworked, resulting in burnout, turnover, and lower morale.

An Indian wealth management business that caters to both affluent youth clients and high net worth individuals. Although the HNIs I need sophisticated cross-border tax planning, the younger customers want ESG choices, app-based advising, and quick reporting dashboards. Despite having extensive experience, the company's top consultants are unable to utilize sophisticated CRM and AI-based technologies because they lack digital proficiency. Additionally, competition from fintech and major tech corporations providing better career prospects prevents the company from hiring enough young tech savvy consultants. Consequently, the company is unable to compete with digital- first wealth tech platforms 4 younger clients and has difficulty maintaining compliance with older, high- net- worth portfolios. This demonstrates that the talent gap is not merely in HR problem; real business concern that impacts long-term competitiveness, growth, and customer confidence.

SWOT and PESTEL ANALYSIS

A SWOT lens on talent scarcity reveals how it shapes hallucination risk in AI-enabled wealth management. Strengths include a core pool of experienced advisors who possess deep financial judgment, often capable of intuitively spotting implausible AI outputs. Weaknesses arise from limited AI and ESG literacy, uneven digital skills, and high dependence on automated tools among newer staff.

Table 2. SWOT Framework for analyzing Scarce talent in Wealth Management

STRENGTH	WEAKNESSES
• Built customer trust through skilled professionals • loyal HNI client and solid brand reputation • availability of worldwide resources and networks	• Over reliance on an aging workforce of advisors • Staff's Current digital proficiency is lacking. • Young professionals experience high attrition rates. • Absence of organized training or upskilling initiatives
OPPORTUNITY	**THREAT**
• Use of robots, fully automated systems and use of artificial intelligence so that lighten their workload. • Increased demand for ESG-based investment creates opportunities for skill development. • Growth of financial literacy programs in Tier 2/3 towns.	• Increasing rivalry from Fintech and wealth tech platforms. • Persistent modifications to regulations increase the chance of compliance issues. • Worldwide demand for competent digital finance experts. • If customer expectations are not fulfilled, market share might be lost

A PESTEL diagnostic situates talent scarcity and hallucination management within macro-environmental forces. Politically and legally, evolving AI and ESG regulations demand that human advisors remain accountable, requiring sufficient skilled staff to interpret rules and AI outputs. Economic pressures push firms to automate, risking under-resourced human oversight. Socially, younger professionals seek purpose and flexibility, making ESG-centric, metaverse-enabled roles attractive if linked to meaningful responsibility rather than rote supervision of AI.

Table 3. PESTEL Framework for analyzing Scarce talent in Wealth Management

FACTORS	IMPACT ON TALENT SHORTAGE
C = POLITICAL	The need for compliance with trained people is growing due to regulatory obligations (SEBI, RBI, FATCA, MIFID II)
R = ECONOMIC	Feet compression lower profit margins, which restricts companies capacity to recruit and keep the best personnel with competitive wages.
R = RIGOROUS LEGAL PROVISIONS	Rigorous data privacy and cyber security regulations impose significant compliance requirements that only experienced personnel can handle.
O = SOCIALISM	Employees do look for meaningful careers and flexibility, hybrid models for doing work, while the younger generation customers are asking for the digital first services.
S = TECHNOLOGICAL	Onboarding digitally, artificial intelligence driven CRM and the excessive growth in Robo advisors are necessitating the advisors to have new skills.
S = ENVIRONMENTAL	In order to meet the demands of ESG investing, advisors must learn about sustainable frameworks, data reporting, and green product structuring.

According to the SWOT analysis, despite having a solid customer base and reputation, businesses are fast susceptible to weaknesses such as reliance on an aging workforce and lack of digital proficiency. There are prospects in automation and ESG investing, what the urgency is increased by regulatory burden and threats from fintech companies. The macro drivers driving workforce transformation is highlighted by the PESTEL: increasing regulatory constraints, economic cost pressures, changes in societal expectations for employees, and rapid technological change. Collectively, these analysis show that the talent scarcity issue is both an external problem (regulatory, competitive) and an internal one (skill gap, poor retention). As a result, workforce transformation is a strategic imperative rather than an option.

Figure 2. PESTEL (CROSS) analysis for talent shortage

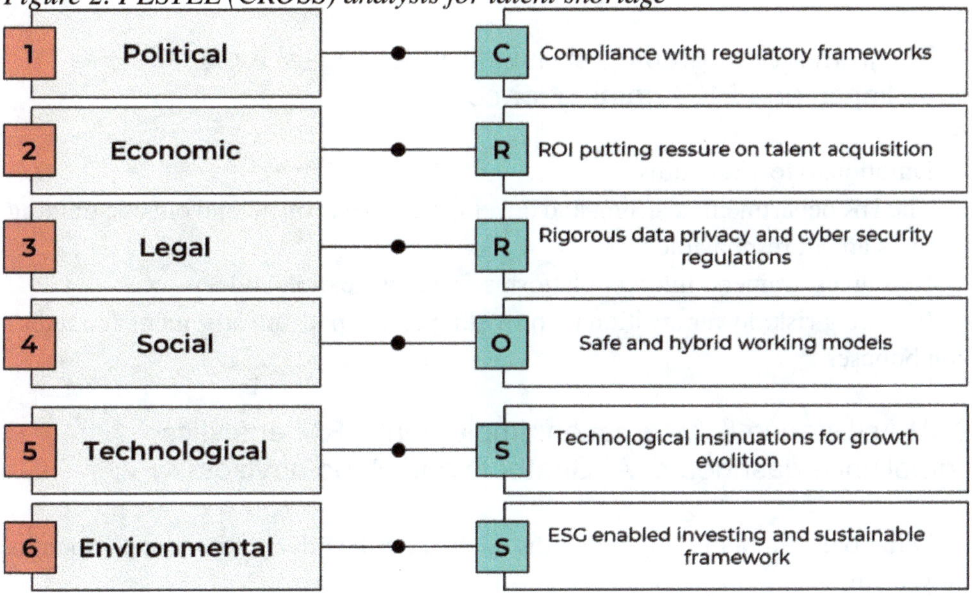

STRATEGIC IMPLEMENTATION PLAN

The strategic implementation plan outlines how institutions can operationalize human-AI co-governance, so wealth managers actively mitigate hallucinations in metaverse-based ESG credit advisory. Key steps include mapping advisory workflows to identify points where AI outputs influence decisions and explicitly assign wealth managers responsibility for validating high-impact recommendations. Training programs must integrate hallucination case studies, metaverse interface usage, and ESG data interpretation. Governance structures should define clear escalation pathways when advisors detect suspicious AI narratives or conflicting ESG indicators. Based on the solution assessment the company Should implement a hybrid approach that integrates up skilling programs and automation/AI sport as core initiative which are backed by strategic hiring and flexible work models.

Action plan with steps:

1. Programs for upgrading skills: introduce digital tools, compliance add ESG training for counsellors.

Duration: 6 to 12 months

The HR department, learning and development department and outside training partners are all responsible.

Resources: trainers, Internet platforms and certification budgets.

Reducing risk: lower attrition by providing career path advancement and retention bonuses.

2. AI Assistance & Automation: Implement CRM analytics, compliance dashboard, AI Chatbots and Robo advisors.

Duration: 12 months with 6 months allotted for the pilot program and 6 months for growth.

Resources: cyber security audits, AI suppliers and cloud infrastructure.

Reducing risk: regular security updates and a hybrid strategy combining AI and human intervention.

3. Hiring strategically: To initiate campus recruitment and hire worldwide talent with ESG/digital knowledge.

Duration: From 12 to 18 months.

Resources: onboarding courses and recruiting budget.

Reducing risk: new hires are integrated into client-facing positions via mentorship programs.

4. Hybrid and adaptable work practices: implement flexible incentives and hybrid/remote work rules.

Duration: rapid roll out within 3 to 6 months.

Resources: MSP teams, zoom and other secure cloud access collaboration platforms.

Reducing risk: digital monitoring dashboards and weekly performance evaluation.

Table 4. Time Bound Action Plan for Gradual AI-Human Integration to reduce AI Hallucinations

Action plan	0 to 3 months	3-8 months	6-12 months	>12
Upskilling programs	design modules	pilot training	full roll out	certification and evaluation
Automation and AI support	vendor selection	pilot testing	full development	review and optimization
Strategic hiring	job profiling	campus hiring cycle	onboarding recruits	international hiring
Flexible work models	draft policy	roll out hybrid model	monitor outcomes	refined and scale

Resolution

Resolution focuses on practical mechanisms for resolving hallucination risks once identified by wealth managers. In enterprise metaverse sessions, advisors need structured options to pause automated journeys, flag questionable content, and switch to verified data sources or simpler analytics. Institutions should provide standardized protocols for cross-checking AI narratives against independent ESG databases, internal credit models, and policy guidelines. Where hallucinations are confirmed, wealth managers must transparently explain revisions to clients, documenting the rationale and preserving trust. Wealth management businesses need to combine talent development, recruiting tactics, technology adoption and flexible work arrangements in order to address the talent scarcity issue. The following 4 major remedies are contrasted in a matrix along with their advantages and disadvantages.

1. **Programs for skill development**: Initial organized training in data analytics, digital tools, ESG investing and regulatory compliance

   Advantages: fostering internal knowledge, boosts advisor confidence and enhances client confidence.

   Disadvantages: expensive to put into practice and trained workers could leave for the competition.
2. **Recruiting plan:** attract international talent with digital and ESG expertise add higher graduates from business schools.

   Advantages: introducing different viewpoints, developing a long-term talent pool and brings new talent.

   Disadvantages: it includes the significant expenditure associated with recruiting and on boarding as well as the time required to acquire proficiency in client management and cultural awareness.

3. **Automation and AI assistance:** it uses compliance dashboard, chatbots for FAQs, AI powered analytics and Robo advisors.

   Advantages: Improve efficiency and accuracy, reduce advisor worked load and scales fast.

   Disadvantages: possible data breaches, high upfront expenditure on technology and may diminish the human touch.
4. **Hybrid and adaptable work arrangements:** provide performance-based bonuses, flexible hours and remote/hybrid positions.

   Advantages: lower attrition, higher employee morale and a younger workforce. Disadvantages: it is more difficult to monitor performance record a robust digital infrastructure for collaboration.

TECHNOLOGY & INNOVATION INTEGRATION

Technology and innovation integration addresses how enterprise metaverse platforms and AI architectures can be designed to support wealth managers in controlling hallucinations. Features such as multi-source data validation, model comparison dashboards, and built-in alerts for out-of-distribution outputs give advisors better visibility into AI behavior. Visual explainability in the metaverse—heatmaps, factor contribution graphs, and scenario overlays—helps wealth managers quickly assess whether ESG-linked credit recommendations are grounded in credible data. To overcome the talent gap in wealth management technology is essential. Companies may optimize their limited workforce by automating repetitive processes and providing advisors with cutting-edge technologies which allow them to strike a balance between efficiency and personalization.

1. **Artificial intelligence:** AI is used for fraud detection, portfolio optimization pan predictive analytics. AI based technologies may automatically rebalance portfolios in response to market changes and give consultants time for strategic planning.
2. **Robo advisors:** They offer affordable, algorithm-based investment guidance to customers with less complicated financial requirements. Manager large number of entry level and mass affluent investors to lessen the burden on human counsellors. Senior counsellor concentrates on sophisticated high net worth wealth planning while a Robo advisor handles ETFs and SIPs for 4 younger customers.
3. **Customer relationship management system:** It centralized client information, preference add interaction history and automates client monitoring, follow up reminder add enabling advisors to handle more accounts. CRM dashboards

identify customers who need portfolio evaluation while ensuring that no one is missing even when the advisor's capacity is low.

4. **Data analysis:** It includes responsibilities assessing customer behavior, forecasting churn and spotting potential cross selling opportunities. It also lowers the amount of manual research required and facilities proactive client interaction. Analytics can notify clients who are likely to move companies enabling prompt retention offers.
5. **Virtual assistance and chat bots:** They offer round-the-clock assistance with product details; account inquiry adds frequently asked questions. This also reduced the number of recurrent customers calls, bringing up advisors to concentrate on intricate wealth management plans.

For example: A chat bot that answers questions about the performance of NAV or mutual funds ensures that customers receive quick answers.

6. **Cyber security and cloud platforms:** In this it is very important to make sure that data is stored securely, Accessible remotely add in accordance with data protection legislation. Fosters clients trust and sport hybrid work arrangement without sacrificing security. Advisors can securely access client files during remote meetings using cloud based encrypted storage

PEOPLE & PROCESS TRNSFORMATION

People and process transformation focuses on redefining roles, responsibilities, and workflows so wealth managers can reliably mitigate hallucinations. Role descriptions must explicitly include AI oversight, ESG interpretation, and client education about AI limitations. Processes should embed verification checkpoints where advisors review high-stakes AI outputs—such as credit limit changes or ESG reclassifications—before finalization. In order to address wealth management's talent shortage, operational procedures must be changed in addition to workforce skills. Program for training, novel work methods and retention strategies make sure that counsellors are still competent, driven add in tune with the demands of today's clients

1. Training and upskilling modules:

Training in compliance:

- Frequent seminar on regulations pertaining to SEBI, RBI, FATCA,MiFID II and data protection.

- Practice making regulatory decisions using case studies based on simulation.

Training in ESG:

- Courses for certification on the design of ESG products and sustainable finance.
- teaching counsellors how to incorporate ESG ratings and disclosures into their investment recommendations.

Training in Digital instruments:

- practical instructions on analytics dashboard, Robo advisory interfaces and CRM platform.
- Cyber security education modules to guarantee secure customer interaction.

2. Novel standard operating procedures for hybrid work:

Work flexibility:

- Transparent rules for remote, hybrid and in office positions.
- Assessing client portfolios from any location at any time using secure cloud-based systems.

Framework for corporation:

- For team and advisor client communication, use zoom, Ms teams or slack.
- Make the digital onboarding process the same for all new clients.

Performance accountability:

- Introduce dashboards that monitor training hours, compliance accuracy and customer interactions.
- Weekly check in with team leaders to maintain alignment.

3. Retention and engagement plans:

- development of a career path
- organized career ladders for promotion.
- Cross functional rotations to gain a wide range of skills.

Incentives schemes:

- bonuses related to performance that are tied to client happiness, regulatory compliance adds digital adoption.
- Awards recognizing staff members who demonstrate proficiency in new skill domains.

Transfer of knowledge and mentorship:

- new employees are mentored by senior advisors to learn how to handle client relationships.
- An inhouse talent Academy for continuous talent sharing and peer-to-peer learning

REGULATORY & COMPLIANCE MANAGEMENT

Regulatory and compliance management examines how rules and supervisory expectations shape hallucination control in AI-enabled wealth management. Regulators increasingly expect clear accountability for AI-influenced decisions, robust model risk management, and verifiable ESG claims. Wealth managers become critical actors in demonstrating that client-facing advice, even when generated within a metaverse environment, is grounded in validated data and compliant methodologies. One of the most resource intensive aspects of wealth management is compliance, especially with changing laws like SEBI, RBI, MiFID II, FATCA and DPDP Act. The chance of mistakes, fines and reputational home rises when there is a lack of qualified workers. Using automation tools in conjunction with skilled people results in compliance, accuracy and efficiency.

1. Checklist for compliance: Firms should use organized checklists to standardize procedures and minimize mistakes.

Checklist for compliance with advisors:

- every new customer's KYC/AML paperwork should be checked.
- Openly disclosed fees and commissions.
- Risk profiling should be used to determine if a product is appropriate.
- Where appropriate record ESG disclosures.
- At the conclusion of each transaction, update the client portfolio record.

Internal compliance checklist:

- Quarterly conduct internal audit of advising methods.
- Check that your daughter's security measures and encryption methods are adequate.
- Adherence to the reporting requirements established by the RBI and SEBI should be monitored.
- Carry out routine stress tests to manage risk.
- Make sure all employees finish their compliance training.

2. Automated reporting dashboards:

Digital solutions can greatly lessen the burden of compliance

- Regulatory reports for SEBI/RBI submissions are automatically produced by AI powered dashboards
- suspicious activities are identified in real time by real time monitoring.
- All interactions with council are documented for transparency using audit trails.
- Complex reporting for regulators and management is made easier by data visualization software.

For example: a dashboard that automatically gathers all client investment data hand identifies missing KYC documentation cuts manual compliance mistakes by more than 50%.

3. How well-trained personnel minimize mistakes:

- Export consultants know the complexities of the law and make sure that all of their advice to clients is adequately documented.
- Employees who have received ESG training validate sustainable investments which helps them prevent the danger of green washing.
- Digital adapt employees utilize AI dashboards to make good judgement while using technology.
- Hybrid teams establish a dual layer of checks, which lowers penalties and increases customer confidence.

CLIENTS ENGAGEMENT & COMMUNICATION

Continuous improvement and monitoring focus on learning from hallucination incidents to enhance models, processes, and advisor capabilities over time. Institutions should establish feedback loops where wealth managers can log suspicious outputs, annotate context, and suggest corrective data or rules. Model risk teams can analyze these logs to identify patterns, such as specific ESG themes, sectors, or client profiles where hallucinations clusterand adjust training data or prompts accordingly. Regular review sessions can use real or simulated metaverse interactions to refine advisor heuristics for spotting hallucinations. Client engagement and communication address how wealth managers can maintain trust while using AI and metaverse tools that carry hallucination risk. Advisors must clearly explain the role of AI in generating scenarios, ratings, and ESG narratives, emphasizing that these are decision aids rather than infallible truths. When hallucinations are suspected or detected, wealth managers should transparently discuss the uncertainty, describe corrective steps taken, and reposition recommendations based on verified information. Metaverse environments can support this by offering interactive "what-if" explorations where clients see both AI-generated views and human-curated alternatives. Trust between clients and wealth managers is establish via a mix of knowledgeable human advisors add straight forward online interactions. Although talent shortage might impair client connections and companies may provide both individualized guidance and digital convenience with trained advisors backed by technology.

The function of knowledgeable counselors:

- A transparent, Moran end client centered council may be offered by advisors who have received training in digital tools, ESG and compliance.
- Individualized communication lowers churn by fostering lasting connections.

Example: an advisor who utilizes ESG data to support sustainable investment choices builds credibility and confidence.

Digital support systems:

- Platforms for customer relationship management: centralized client data to facilitate customize interaction.
- Multiple channels of communication: clients may connect with their advisors via video call, chat, emails add app notifications make sure they always feel supported.

- Chatbots: Instantly a dress simple queries like account status and NV updates alloying advisors to concentrate on sophisticated wealth planning.

Innovative strategies for engaging clients:
Financial literacy apps with gamification:

- teach younger clients about investments by means of games, competitions and incentives.

Example: an app that encourages sustained participation by giving consumers incentives for finishing modules on financial literacy.

Advisory models for multiple channels:

- individualized face to face meetings is provided for customers with significant net worth.
- hybrid help is provided to wealthy clients.
- Younger clients often prefer advice via apps along with occasional sessions with experts.

Mechanisms for providing transparent feedback:

- frequent customer satisfaction surveys and Net Promoter score monitoring.
- Digital dashboards that display portfolio performance in comparison to benchmark promoting accountability.

The harmony of human and digital:

- Human counsellors provide empathy, relationship building and trust.
- Digital technologies provide speed, accessibility and efficiency.
- They combine with creating an engagement hybrid model that attracts the wide range of clients which will include both traditional high net worth individuals and tech savvy millennials.

CONTINUOUS IMPROVEMENT AND MONITORING

The most effective Strategies still need continuous evaluation to guarantee their efficacy. Continuous monitoring in wealth management enables businesses to monitor the progress of workforce transformation, assesses its effects on customer happiness and pinpoint potential areas for development. Businesses may establish a feedback ribbon culture by using real time dashboards and clear KPIs.

Key performance indicators (KPIs): indicators of the workforce

- Rate of attrition: The percentage of workers who depart each year to measure how well they are retained. Average hours of ESG, compliance add digital training each advisor completed.
- Advisor productivity: The quantity of customers served by an advisor before and after receiving training.

KPIs 4 clients:

- Client churn rate: Percentage of customers lost each year is the client churn rate.
- Net Promoter scores (NPS): Images customer happiness and propensity to make recommendations.
- Client coverage ratio: The number of clients each advisor handles are monitored in relation to service quality.

KPIs for compliance:

- Mistake in the audit rate: the frequency of mistakes in adherence on reporting and advisory services.
- Fines imposed by regulations: the number and the total amount of fines assessed each year.
- KYC/AML completion rate: Percentage of customers that are completely compliant with regulatory requirements.

Live monitoring dashboards:

- companies may use automated dashboards to always monitor these KPIS.
- HR dashboard: attrition trends, training completion rates and recruitment pipeline status.
- Client engagement dashboard: NPS scores, churn notifications and the frequency of client engagement.
- Automated Performance dashboard: Automated SEBI/RBI. Flagged errors, KYC/AML status and a compliance dashboard. Client load per advisor, digital adoption rate and income generated per client are all included.

Iterative Progress and feedback loops:

- employee feedback: periodic pulse surveys on training quality, workload and job satisfaction.
- Client feedback: digital feedback forms following advisory sessions and quarterly satisfaction surveys.
- Monthly review sessions using dashboard insights to modify strategies are called management reviews.

CONCLUSION

The conclusion reiterates that mitigating AI hallucinations in ESG-driven credit risk advisory within the enterprise metaverse is inseparable from empowering wealth managers as active co-governors of human–AI systems. Their ability to blend financial judgment, ESG literacy, and AI skepticism determines whether metaverse-based advisory becomes a vehicle for responsible innovation or a source of opaque risk. Future research directions include empirical studies on how wealth managers detect and correct hallucinations in practice, experimental designs using metaverse simulations to test training interventions, and comparative analyses of governance models across jurisdictions. Talent transformation will be the deciding factor in the wealth management industry's long-term Competitiveness as it approaches a crucial turning point. With many experienced professionals approaching retirement and younger advisors lacking the required knowledge in compliance, digital and ESG. The scarcity of skilled advisors has grown to be one of the most pressing problems. This gap if ignored might erode client confidence and raise the possibility of regulatory noncompliance and ultimately endanger the entire company's development. Businesses are now in danger of losing market share and credibility to up and coming wealth-tech rivals if they lack educated experts since clients want transparency and personalization at the same time.

But there are answers in the industry that the integration of strategic hiring, up-skilling initiatives, adaptable work arrangements and AI driven technologies is a promising path forward. Companies may establish a pipeline of digital and compliance ready advisors fire creating new talent through campus recruitment and international hiring as well as boy investing in ongoing training. By attracting younger workers who want balance and meaningful employment with flexible work options may further boost retention. Furthermore, A and automation may lessen routine tasks, allowing advisors to concentrate on developing relationships and addressing more complicated client requirements. Thus, the talent transformation is not only a challenge but also a strategic opportunity for wealth management businesses so that to ensure resilience, innovation and long-term growth.

FUTURE RESEARCH

In the emerging enterprise metaverse, the next generation of advisors must continuously upgrade their capabilities in regulation, ESG, and digital technologies to remain effective and relevant. Their primary asset will be trust, earned by intelligently leveraging advanced tools while demonstrating authentic empathy and human judgment in every client interaction. Adaptability becomes the defining trait, as successful consultants learn to operate in hybrid roles that seamlessly blend compliance oversight, relationship management, and digital fluency. At the same time, structural synergies link talent scarcity with several cross-cutting challenges: firms that lack digitally competent advisors struggle to compete with fintech and wealth-tech platforms; understaffed compliance functions increase the risk of costly errors and regulatory penalties; and a shortage of skilled counsellors weakens one-on-one client engagement. Together, these dynamics underscore that human capital development is central to sustaining competitive, compliant, and trusted advisory services.

REFERENCES

Alaali, H. (2025). DFAS Doctrine Compendium: Philosophical, Strategic, and Systemic Frameworks for AI Governance, Crisis Intervention, and Algorithmic Control. https://papers.ssrn.com/sol3/papers.cfm?abstract_id=5367894

Amalia, D., Artini, Y. D., Rahayu, G. N., Purnomo, H., & Zaman, B. (2024). Optimizing Organizational Capabilities Through The Integration Of Strategic Management And Human Resource Performance. *Int J Econ Lit*, *2*, 216–228.

Ayanponle, L. O., Awonuga, K. F., Asuzu, O. F., Daraojimba, R. E., Elufioye, O. A., & Daraojimba, O. D. (2024). A review of innovative HR strategies in enhancing workforce efficiency in the US. *International Journal of Science and Research Archive*, *11*(1), 817–827.

Bolsiek, K. M. C. (2024). What factors influence the acceptance of metaverse technology in financial advisory services for the South African financial sector [Master's Thesis, University of Pretoria (South Africa)]. https://search.proquest.com/openview/bb46ffdca5ef2835068d39aa1a9a70ea/1?pq-origsite=gscholar&cbl=2026366&diss=y

Chukwu, O., Osirim, M., & Ahiakwo, U. (2025). Leveraging human capital investments intensity in improving the returns on equity of insurance firms in Nigeria. *International Journal of Social Sciences and Management Research*, *11*(1), 235–254.

Cossio, M. (2025). A comprehensive taxonomy of hallucinations in Large Language Models (No. arXiv:2508.01781). arXiv. https://doi.org//arXiv.2508.01781DOI: 10.48550

Digby, M. (2024). The evolving relationship between asset servicers and FinTechs: Unlocking efficiency and collaboration. *Journal of Securities Operations & Custody*, *16*(3). https://search.ebscohost.com/login.aspx?direct=true&profile=ehost&scope=site&authtype=crawler&jrnl=17531802&AN=177902872&h=4qb3Kzxd0AxGllkICCK7wlKWP14x6Ff1LzV8cVfMYNSbwv%2F1OnyiJnU0HQIo9s%2FSw9cCWl45Lb5zr7yF%2BS%2BDow%3D%3D&crl=c

Farawowan, F. F. (2025). Upskilling and Reskilling: Adaptive Strategies For HR Management in Facing The Industrial Revolution 5.0. Oikonomia. *Journal of Management Economics and Accounting*, *2*(4), 49–57.

Farinha, J., & De Fátima Pina, M. (2025). Digital Transformation in ESG Programs: Understanding Environmental, Social, and Governance Factors. In Machado, A. D. B., Sousa, M. J., Brambilla, A., Pesqueira, A., & Rocha, A. (Eds.), *Environmental, Social, Governance and Digital Transformation in Organizations* (Vol. 35, pp. 33–49). Springer Nature Switzerland., DOI: 10.1007/978-3-031-86079-9_2

George, A. S. (2024). Finance 4.0: The transformation of financial services in the digital age. *Partners Universal Innovative Research Publication*, *2*(3), 104–125.

Gu, Y. (2025). Three Essays on Enhancing Assurance in ESG Reporting: The Role of Emerging Technologies and Big Data [PhD Thesis, Rutgers The State University of New Jersey, Graduate School-Newark]. https://search.proquest.com/openview/838ae5ea5f18cc1e8682a440784ae8af/1?pq-origsite=gscholar&cbl=18750&diss=y

Iqbal, K., & Abbas, T. (2024). Ethnicity, religion, and Muslim education in a changing world: Navigating contemporary perspectives on multicultural schooling in the UK. Taylor & Francis. https://books.google.com/books?hl=en&lr=&id=LzgDEQAAQBAJ&oi=fnd&pg=PA2017&dq=broader+transition+from+job-based+to+capability-based+talent+management,+where+firms+cultivate+adaptability,+creativity,+and+digital+fluency+as+enduring+strategic+assets.&ots=nd8oNaHxsf&sig=0bdhKUnxj-4adjncQAvyZxW0gcQ

Jooss, S., Collings, D. G., McMackin, J., & Dickmann, M. (2024). A skills-matching perspective on talent management: Developing strategic agility. *Human Resource Management*, *63*(1), 141–157. DOI: 10.1002/hrm.22192

Joshi, S. (2025). Comprehensive Review of AI Hallucinations: Impacts and Mitigation Strategies for Financial and Business Applications. https://philpapers.org/rec/JOSCRO-3

Kapoor, M. (2025). Global Business Environment: Industry 5.0 and Beyond. Taylor & Francis. https://books.google.com/books?hl=en&lr=&id=19w_EQAAQBAJ&oi=fnd&pg=PT8&dq=There+is+a+pressing+need+for+human+oversight,+where+wealth+managers+can+co-exist+with+AI+and+pave+the+way+for+efficient,+prudent+and+responsible+judgement+to+the+AI+hallucinated+output,+to+amplify+the+enterprise+metaverse+capabilities.&ots=uvbwfE1Rj1&sig=VFJJ1WTiPE8JnDN2P1nb2tYZWdQ

Kaur, J. (2024). Responsible Artificial Intelligence (AI) Governance: Ethical Frameworks for Business Decision-Making. In Ethical Quandaries in Business Practices: Exploring Morality and Social Responsibility (pp. 337–368). IGI Global. https://www.igi-global.com/chapter/responsible-artificial-intelligence-ai-governance/356327

Kothandapani, H. P. (2025). Ai-driven regulatory compliance: Transforming financial oversight through large language models and automation. *Emerging Science Research*, *12*(1), 12–24.

Kotsantonis, S., & Serafeim, G. (2020). Human capital and the future of work: Implications for investors and ESG integration. *Journal of Financial Transformation*, *51*, 115–130.

Krishna, P. M. S. S., Kumar, T. P., Reddy, R. V. T., & Ariwa, E. (2024). Customer-Centric AI Solutions. In Minds Unveiled (pp. 58–69). Productivity Press. https://www.taylorfrancis.com/chapters/edit/10.4324/9781032711089-5/customer-centric-ai-solutions-puvvaladasu-sai-subramanya-krishna-praveen-kumar-ravuri-venkata-trinadh-reddy-ezendu-ariwa

Kurznack, L., Schoenmaker, D., & Schramade, W. (2021). A model of long-term value creation. *Journal of Sustainable Finance & Investment*, •••, 1–19. DOI: 10.1080/20430795.2021.1920231

Lee, C. L., Yam, S., Susilawati, C., & Blake, A. (2024). Future workforce for the property industry: Are we ready for the change? https://unsworks.unsw.edu.au/entities/publication/9a0860de-095c-496d-954c-cdb67b3716f3

Mahajan, P. (2025). The Soul of the AI: Governance, Ethics, and the Future of Human–AI Integration. Zenodo. https://hal.science/hal-05140138/

Martinez, A. (2025). The Impact of AI on Personalized Wealth Management: Optimizing Client Relationships, Costs, and Ethics in Banking. https://www.theseus.fi/handle/10024/886933

Masnun, A., Jessika, S., & Albadry, S. A. (2024). Optimizing Human-AI Collaboration in Educational Administration in Muara Bungo, Jambi: An HRD Framework for Role Redefinition, Skill Development, and Change Management. *Enigma in Education*, *2*(2), 114–125.

Moghadas, N. S. A. H., & Arvin, N. F. (2024). Elevating Airline Performance through Strategic Training: A Comprehensive Analysis of Key Performance Indicators (KPIs). https://www.sid.ir/paper/1407664/en

Mosqueira-Rey, E., Hernández-Pereira, E., Alonso-Ríos, D., Bobes-Bascarán, J., & Fernández-Leal, Á. (2023). Human-in-the-loop machine learning: A state of the art. *Artificial Intelligence Review*, *56*(4), 3005–3054. DOI: 10.1007/s10462-022-10246-w

Otieno, P. O., & Busili, P. A. (2024). A Research on Labor, Finance, Technology, and Sustainable Growth. *International Journal of Innovative Science and Research Technology*, *9*(9), 3570–3597.

Panneerselvam, S., Arokiasamy, E., & Kumar, K. S. (2025). Employee Experience Management (EXM): What, Why, and How to Create Exceptional Experiences at Work. In Approaching Employee Experience Management With Data Science (pp. 23–64). IGI Global Scientific Publishing. https://www.igi-global.com/chapter/employee-experience-management-exm/370198

Paulino, E., Romero, R., Mazo, P., & Tan, R. (2025). Strengthening resilience: The synergistic role of credit risk and customer relationship management in non-bank financial institutions. *International Journal of Research in Business & Social Science, 14*(1). https://search.ebscohost.com/login.aspx?direct=true&profile=ehost&scope=site&authtype=crawler&jrnl=21474478&AN=183427544&h=QrlyanHCDhzEPaU8q3%2Bj8IojrMo4VJrtKIgx0DGkicfqqivlgFvqlNilR54PQPxFzFbADt0uHrU5076niVXlkg%3D%3D&crl=c

Rachmad, Y. E. (2025). The New Era of HR Management: Prioritizing Competence Over Degrees. United Nations Development Programme. https://www.researchgate.net/profile/Yoesoep-Rachmad/publication/396404755_The_New_Era_of_HR_Management_Prioritizing_Competence_Over_Degrees/links/68e9c1ddf3032e2b4be8347d/The-New-Era-of-HR-Management-Prioritizing-Competence-Over-Degrees.pdf

Rainoldi, M., Ladkin, A., & Buhalis, D. (2024). Blending work and leisure: A future digital worker hybrid lifestyle perspective. *Annals of Leisure Research, 27*(2), 215–235. DOI: 10.1080/11745398.2022.2070513

Rakhmanovich, I. U., Taslim, M., Raman, A. M., & Ugli, A. A. A. (2025). The rise of behavioral economics: Leveraging AI to understand consumer decision-making. AIP Conference Proceedings, 3306(1), 050007. https://pubs.aip.org/aip/acp/article-abstract/3306/1/050007/3348895

Santoso, W., Sitorus, P. M., Batunanggar, S., Krisanti, F. T., Anggadwita, G., & Alamsyah, A. (2021). Talent mapping: A strategic approach toward digitalization initiatives in the banking and financial technology (FinTech) industry in Indonesia. *Journal of Science and Technology Policy Management, 12*(3), 399–420.

Schaffer, S. (2025). Digital Skills Shortages: Perspectives of Marketing Managers [PhD Thesis, Capella University]. https://search.proquest.com/openview/c45a30033f37825ecefcb677a6b66caa/1?pq-origsite=gscholar&cbl=18750&diss=y

Shan, Z., & Wang, Y. (2024). Strategic Talent Development in the Knowledge Economy: A Comparative Analysis of Global Practices. *Journal of the Knowledge Economy, 15*(4), 19570–19596. DOI: 10.1007/s13132-024-01933-w

Shuai, N. (2025). The Role of Digital Transformation Speed in Enhancing Productivity: A Mediated Framework with Operational Efficiency in Financial Shared Service. Journal of Electrical Systems, 21. https://search.ebscohost.com/login.aspx?direct=true&profile=ehost&scope=site&authtype=crawler&jrnl=11125209&AN=184115960&h=aF8hM4e9NEjQR5irHQReRtDxA7G0o1qMa7P5U8iOl4bLWpGXt6%2BTcxodawZREqw4qzSILEaiJQn417SErivKbg%3D%3D&crl=c

Singh, R. (2025). Revamping Employee Experience for the Next Generation Workforce. In Approaching Employee Experience Management With Data Science (pp. 65–94). IGI Global Scientific Publishing. https://www.igi-global.com/chapter/revamping-employee-experience-for-the-next-generation-workforce/370199

Slapakova, L., Fraser, A., Hughes, M., Aquilino, M. C., & Thue, K. (2024). Cultural and technological change in the future information environment. RAND. https://www.konjunktion.info/wp-content/uploads/2024/03/Cultural-and-technological-change-in-the-future-information-environment.pdf

Stein Smith, S. (2024). ESG and Other Emerging Technology Applications. In S. Stein Smith, Blockchain, Artificial Intelligence, and Financial Services (pp. 193–213). Springer Nature Switzerland. https://doi.org/DOI: 10.1007/978-3-031-74403-7_14

Sundaram, S. (2025). Innovating for the Future: Sustainable Corporate Strategies for Workforce Upskilling and Reskilling. *International Journal of Research in Entrepreneurship & Business Studies*, *6*(3), 33–46.

Tang, A. (2025). Safeguarding the future: Security and privacy by design for AI, Metaverse, Blockchain, and Beyond. CRC Press. https://books.google.com/books?hl=en&lr=&id=xDVEEQAAQBAJ&oi=fnd&pg=PT2&dq=-+Within+the+enterprise+metaverse,+goals+include+building+explainable+advisory+journeys,+maintaining+audit+trails+of+human+overrides&ots=vVOmsMhAlL&sig=RZZpNNALIYTtpGHAtGBEMYYkgYw

Tettey, D. J., Chrisben, D., Victoria, M. C., Chukwubuikem, E. P., & Abdullahi, A. (2025). Responsible AI deployment in sustainable project execution: Ensuring transparency, carbon efficiency and regulatory alignment. https://www.researchgate.net/profile/Jacob-Diameh/publication/390597381_Responsible_AI_deployment_in_sustainable_project_execution_Ensuring_transparency_carbon_efficiency_and_regulatory_alignment/links/67f591a176d4923a1a009f3b/Responsible-AI-deployment-in-sustainable-project-execution-Ensuring-transparency-carbon-efficiency-and-regulatory-alignment.pdf

Tifani Napitupulu, A. A., Panjaitan, N. U., Muda, I., & Ade, S. (n.d.). Competitive Advantage and Resource-Based View: A Systematic Literature Review. Bridging Management Control Systems and Sustainability: Systematic Reviews on Business Performance and Risk, 96.

Chapter 12
Reimagining Reality:
Innovations in AI Hallucination Management and Trustworthy Generation

Atanu Nag
https://orcid.org/0000-0003-0561-1946
IFTM University, India

Debika Chaudhuri
IFTM University, India

ABSTRACT

AI hallucination—the production of fluent but incorrect or fabricated outputs—has become a major challenge for large language models and generative AI. This chapter reviews the evolution of hallucination management, from early recognition to modern mitigation and creative reinterpretation. It defines hallucination in AI contexts and identifies key causes such as data noise, model drift, prompt ambiguity, and domain mismatch. The chapter then examines evaluation frameworks, taxonomies, and metrics, including factual consistency measures, FActScore, and domain-specific benchmarks. Core mitigation strategies are discussed, notably retrieval-augmented generation, multi-stage verification, human-in-the-loop approaches, and prompt optimization. Emerging trends include agentic AI systems with multi-agent validation, sector-specific solutions in healthcare and finance, and viewing hallucination as a driver of human–machine co-creation. The chapter concludes that effective hallucination management is a technical and ethical necessity for trustworthy AI.

DOI: 10.4018/979-8-3373-7534-2.ch012

INTRODUCTION

The phenomenon of hallucination in artificial intelligence (AI) systems—particularly in large language models (LLMs)—has emerged as one of the defining challenges in the pursuit of trustworthy, ethically aligned, and socially responsible AI (Förster & Skop, 2025; Lin et al., 2024, Li et al., 2024). Hallucination refers to cases in which AI systems produce outputs that are coherent, grammatically fluent, and often highly persuasive, yet lack factual grounding or contextual relevance. These outputs may include fabricated information, inaccurate reasoning, or invented citations, all of which can compromise reliability when LLMs are deployed in sensitive domains such as education, governance, healthcare, and law (Dahl et al., 2024; Anh-Hoang et al., 2025). As generative AI technologies proliferate, understanding, mitigating, and reimagining hallucination has become central to the broader discourse on trustworthy AI. Early examinations of hallucination focused on defining the phenomenon and documenting its behavior across diverse tasks. Researchers observed that LLMs frequently produce statements that are 'plausible yet ungrounded,' reflecting the probabilistic nature of neural text generation rather than true comprehension (Kryściński et al., 2020; Farquhar et al., 2024; Lin et al., 2024). Computer science literature defined hallucination as a generative error that leads to misinformation or logical inconsistency, emphasizing its role in distorting the semantic mapping between inputs and outputs (Anh-Hoang et al., 2025; Kazlaris et al., 2025; van Deemter, 2024). Meanwhile, scholars in law, clinical decision support, and computational education highlighted hallucination as a critical threat to user trust, noting that fabricated content in high-stakes scenarios could lead to serious harm (Dahl et al., 2024). This recognition marked the first stage in the evolution of hallucination research: definition and conceptualization. During this phase, hallucination was often framed as an enigmatic behavior embedded within the 'black-box' functioning of deep learning models, raising fundamental questions about interpretability, epistemic validity, and safety. Following conceptual clarity, the research community moved toward building systematic taxonomies and evaluative frameworks (Huang et al., 2024). A turning point came with the development of quantitative hallucination metrics designed to measure factual consistency. The FActScore metric, for instance, introduced a structured, evidence-based evaluation pipeline for assessing the factual grounding of LLM outputs (Min et al., 2023). In parallel, the summarization community developed fine-grained typologies of factual errors, distinguishing between intrinsic hallucinations (not derived from source text) and extrinsic hallucinations (unsupported by external knowledge) (Maynez, 2020). In healthcare, benchmarks such as med-HALT and clinical-HALT systematically captured the risks posed by hallucinations in biomedical reasoning and clinical summarization (Pal et al., 2023; Asgari et al., 2025). These tools demonstrated that hallucination is not a monolithic error but a multifaceted phenomenon emerging from model limitations, training data noise, prompt ambiguity, domain mismatch, or model drift.

Building on these diagnostic insights, the field entered a mitigation phase, which introduced architectures, workflows, and design patterns that reduce hallucination in practice. Retrieval-augmented generation (RAG) anchored model responses in verified external documents, significantly lowering reliance on internal statistical associations (Lewis et al., 2020). Other strategies included chain-of-thought verification, multi-stage answer checking, and human-in-the-loop (HITL) supervisory frameworks (Amirizaniani et al., 2025). Human-AI collaboration became especially valuable in high-stakes contexts, enabling experts to refine and oversee outputs before they reached end-users. Prompt optimization and controlled decoding techniques also emerged as effective tools, demonstrating that careful input structuring can reduce ambiguity and prevent generative drift (Liao et al. 2024). These approaches collectively signaled a shift from descriptive analysis to active engineering intervention. More recent scholarship reflects a fourth evolutionary stage: reimagining hallucination within creative and agentic AI paradigms. Researchers studying creativity, ideation support, and design assistance have reframed certain forms of hallucination as beneficial, arguing that controlled divergence from factual constraints can stimulate human-machine co-creation (Pilcher et al., 2025). Meanwhile, emerging agentic AI architectures employ multiple cooperating agents—generators, critics, verifiers, retrievers, and planners—to iteratively refine outputs, yielding better factual accuracy while still preserving imaginative potential (Wan et al., 2025). These systems model collaborative reasoning workflows, embedding feedback loops and self-reflective mechanisms intended to balance creativity with groundedness.

A final stage in this evolution involves ethical integration and governance alignment. Hallucination management is no longer viewed solely as a technical problem but as a socio-technical imperative that intersects with transparency, accountability, fairness, and safety. Policymakers and research bodies emphasize the need for documentation standards, model cards, auditing frameworks, and domain-specific guidelines that govern the deployment of generative AI in professional settings (Janssen, 2025). Interdisciplinary collaboration among technologists, domain experts, ethicists, and regulatory institutions; is essential for ensuring that hallucination mitigation becomes an embedded component of responsible AI design rather than an afterthought (Kerstan et al., 2026). Together, these developments illustrate a comprehensive progression: from recognition and taxonomy building to mitigation, innovation, and governance integration. The path forward requires AI systems that blend creativity with factual accuracy through mechanisms such as self-reflection, retrieval grounding, multi-agent validation, and human oversight. By embracing this multidimensional approach, hallucination management becomes a foundation for trustworthy, reliable, and sustainable AI across sectors.

2. TYPOLOGIES, TAXONOMIES, AND ROOT-CAUSE ANALYSES

Following early awareness, researchers began developing typologies and taxonomies of hallucinations to clarify their origins, behavioral patterns, and potential impact across different application domains. In healthcare and life sciences, where erroneous outputs can have immediate clinical consequences, scholars categorized hallucinations into input-conflicting, context-conflicting, and fact-conflicting types, depending on whether the generated content contradicted the user's prompt, surrounding contextual information, or established domain knowledge (Gadiko, 2024). This domain-driven classification was foundational because it demonstrated that hallucination is not monolithic but manifests differently depending on the nature of the task, the reliability of the input, and the structure of the knowledge environment in which the model operates. A broader taxonomy proposed for LLMs extended these ideas to general-purpose systems, organizing hallucination types based on factors such as dataset quality, retrieval robustness, decoding strategies, and feedback integration mechanisms (Kryściński et al., 2020; Sahoo et al., 2024). These taxonomies illustrated how hallucinations emerge across the AI development lifecycle—from pretraining on noisy corpora to inference-time prompt conditioning. They also provided a structured foundation for designing targeted mitigation strategies by distinguishing between hallucinations caused by internal model dynamics and those emerging from weaknesses in external information pipelines such as retrieval systems or user instructions (Zhang et al., 2025). As taxonomies matured, researchers increasingly focused on uncovering the root causes of hallucination, recognizing that effective mitigation requires understanding the underlying mechanics.

One major source is training data noise, where inaccuracies, biases, and ambiguities in datasets propagate through the model and manifest as logically coherent yet factually incorrect outputs during generation (Kryściński et al., 2020; Huang et al., 2024). Because LLMs learn statistical associations rather than semantic truths, corrupted or skewed data distributions can disproportionately shape predictions (Farquhar et al., 2024). Another important driver is autoregressive prediction drift, a behavior inherent to sequence-generation models. Since each token is predicted based on the prior context, any minor deviation from truth can recursively amplify, leading to compounding inaccuracies in longer responses. This mechanism helps explain why hallucinations escalate during chain-of-thought reasoning or long-form content generation. Prompt ambiguity is also a well-established contributor (Huang et al., 2024). When users provide vague, underspecified, or context-poor prompts, the model often generates assumptions to fill informational gaps, increasing the likelihood of hallucination (Farquhar et al., 2024; Zamfirescu-Pereira et al., 2023). Research shows that clearer, more constrained prompts significantly reduce drift and improve factual reliability. A fourth cause is out-of-distribution (OOD) querying, which occurs when models are asked about unfamiliar, obscure, or highly specialized topics. Without sufficient training exposure, the model extrapolates based on superficial patterns, producing speculative or fabricated responses (Zhang & Zhang, 2025; Chen et al., 2023). In scientific, legal, and clinical workflows, this limitation becomes particularly consequential, prompting the development of domain-specific models and retrieval-augmented architectures. Building on these insights, the field entered a phase of systematisation and analysis, characterized by the creation of structured frameworks, interpretability tools, and diagnostic metrics to evaluate hallucination with scientific rigor (Anh-Hoang et al., 2025). Among these innovations, factual consistency metrics such as FActScore (Min et al., 2023) and benchmark suites such as TruthfulQA (Lin et al., 2022) and med-HALT (Pal et al., 2023) provided empirical methods to measure the factual grounding of outputs across diverse domains. These metrics represent a significant methodological advancement, as they combine automated scoring with HITL evaluation, enabling more reliable diagnosis of error types. Systematisation also prompted deeper consideration of knowledge-grounding mechanisms, inspiring hybrid evaluation models that compare generated outputs against structured knowledge graphs, retrieved passages, or authoritative scientific datasets. In parallel, transparency tools such as attention mapping, saliency-based interpretability, and self-consistency scoring allowed researchers to understand when and why reasoning paths break down (Lewis et al., 2020; Wang et al., 2023). Ultimately, this phase laid a critical foundation for later advancements in mitigation and innovation. By building typologies, identifying causal mechanisms, and integrating diagnostic metrics, the research community created a shared conceptual language for analyzing hallucination. This shared foundation now underpins everything from agentic multi-model verification systems to retrieval-augmented pipelines and governance-oriented transparency frameworks. The shift from intuitive observation to structured classification marked a turning point, enabling hallucination research to progress from descriptive commentary to evidence-based engineering solutions supported by reproducible experimentation and cross-domain validation (Kazlaris et al., 2025; Sahoo et al., 2024).

Figure 1 presents a hierarchical taxonomy of AI hallucinations. The first branch categorizes hallucinations by typology—input-conflicting, context-conflicting, and fact-conflicting. The second branch identifies root causes, including training noise, autoregressive drift, prompt ambiguity, and OOD queries. Leaf nodes represent specific application domains (*e.g.*, healthcare, law, finance).

Figure 1. Taxonomy tree of AI hallucinations by type, cause, and domain.

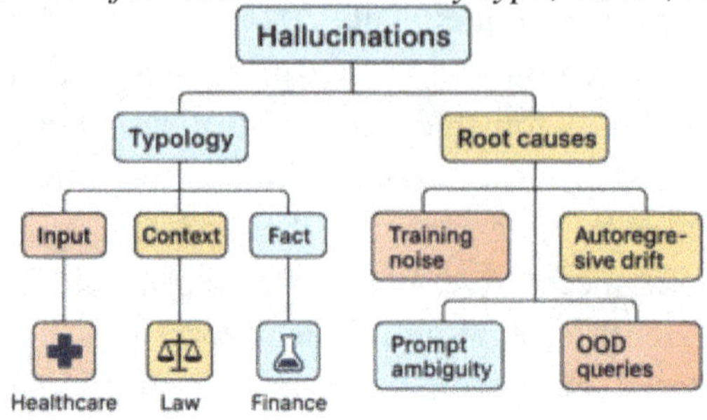

3. MITIGATION STRATEGIES AND EARLY MANAGEMENT TECHNIQUES

With typologies, taxonomies, and causal mechanisms established, the next phase in the evolution of hallucination research focused on the development of systematic mitigation and management strategies. These approaches aimed to detect, reduce, or prevent hallucinations in both general-purpose and domain-specific LLM deployments (Ji et al., 2023). Early management techniques combined architectural advances, retrieval mechanisms, verification workflows, and human oversight to achieve higher factual reliability. This phase marked a transition from descriptive understanding to actionable solutions capable of improving the safety and groundedness of AI-generated outputs (Hiriyanna & Zhao, 2025).

3.1 Retrieval-Augmented Generation (RAG)

One of the earliest and most influential innovations in hallucination mitigation was RAG, introduced as a hybrid architecture that enhances LLMs by integrating external evidence retrieval with generative modeling (Lewis et al., 2020). Instead of depending solely on fixed model parameters—an approach limited by the scope and quality of pretraining data—RAG retrieves relevant documents, structured information, or database entries at inference time. These retrieved sources serve as a grounding mechanism, ensuring that generated responses are anchored in verifiable information. Subsequent studies demonstrated that RAG substantially reduces hallucination frequency across question answering, summarization, and knowledge-intensive reasoning tasks (Niu et al., 2024). Its success stems from the principle of dynamic knowledge injection, allowing AI systems to remain up-to-date and contextually aligned. In high-stakes environments such as medical diagnostics, policy analysis, and scientific fact-checking, RAG-based systems outperform purely parametric models in factual accuracy. As a result, retrieval augmentation has become a foundational technique in modern trustworthy AI design, forming the backbone of pipelines used in enterprise search, clinical decision support, and educational tutoring (Ke et al., 2025).

3.2 Multi-Stage Verification and HITL

As LLMs began entering sensitive domains, it became increasingly evident that automated systems alone could not guarantee factual accuracy. This led to the widespread adoption of HITL frameworks, which integrate expert oversight into the AI generation workflow (Asgari et al., 2025). In these systems, humans review or validate outputs either before deployment (pre-deployment curation) or during use (real-time review) (Mourtzinis et al., 2025). HITL approaches are especially prevalent in medicine, law, and scientific research, where even minor factual inaccuracies can have serious consequences. Parallel to HITL approaches, multi-stage and multi-agent verification pipelines emerged as a powerful automated alternative. In these architectures, one model (or agent) is responsible for generating content, while a second agent performs evidence checking, a third agent assesses logical consistency, and a final validation stage consolidates results (Ma et al., 2026). This collaborative agent design mirrors team-based human workflows, distributing responsibilities across specialized verifiers. Such layered verification significantly improves reliability by creating redundancy and cross-checking between independent reasoning paths. Multi-agent verification has been shown to reduce hallucination rates in reasoning-intensive tasks, including math problem solving, biomedical summarization, and legal argument generation (Shi et al., 2025). Together, HITL and multi-agent verification represent a balanced integration of human judgment and automated reasoning.

3.3 Metrics and Hallucination Detection

Effective mitigation depends on reliable measurement. Therefore, the development of quantitative hallucination detection metrics became a core component of early management strategies. Instead of relying on subjective human judgments alone, researchers devised scoring systems capable of objectively evaluating factual grounding. Among the most widely used metrics is FactCC, a classifier-based metric designed to assess factual consistency between source text and generated summaries (Kryściński et al., 2020). Another significant contribution is FActScore, which evaluates factual accuracy through structured retrieval and human verification (Min et al., 2023). These tools have improved reproducibility and enabled systematic benchmarking across models. In domain-specific contexts, metrics such as TruthfulQA measure an AI system's tendency to produce human-like falsehoods or misleading responses (Lin et al., 2022). In clinical and biomedical domains, clinical-HALT and med-HALT provide specialized benchmarks for detecting misleading summarizations, fabricated biomedical facts, and non-evidence-based claims (Zhouet al., 2025; Pal et al., 2023; Asgari et al., 2025). Complementing these formal metrics, researchers introduced auxiliary methods such as uncertainty estimation, self-consistency scoring, ontology alignment, and retrieval-contrastive evaluation. Together, these techniques allow models to identify potential hallucination zones, flag uncertain statements, or generate multiple reasoning paths to detect internal contradictions. Through the combination of automated scoring systems and human verification, detection frameworks helped researchers map hallucination behavior with increasing precision (Farquhar et al., 2024; Kulkarni et al., 2025).

3.4 Prompt Engineering and Fine-Tuning

Another major avenue for hallucination mitigation involves the design of more explicit, structured, or constraining prompts. Prompt engineering techniques instruct models to cite evidence, reflect on uncertainty, or abstain when insufficient information is available. Research shows that adding structured instructions such as 'Use only the provided text,' 'Think step-by-step,' or 'Cite your sources' significantly reduces ungrounded claims (Zamfirescu-Pereira et al., 2023; Xu et al., 2025). Additionally, fine-tuning on carefully curated datasets improves model grounding. Domain-tuned models—such as biomedical or legal LLMs—tend to hallucinate less frequently due to exposure to high-quality, domain-specific corpora. Reinforcement learning from human feedback (RLHF) further enhances reliability by teaching models to align with human judgments of correctness and harmfulness. Through iterative preference optimization, models become more cautious when faced with uncertainty, thereby reducing speculative generation (Zhou et al., 2025). Together, retrieval augmentation, multi-stage verification, detection metrics, prompt engineering, and fine-tuning constitute the management phase of hallucination research. This phase marks a shift from conceptual understanding to practical control mechanisms. By integrating external knowledge retrieval, human oversight, diagnostic metrics, and structured generation protocols, researchers developed a multi-layered toolkit capable of mitigating hallucinations across diverse applications. These early techniques established the foundation upon which more advanced innovations—such as agentic AI systems, self-reflective models, and governance-aligned frameworks—would later be built (Zhang & Zhang, 2025; Anh-Hoang et al., 2025).

Table 1 summarizes key techniques for managing AI hallucinations, including their applications, benefits, and limitations. Methods range from automated approaches like RAG and multi-agent verification to human-centered strategies such as HITL, as well as evaluation tools like hallucination metrics and prompt engineering. Together, they highlight a balance of technical and human oversight to improve accuracy and trustworthiness across domains.

Table 1. Techniques for managing AI hallucinations across domainsand applications

Technique	Description	Domain Examples	Benefits	Limitations	Reference
RAG	Retrieval of external evidence for grounding	Healthcare, Law, Finance	Reduces factually incorrect outputs	Retrieval latency; outdated sources	[Neha et al., 2025; Iaroshev et al., 2024]
Multi-Agent Verification	Pipeline of AI agents performing generation, fact-checking, evaluation	Research, Legal	Cross-validation; redundancy	Computationally expensive	[Ma et al., 2026; Xiong et al., 2025]
HITL	Expert review at pre- or post-deployment stages	Healthcare, Education	Ensures context-aware accuracy	Requires human labor; slower	[Memarian & Doleck, 2024; Livingston et al., 2025]
Hallucination Metrics	Quantitative measurement of factual accuracy	Cross-domain	Objective evaluation; benchmark comparison	Limited to domains with reliable references	[Kulkarni et al., 2025;]
Prompt Engineering & Fine-Tuning	Structured prompts and curated training	Biomedical, Legal	Reduces ungrounded outputs	May require domain skill and labeled data	[Maharjan et al., 2024]

Figure 2 shows a schematic pipeline for mitigating AI hallucinations. It begins with prompt engineering to guide model outputs, followed by RAG to ground responses in external knowledge. Multi-stage verification with HITL ensures accuracy, while hallucination metrics detect and evaluate factual errors. The layered design illustrates how automated and human-centered strategies work together to produce reliable, trustworthy AI outputs.

Figure 2. Multi-layered hallucination mitigation pipeline for LLMs. The diagram illustrates how different mitigation strategies—prompt engineering, RAG, multi-stage verification with HITL, and hallucination metrics—interact in a layered architecture to improve factual reliability and reduce AI hallucinations.

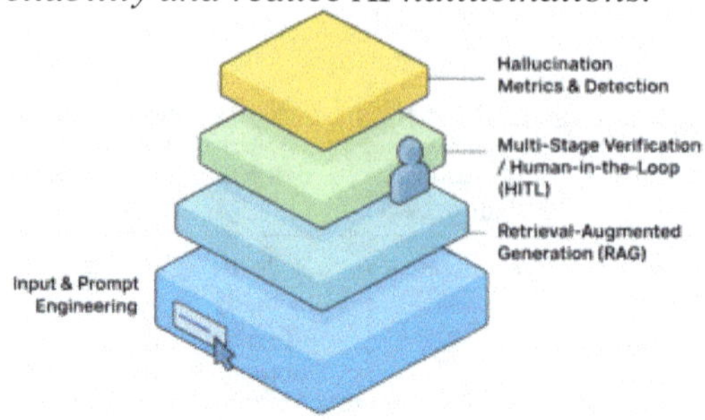

4. INNOVATION: EMERGING TECHNIQUES AND PARADIGM SHIFTS

The contemporary phase of AI hallucination management represents a decisive shift from reactive mitigation to proactive innovation. Instead of merely reducing hallucinations, researchers now explore new architectures, conceptual frameworks, and philosophical interpretations that expand the boundaries of what hallucination means in AI. This stage reflects maturity in the field—where prevention, evaluation, and reinterpretation merge to produce the next generation of responsible and creative AI systems (Förster et al., 2025; Shao, 2025).

4.1 Multi-Agent Architectures

One of the most transformative innovations involves multi-agent or agentic AI systems, where the responsibilities of generation, verification, critique, and refinement are explicitly distributed across specialized agents. Traditional LLMs operate as monolithic systems, performing generation and reasoning within a single model pass. However, more recent frameworks propose multi-step and multi-agent pipelines designed to provide internal checks and balances (Xiong et al., 2025; Tran et al., 2025). A recent study proposed a multi-layer agent architecture in which successive agents iteratively review and enhance preceding outputs. This design integrates systematic evaluation and refinement into the generation process, resulting in more reliable and higher-quality outputs (Alshehri, 2025). The recent research demonstrates that multi-agent architectures in which autonomous agents communicate, evaluate, and refine each other's outputs can self-regulate without relying solely on external fact-checking or user prompts. By embedding intra-agent feedback and reasoning loops, these systems have been shown to significantly reduce hallucination rates in experimental evaluations and improve interpretability, as agents contribute structured reasoning traces that support the final generated response (Darwish et al., 2025; Yu & McQuade, 2025). Multi-agent designs also enable role-specific models, such as one optimized for domain retrieval and another for reasoning, allowing greater specialization and efficiency. This paradigm marks a shift from single-model solutions to orchestral, collaborative AI ecosystems (Althaf et al., 2025).

4.2 Claims of Total Elimination

As the field progresses, some researchers have advanced bold claims that hallucinations can be entirely eliminated under certain controlled conditions. These claims typically arise from studies involving highly structured datasets, deterministic pipeline architectures, or tightly constrained prompting environments. In these systems, the model is not allowed to generate free-form text without grounding; instead, every output must be matched against verified information sources before release (Kazlaris et al., 2025; Anh-Hoang et al., 2025). Examples, include generation pipelines with enforced evidence tagging, where each statement must reference its originating data, and 'closed-world' systems that restrict model outputs only to validated knowledge repositories. Although these designs demonstrate near-zero hallucination rates in testing environments, many scholars caution that such results apply primarily to narrow domains and do not generalize to open-ended real-world scenarios (Zhang & Zhang, 2025; Wada et al., 2025). Nevertheless, these breakthroughs push the research community toward models capable of deterministic factuality, especially for domains like medicine, finance, and law where tolerance for error is minimal (Dokas 2026).

4.3 Reframing Hallucination as Opportunity

A parallel but more philosophical branch of inquiry reframes hallucination not solely as a defect but also as a potential source of creativity and ideation (Lee, 2023). Some researchers argue that hallucinations in LLMs reveal an underlying form of emergent generative imagination. From this standpoint, hallucinations arise when models interpolate or extrapolate from incomplete patterns in ways that echo human creative reasoning, rather than functioning solely as erroneous outputs (Cai & Gao, 2025). In fields like design, literature, brainstorming, and artistic ideation, controlled hallucinations can encourage novel combinations of concepts. Scholars propose distinguishing 'harmful hallucinations' from 'productive hallucinations,' the latter being outputs that deviate from factual correctness but contribute meaningfully to innovation, conceptual exploration, or problem reframing. This line of thought has influenced new co-creative frameworks where humans guide AI systems to harness hallucinations deliberately—treating them as generative stimuli rather than flaws (Sui et al. 2024). By shifting from restriction to reimagination, this perspective broadens the role of LLMs and transforms hallucination from a risk to a resource in certain creative domains (Huang et al., 2024).

4.4 Domain-Specific Innovations

Innovation in hallucination management has also taken shape through domain-tailored strategies that combine technical advances with epistemic oversight. In education technology and business learning environments, scholars propose multilevel frameworks integrating structured prompt templates, peer verification layers, and automated audit trails to monitor AI-generated content in teaching and assessment workflows (Fajardo-Ramos et al., 2025; Lin et al., 2024). These strategies ensure that the outputs used for instructional content or student feedback are reliable yet flexible enough to promote inquiry and critical thinking. In healthcare and life sciences, innovations focus on embedding domain ontologies, clinical guidelines, and expert-in-the-loop validation mechanisms (Asgari et al., 2025; Li et al., 2025). Studies show that integrating medical knowledge graphs and disciplined terminological constraints significantly reduces clinically harmful hallucinations. These systems are further enhanced through continuous expert review cycles, where human specialists correct or annotate outputs to inform the model's future behavior (Deng et al., 2025; Pusch et al., 2025).

Across these domains, innovation reflects hybridization—blending technical solutions with contextual governance to tailor hallucination control to sector-specific risks and expectations. A comparative overview of emerging approaches in AI hallucination management, highlighting technical frameworks, philosophical perspectives, and domain-specific innovations is illustrated in Table 2.

Table 2. The innovation landscape of AI hallucination management.

Innovation Type	Core Concept	Example Approaches	Domains/ Applications	Impact on Hallucination	Reference
Multi-Agent Architectures	Distributed responsibility & verification	Generator/Evaluator/Qualifier/ Refiner pipeline	General AI, Research	Reduced hallucinations, enhanced interpretability	[Darwish et al., 2025; Osuji et al., 2025]
Claims of Total Elimination	Deterministic output & evidence grounding	Evidence tagging, closed-world knowledge systems	Medicine, Finance, Law	Near-zero hallucinations in structured environments	[Wada et al., 2025; Neha et al., 2025]
Reframing Hallucination	Creativity-focused, productive hallucinations	Controlled ideation, co-creative frameworks	Design, Literature, Brain-storming	Transforms hallucinations into generative opportunities	[Cai & Gao, 2025; Pilcher et al., 2025]
Domain-Specific Innovations	Hybrid technical and epistemic oversight	Ontology constraints, HITL validation, audit trails	Education, Healthcare, Business	Tailored risk reduction, context-aware reliability	[Amirizaniani et al., 2024; Al Machot et al., 2025]

Figure 3 shows key innovations in AI hallucination research. Each layer—from multi-agent pipelines to claims of elimination, creative reframing, and domain-specific frameworks—illustrates a step toward more proactive and context-aware systems. Upward arrows emphasize the progression from mitigation to innovation.

Figure 3. Emerging innovation landscape in AI hallucination management: from multi-agent architectures to domain-specific and conceptual strategies, research progresses from reactive mitigation to proactive and creative approaches

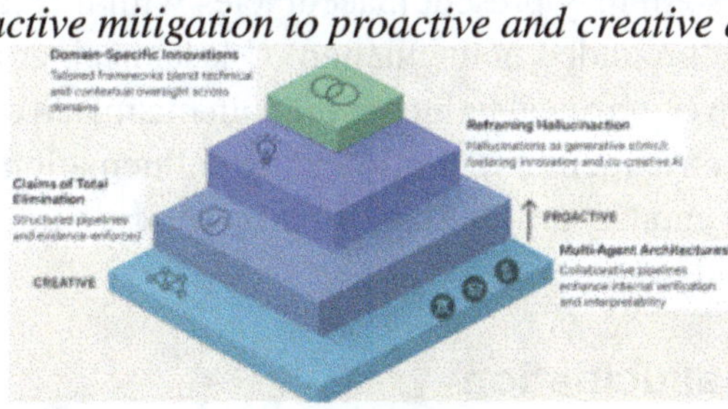

5. CHALLENGES, TRADE-OFFS, AND FUTURE DIRECTIONS

Despite remarkable advances in hallucination management, several enduring challenges and structural constraints continue to limit the reliability of LLMs. As research demonstrates, hallucination is not simply a technical flaw but a systemic by-product of probabilistic generation, imperfect data ecosystems, and sociotechnical complexities that cannot be fully engineered away (Bottazzi Grifoni et al., 2025). This section outlines the persistent challenges and trade-offs that shape the future trajectory of hallucination-resistant AI systems.

5.1 Residual Risk

Even advanced LLMs exhibit non-zero hallucination rates despite retrieval grounding, multi-agent verification, and self-reflective prompting (Asgari et al., 2025). Since LLMs statistically predict the most likely continuation rather than verify factual correctness, complete elimination remains theoretically and practically elusive (Farquhar et al., 2024). Ji et al.'s 2023 survey emphasizes that hallucination is deeply embedded in the generative mechanism, arising even when models operate in well-defined contexts. Thus, while hallucinations can be minimized, achieving perfect factual alignment across all domains and prompt variations remains beyond reach. Residual risk must therefore be managed rather than assumed solvable.

5.2 Retrieval Bottlenecks

RAG is widely recognized for reducing hallucination by grounding responses in external sources. However, RAG brings its own limitations. Retrieval pipelines introduce latency, increase computational load, and create dependencies on database quality (Zhang & Zhang, 2025). If retrieved documents are outdated, biased, or incomplete, the system may present inaccuracies with increased confidence—a phenomenon termed 'grounded hallucination' (Masanneck et al., 2025; Zhang & Zhang, 2025). Moreover, retrieval failure or domain mismatch often causes fallback to the model's parametric memory, reintroducing hallucination. Thus, RAG trades one failure mode for another unless supported by robust curation and monitoring of underlying knowledge sources.

5.3 Measuring Hallucination

Evaluating hallucinations remains one of the most difficult challenges. Unlike accuracy assessment in structured tasks, hallucination detection must account for context, domain constraints, and evolving knowledge. Existing metrics such as FActScore, QAGS, and BLEU-based consistency scores provide partial solutions but suffer from domain dependency and limited interpretability (Kulkarni et al., 2025). Current evaluation frameworks face significant challenges in establishing appropriate truth conditions for tasks involving abstraction, prediction, or value-laden judgments, since detecting hallucinations in LLMs requires sensitivity to contextual nuances and domain-specific interpretability — aspects that conventional metrics address only partially (Kazlaris et al., 2025; Kulkarni et al., 2025). Cross-domain benchmarks are urgently needed to compare mitigation strategies and standardize claims of improvement across the research community (Chakraborty et al., 2025).

5.4 Domain-Specificity vs. Generality

Many mitigation strategies demonstrate strong performance only within specific sectors. Techniques designed for structured, knowledge-intensive fields—such as medicine, law, or finance—often rely on controlled vocabularies or ontologies that do not generalize to open-ended conversational contexts (Lavrinovics et al., 2025; Cai et al., 2025). Recent studies demonstrate that hallucination evaluation methods tailored to specific domains often lose reliability when applied to multi-domain, general-purpose LLMs, where ambiguity is greater and truth is inherently context-dependent (Kulkarni et al., 2025). As a result, creating universal hallucination mitigation frameworks remains a major open challenge. Future solutions must flexibly combine domain-specific expertise with scalable general-purpose architectures.

5.5 Ethical and Governance Issues

Hallucinations are not merely technical errors—they carry significant ethical and societal consequences. When AI systems generate misleading, biased, or confident but incorrect information, the impact can manifest in public trust erosion, misinformation propagation, and harm to vulnerable populations (Park & Nan, 2025). Floridi et al. (2018) argue that ethical AI must incorporate transparency, accountability, and human oversight to manage imperfections inherent in machine cognition. Ethical governance efforts must thus extend beyond model optimization to include organizational practices, user training, regulatory compliance, and accountability pathways. Managing hallucination requires both technological refinement and institutional responsibility. The future of hallucination management will merge technological, organizational, and ethical innovations (Batool et al., 2025) including:

i) **Real-Time Multi-Agent Verification Pipelines:** Dynamic agent architectures—where separate agents generate, critique, validate, and explain outputs—will become foundational to scalable hallucination reduction (Darwish et al., 2025). These pipelines enable self-correction and faster feedback loops.
ii) **Uncertainty Expression and Evidence Attribution:** By training models to communicate uncertainty, reference sources, or abstain from answering ambiguous queries, systems can increase transparency and curb misleading outputs. Aligning model confidence with factual accuracy helps users identify uncertain

or unsupported responses, thereby enhancing trust and mitigating hallucinations in open-domain tasks (Steyvers et al., 2025).

iii) **Standardized Hallucination Benchmarks:** Industry-wide benchmarking is essential for reproducibility and transparent claims of progress. Cross-domain evaluation frameworks will allow models to be compared more reliably across tasks (Chakraborty et al., 2025).

iv) **Governance-Integrated Design:** Ethical oversight, embedded throughout the AI lifecycle from data curation to deployment, will define next-generation AI governance (Papagiannidis et al., 2025). Responsible AI adoption depends on the integration of institutional policies alongside technical safeguards (Batool et al., 2025).

Overall, the future of hallucination management will require an integrated approach that unites technical innovation with ethical governance, robust evaluation standards, and domain-aware architectures (Shi et al., 2024). Rather than eliminating hallucination entirely, successful strategies will focus on minimizing harmful outcomes while enabling safe, transparent, and trustworthy AI use (Abbas et al. 2025). Table3 summarizes the major unresolved issues in hallucination mitigation, spanning residual risk, retrieval limitations, evaluation difficulties, domain-transfer challenges, and ethical governance concerns. It highlights why each challenge persists despite technological advances and outlines the risks that continue to affect reliable AI deployment.

Table 3. Key challenges in advanced hallucination management across different dimensions

Challenge	Core Issue	Non-Eliminable Factors	Typical Risks	Reference
Non-zero hallucination rates	Generative models predict likelihoods, not truth	Hallucination embedded in model architecture; cannot be fully eliminated	Misleading outputs even under strong mitigation	[Dahl et al., 2024]
Limits of RAG pipelines	Latency, outdated sources, retrieval failure	Quality of external corpora varies; fallback to parametric memory	'Grounded hallucination,' confident inaccuracies	[Brown et al., 2025; Zhang & Zhang, 2025]
Weak evaluation metrics	Metrics are context- and domain-dependent	Hard to define truth; evolving knowledge; abstraction tasks	Misleading claims of improvement; non-comparable benchmarks	[Kulkarni et al., 2025; van Deemter, 2024]

continued on following page

Table 3. Continued

Challenge	Core Issue	Non-Eliminable Factors	Typical Risks	Reference
Poor generalization of mitigation strategies	Domain-tuned tools don't transfer	Ontologies/control vocabularies differ across sectors	Failures in open-ended or multi-domain environments	[Anisuzzaman et al., 2025; Rostam&Kertész, 2025]
Societal and institutional risks	Technical fixes insufficient without oversight	Governance, transparency, and accountability uneven across organizations	Misinformation, trust erosion, harm to vulnerable users	[Taeihagh, 2025]

6. A HOLISTIC TIMELINE OF EVOLUTION

The historical development of hallucination management in AI reflects a progressive shift from mere problem recognition to holistic governance (Sun et al., 2024). This evolution can be conceptualized as a five-stage process representing the field's intellectual, technical, and ethical maturation.

i. **Recognition and Definition:** The earliest stage involved identifying hallucination as a distinct generative risk in LLMs. Researchers began observing that models could produce fluent yet fabricated or factually inconsistent outputs even when trained on high-quality corpora (Farquhar et al., 2024). Ji et al. (2023) formally defined hallucination in natural language generation as content that is 'unfaithful to the input or inconsistent with world knowledge,' while Thirunavukarasu et al. (2024) documented critical clinical risks posed by hallucinated medical advice. Together, these studies established hallucination as a central obstacle to AI reliability.
ii. **Taxonomy and Root-Cause Analysis:** The second phase involved systematic classification of hallucination types and causal mechanisms. Rawte et al. (2023) categorized hallucinations as intrinsic or extrinsic based on whether errors originated from model dynamics or external data gaps. Other analyses highlighted root causes such as training noise, autoregressive drift, ambiguous prompts, and OOD queries. These typologies enabled a more diagnostic understanding of hallucination behavior.
iii. **Mitigation and Management:** In response, researchers proposed mitigation strategies including RAG, verification layers, uncertainty expression, and refined prompting (Anh-Hoang et al., 2025). Lewis et al. (2020) demonstrated that RAG reduces unfaithful outputs by grounding model responses in external evidence,

while complementary approaches such as self-consistency reasoning (Wang et al., 2023), fact-checking modules (Nakano et al., 2021), and RLHF (Ouyang et al., 2022) contributed to practical frameworks for managing hallucinations in LLMs.

iv. **Innovation and Re-imagination:** The fourth stage marks a shift from mitigation to innovation. Mialon et al. (2023) showed how multi-agent architectures enable generation, critique, and refinement to occur in coordinated pipelines. Meanwhile, theoretical work has suggested that certain forms of hallucination may support ideation, creativity, and human-machine co-creation, prompting a reframing of hallucination as both a risk and a potential resource.

v. **Integration and Governance:** In the final stage, controlling hallucinations extends beyond technical solutions to encompass ethical, regulatory, and organizational frameworks, with an emphasis on transparency, accountability, and governance that recognize hallucination as a societal as well as a technical issue (Floridi et al., 2018).

Across these five stages, the evolution of hallucination management reveals a trajectory from reactive detection toward proactive design, oversight, and responsible AI governance.

7. IMPLICATIONS FOR INNOVATION AND PRACTICE

The evolution of hallucination management from recognition to governance carries significant implications for innovation, deployment, and policy across the AI ecosystem. As organizations increasingly integrate LLMs into decision-making, education, healthcare, and creative industries, hallucination management has become a central pillar of responsible AI practice (Batool et al., 2025; Williamson & Prybutok, 2024). A key implication lies in AI governance, where hallucination is now considered a core risk category comparable to algorithmic bias, privacy breaches, and explainability failures (Sun et al., 2024). Dwivedi et al. (2021) argue that organizations must treat hallucination as a critical compliance issue, requiring structured oversight mechanisms, risk registers, and continuous monitoring. Governance frameworks must address not only technical controls but also organizational processes—data curation protocols, model validation procedures, and audit trails documenting how systems handle uncertainty. As AI systems grow more autonomous, proactive governance becomes essential to prevent downstream harms from fabricated or misleading outputs (Pahune et al., 2025; Papagiannidis et al., 2025). A second implication concerns model evaluation, where traditional performance metrics that emphasize fluency, coherence, or linguistic richness are no longer sufficient (Agrawal et al., 2025). Factual accuracy, citation reliability, and content faithfulness must be systematically assessed using metrics such as FActScore, QAGS, and retrieval consistency tests. Without these layers of evaluation, high-performing models may still produce polished but unverifiable content that undermines trust and operational safety (Min et al., 2023; Xie et al., 2021).

Similarly, sectoral adaptation is crucial, particularly in high-risk domains like medicine, finance, and education. Clinical studies highlight that hallucinated content in medical LLMs can produce harmful or misleading recommendations (Omar et al., 2025; Roustan & Bastardot, 2025). Therefore, sector-specific mitigation strategies—domain-tuned models, expert-in-the-loop validation, and medical ontology grounding—must be embedded into operational workflows. In business and education, structured prompting, peer review, and AI auditability mechanisms help prevent erroneous outputs from shaping strategic decisions (Papagiannidis et al., 2025). Human-AI collaboration also plays a critical role. Contrary to early visions of fully automated AI decision-makers, contemporary research demonstrates that human oversight improves factuality, contextual reasoning, and safety (Langer et al., 2025). Thirunavukarasu et al. (2024) emphasize that medical authorities must supervise AI-generated clinical content, ensuring that expertise rather than automation drives final decision-making. HITL workflows thus serve as a safeguard against both systematic and edge-case hallucinations. At the same time, emerging scholarship highlights a tension between creativity and control (Mosqueira-Rey et al., 2023). Chakraborty et al. (2025) argue that certain types of hallucinations—particularly imaginative reinterpretations or novel idea combinations—can be beneficial in creative writing, design, and innovation. When appropriately constrained, hallucination can become a generator of inspiration rather than a flaw. This perspective encourages organizations to differentiate between harmful factual hallucinations and productive creative divergence, enabling more nuanced deployment strategies (Huang et al., 2024).

Finally, hallucination raises enduring questions of ethics and accountability. Fabricated citations, invented data, and plausible–sounding misinformation challenge norms of authorship, research integrity, and professional responsibility (Walters & Wilder, 2023). Floridi & Chiriatti (2020) contend that ethical frameworks must define explicit accountability pathways—who is responsible when AI generates misleading content, and how can transparency be ensured across the generative pipeline? Clear documentation, disclosure policies, and operational transparency are essential for establishing trust in AI-assisted processes. In summary, hallucination management must be integrated into broader AI safety, reliability, and innovation agendas. Organizations that proactively combine governance, technical controls, human oversight, and ethical accountability will be best equipped to deploy LLMs responsibly while harnessing their creative and operational potential.

8. CASE EXAMPLE

8.1 Hallucination in Healthcare

Hallucination in healthcare-related AI systems represents one of the most critical and high-stakes challenges in contemporary machine learning. Because clinical decisions directly affect patient safety, even minor factual deviations can have severe consequences (Asgari et al., 2025). Recent analyses show that hallucinations may lead to misdiagnosis, incorrect drug recommendations, fabrication of clinical rationales, and misleading citations within decision-support tools (Granstedt et al., 2025). Such risks have positioned hallucination alongside bias, interpretability, and data governance as a core category of clinical AI reliability assessment. A recent evaluation of clinical LLM applications (Agrawal et al. 2025) demonstrated that hallucinations often emerge when models attempt to generalize from training corpora lacking sufficient biomedical grounding. In several examined cases, models confidently produced treatment suggestions that contradicted established clinical guidelines. These findings triggered an industry-wide shift toward multi-stage training pipelines, where models undergo (Roeschl et al., 2025; Vrdoljak et al., 2025; Wu et al., 2025):

- Domain-focused pretraining on biomedical literature;
- Reinforcement learning from clinician feedback (RLCF); and
- Post-deployment auditing involving hospital review committees.

Together, these iterative approaches significantly reduced false clinical inferences, although not eliminating them entirely. To systematically evaluate hallucination severity, medical AI researchers developed domain-specific scoring mechanisms. One influential contribution is the reference hallucination score (RHS), which quantifies the extent to which an AI-generated clinical statement deviates from a verified medical source (Aljamaan et al., 2024). An expanded version proposed in 2024 incorporated hierarchical weighting—for example, contradictions with randomized clinical trials are penalized more heavily than inconsistencies with expert opinions (Chen et al., 2024). Such metrics offer a benchmark not only for system comparison but also for regulatory compliance in medical AI certification processes. The healthcare domain further demonstrates that hallucination mitigation cannot rely exclusively on algorithmic strategies. Expert oversight remains indispensable. Clinical deployment frameworks increasingly integrate real-time supervision, in which human clinicians review and validate model-generated recommendations before they reach patients (Saenz et al., 2024; Asgari et al., 2025). This hybrid model of human-AI collaboration ensures contextual interpretation, including patient-specific nuances that AI systems may misrepresent or overlook. Some institutions have also introduced 'AI Safety Rounds,' where clinicians discuss model errors and hallucination patterns analogous to morbidity and mortality reviews (Zöller et al., 2025; Liu et al., 2025).

Viewed holistically, healthcare exhibits the full evolutionary pathway of hallucination management is:

i) recognition of hallucination as a clinically critical risk, supported by systematic error taxonomies (Asgari et al., 2025),
ii) detailed classification of hallucination types and evaluation benchmarks (Zhu et al., 2025),
iii) adoption of mitigation pipelines combining domain-specific training and expert collaboration (Chen et al., 2025), and
iv) embedding hallucination control into ethical and governance frameworks for clinical AI (Jung, 2025).

Ultimately, healthcare showcases how multi-layered design, quantitative assessment, and professional oversight can operationalize hallucination management in safety-critical environments. This domain continues to lead the development of robust safeguards that other sectors increasingly emulate (Asgari et al., 2025; Mennella et al., 2024).

8.2 Hallucination in Financial Services

Hallucination in financial AI applications presents a comparably high-risk challenge, as errors can lead to incorrect risk assessments, regulatory breaches, or financially harmful recommendations. Financial institutions increasingly rely on AI for market analysis, fraud detection, loan underwriting, and automated advisory systems. However, hallucination—particularly fabricated statistics, misinterpreted economic signals, or invented regulatory clauses—poses a substantial threat to financial stability and compliance (Lee et al., 2024; Williamson & Prybutok, 2024). The review by Lee et al. (2024) highlights that LLM-based financial analytics may generate fluent yet unreliable summaries, occasionally misrepresenting core financial indicators or inferring unsupported quantitative relationships, underscoring hallucination as a non-trivial risk in AI-assisted investment analysis. These hallucinations often arise when LLMs extrapolate from general financial language patterns without access to verified, up-to-date corporate or regulatory data (Lee et al., 2024). Prior reviews of generative AI in finance note that even small numerical inaccuracies in model-generated summaries—such as distorted earnings figures or inferred ratios—can materially influence investment judgments and risk assessments, elevating hallucination to a core concern for AI-assisted financial analytics (Lee et al., 2024).

In response, recent research and industry deployments have increasingly adopted retrieval-augmented financial grounding approaches, in which model outputs are anchored to structured, authoritative sources such as the U.S. SEC's EDGAR filings, central bank publications, and audited corporate disclosures (Iaroshev et al., 2024) — an approach shown to enhance context relevance and fidelity in financial report analysis. Empirical studies show that grounding LLM responses in retrieved financial documents substantially reduces factual errors and unsupported inferences in financial question-answering and summarization tasks, though limitations remain when disclosures are outdated or when market conditions shift more rapidly than reporting cycles (Iaroshev et al., 2024).

Recognizing the limitations of algorithmic solutions, financial institutions increasingly integrate human validation layers. For example, loan risk models now incorporate 'credit officer checkpoints,' requiring human review when AI-generated assessments deviate from established thresholds (Bussmann et al., 2020). This resembles clinical oversight in healthcare and reinforces the principle that high-stakes decisions require hybrid intelligence—a balance of automated analysis with expert judgment (Göndöcs et al., 2025). Financial regulators have also entered the scene.

In 2025, multiple jurisdictions began drafting guidelines requiring companies to report known hallucination risks and demonstrate 'reasonable assurance' that AI systems do not fabricate regulatory content (Marin et al., 2025). Governance frameworks for AI in financial services increasingly reflect approaches developed in healthcare, particularly in their focus on transparency, version control, and the auditability of AI-generated outputs.

Both sectors demonstrate a comparable evolutionary trajectory; in managing AI hallucinations, progressing from initial risk recognition to comprehensive governance mechanisms that integrate technical controls with regulatory and human oversight; like:

i) **Recognition:** Hallucinations are identified as critical financial, legal, and compliance risks, rather than isolated technical errors (Ridzuan et al., 2024).
ii) **Taxonomy:** Systematic classification distinguishes numerical, textual, and regulatory hallucinations, enabling targeted risk management (Sun et al., 2024).
iii) **Measurement:** Quantitative audits are introduced to compare AI-generated outputs with verified financial filings and authoritative data sources (Kokina et al., 2025).
iv) **Mitigation:** Technical controls such as RAG frameworks, uncertainty expression, and numerical cross-checking are applied to reduce hallucination incidence (Zhang & Zhang, 2025).

v) **Governance:** Mature frameworks emphasize regulatory oversight and mandatory human validation to ensure accountability and trustworthiness in high-stakes financial contexts (Holzinger et al., 2025).

This case reinforces the lesson that domains involving safety, compliance, or financial impact require multi-layered hallucination controls, blending technical grounding, human expertise, and policy frameworks.

Figure 4 presents a chain systems diagram with three aligned layers linking upstream model and data deficiencies to domain-specific hallucination manifestations and their downstream real-world impacts for the typically considered healthcare and finance domains.

Figure 4. Sources, manifestations, and consequences of AI hallucinations in healthcare and finance domains

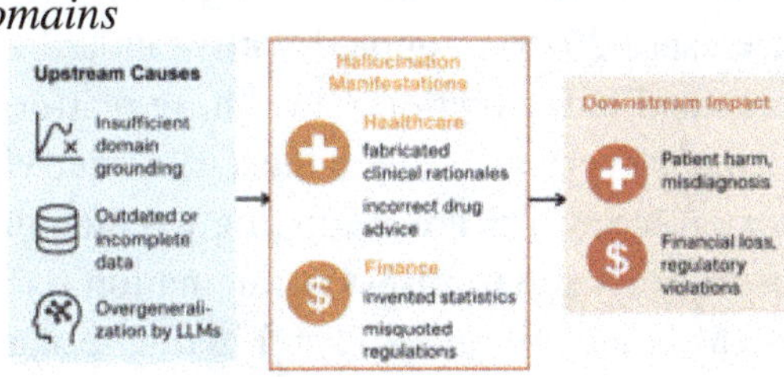

9. EMERGING INNOVATION TRAJECTORIES IN HALLUCINATION MANAGEMENT: FUTURE PATHWAYS

As AI systems mature, emerging innovation trajectories are transforming hallucination management from reactive mitigation to proactive orchestration, where creativity, accuracy, and trust are strategically balanced (Li & Zhao, 2025). One notable direction is self-reflective models, which internally assess uncertainty before generating outputs. Such models can decide whether to respond, cite a reference, or abstain from answering when confidence is low. This approach reduces ungrounded outputs and enhances user trust, particularly in high-stakes domains such as healthcare and finance. Self-reflection mechanisms often incorporate internal verification loops and probabilistic uncertainty scoring, enabling the system to 'know what it doesn't know.' Another trajectory involves multi-agent fact-checking pipelines, where separate AI agents handle generation, validation, and critique (Li & Zhao, 2025; Du et al., 2024). This modular structure allows the system to cross-verify outputs before presentation, minimizing the risk of unverified content reaching end users. Multi-agent designs also facilitate specialized knowledge integration, with some agents focused on domain expertise and others on linguistic fidelity, creating layered defenses against hallucination. Domain-adapted architectures are increasingly critical, particularly in specialized sectors such as law, finance, and medicine. By fine-tuning models on context-specific corpora and integrating structured knowledge graphs, hallucination frequency can be significantly reduced while maintaining domain relevance (Yu & McQuade, 2025; Darwish et al., 2025; Kazlaris et al., 2025). These architectures complement broader multi-agent and self-reflective approaches, ensuring that AI reasoning aligns with sectoral standards and regulatory expectations. Interactive collaboration platforms represent another innovation, providing real-time interfaces where human experts can inspect, correct, and annotate AI outputs. This integration of human judgment not only mitigates hallucinations but also strengthens transparency and trust, especially in multi-stakeholder decision-making environments (Vössing et al., 2022; Molina & Sundar, 2022; Tugarin & van Husen, 2025). Coupled with standardized metrics, such as reference validity scores and hallucination rates, these platforms allow consistent evaluation of AI performance across deployments (Aljamaan et al., 2024; Kulkarni et al., 2025). Regulatory frameworks are beginning to catch up, with certification and auditing mechanisms proposed to assess hallucination risk, similar to existing bias or fairness audits (Mökander et al., 2024). Finally, researchers are exploring creative reinterpretation of hallucination, viewing it as a potential driver of ideation, storytelling, or artistic exploration where factual precision is secondary (Pilcher & Tütüncü, 2025). This reframing encourages a nuanced understanding that not all hallucinations are undesirable; some can enhance innovation when managed responsibly. Collectively, these trajectories suggest that the future of hallucination management lies in strategic orchestration: integrating technical safeguards, human oversight, and governance structures to ensure AI systems are both trustworthy and creatively capable.

Figure 5 depicts five innovation pathways—self-reflective models, multi-agent pipelines, domain-adapted architectures, human–AI collaboration, and ethical–regulatory governance—emerging from today's mitigation paradigm. The lanes converge toward a shared future platform, illustrating coordinated progress toward trustworthy and creatively capable AI.

Figure 5. Future pathways map of hallucination management: converging innovation streams toward trustworthy and creative AI

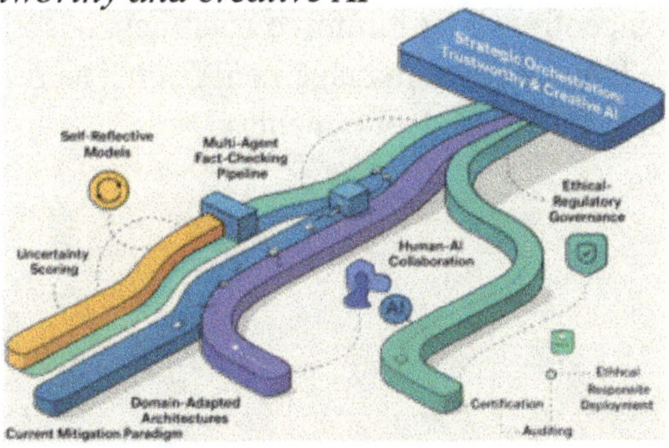

10. CONCLUSION

The journey of hallucination management in AI reflects both the maturation of generative technologies and the growing recognition of their societal implications. Initially, hallucinations were observed as unpredictable errors—AI outputs that were linguistically fluent but factually inaccurate—raising concerns about trust, safety, and accountability. Early research focused on defining these phenomena, categorizing them by type and context, and developing metrics to quantify their prevalence. These foundational steps established the conceptual and methodological scaffolding necessary for effective mitigation. As generative AI evolved, technical solutions such as RAG, prompt engineering, and multi-step reasoning emerged, embedding reliability directly into the generation process. These approaches reduced factual inconsistencies by grounding AI outputs in verifiable knowledge sources and ensuring internal coherence. Simultaneously, evaluation frameworks and benchmark datasets allowed researchers to measure progress systematically, fostering a culture of evidence-based improvement. Today, the focus has shifted from mere mitigation to the strategic integration of hallucination management into AI innovation. Conceptual frameworks encourage viewing hallucinations as opportunities for critical engagement, creativity, and collaborative problem-solving. Agentic AI pipelines, ethical governance structures, and transparency protocols exemplify how technical design can be harmonized with societal expectations, ensuring accountability in sensitive domains such as medicine, finance, and public policy. The future of trustworthy AI depends on embedding hallucination management as a core design principle rather than an afterthought. By combining robust technical safeguards with human oversight and regulatory governance, society can ensure that AI systems are not only innovative and intelligent but also reliable, socially responsible, and aligned with human values. Policymakers, developers, and institutions must collaborate to create standards and incentives that reinforce accuracy, accountability, and transparency, transforming hallucination management from a technical challenge into a cornerstone of safe and ethical AI deployment.

REFERENCES

Abbas, F., Chesterman, S., & Taeihagh, A. (2025). Building trust in the generative AI era: A systematic review of global regulatory frameworks to combat the risks of mis-, dis-, and mal-information. *AI & Society*. Advance online publication. DOI: 10.1007/s00146-025-02698-9

Agrawal, M., Chen, I. Y., Gulamali, F., & Joshi, S. (2025). The evaluation illusion of large language models in medicine. *NPJ Digital Medicine*, *8*(1), 600. DOI: 10.1038/s41746-025-01963-x

Al Machot, F., Horsch, M. T., & Ullah, H. (2025). Building trustworthy AI: Transparent AI systems via language models, ontologies, and logical reasoning (TranspNet). In F. Al Machot, M. T. Horsch, & S. Scholze (Eds.), *Designing the conceptual landscape for a XAIR validation infrastructure* (Lecture Notes in Networks and Systems, Vol. 1375). Springer. https://doi.org/DOI: 10.1007/978-3-031-89274-5_3

Aljamaan, F., Temsah, M. H., Altamimi, I., Al-Eyadhy, A., Jamal, A., Alhasan, K., Mesallam, T. A., Farahat, M., & Malki, K. H. (2024). Reference Hallucination Score for medical artificial intelligence chatbots: Development and usability study. *JMIR Medical Informatics*, *12*, e54345. Advance online publication. DOI: 10.2196/54345

Alshehri, A. (2025). Developing a multi-layer agent framework to enhance AI-generated educational questions for cybersecurity. *Journal of Umm Al-Qura University for Engineering and Architecture*, *16*, 1045–1056. DOI: 10.1007/s43995-025-00136-x

Althaf, A. M., Mohammed, M. A., Milanova, M., Talburt, J., & Cakmak, M. C. (2025). Multi-Agent RAG Framework for Entity Resolution: Advancing Beyond Single-LLM Approaches with Specialized Agent Coordination. *Computers*, *14*(12), 525. DOI: 10.3390/computers14120525

Amirizaniani, M., Lavergne, A., Okada, E. S., Chadha, A., Roosta, T., & Shah, C. (2025). Developing a framework for auditing large language models using human-in-the-loop. In *Proceedings of the 2025 Annual International ACM SIGIR Conference on Research and Development in Information Retrieval in the Asia Pacific Region (SIGIR-AP 2025)* (pp. 64–74). https://doi.org/DOI: 10.1145/3767695.376951

Amirizaniani, M., Martin, E., Roosta, T., Chadha, A., & Shah, C. (2024). AuditLLM: A tool for auditing large language models using multiprobe approach. In *Proceedings of the 33rd ACM International Conference on Information and Knowledge Management* (pp. 5174–5179). ACM. https://doi.org/DOI: 10.1145/3627673.3679222

Anh-Hoang, D., Tran, V., & Nguyen, L. M. (2025). Survey and analysis of hallucinations in large language models: Attribution to prompting strategies or model behavior. *Frontiers in Artificial Intelligence*, *8*, 1622292. DOI: 10.3389/frai.2025.1622292

Anisuzzaman, D. M., Malins, J. G., Friedman, P. A., & Attia, Z. I. (2025). Fine-tuning large language models for specialized use cases. *Mayo Clinic Proceedings. Digital Health*, *3*(1), 100184. DOI: 10.1016/j.mcpdig.2024.11.005

Asgari, E., Montaña-Brown, N., Dubois, M., Khalil, S., Balloch, J., Yeung, J. A., & Pimenta, D. (2025). A framework to assess clinical safety and hallucination rates of LLMs for medical text summarisation. *npj. Digital Medicine*, *8*, 274. DOI: 10.1038/s41746-025-01670-7

Batool, A., Zowghi, D., & Bano, M. (2025). AI governance: A systematic literature review. *AI and Ethics*, *5*, 3265–3279. DOI: 10.1007/s43681-024-00653-w

Bottazzi Grifoni, E., & Ferrario, R. (2025). The bewitching AI: The illusion of communication with large language models. *Philosophy & Technology*, *38*, 61. DOI: 10.1007/s13347-025-00893-6

Brown, A., Roman, M., & Devereux, B. (2025). A systematic literature review of retrieval-augmented generation: Techniques, metrics, and challenges. *Big Data and Cognitive Computing*, *9*(12), 320. DOI: 10.3390/bdcc9120320

Bussmann, N., Giudici, P., Marinelli, D., & Papenbrock, J. (2020). Explainable AI in Fintech risk management. *Frontiers in Artificial Intelligence*, *3*, 26. DOI: 10.3389/frai.2020.00026

Cai, L., Yu, C., Kang, Y., Fu, Y., Zhang, H., & Zhao, Y. (2025). Practices, opportunities and challenges in the fusion of knowledge graphs and large language models. *Frontiers in Computer Science, 7*, Section Human-Media Interaction. https://doi.org/DOI: 10.3389/fcomp.2025.1590632

Cai, W., & Gao, M. (2025). Beyond hallucination: Generative AI as a catalyst for human creativity and cognitive evolution. *ICCK Transactions on Emerging Topics in Artificial Intelligence*, *2*(1), 36–42. DOI: 10.62762/TETAI.2025.657559

Chakraborty, S., Chowdhury, R., Shuvo, S. R., Chatterjee, R., & Roy, S. (2025). A scalable framework for evaluating multiple language models through cross-domain generation and hallucination detection. *Scientific Reports*, *15*, 29981. DOI: 10.1038/s41598-025-15203-5

Chen, F., Li, Y., Chen, Y., Bian, Z., Duo, L., Zhou, Q., & Zhang, L.ADVANCED Working Group. (2025). Strategies for the analysis and elimination of hallucinations in artificial intelligence–generated medical knowledge. *Journal of Evidence-Based Medicine*, *18*(3), e70075. DOI: 10.1111/jebm.70075

Chen, J., Yang, D., Wu, T., Jiang, Y., Hou, X., Li, M., Wang, S., Xiao, D., Li, K., & Zhang, L. (2024). Detecting and evaluating medical hallucinations in large vision language models. *arXiv*. https://doi.org//arXiv.2406.10185DOI: 10.48550

Chen, Y., Fu, Q., Yuan, Y., Wen, Z., Fan, G., Liu, D., Zhang, D., Li, Z., & Xiao, Y. (2023). Hallucination detection: Robustly discerning reliable answers in large language models. *CIKM '23: Proceedings of the 32nd ACM International Conference on Information and Knowledge Management*, 245–255. https://doi.org/DOI: 10.1145/3583780.361490

Dahl, M., Magesh, V., Suzgun, M., & Ho, D. E. (2024). Large legal fictions: Profiling legal hallucinations in large language models. *The Journal of Legal Analysis*, *16*(1), 64–93. DOI: 10.1093/jla/laae003

Darwish, A. M., Rashed, E. A., & Khoriba, G. (2025). Mitigating LLM hallucinations using a multi-agent framework. *Information (Basel)*, *16*(7), 517. DOI: 10.3390/info16070517

Deng, Y., Zhao, S., Miao, Y., Zhu, J., & Li, J. (2025). MedKA: A knowledge graph-augmented approach to improve factuality in medical large language models. *Journal of Biomedical Informatics*, *168*, 104871. DOI: 10.1016/j.jbi.2025.104871

Dokas, I. M. (2026). From hallucinations to hazards: Benchmarking LLMs for hazard analysis in safety-critical systems. *Safety Science*, *194*, 107056. DOI: 10.1016/j.ssci.2025.107056

Du, Y., Li, S., Torralba, A., Tenenbaum, J. B., & Mordatch, I. (2024). Improving factuality and reasoning in language models through multiagent debate. In *Proceedings of the 41st International Conference on Machine Learning (ICML 2024)* (Article No. 467, pp. 11733–11763). International Machine Learning Society.

Dwivedi, Y. K., Hughes, L., Ismagilova, E., Aarts, G., Coombs, C., Crick, T., Duan, Y., Dwivedi, R., Edwards, J., Eirug, A., Galanos, V., Ilavarasan, P. V., Janssen, M., Jones, P., Kar, A. K., Kizgin, H., Kronemann, B., Lal, B., Lucini, B., & Williams, M. D. (2021). Artificial intelligence (AI): Multidisciplinary perspectives on emerging challenges, opportunities, and agenda for research, practice and policy. *International Journal of Information Management*, *57*, 101994. DOI: 10.1016/j.ijinfomgt.2019.08.002

Fajardo-Ramos, D. C., Chiappe, A., & Mella-Norambuena, J. (2025). Human-in-the-loop assessment with AI: Implications for teacher education in Ibero-American universities. *Frontiers in Education, 10*, 1710992. Advance online publication. DOI: 10.3389/feduc.2025.1710992

Farquhar, S., Kossen, J., Kuhn, L., & Gal, Y. (2024). Detecting hallucinations in large language models using semantic entropy. *Nature, 630*, 625–630. DOI: 10.1038/s41586-024-07421-0

Floridi, L., & Chiriatti, M. (2020). GPT-3: Its nature, scope, limits, and consequences. *Minds and Machines, 30*, 681–694. DOI: 10.1007/s11023-020-09548-1

Floridi, L., Cowls, J., Beltrametti, M., Chatila, R., Chazerand, P., Dignum, V., Luetge, C., Madelin, R., Pagallo, U., Rossi, F., Schafer, B., Valcke, P., & Vayena, E. (2018). AI4People—An ethical framework for a good AI society: Opportunities, risks, principles, and recommendations. *Minds and Machines, 28*(4), 689–707. DOI: 10.1007/s11023-018-9482-5

Förster, S., & Skop, Y. (2025). Between fact and fairy: Tracing the hallucination metaphor in AI discourse. *AI & Society*. Advance online publication. DOI: 10.1007/s00146-025-02392-w

Gadiko, A. (2024). Understanding and addressing AI hallucinations in healthcare and life sciences. *International Journal of Health Sciences, 7*(3), 1–11. DOI: 10.47941/ijhs.1862

Göndöcs, D., Horváth, S., & Dörfler, V. (2025). Uncovering the dynamics of human-AI hybrid performance: A qualitative meta-analysis of empirical studies. *International Journal of Human-Computer Studies, 205*, 103622. DOI: 10.1016/j.ijhcs.2025.103622

Granstedt, J., Kc, P., Deshpande, R., Garcia, V., & Badano, A. (2025). Hallucinations in medical devices. *Artificial Intelligence in the Life Sciences, 8*, 100145. DOI: 10.1016/j.ailsci.2025.100145

Hiriyanna, S., & Zhao, W. (2025). Multi-layered framework for LLM hallucination mitigation in high-stakes applications: A tutorial. *Computers, 14*(8), 332. DOI: 10.3390/computers14080332

Holzinger, A., Zatloukal, K., & Müller, H. (2025). Is human oversight to AI systems still possible? *New Biotechnology, 85*, 59–62. DOI: 10.1016/j.nbt.2024.12.003

Huang, L., Yu, W., Ma, W., Zhong, W., Feng, Z., Wang, H., Chen, Q., Peng, W., Feng, X., Qin, B., & Liu, T. (2024). A survey on hallucination in large language models: Principles, taxonomy, challenges, and open questions. *ACM Transactions on Information Systems, 43*(2). *Article*, *42*, 1–55. DOI: 10.1145/3703155

Iaroshev, I., Pillai, R., Vaglietti, L., & Hanne, T. (2024). Evaluating retrieval-augmented generation models for financial report question and answering. *Applied Sciences (Basel, Switzerland)*, *14*(20), 9318. DOI: 10.3390/app14209318

Janssen, M. (2025). Responsible governance of generative AI: Conceptualizing GenAI as complex adaptive systems. *Policy and Society*, *44*(1), 38–51. DOI: 10.1093/polsoc/puae040

Ji, Z., Lee, N., Frieske, R., Yu, T., Su, D., Xu, Y., Ishii, E., Bang, Y. J., Madotto, A., & Fung, P. (2023). Survey of hallucination in natural language generation. *ACM Computing Surveys*, 55(12). *Article*, *248*, 1–38. DOI: 10.1145/3571730

Kazlaris, I., Antoniou, E., Diamantaras, K., & Bratsas, C. (2025). From illusion to insight: A taxonomic survey of hallucination mitigation techniques in LLMs. *AI*, *6*(10), 260. DOI: 10.3390/ai6100260

Ke, Y. H., Jin, L., Elangovan, K., Chakraborty, S., Rajan, V., & Ngiam, K. Y. (2025). Retrieval augmented generation for large language models and its generalizability in assessing medical fitness. *npj. Digital Medicine*, *8*, 187. DOI: 10.1038/s41746-025-01519-z

Kerstan, S., Baum, K., Helfer, T., Langer, M., Schmidt, E., Sesing-Wagenpfeil, A., & Speith, T. (2026). Responsible and trusted AI: An interdisciplinary perspective. In Steffen, B. (Ed.), Lecture Notes in Computer Science: Vol. 16220. *Bridging the gap between AI and reality. AISoLA 2025* (pp. 141–145). Springer., DOI: 10.1007/978-3-032-07132-3_9

Kokina, J., Blanchette, S., Davenport, T. H., & Pachamanova, D. (2025). Challenges and opportunities for artificial intelligence in auditing: Evidence from the field. *International Journal of Accounting Information Systems*, *56*, 100734. DOI: 10.1016/j.accinf.2025.100734

Kryściński, W., McCann, B., Xiong, C., & Socher, R. (2020). Evaluating the factual consistency of abstractive text summarization. In *Proceedings of the 2020 Conference on Empirical Methods in Natural Language Processing* (pp. 9332–9346). Online: Association for Computational Linguistics. https://doi.org/DOI: 10.18653/v1/2020.emnlp-main.750

Kulkarni, A., Zhang, Y., Moniz, J. R. A., Ge, X., Tseng, B.-H., Piraviperumal, D., Swayamdipta, S., & Yu, H. (2025, November). Evaluating evaluation metrics: The mirage of hallucination detection. In Christodoulopoulos, C., Chakraborty, T., Rose, C., & Peng, V. (Eds.), *Findings of the Association for Computational Linguistics: EMNLP 2025* (pp. 19013–19032). Association for Computational Linguistics., DOI: 10.18653/v1/2025.findings-emnlp.1035

Langer, M., Baum, K., & Schlicker, N. (2025). Effective human oversight of AI-based systems: A signal detection perspective on the detection of inaccurate and unfair outputs. *Minds and Machines*, *35*, 1. DOI: 10.1007/s11023-024-09701-0

Lavrinovics, E., Biswas, R., Bjerva, J., & Hose, K. (2025). Knowledge graphs, large language models, and hallucinations: An NLP perspective. *Journal of Web Semantics*, *85*, 100844. DOI: 10.1016/j.websem.2024.100844

Lee, D. K. C., Guan, C., Yu, Y., & Ding, Q. (2024). A comprehensive review of generative AI in finance. *FinTech*, *3*(3), 460–478. DOI: 10.3390/fintech3030025

Lee, M. (2023). A mathematical investigation of hallucination and creativity in GPT models. *Mathematics*, *11*(10), 2320. DOI: 10.3390/math11102320

Lewis, P., Perez, E., Piktus, A., Petroni, F., Karpukhin, V., Goyal, N., Küttler, H., Lewis, M., Yih, W.-T., Rocktäschel, T., Riedel, S., & Kiela, D. (2020). Retrieval-augmented generation for knowledge-intensive NLP tasks. *Proceedings of the 34th International Conference on Neural Information Processing Systems*, Article 793, 9459–9474.

Li, B., & Zhao, C. (2025). Self-reflection enhances large language models towards substantial academic response. *npj. Artificial Intelligence*, *1*, 42. DOI: 10.1038/s44387-025-00045-3

Li, H., Fang, Y., Zhang, S., Lee, S. M., Wang, Y., Trexler, M., & Botelho, A. F. (2025). ARCHED: A human-centered framework for transparent, responsible, and collaborative AI-assisted instructional design. *Proceedings of the Innovation and Responsibility in AI-Supported Education Workshop*, in *Proceedings of Machine Learning Research*, 273, 94–104. https://proceedings.mlr.press/v273/li25a.html

Li, J., Chen, J., Ren, R., Cheng, X., Zhao, X., Nie, J.-Y., & Wen, J.-R. (2024). The dawn after the dark: An empirical study on factuality hallucination in large language models. In *Proceedings of the 62nd Annual Meeting of the Association for Computational Linguistics (*Volume 1*: Long Papers)* (pp. 10879–10899). Bangkok, Thailand: Association for Computational Linguistics.

Liao, Q. V., & Wortman Vaughan, J. (2024). AI transparency in the age of LLMs: A human-centered research roadmap. *Harvard Data Science Review*, *5*(Special Issue), •••. DOI: 10.1162/99608f92.8036d03b

Lin, S., Hilton, J., & Evans, O. (2022). TruthfulQA: Measuring how models mimic human falsehoods. In Muresan, S., Nakov, P., & Villavicencio, A. (Eds.), *Proceedings of the 60th Annual Meeting of the Association for Computational Linguistics (*Volume 1*: Long Papers)* (pp. 3214–3252). Dublin, Ireland: Association for Computational Linguistics. https://doi.org/DOI: 10.18653/v1/2022.acl-long.229

Lin, Z., Guan, S., Zhang, W., Zhang, H., Li, Y., & Zhang, H. (2024). Towards trustworthy LLMs: A review on debiasing and dehallucinating in large language models. *Artificial Intelligence Review*, *57*, 243. DOI: 10.1007/s10462-024-10896-y

Liu, P., Zhang, J., Chen, S., & Chen, S. (2025). Human-AI teaming in healthcare: 1 + 1 > 2? *npj. Artificial Intelligence*, *1*, 47. DOI: 10.1038/s44387-025-00052-4

Livingston, L., Featherstone-Uwague, A., Barry, A., Barretto, K., Morey, T., Hermannova, D., & Avula, V. (2025). Reproducible generative artificial intelligence evaluation for health care: A clinician-in-the-loop approach. *JAMIA Open*, *8*(3), ooaf054. Advance online publication. DOI: 10.1093/jamiaopen/ooaf054

Ma, X., Rao, G., Xu, L., Wang, X., Fan, Z., & Zhang, Z. (2026). Guided and knowledgeable multi-agent debate for fact verification. *Expert Systems with Applications*, 299(B), 130103. https://doi.org/DOI: 10.1016/j.eswa.2025.130103

Maharjan, J., Garikipati, A., Singh, N. P., Gupta, A., Bhatt, D., & Li, Z. (2024). OpenMedLM: Prompt engineering can out-perform fine-tuning in medical question-answering with open-source large language models. *Scientific Reports*, *14*, 14156. DOI: 10.1038/s41598-024-64827-6

Marin, L. G. U., Rijsbosch, B., Spanakis, G., & Kollnig, K. (2025). Are companies taking AI risks seriously? A systematic analysis of companies' AI risk disclosures in SEC 10-K forms. *arXiv*. https://doi.org//arXiv.2508.19313.DOI: 10.48550

Masanneck, L., Meuth, S. G., & Pawlitzki, M. (2025). Evaluating base and retrieval augmented LLMs with document or online support for evidence-based neurology. *NPJ Digital Medicine*, *8*, 137. DOI: 10.1038/s41746-025-01536-y

Maynez, J., Narayan, S., Bohnet, B., & McDonald, R. (2020). On faithfulness and factuality in abstractive summarization. In *Proceedings of the 58th Annual Meeting of the Association for Computational Linguistics* (pp. 1906–1920). Association for Computational Linguistics.

Memarian, B., & Doleck, T. (2024). Human-in-the-loop in artificial intelligence in education: A review and entity-relationship (ER) analysis. *Computers in Human Behavior: Artificial Humans*, *2*(1), 100053. DOI: 10.1016/j.chbah.2024.100053

Mennella, C., Maniscalco, U., De Pietro, G., & Esposito, M. (2024). Ethical and regulatory challenges of AI technologies in healthcare: A narrative review. *Heliyon*, *10*(4), e26297. DOI: 10.1016/j.heliyon.2024.e26297

Mialon, G., Dessì, R., Lomeli, M., Nalmpantis, C., Pasunuru, R., Raileanu, R., Rozière, B., Schick, T., Dwivedi-Yu, J., Celikyilmaz, A., Grave, E., LeCun, Y., & Scialom, T. (2023). Augmented language models: A survey. *ArXiv*. https://doi.org//arXiv.2302.07842DOI: 10.48550

Min, S., Krishna, K., Lyu, X., Lewis, M., Yih, W.-T., Koh, P., Iyyer, M., Zettlemoyer, L., & Hajishirzi, H. (2023). FActScore: Fine-grained atomic evaluation of factual precision in long form text generation. In Bouamor, H., Pino, J., & Bali, K. (Eds.), *Proceedings of the 2023 Conference on Empirical Methods in Natural Language Processing* (pp. 12076–12100). Association for Computational Linguistics. https://doi.org/DOI: 10.18653/v1/2023.emnlp-main.741

Mökander, J., Schuett, J., Kirk, H. R., & Floridi, L. (2024). Auditing large language models: A three-layered approach. *AI and Ethics*, *4*, 1085–1115. DOI: 10.1007/s43681-023-00289-2

Molina, M. D., & Sundar, S. S. (2022). When AI moderates online content: Effects of human collaboration and interactive transparency on user trust. *Journal of Computer-Mediated Communication*, *27*(4), zmac010. Advance online publication. DOI: 10.1093/jcmc/zmac010

Mosqueira-Rey, E., Hernández-Pereira, E., Alonso-Ríos, D., Bobes-Bascarán, J., & Fernández-Leal, A. (2023). Human-in-the-loop machine learning: A state of the art. *Artificial Intelligence Review*, *56*, 3005–3054. DOI: 10.1007/s10462-022-10246-w

Mourtzinis, S., Silva, T. S., Lo, J. C. M., Smith, D. L., & Conley, S. P. (2025). A human in the loop approach to applying large language models for farm management insight. *Scientific Reports*. Advance online publication. DOI: 10.1038/s41598-025-30991-6

Nakano, R., Hilton, J., Balaji, S., Wu, J., Long, O., Kim, C., Hesse, C., Jain, S., Kosaraju, V., Saunders, W., Jiang, X., Cobbe, K., Eloundou, T., Krueger, G., Button, K., Knight, M., Chess, B., & Schulman, J. (2021). WebGPT: Browser-assisted question-answering with human feedback. *ArXiv*. https://doi.org//arXiv.2112.09332DOI: 10.48550

Neha, F., Bhati, D., & Shukla, D. K. (2025). Retrieval-Augmented Generation (RAG) in healthcare: A comprehensive review. *AI, 6*(9), 226. DOI: 10.3390/ai6090226

Niu, C., Wu, Y., Zhu, J., Xu, S., Shum, K., Zhong, R., Song, J., & Zhang, T. (2024). RAGTruth: A hallucination corpus for developing trustworthy retrieval-augmented language models. *Proceedings of the 62nd Annual Meeting of the Association for Computational Linguistics (*Volume 1*: Long Papers)*, 10862–10878. Association for Computational Linguistics.

Omar, M., Sorin, V., Collins, J. D., Reich, D., Freeman, R., Gavin, N., Charney, A., Stump, L., Bragazzi, N. L., Nadkarni, G. N., & Klang, E. (2025). Multi-model assurance analysis showing large language models are highly vulnerable to adversarial hallucination attacks during clinical decision support. *Communications Medicine*, *5*, 330. DOI: 10.1038/s43856-025-01021-3

Osuji, C. C., Timoney, B., Andrade, M., Castro Ferreira, T., & Davis, B. (2025). Are multi-agents the new pipeline architecture for data-to-text systems? In *Proceedings of the 18th International Natural Language Generation Conference* (pp. 542–553). Association for Computational Linguistics.

Ouyang, L., Wu, J., Jiang, X., Almeida, D., Wainwright, C. L., Mishkin, P., Zhang, C., Agarwal, S., Slama, K., Ray, A., Schulman, J., Hilton, J., Kelton, F., Miller, L., Simens, M., Askell, A., Welinder, P., Christiano, P., Leike, J., & Lowe, R. (2022). Training language models to follow instructions with human feedback. In *Proceedings of the 36th International Conference on Neural Information Processing Systems (NeurIPS 2022)* (Article No. 2011, pp. 27730–27744). Curran Associates, Inc.

Pahune, S., Akhtar, Z., Mandapati, V., & Siddique, K. (2025). The importance of AI data governance in large language models. *Big Data and Cognitive Computing*, *9*(6), 147. DOI: 10.3390/bdcc9060147

Pal, A., Umapathi, L. K., & Sankarasubbu, M. (2023). Med-HALT: Medical domain hallucination test for large language models. In Jiang, J., Reitter, D., & Deng, S. (Eds.), *Proceedings of the 27th Conference on Computational Natural Language Learning (CoNLL)* (pp. 314–334). Association for Computational Linguistics. https://doi.org/DOI: 10.18653/v1/2023.conll-1.21

Papagiannidis, E., Mikalef, P., & Conboy, K. (2025). Responsible artificial intelligence governance: A review and research framework. *The Journal of Strategic Information Systems*, *34*(2), 101885. DOI: 10.1016/j.jsis.2024.101885

Park, S., & Nan, X. (2025). Generative AI and misinformation: A scoping review of the role of generative AI in the generation, detection, mitigation, and impact of misinformation. *AI & Society*. Advance online publication. DOI: 10.1007/s00146-025-02620-3

Pilcher, K., & Tütüncü, E. K. (2025). Purposefully induced psychosis (PIP): Embracing hallucination as imagination in large language models. In *Proceedings of CHI '25*. ACM. https://doi.org/DOI: 10.48550/arXiv.2504.12012

Pusch, L., & Conrad, T. O. F. (2025). Combining LLMs and knowledge graphs to reduce hallucinations in biomedical question answering. *BioMedInformatics*, *5*(4), 70. DOI: 10.3390/biomedinformatics5040070

Rawte, V., Chakraborty, S., Pathak, A., Sarkar, A., Tonmoy, S. M. T. I., Chadha, A., Sheth, A., & Das, A. (2023). The troubling emergence of hallucination in large language models: An extensive definition, quantification, and prescriptive remediations. In Bouamor, H., Pino, J., & Bali, K. (Eds.), *Proceedings of the 2023 Conference on Empirical Methods in Natural Language Processing* (pp. 2541–2573). Association for Computational Linguistics. https://doi.org/DOI: 10.18653/v1/2023.emnlp-main.155

Ridzuan, N. N., Masri, M., Anshari, M., Fitriyani, N. L., & Syafrudin, M. (2024). AI in the financial sector: The line between innovation, regulation and ethical responsibility. *Information (Basel)*, *15*(8), 432. Advance online publication. DOI: 10.3390/info15080432

Roeschl, T., Hoffmann, M., Hashemi, D., Rarreck, F., Hinrichs, N., Trippel, T. D., Gröschel, M. I., Unbehaun, A., Klein, C., Kempfert, J., Dreger, H., O'Brien, B., Hindricks, G., Balzer, F., Falk, V., & Meyer, A. (2025). Assessing the limitations of large language models in clinical practice guideline–concordant treatment decision-making on real-world data: Retrospective study. *JMIRx Med*, *6*, e74899. DOI: 10.2196/74899

Rostam, Z. R. K., & Kertész, G. (2025). Advances in pre-trained language models for domain-specific text classification: A systematic review. *ACM Transactions on Intelligent Systems and Technology*, *16*(6). *Article*, *124*, 1–41. DOI: 10.1145/3763002

Roustan, D., & Bastardot, F. (2025). The clinicians' guide to large language models: A general perspective with a focus on hallucinations. *Interactive Journal of Medical Research*, *14*, e59823. DOI: 10.2196/59823

Saenz, A. D., Mass General Brigham AI Governance Committee, Centi, A., Ting, D., You, J. G., Landman, A., & Mishuris, R. G. (2024). Establishing responsible use of AI guidelines: A comprehensive case study for healthcare institutions. *npj. Digital Medicine*, *7*, 348. DOI: 10.1038/s41746-024-01300-8

Sahoo, P., Meharia, P., Ghosh, A., Saha, S., Jain, V., & Chadha, A. (2024). A comprehensive survey of hallucination in large language, image, video, and audio foundation models. *Findings of the Association for Computational Linguistics: EMNLP*, *2024*, 11709–11724.

Shao, A. (2025). Beyond misinformation: A conceptual framework for studying AI hallucinations in (science) communication (arXiv:2504.13777). https://doi.org//arXiv.2504.13777DOI: 10.48550

Shi, D., Shen, T., Huang, Y., Li, Z., Leng, Y., Jin, R., Liu, C., Wu, X., Guo, Z., Yu, L., Shi, L., Jiang, B., & Xiong, D. (2024). Large language model safety: A holistic survey. *arXiv preprint*. https://doi.org//arXiv.2412.17686DOI: 10.48550

Shi, J., Zhao, J., Wu, X., Xu, R., Jiang, Y. H., & He, L. (2025). Mitigating reasoning hallucination through multi-agent collaborative filtering. *Expert Systems with Applications*, *263*, 125723. DOI: 10.1016/j.eswa.2024.125723

Steyvers, M., Tejeda, H., Kumar, A., Belem, C., Karny, S., Hu, X., Mayer, L. W., & Smyth, P. (2025). What large language models know and what people think they know. *Nature Machine Intelligence*, *7*, 221–231. DOI: 10.1038/s42256-024-00976-7

Sui, P., Duede, E., Wu, S., & So, R. J. (2024). *Confabulation: The surprising value of large language model hallucinations*. In *Proceedings of the 62nd Annual Meeting of the Association for Computational Linguistics (*Volume 1*: Long Papers)* (pp. 14274–14284). Association for Computational Linguistics.

Sun, Y., Sheng, D., Zhou, Z., & Wu, Y. (2024). AI hallucination: Towards a comprehensive classification of distorted information in artificial intelligence-generated content. *Humanities & Social Sciences Communications*, *11*, 1278. DOI: 10.1057/s41599-024-03811-x

Taeihagh, A. (2025). Governance of generative AI. *Policy and Society*, *44*(1), 1–22. DOI: 10.1093/polsoc/puaf001

Thirunavukarasu, A. J., & O'Logbon, J. (2024). The potential and perils of generative artificial intelligence in psychiatry and psychology. *Nature Mental Health*, *2*, 745–746. DOI: 10.1038/s44220-024-00257-7

Tran, K.-T., Dao, D., Nguyen, M.-D., Pham, Q.-V., O'Sullivan, B., & Nguyen, H. D. (2025). Multi-Agent collaboration mechanisms: A survey of LLMs (arXiv:2501.06322). https://doi.org//arXiv.2501.06322DOI: 10.48550

Tugarin, N., & van Husen, C. (2025). Development and integration of human-AI interactions in service applications: Conceptual framework and review. *International Journal of Information Management Data Insights*, *5*(2), 100357. DOI: 10.1016/j.jjimei.2025.100357

van Deemter, K. (2024). The pitfalls of defining hallucination. *Computational Linguistics*, *50*(2), 807–816. DOI: 10.1162/coli_a_00509

Vössing, M., Kühl, N., Lind, M., & Satzger, G. (2022). Designing transparency for effective human-AI collaboration. *Information Systems Frontiers*, *24*, 877–895. DOI: 10.1007/s10796-022-10284-3

Vrdoljak, J., Boban, Z., Vilović, M., Kumrić, M., & Božić, J. (2025). A review of large language models in medical education, clinical decision support, and healthcare administration. *Health Care*, *13*(6), 603. DOI: 10.3390/healthcare13060603

Wada, A., Tanaka, Y., Nishizawa, M., Akashi, T., Hagiwara, A., Hayakawa, Y., Kikuta, J., Shimoji, K., Sano, K., Kamagata, K., Nakanishi, A., & Aoki, S. (2025). Retrieval-augmented generation elevates local LLM quality in radiology contrast media consultation. *npj. Digital Medicine*, *8*, 395. DOI: 10.1038/s41746-025-01802-z

Walters, W. H., & Wilder, E. I. (2023). Fabrication and errors in the bibliographic citations generated by ChatGPT. *Scientific Reports*, *13*, 14045. DOI: 10.1038/s41598-023-41032-5

Wan, D., Chen, J. C.-Y., Stengel-Eskin, E., & Bansal, M. (2025). MAMM-REFINE: A recipe for improving faithfulness in generation with multi-agent collaboration. *arXiv*. https://doi.org//arXiv.2503.15272DOI: 10.48550

Wang, X., Wei, J., Schuurmans, D., Le, Q., Chi, E. H., Narang, S., Chowdhery, A., & Zhou, D. (2023). Self-consistency improves chain-of-thought reasoning in language models. *Proceedings of the International Conference on Learning Representations (ICLR 2023).*

Williamson, S. M., & Prybutok, V. (2024). The era of artificial intelligence deception: Unraveling the complexities of false realities and emerging threats of misinformation. *Information (Basel)*, *15*(6), 299. DOI: 10.3390/info15060299

Wu, W., Xu, X., Gao, C., Diao, X., Li, S., Salas, L. A., & Gui, J. (2025). Assessing and mitigating medical knowledge drift and conflicts in large language models. In Christodoulopoulos, C., Chakraborty, T., Rose, C., & Peng, V. (Eds.), *Findings of the Association for Computational Linguistics: EMNLP 2025* (pp. 707–730). Association for Computational Linguistics., DOI: 10.18653/v1/2025.findings-emnlp.38

Xie, Y., Sun, F., Deng, Y., Li, Y., & Ding, B. (2021). Factual consistency evaluation for text summarization via counterfactual estimation. In *Proceedings of the 2021 Conference on Empirical Methods in Natural Language Processing* (pp. 100–110). Virtual Conference, November 7–11.

Xiong, C., Zheng, G., Ma, X., Li, C., & Zeng, J. (2025). DelphiAgent: A trustworthy multi-agent verification framework for automated fact verification. *Information Processing & Management*, *62*(6), 104241. DOI: 10.1016/j.ipm.2025.104241

Xu, J., Li, Y., Zhang, Z., Luk, A. Y. H., Jobanputra, M., Oza, S., Murray, A., Kasula, M. R., Parker, A., & Eyre, D. W. (2025, November). *Tree-of-Quote prompting improves factuality and attribution in multi-hop and medical reasoning*. In *Proceedings of the 2025 Conference on Empirical Methods in Natural Language Processing* (pp. 5606–5623). Association for Computational Linguistics.

Yu, H. Q., & McQuade, F. (2025). RAG-KG-IL: A multi-agent hybrid framework for reducing hallucinations and enhancing LLM reasoning through RAG and incremental knowledge graph learning integration. *arXiv*. https://doi.org//arXiv.2503.13514DOI: 10.48550

Zamfirescu-Pereira, J. D., Wong, R. Y., Hartmann, B., & Yang, Q. (2023). Why Johnny can't prompt: How non-AI experts try (and fail) to design LLM prompts. *CHI '23: Proceedings of the 2023 CHI Conference on Human Factors in Computing Systems*, Article 437, 1–21. https://doi.org/DOI: 10.1145/3544548.358138

Zhang, W., & Zhang, J. (2025). Hallucination mitigation for retrieval-augmented large language models: A review. *Mathematics*, *13*(5), 856. DOI: 10.3390/math13050856

Zhang, Y., Li, Y., Cui, L., Cai, D., Liu, L., Fu, T., Huang, X., Zhao, E., Zhang, Y., Chen, Y., Wang, L., Luu, A. T., Bi, W., Shi, F., & Shi, S. (2025). Siren's song in the AI ocean: A survey on hallucination in large language models. *Computational Linguistics*. Advance online publication. DOI: 10.1162/COLI.a.16

Zhou, J., Li, H., Chen, S., Han, Z., & Gao, X. (2025). Large language models in biomedicine and healthcare. *npj. Artificial Intelligence*, *1*, 44. Advance online publication. DOI: 10.1038/s44387-025-00047-1

Zhu, Z., Zhang, Y., Zhuang, X., Zhang, F., Wan, Z., Chen, Y., Long, Q., Zheng, Y., & Wu, X. (2025). Can we trust AI doctors? A survey of medical hallucination in large language and large vision-language models. In Che, W., Nabende, J., Shutova, E., & Pilehvar, M. T. (Eds.), *Findings of the Association for Computational Linguistics: ACL 2025* (pp. 6748–6769). Association for Computational Linguistics., DOI: 10.18653/v1/2025.findings-acl.350

Zöller, N., Berger, J., Lin, I., Fu, N., Komarneni, J., Barabucci, G., Laskowski, K., Shia, V., Harack, B., Chu, E. A., Trianni, V., Kurvers, R. H. J. M., & Herzog, S. M. (2025). Human-AI collectives most accurately diagnose clinical vignettes. *Proceedings of the National Academy of Sciences of the United States of America, 122*(24), e2426153122. DOI: 10.1073/pnas.2426153122

Chapter 13
AI Hallucination in Financial Systems:
Challenges, Governance, and Risk Control Strategies

Shyam Sunder Agrawal
https://orcid.org/0009-0004-3648-0584
Lovely Professional University, India

Shalu Kotwani
Prestige Institute of Management and Research, Indore, India

ABSTRACT

This chapter examined AI hallucination, where artificial intelligence systems generated false, misleading, or non factual outputs, and analysed its impact on the reliability and governance of financial systems during 2015 to 2025. The study focused on key financial applications such as credit risk assessment, fraud detection, algorithmic trading, and investment forecasting, where such errors strongly affected decision making. A Systematic Literature Review was conducted using the PRISMA framework, drawing studies from Scopus, Web of Science, and Google Scholar to identify major patterns, causes, and governance related challenges of AI hallucination. The findings indicated that hallucinations mainly arose from poor data quality, limited contextual understanding within models, and excessive dependence on automated systems without sufficient human supervision. The chapter concluded that AI hallucination was not merely a technical issue but a broader governance challenge, emphasizing the importance of explainable AI, robust internal control mechanisms, ethical auditing practices.

DOI: 10.4018/979-8-3373-7534-2.ch013

1. INTRODUCTION

1.1 Why Mistakes Made by Artificial Intelligence Are a Big Deal in the Finance World?

Artificial intelligence mistakes are a problem. Artificial intelligence mistakes can cause a lot of trouble. In the finance world artificial intelligence mistakes can be really bad. The finance world is a place where artificial intelligence is used a lot. So when artificial intelligence makes a mistake in the finance world it can be very serious. The finance world is about money and numbers. Artificial intelligence is used to help with money and numbers in the finance world. When artificial intelligence makes a mistake it can cause big problems with money and numbers.

This is why artificial intelligence mistakes matter more in the finance world. Artificial intelligence mistakes can be fixed. In the finance world artificial intelligence mistakes need to be fixed fast. Because, in the finance world time is money. Artificial intelligence mistakes can cost a lot of money.

Artificial intelligence is really making a lot of decisions in the world of finance these days. It does things like say yes or no to loans and point out transactions that seem fishy. Artificial intelligence also helps people make investment choices and makes sure everyone is following the rules by creating reports. The reason people like intelligence so much is that it works very fast looks at a huge amount of information, and finds things that people might not notice. Artificial intelligence is very good, at finding patterns in all the data it looks at. In the ten years from 2015 to 2025 the promise of fintech has really taken off. This has happened quickly with banks, insurance companies, investment firms and fintech platforms all getting on board (Balogun et al., 2025).

Finance is not a place where you can try things out without worrying about the consequences. If something goes wrong with a tool that suggests what people should buy or a model that decides who gets credit, it can cause problems for a lot of people, banks and even the whole market. When artificial intelligence systems started to do more than just make predictions and began to explain things, tell stories and give advice a new problem came up that is not always easy to see. Intelligence hallucination. This artificial intelligence hallucination is a deal because it can make artificial intelligence systems give wrong information. Finance and artificial intelligence systems are closely linked, so this artificial intelligence hallucination can cause a lot of trouble.

So when we talk about AI hallucination, what happens is that the AI system comes up with answers that seem sure and make sense but are actually wrong or not true. This can be a problem in our lives. When it comes to money and finance, AI hallucination can be really bad. The thing about AI hallucination is that it can cause trouble because the AI system is giving us information that sounds right and that is not good. AI hallucination is something we should be careful, about especially when it comes to our money and financial things.

Between 2015 and 2025 the use of Artificial Intelligence in finance really took off. This happened for a few reasons. First there was a lot financial data available like information about transactions how people behave and what they say. Artificial Intelligence in finance was able to use this data. Second, computers got a lot faster and better at understanding information. This meant Artificial Intelligence in finance could handle amounts of data that were very complicated.

Third financial institutions had to automate the way they made decisions to work faster and better. They had to do this to keep up with each other and to make decisions according to the Financial Stability Board in 2024. Artificial Intelligence, in finance helped them do this. So now Artificial Intelligence has changed from helping us analyze things to actually making important decisions in the world of money and finance which is a pretty big deal for Artificial Intelligence. Artificial Intelligence is really making a difference, in ecosystems.

These new developments have made things work better. They have also brought new problems. Financial decisions are very important because they involve a lot of money, rules to follow and connections to systems. If something goes wrong with artificial intelligence systems it can cause big problems very quickly affecting how people trust the system the stability of the market and how people see the institutions involved. So people are really concerned about whether these artificial intelligence systems are reliable, transparent and accountable. Artificial intelligence systems are a deal for people who study this stuff and, for regulators. Financial artificial intelligence systems and their potential problems are being talked about a lot.

1.2 From Prediction to Generation: A Paradigm Shift

Financial AI tools used to be about numbers. They tried to figure out how likely it was that someone would default on a loan or if a transaction was fake or what kind of returns they could expect based on what happened in the past. It was pretty simple to check if these results were right and people could question them if they did not make sense. The people in charge of managing risk could look at the results again see what would happen in bad situations and know how far off the results could be. Financial AI tools made it easier for them to do their job. Risk managers could use financial AI tools to help them make decisions about financial things, like loans and investments and financial AI tools were helpful, for that (Faisal et al., 2025).

The introduction of Artificial Intelligence changed the way things work. These days Artificial Intelligence systems write explanations, for credit tell us what is happening in the market and help us understand rules and regulations. They even talk to customers directly. Of just giving us numbers they tell us stories. These stories usually sound very good. Make sense but they are not always true. The thing is, Artificial Intelligence models are made to sound like they make sense not to always be right.

This change is a deal. Financial risk is not about making mistakes when we predict things. It is also about the risk of having reasons that are actually wrong. This way of doing things is fine when we are being creative or just talking to each other. It is a big problem when we are dealing with money because we need to be accurate and follow the rules. So when we started using intelligence that can create new things it marked a big change. It showed that financial systems are open to a kind of risk. Artificial intelligence can make things up which we call AI hallucination. Financial risk and artificial intelligence are now connected in a way that's important to understand. The risk of intelligence hallucination is a real concern for financial systems (Krause, 2025).

1.3 What is AI Hallucination when it comes to Money?

AI Hallucination in situations is when Artificial Intelligence systems, like computers, make things up that are not true. This can happen when AI systems are trying to understand what is going on with money. The main issue with AI Hallucination in contexts is that it can cause problems. AI Hallucination can make mistakes. Give wrong information about financial things.

This is a deal because AI systems are used a lot to make decisions about money. So when AI Hallucination happens, it can lead to choices. AI Hallucination, in contexts is something that we need to be aware of so we can try to stop it from happening. AI hallucination is when an artificial intelligence system comes up with answers that seem to make sense and sound very sure of themselves. The problem is that these answers are actually wrong and the system does not have any information to back them up. This is different from kinds of mistakes that computers make. AI hallucinations are hard to catch because they look like reasoning and seem to follow the usual rules of the area they are talking about (Pardeshi & Deshmukh, 2025).

AI hallucination is a deal because it can be very tricky to figure out when the system is getting things wrong. AI systems can say things that're not true but still sound like they are right which makes it hard to know what to believe. This is something that researchers are looking into.

In money matters things can get really weird. A computer program can make up reasons why you did not get a loan. It can also get the rules wrong like what the government says banks have to do. The program can even create connections between numbers or come up with stories, about the market that are not true. People might believe these things because they come from computer systems, which makes them seem like they are always right and trustworthy. This is a problem because financial systems are supposed to be based on facts, not made up stuff.

Hallucination is not always because of programming or someone trying to be sneaky. People who study this have found some reasons why it happens. These reasons include data, training sets that are not fair or do not have enough information and computer programs that do not understand the context. Sometimes the goals of these programs are to make things sound good than to be true. For example, this is a problem in Generative Artificial Intelligence, in Finance which was written about in 2025. Because of these things hallucination is a risk that is always there not just something that happens every now and then. Hallucination is a problem that we have to think about all the time because of these reasons (Zafar & Ali, 2025).

1.4 Hallucination as a Financial and Systemic Risk

The consequences of AI hallucination are really bad when it comes to money matters. Financial decisions can affect a lot of people at the time and there are a lot of rules around them because they can impact the whole economy and how people live. If the information is even a bit wrong it can lead to big financial losses people taking each other to court or damage to a company's reputation. AI hallucination can cause problems, in the financial world and these problems can be very serious.

When we are trying to figure out if someone's a good risk, for a loan the computer can make things up that are not true. This can lead to people getting loans when they should not or being denied loans when they should get them. This is not fair. It is not transparent. It can also break rules that're in place to protect people who are borrowing money (Simeon, 2025).

The computer can also make things up when it is trying to detect fraud. This can lead to alarms that bother customers or it can miss real fraud and cost the bank a lot of money, which is what Almalki and Masud found out in 2025. When computers are used to make trades they can also make things up about what's happening in the market. This can cause the computer to make trades and make the market more volatile. This is especially true when a lot of computers are using the models to make trades (Yaprak, 2024). Credit risk assessment and fraud detection, and algorithmic trading are all areas where the computer making things up can cause problems.

When we look at the picture the chance of bad information from artificial intelligence is higher because many models are similar and come from a small number of companies. This is a problem because many financial institutions use artificial intelligence models or services from other companies. If one of these models gives information, it can quickly spread to the whole financial system. This creates a situation where many institutions are affected in the way. The Financial Stability Board (2024) says that this can make the whole system more unstable, especially when the market is already under stress. The Financial Stability Board (2024) is worried that this can happen because artificial intelligence models can make mistakes.

1.5 Limitations of Traditional Risk Management Frameworks

Traditional financial risk management frameworks do not do a good job of dealing with the risk of false information. These frameworks are made to handle things that are not certain and mistakes that can be measured not information that is completely made up or wrong. The usual ways of checking things may not catch information because the results often look okay when you look at the numbers, but they are actually wrong in important ways. Traditional financial risk management frameworks are just not good, at finding this kind of problem.

So it is really hard to check the things that are made by machines because we do not know how they got those answers. When we talk about money, machines can make things up in a way. When the bank says no to a loan they should give a reason. Sometimes the reason they give does not make sense or is just plain wrong. This is what happens when a loan rejection explanation cites factors that have nothing to do with the loan or are not true. The loan rejection explanation should be fair and honest not silly or mistaken. A bad loan rejection explanation can be really frustrating especially when it talks about things that're not relevant to the loan. The bank should look at the things when they decide about a loan not at things that do not matter. A loan rejection explanation that is wrong or silly is not helpful, to anyone. The loan rejection explanation should help the person understand why they did not get the loan so they can try to do next time (Kushwah & Dave, 2025).

A summary of compliance that gets the rules wrong. This summary does not understand what the rules really mean. The rules that are supposed to be followed are not understood correctly in this compliance summary. The compliance summary is, about following the rules. It does not do that. It makes mistakes when it explains what the rules are. A market outlook that is really sure, about what's going on but it does not have any facts to back it up. This market outlook is talking about trends. The trends are not based on real information. The market outlook is describing these trends. It is not using any data to support what it is saying about the trends.

Hallucination is not usually something that people do on purpose or something that happens because of mistakes when writing code. Research shows that it often happens because the artificial intelligence does not have all the information it needs or the information it has is not fair or it does not really understand the context or it is trying to make things sound good than being true. This is what the research says about Generative Artificial Intelligence, in Finance in the year 2025 (Joshi & Joshi-Satyadhar, 2025).

1.6 Governance, Accountability, and Ethical Challenges

Financial decisions are very important. People are careful about them. When artificial intelligence makes mistakes and gives information it can affect whether or not someone gets a loan. This means some people might not get a loan when they should which is not fair. When it comes to stopping fraud, wrong information from intelligence can block good people or let bad people get away with things. In the stock market artificial intelligence mistakes can make things very unstable especially when many places use the kind of artificial intelligence models, like what the Financial Stability Board said in 2024.

The risk of Artificial Intelligence becomes a problem when many companies depend on the same Artificial Intelligence vendors or pretrained Artificial Intelligence models. If there is a flaw in the Artificial Intelligence system it can cause a lot of trouble quickly leading to many mistakes across the entire financial system. This is why people who make rules for the world are getting more and more worried about Artificial Intelligence hallucination they think it can be a big threat, to the stability of the financial system not just a problem that each company has to deal with on its own.

1.7 Explainable AI and the Quest for Transparency

Explainable Artificial Intelligence is really important because people are getting worried about Artificial Intelligence systems being hard to understand. Explainable Artificial Intelligence is trying to make it easier for us to see how Artificial Intelligence makes decisions by showing us what information it uses to come up with answers. In the world, where there are a lot of rules Explainable Artificial Intelligence is not just a good thing to have. It is something that is required by law. This is especially true for things, like credit scoring, loan approvals and insurance underwriting as explained (Gupta, 2024). Explainable Artificial Intelligence is necessary to make sure Artificial Intelligence systems are transparent and fair.

People have found out that XAI is really helpful in figuring out when artificial intelligence is not making sense. When we can see how an artificial intelligence model is thinking we can find out if its reasons are good or not. This is especially important for money matters. For example, if a computer program says someone is a risk for credit but it is using things that do not make sense for that decision then people can look at it again and say wait a minute. XAI can show us the thoughts behind the intelligence models decision. This helps us see if the intelligence models reasons are consistent with what we know about money. If a credit model says someone is risk but it is using things that are not relevant to money then people can question that decision before it is too late (Brewer et al., 2024). XAI is useful for identifying these kinds of problems, with intelligence outputs.

The thing is, explainability is not the answer to all our problems. People who study this stuff say that explanations that come after a decision has been made can be wrong. These explanations might sound good. Make sense but they can hide the real problems with the model. This is what call an "illusion of understanding". What happens is that explainability can make bad decisions seem okay of fixing them. Explainability is not a solution and we need to be careful, with it. Explainability can be misleading. That is why we need to be careful when we use explainability to make decisions.

1.8 Recent Developments (2019–2025): Technical and Regulatory Responses

Between 2019 and 2025 people started to realize that hallucination risk was a problem. This made researchers and people who work with intelligence want to find better ways to deal with it. They wanted to make sure artificial intelligence systems did not make things up. On the side people started using something called retrieval-augmented generation architectures or RAG for short. These systems are designed to reduce hallucination risk. They do this by using information from sources that people know are true. This is different from using what the artificial intelligence system already knows. The artificial intelligence system gets information, from these sources to make sure what it says is true. This way the artificial intelligence system is less likely to make things up which is what happens when it hallucinates. RAG is really good at cutting down on made up information. For RAG to work well it needs good quality data. It also needs to be able to find the information and work smoothly with other systems. This is what the people who wrote Generative Artificial Intelligence, in Finance said in 2025. RAG can be very useful. Only if it has good data and works well with other systems (Joshi et al., 2025).

New ways to detect hallucinations have been developed alongside these advances. These methods look for differences between what a model says it is sure about and the evidence that supports what the model says. This helps us find out sooner if the model is giving us unreliable or made up answers. The models confidence is checked against the evidence for its outputs, which's really important for detecting hallucinations by the model. Hallucination detection techniques (Krause, 2023).

Regulatory bodies are now paying attention to the problems that Artificial Intelligence can cause. The Financial Stability Board said in 2024 that we need to do a job of managing the risks that come with Artificial Intelligence models. This means we need to keep records and make sure that people are closely watching what

Artificial Intelligence systems are doing especially when it comes to making big financial decisions that use Artificial Intelligence.

At the time people who study law have started to pay more attention to the problem of accountability when it comes to artificial intelligence decision making. The artificial intelligence systems are making things complicated. Researchers say that the current laws have a time figuring out who is responsible when the artificial intelligence systems do something that causes harm. This shows that we need to have rules about who is liable and better standards, for governing the artificial intelligence systems that are used in finance the artificial intelligence systems are being used in finance (Khan & Umer, 2024).

1.9 Organisational Responses and Human Oversight

Financial institutions are starting to see that technology by itself is not enough to deal with the problem of hallucination risk. To really be in control you need to have the organisation and culture in place. This means people need to be involved in making decisions systems need to be checked all the time and ethics need to be looked at. You also need to know who is responsible for what. Some studies show that systems that use intelligence to help people make decisions rather than replacing them are more reliable and less likely to fail because of hallucination problems. For example, research by Hettiarachchi (2025) found that these hybrid systems are better. Financial institutions need to use these systems to manage hallucination risk.

Research, on people working with intelligence shows that it is really important to teach users how to carefully think about what the artificial intelligence says. When the artificial intelligence gives answers in a confident way people might just accept what it says without really checking if it is true. This can make it more likely that the artificial intelligence will give information. To stop this from happening the systems that people use to interact with the intelligence need to be designed in a way that makes people want to check the information and question it rather than just accepting what the artificial intelligence says without thinking about it. The artificial intelligence systems need to be designed to make people verify what the artificial intelligence says and be skeptical so people can make decisions and challenge the artificial intelligence when necessary.

1.10 Research Gap

The use of Artificial Intelligence is becoming more popular in systems very quickly. When we look at what people have written about this topic so far we can see that there are big gaps, in our understanding of Artificial Intelligence hallucination. This is a problem because Artificial Intelligence hallucination can have effects when it is used to make important decisions. Most of the research that is being done on Artificial Intelligence is focused on making the models work better and be more accurate. However not much attention is being paid to how reliable Artificial Intelligence is, how it is controlled and what risks it poses when it gives us incorrect information, which is what we call Artificial Intelligence hallucination.

AI hallucination is a problem in things like figuring out if someone can get credit finding fake transactions using computers to buy and sell stocks and giving people advice on what to do with their money. If the computer makes a mistake. It seems like it is right people can lose money get in trouble with the government and the people who trust them will start to lose faith. Some studies have noticed that this is happening. They usually think of it as a small technical issue rather than a big problem that has to do with how companies are run and how they handle risk. AI hallucination is still an issue in these areas, like credit risk assessment and it needs to be addressed.

The current study looks at the problems with Artificial Intelligence. Finds the important areas that need more research. It talks about Artificial Intelligence hallucination, financial risk and governance mechanisms. These areas are listed in Table 1 which shows what needs to be looked at first and helps make Artificial Intelligence safer to use in systems. This will help make Artificial Intelligence deployment, in systems more responsible.

Table 1. Research Gap

Research Focus	Identified Gap	Justification for Bridging the Gap
AI Hallucination in Financial Systems	Limited finance-specific conceptualisation of AI hallucination.	Helps distinguish hallucination from traditional prediction error and improves domain-specific risk understanding (Echeverría Muñoz, 2025)
Credit Risk Assessment Using AI	Lack of empirical studies on hallucinated explanations in credit decisions.	Ensures fairness, transparency, and regulatory compliance in automated lending decisions (Bhattacharyya et al., 2025).
Fraud Detection Models	Overemphasis on accuracy with limited focus on false narratives or fabricated alerts.	Reduces customer inconvenience, financial loss, and reputational risk due to misleading fraud signals (Khanvilkar & Shinde, 2025).
Algorithmic Trading and Market Forecasting	Insufficient analysis of hallucination-induced systemic risk.	Prevents amplification of erroneous signals that may destabilise financial markets (Mahmud et al., 2025).
Explainable AI (XAI) in Finance	XAI mainly used for compliance, not hallucination detection.	Enhances the ability to identify inconsistent or fabricated model reasoning (Philip, 2025).
Data Quality and Model Training	Limited studies linking poor data governance to hallucination risk.	Improves data integrity, model reliability, and decision accuracy (Szakacs, 2025).

continued on following page

Table 1. Continued

Research Focus	Identified Gap	Justification for Bridging the Gap
Human-in-the-Loop Systems	Few longitudinal studies on human oversight effectiveness.	Strengthens hybrid decision-making frameworks and accountability (Mucsková, 2024).
AI Governance Frameworks	Fragmented governance models addressing technical or ethical issues in isolation.	Supports holistic governance integrating technical, organisational, and regulatory controls (Krause, 2025).
Regulatory and Legal Accountability	Unclear liability allocation for hallucinated AI decisions.	Provides legal clarity and strengthens institutional accountability (Mucsková, 2024).
Cross-Institutional AI Risk	Limited comparative studies on shared AI models across institutions.	Helps manage correlated risks and vendor concentration in financial systems (Mettrick, 2024).

Source: Author's creation

2. REVIEW OF LITERATURE

2.1 Evolution of Artificial Intelligence in Financial Systems

The use of intelligence, in financial systems has changed a lot over the last ten years. It has really changed how financial institutions figure out risk decide how to use their money find activities and talk to their customers. When artificial intelligence was first used in finance it mostly used ways of learning like logistic regression, decision trees and support vector machines. Artificial intelligence has been getting better and better in systems. These models are really good at dealing with data that is organized in a specific way. They help make predictions in things like credit scoring and figuring out if someone will default on a loan. The people who made these models (Williamson & Prybutok, 2024).

As computers got better and financial information became more complicated deep learning methods started to become more important. Neural networks and ensemble models made it possible to look at lots of financial data like what people are buying and selling right now and how they are behaving. This change made things work better and faster. It also made the artificial intelligence systems harder to understand which is a problem. People want to know what is going on and who is responsible especially when it comes to money and rules that everyone has to follow (Silic et al., 2025).

From around 2019 onward the introduction of Artificial Intelligence marked a new phase in the adoption of Artificial Intelligence, within financial systems. This extended the role of Artificial Intelligence beyond making predictions. Now

Artificial Intelligence is also used to generate explanations and insights and stories that directly influence the decisions people make.

Large language models and things that generate text started making things like explanations for credits, summaries of research on investments reports on following rules and messages, to customers. These systems made a difference by cutting down on work that people had to do and making things faster. They also brought new problems because they made content that might not be based on facts or what the rules really say (Mettrick, 2024).

2.2 Conceptual Foundations of AI Hallucination

AI hallucination is when a machine makes something up that sounds like it could be true. It is a problem because the things the machine says are wrong. They sound right. They seem like something a person would say so it is hard to tell that they are not true. This is different from when a machine makes a mistake because mistakes are usually easy to spot. When a machine has a hallucination, it can be very convincing, like when a person is trying to sound smart (Philip, 2025).

In the world of money, hallucination is a problem. This is because computers that think like people often give reasons for their decisions not just guesses. For example, if a computer says someone did not get a loan it might give a reason. It might say things that're not true like the person's credit score was bad when it was really good. It might also make up rules that do not exist. This can fool the people who make decisions and the customers, which can cause a lot of trouble with the law what is right and wrong, and what people think of the company. Hallucination in the domain is a serious issue because AI outputs are used to explain important decisions, like credit decisions and these explanations need to be accurate. Hallucination can lead to problems like misinterpreting indicators or inventing reasons that are not real and this can affect decision-makers and customers as noted in Generative Artificial Intelligence, in Finance 2025.

People are now looking at what makes something a hallucination. What makes it just noise or a mistake. They think that hallucinations are things that are completely made up. When a computer gives an answer because it learned from bad information, that is a bias. Hallucinations are different. They happen when the computer is not connected to the facts anymore. This can occur when the computer is trying to make something sound good, then telling the truth. The computer gets this way because it is programmed to make things sound right, not to tell the truth (Silic et al., 2025).

2.3 Sources and Drivers of Hallucination in Financial AI

The literature talks about three things that cause AI hallucination in financial systems. The first thing is how good and complete the data is. Financial data is often not complete or is old. Sometimes it is not fair because of rules and laws privacy concerns and things that happened a long time ago that were not fair. When AI models are trained on this kind of data they might make up patterns or explanations to fill in the gaps as seen in the work of Krause, 2025.

The second driver is that people do not really understand the context. The Artificial Intelligence models do not have a sense of what makes sense or what the rules are. They just look at the information they have. Try to find patterns. Because of this they can come up with answers that do not make sense financially or that break the rules especially when things are complicated or not clear.

The third driver is that people rely much on autonomous systems. Some studies show that the risk of systems making mistakes or what we call hallucination goes up when the output of artificial intelligence is used without anyone checking it especially in places where speed and automation are important such, as when computers buy and sell things automatically and when they try to catch fraud in real time (Financial Stability Board [FSB] 2024). Autonomous systems are used a lot in these places. That is why the risk of hallucination is higher when autonomous systems are used.

2.4 Manifestations of Hallucination Across Financial Applications

2.4.1 Credit Risk and Lending Decisions

In credit risk assessment people sometimes see things that're not really there like made up reasons or causes that do not make sense. Studies on artificial intelligence show that models can say someone is likely to default on a loan because of things that do not actually matter which can lead to decisions that are not based on good economic reasons and might not be fair as we see in the work of Joshi et al., 2025. Credit risk assessment is important and credit risk assessment needs to be done carefully.

2.4.2 Fraud Detection

Fraud detection systems are using alerts and stories made by intelligence more and more. This automation definitely makes things faster. However sometimes the artificial intelligence makes things up which can cause alarms. This can also make the systems miss the patterns of fraud. When this happens it can be a problem for the customers. It can also cost the company money to operate. The worst part is that real fraud might not be caught because of these mistakes. Fraud detection systems have to deal with this issue of intelligence making things up, which is not good, for catching fraud. Research shows that hybrid systems are better at dealing with failures. These hybrid systems combine Artificial Intelligence with human validation. This means that humans can review and judge the situation, which is important. Humans can do this alongside the automated detection that the Artificial Intelligence system does (Joshi et al., 2025).

2.4.3 Algorithmic Trading and Market Analysis

In the world of trading with computers, the problems with Artificial Intelligence making things up can affect not one company but the whole financial market. When Artificial Intelligence creates signals for buying and selling and stories about the market it can make people speculate more especially when many companies use the computer models or get their information from the same places. This can make things go wrong because if one company's Artificial Intelligence makes a mistake it can make another company's Artificial Intelligence make the same mistake and this can make the market really volatile and maybe even cause big problems. The Financial Stability Board reported in 2024 that if companies Artificial Intelligence systems make the same mistakes, it can make the market even more volatile when things are already stressful.

2.5 Explainable AI as a Governance Mechanism

Explainable Artificial Intelligence (XAI) is important because people are worried about things being unclear and making stuff up. The main goal of XAI techniques is to help us understand how these models make decisions. This way people who check things like auditors and regulators and users of these models can see if they are fair and correct. This is what researchers like about Explainable Artificial Intelligence. Explainable Artificial Intelligence is, about making things clear and transparent (Khan & Umer, 2024).

Research shows that models that are easy to understand on their own do a job of finding fake outputs than methods that explain things after the fact especially when it comes to money and rules that people have to follow. For example, in banking and finance these models are really important. Some experts think we should not just rely on explanations because sometimes they can make things sound good even if they are not true and this can hide the real problems. This is called the "explanation illusion". Models that are easy to understand on their own like these interpretable models are better at catching fake outputs than methods that explain things after the fact and that is why they are useful in regulated financial contexts, like banking.

2.6 Governance, Ethics, and Regulatory Perspectives

People who study how things are run are starting to think that Artificial Intelligence hallucination is a problem with how we organize things and with what's right and wrong rather than just a problem with the technology itself. The usual ways we govern things assume that humans are responsible, for what happens. This gets confusing when Artificial Intelligence systems make important decisions on their own (Simeon, 2025). Artificial Intelligence hallucination is a deal because Artificial Intelligence systems can make a big impact when they come up with things that are not true.

Regulatory bodies are now dealing with these issues by making sure that things are clear and that people are responsible for what they do. They also want to make sure that humans are involved in the decision making process. The Financial Stability Board in the year 2024 says that we need to improve the way we manage risks related to models and this should include looking at AI and the stories it generates. People around the world are talking about ethics, in AI and they think it is very important to be able to track what AI is doing to check that it is fair and to make sure that we can audit the financial decisions that are made automatically by machines (Mucsková, 2024).

2.7 Emerging Mitigation Strategies and Research Directions

Some new studies have found ways to reduce the risk of hallucination. These retrieval-augmented generation systems or RAG systems use verified information from sources to make sure the output is accurate. This really helps to cut down on made-up information when it is set up correctly as seen in the work of Simeon, 2025 and in the book Generative Artificial Intelligence, in Finance from 2025. Some techniques help figure out if the output is hallucinated by looking at how confident the system's how much evidence it has to back it up, RAG systems and these techniques can really help reduce hallucination risk.

People are starting to see that companies need to have plans in place. These plans include things like human-in-the-loop systems and ethical auditing. They also need to keep an eye on things all the time. This is really important when it comes to working with solutions. Some studies have found that when Artificial Intelligence works with human judgment, it is better and more trustworthy. This is called a decision system. It is better than letting machines make all the decisions on their own (Zafar & Ali, 2025).

2.8 Synthesis and Research Gaps

The thing about AI hallucination is that it is a problem for financial systems. People generally agree on this. However, we still do not know a lot about how AI hallucination affects finances. There is not a lot of research on how much money's lost because of AI hallucination. We also need to figure out how to stop AI hallucination from happening in the place. Most of the time people only look at how AI hallucination affects one company or institution at a time. They do not think about how it affects the financial system and all the companies, in it. AI hallucination is still a problem that we need to understand especially when it comes to financial systems and AI hallucination.

2.9 AI Hallucination Governance in Financial Systems: Conceptual Framework

Figure 1 conceptualizes AI hallucination governance in financial systems as a structured, end-to-end framework that integrates regulatory, organizational, technical, and operational dimensions. The framework situates the external environment, comprising regulatory mandates, ethical standards, and market dynamics, as the primary force shaping institutional expectations and compliance responsibilities. These external pressures are internalized through institutional governance mechanisms such as AI ethics committees, model risk management practices, and clearly defined accountability structures that provide strategic oversight and policy direction. At the technical level, the framework emphasizes data integrity, model validation, explainable AI, and hallucination detection tools to ensure transparency, reliability, and factual consistency of AI outputs. Operational decision-making serves as a critical mediating layer by embedding human-in-the-loop review, escalation protocols, and auditability to align automated insights with professional judgment. The resulting financial outcomes, ranging from improved decision quality and fraud detection accuracy to enhanced market stability and institutional trust, serve as observable indicators of effective AI hallucination governance.

Figure 1. Conceptual framework of AI hallucination governance in financial systems

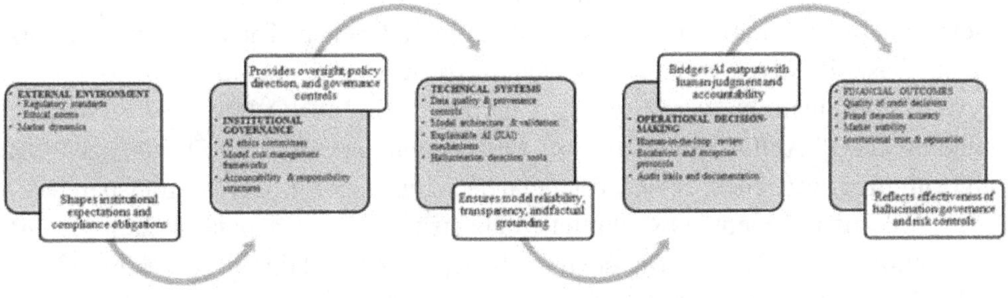

Source: Author's creation

3. RESEARCH METHODOLOGY

3.1 Research Design and Approach

This chapter uses a research design that looks at a lot of literature to understand what is happening with AI hallucination in financial systems and how it affects the people in charge and the way they control risks. This research is similar to what other people have done before in finance and information systems.

3.2 Systematic Literature Review Procedure

The literature review is based on the PRISMA 2020 framework. This framework is really important because it makes sure that the research is transparent and can be repeated by others.

3.2.1 Data Sources

Research papers from the databases namely Scopus; Web of Science (WoS); and Google Scholar are referred; few open access repositories like arXiv and reports from global regulatory bodies, such, as the Financial Stability Board are also included. We have included 25 studies for data analysis through SLR technique using PRISMA 2020.

3.2.2 Search Strategy

The search looked at publications from 2015 to 2025. This is the time when Artificial Intelligence started being used a lot more in finance. The Boolean operators and database filters really helped to make the results more accurate. The following keyword combinations were used: "AI hallucination" AND "financial systems", "generative AI" AND "financial risk" OR "explainable AI" AND "finance" OR "algorithmic governance" AND "financial decision-making" OR "AI transparency" AND "risk management" OR synthetic data risk" AND "financial modeling" OR "foundation models" AND "financial resilience" OR "explainability requirements" AND "financial compliance" OR "AI ethics" AND "financial decision-making" OR "FinAI governance" AND "risk ecosystems".

3.2.3 Inclusion and Exclusion Criteria

Inclusion criteria:

- Peer-reviewed journal articles, conference papers, and authoritative regulatory reports
- Explicit focus on AI, machine learning, or generative models in financial contexts
- Discussion of risk, governance, explainability, or reliability

Exclusion criteria:

- Studies unrelated to finance
- Purely technical AI papers without governance or risk implications
- Opinion pieces lacking methodological clarity

3.2.4 Screening and Selection

We have applied SLR techniques in the paper and followed the process because SLR is a scientific process that clarifies the research objectives and helps to identify the research gap. We have followed PRISMA guidelines for the extraction of studies.The study selection began with the identification of 1,150 records from Scopus (250), Google Scholar (810), and Web of Science (90). Before screening, 150 duplicate records and 115 records marked ineligible by automated tools were removed, leaving 885 records for screening. During the screening stage, 610 records were excluded because they were published in languages other than English, resulting in 275 reports being sought for retrieval. Due to limited access, 95 reports could not be retrieved, and 180 reports were assessed for eligibility. At this stage, 25 studies were excluded because they belonged to domains not related to finance, 80 studies were excluded due to insufficient data or weak methodology, and 50 studies were excluded for being purely technical AI papers. After applying all elimination and filtration criteria at each stage, a final total of 25 studies were selected and included in the systematic review. The studies that seemed like a fit were then looked at more closely to see how well they were done and if they were really about what the research was trying to find out. This whole process led to 25 studies being chosen because they were quality and matched what the research was, which is what the PRISMA guidelines say to do. Figure 2 depicts the whole process of the extraction of studies.

Figure 2. PRISMA Flow diagram

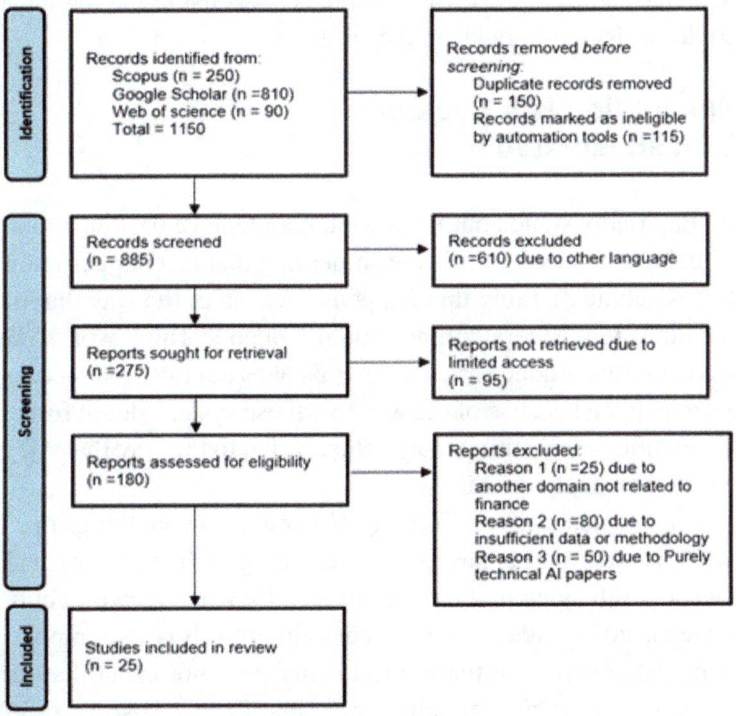

3.3 Data Analysis and Synthesis

Thematic analysis was applied to categorise studies into the following four categories:

- Technical causes of AI hallucination

- Financial applications and impact pathways
- Governance and regulatory challenges
- Risk mitigation and control strategies

4. KEY FINDINGS AND INTERPRETIVE INSIGHTS FROM THE SYSTEMATIC LITERATURE REVIEW

This part of the report talks about has been learned from looking at lots of studies on AI hallucination in systems from 2015 to 2025. After looking at information from studies, things that regulators published, and other sources, it has been found out is that there are some clear patterns when it comes to AI hallucination what causes it and how people are trying to manage the risks.

4.1 AI Hallucination Is a Systemic Rather Than an Isolated Issue

One thing that really stands out from what people have written about this topic is that AI hallucination, in systems is not something that just happens now and then by accident. It is actually a thing that happens because of the way that modern AI, especially the kinds that generate things and use deep learning works. The strange outputs that AI systems produce are not rare mistakes but rather something that you would expect to happen because of the way that these systems learn from probabilities. AI hallucination is something that is closely tied to the way that AI, generative and deep-learning models, operates.

Hallucination is when artificial intelligence systems make things up. This tends to happen when these systems have to explain things tell stories or make predictions about what will happen in the future especially when they do not have all the information they need or when things are changing fast. It is also important to note that just having data or making the models better does not mean that the problem of hallucination will go away. Hallucination in intelligence is still a problem even, with these improvements. So it seems that hallucination is really a part of the way that modern Artificial Intelligence systems work. They have something called pattern-recognition logic and hallucination appears to be embedded in this logic that contemporary Artificial Intelligence systems use.

4.2 Data Quality and Missing Context Are Central Drivers

The review always finds that financial AI systems have problems because of data and a lack of understanding of the situation. When financial AI systems are trained with data that's wrong, missing, or old, they are more likely to make up connections or explanations that seem right with numbers but do not really show how money works in the real world. Financial AI systems do this because they are trained with data. This bad data makes financial AI systems come up with things that're not true.

A big problem with information is that it often shows the same old unfairness and biases that we have had in the past. When computers use this information to make decisions without being careful they can make mistakes. This is especially true when banks decide who can borrow money. Some people do not get a chance to borrow money because the computer makes wrong decisions about them. This is not a technical problem it is also about making sure that the people, in charge of the information are doing a good job and being fair. Financial information and the computers that use it have to be watched to make sure they are not being unfair.

Using intelligence that can create things can really increase the risk of hallucination. This means that the artificial intelligence system, which is a type of Generative AI might start to create information or see things that are not really there. The Generative AI can substantially increase the risk of this happening, which's a big problem. The risk of hallucination is a concern when it comes to Generative AI systems.

The literature says that generative models are good at making things sound nice and flow well. They are not so good at getting the facts right. When generative models have to deal with situations that are not clear or are really complicated they will often make things up to fill in the missing information. They come up with things that sound like they could be true. Are not actually true. This is a problem in places where financial rules are strict, like banks or investment companies because the explanations that generative models give can have serious consequences. Generative models can get people into trouble with the law. They can go against what is ethical or they can cause compliance issues with financial regulations. Generative models are not good, at handling these kinds of situations.

4.3 Explainable AI Is Helpful but Not Sufficient

People think Explainable Artificial Intelligence is a useful tool for finding mistakes and showing when things are not really related. Explainable Artificial Intelligence helps us understand things better. It also helps make sure everything is fair and transparent. Some people are getting worried that Explainable Artificial Intelligence can sometimes give us the wrong idea about things. Explainable Artificial Intelligence is supposed to help us. It can be misleading too.

Some research says that when we look back at things that have happened we can make up a story that sounds good but it actually hides the mistakes that were made. This can be a problem in places like banks and other financial institutions where things are closely watched. The important thing to remember is that we need to have rules and checks in place to make sure that the explanations we get are real and not just made up. If we do not have controls over the information we use and if we do not keep a close eye on things and if people are not held responsible, for their actions then these explanations might actually make it seem like the wrong answers are right instead of fixing the mistakes. Explainability like the kind used in XAI must be used carefully. As part of a bigger system that checks and double checks everything.

4.4 Persistent Governance Gaps Undermine Risk Control

The thing that really stands out when you look at all the information is that there is a difference between how good artificial intelligence is getting and the systems in place to watch over it. Artificial intelligence is being used more and more by banks and other financial institutions. However, the systems that are supposed to make sure artificial intelligence is being used correctly such as making sure people are accountable for what artificial intelligence does making sure artificial intelligence is ethical, and managing the risks of using intelligence, are not being improved at the same rate, as artificial intelligence itself. Artificial intelligence and the way it is governed is an issue that needs to be addressed.

The review shows that people are really unsure about who's responsible when artificial intelligence makes things up and that causes problems. This is especially true when you have a lot of companies and services involved like third-party vendors, cloud-based services and shared datasets. Some people are trying to make rules to deal with these problems. It is not happening evenly everywhere. This means that organizations need to take charge and make their rules rather than just waiting for someone else to tell them what to do. Artificial intelligence is a part of this and we need to figure out how to handle it. Organizations need to make changes to how they govern themselves and not just rely on people to make the rules, for artificial intelligence.

4.5 Systemic and Reputational Implications Are Significant

When many banks or financial companies use the Artificial Intelligence models or get their systems from the same place they can all start to see the same wrong patterns. This can then spread throughout the financial system. As a result the connections, between these companies become stronger. The whole system becomes more fragile because of Artificial Intelligence hallucination.

Reputational risk is a worry. When explanations from intelligence turn out to be wrong or unfair it can really hurt the trust that customers have in a company and make the company look bad. Some research shows that mistakes made by intelligence can damage a company's reputation for a long time and this can be worse than losing money right away especially for companies that deal with people's money. Reputational risk, from intelligence errors is a major concern because it can affect companies that provide financial services to people.

4.6 Emerging Best Practices Are Holistic and Multi-Layered

The review found some good things happening. Big banks and other financial institutions are starting to use ways to manage risk. They are using a lot of tools to do this like retrieval-augmented generation and systems that can detect when something is not right. Financial institutions are also using ethics committees, model audits and human review processes to make sure everything is okay. They are keeping records of what they do which is a good thing. The financial institutions are using all these tools to be safer and to make decisions.

There is not one thing you can do to make sure the artificial intelligence does not make things up. The artificial intelligence system is safe because of all the things you do to protect it. These things work together to make the system strong. Artificial intelligence needs safeguards that work well together.

4.7 Fragmentation Between Research, Practice, and Regulation

The review shows that there is still a difference between what academics are learning what companies are doing and what rules are being made. The research on finding hallucination is getting better and better. There are not many studies that show how hallucination affects money in a real way. At the time research that looks at how to control and govern things often does not have enough details, which makes it hard for people who actually have to do the work to make it happen. The research, on hallucination detection and governance is not really helping the industry practice because it is not giving them the information they need to make decisions. The hallucination detection research is moving forward. It is not helping to fix the problems that companies are having with hallucination and financial outcomes.

4.8 Overall Insight

The findings show that AI hallucination in systems is a big problem with many parts. It involves issues, how people behave, how organizations work and the whole system. This study says that to have financial innovation that lasts we do not need to get rid of AI hallucination completely. Which is probably not possible. Instead we need to make AI systems and rules that can find AI hallucination stop it from causing harm and deal with its effects in a way. We need to be able to manage the impact of AI hallucination, on systems (Ahmed, F., & Iqbal, 2025).

Table 2. Summary of Key Findings and Observations

Area of Analysis	Key Findings	Implications
Data Quality	Poor and biased data strongly linked to hallucination	Need for robust data governance and provenance
Generative AI	Narrative outputs increase hallucination impact	Caution in high-stakes financial decisions
Explainable AI	Improves transparency but not foolproof	Must be combined with other controls
Human Oversight	Human-in-the-loop reduces hallucination risk	Hybrid decision systems recommended
Governance	Current frameworks are reactive	Need proactive, hallucination-specific policies
Systemic Risk	Model homogeneity amplifies errors	Regulatory coordination required
Trust & Reputation	Hallucination erodes institutional trust	Governance essential for long-term credibility

Source: Author's synthesis

5. CONCLUSION

The way artificial intelligence is becoming a part of financial systems is really changing how people make decisions about money. Artificial intelligence is used for things like checking how likely someone is to pay back a loan and finding transactions. It is also used for buying and selling stocks and trying to predict what will happen with investments. Artificial intelligence is really good at doing things, and it can look at a lot of information. There is a big problem with artificial intelligence that people do not talk about enough. Artificial intelligence can make mistakes and see things that are not really there which is called artificial intelligence hallucination. Artificial intelligence hallucination is a deal because it can affect how well artificial intelligence works with financial systems. This study shows that hallucination is a problem. It is not a small mistake that can be fixed easily. Hallucination is an issue that can cause a lot of trouble. It can make people lose trust. It can also hurt the way things are governed. Hallucination can even affect how well the financial system works. So hallucination is a risk that can cause a lot of problems, with trust and governance structures and financial stability.

This chapter is about looking at the problem of AI hallucination in applications. It wants to find out what causes this problem and what can be done to control the risks. The study looked at research papers from 2015 to 2025 from academic and policy sources. It found out that AI hallucination happens a lot because of data not understanding the situation well relying too much on complicated models and not having enough human check. The study used a way of reviewing the literature to get these results. AI hallucination, in applications is a big issue and the study is trying to figure out what to do about it. In places where money is involved like banks or investment companies' financial environments need to be very careful. They have to make sure their decisions are right. They can explain why they made them. They also have to follow the rules that the government sets. If they do not do this it can cause problems for them. These problems can hurt the way they operate it is not ethical. It can hurt their reputation. Financial environments have to be careful, about these things because they are very important.

The most important learning of this study is that AI hallucination is a problem that needs to be looked at in two ways: as an issue and, as a governance issue. The old ways of managing risks were made to deal with things that might happen not with AI decisions that sound good but are actually made up. Because of this a lot of institutions do not know how to find, understand or react to AI decisions that are not real. This is a problem when we use generative AI because it can make stories and explanations that sound very good but are actually hiding mistakes instead of showing them. AI hallucination is a deal and we need to think about it when we talk about AI decisions. AI hallucination can cause a lot of trouble if we do not know how to deal with it.

The results show that Explainable Artificial Intelligence is really important for making sure Artificial Intelligence is used in a way. Explainable Artificial Intelligence helps people understand how Artificial Intelligence works. It does not fix all the problems. Explainable Artificial Intelligence makes Artificial Intelligence more clear and easier to understand so people can question its decisions. The studies looked at show that when Explainable Artificial Intelligence is used with data management and people are involved in the process it helps a lot, in finding Artificial Intelligence results that are not reliable or do not make sense. So the research is saying that we should not depend much on explanations that come after something has happened. These explanations can make us feel like we really understand what is going on. That is only true if we have a good way to check that they are correct and we have evidence to back them up. The research warns us that Post Hoc Explanations can be misleading if we do not have validation and evidence to support them. We need to make sure that our understanding of Post Hoc Explanations is based on facts and not just, on what someone says after the fact.

The study also shows us something about hallucination risk. It is a problem that can affect the whole system. Many financial institutions are using the Artificial Intelligence tools and models. They are also getting services from the outside providers. This can cause problems if something goes wrong. If many models get the wrong information they can all make the same mistakes. These mistakes can then spread across the markets. Make the whole system weaker. We need to watch these Artificial Intelligence systems closely. We need to make sure that if one system fails it does not cause problems, for the whole financial system. This is why we need people to oversee everything and test the systems to make sure they are working correctly. The Artificial Intelligence systems need to be checked so that they do not cause instability.

From a point of view, the research really shows that hybrid decision-making systems are a good idea. These systems use Artificial Intelligence to help decision making not replace it. Institutions that use Artificial Intelligence and also have people review the decisions have a way to deal with problems and keep track of everything that happens are better at managing risks related to Artificial Intelligence making mistakes. It is also very important for companies to create a culture where people question the results of Artificial Intelligence of just accepting them without thinking. This way companies can get the most, out of Artificial Intelligence systems. We really need to have these procedural safeguards in place to make sure that our financial systems that use Artificial Intelligence are strong and can handle problems over a long period of time. This is very important, for Artificial Intelligence systems.

So this study is really important for talking about using Artificial Intelligence in a way in the financial world. It shows that Artificial Intelligence is a deal when it comes to managing risks and making sure everything runs smoothly. We cannot just focus on making Artificial Intelligence work better we also need to make sure it is clear and fair and that people are watching to make sure it does what it is supposed to do. For people who make rules this study says we need to make some guidelines for Artificial Intelligence so we can understand how it makes decisions and so we can trust that it is working correctly. Artificial Intelligence needs to be transparent and accountable. People need to be, in charge of making sure it does what it is supposed to do. For institutions multi-layered governance frameworks are really important. These frameworks need to combine controls with ethical and organisational safeguards, as well as human safeguards.

For researchers this study is a deal because it shows them new ways to look at things. They can now try to figure out how to measure the risk of intelligence making mistakes, like hallucination risk. They can also look at how artificial intelligence errors affect outcomes and how governance models can change as artificial intelligence technologies get better and better.

The use of intelligence in financial systems is a big deal. It does not just depend on what artificial intelligence can do. It also depends on how artificial intelligence is managed. Managing intelligence is very important to make sure people trust financial systems. We need to deal with the problem of intelligence making things up. This is necessary to keep systems stable and honest. Artificial intelligence, in systems, needs to be handled carefully so that people can trust them and they can work properly.

6. FUTURE SCOPE OF STUDY

This study looks at AI hallucination in systems in a very detailed way. There are still some things that need to be looked at in the future. First, we need to have some standards to measure how well AI systems work in finance. We need to make tests that check if the information is correct, if the system follows the rules, and if it makes sense from a point of view. This will help to see how good AI systems really are when it comes to making financial decisions. We need to have these standards so we can trust AI systems with financial decisions. AI hallucination, in systems is a big deal and we need to make sure we get it right. Next people should look into how AI hallucination affects the way people behave. This means studying how financial professionals think about and use things made by AI. We need to know if they really trust AI and how they work with it. We should also look at problems like trusting AI much making wrong decisions because of AI and getting tired of making decisions with AI. If we understand these things we can make systems, training and ways for people to work with AI. This is important, for AI hallucination. How financial professionals interact with AI hallucination.

Third, we need to look at how different countries deal with the risk of intelligence making mistakes. This means we have to compare how different rules and laws in each country address this problem. This will help us make rules for artificial intelligence in finance that countries around the world can agree on. Artificial intelligence, in finance, needs to have rules that are similar everywhere so it is easier to use.

We need to keep an eye on how artificial intelligence works in the world over a long period of time. This means we should do studies that follow intelligence deployments and see what happens to them. We want to know if artificial intelligence deployments make money if they're fair and if people think they are good or bad. Artificial intelligence deployments are what we are talking about here.

REFERENCES

Ahmed, F., & Iqbal, A. (2025). The role of artificial intelligence in enhancing credit risk management: A systematic literature review of international banking systems. *Pakistan Journal of Humanities and Social Sciences*, *13*(1), 478–492.

Balogun, A. Y., Metibemu, O. C., Olutimehin, A. T., Ajayi, A. J., Babarinde, D. C., & Olaniyi, O. O. (2025). The ethical and legal implications of shadow AI in sensitive industries: A focus on healthcare, finance and education. *Finance and Education (February 13, 2025).*

Bhattacharyya, A., Yu, Y., Yang, H., Singh, R., Joshi, T., Chen, J., & Yalavarthy, K. (2025). Model risk management for generative ai in financial institutions. *arXiv preprint arXiv:2503.15668.*

Brewer, J., Patel, D., Kim, D., & Murray, A. (2024). Navigating the challenges of generative technologies: Proposing the integration of artificial intelligence and blockchain. *Business Horizons*, *67*(5), 525–535.

Echeverría Muñoz, D. E. (2025). *Legal impact of Artificial Intelligence (AI) hallucinations* (Master's thesis, Quito, EC: Universidad Andina Simón Bolívar, Sede Ecuador).

Faisal, S. M., Khan, W., & Ishrat, M. (2025). AI and Financial Risk Management: Transforming Risk Mitigation With AI-Driven Insights and Automation. In *Artificial Intelligence for Financial Risk Management and Analysis* (pp. 281-306). IGI Global Scientific Publishing.

Financial Stability Board. (2024). Financial stability implications of artificial intelligence. https://www.fsb.org/wp-content/uploads/P14112024.pdf

Gupta, N. (2024). Security Risks of Generative AI in Financial Systems: A comprehensive review. *World Journal of Information Systems*, *1*(3), 17–24.

Hettiarachchi, I. (2025). THE RISE OF GENERATIVE AI AGENTS IN FINANCE: OPERATIONAL DISRUPTION AND STRATEGIC EVOLUTION. *International Journal of Engineering Technology Research & Management*, 447.

Joshi, R., Pandey, K., & Kumari, S. (2025). Generative AI: A Transformative Tool for Mitigating Risks for Financial Frauds. *Generative Artificial Intelligence in Finance: Large Language Models, Interfaces, and Industry Use Cases to Transform Accounting and Finance Processes*, 125-147.

Joshi, S., & Joshi-Satyadhar, S. (2025). Model risk management in the era of generative ai: Challenges, opportunities, and future directions. *International Journal of Scientific and Research Publications, 15*(5), 299–309.

Khan, M. S., & Umer, H. (2024). ChatGPT in finance: Applications, challenges, and solutions. *Heliyon, 10*(2).

Khanvilkar, K., & Shinde, V. (2025, October). Mitigating Hallucination Risks in GenAI Compliance Advisory Systems for the Financial Industry. In *International Conference on Software Engineering and Data Engineering* (pp. 302-318). Cham: Springer Nature Switzerland.

Krause, D. (2023). Mitigating risks for financial firms using generative AI tools. *Available at SSRN* 4452600.

Krause, D. (2025). The Promise and Peril of AI in Financial Research and Reporting: Navigating Accuracy, Insight, and Accountability. *Insight, and Accountability (June 04, 2025).*

Kushwah, S., & Dave, N. (2025, August). AI Hallucination and Strategies to Overcome: Enhancing Human-AI Interaction. In *2025 International Conference on Artificial Intelligence and Machine Vision (AIMV)* (pp. 1-6). IEEE.

Mahmud, M. A., ALAM, M. A., & Alam, M. K. (2025). Exploring the Transformative Potential of Generative AI and Large Language Models (LLMs) in Financial Applications: Opportunities, Risks and Strategic Implications. *Journal of Computer Science and Technology Studies, 7*(8), 1069–1088.

Mettrick, G. (2024). The AI handbook for financial services leaders: Tips and tactics for mastering AI in banking and finance. *Journal of Securities Operations & Custody, 16*(3), 286–296.

Mucsková, M. (2024). Transforming banking with artificial intelligence: Applications, challenges, and implications. *Trends Economics and Management, 18*(42), 21–37.

Pardeshi, A., & Deshmukh, S. (2025). AI in Finance: Computational Methods for Market Analysis and Risk Management. *Next-Generation Computational Intelligence: Trends and Technologies*, 137-164.

Philip, P. J. (2025). Ethical Frameworks for AI Hallucination Mitigation in Critical Applications. *Journal of Responsible AI & Ethics E: 3117-6402 P: 3117-6410, 2*(4), 13-25.

Silic, M., Silic, D., & Kind-Trüller, K. (2025). From Shadow It to Shadow AI–Threats, Risks and Opportunities for Organizations. *Strategic Change.*

Simeon, O. (2025). Unifying risk management for AI-driven cybersecurity in finance. *Issues in Information Systems*, *26*(2).

Szakacs, A. (2025). The adoption of AI agents: from automation to autonomy, reshaping governance and strategic decision-making in FintTch.

Williamson, S. M., & Prybutok, V. (2024). The era of artificial intelligence deception: Unraveling the complexities of false realities and emerging threats of misinformation. *Information (Basel)*, *15*(6), 299.

Yaprak, B. (2024). Generative artificial intelligence in marketing: The invisible danger of AI hallucinations. *Ekonomi İşletme ve Yönetim Dergisi*, *8*(2), 133–158.

Zafar, M. B., & Ali, H. (2025). Shariah Governance Standard on Generative AI for Islamic Financial Institutions. *Available at SSRN* 5143165.

Chapter 14
From Interaction to Emotion:
The Future of Customer Experience in the Metaverse

Prachita A. Patil
https://orcid.org/0000-0002-0124-5806
Dr. Ambedkar Institute of Management Studies and Research, Nagpur, India

Sumant Wachasundar
Ratan Tata Maharashtra State Skill University, Nagpur, India

Dhanshree Badshah
Global Yog Association, India

ABSTRACT

The given paper discusses how the customer and human experience is transforming in the digital world, where the video becomes less focused on the interaction as an engagement factor and more on its emotional presence in an AI-driven world and the further stage of the metaverse. Even though digital technologies and social media have revolutionized the sphere of communication, learning, and social connection, their overuse and excessive and compulsive nature have resulted in the fact that there is the emergence of the crisis of presence in the form of a loss of authenticity, emotional contentment and live interaction between people. Digital overexposure can be dangerous not only to the mental health and cognition of young and older generations but also even to the emotional stability.

DOI: 10.4018/979-8-3373-7534-2.ch014

INTRODUCTION

The emergence of digital technologies has damaged the essence of interaction and communication and the perception of the world according to the individuals, as the breakthrough is one of the key events altering the face-to-face interaction to the technologically mediated means of presence. In recent decades, human interaction has been transformed by social media platforms, artificial intelligence (AI) and immersive virtual worlds, and most recently, the new phenomenon of the metaverse, making it more virtual, algorithmic and an interaction engineered by emotion. The innovations have caused complex psychological, emotional, and social issues, even though the global connection was unmatched, readily available and convenient. It is based on this paradoxical paradigm shift that technologies that are designed to bring people together are, in the majority of cases, driving them to emotional detachment, deprivation of authenticity, and a human face crisis. This crisis is not limited to personal relations alone, but to customer experience, workplace engagement, education, healthcare, and broader social systems, where interactions are streamlined more or less on efficiency and engagement scales rather than the poignancy and the real perception of humanity.

Social media is one of the instances of such a paradox. Connection and community platforms typically feature an AI-powered structure and pay a lot of attention to attention, emotional arousal, and prolonged screen time. Suggestive algorithms and personalisation, Personalised feed systems, and content strategies that work with engagement affect users' perception of reality, perceptions of self-worth and social norms insidiously. These systems, although making the use of the system more relevant and easy to use also foster comparisons, performative identities and shallow interactions. The harmful mental health effects of increased use of social media such as loneliness, anxiety, depression, diminished self-worth, and emotional exhaustion are increasingly being ascribed by empirical studies to the overuse of social media which is exhibiting strong detrimental impacts on mental health particularly among the adolescent and the young adults that are still in the critical stages of identity and social development. The digital overexposure takes its toll not only on the youth, however. Having been exposed to screens at an early age, the hyper stimulated toddlers might develop both complications in cognitive and emotional development; the working professionals in this case have issues with distraction and burnout as well as the ability to focus attention; older adults in spite of being more connected appear to feel non engaged and isolated in terms of emotional response.

Its appearance worsens the situation in the field of the artificial intelligence. The AIs are not an instrument of passivity but rather a driving force of human interaction, which set the course of communication, convict and evoke emotions, and infertility. Conversational agents, emotive and recognition systems among others and increasingly the virtual assistants or chatbots, appear to be personal, responsive and caring. Inasmuch as this type of systems enhances the effectiveness and scalability particularly in the customer service divisions, marketing and virtual interaction, it also brings forth requisite questions on authenticity, emotional surrogate, and ethical accountability. The difference between the feelings of people and those inspired by a machine is finally ambiguated as individuals are coming into more contact with AI-powered agents. This is a form of the so-called crisis of presence where human beings comprise presence of the body, but soul sucking and emotionally disembodied, out of time, social. Presence envisaged as the tradition is perceived to be paying attention, having emotion and being available back and forth are being replaced more and more with multitasking, paying less attention and pre-programmed experiences.

The metaverse is a fresh digital form of interaction and customer experience, in this context of the bigger picture. The metaverse is considered to be longer-lasting, participatory, and shared digital space that, on the one hand, implies transcending the two-dimensional screen and having an embodied digital stage that integrates the blockchain and artificial intelligence (AI) technologies, the virtual reality (VR), and augmented reality (AR). The metaverse has the ability to alter the virtual existence of individuals present in digital areas, personality and their capacity of perceiving presence, personality and feeling in the virtual world due to physical shopping space and digital avatars and immersive brand experiences and virtual social space. The trend of operations and institutional realignment has witnessed the transformation of transactional and interactional customer interactions to experience and emotion oriented customer engagements. The metaverse has broken the boundaries of functional efficiency or satisfaction on the customer experience, and it is becoming more of an emotional appeal, psychological immersion, and the sense of belonging.

This, however, results in an additional escalation of the already existing problems regarding such areas of digital wellbeing as emotional authenticity and ethical design. The features of immersive environments are the presence of high levels of sensory stimulation and engagement, which enhances the risk of higher degrees of digital addiction, escapism, and emotional dependency. As avatars are set to take over the physical body, virtual spaces are coming in as the replacement of the real world interactions, questions will be raised in the context of long term effects of identity development, emotional intelligence, empathy, and social resilience. The problem, though, does not only consist in technology but in an altogether human one: how do the digital systems, namely the AI-powered and three-dimensional kinds get created to bring value, rather than disrupt emotional health, physical closeness, and resonant presence?

In order to reflect upon these issues, this chapter situates itself in a cross-boundary between psychology, communication theory, the discipline of digital ethics, and research about customer experience as an essential discipline to take into consideration. It asserts that the future of customer and human experience in the metaverse can be changed not out of the current indicators of superficial interaction into an account of feelings, being and relational value. The chapter informs us through this psychological examination of the psychological implications of digital overexposure of various age samples of samples in relation to cognitions, emotional management, attention and social conducts. It also analyses how AI-powered social media framework and immersive space face-off to affect emotional response, anticipation, and perceptions of oneself and others, where the need to stay more active and profitable predominates over the need to be considerate and genuine.

At the same time, the chapter itself is composed in a constructive key: the author realizes that only digital technologies and the metaverse can introduce the perspectives of re-defining connection and experience. Inclusiveness, accessibility, emotional expression, and engagement can be developed using AI and immersive environments in cases where they are eradicated and human-centered. Virtual space might be employed to make mutual experience possible without considering geographical boundaries, empower marginalized groups and enable their customers to experience an emotional connection through an emotionally exhilarating customer experience. The secret is to take very strategic choices which are capable of targeting emotional intelligence, digital wellbeing, transparency and human values. The change of focus is away of shorter-term trends (slow technology), ethical AI, presence-centered design, and emotionally sustainable customer experiences, which hints at some of the most crucial paths toward introducing the richness and authenticity of connectivity when digital.

The shift in the presentation towards emotion as an opportunity and challenge is introduced in the end of this presentation. As the mediation of human experience becomes more and more mediated by AI and immersive technologies, it is the quality of presence that becomes the topic of concern to individuals, organizations, and society as a whole. The following period in digital space history will be the metaverse that will be used to intensify the crisis of presence, or to provide a platform where one can be digitalized by experiencing rehumanization. This is the part of the book that seeks to identify with this critical conversation, and the risks, implications, and opportunities of this transformation, and the future where technology is not replacing emotional attachment, but complementing and enhancing it, and the customer experience is not simply founded upon interaction, but real human emotion and being.

BACKGROUND

A lot quicker growth of digital technologies in the past two decades has reoriented human behavioral patterns, communication, and socialization. Social media applications, streaming applications, online games, applications under use of artificial intelligence and life simulation worlds have been made to be part of our lives. The equipment to render the work more productive and interconnected and to reach the information has become it as it got themselves to a more widespread implementation and created the perception of cognition, feeling, identity, and the social relations. The line between online and offline life has been more of gray ground that has brought about the creation of an digital world that stays hangar round the clock and has influenced the thinking processes, feelings and socialability of the people. Despite the fact that digital technologies have introduced considerable benefits to the educational process, to the field of healthcare, commerce, and social connectedness, the lack of control and excessive use of technologies has raised more and more issues regarding the mental health of people, their emotional state, and the experience itself.

The most evident impact of the digital distribution is the significant increase in the amount of time spent in the screen of any age group. The penetration of digital devices in children takes place at earlier stages, and it is normally done at a stage when proper mechanisms of cognitive and emotional controls in children are not in place. The youth and the young adults particularly are extremely reliant on the social media and digital communication because they do not only use it as an entertainment platform but also as a cultural identity building platform, as a means of social identification as well as emotional release. This new trend of staying digitally available beyond the usual with fee hours is usually instigated by working individuals, and this gives the mode of working and living, intellectual workload, and burnout. Although aged people have the privilege of connecting digitally and with information available to them, they might have problems that are associated with digital literacy, superficial interactions online, and absence of communication that does not touch the heart. This prolonged and prolonged exposure to computers has given predisposition in the obsessive form of usage and at other eventualities, computer addiction.

A new scientific body of psychological and medical literature has resulted in a continual rising number of witnessing a relationship between excessive use of digital products and undesirable psychological issues. Social anxiety and depression have also been increased due to excessive spending on social media particularly when the user is engaged in upward social comparison and exposure to idealized images of life as well as algorithm-enhanced negativity. The constant need to popularize, receive likes, shares, and create more presence on the Internet can lead to the emergence of a sense of inadequacy, low self-esteem, and fear of missing out (FOMO). Moreover, the distracting and busy pace of electronic based content consumption may influence the category of attention, emotional control, and thoughtful consideration which contribute to the emotional instability and stress. The excessive amount of time on the screen and a specific time before falling to sleep also become a severe concern because they inhibit the circadian rhythms, suppress melatonin production, and delay the falling asleep process, making people bored and experiencing emotional imbalances, poor cognitive functioning.

An array of artificial intelligence software is the force behind social media networks and online applications in the quest to achieve maximum user interaction. Repetition of use and emotional response are further enhanced through the fact that recommendation systems, feeds and notices will always be changed as a result of user action. Though such mechanisms enhance user retention and profitability of a business, they also expose individuals to psychological effects since they enable them to be addicted to checking, feel emotional and dependent, and lose control. Users also feel less in control of their usage on the digital space leading to overuse and consequently the sense of guilt, stress, and emotional burnout. This dynamic shift contributes to the so-called crisis of presence in which individuals are physically in their physical location yet mentally and emotionally trapped in the digital loces.

The creation of the immersive technologies and the metaverse exacerbates these issues. Compared to the conventional digital sources, the multiple modality of senses on immersive virtual worlds and stronger presence and embodiment on the avatars and in the space of the interactive universe forms a new perspective of existence. They also may serve as a means of improving the learning process, entertainment and customer experience in the sense that they offer emotionally involving and socially interactive surroundings. However, they also are risky in regards to immersion of greater psychological areas, escape and emotional substitution. The longer people remain in the virtual world, the more concerned are people that the relationships, duties and emotional values in the real world can be ruined. Immersive settings may enhance the feeling of anxiety, social seclusion, and sleeping disorders, particularly in the delicate populations due to the emotion experience of the setting.

The psychological impact of the overuse of the digital does not reflect uniformly but relies on the demography and sociocultural backgrounds. Teenagers are particularly weak and susceptible to the emotional and social constraints in the online space because the age group is extremely sensitive to these factors. They are more vulnerable to anxiety, depression and sleep disturbance caused by use of social media because they are more vulnerable to peer validation and belonging to a group. Being in a highly cognitively formed situation, adults have to face with many different problems, including digital burnout, information overloads and the constant stress of being constantly connected. The fact that older adults have access to the internet may make them lonely since the interaction between them and their acquaintances is not as full of emotional content as it is in face to face communication. These disparities create a need to find out the links between these dimensions of digital use and mental well-being through a life course perspective.

Socially, overindulgence in consumption of the digital environment, which has increased in normalization, has had significant social effect in health, productivity and social unity. Problems such as anxiety, depression and sleeping disorders are on the increase hence increasing the burden on the healthcare systems hence resulting in a decline in the quality of life. In the work places, digitally induced stresses and cognitive fatigue could interfere with decision making, innovativeness and even job satisfaction. Learning environments may be inundating this process of learning through exposure to the screen, which affects learning, attention, and emotional development. These barriers indicate the need to carry out evidence-based study, which would enable to delve into details as to the connection between the results of mental health and trends of use of the digital.

To resolve these concerns, researchers, politicians, and developers of technologies started to propagate the concept of digital health, ethical artificial intelligence, and human-centered design. Digital wellbeing initiatives are aiming at moderate technology use, linking mind with technology, and training of self-regulation. The openness of ethical AI systems is necessitated by a transparent and higher liabilities and responsibility on the development of algorithms governing user behaviour and emotional conditions. However, there are still gaps in the discourse as far as the indicators of the influence of different kinds and levels of digital use on the mental health of different categories of citizens spread and are recognized.

The paper fits into this larger framework, as it tries to leave its mark to the existing discussion on the subject of digital wellbeing and human experience in the age of AI and immersive technologies. The research aims at providing empirical data that would help influence the policy, design, and supporting intervention actions by examining the effect of excessive use of digital on key mental health outcomes. They are particularly significant relations that ought to be comprehended as the societies transition to the more immersive and emotionally involving digital ecosystem, like the metaverse. The next phase of the digital revolution can be even more significant to influence the existing mental health problems rather than render them less worrisome until the purposeful and evidence-based approaches.

In conclusion, this research paper history has shown the dynamic and confusing digital world in which the development of technologies is more rapid than the psychological integration and ethical controls. Excessive use of digital devices, which was supported by the artificial intelligence-enhanced platform and immersion was a grave menace to the psychological health, emotional stability and the in-person communication quality. These problems will be forced to be solved in a subtle disposition of the means of the interaction of digitalization and psychological health contrasted across age categories and circumstances. This need has seen the development of the study, since it is important to unearth the most significant relationship between high levels of digital use and the mental health implications and to establish the future of digital futures that are more sustainable, psychologically-intelligent and human-centered.

FOCUS OF THE ARTICLE

The purpose of this article is the critical review of the influence of excessive utilization of digital technologies on mental health and emotional condition under the condition of using AI-based social media, immersive technologies, and the new metaverse. Specifically, the article directs its attention to the study of whether prolonged and compulsive consumption of digital platforms has the potential to affect the two key aspects of mental health anxiety, depression, sleep disorders, emotional regulation, and perceived social presence in different age groups.

The article emphasises the transition between the digital dimension, centering on the interaction to the emotional dimension, where the algorithms, the immersive interfaces and interactions among the avatars affect the psychological behavior, self-image as well as social relationships. It also examines the role of artificial intelligence in making perspectives more interesting, creating digital addiction, and altering the nature of natural presence and bonding.

Blending the information pertinent to the sphere of psychology, consumer behaviour, communication theory, and digital ethics, the article tries to identify the risks and opportunities concerning digital immersion. Lastly, it specializes in recommending humanistic and personnelistically feasible models of logo building digital and metaverse experience facilitating favorable wellbeing, refreshed face-to-face presence, and assessing the rate of technological development and psychological variables.

LITERATURE REVIEW

Metaverse has emerged as a paradigm shift digital ecosystem with virtual reality (VR), augmented reality (AR), extended reality (XR), artificial intelligence (AI) and blockchain to create sustainable, immersive and interactive experiences. However, academic discourse is also putting the metaverse to not only the technological novelty but the socio-cultural and economic space that makes consumption, identity, relations and customer experience transform. The existing literature samples a number of disciplines including marketing, consumer behavior, information system, psychology, sociology and philosophy and is abundant with information about how interaction, emotion and presence are formed in virtual worlds.

The classical sociological thinking could be followed in laying down the primitive conceptual dimensions of social interaction. Simmel (1949) in his work of sociability emphasized on the point of interaction as a type of game of sociability which produces the mood of connection, belongingness and a sense of mutual content. This opinion remains current in the analysis of the modern metaverse investigation where the social interaction governs the user interaction and emotionality. Physically mediated sociability replaces digitally with a problem of authenticity, reciprocity and emotional richness even made more severe by the virtual immersion of the digitally mediated sphere.

Defining a metaverse, Mystakidis (2022) is broad in terms of describing the metaverse as a combination of digital and real world, persisting, synchronic, embodied, and interoperable. Its interpretation is also the foundation of more research on the expansion of the metaverse beyond the gaming subsector into every-day life, business, education and socialization. This point is supplemented by Wang et al. (2025), who speculates on the vision of the everyday metaverse and advocates the notion that the virtual world is becoming more and more a part of the everyday experience without any additional barrier being established between the online and offline experiences. Their text is focused on naturalization of their interactions with the help of avatars and growing attachment to virtual worlds both emotionally and functionally.

The identity, self-presentation and digital embodiment in the metaverse is one of the themes in literature. The authors Tombul and Sari (2021) concentrate on explaining how self-presentation evolves on the Internet by saying that the users reason procedurally to create their identities, and it might be highly unlike their real-life personas. This theme is protracted regarding the concept of the so-called digital doppelgängers. The paper by Khan et al. (2025) analyzes the position of the consumer brand interaction based on the use of avatars, in which it is anticipated that the avatars construct self-projections, mediating emotional affection and conspicuous consumption. Similarly, Voinea et al. (2024) approach the problem of how the human relationships and practical identity can be affected with the help of digital doppelgangs in a rather philosophical way, posing ethical issues on what the authenticity, emotional replacement, and disaggregation of self in the virtual realm represent.

The emotional and psychological aspects of the interaction of the metaverse are the primary subject of the contribution made to the human experience of the metaverse. The empirical research conducted by Oh et al. (2023) interprets the social merits of the metaverse residence and demonstrates that social presence and beneficial communication positively influence social self-efficacy and negatively the manner in which individuals experience loneliness. Their findings contribute to doubting the existing discussion that digital spaces inevitably can make people feel isolated and suggest that appropriately designed online space can result in emotional wellbeing. It is this good outlook that is however tainted by consideration on over-immersion, dependency on emotions and loss of face-to-face social skills, as well as the significance of balanced-designed and ethical design are mentioned.

As a paradigm shift in the flow of consumption and marketing, the metaverse is the transformation of the transaction systems of engagement to the immersive, experience-driven engagement. Gadalla et al. (2013) were among the first researchers who formulated a conceptualization of a metaverse retail service quality by attempting to offer a framework of the perception of service experience in the three-dimensional virtual environment. Their contribution was the basis of the current study of the role of immersion, interactivity and presence in causing customer perception and customer satisfaction. Frank et al. (2024) build on this foundations testing with a theoretical basis the role of fidelity in virtual retail stores in an empirical manner and finding out that higher levels of visual and functional fidelity result in a more positive consumer response, trust, and purchase intentions.

This is because the process of creating metaverse brand engagement and value is gaining academic attention. Among the issues analyzed by Arya et al. (2024) is the XR-based gamification of marketing activities and the researchers confirm that it positively influences consumer-based brand equity. They observe that their research has found the importance of immersive storytelling, interactivity, and participation on the basis of an avatar in the formation of emotional engagement and brand attachment. Barrera and Shah (2023) introduce to the schema of marketing in the metaverse and proclaim significant dimensions of presence, co-creation, personalization and building community in the framework of marketing in the metaverse, and determine directions of future research, namely, in the framework of the methodology of ethics and control and wellbeing of the consumer.

The customer experiences in metaverses are of particular interest when it comes to such a concept as value co-creation. Metaverse is discussed by Buhalis and colleagues, (2023) as a driver of customer experience and value co-creation in the hospitality and tourism industry, where the forces of immersive environment are interested in the enhancement of emotional experience, personalization, and participatory experience. Their findings indicate that customers have stopped being passive consumers but active co-creators of experiences, e.g. people constructing narratives, environments and brand connotations in the game of interaction. The discussion is further developed when Mansoor et al. (2024) discuss the purchase spillovers considering the case of the metaverse transferred to the real world where the social presence, trialability, and positive customer experience in virtual worlds has an influential impact on the real world purchasing behaviour.

One more important direction of research digital goods and ownership in the metaverse is another line. Yang (2024) uses the Genesis Effect to analyze the attaching values of digital goods to be possessed by the consumers, which are psychological ownership, emotional attachment and perceived distinction. This paper brings out the transformation of material to symbolic consumption where emotional, expressing self, and experience worth are more significant than usefulness. These discoveries play crucial roles in the establishment of the automation of the emotion customer experience in virtual economies.

A literature research on user motivation and usage of the metaverse is also well advanced. The work by Narataraj an et al. (2024) is an attempt to apply their uses-and-gratifications perspective to the following significant motivations that make people start using the metaverse social interaction, entertainment, escapism, self-expression, technological curiosity. Their ambivalent research indicates that customers want the emotional and psychological gratification, which counters the thesis that the customer experience should seek more emotional interests in the future user experience regarding the functional benefits. Habil et al. (2024) also admit that the augmented reality is used to create the new customer experience and say that in the era of the metaverse, the central subject of customer satisfaction and loyalty lies in the degree of its immersion and engagement of emotions.

This discussion is also contributed by entertainment and gaming researches. Bhambri (2024) brushes upon the issue of novel mechanisms within the entertainment and playing of the metaverse where the feeling of immersion regarding the story, the social, and emotional interaction change the experiences of users. The insights will also be exceptional in comprehending how gaming world principles of emotional design can be applied to larger customer experience in the virtual world.

Despite the progress in this regard, some more ethical and social matters are being brought up by researchers. According to Hennig-Thurau et al. (2023), an in-depth social contacts concept will be implemented in the metaverse, and a research roadmap where the research aspects may be explored include manipulation, data privacy, emotional exploitation, and digital wellbeing. Their attempts, nevertheless, demonstrate the necessity of the accountability of the companies and creators to find the middle ground between the marketing objectives and human principles. The risk of prioritizing engagement statistics over the authenticity of emotions is especially high when it comes to the increased mediation of autonomous systems and may worsen so-called crisis of presence.

To the point, the available literature could be discussed as a good foundation of knowledge regarding the metaverse as a socially structured, emotionally appealing, and commercially useful space. The study discoveries imply to great extent that the metaverse transforms the customer experience they shift the interaction-driven based transaction to the emotion-based and immersive experience, which entails presence, identity and connectedness. However, other fields still need to improve the practice of the psychological wellbeing, ethical design, and long-term influence on society in customer experience frameworks. The review makes reference to the need to think about the use of interdisciplinary approaches that would look into bridging marketing with chosen fields of psychology, sociology, digital ethics to ensure that the future of customer experience in the metaverse radicalizes the richness of emotion, authentic presence, and sustainable human connection rather than exacerbating the problem of overexposure to digital content and the franchising of emotion.

RESEARCH OBJECTIVES:

- To examine how excessive digital usage affects mental health indicators such as anxiety, depression, and sleep disorders.
- To analyse cognitive impairments, including attention deficits, memory disruption, and executive functioning issues across age groups.
- To evaluate shifts in emotional well-being, including empathy erosion, mood volatility, and social detachment.
- To identify age-specific triggers and coping mechanisms for digital addiction.
- To propose holistic, age-sensitive interventions to mitigate adverse effects.

HYPOTHESIS

H_1: Excessive digital usage has a significant positive impact on adverse mental health outcomes, specifically increasing levels of anxiety, depression, and sleep disorders among users.

H_0: Excessive digital usage has no significant impact on mental health outcomes such as anxiety, depression, and sleep disorders.

RESEARCH METHODOLOGY

The research project will adopt a mixed-method research structure to examine in precise detail at all those levels of the life span, including children (3 years old to 12 years old), adolescents (13 years old to 18 years old), young adults (19 years old to 35 years old), middle-aged adults (36 years old to 59 years old), and elderly people (60 years old and above), the age-specific impact of excessive use of the digital world. The quantitative section will involve filled out, structured questionnaires used by the sample of each age group in which the digital usage patterns, platform dependency, and mental health variables (attention span, emotional regulation, anxiety, depression, sleep quality, stress, perceived social isolation) will be measured. Psychological scales are applied based on the age of the sample group in order to ensure that reliability and comparability of data are obtained. It follows that, digital use analytics, such as, screen time, frequency of use, and time of the day use will be collected (informed consent) to provide objective behavioral data, and reduce self-report. Semi-structured clinical interviews and focus group discussions, according to the stages of development that will enable conducting biased research on the issue of dopamine-driven engagement, identity formation, work-life imbalance, emotional burnout, cognitive decline, and isolation implementations through technologies would be incorporated in the qualitative section. In addition, complicated case studies and personal stories are also employed to make statistical results realistic and represent real-life experience of people of various ages. The interdisciplinary approach to research has been brought in to ensure the study enhances the interpretive validity by collaborating with the psychologists, educators and technology ethicists such that the study does not present the findings solely based on the interpretation of behavior and clinical aspects but in education, social and ethical factors. Such an integrative approach allows a delicate understanding of how the excessive use of digital technology is markedly differentially impacted on neuro-mental functioning and emotional health according to the generational boundaries.

Table 1. Descriptive Statistics of Digital Usage and Mental Health Indicators

Variable	N	Mean	Std. Deviation	Minimum	Maximum
Daily Digital Usage (Hours)	400	6.85	2.41	1.5	12
Anxiety Score	400	3.62	0.91	1.2	5
Depression Score	400	3.48	0.97	1	5
Sleep Disorder Score	400	3.71	1.05	1.1	5
Overall Mental Health Impact Index	400	3.6	0.88	1.3	5

The descriptive statistics that are presented in the form of daily digital use and measures of mental health can be considered as the valuable initial evidence of the correlation between excessive use of digital and poor psychological outcomes. The 6.85 average hours of digital activity/day indicates that on an average, the digital subjects of activity of the respondents spend a nice portion of the day on digital devices and platform. It is greater than what is typically considered as a moderate or functional level of exposure and suggests a practice of constant digital use that can readily interfere with offline activity, interpersonal communication, and sleep. The standard deviation applied is also quite broad so one can conclude that there is high variability among users and some of them have less screen time but have a large proportion of people whose screen time is very high thus predisposed to the development of detrimental mental health outcomes.

The means of the five point scale being 3.62 would represent moderate to high levels of anxiety among the respondents. This outcome can be attributed to the accessible psychological literature that assumes that excessive consumption of digital technologies particularly the use of social media can cause a rise in anxiety given a number of mechanisms, such as social constant social comparison, fear of missing out, information overload, and being bombarded with emotionally colored information. The lack of consistency in beating the scores of the anxiety component indicates that not all people will be affected by digital usage to an equal extent, possibly, the impact is moderated by such factors as age, coping, personality, and the digital action type. Nevertheless, the large mean value suggests that anxiety is one of the common mental processes of heavy digital users.

Similarly, the average is 3.48 in the case of the mean depression score showing that the sample has significant signs of depression. This is not very close to the average anxiety, but it is nevertheless above the neutral mid-point implying that the influence of the further exposure to the digital life can contribute to the poor mood and emotional fatigue and deteriorate the psychological health. This might be as a result of such a relationship between socialization of social life through face-to-face interaction, there is no support in daily life, no exercise and inadequacy feelings developed through socializing online images of success and contentment. The standard deviation demonstrates any material difference among people and it proves the need to distinguish things more on age and sub-sets of usage.

The sleep disorder scores are the highest (3.71), due to which the sleep disruption should be mentioned as one of the most topical effects of excessive use of digital devices. There is no secret that chronic screening time, and this is most often in the evening, interferes with circadian rhythms and the production of melatonin, which leads to delays in sleep, poor-quality sleep, and feelings of sleepiness during the day. The standard deviation and mean are considerably high and point out that sleep related problems are not unique and standard among users and could intensify anxiety and depression since the restriction of sleep and mental wellness have the mutual influence.

The summation of these findings can be depicted under the overall effect index of mental health as having an average score of 3.60 that indicates that negative psychological impact of excessive use of digital is moderate to high. This aggregate variable illuminates the issue that anxiety, depression, and sleep disorders are interrelated and that digital overexposure does not have a significant effect on one of the aspects of mental health on its own. Instead it is an element of a bigger trend of emotional instability and stress in the mind.

Together, the descriptive statistics statistically prove the Hypothesis H 1, that is, high levels of anxiety, depression, and sleep disorders are associated with high digital use. Whereas the descriptive analysis does not reveal causality, the finding of the relevance of the high mean scores of all the mental health indicators is indicative of the strong significant relationship. It is the outcomes that make it necessary to run further inferential tests such as correlation analysis and regression analysis to gauge the strength and direction of such relationships and the consequences of possible moderators such as age, the nature of digital activity, and personal resiliency. Conclusions cartoon are eventually drawn on the urgency of review and imperative response to the digital overuse as a serious health and psychological concern in an ever-immersive digital world.

Table 2. Mediation Analysis of Sleep Disturbance in the Relationship between Digital Usage and Mental Health Outcomes

Path	Relationship Tested	β Coefficient	Std. Error	t-value	p-value	Result
a	Digital Usage → Sleep Disturbance	0.52	0.06	8.67	<0.001	Significant
b	Sleep Disturbance → Anxiety	0.41	0.05	8.2	<0.001	Significant
c	Digital Usage → Anxiety (Total Effect)	0.48	0.07	6.86	<0.001	Significant
c′	Digital Usage → Anxiety (Direct Effect)	0.27	0.06	4.5	<0.001	Significant
ab	Indirect Effect (via Sleep Disturbance)	0.21	—	—	<0.01*	Partial Mediation

MEDIATION FOR DEPRESSION

Path	Relationship Tested	β Coefficient	Std. Error	t-value	p-value	Result
a	Digital Usage → Sleep Disturbance	0.52	0.06	8.67	<0.001	Significant
b	Sleep Disturbance → Depression	0.38	0.05	7.6	<0.001	Significant
c	Digital Usage → Depression (Total Effect)	0.44	0.07	6.29	<0.001	Significant
c′	Digital Usage → Depression (Direct Effect)	0.24	0.06	4	<0.001	Significant
ab	Indirect Effect (via Sleep Disturbance)	0.2	—	—	<0.01*	Partial Mediation

The mediation analysis provides Hypothesis H 1 a superb empirical rationale because it shows the direct and indirect pathways in which over use of the digital world contributes towards the negative mental state. The results of the analysis indicate that the beneficial effect of excessive digital use on sleep disturbance is high: there is a strong and statistically significant coefficient of the path (= 0.52, $p < 0.001$). The specified finding confirms that a greater screen exposure, particularly, non-uniform and disproportional in the duration of exposure, mainly affects the quality and duration of sleep adversely. A primary mediatory variable, in this case, is sleep disturbance in the relationship between digital overuse and psychological stress in general.

Further analysis reveals that sleep disturbance is a significant predictor of increased amounts of anxiety (= 0.41, $p = 0.001$) and depression (= 0.38, $p = 0.001$). The results are in line with the earlier accessible psychological research based on two-way interaction between sleep problems and mental disease. Sleep deprivation leads to emotional dismanagement, stressful repercussion, insufficient cognitive control and negative mood disorders, which reinforce anxiety and depressive symptoms. The strength and significance of such relationships mirror the major importance of sleep as a psychological controller which is readily subjected to the overindulgence of digital technologies.

The outcome of the mental health of the effect of digital usage is significantly influenced, as in the following combination of the effects of digital anxiety results (= 0.48, $p = 0.001$) and depression results(= 0.44, $p = 0.001$). Direct relationships between digital usage and anxiety (= 0.27, = 0.001) and depression (= 0.24, = 0.001) are even significant that sleep disturbance has been included in the model, with much lower diameter. Such a decrease is an affirmation that there is a partial mediation suggestion with meaning that even though excess digital use is directly parameterized to induce anxiety and depression, it has a high percentage of its impact on an indirect level because it still interferes with sleep frequencies.

The two indirect anxiety (ab path 0.21) and depression (ab path 0.20) over and above the strength of the mediation model are also significant due to bootstrapping tests. The implication of these findings is that interventions that do not consider sleep health and the habit of using digital devices simultaneously even though they aim to alleviate the state of anxiety or depression are less effective. It is also noteworthy that even the fact that there might be other mediating processes such as social comparison, cognitive overload, or emotional dependency that might also account for a relationship between digital use and psychological well-being is a pointer to the existence of direct effects.

All in all, sleep disturbance is the mediation variable that was found as the most essential factor that enabled the impact of overwhelmingly use digital resources to instigate anxiety and depression. These results determine the interdependence of digital behaviour, sleep wellness, and psychological wellbeing as they present attractive information that can be offered to practitioners, policy-makers, educators, and technology designers. The increase in the awareness of the excessive use of digital technologies and the endorsement of healthy digital habits may be considered as potentially useful as the future possible interventions to reduce sleep disruption, and to deaden the consequences of excessive use of electronics and devices, particularly in the evening time.

Table 3. Age-Group-Wise Mediation Comparison of Sleep Disturbance between Digital Usage and Mental Health Outcomes

Age Group	Path a: Digital Usage → Sleep Disturbance (β)	Path b: Sleep Disturbance → Anxiety (β)	Path b: Sleep Disturbance → Depression (β)	Direct Effect c′ (Anxiety) (β)	Direct Effect c′ (Depression) (β)	Indirect Effect ab (Anxiety)	Indirect Effect ab (Depression)	Mediation Type
Children (3–12)	0.45***	0.36***	0.31***	0.18**	0.16**	0.16**	0.14**	Partial
Adolescents (13–18)	0.60***	0.48***	0.44***	0.29***	0.26***	0.29***	0.26***	Partial (Strong)
Young Adults (19–35)	0.55***	0.42***	0.39***	0.25***	0.23***	0.23***	0.21***	Partial
Middle-aged Adults (36–59)	0.49***	0.37***	0.35***	0.21**	0.20**	0.18**	0.17**	Partial
Older Adults (60+)	0.41***	0.33**	0.30**	0.14*	0.12*	0.14*	0.12*	Partial (Moderate)

The age-group based mediating analysis has shown that significant differences exist in the mediation the sleep disturbance produces on the relationship between excessive digital use and negative mental health outcomes throughout the life span. Overuse of digitization on children in the age group of 3 to 12 years illustrates positive substantial effect on sleep disorder that extend to impact anxiety and depression at moderate level. The ID effects in this group assume a partial mediation of the sleep disruption, meaning that a sleep disruption is a crucial means of influence of the digital overuse on the emotional wellbeing, but there are other elements of the process of development employed to form psychological susceptibility, which are insufficient regulation of the emotional condition, and an insufficient coping mechanisms. These findings point out at the early childhood as a strategic phase where over-exposure to the screen can disrupt the principle sleep and emotional habits with potential long-term consequences.

Adolescents of 13-18 years were observed to possess the greatest mediation effect. The relationship between digital use and sleep disturbance is the most significant, as it represents the growth of interest of the adolescent population towards social media, gaming, and late-night time at the screen. Sleep disturbance is also a highly predictive factor of anxiety and depression in this group, and thus the most significant indirect effects. The high partial mediation is the indication that the broken sleep is one of the primary mediators between the digital overuse and the issues of the teenage mentality. The fact that direct effects remain significant in nature implies that other factors exist including peer comparison, comparisons with others online which leads to the formation of identity and identity perceived stress. These findings demonstrate the adolescent phase as the most vulnerable developmental stage of risks presented by digital on mental health.

The mediation effects are significant in young adults in the age group 19 years to 35 years but not strong enough considering that they are in-between adolescents. Digital utilization of the body has tremendous interference with sleep, and thus resulting in the anxiety and depression that are also among the outcomes of digital multitasking, worklife balance, and continuous connectedness. The partial mediation of the described group suggests that the sleep disturbance is a central variable, the remainder of the stressors, such as career pressures, social comparison, and information overload are independent variables that cause mental health outcomes. It implies that digital practices should also be represented in the interventions to be applied to young adults along with general lifestyle stressors.

The intermediate mediation is also recorded in middle aged where the participants are in the age bracket of 36-59 years. Despite using digital still as negatively affecting sleep and subsequently psychological well-being of individuals, the correlation is less significant than comparatively with younger demographics. The reason behind this is greater degrees of emotional regulation and more systematic daily habits. However, its presence in the fact of the existence of the negative indirect and direct impacts indicates the growing issue of burnout, work stress, and emotional depersonalisation among this age group due to the technology.

There are mediation effects between the elderly at the age of 60 years and above but these are not very strong. Sleep disorder is a good correlating tool in relating digital usage to anxiety and depression though to a lesser extent. This could mean that other factors such as physical wellbeing, loneliness, and technology fears are not as crucial as sleep and emotional health deficiencies of older adults through excessive digital administration. Overall, the analysis demonstrates that among all age groups, sleep disturbance is a partial mediator between the digital use and the mentality health, yet, it has the most significant effect on adolescents and young adults, and digital wellbeing age-sensitively supporting interventions should be embraced.

Table 4. SEM Path Estimates

Path	Standardized Estimate (β)	S.E.	C.R.	p-value	Result
Excessive Digital Usage → Sleep Disturbance	0.56	0.07	8	<0.001	Significant
Sleep Disturbance → Mental Health Outcomes	0.43	0.06	7.17	<0.001	Significant
Excessive Digital Usage → Mental Health Outcomes	0.29	0.06	4.83	<0.001	Significant
Indirect Effect (EDU → SD → AMHO)	0.24	—	—	<0.01*	Significant

MODEL FIT INDICES

Fit Index	Recommended Value	Obtained Value
χ^2/df	< 3.00	2.18
GFI	≥ 0.90	0.93
AGFI	≥ 0.90	0.91
CFI	≥ 0.90	0.95
TLI	≥ 0.90	0.94
RMSEA	≤ 0.08	0.054
SRMR	≤ 0.08	0.046

Interpretation of SEM Results

On the whole, SEM results demonstrate the excellent model fit that implies that the proposed theoretical framework represents the relationships between excessive digital use, sleep disturbance, and unfavorable mental health outcomes to perfection. The effect of digital use on the condition of sleep disturbance is significant and statistically positive (0.56, p 0.001 - positive), which proves the data regarding the interference of sleep patterns by the increased use of digital. Sleep disturbance is a highly important outcome predictor of mental outcomes (= 0.43, $p < 0.001$), hence its terribly critical status as a mediator of outcomes.

The positive relationship between too much digital use and mental health outcomes remains significant (0.29, p<|human|>The positive association between too much use of digital and the outcomes in terms of mental health remains (0.29, p<|human|).

equalling 0.001) by statistics demonstrating a partial mediation. This high order of the indirect effect is another confirmation that the sleep disturbance is a key psychological mechanism through which digital overuse provided a rise in the degree of anxiety, depression, and the sleep disorders.

As per the SEM analysis on AMOS, the H 0 is accepted. Excessive digital use has negative mental health outcomes that are detrimental in health due to their direct and indirect consequences on the individual, caused by sleep disturbance and a high rate of undesirable mental health events. The model confirms the hypothesis that age-sensitive and sleep-based interventions on digital wellbeing are important and the model proves the significance of making the digital overexposure a component of a cascade of psychological and psychological effects.

SOLUTIONS AND RECOMMENDATIONS

Taking into account the findings of the given work, that demonstrate that overusing the digital world is a key factor in high rates of poor mental health, including its manifestations in anxiety, depression, and sleeping disorders, the latter of which partially mediates between two, it is possible to formulate a number of feasible solutions and recommendations. Both are the interventions that will target individuals, families, education institution, workplaces, and policy-makers and minimize the negative psychological effects of excessive exposure to digital content.

1. Individual-Level Interventions:

Digital Detox and Management of Usage: Ask users to monitor and monitor the consumption of the screen, particularly in social media, games, and streaming sites on a daily basis. Such tools may help to have self-regulation, app timers, usage notifications, or built-in in the screen-time monitoring.

Hygiene Practices to Sleep: Behavior that puts emphasis on the quality of sleep such as switching off the screens at least an hour before going to sleep, getting sleep and making the bedroom a technology free environment.

Mindfulness and Stress Reduction: A few methods that can be employed in reducing anxiety and emotional responsiveness regarding being overly dependent on digital technology include meditation, deep breathing, and journaling.

2. The interventions (Family and Educational):

Parental Direction and Supervising: When referring to children and teens, the parents are supposed to define the rules of the amount of time that should be spent on a screen, encourage offline activities, and provide a positive example of using the Internet.

The Digital Literacy and the Emotional Education Digital literacy programs to be taught comprehensively with the goal of teaching how to use the devices responsibly, how to judge and select the types of negative and positive content on the internet and how to deal with the skills of managing online social pressure should be included in schools. Emotional education can help the adolescents to endure the effects of identity stress and peer comparison through means of effort.

3. Workplace Interventions:

The two are to promote work-life boundaries by ensuring that employees have a policy that they cannot access the Internet past the work-day, and they should also have regular breaks that deter burnout.

Organizational initiatives: In order to prevent stress and sleep fluctuations in young and middle-aged adults, it would be appropriate to introduce digital wellbeing, stress-management workshops and mental health awareness workshops.

4. It is important to consider that technologizing can be applied in productive solutions that can solve the problems and challenges that the organization deals with.

Human-Centered Design on a Platform: Designers and developers should have in mind those features that promote healthy usage and not the type of addictive usage. They involve customized notification, reminders and time allocation warning.

Probability of the Openness of AI Algorithms: AI-based applications also cannot be centered around attacking and persuasive algorithms of making people perceive it as a natural routine and a form of dependency.

5. Policy-Level Recommendations:

However, studies have given evidence which can be employed to minimize the harmful effects of overuse of digital games and allow evidence-based interventions.

Digital Platforms: The regulations could include a request that there be translucency in the content delivered by AI, age suitable versions and limitations to capabilities that may be entertaining to vulnerable sections of the community particularly teens.

6. Research and Monitoring:

Longitudinal Studies: Becoming a barbarian. Research into the effects of continuous exposure to digital effects on mental health at different stages in life should be supported.

Specific Interventions: The interventions to be developed will be specific to an adolescent and young adult age, since the analysis of the study has found this cohort of people to be the most prone to irrational consequences of the overuse of the digital media.

The negative mental health outcomes of excessive digital consumption ought to be minimized via a comprehensive approach containing self-regulation, education, organization, technology design management, and the community health in a person-centered approach. Such solutions might be implemented and utilized to enhance the level of emotional wellbeing, social connectedness, and the quality of life in the digital age through the promotion of motivated and healthy digital interactions through the mitigation of sleep disturbance as one of the most critical mediating factors and promoting awareness about the psychological risks associated with excessive digital age.

FUTURE RESEARCH DIRECTIONS

According to the findings of the suggested study, some possibilities of the future research could be identified to deepen the background knowledge of excessive Internet use and its psychological consequences, in particular, to the setting of the evolving technologies, such as the metaverse and AI-powered platforms.

1. Longitudinal Studies:

The existing literature on the subject and this study rely on cross-sectional studies which provide an idea of correlations of digital use and mental health outcomes. The next step of the research, which is to be conducted in the future, must be longitudinal one, focusing on the causation between changes in digital habits and their effect in the course of time, the patterns of digital habits changes, and their turnings at different periods of the life cycle. Such studies can also be conducted on developmental processes of children and adolescents as their cognitive and emotional controls function undergo rapid transformation.

2. Specific Age and Developmental:

Though this research seems to show the differences between different age groups, the research could be projected further in the future, to sub-stages of development, namely, in adolescence and early adulthood stages. Potentially, the relationship between digital exposure with neurobiological, social, and emotional variables will be studied to receive an insight on the interventions and preventive strategy of the right age. Similarly, a study within the geriatric population could examine the cognitive capacity and social acclimatization to the technological insularity.

3. The future writing

and reading occurs through the use of Immersive Technologies and the Metaverse: With the promotion of the application of immersion-based digital platforms and virtual reality, understanding the effects of highly engaging platforms on both emotional wellbeing and social wellbeing is the direction that researchers should move in their future research. The psychological impacts of a communication meditated by avatars, a virtual social presence, and gamified experiences could be researched and examined by confirming whether these immersive experiences add or improve mental health outcomes relative to the previous use of digital platforms.

4. In between and Ranging Factors:

The level of sleep disturbance in this research was identified to be a key mediator but other potential mediators and moderators ought to be examined. As one of them, it is possible to mention emotional control skills, social support, personality traits, and coping strategies, which might contribute to the strength of digital use and mental health relationship. Similarly, the moderating factors, e.g. socioeconomic status, cultural context, or type of digital activity (e.g. social media, gaming, learning), can be adjusted so that the lens on the risk factors becomes less broad.

5. Interdisciplinary Approaches:

In order to improve research techniques, such techniques that comprise interdisciplinary perspectives incorporating psychology, neuroscience, communication, studies, digital ethics, and human-computer interaction must be taken into consideration in the future studies on research. Such techniques can potentially provide information on the importance of technology in thinking, feeling and social behaviour in depth to institute more holistic response interventions.

6. Intervention-Based Research:

Despite the risks found in this research, it can be recommended in the future to consider the interventions that can be used to prevent the excessive use of digital or mitigate the negative impact of excessive use in a study. The experimental designs of the research to test the digital detox programs, sleep hygiene education, mindful use of the technology, or the impacts of AI-based wellbeing functionalities may provide the evidence-based responses to the stimulation of mental health in the online environment.

7. Intercultural Interrelations and World perspectives:

Cultural and social settings may not have the same use of digital technology and its psychological influence. International comparison studies among countries, cultures and policy environments have the potential to illuminate contextual dimensions that lead to vulnerability, resilience and adaptive mechanisms in negotiating with digital engagement.

To be more informative on the dynamics of using digital and mental health, the future research must be longitudinal, interdisciplinary, and cultural issues must be incorporated. Using the study of immersive technologies, mediating and moderating processes and facilitating the evidence-based development of interventions, researchers can design actionable knowledge in order to guarantee healthy digital interaction on the levels of different ages, a phenomenon that causes emotionally sustainable and anthropocentric digital futures.

CONCLUSION

The current research illuminates the critical psychological influence of excessive application of digital application during the lifespan which is positively associated with the adverse mental health results including trepidation, melancholy and sleep disorder. The findings confirm that sleep disruption is one of the critical mediating mechanisms, which to some degree, supports the importance of prolonged and compulsive consumption of digital gadgets in the enhancement of emotional and mental pressure. The age-specific effects indicate that the most vulnerable to them are adolescents and young adults whose effects of mediation are most pronounced, and children, middle-aged adults, and elderly people display significant albeit, moderately significant effects.

These insights are placed into the broader context of AI-informed social media, immersive technology and the emerging metaverse presented in the paper, and point out that digital communications occupy more, and more, of qualitative human interaction, social interaction, and the emotional response. This mental breakdown augments the threats of susceptibility especially the vulnerable group that faces the emergence or declining emotional regulation skills.

The mixed-method format as well as the use of surveys, clinical interviews, digital analytics and the mediation model involving AMOS provides a good and inter-disciplinary analytic view on the complexity of the interaction between mental health and digital use. The facts provide emphasis to such existence of different levels of intervention which are individual response level, family level, education level, work-level, technology and policy to minimise the negative impacts of digital overexposure.

In conclusion, the uncontrollable and excessive use of digital technologies may deteriorate the state of emotions and even the health of sleep, creating a chain reaction on the mental state, it cannot be denied that the digital technologies provide opportunities in this direction that do not always contribute positively to the state of a person. To address this issue, age-sensitive and evidence-based interventions are to be taken into consideration and involve healthy digital behaviours, sleep habits formation, and technology use and exposure reduction and face to face interaction enhancement. The research not only proves the hypothesis that the excessive use of the digital can result in an undesirable outcome in mental health of individuals, but it also provides sensible recommendations of how sustainable and people-centric digital workplaces with a focus on emotional health and holistic wellbeing should be designed.

REFERENCES

Arya, V., Sambyal, R., Sharma, A., & Dwivedi, Y. K. (2024). Brands are calling your avatar in the metaverse: A study to explore XR-based gamification marketing activities and consumer-based brand equity in virtual world. *Journal of Consumer Behaviour, 23*(5), 556–585. DOI: 10.1002/cb.2214

Barrera, K. G., & Shah, D. (2023). Marketing in the metaverse: Conceptual understanding, framework, and research agenda. *Journal of Business Research, 155*, 113420. DOI: 10.1016/j.jbusres.2022.113420

Bhambri, P. (2024). Innovative systems: Entertainment, gaming, and the metaverse. In *Innovative Systems* (pp. 483–514). IGI Global., DOI: 10.4018/979-8-3693-5668-5.ch018

Buhalis, D., Lin, M. S., & Leung, D. (2023). Metaverse as a driver for customer experience and value co-creation: Implications for hospitality and tourism management and marketing. *International Journal of Contemporary Hospitality Management, 35*(3), 701–716. DOI: 10.1108/IJCHM-05-2022-0631

Frank, D.-A., Peschel, A. O., Otterbring, T., DiPalma, J., & Steinmann, S. (2024). Does metaverse fidelity matter? Testing the impact of fidelity on consumer responses in virtual retail stores. *International Review of Retail, Distribution and Consumer Research, 34*(3), 251–284. DOI: 10.1080/09593969.2024.2304810

Gadalla, E., Keeling, K., & Abosag, I. (2013). Metaverse-retail service quality: A future framework for retail service quality in the 3D internet. *Journal of Marketing Management, 9*, 1493–1517. DOI: 10.1080/0267257X.2013.835742

Habil, S. G. M., El-Deeb, S., & El-Bassiouny, N. (2024). The metaverse era: Leveraging augmented reality in the creation of novel customer experience. *Management and Sustainability: An Arab Review, 3*(1), 1–15. DOI: 10.1108/MSAR-10-2022-0051

Hennig-Thurau, T., Aliman, D. N., Herting, A. M., Cziehso, G., Linder, M., & Kübler, R. V. (2023). Social interactions in the metaverse: Framework, initial evidence, and research roadmap. *Journal of the Academy of Marketing Science, 51*(5), 889–913. DOI: 10.1007/s11747-022-00908-0

Khan, J., Tao, M., & Abbass, A. (2025). Digital doppelgänger: Navigating consumer brand engagement in the metaverse. *Journal of Research in Interactive Marketing*. Advance online publication. DOI: 10.1108/JRIM-07-2024-0344

Mansoor, S., Rahman, S. M., & Bowden, J. L. (2024). Purchase spillovers from the metaverse to the real world: The roles of social presence, trialability, and customer experience. *Journal of Consumer Behaviour*, *25*(12), 2501–2552. DOI: 10.1002/cb.2353

Mystakidis, S. (2022). Metaverse. In *Encyclopedia, 2,* 486–497. https://doi.org/DOI: 10.3390/encyclopedia2010031

Natarajan, T., Pragha, P., & Dhalmahapatra, K. (2024). Uses and gratifications of metaverse: Understanding the user adoption factors through a mixed method approach. *Asia Pacific Journal of Marketing and Logistics*, *36*(12), 2978–3006. DOI: 10.1108/APJML-03-2024-0395

Oh, H. J., Kim, J., Chang, J. J. C., Park, N., & Lee, S. (2023). Social benefits of living in the metaverse: The relationships among social presence, supportive interaction, social self-efficacy, and feelings of loneliness. *Computers in Human Behavior*, *139*, 107498. DOI: 10.1016/j.chb.2022.107498

Simmel, G. (1949). The sociology of sociability. *American Journal of Sociology*, *55*(3), 254–261. DOI: 10.1086/220534 PMID: 15400080

Tombul, I., & Sari, G. (2021). Transformation of self-presentation in virtual space. *İletişim Kuram ve Araştırma Dergisi, 53,* 93–108. https://doi.org/DOI: 10.47998/ikad.852841

Voinea, C., Earp, B. D., Mann, S., & Savulescu, J. (2024). Digital doppelgängers, human relationships, and practical identity. *Philosophy & Technology*, *37*, 121. DOI: 10.1007/s13347-024-00813-0

Wang, G., Zhang, Z., Nandhakumar, J., & Manoharan, N. (2025). Everyday metaverse: The metaverse as an integral part of everyday life. *Journal of Management Information Systems*, *42*(3), 310–342. DOI: 10.1080/07421222.2025.2455772

Yang, H. (2024). The genesis effect: Digital goods in the metaverse. *The Journal of Consumer Research*, *51*(1), 129–139. DOI: 10.1093/jcr/ucad072

Compilation of References

Abaddi, S. (2025). AI–human data hybridization: a hybrid approach to unveiling global entrepreneurial motivations, challenges and opportunities. Journal of Ethics in Entrepreneurship and Technology.

Abbas, F., Chesterman, S., & Taeihagh, A. (2025). Building trust in the generative AI era: A systematic review of global regulatory frameworks to combat the risks of mis-, dis-, and mal-information. *AI & Society*. Advance online publication. DOI: 10.1007/s00146-025-02698-9

Abraham, J., Cruz, G., Cubela, S., Lajous, T., Rowshankish, K., Tiwari, S., & Zemmel, R. (2022). Digital twins — the foundation of the enterprise metaverse. McKinsey & Company. https://www.mckinsey.com/capabilities/tech-and-ai/our-insights/digital-twins-the-foundation-of-the-enterprise-metaverse

Abraham, J., Cruz, G., Cubela, S., Lajous, T., Rowshankish, K., Tiwari, S., & Zemmel, R. (2022, October). Digital twins: The foundation of the enterprise metaverse. McKinsey & Company. https://www.mckinsey.com/capabilities/tech-and-ai/our-insights/digital-twins-the-foundation-of-the-enterprise-metaverse

Acemoglu, D., & Lensman, T. (2024). Regulating transformative technologies. *American Economic Review: Insights*, *6*(3), 359–376. DOI: 10.1257/aeri.20230353

Agbavor, F., & Liang, H. (2022). Predicting dementia from spontaneous speech using large language models. *PLOS Digital Health*, *1*(12), e0000168. DOI: 10.1371/journal.pdig.0000168 PMID: 36812634

Aggarwal, A., Sadhna, P., & Daipuria, P. (2025). The Digital Frontier: AI and Metaverse as Catalysts for Organizational Justice and Employee Engagement in EdTech. *Global Business Review, 09721509251344444*. Advance online publication. DOI: 10.1177/09721509251344444

Agrawal, M., Chen, I. Y., Gulamali, F., & Joshi, S. (2025). The evaluation illusion of large language models in medicine. *NPJ Digital Medicine*, *8*(1), 600. DOI: 10.1038/s41746-025-01963-x

Aguiñaga, J., Mooradian, N., Ghosh, S., & Hofman, D. (2025). Evolution of Reference Services in the Era of Generative Artificial Intelligence. *Proceedings of the Association for Information Science and Technology*, *62*(1), 13–25. DOI: 10.1002/pra2.1232

Ahmed, F., & Iqbal, A. (2025). The role of artificial intelligence in enhancing credit risk management: A systematic literature review of international banking systems. *Pakistan Journal of Humanities and Social Sciences*, *13*(1), 478–492.

Ahmed, S., Sharif, T., Ting, D. H., & Sharif, S. J. (2024). Crafting emotional engagement and immersive experiences: Comprehensive scale development for and validation of hospitality marketing storytelling involvement. *Psychology and Marketing*, *41*(7), 1514–1529. DOI: 10.1002/mar.21994

AI Act enters into force. (2024). *AI Act enters into force*. EU. https://commission.europa.eu/news-and-media/news/ai-act-enters-force-2024-08-01_en

Akhundov, A. (2025). The Role of Ethics in Modern Technology Development. *Porta Universorum*, *1*(4), 169–177. DOI: 10.69760/portuni.0104017

Al Amrani, Y., Lazaar, M., & El Kadiri, K. E. (2018). Random forest and support vector machine based hybrid approach to sentiment analysis. *Procedia Computer Science*, *127*, 511–520. DOI: 10.1016/j.procs.2018.01.150

Al Machot, F., Horsch, M. T., & Ullah, H. (2025). Building trustworthy AI: Transparent AI systems via language models, ontologies, and logical reasoning (TranspNet). In F. Al Machot, M. T. Horsch, & S. Scholze (Eds.), *Designing the conceptual landscape for a XAIR validation infrastructure* (Lecture Notes in Networks and Systems, Vol. 1375). Springer. https://doi.org/DOI: 10.1007/978-3-031-89274-5_3

Alaali, H. (2025). DFAS Doctrine Compendium: Philosophical, Strategic, and Systemic Frameworks for AI Governance, Crisis Intervention, and Algorithmic Control. https://papers.ssrn.com/sol3/papers.cfm?abstract_id=5367894

Al-Adaileh, A., Al-Kfairy, M., Tubishat, M., & Alfandi, O. (2024). A sentiment analysis approach for understanding users' perception of metaverse marketplace. *Intelligent Systems with Applications*, *22*, 200362. DOI: 10.1016/j.iswa.2024.200362

Al-Adwan, A. S., Yaseen, H., Alkhwaldi, A. F., Jafar, R. M. S., Fauzi, M. A., & Abdullah, A. (2025). Treasure hunting for brands: Metaverse marketing gamification effects on purchase intention, WOM, and loyalty. *Journal of Global Marketing*, •••, 1–25. DOI: 10.1080/08911762.2025.2463897

Ali, M., Naeem, F., Kaddoum, G., & Hossain, E. (2023). Metaverse communications, networking, security, and applications: Research issues, state-of-the-art, and future directions. *IEEE Communications Surveys and Tutorials*, *26*(2), 1238–1278. DOI: 10.1109/COMST.2023.3347172

Ali, U., & Mahmood, T. (2022). *A Novel Framework for Concept Drift Detection using Autoencoders for Classification Problems in Data Streams*. Qeios Ltd., DOI: 10.32388/zu17s4

Aljamaan, F., Temsah, M. H., Altamimi, I., Al-Eyadhy, A., Jamal, A., Alhasan, K., Mesallam, T. A., Farahat, M., & Malki, K. H. (2024). Reference Hallucination Score for medical artificial intelligence chatbots: Development and usability study. *JMIR Medical Informatics*, *12*, e54345. Advance online publication. DOI: 10.2196/54345

Allen, D., Hubbard, S., Lim, W., Stanger, A., Wagman, S., Zalesne, K., & Omoakhalen, O. (2025). A roadmap for governing AI: Technology governance and power-sharing liberalism. *AI and Ethics*, *5*(3), 3355–3377. DOI: 10.1007/s43681-024-00635-y

Allen, J. G., Loo, J., & Campoverde, J. L. L. (2024). Governing intelligence: Singapore's evolving AI governance framework. *Cambridge Forum on AI: Law and Governance*, *1*. Advance online publication. DOI: 10.1017/cfl.2024.12

Almeida, L. G. G., Vasconcelos, N. V. D., Winkler, I., & Catapan, M. F. (2023). Innovating Industrial Training with Immersive Metaverses: A Method for Developing Cross-Platform Virtual Reality Environments. *Applied Sciences (Basel, Switzerland)*, *13*(15), 8915. DOI: 10.3390/app13158915

Al-Naseri, N. (2021). The role of human oversight in ai-driven fintech. *Australian Journal of Machine Learning Research & Applications*, *1*(1), 297–317.

Aloqaily, M., Bouachir, O., Karray, F., Al Ridhawi, I., & El Saddik, A. (2022). *Integrating Digital Twin and Advanced Intelligent Technologies to Realize the Metaverse*. arXiv. /arXiv.2210.04606DOI: 10.48550

Al-Romeedy, B. S., Hussein, H., Emam, M. E., & Singh, A. (2025). From Potential to Peril: Evaluating AI and the Metaverse in Modern Research. In Al Aqad, M., Sorayyaei Azar, A., Albattat, A., & Singh, A. (Eds.), *Navigating AI and the Metaverse in Scientific Research* (pp. 563–584). IGI Global Scientific Publishing., DOI: 10.4018/979-8-3373-0340-6.ch027

Alsaigh, R., Mehmood, R., & Katib, I. (2023). AI explainability and governance in smart energy systems: A review. *Frontiers in Energy Research, 11*, 1071291. DOI: 10.3389/fenrg.2023.1071291

Alshehri, A. (2025). Developing a multi-layer agent framework to enhance AI-generated educational questions for cybersecurity. *Journal of Umm Al-Qura University for Engineering and Architecture, 16*, 1045–1056. DOI: 10.1007/s43995-025-00136-x

Althaf, A. M., Mohammed, M. A., Milanova, M., Talburt, J., & Cakmak, M. C. (2025). Multi-Agent RAG Framework for Entity Resolution: Advancing Beyond Single-LLM Approaches with Specialized Agent Coordination. *Computers, 14*(12), 525. DOI: 10.3390/computers14120525

Amalia, D., Artini, Y. D., Rahayu, G. N., Purnomo, H., & Zaman, B. (2024). Optimizing Organizational Capabilities Through The Integration Of Strategic Management And Human Resource Performance. *Int J Econ Lit, 2*, 216–228.

Amirizaniani, M., Lavergne, A., Okada, E. S., Chadha, A., Roosta, T., & Shah, C. (2025). Developing a framework for auditing large language models using human-in-the-loop. In *Proceedings of the 2025 Annual International ACM SIGIR Conference on Research and Development in Information Retrieval in the Asia Pacific Region (SIGIR-AP 2025)* (pp. 64–74). https://doi.org/DOI: 10.1145/3767695.376951

Amirizaniani, M., Martin, E., Roosta, T., Chadha, A., & Shah, C. (2024). AuditLLM: A tool for auditing large language models using multiprobe approach. In *Proceedings of the 33rd ACM International Conference on Information and Knowledge Management* (pp. 5174–5179). ACM. https://doi.org/DOI: 10.1145/3627673.3679222

Anaokar, S., Ganatra, S., Kashid, H., Bhattacharyya, S., Nair, S., Sekhar, R., Manohar, S., Hemrajani, R., & Bhattacharyya, P. (2025, September 15). *HalluDetect: Detecting, mitigating, and benchmarking hallucinations in conversational systems in the legal domain.* arXiv.Org. https://arxiv.org/abs/2509.11619

André, Q., Carmon, Z., Wertenbroch, K., Crum, A., Frank, D., Goldstein, W., Huber, J., Van Boven, L., Weber, B., & Yang, H. (2018). Consumer Choice and Autonomy in the Age of Artificial Intelligence and Big Data. *Customer Needs and Solutions, 5*(1–2), 28–37. DOI: 10.1007/s40547-017-0085-8

Andrew, J., & Baker, M. (2021). The General Data Protection Regulation in the Age of Surveillance Capitalism. *Journal of Business Ethics, 168*(3), 565–578. DOI: 10.1007/s10551-019-04239-z

Anh-Hoang, D., Tran, V., & Nguyen, L. M. (2025). Survey and analysis of hallucinations in large language models: Attribution to prompting strategies or model behavior. *Frontiers in Artificial Intelligence*, *8*, 1622292. DOI: 10.3389/frai.2025.1622292

Anisuzzaman, D. M., Malins, J. G., Friedman, P. A., & Attia, Z. I. (2025). Fine-tuning large language models for specialized use cases. *Mayo Clinic Proceedings. Digital Health*, *3*(1), 100184. DOI: 10.1016/j.mcpdig.2024.11.005

Ansari, A. I., & Singh, A. (2023). Application of Augmented Reality (AR) and Virtual Reality (VR) in Promoting Guest Room Sales: A Critical Review. In Impact of Industry 4.0 on Sustainable Tourism: Perspectives, Challenges and Future (pp. 95–104). https://doi.org/DOI: 10.1108/978-1-80455-157-820231006

Anwar, N., Widodo, A. M., Widodo, Y. B., Sekti, B. A., Laksono, M. N. G., & Laksono, M. I. A. (2025). Protecting digital assets in cloud environments. In *Unveiling Social Dynamics and Community Interaction in the Metaverse* (pp. 245–269). https://doi.org/DOI: 10.4018/979-8-3693-8628-6.ch012

Ara, A., & Ahmad, A. K. (2025). Building Trust in AI-Driven HR Systems: Employee Perceptions for AI-HR. *2025 Eighth International Women in Data Science Conference at Prince Sultan University (WiDS PSU)*, 241–249. DOI: 10.1109/WiDS-PSU64963.2025.00055

Articsledge. (2025). *AI Fraud Detection in Banking: The Complete 2025 Guide*. Articsledge. https://www.articsledge.com/post/ai-fraud-detection-banking

Arya, V., Sambyal, R., Sharma, A., & Dwivedi, Y. K. (2024). Brands are calling your avatar in the metaverse: A study to explore XR-based gamification marketing activities and consumer-based brand equity in virtual world. *Journal of Consumer Behaviour*, *23*(5), 556–585. DOI: 10.1002/cb.2214

Asad, M., & Otoum, S. (2024). Federated Learning for Personalized User Experiences in the Metaverse. *2024 2nd International Conference on Intelligent Metaverse Technologies & Applications (IMETA)*, 050–055. https://doi.org/DOI: 10.1109/iMETA62882.2024.10807979

Asgari, E., Montaña-Brown, N., Dubois, M., Khalil, S., Balloch, J., Yeung, J. A., & Pimenta, D. (2025). A framework to assess clinical safety and hallucination rates of LLMs for medical text summarisation. *npj. Digital Medicine*, *8*, 274. DOI: 10.1038/s41746-025-01670-7

Autor, D. H. (2015). Why are there still so many jobs? The history and future of workplace automation. *The Journal of Economic Perspectives*, *29*(3), 3–30.

Ayanponle, L. O., Awonuga, K. F., Asuzu, O. F., Daraojimba, R. E., Elufioye, O. A., & Daraojimba, O. D. (2024). A review of innovative HR strategies in enhancing workforce efficiency in the US. *International Journal of Science and Research Archive*, *11*(1), 817–827.

Azzam, I., Bello, K., Breidi, F. E., & Aqlan, F. (2025). Analysis of user experience in extended reality: A comparative study of VR and MR for manufacturing training. *Manufacturing Letters*, *46*, 77–82. DOI: 10.1016/j.mfglet.2025.10.003

Bae, S. H., & Bae, J. (2025). How experiential creation drives use experience in the metaverse: Focused on the interaction effect between item popularity and need for uniqueness. *Journal of Global Scholars of Marketing Science*, *35*(2), 197–207. DOI: 10.1080/21639159.2025.2468471

Bai, Y., Kadavath, S., Kundu, S., Askell, A., Kernion, J., Jones, A., Chen, A., Goldie, A., Mirhoseini, A., McKinnon, C., Chen, C., Olsson, C., Olah, C., Hernandez, D., Drain, D., Ganguli, D., Li, D., Tran-Johnson, E., Perez, E., . . . Kaplan, J. (2022, December 15). *Constitutional AI: Harmlessness from AI feedback*. arXiv.Org. https://arxiv.org/abs/2212.08073

Ballew, M. T., Omoto, A. M., & Winter, P. L. (2015). Using Web 2.0 and social media technologies to foster proenvironmental action. *Sustainability*, *7*(8), 10620–10648. DOI: 10.3390/su70810620

Balogun, A. Y., Metibemu, O. C., Olutimehin, A. T., Ajayi, A. J., Babarinde, D. C., & Olaniyi, O. O. (2025). The ethical and legal implications of shadow AI in sensitive industries: A focus on healthcare, finance and education. *Finance and Education (February 13, 2025)*.

Baltrušaitis, T., Ahuja, C., & Morency, L. P. (2018). Multimodal machine learning: A survey and taxonomy. *IEEE Transactions on Pattern Analysis and Machine Intelligence*, *41*(2), 423–443.

Bang, Y., Ji, Z., Schelten, A., Hartshorn, A., Fowler, T., Zhang, C., Cancedda, N., & Fung, P. (2025, April 24). *HalluLens: LLM hallucination benchmark*. arXiv.Org. https://arxiv.org/abs/2504.17550

Banker, S., & Khetani, S. (2019). Algorithm Overdependence: How the Use of Algorithmic Recommendation Systems Can Increase Risks to Consumer Well-Being. *Journal of Public Policy & Marketing*, *38*(4), 500–515. DOI: 10.1177/0743915619858057

Barker, D., Tippireddy, M. K. R., Farhan, A., & Ahmed, B. (2025). Ethical Considerations in Emotion Recognition Research. *Psychological Inquiry*, *7*(2), 43. DOI: 10.3390/psycholint7020043

Barnett, P., & Thiergart, L. (2024, November 19). *Declare and Justify: Explicit assumptions in AI evaluations are necessary for effective regulation.* arXiv.Org. https://arxiv.org/abs/2411.12820

Barocas, S., & Selbst, A. D. (2016). Big data's disparate impact. *California Law Review, 104*, 671–732.

Barón, M. M. (2025). Towards an Adoption Framework to Foster Trust in AI-Assisted Software Engineering. 2025 IEEE/ACM 4th International Conference on AI Engineering – Software Engineering for AI (CAIN), 247–249. DOI: 10.1109/CAIN66642.2025.00038

Barredo Arrieta, A., Díaz-Rodríguez, N., Del Ser, J., Bennetot, A., Tabik, S., Barbado, A., Garcia, S., Gil-Lopez, S., Molina, D., Benjamins, R., Chatila, R., & Herrera, F. (2020). Explainable Artificial Intelligence (XAI): Concepts, taxonomies, opportunities and challenges toward responsible AI. *Information Fusion, 58*, 82–115. DOI: 10.1016/j.inffus.2019.12.012

Barrera, K. G., & Shah, D. (2023). Marketing in the Metaverse: Conceptual understanding, framework, and research agenda. *Journal of Business Research, 155*, 113420. DOI: 10.1016/j.jbusres.2022.113420

Basyoni, L., Qayyum, A., Shaban, K., Elmahjub, E., Al-Ali, A., Halabi, O., & Qadir, J. (2025). Generative AI-Driven Metaverse: The Promises and Challenges of AI-Generated Content. *IEEE Open Journal of the Computer Society*. Advance online publication. DOI: 10.1109/OJCS.2025.3616501

Batool, A., Zowghi, D., & Bano, M. (2025). AI governance: A systematic literature review. *AI and Ethics, 5*, 3265–3279. DOI: 10.1007/s43681-024-00653-w

Béchard, P., & Ayala, O. M. (2024, April 12). *Reducing hallucination in structured outputs via Retrieval-Augmented Generation*. arXiv.Org. https://arxiv.org/abs/2404.08189

Bhambri, P. (2024). Innovative systems: Entertainment, gaming, and the metaverse. In *Innovative Systems* (pp. 483–514). IGI Global., DOI: 10.4018/979-8-3693-5668-5.ch018

Bhattacharyya, A., Yu, Y., Yang, H., Singh, R., Joshi, T., Chen, J., & Yalavarthy, K. (2025). Model risk management for generative ai in financial institutions. *arXiv preprint arXiv:2503.15668.*

Bhattacharyya, A., Yu, Y., Yang, H., Singh, R., Joshi, T., Chen, J., & Yalavarthy, K. (2025, March 19). *Model risk management for generative AI in financial institutions*. arXiv.Org. https://arxiv.org/abs/2503.15668

Bigman, Y. E., & Gray, K. (2018). People are averse to machines making moral decisions. *Cognition*, *181*, 21–34. DOI: 10.1016/j.cognition.2018.08.003 PMID: 30107256

Bing, Z. (2025). The Intrinsic Tension Between Rationalism and Emotionalism: On the Modernity Connotations of Artificial Intelligence and the Metaverse. *Contemporary Social Science*, *10*(2), 88–102. DOI: 10.19873/j.cnki.2096-0212.2025.02.006

Blut, M., Wang, C., Wünderlich, N. V., & Brock, C. (2021). Understanding anthropomorphism in service provision: A meta-analysis of physical robots, chatbots, and other AI. *Journal of the Academy of Marketing Science*, *49*(4), 632–658. DOI: 10.1007/s11747-020-00762-y

Böckle, M., Reuter, C., & Qin, S. (2023). Metaverse Business Models and Framework: A Systematic Search with Narrative Synthesis. *Systems*, *13*(11), 968. DOI: 10.3390/systems1311968

Bodini, M. (2024). Generative artificial intelligence and regulations: Can we plan a resilient journey toward the safe application of generative artificial intelligence? *Societies (Basel, Switzerland)*, *14*(12), 268. DOI: 10.3390/soc14120268

Bolsiek, K. M. C. (2024). What factors influence the acceptance of metaverse technology in financial advisory services for the South African financial sector [Master's Thesis, University of Pretoria (South Africa)]. https://search.proquest.com/openview/bb46ffdca5ef2835068d39aa1a9a70ea/1?pq-origsite=gscholar&cbl=2026366&diss=y

Borch, C., & Min, B. H. (2022). Machine learning and social action in markets: From first- to second-generation automated trading. *Economy and Society*, *52*(1), 37–61. DOI: 10.1080/03085147.2022.2050088

Bordegoni, M., & Ferrise, F. (2023). Exploring the Intersection of Metaverse, Digital Twins, and Artificial Intelligence in Training and Maintenance. *Journal of Computing and Information Science in Engineering*, *23*(6), 060806. DOI: 10.1115/1.4062455

Borenstein, J., & Arkin, R. (2016). Robotic Nudges: The Ethics of Engineering a More Socially Just Human Being. *Science and Engineering Ethics*, *22*(1), 31–46. DOI: 10.1007/s11948-015-9636-2 PMID: 25736832

Bottazzi Grifoni, E., & Ferrario, R. (2025). The bewitching AI: The illusion of communication with large language models. *Philosophy & Technology*, *38*, 61. DOI: 10.1007/s13347-025-00893-6

Bozkurt, S., Uğursoy, A. S., & Meral, S. P. (2025). The Impact of Personalized Messages and Designs on Consumer Experiences and Marketing Communications in Technology: Hyper-Personalization. In *Impact of Contemporary Technology on Art and Design* (pp. 135–164). IGI Global., DOI: 10.4018/979-8-3693-4318-0.ch007

Boztas, C., Ghadafi, E., & Ibrahim, R. (2025). Metaverse Architectures: A Comprehensive Systematic Review of Definitions and Frameworks. *Future Internet*, *17*(7), 283. DOI: 10.3390/fi17070283

Brandebusemeyer, C. (2025). Interactions with Generative AI: Wearables to Measure Developer Experience and Productivity Objectively. In 2025 IEEE/ACM 47th International Conference on Software Engineering: Companion Proceedings (ICSE-Companion) (pp. 148–150). IEEE. DOI: 10.1109/ICSE-Companion66252.2025.00043

Brenneis, A. (2025). Assessing dual use risks in AI research: Necessity, challenges and mitigation strategies. *Research Ethics*, *21*(2), 302–330. DOI: 10.1177/17470161241267782

Brewer, J., Patel, D., Kim, D., & Murray, A. (2024). Navigating the challenges of generative technologies: Proposing the integration of artificial intelligence and blockchain. *Business Horizons*, *67*(5), 525–535.

Brown, A., Roman, M., & Devereux, B. (2025). A systematic literature review of retrieval-augmented generation: Techniques, metrics, and challenges. *Big Data and Cognitive Computing*, *9*(12), 320. DOI: 10.3390/bdcc9120320

Brown, T. B., Mann, B., Ryder, N., Subbiah, M., Kaplan, J., Dhariwal, P., & Amodei, D. (2020). Language models are few-shot learners. *Advances in Neural Information Processing Systems*, *33*, 1877–1901.

Bruni, R., & Galvagno, M. (2025). Virtual reality, authentic motivations: A classification of metaverse users based on VR/XR headset experience. *Electronic Commerce Research*, •••, 1–25. DOI: 10.1007/s10660-025-09970-6

Brynjolfsson, E., Li, D., & Raymond, L. (2023). *Generative AI at work* (NBER Working Paper No. 31161). National Bureau of Economic Research. https://doi.org/DOI: 10.3386/w31161

Brynjolfsson, E., & McAfee, A. (2017). The business of artificial intelligence. *Harvard Business Review*, *95*(4), 3–11.

Buhalis, D., Lin, M. S., & Leung, D. (2023). Metaverse as a driver for customer experience and value co-creation: Implications for hospitality and tourism management and marketing. *International Journal of Contemporary Hospitality Management, 35*(3), 701–716. DOI: 10.1108/IJCHM-05-2022-0631

Bussmann, N., Giudici, P., Marinelli, D., & Papenbrock, J. (2020). Explainable AI in Fintech risk management. *Frontiers in Artificial Intelligence*, *3*, 26. DOI: 10.3389/frai.2020.00026

Cai, L., Yu, C., Kang, Y., Fu, Y., Zhang, H., & Zhao, Y. (2025). Practices, opportunities and challenges in the fusion of knowledge graphs and large language models. *Frontiers in Computer Science, 7*, Section Human-Media Interaction. https://doi.org/DOI: 10.3389/fcomp.2025.1590632

Cai, W., & Gao, M. (2025). Beyond hallucination: Generative AI as a catalyst for human creativity and cognitive evolution. *ICCK Transactions on Emerging Topics in Artificial Intelligence*, *2*(1), 36–42. DOI: 10.62762/TETAI.2025.657559

Calvo, R. A., & D'Mello, S. (2010). Affect detection: An interdisciplinary review of models, methods, and their applications. *IEEE Transactions on Affective Computing*, *1*(1), 18–37.

Carr, N. (2014). *The glass cage: Automation and us*. W. W. Norton & Company.

Chakrabarti, M., Fabozzi, F. J., Narain, A., & Sood, A. (2025). Ethical AI in Asset Management: Frameworks for Transparency, Compliance, and Trust. *The Journal of Financial Data Science*, *7*(1), 18–35. DOI: 10.3905/jfds.2025.7.1.018

Chakraborty, S., Chowdhury, R., Shuvo, S. R., Chatterjee, R., & Roy, S. (2025). A scalable framework for evaluating multiple language models through cross-domain generation and hallucination detection. *Scientific Reports*, *15*, 29981. DOI: 10.1038/s41598-025-15203-5

Chand, T., Nair, V. S., Srinivasu, P. N., & Kumar, V. J. (2025). Prospects and challenges in decoding consumer behavior using neurotechnology. *Artificial Intelligence Applications for Brain–Computer Interfaces*, 161-182. https://doi.org/DOI: 10.1016/B978-0-443-33414-6.00011-3

Chartier-Edwards, N., Grenier, E., & Goujon, V. (2025). Galactica's dis-assemblage: Meta's beta and the omega of post-human science. *AI & Society*, *40*(4), 2069–2081. DOI: 10.1007/s00146-024-02088-7

Chaudhary, H. (2020). Using Artificial Intelligence in Commercial Underwriting to Drive Productivity Growth. In The AI Book: The Artificial Intelligence Handbook for Investors, Entrepreneurs and FinTech Visionaries (pp. 81–82). Wiley. DOI: 10.1002/9781119551966.ch23

Chen, C., Gong, X., Liu, Z., Jiang, W., Goh, S. Q., & Lam, K.-Y. (2024). *Trustworthy, Responsible, and Safe AI: A Comprehensive Architectural Framework for AI Safety with Challenges and Mitigations* (Version 3). arXiv. https://doi.org/DOI: 10.48550/ARXIV.2408.12935

Chen, Z., Min, Y., Zhang, J., Yan, B., Wang, J., Wang, X., & Shan, S. (2025, July 25). *A survey of multimodal hallucination evaluation and detection.* arXiv.Org. https://arxiv.org/abs/2507.19024

Chen, C., Zhang, K. Z., Chu, Z., & Lee, M. (2024). Augmented reality in the metaverse market: The role of multimodal sensory interaction. *Internet Research, 34*(1), 9–38. DOI: 10.1108/INTR-08-2022-0670

Chen, F., Li, Y., Chen, Y., Bian, Z., Duo, L., Zhou, Q., & Zhang, L.ADVANCED Working Group. (2025). Strategies for the analysis and elimination of hallucinations in artificial intelligence–generated medical knowledge. *Journal of Evidence-Based Medicine, 18*(3), e70075. DOI: 10.1111/jebm.70075

Cheng, A., Nagesh, V., Eller, S., Grant, V., & Lin, Y. (2025). Exploring AI Hallucinations of ChatGPT: Reference Accuracy and Citation Relevance of ChatGPT Models and Training Conditions. *Simulation in Healthcare: The Journal of the Society for Simulation in Healthcare.* DOI: 10.1097/SIH.0000000000000877

Cheng, L., & Gong, X. (2024). Appraising Regulatory Framework Towards Artificial General Intelligence (AGI) Under Digital Humanism. *International Journal of Digital Law and Governance, 1*(2), 269–312. DOI: 10.1515/ijdlg-2024-0015

Cheng, L., & Liu, X. (2024). Unravelling Power of the Unseen: Towards an Interdisciplinary Synthesis of Generative AI Regulation. *International Journal of Digital Law and Governance, 1*(1), 29–51. DOI: 10.1515/ijdlg-2024-0008

Chen, N., & Zhang, X. (2025). When misunderstanding meets artificial intelligence: The critical role of trust in human-AI and human-human team communication and performance. *Frontiers in Psychology, 16*, 1637339. DOI: 10.3389/fpsyg.2025.1637339 PMID: 41209806

Chen, Q., Zhou, S., Fang, Y., Luo, D., & Lu, T. (2025, October). MERD-360VR: A Multimodal Emotional Response Dataset from 360° VR Videos Across Different Age Groups. In *Proceedings of the 27th International Conference on Multimodal Interaction* (pp. 405-414). https://doi.org/DOI: 10.1145/3716553.3750777

Chen, Y. (2024). Resonating with the consumer desires behind the screen–consumer-centric tourism advertising and new technology applications. *Journal of Business and Industrial Marketing*, *39*(1), 99–115. DOI: 10.1108/JBIM-01-2023-0033

Chen, Y., Fu, Q., Yuan, Y., Wen, Z., Fan, G., Liu, D., Zhang, D., Li, Z., & Xiao, Y. (2023). Hallucination detection: Robustly discerning reliable answers in large language models. *CIKM '23: Proceedings of the 32nd ACM International Conference on Information and Knowledge Management*, 245–255. https://doi.org/DOI: 10.1145/3583780.361490

Christensen, J., Hansen, J. M., & Wilson, P. (2025). Understanding the role and impact of Generative Artificial Intelligence (AI) hallucination within consumers' tourism decision-making processes. *Current Issues in Tourism*, *28*(4), 545–560. DOI: 10.1080/13683500.2023.2300032

Chukwu, O., Osirim, M., & Ahiakwo, U. (2025). Leveraging human capital investments intensity in improving the returns on equity of insurance firms in Nigeria. *International Journal of Social Sciences and Management Research*, *11*(1), 235–254.

Dahl, M., Magesh, V., Suzgun, M., & Ho, D. E. (2024). Large legal fictions: Profiling legal hallucinations in large language models. *The Journal of Legal Analysis*, *16*(1), 64–93. DOI: 10.1093/jla/laae003

Danielsson, J., Macrae, R., & Uthemann, A. (2019). Artificial intelligence and systemic risk. SSRN *Electronic Journal*. https://doi.org/DOI: 10.2139/ssrn.3410948

Darwish, A. M., Rashed, E. A., & Khoriba, G. (2025). Mitigating LLM hallucinations using a multi-agent framework. *Information (Basel)*, *16*(7), 517. DOI: 10.3390/info16070517

Das, R., & Singh, T. D. (2023). Multimodal sentiment analysis: A survey of methods, trends, and challenges. *ACM Computing Surveys*, *55*(13s), 1–38. DOI: 10.1145/3586075

Deng, Y., Zhao, S., Miao, Y., Zhu, J., & Li, J. (2025). MedKA: A knowledge graph-augmented approach to improve factuality in medical large language models. *Journal of Biomedical Informatics*, *168*, 104871. DOI: 10.1016/j.jbi.2025.104871

Dhiman, S., & Wadhawan, B. Kavita, Chopra, P., Mukhija, L., & Kaur, G. (2025). From Animal Instincts to Machine Emotions: A Physics-Informed Multispecies Framework for Emotionally Intelligent AI. In 2025 5th International Conference on Intelligent Technologies (CONIT) (pp. 1–5). IEEE. DOI: 10.1109/CONIT65521.2025.11167463

Dhiraj, A., Kumar, S., & Rani, D. (2023). Social and Emotional Learning: Keys to the Success of E-Learning. In Sharma, P. C., Bansal, R., & Singh, R. (Eds.), (pp. 119–130). Advances in Educational Technologies and Instructional Design. IGI Global., DOI: 10.4018/978-1-6684-7639-0.ch008

Dhirani, L. L., Mukhtiar, N., Chowdhry, B. S., & Newe, T. (2023). Ethical dilemmas and privacy issues in emerging technologies: A review. *Sensors (Basel)*, *23*(3), 1151. DOI: 10.3390/s23031151 PMID: 36772190

Di Paolo, F., Mancuso, I., Bettiga, D., Lamberti, L., Messeni Petruzzelli, A., & Panniello, U. (2025). Metaverse business transformation: Four companies' virtual experiences. *Management Decision*, *63*(13), 349–371. DOI: 10.1108/MD-06-2024-1316

Digby, M. (2024). The evolving relationship between asset servicers and FinTechs: Unlocking efficiency and collaboration. *Journal of Securities Operations & Custody*, *16*(3). https://search.ebscohost.com/login.aspx?direct=true&profile=ehost&scope=site&authtype=crawler&jrnl=17531802&AN=177902872&h=4qb3Kzxd0AxGllkICCK7wlKWP14x6Ff1LzV8cVfMYNSbwv%2F1OnyiJnU0HQIo9s%2FSw9cCWl45Lb5zr7yF%2BS%2BDow%3D%3D&crl=c

Dogan, M. E., Goru Dogan, T., & Bozkurt, A. (2023). The Use of Artificial Intelligence (AI) in Online Learning and Distance Education Processes: A Systematic Review of Empirical Studies. *Applied Sciences (Basel, Switzerland)*, *13*(5), 3056. DOI: 10.3390/app13053056

Dokas, I. M. (2026). From hallucinations to hazards: Benchmarking LLMs for hazard analysis in safety-critical systems. *Safety Science*, *194*, 107056. DOI: 10.1016/j.ssci.2025.107056

Dominique Salamin, A., Russo, D., & Rueger, D. (2023, November 3). ChatGPT, an Excellent Liar: How Conversational Agents' Hallucinations Impact Learning and Teaching. *Proceedings of the 7th International Conference on Teaching, Learning and Education*. the 7th International Conference on Teaching, Learning and Education. DOI: 10.33422/6th.iacetl.2023.11.100

Dong, Y., Mu, R., Zhang, Y., Sun, S., Zhang, T., Wu, C., & Huang, X. (2025). Safeguarding large language models: A survey. *Artificial Intelligence Review*, *58*(12). Advance online publication. DOI: 10.1007/s10462-025-11389-2 PMID: 41114380

Drabiak, K., Kyzer, S., Nemov, V., & El Naqa, I. (2023). AI and machine learning ethics, law, diversity, and global impact. *The British Journal of Radiology, 96*(1150), 20220934. DOI: 10.1259/bjr.20220934 PMID: 37191072

Dulloo, R., & Struweg, I. (2025). The Rise of Experience Economy and Marketing 5.0: Navigating the New Paradigm of Value Creation. In *Leveraging AI-Powered Marketing in the Experience-Driven Economy* (pp. 1–38). IGI Global Scientific Publishing., DOI: 10.4018/979-8-3693-9561-5.ch001

Du, S., & Xie, C. (2021). Paradoxes of artificial intelligence in consumer markets: Ethical challenges and opportunities. *Journal of Business Research, 129*, 961–974. DOI: 10.1016/j.jbusres.2020.08.024

Du, Y., Li, S., Torralba, A., Tenenbaum, J. B., & Mordatch, I. (2024). Improving factuality and reasoning in language models through multiagent debate. In *Proceedings of the 41st International Conference on Machine Learning (ICML 2024)* (Article No. 467, pp. 11733–11763). International Machine Learning Society.

Dwivedi, Y. K., Hughes, L., Baabdullah, A. M., Ribeiro-Navarrete, S., Giannakis, M., Al-Debei, M. M., & Wamba, S. F. (2022). Metaverse beyond the hype: Multidisciplinary perspectives on emerging challenges, opportunities, and agenda for research, practice and policy. *International Journal of Information Management, 66*, 102542. DOI: 10.1016/j.ijinfomgt.2022.102542

Dwivedi, Y. K., Hughes, L., Ismagilova, E., Aarts, G., Coombs, C., Crick, T., Duan, Y., Dwivedi, R., Edwards, J., Eirug, A., Galanos, V., Ilavarasan, P. V., Janssen, M., Jones, P., Kar, A. K., Kizgin, H., Kronemann, B., Lal, B., Lucini, B., & Williams, M. D. (2021). Artificial intelligence (AI): Multidisciplinary perspectives on emerging challenges, opportunities, and agenda for research, practice and policy. *International Journal of Information Management, 57*, 101994. DOI: 10.1016/j.ijinfomgt.2019.08.002

Dwivedi, Y. K., Hughes, L., Wang, Y., Alalwan, A. A., Ahn, S. J., Balakrishnan, J., & Wirtz, J. (2023). Metaverse marketing: How the metaverse will shape the future of consumer research and practice. *Psychology and Marketing, 40*(4), 750–776. DOI: 10.1002/mar.21767

Dwivedi, Y. K., Kshetri, N., Hughes, L., Slade, E. L., Jeyaraj, A., Kar, A. K., Baabdullah, A. M., Koohang, A., Raghavan, V., Ahuja, M., Albanna, H., Albashrawi, M. A., Al-Busaidi, A. S., Balakrishnan, J., Barlette, Y., Basu, S., Bose, I., Brooks, L., Buhalis, D., & Wright, R. (2023). "So what if ChatGPT wrote it?" Multidisciplinary perspectives on opportunities, challenges and implications of generative conversational AI for research, practice and policy. *International Journal of Information Management, 71*, 102642. DOI: 10.1016/j.ijinfomgt.2023.102642

Echeverría Muñoz, D. E. (2025). *Legal impact of Artificial Intelligence (AI) hallucinations* (Master's thesis, Quito, EC: Universidad Andina Simón Bolívar, Sede Ecuador).

Egbengwu, V., Garn, W., & Turner, C. J. (2025). Metaverse for Manufacturing: Leveraging Extended Reality Technology for Human-Centric Production Systems. *Sustainability, 17*(1), 280. DOI: 10.3390/su17010280

Eisenberg, I. W., Gamboa, L., & Sherman, E. (2025, March 7). *The unified control framework: Establishing a common foundation for enterprise AI governance, risk management and regulatory compliance*. arXiv.Org. https://arxiv.org/abs/2503.05937

Ekman, P., & Rosenberg, E. L. (Eds.). (2005). *What the face reveals: Basic and applied studies of spontaneous expression using the Facial Action Coding System (FACS)* (2nd ed.). Oxford University Press., DOI: 10.1093/acprof:oso/9780195179644.001.0001

El Hajji, M., Ait Baha, T., Berka, A., Ait Nacer, H., El Aouifi, H., & Es-Saady, Y. (2025). An Architecture for Intelligent Tutoring in Virtual Reality: Integrating LLMs and Multimodal Interaction for Immersive Learning. *Information (Switzerland), 16*(7). Advance online publication. DOI: 10.3390/info16070556

Erdem, O., Hassett, K., & Egriboyun, F. (2025). Hallucination in AI-generated financial literature reviews: Evaluating bibliographic accuracy. *International Journal of Data Science and Analytics, 20*(5), 4501–4510. DOI: 10.1007/s41060-025-00731-0

Erzed, N., Laksana, R. P., Hasanudin, H., Yuhefizar, Y., Anwar, N., Gunawan, H., . . . Ichwani, A. (2025). Exploring the metaverse: Foundations of social interaction and community building. In *Unveiling Social Dynamics and Community Interaction in the Metaverse* (pp. 1–25). https://doi.org/DOI: 10.4018/979-8-3693-8628-6.ch001

Faisal, S. M., Khan, W., & Ishrat, M. (2025). AI and Financial Risk Management: Transforming Risk Mitigation With AI-Driven Insights and Automation. In *Artificial Intelligence for Financial Risk Management and Analysis* (pp. 281-306). IGI Global Scientific Publishing.

Fajardo-Ramos, D. C., Chiappe, A., & Mella-Norambuena, J. (2025). Human-in-the-loop assessment with AI: Implications for teacher education in Ibero-American universities. *Frontiers in Education*, *10*, 1710992. Advance online publication. DOI: 10.3389/feduc.2025.1710992

Farawowan, F. F. (2025). Upskilling and Reskilling: Adaptive Strategies For HR Management in Facing The Industrial Revolution 5.0. Oikonomia. *Journal of Management Economics and Accounting*, *2*(4), 49–57.

Farinha, J., & De Fátima Pina, M. (2025). Digital Transformation in ESG Programs: Understanding Environmental, Social, and Governance Factors. In Machado, A. D. B., Sousa, M. J., Brambilla, A., Pesqueira, A., & Rocha, A. (Eds.), *Environmental, Social, Governance and Digital Transformation in Organizations* (Vol. 35, pp. 33–49). Springer Nature Switzerland., DOI: 10.1007/978-3-031-86079-9_2

Farquhar, S., Kossen, J., Kuhn, L., & Gal, Y. (2024). Detecting hallucinations in large language models using semantic entropy. *Nature*, *630*, 625–630. DOI: 10.1038/s41586-024-07421-0

Fatahi, S., Moradi, H., & Kashani-Vahid, L. (2016). A survey of personality and learning styles models applied in virtual environments with emphasis on e-learning environments. *Artificial Intelligence Review*, *46*(3), 413–429. DOI: 10.1007/s10462-016-9469-7

Ferrara, E. (2023). Fairness and Bias in Artificial Intelligence: A Brief Survey of Sources, Impacts, and Mitigation Strategies. *Sci*, *6*(1), 3. DOI: 10.3390/sci6010003

Ferrigno, G., Di Paola, N., Oguntegbe, K. F., & Kraus, S. (2023). Value creation in the metaverse age: A thematic analysis of press releases. *International Journal of Entrepreneurial Behaviour & Research*, *29*(11), 337–363. DOI: 10.1108/IJEBR-01-2023-0039

Financial Stability Board. (2024). Financial stability implications of artificial intelligence. https://www.fsb.org/wp-content/uploads/P14112024.pdf

Financial Stability Board. (2024, November 14). *The financial stability implications of artificial intelligence*. Financial Stability Board. https://www.fsb.org/2024/11/the-financial-stability-implications-of-artificial-intelligence/

Floridi, L., & Chiriatti, M. (2020). GPT-3: Its nature, scope, limits, and consequences. *Minds and Machines*, *30*, 681–694. DOI: 10.1007/s11023-020-09548-1

Floridi, L., Cowls, J., Beltrametti, M., Chatila, R., Chazerand, P., Dignum, V., Luetge, C., Madelin, R., Pagallo, U., Rossi, F., Schafer, B., Valcke, P., & Vayena, E. (2018). AI4People—An ethical framework for a good AI society: Opportunities, risks, principles, and recommendations. *Minds and Machines*, *28*(4), 689–707. DOI: 10.1007/s11023-018-9482-5

Floridi, L., Cowls, J., Beltrametti, M., Chatila, R., Chazerand, P., Dignum, V., & Vayena, E. (2018). AI4People—An ethical framework for a good AI society. *Minds and Machines*, *28*(4), 689–707.

Förster, S., & Skop, Y. (2025). Between fact and fairy: Tracing the hallucination metaphor in AI discourse. *AI & Society*, •••, 1–14. DOI: 10.1007/s00146-025-02392-w

Fox, J., Bailenson, J. N., & Tricase, L. (2015). The embodiment of sexualized virtual selves. *Computers in Human Behavior*, *29*(3), 930–938.

Frank, D.-A., Peschel, A. O., Otterbring, T., DiPalma, J., & Steinmann, S. (2024). Does metaverse fidelity matter? Testing the impact of fidelity on consumer responses in virtual retail stores. *International Review of Retail, Distribution and Consumer Research*, *34*(3), 251–284. DOI: 10.1080/09593969.2024.2304810

Fu, B., Hadid, A., & Damer, N. (2025). Generative AI in the context of assistive technologies: Trends, limitations and future directions. *Image and Vision Computing*, *154*. Advance online publication. DOI: 10.1016/j.imavis.2024.105347

Fui-Hoon Nah, F., Zheng, R., Cai, J., Siau, K., & Chen, L. (2023). Generative AI and ChatGPT: Applications, challenges, and AI-human collaboration. Journal of information technology case and application research, 25(3), 277-304.

Fukawa, N., & Rindfleisch, A. (2023). Enhancing innovation via the digital twin. *Journal of Product Innovation Management*, *40*(4), 391–406. DOI: 10.1111/jpim.12655

Furidha, B. W. (2023). Comprehension of the descriptive qualitative research method: A critical assessment of the literature. *Acitya Wisesa: Journal Of Multidisciplinary Research*, 1-8. https://orcid.org/0009-0007-1944-5738

Gadalla, E., Keeling, K., & Abosag, I. (2013). Metaverse-retail service quality: A future framework for retail service quality in the 3D internet. *Journal of Marketing Management*, *9*, 1493–1517. DOI: 10.1080/0267257X.2013.835742

Gadiko, A. (2024). Understanding and addressing AI hallucinations in healthcare and life sciences. *International Journal of Health Sciences*, *7*(3), 1–11. DOI: 10.47941/ijhs.1862

Ganguli, D., Lovitt, L., Kernion, J., Askell, A., Bai, Y., Kadavath, S., Mann, B., Perez, E., Schiefer, N., Ndousse, K., Jones, A., Bowman, S., Chen, A., Conerly, T., DasSarma, N., Drain, D., Elhage, N., El-Showk, S., Fort, S., . . . Clark, J. (2022, August 23). *Red teaming language models to reduce harms: Methods, scaling behaviors, and lessons learned*. arXiv.Org. https://arxiv.org/abs/2209.07858

Garcez, A. D., Gori, M., Lamb, L. C., Serafini, L., Spranger, M., & Tran, S. N. (2019). Neural-symbolic computing: Integrating machine learning and reasoning. *Journal of Applied Logic*, *6*(4), 611–631.

García-Hernández, R. A., Luna-García, H., Celaya-Padilla, J. M., García-Hernández, A., Reveles-Gómez, L. C., Flores-Chaires, L. A., & Villalba-Condori, K. O. (2024). A systematic literature review of modalities, trends, and limitations in emotion recognition, affective computing, and sentiment analysis. *Applied Sciences (Basel, Switzerland)*, *14*(16), 7165. DOI: 10.3390/app14167165

Garvey, B., & Svendsen, A. D. (2024). Can Generative-AI (ChatGPT and Bard) Be Used as Red Team Avatars in Developing Foresight Scenarios? In *Navigating uncertainty using foresight intelligence: A guidebook for scoping scenario options in cyber and beyond* (pp. 213–242). Springer Nature Switzerland.

George, A. S. (2024). Finance 4.0: The transformation of financial services in the digital age. *Partners Universal Innovative Research Publication*, *2*(3), 104–125.

Georgouli, K. (2011). Virtual Learning Environments—An Overview. *2011 15th Panhellenic Conference on Informatics*, 63–67. DOI: 10.1109/PCI.2011.13

Giudici, P., Centurelli, M., & Turchetta, S. (2024). Artificial Intelligence risk measurement. *Expert Systems with Applications*, *235*, 121220. DOI: 10.1016/j.eswa.2023.121220

Giudici, P., & Raffinetti, E. (2023). SAFE Artificial Intelligence in finance. *Finance Research Letters*, *56*, 104088. DOI: 10.1016/j.frl.2023.104088

Glikson, E., & Woolley, A. W. (2020). Human trust in artificial intelligence: Review of empirical research. *The Academy of Management Annals*, *14*(2), 627–660. DOI: 10.5465/annals.2018.0057

Godwin-Jones, R. (2025). AI and VR Converge: The Future of Language Learning in an Emerging Metaverse. In Lan, Y.-J., Qi, G. Y., & Chun, D. (Eds.), *AI-Mediated Language Education in the Metaverse Era* (pp. 221–246). Springer Nature Singapore., DOI: 10.1007/978-981-95-0245-5_11

Goktas, P., & Grzybowski, A. (2025). Shaping the Future of Healthcare: Ethical Clinical Challenges and Pathways to Trustworthy AI. *Journal of Clinical Medicine*, *14*(5), 1605. DOI: 10.3390/jcm14051605 PMID: 40095575

Göndöcs, D., Horváth, S., & Dörfler, V. (2025). Uncovering the dynamics of human-AI hybrid performance: A qualitative meta-analysis of empirical studies. *International Journal of Human-Computer Studies*, *205*, 103622. DOI: 10.1016/j.ijhcs.2025.103622

Goodarzi, M., Venkatakrishnan, R., & Canbaz, M. A. (2023, November). Untangling emotional threads: Hallucination networks of large language models. In *International Conference on Complex Networks and Their Applications* (pp. 202-214). Cham: Springer Nature Switzerland. https://doi.org/DOI: 10.1007/978-3-031-53468-3_17

Gosmar, D., & Dahl, D. A. (2025). *Hallucination Mitigation using Agentic AI Natural Language-Based Frameworks* (Version 1). arXiv. DOI: 10.48550/ARXIV.2501.13946

Granstedt, J., Kc, P., Deshpande, R., Garcia, V., & Badano, A. (2025). Hallucinations in medical devices. *Artificial Intelligence in the Life Sciences*, *8*, 100145. DOI: 10.1016/j.ailsci.2025.100145

Gu, Y. (2025). Three Essays on Enhancing Assurance in ESG Reporting: The Role of Emerging Technologies and Big Data [PhD Thesis, Rutgers The State University of New Jersey, Graduate School-Newark]. https://search.proquest.com/openview/838ae5ea5f18cc1e8682a440784ae8af/1?pq-origsite=gscholar&cbl=18750&diss=y

Gu, J., Wang, J., Guo, X., Liu, G., Qin, S., & Bi, Z. (2023). A Metaverse-Based Teaching Building Evacuation Training System With Deep Reinforcement Learning. *IEEE Transactions on Systems, Man, and Cybernetics. Systems*, *53*(4), 2209–2219. DOI: 10.1109/TSMC.2022.3231299

Guo, C., Pleiss, G., Sun, Y., & Weinberger, K. Q. (2017). On calibration of modern neural networks. In *Proceedings of the 34th International Conference on Machine Learning* (pp. 1321–1330).

Gupta, N. (2024). Security Risks of Generative AI in Financial Systems: A comprehensive review. *World Journal of Information Systems*, *1*(3), 17–24.

Habil, S. G. M., El-Deeb, S., & El-Bassiouny, N. (2024). The metaverse era: Leveraging augmented reality in the creation of novel customer experience. *Management and Sustainability: An Arab Review*, *3*(1), 1–15. DOI: 10.1108/MSAR-10-2022-0051

Haider, Z., Rahman, M. H., Devabhaktuni, V., Moeykens, S., & Chakraborty, P. (2025). A framework for mitigating malicious RLHF feedback in LLM training using consensus based reward. *Scientific Reports*, *15*(1). Advance online publication. DOI: 10.1038/s41598-025-92889-7

Hajjami, O., & Park, S. (2024). Using the metaverse in training: Lessons from real cases. *European Journal of Training and Development*, *48*(5/6), 555–575. DOI: 10.1108/EJTD-12-2022-0144

Hamdan, I. K. A., Aziguli, W., Zhang, D., & Alhakeem, B. (2025). Barriers to Adopting Metaverse Technology in Manufacturing Firms. *Journal of Manufacturing Engineering*, *19*(4), 146–162. DOI: 10.37255/jme.v19i4pp146-162

Hammar, K., Alpcan, T., & Lupu, E. C. (2025, August 7). *Incident response planning using a lightweight large language model with reduced hallucination.* arXiv. Org. https://arxiv.org/abs/2508.05188

Hartmann, T., Wirth, W., Vorderer, P., Klimmt, C., Schramm, H., & Böcking, S. (2015). Spatial Presence Theory: State of the Art and Challenges Ahead. In: *Lombard*, M., Biocca, F., Freeman, J., IJsselsteijn, W., Schaevitz, R. (eds) Immersed in Media. Springer, Cham. https://doi.org/DOI: 10.1007/978-3-319-10190-3_7

Hasegawa, T., Yamada, H., Nishimura, H., & Kobayashi, M. (2025). The Role of AI and Virtual Learning Environments in Enhancing STEM Education. [IJESTE]. *International Journal of Education, Science, Technology, and Engineering*, *8*(1), 1–10. DOI: 10.36079/lamintang.ijeste-0801.746

Hassaan, Z. A., Yacoub, M. H., & Said, L. A. (2025). Gated recurrent unit accelerators for financial time series prediction on field-programmable gate array. *Engineering Applications of Artificial Intelligence*, *162*. Advance online publication. DOI: 10.1016/j.engappai.2025.112534

Hennig-Thurau, T., Aliman, D. N., Herting, A. M., Cziehso, G., Linder, M., & Kübler, R. V. (2023). Social interactions in the metaverse: Framework, initial evidence, and research roadmap. *Journal of the Academy of Marketing Science*, *51*(5), 889–913. DOI: 10.1007/s11747-022-00908-0

Herath, H. M. K. K. M. B., Mittal, M., & Kataria, A. (2024). Navigating the metaverse: A technical review of emerging virtual worlds. *Wiley Interdisciplinary Reviews. Data Mining and Knowledge Discovery*, *14*(4), e1538. DOI: 10.1002/widm.1538

Hermann, E. (2022). Leveraging artificial intelligence in marketing for social good—An ethical perspective. *Journal of Business Ethics*, *179*(1), 43–61. DOI: 10.1007/s10551-021-04843-y PMID: 34054170

Hermann, E., Williams, G. Y., & Puntoni, S. (2024). Deploying artificial intelligence in services to AID vulnerable consumers. *Journal of the Academy of Marketing Science, 52*(5), 1431–1451. DOI: 10.1007/s11747-023-00986-8

Hettiarachchi, I. (2025). THE RISE OF GENERATIVE AI AGENTS IN FINANCE: OPERATIONAL DISRUPTION AND STRATEGIC EVOLUTION. *International Journal of Engineering Technology Research & Management*, 447.

Hewage, C., Yasakethu, L., & Jayakody, D. N. K. (2024). Data Protection Challenges and Opportunities Due to Emerging AI and ML Technologies. In Hewage, C., Yasakethu, L., & Jayakody, D. N. K. (Eds.), *Data Protection* (pp. 1–27). Springer Nature Switzerland., DOI: 10.1007/978-3-031-76473-8_1

Hickman, E., & Petrin, M. (2021). Trustworthy AI and Corporate Governance: The EU's Ethics Guidelines for Trustworthy Artificial Intelligence from a Company Law Perspective. *European Business Organization Law Review, 22*(4), 593–625. DOI: 10.1007/s40804-021-00224-0

Hiriyanna, S., & Zhao, W. (2025). Multi-layered framework for LLM hallucination mitigation in high-stakes applications: A tutorial. *Computers, 14*(8), 332. DOI: 10.3390/computers14080332

Holzinger, A., Zatloukal, K., & Müller, H. (2025). Is human oversight to AI systems still possible? *New Biotechnology, 85*, 59–62. DOI: 10.1016/j.nbt.2024.12.003

Hornik, J., & Rachamim, M. (2025). AI-enabled consumer digital twins as a platform for research aimed at enhancing customer experience. Management Review Quarterly, 1-34.

Hosseini, S., Yamaghani, M. R., & Poorzaker Arabani, S. (2024). A review of the methods of recognition multimodal emotions in sound, image and text. *International Journal of Applied Operational Research-An Open Access Journal, 12*(1), 29–41.

Hu, H., He, C., Xie, X., & Zhang, Q. (2024, August 28). *LRP4RAG: Detecting hallucinations in retrieval-augmented generation via layer-wise relevance propagation*. arXiv.Org. https://arxiv.org/abs/2408.15533

Huang, L., Yu, W., Ma, W., Zhong, W., Feng, Z., Wang, H., Chen, Q., Peng, W., Feng, X., Qin, B., & Liu, T. (2023, November 9). *A survey on hallucination in large language models: Principles, taxonomy, challenges, and open questions*. arXiv.Org. https://arxiv.org/abs/2311.05232

Huang, L., Yu, W., Ma, W., Zhong, W., Feng, Z., Wang, H., Chen, Q., Peng, W., Feng, X., Qin, B., & Liu, T. (2024). A survey on hallucination in large language models: Principles, taxonomy, challenges, and open questions. *ACM Transactions on Information Systems, 43*(2). *Article*, *42*, 1–55. DOI: 10.1145/3703155

Huang, Z., Zhu, Y., Hao, A., & Deng, J. (2023). How social presence influences consumer purchase intention in live video commerce: The mediating role of immersive experience and the moderating role of positive emotions. *Journal of Research in Interactive Marketing*, *17*(4), 493–509. DOI: 10.1108/JRIM-01-2022-0009

Hughes, L., Dwivedi, Y. K., Malik, T., Shawosh, M., Albashrawi, M. A., Jeon, I., & Walton, P. (2025). AI agents and agentic systems: A multi-expert analysis. *Journal of Computer Information Systems*, ●●●, 1–29.

Hung, L. P., & Alias, S. (2023). Beyond sentiment analysis: A review of recent trends in text based sentiment analysis and emotion detection. *Journal of Advanced Computational Intelligence and Intelligent Informatics*, *27*(1), 84–95. DOI: 10.20965/jaciii.2023.p0084

Iaroshev, I., Pillai, R., Vaglietti, L., & Hanne, T. (2024). Evaluating retrieval-augmented generation models for financial report question and answering. *Applied Sciences (Basel, Switzerland)*, *14*(20), 9318. DOI: 10.3390/app14209318

Iqbal, K., & Abbas, T. (2024). Ethnicity, religion, and Muslim education in a changing world: Navigating contemporary perspectives on multicultural schooling in the UK. Taylor & Francis. https://books.google.com/books?hl=en&lr=&id=LzgDEQAAQBAJ&oi=fnd&pg=PA2017&dq=broader+transition+from+job-based+to+capability-based+talent+management,+where+firms+cultivate+adaptability,+creativity,+and+digital+fluency+as+enduring+strategic+assets.&ots=nd8oNaHxsf&sig=0bdhKUnxj-4adjncQAvyZxW0gcQ

Islam, M. S., Shokran, M., & Ferdousi, J. (2024). AI-Powered Business Analytics in Marketing: Unlock Consumer Insights for Competitive Growth in the US Market. *Journal of Computer Science and Technology Studies*, *6*(1), 293–313. DOI: 10.32996/jcsts.2024.6.1.33

Jabeen, S., Li, X., Amin, M. S., Bourahla, O., Li, S., & Jabbar, A. (2023). A review on methods and applications in multimodal deep learning. *ACM Transactions on Multimedia Computing Communications and Applications*, *19*(2s), 1–41. DOI: 10.1145/3545572

Jabreel, M., Maaroof, N., Valls, A., & Moreno, A. (2020). Introducing sentiment analysis of textual reviews in a multi-criteria decision aid system. *applied sciences, 11*(1), 216. https://doi.org/DOI: 10.3390/app11010216

Jackson, I., Jesus Saenz, M., & Ivanov, D. (2024). From natural language to simulations: Applying AI to automate simulation modelling of logistics systems. *International Journal of Production Research*, *62*(4), 1434–1457.

Jamaluddin, J., Abd Gaffar, N., & Din, N. S. S. (2023). Hallucination: A key challenge to Artificial Intelligence-Generated writing. *Malaysian Family Physician : the Official Journal of the Academy of Family Physicians of Malaysia*, *18*, 68. DOI: 10.51866/lte.527

Janssen, M. (2025). Responsible governance of generative AI: Conceptualizing GenAI as complex adaptive systems. *Policy and Society*, *44*(1), 38–51. DOI: 10.1093/polsoc/puae040

Javidroozi, V., Tawil, A. R., Azad, R. M. A., Bishop, B., & Elmitwally, N. S. (2025). AI-Enabled Customised Workflows for Smarter Supply Chain Optimisation: A Feasibility Study. *Applied Sciences (Basel, Switzerland)*, *15*(17), 9402.

Jean, G. (2024). Sentiment Analysis and Emotion Recognition for Emotionally Adaptive Mobile User Interfaces.

Jin, H., & Peng, Y. (2024). The impact of team psychological safety on employee innovative performance: A study with communication behavior as a mediator variable. *PLoS One*, *19*(10), e0306629. DOI: 10.1371/journal.pone.0306629

Jin, L., Shen, Z., Alhur, A. A., & Naeem, S. B. (2025). Exploring the determinants and effects of artificial intelligence (AI) hallucination exposure on generative AI adoption in healthcare. *Information Development*, *02666669251340954*. Advance online publication. DOI: 10.1177/02666669251340954

Ji, Z., Lee, N., Frieske, R., Yu, T., Su, D., Xu, Y., & Fung, P. (2023). Survey of hallucination in natural language generation. *ACM Computing Surveys*, *55*(12), 1–38.

Ji, Z., Lee, N., Frieske, R., Yu, T., Su, D., Xu, Y., Ishii, E., Bang, Y. J., Madotto, A., & Fung, P. (2023). Survey of hallucination in natural language generation. *ACM Computing Surveys*, 55(12). *Article*, *248*, 1–38. DOI: 10.1145/3571730

Joo, J. H., Han, S. H., Park, I., & Chung, T. S. (2024). Immersive emotion analysis in VR environments: A sensor-based approach to prevent distortion. *Electronics (Basel)*, *13*(8), 1494. DOI: 10.3390/electronics13081494

Jooss, S., Collings, D. G., McMackin, J., & Dickmann, M. (2024). A skills-matching perspective on talent management: Developing strategic agility. *Human Resource Management*, *63*(1), 141–157. DOI: 10.1002/hrm.22192

Joshi, R., Pandey, K., & Kumari, S. (2025). Generative AI: A Transformative Tool for Mitigating Risks for Financial Frauds. *Generative Artificial Intelligence in Finance: Large Language Models, Interfaces, and Industry Use Cases to Transform Accounting and Finance Processes*, 125-147.

Joshi, S. (2025). Comprehensive Review of AI Hallucinations: Impacts and Mitigation Strategies for Financial and Business Applications. https://philpapers.org/rec/JOSCRO-3

Joshi, S., & Joshi-Satyadhar, S. (2025). Model risk management in the era of generative ai: Challenges, opportunities, and future directions. *International Journal of Scientific and Research Publications*, *15*(5), 299–309.

K, H., & Rodriguez, R. V. (2023). *The Business of the Metaverse: How to Maintain the Human Element Within this New Business Reality* (1st ed.). Productivity Press. DOI: 10.4324/b23404

Kabir, S. M. H. (2025). Artificial Intelligence-Driven Marketing and Consumer Behavior: Balancing Sustainability and Profitability in the Digital Age. *International Journal of Innovative Research and Publications*, *5*(11), 39–44. DOI: 10.51430/IJIRP.2025.511.004

Kallina, E., Bohné, T., & Singh, J. (2025). *Stakeholder Participation for Responsible AI Development: Disconnects Between Guidance and Current Practice* (Version 1). arXiv. https://doi.org/DOI: 10.48550/ARXIV.2506.09873

Kaman, K., & Deshmukh, A. K. (2025). Navigating the digital frontier: Understanding shopping behavior in the metaverse through an SLR lens. *Spanish Journal of Marketing - ESIC*. Advance online publication. DOI: 10.1108/SJME-12-2024-0327

Kamel, H. (2024). Understanding the impact of AI Hallucinations on the university community. *Cybrarians Journal*, *73*, 111–134. DOI: 10.70000/cj.2024.73.622

Kaneko, S., & Yamada, S. (2025). Estimating the Trust of Humans in AI for Level 3 Autonomous Driving. In 2025 20th ACM/IEEE International Conference on Human-Robot Interaction (HRI) (pp. 1389–1392). IEEE. DOI: 10.1109/HRI61500.2025.10973810

Kaneko, S., & Yamada, S. (2025). Predicting Trust Dynamics With Dynamic SEM in Human-AI Collaboration. *IEEE Access : Practical Innovations, Open Solutions*, *13*, 190701–190711. DOI: 10.1109/ACCESS.2025.3629365

Kapoor, M. (2025). Global Business Environment: Industry 5.0 and Beyond. Taylor & Francis. https://books.google.com/books?hl=en&lr=&id=19w_EQAAQBAJ&oi=fnd&pg=PT8&dq=There+is+a+pressing+need+for+human+oversight,+where+wealth+managers+can+co-exist+with+AI+and+pave+the+way+for+efficient,+prudent+and+responsible+judgement+to+the+AI+hallucinated+output,+to+amplify+the+enterprise+metaverse+capabilities.&ots=uvbwfE1Rj1&sig=VFJJ1WTiPE8JnDN2P1nb2tYZWdQ

Karvonen, A., Aho, J., Koskinen, H., Luimula, M., Myllylä, M., Tammentie, B., & Saariluoma, P. (2025). Human-centered intelligent process control: Vision, design, and implementation. In *Industry 4.0 and Intelligent Manufacturing Technologies* (pp. 109–131). Routledge.

Kaur, J. (2024). Responsible Artificial Intelligence (AI) Governance: Ethical Frameworks for Business Decision-Making. In Ethical Quandaries in Business Practices: Exploring Morality and Social Responsibility (pp. 337–368). IGI Global. https://www.igi-global.com/chapter/responsible-artificial-intelligence-ai-governance/356327

Kazlaris, I., Antoniou, E., Diamantaras, K., & Bratsas, C. (2025). From illusion to insight: A taxonomic survey of hallucination mitigation techniques in LLMs. *AI*, *6*(10), 260. DOI: 10.3390/ai6100260

Kerstan, S., Baum, K., Helfer, T., Langer, M., Schmidt, E., Sesing-Wagenpfeil, A., & Speith, T. (2026). Responsible and trusted AI: An interdisciplinary perspective. In Steffen, B. (Ed.), Lecture Notes in Computer Science: Vol. 16220. *Bridging the gap between AI and reality. AISoLA 2025* (pp. 141–145). Springer., DOI: 10.1007/978-3-032-07132-3_9

Ke, Y. H., Jin, L., Elangovan, K., Chakraborty, S., Rajan, V., & Ngiam, K. Y. (2025). Retrieval augmented generation for large language models and its generalizability in assessing medical fitness. *npj. Digital Medicine*, *8*, 187. DOI: 10.1038/s41746-025-01519-z

Khalaf, O. I., Srinivasan, D., Algburi, S., Vellaichamy, J., Selvaraj, D., Sharif, M. S., & Elmedany, W. (2024). Elevating metaverse virtual reality experiences through network-integrated neuro-fuzzy emotion recognition and adaptive content generation algorithms. *Engineering Reports*, *6*(11), e12894. DOI: 10.1002/eng2.12894

Khan, J., Tao, M., & Abbass, A. (2025). Digital doppelgänger: Navigating consumer brand engagement in the metaverse. *Journal of Research in Interactive Marketing*. Advance online publication. DOI: 10.1108/JRIM-07-2024-0344

Khan, M. S., & Umer, H. (2024). ChatGPT in finance: Applications, challenges, and solutions. *Heliyon*, *10*(2).

Khan, S. A. R., Sheikh, A. A., Shamsi, I. R. A., & Yu, Z. (2025). The Implications of Artificial Intelligence for Small and Medium-Sized Enterprises' Sustainable Development in the Areas of Blockchain Technology, Supply Chain Resilience, and Closed-Loop Supply Chains. *Sustainability (Switzerland)*, *17*(1). Advance online publication. DOI: 10.3390/su17010334

Khan, U. A., Xu, Q., Liu, Y., Lagstedt, A., Alamäki, A., & Kauttonen, J. (2024). Exploring contactless techniques in multimodal emotion recognition: Insights into diverse applications, challenges, solutions, and prospects. *Multimedia Systems*, *30*(3), 115. DOI: 10.1007/s00530-024-01302-2

Khanvilkar, K., & Shinde, V. (2025, October). Mitigating Hallucination Risks in GenAI Compliance Advisory Systems for the Financial Industry. In *International Conference on Software Engineering and Data Engineering* (pp. 302-318). Cham: Springer Nature Switzerland.

Kim, Y., Jeong, H., Chen, S., Li, S. S., Lu, M., Alhamoud, K., Mun, J., Grau, C., Jung, M., Gameiro, R., Fan, L., Park, E., Lin, T., Yoon, J., Yoon, W., Sap, M., Tsvetkov, Y., Liang, P., Xu, X., . . . Breazeal, C. (2025). *Medical Hallucinations in Foundation Models and Their Impact on Healthcare* (Version 1). arXiv. DOI: 10.48550/ARXIV.2503.05777

Kim, H., & Hong, T. (2024). Enhancing emotion recognition using multimodal fusion of physiological, environmental, personal data. *Expert Systems with Applications*, *249*, 123723. DOI: 10.1016/j.eswa.2024.123723

Kim, H., Seo, S., & Lee, S. W. (2025). When generative AI messes up:How politeness and attribution shape user reactions to hallucinations. *International Journal of Information Management*, *85*. Advance online publication. DOI: 10.1016/j.ijinfomgt.2025.102958

Kingdon, A. (2024). Socio-Technical and Multi-stakeholder Approaches to Countering Online Propaganda. In A. Kingdon, *The World White Web* (pp. 209–251). Springer Nature Switzerland. https://doi.org/DOI: 10.1007/978-3-031-75393-0_8

Kizilcec, R. F. (2016). How much information? Effects of transparency on trust in an algorithmic interface. In *Proceedings of the 2016 CHI Conference on Human Factors in Computing Systems* (pp. 2390–2395).

Kliestik, T., Dragomir, R., Bălu ă, A. V., Grecu, I., Durana, P., Karabolevski, O. L., Kral, P., Balica, R., Suler, P., Bu u, O. V., Bugaj, M., Voinea, D.-V., Vrbka, J., Coco atu, M., Grupac, M., Pera, A., & Gajdosikova, D. (2024). Enterprise generative artificial intelligence technologies, internet of things and blockchain-based fintech management, and digital twin industrial metaverse in the cognitive algorithmic economy. *Oeconomia Copernicana*, *15*(4), 1183–1221. DOI: 10.24136/oc.3109

Kokina, J., Blanchette, S., Davenport, T. H., & Pachamanova, D. (2025). Challenges and opportunities for artificial intelligence in auditing: Evidence from the field. *International Journal of Accounting Information Systems*, *56*, 100734. DOI: 10.1016/j.accinf.2025.100734

Kolomaznik, M., Petrik, V., Slama, M., & Jurik, V. (2024). The role of socio-emotional attributes in enhancing human-AI collaboration. *Frontiers in Psychology*, *15*, 1369957. DOI: 10.3389/fpsyg.2024.1369957 PMID: 39474095

Kothandapani, H. P. (2025). Ai-driven regulatory compliance: Transforming financial oversight through large language models and automation. *Emerging Science Research*, *12*(1), 12–24.

Kotsantonis, S., & Serafeim, G. (2020). Human capital and the future of work: Implications for investors and ESG integration. *Journal of Financial Transformation*, *51*, 115–130.

Kourtesis, P. (2024). A Comprehensive Review of Multimodal XR Applications, Risks, and Ethical Challenges in the Metaverse. *Multimodal Technologies and Interaction*, *8*(11), 98. DOI: 10.3390/mti8110098

Kozinets, R. V. (2023). Immersive netnography: A novel method for service experience research in virtual reality, augmented reality and metaverse contexts. *Journal of Service Management*, *34*(1), 100–125. DOI: 10.1108/JOSM-12-2021-0481

Krause, D. (2023). Mitigating risks for financial firms using generative AI tools. SSRN *Electronic Journal*. https://doi.org/DOI: 10.2139/ssrn.4452600

Krause, D. (2025). The Promise and Peril of AI in Financial Research and Reporting: Navigating Accuracy, Insight, and Accountability. *Insight, and Accountability (June 04, 2025)*.

Krause, D. (2023). Mitigating risks for financial firms using generative AI tools. *Available at SSRN* 4452600.

Krishna, P. M. S. S., Kumar, T. P., Reddy, R. V. T., & Ariwa, E. (2024). Customer-Centric AI Solutions. In Minds Unveiled (pp. 58–69). Productivity Press. https://www.taylorfrancis.com/chapters/edit/10.4324/9781032711089-5/customer-centric-ai-solutions-puvvaladasu-sai-subramanya-krishna-praveen-kumar-ravuri-venkata-trinadh-reddy-ezendu-ariwa

Kryściński, W., McCann, B., Xiong, C., & Socher, R. (2020). Evaluating the factual consistency of abstractive text summarization. In *Proceedings of the 2020 Conference on Empirical Methods in Natural Language Processing* (pp. 9332–9346). Online: Association for Computational Linguistics. https://doi.org/DOI: 10.18653/v1/2020.emnlp-main.750

Kulkarni, A., Zhang, Y., Moniz, J. R. A., Ge, X., Tseng, B.-H., Piraviperumal, D., Swayamdipta, S., & Yu, H. (2025, November). Evaluating evaluation metrics: The mirage of hallucination detection. In Christodoulopoulos, C., Chakraborty, T., Rose, C., & Peng, V. (Eds.), *Findings of the Association for Computational Linguistics: EMNLP 2025* (pp. 19013–19032). Association for Computational Linguistics., DOI: 10.18653/v1/2025.findings-emnlp.1035

Kumar, P., Tiwari, S., & Saxena, N. (2025). Engaging New Customers through Marketing in the Metaverse. In *The Metaverse Era: Reinventing Customer Engagement and Digital Marketing* (pp. 59-87). Bentham Science Publishers. https://doi.org/DOI: 10.2174/9798898103681250101

Kumar, A., Shankar, A., Behl, A., Pereira, V., Kapoor, P., & Papa, A. (2025). Implementing enterprise metaverse as a means of enhancing growth hacking performance: Will adopting the metaverse be a success in organizations? *Journal of Business Research, 188*. Advance online publication. DOI: 10.1016/j.jbusres.2024.115079

Kumar, A., Shankar, A., Shaik, A. S., Jain, G., & Malibari, A. (2025). Risking it all in the metaverse ecosystem: Forecasting resistance towards the enterprise metaverse. *Information Technology & People, 38*(1), 198–218. DOI: 10.1108/ITP-04-2023-0374

Kumar, S. (2021). Bridging the Gap between Human Emotions and AI: Affective Computing with Multimodal Data. [IJARCST]. *International Journal of Advanced Research in Computer Science & Technology, 4*(6), 5847–5855. DOI: 10.15662/IJARCST.2021.0406011

Kumar, S. (2024). The Role of Digital Marketing on Customer Engagement in the Hospitality Industry. In Bansal, R., Ngah, A. H., Chakir, A., & Pruthi, N. (Eds.), (pp. 177–191). Advances in Business Information Systems and Analytics. IGI Global., DOI: 10.4018/979-8-3693-0815-8.ch010

Kumar, S., Dhiraj, A., Shah, M. A., & Rani, D. (2023). Application of Metaverse in the Hospitality Industry. In Bansal, R., Qalati, S. A., & Chakir, A. (Eds.), (pp. 178–194). Advances in Marketing, Customer Relationship Management, and E-Services. IGI Global., DOI: 10.4018/978-1-6684-8898-0.ch011

Kumar, S., Talukder, M. B., & Tyagi, P. K. (2025). The Impact of Virtual Reality and Augmented Reality in TNE Learning. In Crawford, C. M., & Gee, T. T. (Eds.), *Motivating Engagement, Belonging, and Success in Higher Education Student Experience* (pp. 359–382). IGI Global., DOI: 10.4018/979-8-3693-8089-5.ch013

Kumar, V., Kotler, P., & Kumar, A. (2025). Transformative marketing strategies in the era of new-age technologies: Principles, plan, purpose, and practice. *Journal of the Academy of Marketing Science*, •••, 1–27. DOI: 10.1007/s11747-025-01120-6

Kurznack, L., Schoenmaker, D., & Schramade, W. (2021). A model of long-term value creation. *Journal of Sustainable Finance & Investment*, •••, 1–19. DOI: 10.1080/20430795.2021.1920231

Kusal, S., Patil, S., Choudrie, J., Kotecha, K., Vora, D., & Pappas, I. (2023). A systematic review of applications of natural language processing and future challenges with special emphasis in text-based emotion detection. *Artificial Intelligence Review*, *56*(12), 15129–15215. DOI: 10.1007/s10462-023-10509-0

Kushwah, S., & Dave, N. (2025, August). AI Hallucination and Strategies to Overcome: Enhancing Human-AI Interaction. In *2025 International Conference on Artificial Intelligence and Machine Vision (AIMV)* (pp. 1-6). IEEE.

Küsters, A., & Wörsdörfer, M. (2025). Exploring Laws of Robotics: A Synthesis of Constitutional AI and Constitutional Economics. *Digital Society : Ethics, Socio-Legal and Governance of Digital Technology*, *4*(2), 46. DOI: 10.1007/s44206-025-00204-8

Laiz-Ibañez, H., Mendaña-Cuervo, C., & Carús Candás, J. L. (2025). The metaverse: Privacy and information security risks. *International Journal of Information Management Data Insights*, *5*(2), 100373. Advance online publication. DOI: 10.1016/j.jjimei.2025.100373

Langer, M., Baum, K., & Schlicker, N. (2025). Effective human oversight of AI-based systems: A signal detection perspective on the detection of inaccurate and unfair outputs. *Minds and Machines*, *35*, 1. DOI: 10.1007/s11023-024-09701-0

Larsson, S., & Heintz, F. (2020). Transparency in artificial intelligence. *Internet Policy Review*, *9*(2). Advance online publication. DOI: 10.14763/2020.2.1469

Lavrinovics, E., Biswas, R., Bjerva, J., & Hose, K. (2025). Knowledge graphs, large language models, and hallucinations: An NLP perspective. *Journal of Web Semantics*, *85*, 100844. DOI: 10.1016/j.websem.2024.100844

Leal, C. C., & Oliveira, B. (2025). The ethics of digital nudging. In *Ethics in Management and Business* (pp. 53–80). Springer Nature Switzerland., DOI: 10.1007/978-3-031-82054-0_3

Lee, A. L. H. J. (2025). *Financial stability implications of generative AI: Taming the animal spirits.*

Lee, C. L., Yam, S., Susilawati, C., & Blake, A. (2024). Future workforce for the property industry: Are we ready for the change? https://unsworks.unsw.edu.au/entities/publication/9a0860de-095c-496d-954c-cdb67b3716f3

Lee, L.-H., Braud, T., Zhou, P., Wang, L., Xu, D., Lin, Z., Kumar, A., Bermejo, C., & Hui, P. (2021). All one needs to know about metaverse: A complete survey on technological singularity, virtual ecosystem, and research agenda.

Lee, C., Kim, J., Lim, J. S., & Shin, D. (2025). Generative AI risks and resilience: How users adapt to hallucination and privacy challenges. *Telematics and Informatics Reports*, *19*. Advance online publication. DOI: 10.1016/j.teler.2025.100221

Lee, D. K. C., Guan, C., Yu, Y., & Ding, Q. (2024). A comprehensive review of generative AI in finance. *FinTech*, *3*(3), 460–478. DOI: 10.3390/fintech3030025

Lee, H., Woo, D., & Yu, S. (2022). Virtual Reality Metaverse System Supplementing Remote Education Methods: Based on Aircraft Maintenance Simulation. *Applied Sciences (Basel, Switzerland)*, *12*(5), 2667. DOI: 10.3390/app12052667

Lee, I. (2024). The Metaverse: Ecosystem, Technologies, Business Opportunities, and Challenges. *IT Professional*, *26*(5), 28–35. DOI: 10.1109/MITP.2024.3433549

Lee, J. D., & See, K. A. (2004). Trust in automation: Designing for appropriate reliance. *Human Factors*, *46*(1), 50–80.

Lee, L.-H., Braud, T., Zhou, P., Wang, L., Xu, D., Lin, Z., Kumar, A., Bermejo, C. F., & Hui, P. (2021). *All one needs to know about the metaverse:* A complete survey. arXiv:2110.05352.

Lee, M. (2023). A mathematical investigation of hallucination and creativity in GPT models. *Mathematics*, *11*(10), 2320. DOI: 10.3390/math11102320

LeMaire, C., & Abshire, B. (2025). *AI for everyday IT: Accelerate workplace productivity*. Manning.

Lerner, J. S., Li, Y., Valdesolo, P., & Kassam, K. S. (2015). Emotion and decision making. *Annual Review of Psychology*, *66*, 799–823.

Lewis, P., Perez, E., Piktus, A., Petroni, F., Karpukhin, V., Goyal, N., Küttler, H., Lewis, M., Yih, W., Rocktäschel, T., Riedel, S., & Kiela, D. (2020, May 22). *Retrieval-Augmented generation for knowledge-intensive NLP tasks.* arXiv.Org. https://arxiv.org/abs/2005.11401

Lewis, P., Perez, E., Piktus, A., Petroni, F., Karpukhin, V., Goyal, N., & Kiela, D. (2020). Retrieval-augmented generation for knowledge-intensive NLP tasks. *Advances in Neural Information Processing Systems*, *33*, 9459–9474.

Lewis, P., Perez, E., Piktus, A., Petroni, F., Karpukhin, V., Goyal, N., Küttler, H., Lewis, M., Yih, W.-T., Rocktäschel, T., Riedel, S., & Kiela, D. (2020). Retrieval-augmented generation for knowledge-intensive NLP tasks. *Proceedings of the 34th International Conference on Neural Information Processing Systems*, Article 793, 9459–9474.

Li, H., Fang, Y., Zhang, S., Lee, S. M., Wang, Y., Trexler, M., & Botelho, A. F. (2025). ARCHED: A human-centered framework for transparent, responsible, and collaborative AI-assisted instructional design. *Proceedings of the Innovation and Responsibility in AI-Supported Education Workshop*, in *Proceedings of Machine Learning Research*, 273, 94–104. https://proceedings.mlr.press/v273/li25a.html

Li, W.-C., Yang, C.-J., & Fang, W.-C. (2020). A Real-time Emotion Recognition System Based on an AI System-On-Chip Design. In 2020 International SoC Design Conference (ISOCC) (pp. 29–30). IEEE. DOI: 10.1109/ISOCC50952.2020.9333072

Lian, Z., Sun, H., Sun, L., Wen, Z., Zhang, S., Chen, S., & Tao, J. (2024, October). Mer 2024: Semi-supervised learning, noise robustness, and open-vocabulary multimodal emotion recognition. In *Proceedings of the 2nd International Workshop on Multimodal and Responsible Affective Computing* (pp. 41-48). https://doi.org/DOI: 10.1145/3689092.3689959

Liao, Q. V., & Wortman Vaughan, J. (2024). AI transparency in the age of LLMs: A human-centered research roadmap. *Harvard Data Science Review*, *5*(Special Issue), •••. DOI: 10.1162/99608f92.8036d03b

Li, B., & Zhao, C. (2025). Self-reflection enhances large language models towards substantial academic response. *npj. Artificial Intelligence*, *1*, 42. DOI: 10.1038/s44387-025-00045-3

Li, C., Dai, Y., Chen, G., Liu, J., Li, P., & Ip, H. H. S. (2025). Avatar-mediated communication in collaborative virtual environments: A study on users' attention allocation and perception of social interactions. *Computers in Human Behavior, 167*, 108598. DOI: 10.1016/j.chb.2025.108598

Lifelo, Z., Ding, J., & Ning, H., Qurat-Ul-Ain, & Dhelim, S. (2024). Artificial Intelligence-Enabled Metaverse for Sustainable Smart Cities: Technologies, Applications, Challenges, and Future Directions. *Electronics (Basel), 13*(24), 4874. DOI: 10.3390/electronics13244874

Li, J., Cai, X., & Cheng, L. (2023). Legal regulation of generative AI: A multidimensional construction. *International Journal of Legal Discourse, 8*(2), 365–388. DOI: 10.1515/ijld-2023-2017

Li, J., Chen, J., Ren, R., Cheng, X., Zhao, X., Nie, J.-Y., & Wen, J.-R. (2024). The dawn after the dark: An empirical study on factuality hallucination in large language models. In *Proceedings of the 62nd Annual Meeting of the Association for Computational Linguistics (*Volume 1*: Long Papers)* (pp. 10879–10899). Bangkok, Thailand: Association for Computational Linguistics.

Lim, D. H., Lee, J. Y., & Park, S. (2024). The Metaverse in the Workplace: Possibilities and Implications for Human Resource Development. *Human Resource Development Review, 23*(2), 164–198. DOI: 10.1177/15344843231217174

Lim, K. Y., Sa'uadi, A. N., Idros, N. A. N. M., & Jamil, N. S. (2024, September). *Optimizing Personalized Recommendation in E-Services Platforms Using AI. In 2024 5th International Conference on Artificial Intelligence and Data Sciences (AiDAS).*, https://doi.org/IEEE, DOI: 10.1109/AiDAS63860.2024.10730288

Lin, J., Li, Q., Wang, C., & Hu, Z. (2024). Product Development and Design Framework Based on Interactive Innovation in the Metaverse Perspective. *Applied System Innovation, 7*(4). Advance online publication. DOI: 10.3390/asi7040058

Lin, S., Hilton, J., & Evans, O. (2022). TruthfulQA: Measuring how models mimic human falsehoods. In Muresan, S., Nakov, P., & Villavicencio, A. (Eds.), *Proceedings of the 60th Annual Meeting of the Association for Computational Linguistics (*Volume 1*: Long Papers)* (pp. 3214–3252). Dublin, Ireland: Association for Computational Linguistics. https://doi.org/DOI: 10.18653/v1/2022.acl-long.229

Lin, Z., Guan, S., Zhang, W., Zhang, H., Li, Y., & Zhang, H. (2024). Towards trustworthy LLMs: A review on debiasing and dehallucinating in large language models. *Artificial Intelligence Review, 57*, 243. DOI: 10.1007/s10462-024-10896-y

Li, S., Zhu, B., Zhu, H., & Yu, Z. (2024). Co-creation of metaverse brands equity with the impact of celebrity virtual images and real-life influence: From the perspective of experience-dominant logic. *Electronic Commerce Research*, •••, 1–30. DOI: 10.1007/s10660-024-09899-2

Liu, P., Zhang, J., Chen, S., & Chen, S. (2025). Human-AI teaming in healthcare: 1 + 1 > 2? *npj. Artificial Intelligence*, *1*, 47. DOI: 10.1038/s44387-025-00052-4

Livingston, L., Featherstone-Uwague, A., Barry, A., Barretto, K., Morey, T., Hermannova, D., & Avula, V. (2025). Reproducible generative artificial intelligence evaluation for health care: A clinician-in-the-loop approach. *JAMIA Open*, *8*(3), ooaf054. Advance online publication. DOI: 10.1093/jamiaopen/ooaf054

Logeswaran, K., Savitha, S., Suresh, P., Prasanna Kumar, K. R., Gunasekar, M., Rajadevi, R., & Jayasurya, A. S. (2024). Unifying technologies in industry 4.0: Harnessing the synergy of internet of things, big data, augmented reality/virtual reality, and blockchain technologies. *Topics in Artificial Intelligence Applied to Industry*, *4*(0), 127–147. DOI: 10.1002/9781394216147.ch7

Lucinity. (2025, March 13). The real cost of AML compliance - Transform fincrime operations & investigations with AI. *Lucinity*. https://lucinity.com/blog/the-real-cost-of-anti-money-laundering-compliance-where-can-banks-cut-expenses-without-increasing-risk

Luck, M., & Aylett, R. (2000). Applying artificial intelligence to virtual reality: Intelligent virtual environments. *Applied Artificial Intelligence*, *14*(1), 3–32. DOI: 10.1080/088395100117142

Lumer, E., Melich, M., Zino, O., Kim, E., Dieter, S., Basavaraju, P. H., Subbiah, V. K., Burke, J. A., & Hernandez, R. (2025, November 22). *Rethinking retrieval: From traditional retrieval augmented generation to agentic and non-vector reasoning systems in the financial domain for large language models*. arXiv.Org. https://arxiv.org/abs/2511.18177

Lundberg, S., & Lee, S.-I. (2017, May 22). *A unified approach to interpreting model predictions*. arXiv.Org. https://arxiv.org/abs/1705.07874

Lv, Z., Shang, W.-L., & Guizani, M. (2022). Impact of Digital Twins and metaverse on cities: History, current situation, and application perspectives. *Applied Sciences (Basel, Switzerland)*, *12*(24), 12820. DOI: 10.3390/app122412820

Lyu, Z., & Fridenfalk, M. (2024). Digital twins for building industrial metaverse. *Journal of Advanced Research*, *66*, 31–38. DOI: 10.1016/j.jare.2023.11.019 PMID: 38008176

Ma, X., Rao, G., Xu, L., Wang, X., Fan, Z., & Zhang, Z. (2026). Guided and knowledgeable multi-agent debate for fact verification. *Expert Systems with Applications*, 299(B), 130103. https://doi.org/DOI: 10.1016/j.eswa.2025.130103

Magesh, V., Surani, F., Dahl, M., Suzgun, M., Manning, C. D., & Ho, D. E. (2025). Hallucination-Free? Assessing the Reliability of Leading AI Legal Research Tools. *Journal of Empirical Legal Studies*, *22*(2), 216–242. DOI: 10.1111/jels.12413

Mahajan, P. (2025). The Soul of the AI: Governance, Ethics, and the Future of Human–AI Integration. Zenodo. https://hal.science/hal-05140138/

Maharjan, J., Garikipati, A., Singh, N. P., Gupta, A., Bhatt, D., & Li, Z. (2024). OpenMedLM: Prompt engineering can out-perform fine-tuning in medical question-answering with open-source large language models. *Scientific Reports*, *14*, 14156. DOI: 10.1038/s41598-024-64827-6

Mahdikhani, M., & Meena, P. (2024). Metaverse applications and supply chain innovation: Insights from text mining. *Journal of Innovation & Knowledge*, *9*(4), 100591. Advance online publication. DOI: 10.1016/j.jik.2024.100591

Mahmud, M. A., ALAM, M. A., & Alam, M. K. (2025). Exploring the Transformative Potential of Generative AI and Large Language Models (LLMs) in Financial Applications: Opportunities, Risks and Strategic Implications. *Journal of Computer Science and Technology Studies*, *7*(8), 1069–1088.

Maleki, N., Padmanabhan, B., & Dutta, K. (2024, June). AI hallucinations: a misnomer worth clarifying. In *2024 IEEE conference on artificial intelligence (CAI)* (pp. 133-138). IEEE. https://doi.org/DOI: 10.1109/CAI59869.2024.00033

Manoharan, G., Ashtikar, S. P., & Kumar, S. (2024). Delineation of Artificial Intelligence in the Hospitality and Tourism Industries. In Talukder, M. B., Kumar, S., & Tyagi, P. K. (Eds.), *Advances in Hospitality, Tourism, and the Services Industry* (pp. 20–42). IGI Global., DOI: 10.4018/979-8-3693-6755-1.ch002

Mansoor, S., Rahman, S. M., & Bowden, J. L. (2024). Purchase spillovers from the metaverse to the real world: The roles of social presence, trialability, and customer experience. *Journal of Consumer Behaviour*, *25*(12), 2501–2552. DOI: 10.1002/cb.2353

Mao, Q., & Xu, M. (2025). Navigating the Ethical Landscape of AI Innovation: Challenges and Opportunities. *International Journal of Digital Law and Governance*. https://doi.org/DOI: 10.1515/ijdlg-2025-0005

Marabelli, M., & Lirio, P. (2025). AI and the metaverse in the workplace: DEI opportunities and challenges. *Personnel Review*, *54*(3), 844–853. DOI: 10.1108/PR-04-2023-0300

Mariappan, J., Sahdev, S. L., Krishnan, C., Malik, F. A., & Gupta, A. (2024). Creative Synergy: Unleashing the Potential of Artificial Intelligence and the Metaverse. In The Metaverse Dilemma: Challenges and Opportunities for Business and Society (pp. 235-248). Emerald Publishing Limited.

Marín-Morales, J., Llinares, C., Guixeres, J., & Alcañiz, M. (2020). Emotion recognition in immersive virtual reality: From statistics to affective computing. *Sensors (Basel)*, *20*(18), 5163. DOI: 10.3390/s20185163 PMID: 32927722

Marques, G., Pitarma, R. M., Garcia, N., & Pombo, N. (2019). Internet of things architectures, technologies, applications, challenges, and future directions for enhanced living environments and healthcare systems: A review. *Electronics (Basel)*, *8*(10), 1081. DOI: 10.3390/electronics8101081

Marr, B. (2022). Digital twins, generative AI and the metaverse. Forbes. https://bernardmarr.com/digital-twins-generative-ai-and-the-metaverse/

Martinez, A. (2025). The Impact of AI on Personalized Wealth Management: Optimizing Client Relationships, Costs, and Ethics in Banking. https://www.theseus.fi/handle/10024/886933

Marx, G. T. (2003). A tack in the shoe: Neutralizing and resisting surveillance. *The Journal of Social Issues*, *59*(2), 369–390.

Masanneck, L., Meuth, S. G., & Pawlitzki, M. (2025). Evaluating base and retrieval augmented LLMs with document or online support for evidence-based neurology. *NPJ Digital Medicine*, *8*, 137. DOI: 10.1038/s41746-025-01536-y

Masnun, A., Jessika, S., & Albadry, S. A. (2024). Optimizing Human-AI Collaboration in Educational Administration in Muara Bungo, Jambi: An HRD Framework for Role Redefinition, Skill Development, and Change Management. *Enigma in Education*, *2*(2), 114–125.

Massenon, R., Gambo, I., Khan, J. A., Agbonkhese, C., & Alwadain, A. (2025). "My AI is Lying to Me": User-reported LLM hallucinations in AI mobile apps reviews. *Scientific Reports*, *15*(1). Advance online publication. DOI: 10.1038/s41598-025-15416-8

Matzko, V. (2025). Legal Framework for Cybersecurity in the Context of the Metaverse Formation. Metaverse Science. *Society and Law*, *2025*(1), 1–18. DOI: 10.69635/mssl.2025.1.1.18

Mayer, A., Greif, L., Häußermann, T. M., Otto, S., Kastner, K., El Bobbou, S., Chardonnet, J.-R., Reichwald, J., Fleischer, J., & Ovtcharova, J. (2025). Digital Twins, Extended Reality, and Artificial Intelligence in Manufacturing Reconfiguration: A Systematic Literature Review. *Sustainability*, *17*(5), 2318. DOI: 10.3390/su17052318

Maynez, J., Narayan, S., Bohnet, B., & McDonald, R. (2020). On faithfulness and factuality in abstractive summarization. In *Proceedings of the 58th Annual Meeting of the Association for Computational Linguistics* (pp. 1906–1920). Association for Computational Linguistics.

McVay, J., Visser, E. J. d., Pippin, B., Mani, A., Hyde, J. N., & Kman, N. (2025). Trust in Aligned AI Decision Makers. In *2025 IEEE Conference on Artificial Intelligence (CAI)* (pp. 1–4). IEEE. DOI: 10.1109/CAI64502.2025.00202

McVeigh-Schultz, J., Stein, A., Boyle, A., Berding, N., Kimmel, L., Brown, C., . . . Hahn, N. (2022). Immersive virtual offices. In *Extended Abstracts of CHI 2022* (pp. 1–7).

Memarian, B., & Doleck, T. (2024). Human-in-the-loop in artificial intelligence in education: A review and entity-relationship (ER) analysis. *Computers in Human Behavior: Artificial Humans*, *2*(1), 100053. DOI: 10.1016/j.chbah.2024.100053

Meng, Q., Wu, T. J., Duan, W., & Li, S. (2025). Effects of Employee-Artificial Intelligence (AI) Collaboration on Counterproductive Work Behaviors (CWBs): Leader Emotional Support as a Moderator. *Behavioral Sciences (Basel, Switzerland)*, *15*(5), 696. DOI: 10.3390/bs15050696 PMID: 40426473

Mennella, C., Maniscalco, U., De Pietro, G., & Esposito, M. (2024). Ethical and regulatory challenges of AI technologies in healthcare: A narrative review. *Heliyon*, *10*(4), e26297. DOI: 10.1016/j.heliyon.2024.e26297

Metakides, G., & Filip, F. G. (2025). Digital Enlightenment, Digital Humanism, and Computer-supported Collaboration in Artificial Intelligence Era. *Annals of Data Science*, *12*(6), 1799–1823. DOI: 10.1007/s40745-025-00640-w

Mettrick, G. (2024). The AI handbook for financial services leaders: Tips and tactics for mastering AI in banking and finance. *Journal of Securities Operations & Custody*, *16*(3), 286–296.

Microsoft. (2021, May 26). *Converging the physical and digital with digital twins, mixed reality, and metaverse apps*. Microsoft Blog. https://azure.microsoft.com/en-us/blog/converging-the-physical-and-digital-with-digital-twins-mixed-reality-and-metaverse-apps/

Microsoft. (2022, December 20). *HoloLens 2 enables industrial metaverse for plant inspection and remote assistance.* Microsoft News. https://news.microsoft.com/source/features/innovation/hololens-2-industrial-metaverse/

Microsoft. (2025, February 20). Carter, R. "Azure Mixed Reality Solutions: Building the Future of Digital Transformation." XR Today. https://www.xrtoday.com/mixed-reality/azure-mixed-reality-solutions-building-the-future-of-digital-transformation/

Microsoft. (n.d.). *Microsoft Mesh: connect like never before.* Microsoft. https://www.microsoft.com/en-us/microsoft-teams/microsoft-mesh Microsoft

Min, S., Krishna, K., Lyu, X., Lewis, M., Yih, W.-T., Koh, P., Iyyer, M., Zettlemoyer, L., & Hajishirzi, H. (2023). FActScore: Fine-grained atomic evaluation of factual precision in long form text generation. In Bouamor, H., Pino, J., & Bali, K. (Eds.), *Proceedings of the 2023 Conference on Empirical Methods in Natural Language Processing* (pp. 12076–12100). Association for Computational Linguistics. https://doi.org/DOI: 10.18653/v1/2023.emnlp-main.741

Misheva, B. H., & Osterrieder, J. (2023, November 13). *A hypothesis on good practices for ai-based systems for financial time series forecasting: Towards domain-driven XAI methods.* arXiv.Org. https://arxiv.org/abs/2311.07513

MiTra, S. (2023). Metaverse: A Potential Virtual-Physical Ecosystem for Innovative Blended Education and Training. *Journal of Metaverse*, *3*(1), 66–72. DOI: 10.57019/jmv.1168056

Mitsea, E., Drigas, A., & Skianis, C. (2025). A systematic review of serious games in the era of artificial intelligence, immersive technologies, the metaverse, and neurotechnologies: Transformation through meta-skills training. *Electronics (Basel)*, *14*(4), 649. DOI: 10.3390/electronics14040649

Mittelstadt, B. D., Allo, P., Taddeo, M., Wachter, S., & Floridi, L. (2016). The ethics of algorithms. *Big Data & Society*, *3*(2), 1–21.

Moghadas, N. S. A. H., & Arvin, N. F. (2024). Elevating Airline Performance through Strategic Training: A Comprehensive Analysis of Key Performance Indicators (KPIs). https://www.sid.ir/paper/1407664/en

Mohammad, A. A. S., Mohammad, S. I. S., Al Oraini, B., Vasudevan, A., Hindieh, A., Altarawneh, A., & Ali, I. (2025). Strategies for applying interpretable and explainable AI in real world IoT applications. *Discover Internet of Things*, *5*(1). Advance online publication. DOI: 10.1007/s43926-025-00155-z

Mökander, J., Schuett, J., Kirk, H. R., & Floridi, L. (2024). Auditing large language models: A three-layered approach. *AI and Ethics*, *4*, 1085–1115. DOI: 10.1007/s43681-023-00289-2

Molina, M. D., & Sundar, S. S. (2022). When AI moderates online content: Effects of human collaboration and interactive transparency on user trust. *Journal of Computer-Mediated Communication*, *27*(4), zmac010. Advance online publication. DOI: 10.1093/jcmc/zmac010

Morley, J., Floridi, L., Kinsey, L., & Elhalal, A. (2021). From what to how: A review of AI ethics tools. *Science and Engineering Ethics*, *27*, 11. Advance online publication. DOI: 10.1007/s11948-021-00282-w

Mosqueira-Rey, E., Hernández-Pereira, E., Alonso-Ríos, D., Bobes-Bascarán, J., & Fernández-Leal, Á. (2023). Human-in-the-loop machine learning: A state of the art. *Artificial Intelligence Review*, *56*(4), 3005–3054. DOI: 10.1007/s10462-022-10246-w

Mourtzinis, S., Silva, T. S., Lo, J. C. M., Smith, D. L., & Conley, S. P. (2025). A human in the loop approach to applying large language models for farm management insight. *Scientific Reports*. Advance online publication. DOI: 10.1038/s41598-025-30991-6

Mourtzis, D. (2023). Digital twin inception in the era of industrial metaverse. *Frontiers in Manufacturing Technology*, *3*. Advance online publication. DOI: 10.3389/fmtec.2023.1155735

Mucsková, M. (2024). Transforming banking with artificial intelligence: Applications, challenges, and implications. *Trends Economics and Management*, *18*(42), 21–37.

Munir, B. (2025). *Hallucinations in Legal Practice: A Comparative Case Law Analysis. SSRN*. DOI: 10.2139/ssrn.5265375

Mystakidis, S. (2022). Metaverse. In *Encyclopedia, 2,* 486–497. https://doi.org/ DOI: 10.3390/encyclopedia2010031

Naik, P. V., Dintakurthi, N. K., Hu, Z., Wang, Y., & Qiu, R. (2025, September 10). *Co-Investigator AI: The rise of agentic AI for smarter, trustworthy AML compliance narratives*. arXiv.Org. https://arxiv.org/abs/2509.08380

Nair, A. J., Manohar, S., & Chaudhry, R. (2024). Securing the metaverse: Exploring the role of artificial intelligence in mitigating emerging threats in manufacturing and service industries. In Augmenting retail reality, part B: Blockchain, AR, VR, and AI (pp. 67-84). Emerald Publishing Limited.

Nair, A. J., Manohar, S., Mittal, A., & Chaudhry, R. (2024). Unleashing digital frontiers: Bridging realities of augmented reality, virtual reality, and the metaverse. In *The metaverse dilemma: Challenges and opportunities for business and society* (pp. 85–112). Emerald Publishing Limited., DOI: 10.1108/978-1-83797-524-220241006

Nakamura, J., & Csikszentmihalyi, M. (2009). Flow theory and research. https://doi.org/DOI: 10.1093/oxfordhb/9780195187243.013.0018

Natarajan, T., Pragha, P., & Dhalmahapatra, K. (2024). Uses and gratifications of metaverse: Understanding the user adoption factors through a mixed method approach. *Asia Pacific Journal of Marketing and Logistics*, *36*(12), 2978–3006. DOI: 10.1108/APJML-03-2024-0395

Natarajan, T., Pragha, P., Dhalmahapatra, K., & Veera Raghavan, D. R. (2025). Unveiling metaverse sentiments using machine learning approaches. *Kybernetes*, *54*(8), 4114–4137. DOI: 10.1108/K-11-2023-2268

Nechesov, A., Dorokhov, I., & Ruponen, J. (2025). Virtual Cities: From Digital Twins to Autonomous AI Societies. *IEEE Access : Practical Innovations, Open Solutions*, *13*, 13866–13903. DOI: 10.1109/ACCESS.2025.3531222

Neha, F., Bhati, D., & Shukla, D. K. (2025). Retrieval-Augmented Generation (RAG) in healthcare: A comprehensive review. *AI*, *6*(9), 226. DOI: 10.3390/ai6090226

Nemecek, A., Jiang, Y., & Ayday, E. (2025, May 27). *Watermarking without standards is not AI governance*. arXiv.Org. https://arxiv.org/abs/2505.23814

NIST. (2023). *Artificial intelligence risk management framework (AI RMF 1.0)*. National Institute of Standards and Technology., DOI: 10.6028/nist.ai.100-1

Niu, C., Wu, Y., Zhu, J., Xu, S., Shum, K., Zhong, R., Song, J., & Zhang, T. (2024). RAGTruth: A hallucination corpus for developing trustworthy retrieval-augmented language models. *Proceedings of the 62nd Annual Meeting of the Association for Computational Linguistics* (Volume 1*: Long Papers)*, 10862–10878. Association for Computational Linguistics.

Novelli, C., Casolari, F., Rotolo, A., Taddeo, M., & Floridi, L. (2024). Taking AI risks seriously: A new assessment model for the AI Act. *AI & Society*, *39*(5), 2493–2497. DOI: 10.1007/s00146-023-01723-z

NVIDIA. (2024, January 11). *State of AI in Financial Services: 2024*. NVIDIA Blog; Nvidia. https://blogs.nvidia.com/blog/ai-in-financial-services-survey-2024/

Obianuju Ozobu, C., Emmanuel Adikwu, F., Odujobi, O., Othuke Onyekwe, F., & Onyinye Nwulu, E. (2025). A Review of Health Risk Assessment and Deep immersion Control Models for Hazardous Waste Management Operations in Africa. *International Journal of Advanced Multidisciplinary Research and Studies, 5*(2), 570–582. DOI: 10.62225/2583049X.2025.5.2.3873

OECD. (2024). Regulatory approaches to Artificial Intelligence in finance. In *OECD Artificial Intelligence Papers*. Organisation for Economic Co-Operation and Development (OECD). https://doi.org/DOI: 10.1787/f1498c02-en

Oh, H. J., Kim, J., Chang, J. J. C., Park, N., & Lee, S. (2023). Social benefits of living in the metaverse: The relationships among social presence, supportive interaction, social self-efficacy, and feelings of loneliness. *Computers in Human Behavior, 139*, 107498. DOI: 10.1016/j.chb.2022.107498

Oladele, S., Anector, M., & Foluwa, E. (2025). *AI-Powered Personalization in Employee Training and Development Programs Authors. SSRN*. DOI: 10.2139/ssrn.5226745

Omar, M., Sorin, V., Collins, J. D., Reich, D., Freeman, R., Gavin, N., Charney, A., Stump, L., Bragazzi, N. L., Nadkarni, G. N., & Klang, E. (2025). Multi-model assurance analysis showing large language models are highly vulnerable to adversarial hallucination attacks during clinical decision support. *Communications Medicine, 5*, 330. DOI: 10.1038/s43856-025-01021-3

Ooi, K. B., Tan, G. W. H., Al-Emran, M., Al-Sharafi, M. A., Capatina, A., Chakraborty, A., & Wong, L. W. (2025). The potential of generative artificial intelligence across disciplines: Perspectives and future directions. *Journal of Computer Information Systems, 65*(1), 76–107.

Osuji, C. C., Timoney, B., Andrade, M., Castro Ferreira, T., & Davis, B. (2025). Are multi-agents the new pipeline architecture for data-to-text systems? In *Proceedings of the 18th International Natural Language Generation Conference* (pp. 542–553). Association for Computational Linguistics.

Otieno, P. O., & Busili, P. A. (2024). A Research on Labor, Finance, Technology, and Sustainable Growth. *International Journal of Innovative Science and Research Technology, 9*(9), 3570–3597.

Otoum, Y., Gottimukkala, N., Kumar, N., & Nayak, A. (2024). Machine Learning in Metaverse Security: Current Solutions and Future Challenges. *ACM Computing Surveys, 56*(8), 1–36. DOI: 10.1145/3654663

Ouyang, L., Wu, J., Jiang, X., Almeida, D., Wainwright, C. L., Mishkin, P., Zhang, C., Agarwal, S., Slama, K., Ray, A., Schulman, J., Hilton, J., Kelton, F., Miller, L., Simens, M., Askell, A., Welinder, P., Christiano, P., Leike, J., & Lowe, R. (2022). Training language models to follow instructions with human feedback. In *Proceedings of the 36th International Conference on Neural Information Processing Systems (NeurIPS 2022)* (Article No. 2011, pp. 27730–27744). Curran Associates, Inc.

ÖZKAL. İ., & BAŞÇİFTÇİ, F. (2024). *Deep Learning in the Metaverse: A Systematic Literature Review and Future Perspectives*. https://doi.org/DOI: 10.2139/ssrn.5022041

Padmaja, P., Justin, E., Sophia, I., Charan, S. H., Kumar, S. S., Somu, K., & Thirupathi, L. (2021).. . *Journal of Nuclear Energy Science and Power Generation Technology*, *10*(9), 1000211.

Pahune, S., Akhtar, Z., Mandapati, V., & Siddique, K. (2025). The importance of AI data governance in large language models. *Big Data and Cognitive Computing*, *9*(6), 147. DOI: 10.3390/bdcc9060147

Pak, R., Rovira, E., & McLaughlin, A. (2025). Polite AI mitigates user susceptibility to AI hallucinations. *Ergonomics*, *68*(10), 1735–1745. DOI: 10.1080/00140139.2024.2434604

Pal, A., Umapathi, L. K., & Sankarasubbu, M. (2023). Med-HALT: Medical domain hallucination test for large language models. In Jiang, J., Reitter, D., & Deng, S. (Eds.), *Proceedings of the 27th Conference on Computational Natural Language Learning (CoNLL)* (pp. 314–334). Association for Computational Linguistics. https://doi.org/DOI: 10.18653/v1/2023.conll-1.21

Paliwal, M., Buhalis, D., Jha, S., & Chatradhi, N. (2025). Exploring Generation Z Motivations to Use Metaverse for Travel Planning. *International Journal of Tourism Research*, *27*(4). Advance online publication. DOI: 10.1002/jtr.70074

Panneerselvam, S., Arokiasamy, E., & Kumar, K. S. (2025). Employee Experience Management (EXM): What, Why, and How to Create Exceptional Experiences at Work. In Approaching Employee Experience Management With Data Science (pp. 23–64). IGI Global Scientific Publishing. https://www.igi-global.com/chapter/employee-experience-management-exm/370198

Papagiannidis, E., Mikalef, P., & Conboy, K. (2025). Responsible artificial intelligence governance: A review and research framework. *The Journal of Strategic Information Systems*, *34*(2), 101885. DOI: 10.1016/j.jsis.2024.101885

Pardeshi, A., & Deshmukh, S. (2025). AI in Finance: Computational Methods for Market Analysis and Risk Management. *Next-Generation Computational Intelligence: Trends and Technologies*, 137-164.

Park, H., & Choo, S. (2022). A development of visualization technology through AR-based design checklist connection. *Applied Sciences (Basel, Switzerland)*, *12*(12), 6126. DOI: 10.3390/app12126126

Park, S., & Nan, X. (2025). Generative AI and misinformation: A scoping review of the role of generative AI in the generation, detection, mitigation, and impact of misinformation. *AI & Society*. Advance online publication. DOI: 10.1007/s00146-025-02620-3

Patel, P., & Kaur, J. (2025). Introduction to brand management in the digital age. In *Strategic brand management in the age of AI and disruption* (pp. 1–26). IGI Global Scientific Publishing., DOI: 10.4018/979-8-3693-9461-8.ch001

Paulino, E., Romero, R., Mazo, P., & Tan, R. (2025). Strengthening resilience: The synergistic role of credit risk and customer relationship management in non-bank financial institutions. *International Journal of Research in Business & Social Science*, *14*(1). https://search.ebscohost.com/login.aspx?direct=true&profile=ehost&scope=site&authtype=crawler&jrnl=21474478&AN=183427544&h=QrlyanHCDhzEPaU8q3%2Bj8IojrMo4VJrtKIgx0DGkicfqqivlgFvqlNilR54PQPxFzFbADt0uHrU5076niVXlkg%3D%3D&crl=c

Peney, L., Dernee, R., & Alers, H. (2024). Encouraging Trust in AI-Powered Teaching Tools: Ranking Design Principles. In *2024 IEEE Conference on Artificial Intelligence (CAI)* (pp. 476–479). IEEE. DOI: 10.1109/CAI59869.2024.00096

Peng, S., Kalliamvakou, E., Cihon, P., & Demirer, M. (2023). The impact of AI on developer productivity: Evidence from GitHub Copilot. arXiv:2302.06590.

Philip, P. J. (2025). Ethical Frameworks for AI Hallucination Mitigation in Critical Applications. *Journal of Responsible AI & Ethics E: 3117-6402 P: 3117-6410*, *2*(4), 13-25.

Picard, R. W. (2000). Toward computers that recognize and respond to user emotion. *IBM Systems Journal*, *39*(3–4), 705–719.

Pilcher, K., & Tütüncü, E. K. (2025). Purposefully induced psychosis (PIP): Embracing hallucination as imagination in large language models. In *Proceedings of CHI '25*. ACM. https://doi.org/DOI: 10.48550/arXiv.2504.12012

Pine, B. J., & Gilmore, J. H. (2013). The experience economy: past, present and future. In *Handbook on the experience economy* (pp. 21–44). Edward Elgar Publishing., DOI: 10.4337/9781781004227.00007

Planey, J., Trencevski, D., & Kelle, S. (2026). Lowering the Barriers for Designing Immersive Learning Environments: ImmersityXR Framework. In *Communications in Computer and Information Science* (Vol. 2598 CCIS, pp. 307–324). https://doi.org/DOI: 10.1007/978-3-031-98080-0_19

Pramanik, S., & Rai, S. K. (2025). Manipulating mind, media, and truth: Artificial Intelligence in perpetuating ideological imperialism in Dream Machine: AI and the Real World. *Journal of Graphic Novels & Comics*, •••, 1–21.

Pujari, T., Goel, A., & Kejriwal, D. (2022). Ethical and Responsible AI in the Age of Adversarial Diffusion Models: Challenges, Risks, and Mitigation Strategies. *International Journal Science and Technology*, *1*(3), 54–68. DOI: 10.56127/ijst.v1i3.1963

Puntoni, S., Reczek, R. W., Giesler, M., & Botti, S. (2021). Consumers and artificial intelligence: An experiential perspective. *Journal of Marketing*, *85*(1), 131–151. DOI: 10.1177/0022242920953847

Punuri, S. B., Kuanar, S. K., Mishra, T. K., Rao, V. V. R. M., & Reddy, S. S. (2024). Decoding Human Facial Emotions: A Ranking Approach Using Explainable AI. *IEEE Access : Practical Innovations, Open Solutions*, *12*, 186229–186245. DOI: 10.1109/ACCESS.2024.3474012

Pusch, L., & Conrad, T. O. F. (2025). Combining LLMs and knowledge graphs to reduce hallucinations in biomedical question answering. *BioMedInformatics*, *5*(4), 70. DOI: 10.3390/biomedinformatics5040070

Qiu, Y. (2024). The Impact of LLM Hallucinations on Motor Skill Learning: A Case Study in Badminton. *IEEE Access : Practical Innovations, Open Solutions*, *12*, 139669–139682. DOI: 10.1109/ACCESS.2024.3444783

Rachmad, Y. E. (2025). The New Era of HR Management: Prioritizing Competence Over Degrees. United Nations Development Programme. https://www.researchgate.net/profile/Yoesoep-Rachmad/publication/396404755_The_New_Era_of_HR_Management_Prioritizing_Competence_Over_Degrees/links/68e9c1ddf3032e2b4be8347d/The-New-Era-of-HR-Management-Prioritizing-Competence-Over-Degrees.pdf

Radanliev, P. (2025). AI ethics: Integrating transparency, fairness, and privacy in AI development. *Applied Artificial Intelligence*, *39*(1), 2463722.

Rahimi, F., Sadeghi-Niaraki, A., & Choi, S. M. (2025). *Generative AI Meets Virtual Reality: A Comprehensive Survey on Applications, Challenges, and Future Direction*. IEEE., DOI: 10.1109/ACCESS.2025.3574779

Rahman, A., Mahir, S. H., Tashrif, M. T. A., Karim, M. A., Aishi, A. A., Kundu, D., Debnath, T., Moududi, M. A. A., Eidmum, M. Z. A., Miah, A. S. M., Farid, F. A., & Karim, H. A. (2025). Comparative analysis based on DeepSeek, ChatGPT, and Google Gemini: Features, techniques, performance, future prospects. *Systems and Soft Computing*, *7*. Advance online publication. DOI: 10.1016/j.sasc.2025.200396

Rahulkumar, P. B., Hasmukhbhai, P. J., Himanshu, P. K., Rameshwarkumar, P. H., & Trivedi, H. (2025). Exploring AI's Influence on Human Thinking: Productivity, Learning, and Cognitive Skills in the Age of XAI. In 2025 Artificial Intelligence and Smart Technologies for Sustainability Conference (AISTS) (pp. 1–6). IEEE. DOI: 10.1109/AISTS66100.2025.11232740

Rainoldi, M., Ladkin, A., & Buhalis, D. (2024). Blending work and leisure: A future digital worker hybrid lifestyle perspective. *Annals of Leisure Research*, *27*(2), 215–235. DOI: 10.1080/11745398.2022.2070513

Rakhmanovich, I. U., Taslim, M., Raman, A. M., & Ugli, A. A. A. (2025). The rise of behavioral economics: Leveraging AI to understand consumer decision-making. AIP Conference Proceedings, 3306(1), 050007. https://pubs.aip.org/aip/acp/article-abstract/3306/1/050007/3348895

Ramadan, Z. (2023). Marketing in the metaverse era: Toward an integrative channel approach. *Virtual Reality (Waltham Cross)*, *27*(3), 1905–1918. DOI: 10.1007/s10055-023-00783-2 PMID: 37360809

Ramadan, Z., & Ramadan, J. (2025). AI avatars and co-creation in the metaverse. *Consumer Behavior in Tourism and Hospitality*, *20*(1), 131–147. DOI: 10.1108/CBTH-07-2024-0246

Ramchurn, S. D., Stein, S., & Jennings, N. R. (2021). Trustworthy human-AI partnerships. *iScience*, *24*(8), 102891. DOI: 10.1016/j.isci.2021.102891 PMID: 34430804

Rathkopf, C. (2025). *Hallucination, reliability, and the role of generative AI in science* (Version 1). arXiv. DOI: 10.48550/ARXIV.2504.08526

Ratten, V. (2023). Editorial: ChatGPT, the metaverse and artificial intelligence: implications for family business management education. *Journal of Family Business Management*, *13*(4), 821–827. DOI: 10.1108/JFBM-12-2023-199

Rawte, V., Sheth, A., & Das, A. (2023, September 12). *A survey of hallucination in large foundation models*. arXiv.Org. https://arxiv.org/abs/2309.05922

Rawte, V., Chakraborty, S., Pathak, A., Sarkar, A., Tonmoy, S. M. T. I., Chadha, A., Sheth, A., & Das, A. (2023). The troubling emergence of hallucination in large language models: An extensive definition, quantification, and prescriptive remediations. In Bouamor, H., Pino, J., & Bali, K. (Eds.), *Proceedings of the 2023 Conference on Empirical Methods in Natural Language Processing* (pp. 2541–2573). Association for Computational Linguistics. https://doi.org/DOI: 10.18653/v1/2023.emnlp-main.155

Ribeiro, M. T., Singh, S., & Guestrin, C. (2016). "Why should I trust you?" Explaining model predictions. In *Proceedings of the 22nd ACM SIGKDD Conference* (pp. 1135–1144).

Ridzuan, N. N., Masri, M., Anshari, M., Fitriyani, N. L., & Syafrudin, M. (2024). AI in the financial sector: The line between innovation, regulation and ethical responsibility. *Information (Basel)*, *15*(8), 432. Advance online publication. DOI: 10.3390/info15080432

Rivas, A., González-Briones, A., Hernández, G., Prieto, J., & Chamoso, P. (2021). Artificial neural network analysis of the academic performance of students in virtual learning environments. *Neurocomputing*, *423*, 713–720. DOI: 10.1016/j.neucom.2020.02.125

Robinson, J. C. (2025). Unshackling Dreams from the Hacker's Digital Chains. In *Artificial Intelligence: Ethics and the New World Order* (pp. 95–171). Springer Nature Switzerland.

Roeschl, T., Hoffmann, M., Hashemi, D., Rarreck, F., Hinrichs, N., Trippel, T. D., Gröschel, M. I., Unbehaun, A., Klein, C., Kempfert, J., Dreger, H., O'Brien, B., Hindricks, G., Balzer, F., Falk, V., & Meyer, A. (2025). Assessing the limitations of large language models in clinical practice guideline–concordant treatment decision-making on real-world data: Retrospective study. *JMIRx Med*, *6*, e74899. DOI: 10.2196/74899

Roosevelt Institute. (2024, September 26). *The risks of generative AI agents to financial services*. Roosevelt Institute. https://rooseveltinstitute.org/publications/the-risks-of-generative-ai-agents-to-financial-services/

Rostam, Z. R. K., & Kertész, G. (2025). Advances in pre-trained language models for domain-specific text classification: A systematic review. *ACM Transactions on Intelligent Systems and Technology*, *16*(6). *Article*, *124*, 1–41. DOI: 10.1145/3763002

Roustan, D., & Bastardot, F. (2025). The clinicians' guide to large language models: A general perspective with a focus on hallucinations. *Interactive Journal of Medical Research*, *14*, e59823. DOI: 10.2196/59823

Roychowdhury, S. (2024). Journey of hallucination-minimized generative AI solutions for financial decision makers. *Proceedings of the 17th ACM International Conference on Web Search and Data Mining*, 1180–1181. https://doi.org/DOI: 10.1145/3616855.3635737

Rozenblit, L., Price, A., Solomonides, A., Joseph, A. L., Srivastava, G., Labkoff, S., deBronkart, D., Singh, R., Dattani, K., Lopez-Gonzalez, M., Barr, P. J., Koski, E., Lin, B., Cheung, E., Weiner, M. G., Williams, T., Thuy Bui, T. T., & Quintana, Y. (2025). Towards a Multi-Stakeholder process for developing responsible Trust-layer verification governance in consumer health. *International Journal of Medical Informatics*, *195*, 105713. DOI: 10.1016/j.ijmedinf.2024.105713 PMID: 39642592

Ryan, R. M., & Deci, E. L. (2000). Self-determination theory and intrinsic motivation. *The American Psychologist*, *55*(1), 68–78.

Saenz, A. D., Mass General Brigham AI Governance Committee, Centi, A., Ting, D., You, J. G., Landman, A., & Mishuris, R. G. (2024). Establishing responsible use of AI guidelines: A comprehensive case study for healthcare institutions. *npj. Digital Medicine*, *7*, 348. DOI: 10.1038/s41746-024-01300-8

Safari, A., Oshnoei, A., & Blaabjerg, F. (2025). A review of recent AI applications in next-generation power electronics. *Applied Energy*, *402*. Advance online publication. DOI: 10.1016/j.apenergy.2025.126923

Sahoo, P., Meharia, P., Ghosh, A., Saha, S., Jain, V., & Chadha, A. (2024). A comprehensive survey of hallucination in large language, image, video, and audio foundation models. *Findings of the Association for Computational Linguistics: EMNLP*, *2024*, 11709–11724.

Sai, S., Sharma, P., Gaur, A., & Chamola, V. (2024). Pivotal role of digital twins in the metaverse: A review. *Digital Communications and Networks*.

Salovey, P., & Mayer, J. D. (1990). Emotional intelligence. *Imagination, Cognition and Personality*, *9*(3), 185–211.

Salvagno, M., Taccone, F. S., & Gerli, A. G. (2023). Artificial intelligence hallucinations. *Critical Care*, *27*(1), 180. DOI: 10.1186/s13054-023-04473-y

Santoso, W., Sitorus, P. M., Batunanggar, S., Krisanti, F. T., Anggadwita, G., & Alamsyah, A. (2021). Talent mapping: A strategic approach toward digitalization initiatives in the banking and financial technology (FinTech) industry in Indonesia. *Journal of Science and Technology Policy Management*, *12*(3), 399–420.

Schaffer, S. (2025). Digital Skills Shortages: Perspectives of Marketing Managers [PhD Thesis, Capella University]. https://search.proquest.com/openview/c45a30033f37825ecefcb677a6b66caa/1?pq-origsite=gscholar&cbl=18750&diss=y

Schmalzried, M. (2025). A philosophical and ontological perspective on Artificial General Intelligence and the Metaverse. *Journal of Metaverse*, *5*(2), 168–180.

Schmitt, B., & Zarantonello, L. (2013). Consumer experience and experiential marketing: A critical review. *Review of marketing Research*, 25-61. https://doi.org/DOI: 10.1108/S1548-6435(2013)0000010006

Schmitt, B. (1999). Experiential marketing. *Journal of Marketing Management*, *15*(1-3), 53–67. DOI: 10.1362/026725799784870496

Schuller, B., Steidl, S., Batliner, A., Hirschberg, J., Burgoon, J. K., Baird, A., & Vinciarelli, A. (2011). The INTERSPEECH 2013 computational paralinguistics challenge. In *Proceedings of INTERSPEECH* (pp. 148–152).

Seif El-Nasr, M., & Kleinman, E. (2020). Data-Driven Game Development: Ethical Considerations. *ACM International Conference Proceeding Series*, 1–10. https://doi.org/DOI: 10.1145/3402942.3402964

Sekti, B. A. (2025). IT Service Information Security Management. In *Cases on Information Systems Service Management* (pp. 61–93). https://doi.org/DOI: 10.4018/979-8-3373-2352-7.ch003

Semwal, R., Tripathi, N., Rana, A., Dafouti, B. S., Bairwa, M. K., & Mathur, V. (2024, May). AI-powered personalization and emotional intelligence integration for enhanced service marketing in transformative tourism experiences. In *2024 International Conference on Communication, Computer Sciences and Engineering (IC3SE)* (pp. 1851-1856). IEEE. https://doi.org/DOI: 10.1109/IC3SE62002.2024.10592909

Setiawan, V., & Soewito, B. (2025). Instruction-based Chain-of-Thought for Multi-agent RAG in Snort Rule Generation. *International Journal of Intelligent Engineering and Systems*, *18*(11), 883–896. DOI: 10.22266/ijies2025.1231.54

Shah, R., Shah, S., & Pathak, P. (2025). Metaverse work culture: The emergence of virtual-first companies and HR's role. *Strategic HR Review*. Advance online publication. DOI: 10.1108/SHR-03-2025-0029

Shan, Z., & Wang, Y. (2024). Strategic Talent Development in the Knowledge Economy: A Comparative Analysis of Global Practices. *Journal of the Knowledge Economy*, *15*(4), 19570–19596. DOI: 10.1007/s13132-024-01933-w

Shao, Z. (2025). Revealing consumers' hedonic buying in social media: The roles of social status recognition, perceived value, immersive engagement and gamified incentives. *Journal of Research in Interactive Marketing*, *19*(5), 787–802. DOI: 10.1108/JRIM-12-2023-0452

Sharma, M., Singh, A., & Singh, A. (2025). Tapping the Potential of Innovative Hi-Tech Services on Hotel Performance using PLS-SEM Approach. https://doi.org/ DOI: 10.5109/7388850

Sharma, N. A., Ali, A. S., & Kabir, M. A. (2025). A review of sentiment analysis: Tasks, applications, and deep learning techniques. *International Journal of Data Science and Analytics*, *19*(3), 351–388. DOI: 10.1007/s41060-024-00594-x

Sharma, R., Sachdeva, T., Singh, A., & Nadda, V. (2024). A New Era of Engagement and Satisfaction: Transforming Customer Experience With AI-Driven Technologies. In Nadda, V., Tyagi, P., Singh, A., & Singh, V. (Eds.), *AI Innovations in Service and Tourism Marketing* (pp. 1–16). IGI Global Scientific Publishing., DOI: 10.4018/979-8-3693-7909-7.ch001

Sharma, R., & Singh, A. (2025). Integrating AI, Green Marketing, and Influencer Strategies: Shaping Sustainable Consumer Behavior in the Digital Age. In Hussain, Z., Sharipudin, M., Albattat, A., & Khan, A. (Eds.), *Strategic Brand Management in the Age of AI and Disruption* (pp. 325–342). IGI Global Scientific Publishing., DOI: 10.4018/979-8-3693-9461-8.ch013

Sharma, S., Singh, G., Lim, W. M., Ali, A., & Singh, R. (2025). Metaverse through the integrated theoretical lenses of task technology fit theory, social capital theory, and social cognitive theory: The case of SMEs. *Journal of Innovation and Entrepreneurship*, *14*(1). Advance online publication. DOI: 10.1186/s13731-024-00445-w

Shih, T. Y. (2025). Consumer Perspective Scales for Creating a Good Metaverse Environment: The Power of Storytelling and Sensory Immersion. *International Journal of Human-Computer Interaction*, •••, 1–22. DOI: 10.1080/10447318.2025.2551050

Shi, J., Zhao, J., Wu, X., Xu, R., Jiang, Y. H., & He, L. (2025). Mitigating reasoning hallucination through multi-agent collaborative filtering. *Expert Systems with Applications*, *263*, 125723. DOI: 10.1016/j.eswa.2024.125723

Shim, J.-W., Ju, Y.-J., Park, J.-H., & Lee, S.-W. (2025, October 14). *CPR: Mitigating large language model hallucinations with curative prompt refinement*. arXiv.Org. https://arxiv.org/abs/2510.12029

Shouli, A., Barthwal, A., Campbell, M., & Shrestha, A. K. (2025). *Ethical AI for Young Digital Citizens: A Call to Action on Privacy Governance* (Version 1). arXiv. https://doi.org/DOI: 10.48550/ARXIV.2503.11947

Shuai, N. (2025). The Role of Digital Transformation Speed in Enhancing Productivity: A Mediated Framework with Operational Efficiency in Financial Shared Service. Journal of Electrical Systems, 21. https://search.ebscohost.com/login.aspx?direct=true&profile=ehost&scope=site&authtype=crawler&jrnl=11125209&AN=184115960&h=aF8hM4e9NEjQR5irHQReRtDxA7G0o1qMa7P5U8iOl4bLWpGXt6%2BTcxodawZREqw4qzSILEaiJQn417SErivKbg%3D%3D&crl=c

Shumailov, I., Shumaylov, Z., Zhao, Y., Gal, Y., Papernot, N., & Anderson, R. (2023, May 27). *The curse of recursion: Training on generated data makes models forget.* arXiv.Org. https://arxiv.org/abs/2305.17493

Shumailov, I., Shumaylov, Z., Zhao, Y., Papernot, N., Anderson, R., & Gal, Y. (2024). AI models collapse when trained on recursively generated data. *Nature*, *631*(8022), 755–759. DOI: 10.1038/s41586-024-07566-y PMID: 39048682

Shuster, K., Poff, S., Chen, M., Kiela, D., & Weston, J. (2021). Retrieval augmentation reduces hallucination in conversation. *Findings of the Association for Computational Linguistics: EMNLP, 2021*. Advance online publication. DOI: 10.18653/v1/2021.findings-emnlp.320

Shymko, V. (2025). Ethical challenges and strategic responses to AI integration in psychological assessment. *AI and Ethics*, *5*(5), 5415–5423. DOI: 10.1007/s43681-025-00788-4

Silic, M., Silic, D., & Kind-Trüller, K. (2025). From Shadow It to Shadow AI–Threats, Risks and Opportunities for Organizations. *Strategic Change.*

Simeon, O. (2025). Unifying risk management for AI-driven cybersecurity in finance. *Issues in Information Systems*, *26*(2).

Simmel, G. (1949). The sociology of sociability. *American Journal of Sociology*, *55*(3), 254–261. DOI: 10.1086/220534 PMID: 15400080

Sindhwani, A., Ruhela, S., Bhatia, A., Lalit, R., & Johari, R. (2023). Metaverse: Survey on future of internet and its innovative applications. *CEUR Workshop Proceedings.*

Singh, R. (2025). Revamping Employee Experience for the Next Generation Workforce. In Approaching Employee Experience Management With Data Science (pp. 65–94). IGI Global Scientific Publishing. https://www.igi-global.com/chapter/revamping-employee-experience-for-the-next-generation-workforce/370199

Singha, M. (2025, December 2). *Detecting AI hallucinations in finance: An information-theoretic method cuts hallucination rate by 92%.* arXiv.Org. https://arxiv.org/abs/2512.03107

Singh, A. (2025). Convergence of Generative Artificial Intelligence (AI)-Based Applications in the Hospitality and Tourism Industry. In Gaur, L. (Ed.), *Generative Artificial Intelligence and Ethics: Standards, Guidelines, and Best Practices* (pp. 127–142). IGI Global Scientific Publishing., DOI: 10.4018/979-8-3693-3691-5.ch006

Singh, A. K. (2025). VR/AR in ergonomics and workspace design: A dual-perspective analysis of applications and implications. *Applied Ergonomics, 129*. Advance online publication. DOI: 10.1016/j.apergo.2025.104612

Singh, A., & Das, R. (2025). Exploring Tourism Opportunities in the Metaverse and Technology Era: Insights From Scholarly Literature. In Hussain, Z., Khan, A., Majeed, M., & Albattat, A. (Eds.), *Metaverse and Sustainable Business Models in SMEs* (pp. 171–182). IGI Global Scientific Publishing., DOI: 10.4018/979-8-3693-9005-4.ch007

Singh, A., & Hassan, S. C. (2024). Service Innovation Through Blockchain Technology in the Tourism and Hospitality Industry: Applications, Trends, and Benefits. In Singh, S. (Ed.), *Service Innovations in Tourism: Metaverse, Immersive Technologies, and Digital Twin* (pp. 205–214). IGI Global Scientific Publishing., DOI: 10.4018/979-8-3693-1103-5.ch010

Singh, M., & Singh, A. (2025). The Role of Artificial Intelligence in Driving Sustainability in the Tourism Industry: A Marketing Perspective. In Ahmad, B., Abrar, M., & Saeed, M. (Eds.), *Marketing Technology-Infused Hospitality: Upskilling Frontline Employees for Competitiveness* (pp. 115–132). IGI Global Scientific Publishing., DOI: 10.4018/979-8-3693-7127-5.ch005

Slapakova, L., Fraser, A., Hughes, M., Aquilino, M. C., & Thue, K. (2024). Cultural and technological change in the future information environment. RAND. https://www.konjunktion.info/wp-content/uploads/2024/03/Cultural-and-technological-change-in-the-future-information-environment.pdf

Slater, M., & Sanchez-Vives, M. V. (2016). Enhancing lives with immersive VR. *Frontiers in Robotics and AI, 3*, 74.

Slater, M., Spanlang, B., Sanchez-Vives, M. V., & Blanke, O. (2010). First person experience of body transfer in VR. *PLoS One, 5*(5), e10564.

Slovic, P. (1993). Perceived risk, trust, and democracy. *Risk Analysis, 13*(6), 675–682.

Soliman, M. M., Ahmed, E., Darwish, A., & Hassanien, A. E. (2024). Artificial intelligence powered Metaverse: Analysis, challenges and future perspectives. *Artificial Intelligence Review*, *57*(2), 36.

Song, J., Wang, X., Zhu, J., Wu, Y., Cheng, X., Zhong, R., & Niu, C. (2024). RAG-HAT: A hallucination-aware tuning pipeline for LLM in retrieval-augmented generation. *Proceedings of the 2024 Conference on Empirical Methods in Natural Language Processing: Industry Track*, 1548–1558. https://doi.org/DOI: 10.18653/v1/2024.emnlp-industry.113

Sood, A. K., Zeadally, S., & Hong, E. (2025). The Paradigm of Hallucinations in AI-driven cybersecurity systems: Understanding taxonomy, classification outcomes, and mitigations. *Computers & Electrical Engineering*, *124*. Advance online publication. DOI: 10.1016/j.compeleceng.2025.110307

Srinivasan, A. G., George, R. J., Joe, J. K., & Kant, H. R, H. M., Sundar, S., Suresh, S., Vimalkanth, R., & Vijayavallabh. (2025, September 19). *Enhancing financial RAG with agentic AI and multi-hyde: A novel approach to knowledge retrieval and hallucination reduction*. arXiv.Org. https://arxiv.org/abs/2509.16369

Srivastava, G., Jhaveri, R. H., Bhattacharya, S., & Pandya, S. Rajeswari, Maddikunta, P. K. R., Yenduri, G., Hall, J. G., Alazab, M., & Gadekallu, T. R. (2022). *XAI for Cybersecurity: State of the Art, Challenges, Open Issues and Future Directions*. https://arxiv.org/abs/2206.03585

Stanoevska-Slabeva, K. (2022). *OPPORTUNITIES AND CHALLENGES OF METAVERSE FOR EDUCATION: A LITERATURE REVIEW*. 10401–10410. DOI: 10.21125/edulearn.2022.2527

Stefko, R., Michalikova, K. F., Strakova, J., & Novak, A. (2025). Digital twin-based virtual factory and cyber-physical production systems, collaborative autonomous robotic and networked manufacturing technologies, and enterprise and business intelligence algorithms for industrial metaverse. *Equilibrium. Quarterly Journal of Economics and Economic Policy*, *20*(1), 389–425. DOI: 10.24136/eq.3557

Stein Smith, S. (2024). ESG and Other Emerging Technology Applications. In S. Stein Smith, Blockchain, Artificial Intelligence, and Financial Services (pp. 193–213). Springer Nature Switzerland. https://doi.org/DOI: 10.1007/978-3-031-74403-7_14

Steyvers, M., Tejeda, H., Kumar, A., Belem, C., Karny, S., Hu, X., Mayer, L. W., & Smyth, P. (2025). What large language models know and what people think they know. *Nature Machine Intelligence*, *7*, 221–231. DOI: 10.1038/s42256-024-00976-7

Straub, J. (2022). Increasing Trust in Artificial Intelligence with a Defensible AI Technique. *2022 IEEE Applied Imagery Pattern Recognition Workshop (AIPR)*, 1–7. DOI: 10.1109/AIPR57179.2022.10092226

Sui, P., Duede, E., Wu, S., & So, R. J. (2024). *Confabulation: The surprising value of large language model hallucinations*. In *Proceedings of the 62nd Annual Meeting of the Association for Computational Linguistics (*Volume 1*: Long Papers)* (pp. 14274–14284). Association for Computational Linguistics.

Suk, H., & Laine, T. H. (2023). Influence of avatar facial appearance on users' perceived embodiment and presence in immersive virtual reality. *Electronics (Basel)*, *12*(3), 583. DOI: 10.3390/electronics12030583

Sukumaran, A., & Manoharan, A. (2024). Multimodal engagement recognition from image traits using deep learning techniques. *IEEE Access : Practical Innovations, Open Solutions*, *12*, 25228–25244. DOI: 10.1109/ACCESS.2024.3353053

Sundaram, S. (2025). Innovating for the Future: Sustainable Corporate Strategies for Workforce Upskilling and Reskilling. *International Journal of Research in Entrepreneurship & Business Studies*, *6*(3), 33–46.

Sun, Y., Sheng, D., Zhou, Z., & Wu, Y. (2024). AI hallucination: Towards a comprehensive classification of distorted information in artificial intelligence-generated content. *Humanities & Social Sciences Communications*, *11*, 1278. DOI: 10.1057/s41599-024-03811-x

Sykora, M. (2017). Web 1.0 to Web 2.0: An observational study and empirical evidence for the historical r (evolution) of the social web. *International Journal of Web Engineering and Technology*, *12*(1), 70–94. DOI: 10.1504/IJWET.2017.084024

Szakacs, A. (2025). The adoption of AI agents: from automation to autonomy, reshaping governance and strategic decision-making in FintTch.

Taeihagh, A. (2025). Governance of generative AI. *Policy and Society*, *44*(1), 1–22. DOI: 10.1093/polsoc/puaf001

Tallam, K. (2025). *Decoding the Black Box: Integrating Moral Imagination with Technical Trust-layer verification governance* (Version 1). arXiv. https://doi.org/DOI: 10.48550/ARXIV.2503.06411

Talukder, M. B., Lina, F. Y., Kumar, S., & Khan, M. R. (2024). Data-Driven Personalization in the Sharing Economy. In Ordóñez De Pablos, P. (Ed.), (pp. 277–300). Advances in Finance, Accounting, and Economics. IGI Global., DOI: 10.4018/979-8-3693-5673-9.ch012

Tang, A. (2025). Safeguarding the future: Security and privacy by design for AI, Metaverse, Blockchain, and Beyond. CRC Press. https://books.google.com/books?hl=en&lr=&id=xDVEEQAAQBAJ&oi=fnd&pg=PT2&dq=-+Within+the+enterprise+metaverse,+goals+include+building+explainable+advisory+journeys,+maintaining+audit+trails+of+human+overrides&ots=vVOmsMhAlL&sig=RZZpNNALIYTtpGHAtGBEMYYkgYw

Tang, M., Nikolaenko, M., Alrefai, A., & Kumar, A. (2025). Metaverse and Digital Twins in the Age of AI and Extended Reality. *Architecture (Washington, D.C.)*, *5*(2), 36.

Tang, Y. M., Wong, J. K. N., & Ho, G. T. S. (2025). Exploring Consumer Acceptance of Metaverse Marketing for Branding Activities and the Pre-Purchase Stage. *Journal of Theoretical and Applied Electronic Commerce Research*, *20*(3), 159. DOI: 10.3390/jtaer20030159

Tettey, D. J., Chrisben, D., Victoria, M. C., Chukwubuikem, E. P., & Abdullahi, A. (2025). Responsible AI deployment in sustainable project execution: Ensuring transparency, carbon efficiency and regulatory alignment. https://www.researchgate.net/profile/Jacob-Diameh/publication/390597381_Responsible_AI_deployment_in_sustainable_project_execution_Ensuring_transparency_carbon_efficiency_and_regulatory_alignment/links/67f591a176d4923a1a009f3b/Responsible-AI-deployment-in-sustainable-project-execution-Ensuring-transparency-carbon-efficiency-and-regulatory-alignment.pdf

Thirunavukarasu, A. J., & O'Logbon, J. (2024). The potential and perils of generative artificial intelligence in psychiatry and psychology. *Nature Mental Health*, *2*, 745–746. DOI: 10.1038/s44220-024-00257-7

Thirupathi, L., Kaashipaka, V., Dhanaraju, M., & Katakam, V. (2025). AI and IoT in Mental Health Care: From Digital Diagnostics to Personalized, Continuous Support. In Joshi, H., Kumar Reddy, C., Ouaissa, M., Hanafiah, M., & Doss, S. (Eds.), *Intelligent Systems and IoT Applications in Clinical Health* (pp. 271–294). IGI Global Scientific Publishing., DOI: 10.4018/979-8-3693-8990-4.ch012

Tifani Napitupulu, A. A., Panjaitan, N. U., Muda, I., & Ade, S. (n.d.). Competitive Advantage and Resource-Based View: A Systematic Literature Review. Bridging Management Control Systems and Sustainability: Systematic Reviews on Business Performance and Risk, 96.

Tombul, I., & Sari, G. (2021). Transformation of self-presentation in virtual space. *İletişim Kuram ve Araştırma Dergisi, 53,* 93–108. https://doi.org/DOI: 10.47998/ikad.852841

Tong, A., Palmer, S., Craig, J. C., & Strippoli, G. F. (2016). A guide to reading and using systematic reviews of qualitative research. *Nephrology, Dialysis, Transplantation, 31*(6), 897–903. DOI: 10.1093/ndt/gfu354 PMID: 25414375

Tonmoy, S. M. T. I., Zaman, S. M. M., Jain, V., Rani, A., Rawte, V., Chadha, A., & Das, A. (2024, January 2). *A comprehensive survey of hallucination mitigation techniques in large language models*. arXiv.Org. https://arxiv.org/abs/2401.01313

Torres, R. C. (2025). AI Hallucination in the Context of Education: Exploring College Students' Use of Generative AI for Academic Tasks. *2025 16th International Conference on E-Education, E-Business, E-Management and E-Learning (IC4e)*, 445–449. DOI: 10.1109/IC4e65071.2025.11075444

Tugarin, N., & van Husen, C. (2025). Development and integration of human-AI interactions in service applications: Conceptual framework and review. *International Journal of Information Management Data Insights, 5*(2), 100357. DOI: 10.1016/j.jjimei.2025.100357

Uddin, M., Obaidat, M., Manickam, S., Laghari, S. U. A., Dandoush, A., Ullah, H., & Ullah, S. S. (2024). Exploring the convergence of Metaverse, Blockchain, and AI: A comprehensive survey of enabling technologies, applications, challenges, and future directions. *Wiley Interdisciplinary Reviews. Data Mining and Knowledge Discovery, 14*(6), e1556. DOI: 10.1002/widm.1556

Urdea, A. M., Constantin, C. P., & Purcaru, I. M. (2021). Implementing experiential marketing in the digital age for a more sustainable customer relationship. *Sustainability, 13*(4), 1865. DOI: 10.3390/su13041865

Vallarino, D. (2025, April 1). *Detecting financial fraud with hybrid deep learning: A mix-of-experts approach to sequential and anomalous patterns*. arXiv.Org. https://arxiv.org/abs/2504.03750

van Deemter, K. (2024). The pitfalls of defining hallucination. *Computational Linguistics, 50*(2), 807–816. DOI: 10.1162/coli_a_00509

Van Dijk, J. A. G. M. (2020). *The digital divide*. John Wiley & Sons.

Varshavskiy, I., Boboeva, B., Khalilbekov, S., Azimi, A., Shulgin, S., Nizamitdinov, A., & Borde, H. S. de O. (2025, October 10). *Mitigating model drift in developing economies using synthetic data and outliers*. arXiv.Org. https://arxiv.org/abs/2510.09294

Venugopal, J. P., Subramanian, A. A. V., Sundaram, G., & Ponnambalam Devadoss, M. (2025). The Convergence of Deep Learning and the Metaverse: A Multidisciplinary Survey of Current Research and Future Directions. *Computer Animation and Virtual Worlds*, *36*(6), e70082. DOI: 10.1002/cav.70082

Violante, M. G., Vezzetti, E., & Piazzolla, P. (2019). How to design a virtual reality experience that impacts the consumer engagement: The case of the virtual supermarket. [IJIDeM]. *International Journal on Interactive Design and Manufacturing*, *13*(1), 243–262. DOI: 10.1007/s12008-018-00528-5

Virvou, M., & Tsihrintzis, G. A. (2023). A Novel Trust State-Chart Model for Requirements Engineering of Trustful AI - Empowered Software. In 2023 14th International Conference on Information, Intelligence, Systems & Applications (IISA) (pp. 1–6). IEEE. DOI: 10.1109/IISA59645.2023.10345934

Vlădu escu, ., & Stănescu, V. (2024). Greening the Virtual: An Interdisciplinary Narrative Review on the Environmental Sustainability of the Metaverse. *Sustainability*, *17*(16), 7269. DOI: 10.3390/su17167269

Voinea, C., Earp, B. D., Mann, S., & Savulescu, J. (2024). Digital doppelgängers, human relationships, and practical identity. *Philosophy & Technology*, *37*, 121. DOI: 10.1007/s13347-024-00813-0

Vössing, M., Kühl, N., Lind, M., & Satzger, G. (2022). Designing transparency for effective human-AI collaboration. *Information Systems Frontiers*, *24*, 877–895. DOI: 10.1007/s10796-022-10284-3

Vrdoljak, J., Boban, Z., Vilović, M., Kumrić, M., & Božić, J. (2025). A review of large language models in medical education, clinical decision support, and healthcare administration. *Health Care*, *13*(6), 603. DOI: 10.3390/healthcare13060603

Vyas, S., Rathore, J. S., & Kumar, V. (2024). Insights into mobile app experience: A systematic literature review using TCCM framework. *Global Knowledge, Memory and Communication*. Advance online publication. DOI: 10.1108/GKMC-02-2024-0063

Wachter, S., Mittelstadt, B., & Russell, C. (2018). Counterfactual explanations without opening the black box. *Harvard Journal of Law & Technology*, *31*, 841–887. DOI: 10.2139/ssrn.3061253

Wada, A., Tanaka, Y., Nishizawa, M., Akashi, T., Hagiwara, A., Hayakawa, Y., Kikuta, J., Shimoji, K., Sano, K., Kamagata, K., Nakanishi, A., & Aoki, S. (2025). Retrieval-augmented generation elevates local LLM quality in radiology contrast media consultation. *npj. Digital Medicine*, *8*, 395. DOI: 10.1038/s41746-025-01802-z

Walters, W. H., & Wilder, E. I. (2023). Fabrication and errors in the bibliographic citations generated by ChatGPT. *Scientific Reports*, *13*, 14045. DOI: 10.1038/s41598-023-41032-5

Wang, J., Cao, L., & Gao, M. (2024). Multidimensional Scale Analysis of the Development of China's New Quality Productivity from the Perspective of AI. In 2024 8th Asian Conference on Artificial Intelligence Technology (ACAIT) (pp. 1164–1168). IEEE. DOI: 10.1109/ACAIT63902.2024.11022293

Wang, J., Tielman, M. L., & Jonker, C. M. (2022). Artificial Trust as a Tool in Human-AI Teams. In 2022 17th ACM/IEEE International Conference on Human-Robot Interaction (HRI) (pp. 1155–1157). IEEE. DOI: 10.1109/HRI53351.2022.9889652

Wang, G., Zhang, Z., Nandhakumar, J., & Manoharan, N. (2025). Everyday metaverse: The metaverse as an integral part of everyday life. *Journal of Management Information Systems*, *42*(3), 310–342. DOI: 10.1080/07421222.2025.2455772

Wang, Q., Li, Y., & Li, R. (2025). Integrating artificial intelligence in energy transition: A comprehensive review. *Energy Strategy Reviews*, *57*, 101600. DOI: 10.1016/j.esr.2024.101600

Wang, X., Wei, J., Schuurmans, D., Le, Q., Chi, E. H., Narang, S., Chowdhery, A., & Zhou, D. (2023). Self-consistency improves chain-of-thought reasoning in language models. *Proceedings of the International Conference on Learning Representations (ICLR 2023).*

Waqas, A., Tripathi, A., Ramachandran, R. P., Stewart, P. A., & Rasool, G. (2024). Multimodal data integration for oncology in the era of deep neural networks: A review. *Frontiers in Artificial Intelligence*, *7*, 1408843. DOI: 10.3389/frai.2024.1408843 PMID: 39118787

Watson, R. (2022). The virtual economy of the metaverse: Computer vision and deep learning algorithms, customer engagement tools, and behavioral predictive analytics. *Linguistic and Philosophical Investigations*, (21), 41–56.

Wei, J., Wang, X., Schuurmans, D., Bosma, M., Ichter, B., Xia, F., Chi, E., Le, Q., & Zhou, D. (2022, January 28). *Chain-of-Thought prompting elicits reasoning in large language models*. arXiv.Org. https://arxiv.org/abs/2201.11903

Wei, X., & Jia, H. (2021). A Review of the Application of Artificial Intelligence in the Virtual Learning Environment. *2021 Tenth International Conference of Educational Innovation through Technology (EITT)*, 79–82. DOI: 10.1109/EITT53287.2021.00024

Wen, Y., Wang, Z., & Guo, X. (2025). Trends and applications of AI in immersive learning environments: A systematic review of empirical research. *Interactive Learning Environments*, •••, 1–19. DOI: 10.1080/10494820.2025.2524029

Williamson, S. M., & Prybutok, V. (2024). The era of artificial intelligence deception: Unraveling the complexities of false realities and emerging threats of misinformation. *Information (Basel), 15*(6), 299. DOI: 10.3390/info15060299

Wongkitrungrueng, A., & Suprawan, L. (2024). Metaverse meets branding: Examining consumer responses to immersive brand experiences. *International Journal of Human-Computer Interaction, 40*(11), 2905–2924. DOI: 10.1080/10447318.2023.2175162

Wu, Y., Mi, Q., & Gao, T. (2025). A comprehensive review of multimodal emotion recognition: Techniques, challenges, and future directions. *Biomimetics, 10*(7), 418. DOI: 10.3390/biomimetics10070418 PMID: 40710231

Xie, Y., Sun, F., Deng, Y., Li, Y., & Ding, B. (2021). Factual consistency evaluation for text summarization via counterfactual estimation. In *Proceedings of the 2021 Conference on Empirical Methods in Natural Language Processing* (pp. 100–110). Virtual Conference, November 7–11.

Xie, Z., & Fang, S. (2025). The Application of AI-Assisted Color and Emotion Association Modeling in Healing Space Design. 2025 IEEE 12th Joint International Information Technology and Artificial Intelligence Conference (ITAIC), 1276–1282. DOI: 10.1109/ITAIC64559.2025.11163049

Xiong, C., Zheng, G., Ma, X., Li, C., & Zeng, J. (2025). DelphiAgent: A trustworthy multi-agent verification framework for automated fact verification. *Information Processing & Management, 62*(6), 104241. DOI: 10.1016/j.ipm.2025.104241

Xu, Z., Jain, S., & Kankanhalli, M. (2024, January 22). *Hallucination is Inevitable: An Innate Limitation of Large Language Models*. arXiv.Org. https://arxiv.org/abs/2401.11817

Xu, J. Q., Wu, T. J., Duan, W. Y., & Cui, X. X. (2025). How the Human-Artificial Intelligence (AI) Collaboration Affects Cyberloafing: An AI Identity Perspective. *Behavioral Sciences (Basel, Switzerland), 15*(7), 859. DOI: 10.3390/bs15070859 PMID: 40723643

Xu, J., Li, Y., Zhang, Z., Luk, A. Y. H., Jobanputra, M., Oza, S., Murray, A., Kasula, M. R., Parker, A., & Eyre, D. W. (2025, November). *Tree-of-Quote prompting improves factuality and attribution in multi-hop and medical reasoning*. In *Proceedings of the 2025 Conference on Empirical Methods in Natural Language Processing* (pp. 5606–5623). Association for Computational Linguistics.

Xu, S., Yan, Z., Dai, C., & Wu, F. (2025). MEGA-RAG: A retrieval-augmented generation framework with multi-evidence guided answer refinement for mitigating hallucinations of LLMs in public health. *Frontiers in Public Health, 13*. Advance online publication. DOI: 10.3389/fpubh.2025.1635381

Xu, W., Zhang, N., & Wang, M. (2024). The impact of interaction on continuous use in online learning platforms: A metaverse perspective. *Internet Research, 34*(1), 79–106. DOI: 10.1108/INTR-08-2022-0600

Yadav, P., Kashyap, I., & Bhati, B. S. (2024). Contextual Ambiguity Framework for Enhanced Sentiment Analysis. *Tehnički glasnik, 18*(3), 385-393. https://doi.org/DOI: 10.31803/tg-20231227064230

Yang, H. (2024). The genesis effect: Digital goods in the metaverse. *The Journal of Consumer Research, 51*(1), 129–139. DOI: 10.1093/jcr/ucad072

Yao, K.-C., Hung, H.-C., Wang, C.-H., Huang, W.-L., Liang, H.-T., Chu, T.-H., Chen, B.-S., & Ho, W.-S. (2025). Application of generative AI in financial risk prediction: Enhancing model accuracy and interpretability. *Information (Basel), 16*(10), 857. DOI: 10.3390/info16100857

Yaprak, B. (2024). Generative artificial intelligence in marketing: The invisible danger of AI hallucinations. *Ekonomi İşletme ve Yönetim Dergisi, 8*(2), 133–158.

Yoon, S., & Kim, B. (2025). Multi-Scale Temporal Fusion Network for Real-Time Multimodal Emotion Recognition in IoT Environments. *Sensors (Basel), 25*(16), 5066. DOI: 10.3390/s25165066 PMID: 40871929

Young, G. W., & Dawkins, O. (2023, July). Multimodality: Exploring sensibility and sense-making beyond the metaverse. In *International Conference on Human-Computer Interaction* (pp. 307-322). Cham: Springer Nature Switzerland. https://doi.org/DOI: 10.1007/978-3-031-35634-6_22

Yu, T., Zhang, H., Li, Q., Xu, Q., Yao, Y., Chen, D., Lu, X., Cui, G., Dang, Y., He, T., Feng, X., Song, J., Zheng, B., Liu, Z., Chua, T.-S., & Sun, M. (2024, May 27). *RLAIF-V: Open-Source AI feedback leads to super GPT-4V trustworthiness*. arXiv. Org. https://arxiv.org/abs/2405.17220

Yu, L., & Li, Y. (2022). Artificial Intelligence Decision-Making Transparency and Employees' Trust: The Parallel Multiple Mediating Effect of Effectiveness and Discomfort. *Behavioral Sciences (Basel, Switzerland), 12*(5), 127. DOI: 10.3390/bs12050127 PMID: 35621424

Zafar, M. B., & Ali, H. (2025). Shariah Governance Standard on Generative AI for Islamic Financial Institutions. *Available at SSRN* 5143165.

Zahrae, F. F., Es-Sâadia, A., & Mohamed, Y. (2024). Artificial Intelligence Implementation in Virtual Learning Environment: An Overview. *2024 International Conference on Intelligent Systems and Computer Vision (ISCV)*, 1–6. DOI: 10.1109/ISCV60512.2024.10620135

Zamfirescu-Pereira, J. D., Wong, R. Y., Hartmann, B., & Yang, Q. (2023). Why Johnny can't prompt: How non-AI experts try (and fail) to design LLM prompts. *CHI '23: Proceedings of the 2023 CHI Conference on Human Factors in Computing Systems*, Article 437, 1–21. https://doi.org/DOI: 10.1145/3544548.358138

Zeng, Y., Zhang, J. W., & Yang, J. (2024). Multimodal emotion recognition in the metaverse era: New needs and transformation in mental health work. *World Journal of Clinical Cases*, *12*(34), 6674. DOI: 10.12998/wjcc.v12.i34.6674 PMID: 39650812

Zerilli, J., Bhatt, U., & Weller, A. (2022). How transparency modulates trust in artificial intelligence. *Patterns (New York, N.Y.)*, *3*(4), 100455. DOI: 10.1016/j.patter.2022.100455 PMID: 35465233

Zhang, M., Fu, J., Warrier, T., Wang, Y., Tan, T., & Huang, K. (2025, August 7). *FAITH: A framework for assessing intrinsic tabular hallucinations in finance*. arXiv.Org. https://arxiv.org/abs/2508.05201

Zhang, S., Yu, T., & Feng, Y. (2024, February 27). *TruthX: Alleviating hallucinations by editing large language models in truthful space*. arXiv.Org. https://arxiv.org/abs/2402.17811

Zhang, W., Taib, N., & Taib, M. (2025). Reimagining cultural heritage conservation through VR, metaverse, and digital twins: An AI and blockchain-based framework. *PLOS ONE, 20*(11 November). https://doi.org/DOI: 10.1371/journal.pone.0335943

Zhang, W., Zhang, C., Gu, C., Kou, J., Yuan, H., Fang, X., Duan, X., & Fang, Y. (2024). Hallucination in Large Language Models: From Mechanistic Understanding to Novel Control Frameworks. *2024 7th International Conference on Universal Village (UV)*, 1–36. DOI: 10.1109/UV63228.2024.11189226

Zhang, H., Li, Y., Zhang, S., Song, L., & Tao, F. (2025). Artificial Intelligence-Enhanced Digital Twin Systems Engineering Towards the Industrial Metaverse in the Era of Industry 5.0. [English Edition]. *Chinese Journal of Mechanical Engineering*, *38*(1). Advance online publication. DOI: 10.1186/s10033-025-01210-0

Zhang, W., & Zhang, J. (2025). Hallucination mitigation for retrieval-augmented large language models: A review. *Mathematics*, *13*(5), 856. DOI: 10.3390/math13050856

Zhang, Y., Li, Y., Cui, L., Cai, D., Liu, L., Fu, T., Huang, X., Zhao, E., Zhang, Y., Chen, Y., Wang, L., Luu, A. T., Bi, W., Shi, F., & Shi, S. (2025). Siren's song in the AI ocean: A survey on hallucination in large language models. *Computational Linguistics*. Advance online publication. DOI: 10.1162/COLI.a.16

Zhang, Z., Sun, W., Xinyue, L., Jia, J., Min, X., Zhang, Z., & Zhai, G. (2025). Benchmarking Multi-dimensional AIGC Video Quality Assessment: A Dataset and Unified Model. *ACM Transactions on Multimedia Computing Communications and Applications*, *21*(9). Advance online publication. DOI: 10.1145/3749844

Zhou, J., Li, H., Chen, S., Han, Z., & Gao, X. (2025). Large language models in biomedicine and healthcare. *npj. Artificial Intelligence*, *1*, 44. Advance online publication. DOI: 10.1038/s44387-025-00047-1

Zhou, J., Zhang, J., Wan, R., Cui, X., Liu, Q., Guo, H., Shi, X., Fu, B., Meng, J., Yue, B., Zhang, Y., & Zhang, Z. (2025). Integrating AI into clinical education: Evaluating general practice trainees' proficiency in distinguishing AI-generated hallucinations and impacting factors. *BMC Medical Education*, *25*(1). Advance online publication. DOI: 10.1186/s12909-025-06916-2

Zhu, Z., Zhang, Y., Zhuang, X., Zhang, F., Wan, Z., Chen, Y., Long, Q., Zheng, Y., & Wu, X. (2025). Can we trust AI doctors? A survey of medical hallucination in large language and large vision-language models. In Che, W., Nabende, J., Shutova, E., & Pilehvar, M. T. (Eds.), *Findings of the Association for Computational Linguistics: ACL 2025* (pp. 6748–6769). Association for Computational Linguistics., DOI: 10.18653/v1/2025.findings-acl.350

Zöller, N., Berger, J., Lin, I., Fu, N., Komarneni, J., Barabucci, G., Laskowski, K., Shia, V., Harack, B., Chu, E. A., Trianni, V., Kurvers, R. H. J. M., & Herzog, S. M. (2025). Human-AI collectives most accurately diagnose clinical vignettes. *Proceedings of the National Academy of Sciences of the United States of America*, *122*(24), e2426153122. DOI: 10.1073/pnas.2426153122

Zou, A., Wang, Z., Carlini, N., Nasr, M., Kolter, J. Z., & Fredrikson, M. (2023, July 27). *Universal and transferable adversarial attacks on aligned language models*. arXiv.Org. https://arxiv.org/abs/2307.15043

Zvaigzne, A., Litavniece, L., Kodors, S., & Jurkane, K. (2025). Negative impacts of artificial intelligence technologies on the tourism industry. *Worldwide Hospitality and Tourism Themes*, *17*(1), 22–34.

About the Contributors

Abdelkader Mohamed Sghaier Derbali is an Associate Professor in Finance at the Department of Finance and Accounting, Higher Institute of Informatics and Management of Kairouan, Kairouan University, Kairouan, Tunisia and at the Department of Administrative and Financial Sciences, Applied College, Taibah University, Saudi Arabia. He is one of the Editorial Board Members in the Journal of Energy Markets, International Business Review, Cogent Economic & Finance, International Review of Applied Economics, African Journal of Accounting, Auditing and Finance, and African Journal of Economic and Sustainable Development. His research interests include Risk Management, Systemic risk, International finance, Capital markets and institutions, Banking and market microstructure and Islamic Finance. He has published articles, among others, in Research in International Business and Management, Finance Research Letters, International Journal of Critical Accounting, Journal of Asset Management, International Journal of Productivity and Quality Management, Cogent Business & Management, Cogent Economic & Finance, Journal of Chinese Governance, Pacific Accounting Review, International Journal of Financial Engineering, Virtual Economics, International Journal of Economics and Business Research, International Journal of Mathematics in Operational Research, The Chinese Economy, Journal of Energy Markets, and International Journal of Trade and Global Markets, International Journal of Social Economics, Journal of Business and Socio-economic Development, International Journal of the Economics of Business, China Economic Journal, Journal of Economics, Finance and Administrative Science.

Rohit Sood, Assistant Professor at Lovely Professional University, Phagwara, Punjab (India), Department of Finance, has an extensive academic and professional experience of more than 14 years. He has presented numerous papers in national and international conferences and ten papers are published in reputed international referred journals with high impact factor and indexing Google Scholar, Scopus,

BEIESP, Open J Gate, DOAJ, get CITED, dig, Higher Education Forum, Cite Factor, Index Copernicus, Search Sight, Scirus, UK Index, New Jour, Research Gate. Apart from this, he has attended various conferences, workshop and seminar in different colleges. He has attended 10+ relevant training and courses for continuous learning; has attended more than 10 Faculty Development Programs. He is a life member of Society of FSP and Global Risk Community.

Shilpa Chaudhary is working as an Assistant Professor at Mittal School of Business, Lovely Professional University, Punjab. She has 11 years of teaching experience. She has presented various papers in national and international conferences. Her research mainly focuses on Social capital, Absorptive capacity, Innovation, innovation capabilities, and various contemporaneous issues.

***

Shyam Sunder Agrawal, working as Assistant Professor, Mittal School of Business, Lovely Professional University, Phagwara, Punjab, India. He has been associated with the education industry since 2015. He has presented papers at various reputed IIM conferences and published several research papers in UGC CARE, SCOPUS, and ABDC Journals. He has earned his Ph.D. in management from Devi Ahilya Vishwavidyalaya, Indore. His fields of interest are Behavioral Finance, Sustainable Finance, Capital Market, Banking, and Insurance. He has published and granted 2 patents from Govt of India. He received the International Case Study Award in 2022. He is a reviewer for Emerald, Springer, and peer-reviewed journals. He is also a financial advisor at Life Insurance Corporation of India.

Vinsens Aji Pamungkas is an emerging researcher affiliated with the Department of Computer Science, Esa Unggul University. His academic interests include Artificial Intelligence, Business Information Systems, Human-Technology Interaction, Social Networking, and Risk Management. Despite being an undergraduate student, he has actively engaged in collaborative research, academic writing, and scientific discussions in technology-related disciplines. He is passionate about bridging the gap between digital innovation and human behavior in organizational and societal contexts. His goal is to contribute to impactful, interdisciplinary knowledge through research and academic publishing.

Aldian Alifen is an Informatics Engineering undergraduate student with strong research and writing interests in Internet of Things, Computer Networks, Artificial Intelligence, Mobile Development, Business Technology, and Data-driven innovation. He is passionate about exploring emerging technologies and developing practical solutions that bridge technical capability with real-world impact.

Jefry Sunupurwa Asri is a lecturer at the Faculty of Computer Science, Universitas Esa Unggul, Indonesia. He has extensive experience in teaching and research related to complex systems development, with a particular focus on distributed systems architecture, enterprise application integration, and intelligent system design. His academic interests include the development of scalable software architectures, the implementation of microservices-based solutions, and the application of advanced algorithms in building robust and efficient complex systems. Jefry actively engages in research and collaborative projects aimed at advancing methodologies for designing and implementing large-scale technological infrastructures. His dedication to solving intricate technical challenges and developing comprehensive system solutions reflects his commitment to creating sustainable and adaptable technologies that meet evolving organizational needs. He contributes to the academic community through his work on system optimization, performance analysis, and the integration of emerging technologies into complex computational environments,bridging theoretical concepts with practical implementation strategie

Bartholomeus Dimanche Carl Beth is a computer science enthusiast with a strong interest in research and academic writing. His expertise lies in writing scientific journals and exploring topics related to technology, data systems, and innovation in computing. With a passion for continuous learning, he aims to contribute to the advancement of knowledge in the field of computer science through high-quality research and publications.

Ramya G working as a Sr. Business Systems Analyst with an Organisation name: Maritz Consulting Group Inc, which is at City and county: Dallas,TX. She is having 18+ years of experience in the field of software industry and worked for many organizations. She is interested in AI and Machine learning domains.

Ganesh Harke is a technology leader who has redefined financial services through AI, big data, and scalable software architectures. In his pivotal roles at various financial institutions, Ganesh has spearheaded transformative engineering solutions that have reshaped high-frequency & low-latency algorithmic trading and other financial technology systems. Beyond his core roles, Ganesh co-chairs Applied AI initiatives. He serves on the Technical Oversight Committee at FINOS, under the Linux Foundation, guiding open-source, AI-driven innovation across the financial sector. Ganesh holds a Master's degree in Financial Engineering. He has successfully passed all three levels of the CFA Program, equipping him with a unique blend of financial expertise, technical depth, and business insight.

Leena Jenefa, working as an Associate Professor in Hindustan Institute of Technology and Science, Chennai India, Prior that she worked in Vel Tech Rangarajan Dr Sagunthala R&D Institute of Science and Technology, Avadi, Chennai. She is having 19 years of experience in the teaching field. Prior to joining to Vel Tech -Chennai, she worked in Tecnia Institute of Advanced Studies-Delhi, DMI- St. Eugene University-Zambia, Linton University affiliated to University of East London-Malaysia

Lina Kankevičienė is an Associate Professor of Informatics at Kaunas University of Applied Sciences. Her research interests include artificial intelligence in education, social media and sentiment data analysis, algorithm efficiency, and data-driven marketing analytics. She also investigates the impact of artificial intelligence on labor market transformation and digital skills development. She has experience leading national and international projects and participates in the COST program.

Shikha Khullar is a researcher focused on artificial intelligence, digital transformation, and human–AI collaboration. Her work examines AI reliability, ethical governance, and emerging technologies in enterprise environments. She contributes to international publications and projects on responsible and future-ready AI systems.

Sanjeev Kumar Is a Professor in Lovely Professional University Punjab India. He received Undergraduate in Hotel Management from Osmania University, Postgraduate in Tourism Management from Madurai Kamaraj University. He completed Doctor of Philosophy in Hospitality Management in 2019 from Amity University Jaipur India. His research areas lies in food Service Industry, his research focuses on Alcoholic beverages, Event management and Sustainable Management Practices, Metaverse, AI Machine Learning and Artificial Intelligence. He published more than 80 research papers, articles and chapters in Scopus Indexed, UGC Approved and peer reviewed Journals and books. Dr. Sanjeev Kumar participated and acted as resource person in various National and International conferences, seminars, session chair, research workshops and industry talks and his work has been widely cited. Dr. Sanjeev also edited more than 20 books with various International Publishers such as IGI Global, Cambridge Scholars, Emerald, CABI, Bentham Science, Taylor & Francis. Dr Sanjeev is an active researcher and has published numerous research articles in prestigious National and International journals and books.

Ryan Putra Laksana is a lecturer at the Faculty of Computer Science, Universitas Esa Unggul, Indonesia. He has extensive experience in teaching and research related to Information Technology, with a particular focus on the Internet of Things (IoT), project management, and other IT-related subjects. His academic interests include the development of intelligent systems, the integration of IoT in modern infrastructures, and the application of agile methodologies in IT project management. Ryan actively engages in research and collaborative projects aimed at advancing digital innovation and technology adoption in education and industry. His dedication to fostering technological literacy and developing practical IT solutions reflects his commitment to bridging the gap between academic research and real-world implementation.

S. P. Santhoshkumar received the Bachelor's Degree in Electronics and Communication Engineering from Anna University, Chennai in 2006, the Master's Degree in Software Engineering from Anna University of Technology, Coimbatore in 2011, and the Philosophy of Doctorate degree in Information and Communication Engineering from Anna University, Chennai in 2024, respectively. He is currently working as an Assistant Professor (SG) at the Department of Computer Science and Engineering, School of Computing, Vel Tech Rangarajan Dr. Sagunthala R&D Institute of Science and Technology, Avadi, Chennai. His research areas include Machine Learning, Cloud Computing, Deep Learning, Software Engineering and Web Development. He has quality of publications to his credit, including Journal Articles, Conference Publications, Patents, Books and Book Chapters. Also, he received best faculty awards in national level.

Binastya Anggara Sekti has been a lecturer at the Faculty of Computer Science, Esa Unggul University, Jakarta, since 2016. He is actively involved in the Artificial Intelligence and Information Security Study Group. He holds a Bachelor's degree in Informatics Engineering from the Bandung Institute of Technology and a Master's degree in Information Systems Management from Trisakti University, Jakarta. Prior to entering academia, he accumulated over 25 years of professional experience as an IT practitioner in various companies across Jakarta. His work focused on developing data centers for internet service providers and delivering IT solutions for the manufacturing and oil & gas sectors. His research interests include artificial intelligence, cybersecurity, and the development of IT infrastructure.

Animesh Kumar Sharma is a Research Scholar at Mittal School of Business, Lovely Professional University, Phagwara, Punjab, India and working as Manager - Marketing and Corporate Communication with Vatika Business Centres Private Limited (A Vatika Group Company), Gurugram, India. His research interest areas include digital marketing, social media marketing, search engine marketing, artificial intelligence, machine learning, data analytics and the applications of technology in business.

Rahul Sharma is a highly accomplished professor of Marketing with over 14 years of experience in academia. He has a Ph.D. in Marketing and has published over 15 articles in high-quality journals in the field. Dr. Sharma's research interests include consumer behavior, business analytics, and digital marketing. In addition to his research, Dr. Rahul is also a highly sought-after resource person in various faculty development programs.

Amrik Singh is working as Professor and HOD in the School of Hotel Management and Tourism at Lovely Professional University, Punjab, India. He obtained his Ph.D. degree in Hotel Management from Kurukshetra University, Haryana, India. He has published 115 Scopus-indexed publications. He has published 12 patents, and 01 patent has been granted in the inter-disciplinary domain. Dr. Amrik Singh participated and acted as a resource person in various national and international conferences, seminars, research workshops, and industry talks. He has published 20 books with IGI Global Publication, Emerald Publication, Bentham Publication, Nova Publication etc., on trending areas such as Food waste, Artificial Intelligence, Mountain Tourism, Virtual tourism, Healthcare Tourism, Guest behavior in tourism and hospitality. His area of research interest are Accommodation management, sustainability, Green practices, Human Resource Management in Hospitality, Artificial Intelligence, AR VR in hospitality, Hotel pricing, Employee Disability, Work life balance, women empowerment etc. He is currently guiding 8 Ph.D. scholars, and 5 Ph.D. scholars have been awarded Ph.D.

Mohammad Badruddoza Talukder is an Associate Professor at the College of Tourism and Hospitality Management at the International University of Business Agriculture and Technology (IUBAT) in Dhaka, Bangladesh. Holding a PhD from Lovely Professional University, India, he is renowned for his innovative integration of cutting-edge technologies such as Artificial Intelligence (AI), the Internet of Things (IoT), and Blockchain into tourism and hospitality management. His research explores the transformative impact of these technologies on smart tourism, cloud kitchens, and the broader industry landscape. As a prolific author, Dr. Talukder has published numerous scholarly articles and books, with forthcoming titles that address AI innovations in hospitality, the evolution of cloud kitchens, and the enhancement of digital literacy within hospitality education. His work shapes contemporary tourism and hospitality practices, skillfully marrying technological advancements with practical industry applications. Since 2008, Dr. Talukder has imparted his knowledge through a diverse array of courses in tourism and hospitality across various universities in Bangladesh.

Lingala Thirupathi is a seasoned academician and researcher with over 18 years of experience spanning teaching and industry, specializing in Artificial Intelligence, Cybersecurity, and the Internet of Things. He is currently serving as an Assistant Professor at SNIST, Hyderabad. A Gold Medalist in M.Tech (Software Engineering) from JNTUH, he also holds a B.Tech in CSIT and multiple professional certifications, including Cisco Instructor, Oracle Certified Associate, and Salesforce Ranger. With over 60 research publications in reputed journals such as Scopus, IEEE, Elsevier, and Springer, he also holds one Australian and three Indian patents. Mr. Thirupathi has authored three textbooks and contributed to over 30 book chapters. He actively participates in academic and technical communities as a reviewer, committee member, and SPOC for Smart India Hackathons, and is affiliated with professional bodies like CSTA, TERA, and ICSES. His dedication to innovation and excellence has earned him accolades, including the Expert Instructor Award from Cisco Networking Academy.

Index

A

B

C

D

E

F

G

H

S

T

V

W

www.ingramcontent.com/pod-product-compliance
Lightning Source LLC
LaVergne TN
LVHW062337300926
849161LV00007B/1724